FROMMERS

COMPREHENSIVE TRAVEL GUIDE

ALASKA '94 -'95

by John Gottberg

PRENTICE HALL TRAVEL

NEW YORK • LONDON • TORONTO • SYDNEY • TOKYO • SINGAPORE

FROMMER BOOKS

Published by Prentice Hall General Reference
A division of Simon & Schuster Inc.
15 Columbus Circle
New York, NY 10023

ISBN 0-671-84672-8
ISSN 1042-8283

Design by Robert Bull Design
Maps by Ortelius Design

FROMMER'S EDITORIAL STAFF
Editorial Director: Marilyn Wood
Editorial Manager/Senior Editor: Alice Fellows
Senior Editor: Lisa Renaud
Editors: Charlotte Allstrom, Thomas F. Hirsch, Peter Katucki, Sara Hinsey Raveret, Theodore Stavrou
Assistant Editors: Margaret Bowen, Christopher Hollander, Alice Thompson, Ian Wilker
Editorial Assistant: Gretchen Henderson
Managing Editor: Leanne Coupe

SPECIAL SALES
Bulk purchases (10+ copies) of Frommer's Travel Guides are available to corporations at special discounts. The Special Sales Department can produce custom editions to be used as premiums and/or for sales promotion to suit individual needs. Existing editions can be produced with custom cover imprints such as a corporate logo. For more information write to: Special Sales, Prentice Hall Travel, 15 Columbus Circle, New York, New York 10023.

Manufactured in the United States of America

CONTENTS

LIST OF MAPS

INVITATION TO THE READER

In this guide to Alaska, I've selected what I consider to be the best of the many fine establishments that I came across while conducting my research. You, too, in the course of your visit to Alaska, may come across a hotel, restaurant, shop, or attraction that you feel should be included here; or you may find that a place I've selected has since changed for the worse. In either case, let me know of your discovery. Write to me also if you have any other comments on this edition or suggestions for future editions. Address your letter to:

John Gottberg
Frommer's Alaska '94–'95
c/o Prentice Hall Travel
15 Columbus Circle
New York, NY 10023

DISCLAIMERS

(1) I've made every effort to ensure the accuracy of the prices as well as of the other information contained in this guide. Yet I advise you to keep in mind that prices fluctuate over time and that some of the other information herein may also change as a result of the various volatile factors affecting the travel industry.

(2) Neither the author nor the publisher can be held responsible for the experiences of the reader while traveling.

SAFETY ADVISORY

Inhabited Areas While traveling in Alaska, follow the same basic safety precautions as you would anywhere else. Be aware of your immediate surroundings. Wear a moneybelt and keep a close eye on your possessions. *Be especially careful with cameras, purses, and wallets*—all favorite targets of thieves and pickpockets. Although Alaska is relatively safe, you should keep in mind that every society has its criminals (see the section on safety, under "Preparing for Your Trip," in Chapter 3). It's therefore your responsibility to exercise caution at all times, in heavily touristed areas no less than in secluded areas (which you should avoid, particularly after dark).

Remote Areas More specific to Alaska is the importance of safety in the natural environment. Here, too, commonsense precautions should be followed. If you're traveling in a car or bus and come across a bear, moose, or any other wild animal on or near the road, *stay in your vehicle!* A bear can become dangerous when spooked or threatened. If you're camping or hiking in the wild, observe the standard rules of dealing with wildlife. For more safety tips, see "Fast Facts: Safety" in Chapter 2.

CHAPTER 1

GETTING TO KNOW ALASKA

The only way to speak of Alaska is in superlatives. Larger than one-fifth of the continental United States, with more miles of coastline than the other 49 states combined, Alaska is bigger than all but 16 of the world's nations.

Visitors are awed by the sheer enormity of the landscape: Everything seems to be on a grand scale, as if the physical features of America's Lower 48 (contiguous) states are mere miniatures. Not only is Mount McKinley, at 20,320 feet, the highest mountain in North America, but it rises directly from 2,000-foot lowlands to be joined by six other peaks over 14,500 feet. Not only does Alaska contain great glaciers like the Malaspina, itself larger than Rhode Island, but it has some 100,000 glaciers covering over 28,000 square miles, more than 125 times the area covered by glaciers in the rest of the United States combined. Its bears are not just bears, but the biggest bears. And so on.

Superimpose a map of Alaska over one of the contiguous states and you'll begin to get an idea of its scale. If Ketchikan, the southeasternmost town, falls over Charleston, S. C., then Attu Island, the westernmost point of the Aleutians, will be near Yuma, Ariz., and Point Barrow, in the north, will fall somewhere near Bemidji, Minn. The state is about 2,400 miles from east to west, about 1,420 miles from north to south.

The name Alaska derives from the Aleut word *alaxsxag*, meaning "mainland" (a list of other regional terms appears in the appendix, "Glossary of Alaskana"). Early Russian fur traders, however, finding the word difficult to pronounce, called the territory Bolshaya Zemlya, "Great Land."

✪ "Alaska" comes from the Aleut word for "mainland."

The name fits. Some 590,000 square miles in size, but with a population of barely half a million, Alaska spans an awesome diversity of geographical zones and lifestyles. Commercial fishermen's homes cling to the slopes of densely forested southeastern fjords, while Eskimo walrus hunters live in Arctic villages where summers have no nights and winters no days. Solitary gold prospectors pan streams and chip rocks in the shadow of Mount McKinley as young executives in three-piece suits commute to offices in Anchorage high-rises. Descendants of Russian colonists go to onion-domed Russian Orthodox churches in Sitka, Kodiak, and other towns, while U.S. military families in the stark, windswept Aleutians pray for a safe delivery home from their temporary exile.

Although construction of the Trans Alaska Pipeline in the mid-1970s opened up many parts of Alaska that had previously been inaccessible and drew many younger people from the Lower 48 to partake of Alaska's new wealth, the state remains

? DID YOU KNOW . . . ?

- Alaska is by far the largest of the 50 states—more than twice the size of Texas—but ranks 49th in population.
- Alaska has the northernmost, westernmost, and easternmost points in the United States.
- Alaska is only three miles from Russia.
- Alaska has more coastline than the rest of the U.S. combined.
- Barrow, America's northernmost city, has 84 straight summer days during which the sun never sets; in winter, it has 67 straight days when the sun never rises.
- The United States paid 2¢ per acre to buy Alaska from Russia in 1867.
- Mount McKinley, at 20,320 feet, is the highest mountain in North America.
- The Malaspina Glacier is larger in area than Rhode Island.
- Some 90% of all American bald eagles (about 27,000) live in Alaska.
- Alaska has more than 1,400 miles of ferry routes, known as "marine highways."
- Alaska has more planes and pilots per capita than any other state.
- The Iditarod Trail Sled Dog Race from Anchorage to Nome, held every February, is the world's longest and richest dog-sledding event.
- Anchorage is almost equidistant between New York and Tokyo.
- Sitka was once the largest city on the west coast of North America.
- Turnagain Arm, in the Cook Inlet near Anchorage, has a bore tide that can approach 39 feet—the second greatest in North America.

America's "last frontier." Despite its vastness, Alaska has less than 12,000 miles of roads, about one-third unpaved. (By contrast, the country of Austria, 5.5% the size of Alaska, has some 25,000 miles of roads.) Most "bush" settlements—those inaccessible by road—depend on planes and air taxis to connect them with the outside world. Thus Alaska has far more planes and pilots per capita than any other state. Alaska also has more than 1,400 miles of ferry routes, or "marine highways."

Don't stay indoors on your visit to Alaska. The state beseeches you to get out-of-doors and take part in whatever activities you are physically capable of. If you're young in body and spirit, indulge yourself in some river rafting, sea kayaking, or glacier skiing. If you've reached an age when the spirit is willing but the body is not, you can still go in for a fishing expedition, a hot-air balloon trip, or a flightseeing excursion.

Alaska's rich wildlife is best seen by getting away from the highways, either by backpacking into the bush or by arranging to be dropped off (and picked up later) by a small plane or chartered boat. The extensive national park and wildlife refuge system is set up to allow just such opportunities.

The towns and cities themselves have a modicum of attractions, such as museums and historic sites. Each has a character of its own. Sitka and Kodiak, for instance, have a rich Russian heritage; Skagway, Nome, and Fairbanks still ooze with the atmosphere of the gold rushes; frozen, isolated Barrow and rainy, bustling Ketchikan are as different as two towns can be. Part of the pleasure of visiting Alaska is in discovering the tremendous variety that comprises the whole.

By the way, don't expect Alaska to look anything like the place portrayed in the CBS television series "Northern Exposure." That program is filmed entirely in the state of Washington.

1. THE NATURAL ENVIRONMENT

Alaska is a young land. Its oldest rocks date back only about 600 million years. Because of its youth, it is geologically volatile, as its volcanoes and earthquakes attest. It is also the most glacially active landscape in the inhabited world. Add to this the phenomena of permafrost and the aurora borealis (the "northern lights") and you can begin to appreciate the fascination many earth scientists have with Alaska.

Three major mountain ranges cross the state in roughly east-west strips. A coastal range arcs widely around the Gulf of Alaska, forming the Alexander Archipelago in the southeast, Kodiak Island in the southwest, and the St. Elias, Chugach, and Kenai Mountains in between. The massive Alaska Range, capped by Mount McKinley, rises in the middle of the state, continuing east to the Wrangell Mountains and to the southwest as the long, volcanic Aleutian Range. The considerably lower Brooks Range lies to the north of the Arctic Circle, giving way to the broad North Slope which descends gradually to the Beaufort Sea. Between the Brooks and Alaska Ranges, the vast plateau called "The Interior" is drained by North America's third-longest stream, the Yukon River, and its tributaries. Much of the terrain here is muskeg, deep boglike areas favored by wildlife.

The Aleutian Trench, some 25,000 feet deep along the archipelago's southern shore, marks the spot where (according to the current theory of plate tectonics) the Pacific plate is sliding under the North American plate, causing tremendous geologic changes. More than half the state is seismically active: About 10% of the world's earthquakes occur annually in Alaska, most of them in the Aleutian Islands. The Aleutian Range has 47 active volcanoes, the northernmost of which—10,197-foot Mount Redoubt—is visible from Anchorage. As recently as 1990, ash from Mount Redoubt forced cancellation of flights to and from Anchorage International Airport. Mount Augustine, an island only 70 miles from Homer, was very active in 1986.

ICE & SNOW

Because of its northern latitudes, an unusual feature of Alaska's terrain is permafrost, or permanently frozen ground. In the Arctic region, continuous permafrost underlies surface dirt to depths of more than 2,000 feet. Pockets of permafrost exist through the Interior to the southern slopes of the Alaska Range.

The nature of permafrost has created special problems for construction in much of Alaska. Because buildings and highways erected on permafrost can cause it to thaw and the structures to sink, layers of malleable gravel several feet thick are typically used as a foundation. Nevertheless the cracks in the Alaska Highway after spring thaw bear witness to the limited success of this technique. Other innovations, such as Styrofoam slabs, are being tried.

Glaciers are a far less permanent manifestation of the Alaskan climate. Only about 15,000 years ago, in the middle of the last Ice Age, all of Alaska was covered by ice and snow thousands of feet thick. As the cold weather gradually subsided, the ice receded, gouging fjords, lakes, and valleys as it went.

○ Some 15,000 years ago, Alaska was covered by ice and snow thousands of feet deep.

Today less than 5% of Alaska is covered by ice fields or glaciers. The 28,800-square-mile glacial area remaining is still larger than any other area in the world outside Antarctica or the ice cap of Greenland. Two glaciers, the Malaspina and the Bering near Yakutat, are bigger than the state of Rhode Island, and several other of these moving rivers of ice approach them in size.

Glaciers are formed when the intense pressure of snow buildup on an alpine icefield causes underlying layers to compress into an almost plastic glacial ice—extremely hard, but able to flow like viscous water. This ice squeezes out between mountain peaks like toothpaste from a tube. Once started on its way, gravity keeps the glacier tumbling downward, grinding its way downhill at speeds that can reach several miles a day. Its terminus is the point at which the rate of melting equals the rate of accumulation. As these factors change, the glacier can advance or retreat.

The glacier may act like a giant conveyor belt as it moves down its valley, tearing rocks from mountain walls and depositing them at its terminus. These loads of debris, called moraines, tell geologists how far glaciers advanced before receding to current limits.

MILEAGE CHART

Approximate driving distances in miles between cities.

	Anchorage	Circle	Eagle	Fairbanks	Haines	Homer	Prudhoe Bay	Seward	Skagway	Tok	Valdez
Anchorage		520	501	358	775	226	847	126	832	328	304
Circle	520		541	162	815	746	1972	646	872	368	526
Eagle	501	541		379	620	727	868	627	579	173	427
Fairbanks	358	162	379		653	584	489	484	710	206	364
Haines	775	815	620	653		1001	1142	901	359	447	701
Homer	226	746	727	584	1001		1073	173	1058	554	530
Prudhoe Bay	847	1972	868	489	1142	1073		973	1199	695	853
Seward	126	646	627	484	901	173	973		958	454	430
Skagway	832	872	579	710	359	1058	1199	958		504	758
Tok	328	368	173	206	447	554	695	454	504		254
Valdez	304	526	427	364	701	530	853	430	758	254	

200 mi
322 km

Chukchi Sea

RUSSIA

Little
Diomede
Island

Nome

Norton Sound

St. Lawrence
Island

Yukon Delta
National Wildlife
Refuge

St. Matthew Island

Bering Sea

Nunivak
Island

Bethel

Yukon Delta
National Wildlife
Refuge

Attu Island

Pribilof
Islands

Bristol Bay

Cape
St. Stephen

Rat Islands

Alaska Peninsula

Unimak Cold
Island Bay

Dutch
Harbor

Adak

Atka Island

Atka

Fort Glen

Unimak

Adak Island

Unalaska

Aleutian Islands

Pacific Ocean

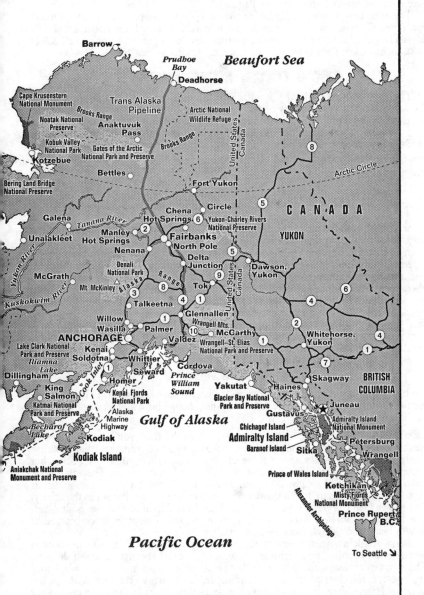

ALASKA

Arctic Ocean

Beaufort Sea

Barrow

Prudhoe Bay

Deadhorse

Cape Krusenstern National Monument

Trans Alaska Pipeline

Brooks Range

Anaktuvuk Pass

Arctic National Wildlife Refuge

Noatak National Preserve

Kobuk Valley National Park

Gates of the Arctic National Park and Preserve

Brooks Range

United States / Canada

8

Kotzebue

Bettles

Fort Yukon

Arctic Circle

Bering Land Bridge National Preserve

Circle

C A N A D A

Galena

Tanana River

Chena Hot Springs

6

Yukon-Charley Rivers National Preserve

5

YUKON

Unalakleet

Manley Hot Springs

2

Fairbanks

North Pole

Yukon River

Nenana

Denali National Park

Delta Junction

5

Dawson, Yukon

McGrath

Mt. McKinley

Alaska Range

9

Tok

United States / Canada

6

Kuskokwim River

3

8

4

1

Talkeetna

Glennallen

Willow

Wrangell Mts.

Dawson, Yukon

Wasilla

Palmer

10

McCarthy

4

ANCHORAGE

Valdez

Wrangell–St. Elias National Park and Preserve

1

Whitehorse, Yukon

4

Lake Clark National Park and Preserve

Kenai

Soldotna

1

Cordova

2

Iliamna Lake

Whittier

Seward

Prince William Sound

7

1

Dillingham

Homer

Kenai Fjords National Park

Yakutat

Skagway

BRITISH COLUMBIA

King Salmon

Glacier Bay National Park and Preserve

Haines

Katmai National Park and Preserve

Alaska Marine Highway

Gulf of Alaska

Gustavus

Juneau

Becharof Lake

Chichagof Island

Admiralty Island National Monument

Kodiak

Admiralty Island

Petersburg

Kodiak Island

Baranof Island

Sitka

Wrangell

Aniakchak National Monument and Preserve

Prince of Wales Island

Ketchikan

Misty Fjords National Monument

Alexander Archipelago

Prince Rupert B.C.

Pacific Ocean

To Seattle ↘

Often a glacier will tumble into the sea, calving huge icebergs into the frigid water with thunderous roars. This is known as a tidewater glacier. Columbia Glacier in Prince William Sound is the best known; LeConte Glacier near Petersburg is the world's southernmost tidewater glacier. Other glaciers end in lakes (like the Portage Glacier at Anchorage or the Mendenhall Glacier at Juneau) or simply end in a valley (like the Matanuska Glacier east of Palmer).

The great compression of glacial ice gives it a deep-blue appearance to the human eye, especially where it has fractured. This remarkable color is intensified on cloudy days. The glacial ice crystals are so dense that they act as prisms, absorbing all colors of sunlight except the blue wavelength, which is reflected back.

LONG DAYS, LONG NIGHTS

The Arctic Circle marks the point at which there is no sunrise on December 21, the winter solstice (shortest day of the year), and no sunset on June 21, the summer solstice (longest day). This gives rise to a unique phenomenon: When the sun rises on May 10 in Barrow, North America's northernmost city, it doesn't set until August 2. There are 84 days of continuous daylight. Yet when the sun sets on November 18, it doesn't rise again until January 24; thus Barrow residents tolerate 67 days of continuous darkness—something a first-time visitor may find disconcerting.

○ **Barrow, North America's northernmost city, has 84 days of continuous daylight.**

All Alaskans get used to long summer days and long winter nights, which are increasingly less so the farther south you go. Fairbanks has nearly 22 hours of daylight on June 21, but fewer than 4 hours on December 21, while days in Anchorage range from 19½ to 5½ hours in length and those in Juneau from 18½ to 6½ hours.

Many Alaskans will tell you that the best thing about long nights is that they give you more opportunity to view the aurora borealis, the "northern lights." This phenomenon is produced by protons and electrons, charged and released by sunspot activity, colliding with gas particles in the earth's upper atmosphere. Some of them are pulled by the planet's magnetic forces into the northern and southern latitudes, where they become visible to the naked eye. The colors and shapes of the magnetic waves vary greatly, from simple arcs of rainbow hues to hemispheric draperies. Viewing is good in the fall but best when the heavens are darkest, between January and March.

WILDLIFE

For many Alaska visitors, the no. 1 reason to visit the state is to see its rich and varied wildlife. Land mammals take first spot on the list, though birds and marine life are not far behind.

LAND MAMMALS No matter where you go in the state, you'll be cautioned to beware of **bears.** Three principal species make their homes in Alaska. Polar bears are rarely troublesome—they spend most of their lives on the Arctic ice pack—but brown and black bears inhabit almost all the state's forested areas. The adult black bear, which typically weighs 200 pounds and stands 4½ feet at the shoulder, is positively puny compared with the dangerous brown bear, also known as the grizzly. The brown bear can weigh over 1,200 pounds and stand eight feet tall on its hind legs. The Kodiak brown bear is the largest carnivore on earth. Unlike the black bear, adult brown bears don't climb trees—but then, they don't need to.

Many Alaskans, hunters or not, insist on carrying a high-caliber rifle or shotgun whenever they venture off a highway. It's legal to shoot a bear anytime in self-defense. The best way to deal with a bear in the wild is simply to avoid it, especially when cubs are involved. If a close encounter is unavoidable, don't surprise the bear. Make plenty of noise: Hikers often tie bells or cans of rocks to their packs. If you face a bear, don't turn your back and run, for that can invite pursuit. Instead, back away slowly.

If you're planning a camping or backpacking trip, be sure to obtain an excellent pamphlet, "The Bears and You," from any office of the U.S. Forest Service or the Alaska Department of Fish and Game. The state has three designated viewing areas for folks fascinated by bears: Pack Creek on Admiralty Island, near Juneau; Anan Creek at Ernest Sound, south of Wrangell; and McNeil River, adjacent to Katmai National Park in southwestern Alaska.

Another animal that can be dangerous when irritated is the **moose.** This largest member of the deer family (up to eight feet at the shoulder) is frequently seen crossing or grazing beside busy highways, especially in winter; every year commuter traffic leaving Anchorage on the Glenn Highway is inevitably backed up once or twice by a traffic accident caused by a moose. They are not the most intelligent of animals, and will stand their ground against a locomotive rather than give up a blade of grass between the rails. Moose appear ungainly, but they can run quickly and kick hard. Avoid approaching them too closely. Moose are found on the Alaskan mainland from Misty Fjords National Monument all the way to the North Slope, especially in birch forests.

Experts have identified at least 13 distinct herds of **caribou** on tundralike grazing lands from the Aleutian Islands to the Kenai Peninsula to the Brooks Range and beyond. They number over 800,000, but they shun civilized areas. Unless you're flying, Denali National Park is the best place to see them. **Reindeer** are caribou that have been domesticated for their milk, meat, and hides.

The **musk ox** was once native to Alaska, but none remained in 1929 when the woolly buffalolike animal was reintroduced to Nunivak Island, in the Bering Sea. It has flourished since, and small herds now roam in several areas of western Alaska, including the Seward Peninsula near Nome. Basically docile animals, musk oxen were easy pickings for guns because of their behavior under attack: They form a circle with their young in the middle and challenge aggressors with their long horns. Some colonies have now been domesticated for their soft underwool, called *qiviut* by Eskimos.

Other large land animals in Alaska include the Dall sheep, found in all major mountain ranges except the southern Aleutian Range; the mountain goat, common in higher elevations south and east of Anchorage; the Sitka black-tailed deer, a denizen of dense rain forests in the Southeast, Prince William Sound, and Kodiak Island; and the American bison, several hundred of which graze near Delta Junction. Alaska also boasts many wolves, elk, wolverines, foxes, and beavers, as well as a great variety of smaller fur-bearing mammals.

MARINE MAMMALS There are few sights more spectacular than a **humpback whale** breaching—leaping high above the water and coming down with an explosive splash. These massive acrobats average 40–50 feet in length, weigh 30 tons or more, and are found in all oceans. But they are an endangered species, their numbers today only about 7% of those of a few hundred years ago. The 850 or so that make their homes in the North Pacific might be spotted anywhere in the Gulf of Alaska, but especially in Prince William Sound or Glacier Bay. Alaskan waters boast nine other species of great whales and five smaller whales, plus porpoises and dolphins.

There are also eight species of **seals,** including the harbor seal so common at the foot of tidewater glaciers and the bearded seal (*oogruk*) whose meat the Eskimos love. The **Steller sea lion** and **Pacific walrus** are commonly found in the Bering and Chukchi Seas, with the sea lion's rapidly dwindling range extending to the Kenai Peninsula and through the Aleutians. The lovable little **sea otters,** whose fur almost caused their demise two centuries ago, have made a comeback, and now are frequent visitors to harbors and commercial fishing enterprises. You'll frequently see them far offshore, dining while floating on their backs.

○ **Alaskan waters boast 10 species of great whales, among them the humpback.**

BIRDS According to the University of Alaska, documented sightings of 405 different species of birds have been made in Alaskan air space. Fewer than half of those make their homes in Alaska year-round; the others migrate, some—like the arctic tern—from as far away as Antarctica.

In terms of sheer numbers, **sea birds** are by far the most common species. Ornithologists estimate that there are more than 40 million here. Who doesn't love the colorful, big-beaked little puffin? Auklets, kittiwakes, murres, cormorants, and dozens of other birds have rookeries (nesting grounds and breeding places) along many of the Gulf of Alaska's rocky shores. The **trumpeter swan**, which has a major nesting colony in the Copper River Delta, has rebounded from endangered status in the past couple of decades and now numbers about 8,000.

And of course there's the **American bald eagle,** of which Alaska has nine times more in residence (an estimated 27,000) than all the other states combined. This magnificent bird, a national symbol of the United States of America, has a length of up to three feet, a wingspan of seven feet, and a life span in the wild of 20–30 years. It mates for life, and returns each year to the same treetop or cliffside to build its nest or reoccupy its old one. National law prohibits killing, injuring, or disturbing a bald eagle in any way.

No less a statesman than Benjamin Franklin, however, offered this honest assessment of the bald eagle, in promoting the wild turkey as our national bird: "He is a bird of low moral character; he does not get his living honestly." Franklin was right in calling the bald eagle a scavenger. But fish, taken "honestly" from streams and rivers, is the main component of its diet. Visitors to the Chilkat River near Haines have counted, in a single fall day, as many as 3,000 eagles—that's about 10% of the species—pursuing huge runs of spawning chum salmon.

Bald eagles don't get "bald"—that is, they don't develop their white head and tail feathers—until they reach an age of four years. Prior to that they're classified as immature and are not yet ready for breeding.

FEDERALLY PROTECTED LANDS

Approximately 40% of Alaskan land is protected under various categories by the federal government. This includes some 77 million acres of national wildlife refuges, 50 million acres of national parks and preserves, and 23 million acres of national forests. Hunting and mining are permitted in national forests, wildlife refuges, and preserves, but not in national parks. Timber harvesting is also allowed in national forests, but not in the other divisions.

✪ About 40% of Alaska consists of federally protected wildlife refuges and national forests, parks, and preserves.

Alaska has 13 **national parks and preserves.** The most famous are Denali National Park, encompassing Mount McKinley, and Glacier Bay, with its great numbers of tidewater glaciers and impressive marine life. The others are Kenai Fjords and Wrangell–St. Elias in south-central Alaska; Yukon-Charley Rivers on the Canadian border in the Interior; Gates of the Arctic, Kobuk Valley, and Noatak in the Brooks Range; Cape Krusenstern and Bering Land Bridge on the Chukchi Sea; and Lake Clark, Katmai, and Aniakchak in the Aleutian Range. In addition, there are two **national historic parks:** Sitka and Klondike Gold Rush. Each has its unique features; each is discussed in the regional chapters following.

Two enormous **national wildlife refuges,** each comprising more than 19 million acres, are included in the state's refuge system: Arctic National Wildlife Refuge and Yukon Delta National Wildlife Refuge. Alaska Maritime National Wildlife Refuge, though not the largest in land area, encompasses more than 2,500 headlands and offshore islands from Ketchikan to Barrow, including most of the Aleutian chain. Alaska's 13 other national wildlife refuges include the Kenai, which covers a large portion of that peninsula, and the Kodiak, which takes in a good two-thirds of that island.

Alaska has only two **national forests,** but they are the two largest in the United States. Tongass National Forest, with its 16.9 million acres, covers the entire panhandle with the exception of Glacier Bay National Park, small areas near the major towns, and a few other anomalies. It also encompasses Misty Fjords and Kootznoowoo (Admiralty Island) National Monuments and 12 additional wilderness areas totaling 5.4 million acres. Chugach National Forest, with 5.9 million acres, includes all of Prince William Sound, the northeastern third of the Kenai Peninsula, and most of Afognak Island near Kodiak Island.

The **Alaska State Parks** also manages about 3 million acres of recreational land in 85 units around the state, half of it accessible by road. The half that isn't is the primitive but beautiful 1.4-million-acre Wood-Tikchik State Park near Bristol Bay. Other major units include Chugach State Park abutting Anchorage, Denali State Park, Kachemak Bay State Park, and Chena River State Recreation Area, each with more than 250,000 acres.

2. HISTORY

Human habitation began in Alaska sometime between 10,000 and 50,000 years ago, when nomadic Asiatic tribes crossed the Bering land bridge in pursuit of game. They spread south and east—first the ancestors of today's Indians, then early Aleuts and Eskimos—gradually establishing homelands where they could eke out a living from the alien land.

The first white man known to have visited Alaska was Vitus Bering, a Dane commissioned in 1725 by Russian Tsar Peter the Great to explore the North Pacific. In 1728 he sighted St. Lawrence Island and sailed through the strait now bearing the Bering name.

In the following three decades visitors to Alaskan waters were almost exclusively Russian fur traders. Other European powers made tentative voyages north from the American west coast—Juan Perez of Spain in 1774, James Cook of England in 1776–78, George Vancouver of England in 1791–94—but it was left for the Russians to found a colony.

RUSSIAN AMERICA

Siberian fur merchant Grigori Shelekhov established the first Russian settlement in North America when he came to Three Saints Bay, Kodiak Island, in 1784 with 192 men and one woman (his wife, Natalie). In 1791 he turned management of the post over to Alexander Baranov (Baranof), a colorful businessman who emerged as the dominant personality of Russian Alaska.

Many stories are told about Baranov's capacity for drink and of his taking a Kenai princess as his mistress. His most important action, historically, was founding Sitka as the capital of Russian America. Concerned about British activity in what he regarded as Russian territory, he took about 1,000 Aleuts and 100 Russians with him to build Redoubt Arkhangelsk Mikhailovsk (Fort St. Michael) in 1799. It was destroyed and its occupants were massacred three years later by hostile Tlingit natives, but in 1804 Baranov—accompanied by a Russian warship—returned to the site,

DATELINE

- **1728** Vitus Bering makes first European visit to Alaska.
- **1778** Capt. James Cook sails into Cook Inlet.
- **1784** Russians establish fur-trading post on Kodiak Island.
- **1804** Sitka founded as capital of Russian America.
- **1824** Boundary set between Russian America and British Canada.
- **1867** U.S. Secretary of State William Seward buys Alaska from Russia for $7.2 million.
- **1879** Naturalist John Muir visits Glacier Bay and southeast Alaska.
- **1880** Gold strike leads to founding of Juneau.
- **1896** Gold discovered in Klondike, beginning first great gold rush.
- **1898** Second major gold rush, in Nome.
- **1902** Gold strike results in founding of Fairbanks.

(continues)

DATELINE

- **1906** Territorial capital moves from Sitka to Juneau.
- **1912** First territorial legislature established.
- **1915** Construction of Alaska Railroad begins; Anchorage is founded as a rail center.
- **1917** Mount McKinley (now Denali) National Park established.
- **1925** Glacier Bay National Park established.
- **1935** Matanuska Colony created by "New Deal" for Depression-stricken farm families.
- **1942** Alaska-Canada Highway built.
- **1943** U.S. troops drive Japanese from Aleutian Islands.
- **1959** Alaska becomes 49th state of the Union.
- **1964** Good Friday earthquake devastates Anchorage and much of south-central Alaska.
- **1968** Huge oil field discovered at Prudhoe Bay.
- **1971** Alaska Native Claims Settlement Act passed.
- **1977** Trans Alaska Pipeline completed.
- **1980** Alaska Lands Act preserves 100 million acres.

(continues)

drove the natives from what today is Baranof Island, and built Novoarkhangelsk (New Arkhangelsk), now Sitka, which grew to become (for a time) the largest city on the west coast of North America.

In Russia, meanwhile, Shelekhov's son-in-law and heir, Nikolai Rezanov, had merged with rival fur merchants and obtained a royal charter granting the new Russian-American Company sole rights in the New World. Baranov was appointed the company's chief manager in America. Under his guidance it became a highly profitable venture. Baranov's interests did not extend far beyond business, although in 1808 he initiated the establishment of a Russian fort (now known as Fort Ross) on the California coast north of San Francisco, which remained in Russian hands until 1841. Baranov retired in 1817, and died of fever in the tropics while aboard a ship headed back to St. Petersburg.

Other Russian-American Company managers who succeeded Baranov were not as competent, nor did they demonstrate the capacity for self-sufficiency so necessary for survival in an isolated colony. Their most critical political action was an 1824 treaty setting the boundary (basically the one used today) between Russian America and British Canada, thus effectively ending Russian expansion in North America.

Less dramatic accomplishments had an equally lasting effect. As more Russian women moved to the colony, an ordered social life evolved, marked by the growth of schools, hospitals, and Orthodox churches. Native warfare and slavery became memories as Aleuts and some Eskimos and Indians were Christianized. Western and interior Alaska were explored and Russian settlements sprang up all over the territory. Coal was discovered on the Kenai Peninsula.

But by the middle of the 19th century the company was struggling financially and falling back on elaborate economic schemes like towing icebergs to San Francisco. The Crimean War and other pressing obligations in Europe convinced the Russian government to dispense with its North American possessions.

SEWARD'S FOLLY

Negotiations to sell Alaska to the United States began in 1859, when Baron Eduard de Stoeckel, Russian ambassador to the United States, was granted the authority by Tsar Alexander II to engineer a transaction. The American Civil War impeded progress on an agreement, but U.S. Secretary of State William H. Seward, acting for an ambivalent President Andrew Johnson, finally signed a treaty on March 30, 1867. Formal transfer took place on October 18 of that year at Sitka after ratification of the treaty by both governments.

The purchase price was $7.2 million, about 2¢ an acre. Seward was an ardent imperialist who envisioned Alaska as the first possession of a Pacific empire; many of his countrymen, believing that any available monies should be channeled into rebuilding the post–Civil War South, felt the price paid was exorbitant for what they imagined to be a frozen wasteland. Indeed, the purchase was labeled "Seward's Folly" by the nation's press.

For the next 30 years the territory languished as it hadn't done since the early years of Russian visitation. Population dropped sharply as the Russians headed home, while only a small number of Americans moved in. The federal government created the Department of Alaska and put the army (and later the navy) in charge. There was some interest in the fur trade and salmon fishing, but with greater investment opportunities in the Lower 48 few Americans risked their capital this far north.

DATELINE

• 1989 Supertanker *Exxon Valdez* runs aground, causing world's greatest oil spill.

Gold was the element that shook Americans out of their Alaskan doldrums. Minor gold rushes hit Sitka and Wrangell in 1872, Juneau in 1880, and the Kenai Peninsula in 1895. The great Treadwell mine boomed outside Juneau, the first oil claims were staked in the Cook Inlet area, several corporate salmon canneries opened, and rough-and-ready frontier towns began to grow to serve the miners and fishermen. But these minibooms were minor compared with what was to follow.

○ **The first white man known to have visited Alaska was a Dane, Vitus Bering, in 1728; shortly afterward the Russians came.**

THE GREAT GOLD RUSHES

Ironically, the gold discovery that really established Alaska's name in the mind of the American public was one that didn't even occur on Alaskan soil. On August 17, 1896, a down-on-his-luck prospector named George Washington Carmack and two Indian companions—known to history as Tagish Charlie and Skookum Jim—found gold on Bonanza Creek, a tributary of the Klondike River near present-day Dawson City in Canada's Yukon Territory. A few months later, when a supply ship laden with gold dust arrived in Seattle, the cry arose: "There's gold in the Klondike!" And by the following summer some 30,000 fortune-hungry gold diggers were en route north.

A few of them did get wealthy. But for the most part, by the time these argonauts arrived in the Klondike they found the best claims long since staked by those prospectors already on the scene. And the people who got rich were the entrepreneurs and confidence men who provided services, scams, and entertainment in towns like Skagway, where most of the gold-seekers disembarked from steamers before heading inland.

Within a year of the start of the gold rush, Skagway, at the foot of the Chilkoot Trail to the Yukon, had become the largest city in Alaska, with a population of nearly 20,000. (Fewer than 1,000 year-round residents live there today.) It was truly the great city of the north. Yet men can indeed be fickle when their minds are set on making a fortune. So when word came from far-off Nome that a new major gold strike had been made in September 1898, it was again "off to the races."

Few of the would-be miners imagined how hard life would be in Nome. Though much more accessible than the Klondike, this windswept Bering Sea port was devoid of trees for houses or fuel, and its harsh climate was alien to agriculture and animals alike. Most of the gold-seekers established temporary homes in tents on the frigid beach—a beach whose sands, it was soon discovered, were almost as rich in gold as the nearby hills being sluiced. With competition for riches so fierce, Nome developed a reputation for lawlessness that exceeded even Skagway's, notwithstanding John Wayne and *North to Alaska* (1960).

○ **The U.S. purchase of Alaska in 1867 was regarded as a "folly"—until gold was discovered.**

Another big gold strike near modern Fairbanks in 1902 helped establish that city, the second-largest in modern Alaska. But the main effects of the gold rushes were more far-reaching. Federal legislation extended the reach of several government agencies, most prominently justice and revenue, to the territory. Surveys and road construction got under way. Accorded a limited degree of self-government, Alaskans incorporated towns and elected their own officials. The territorial capital was moved from Sitka to Juneau in 1906, Alaskans were authorized a congressional delegate in 1906, and the U.S. Congress granted the territory its own legislature in 1912.

By World War I, Alaska's population had stabilized at between 60,000 and 70,000, about half of the inhabitants Natives. More than 80% of the non-Natives were males. Copper surpassed gold as the chief economic base, then was itself supplanted by commercial fishing. Construction of the Alaska Railroad began in 1915 (it was completed in 1923) and resulted in the founding of Anchorage, now a thriving city of a quarter million people. The following year, 1916, the first bill for Alaska statehood was introduced in Congress by Delegate James Wickersham, one of the most famous names in 20th-century Alaskan history. But statehood was still many years away.

WORLD WAR II

The watershed years for Alaska's leap to modernity were those of World War II. Because of its proximity to Japan (Anchorage is almost equidistant between Washington and Tokyo, and the westernmost Aleutian island of Attu is a scant 650 miles from the Kuril Islands, then a Japanese possession), Alaska was regarded as a key link in the American military defense system.

Fort Richardson was established at Anchorage in 1940, and construction began on Elmendorf Air Base in the same year. As tensions grew on opposite sides of the Pacific, additional army and navy bases were built in Sitka, Kodiak, Fairbanks, and Dutch Harbor (Unalaska Island) at the eastern end of the Aleutian chain, while smaller garrisons were established in other locations. With the bombing of Pearl Harbor in December 1941, tens of thousands of troops rushed north. Government workers, meanwhile, required a mere eight months to construct the Alaska-Canada Highway in 1942.

The troop presence didn't stop the Japanese aggressors. In early June 1942, Dutch Harbor was attacked by a good-sized air and naval force intended to paralyze the American fleet while occupational forces landed on Adak, Kiska, and Attu islands farther to the west. Alerted to the Japanese invasion by a vigilant patrol plane, Dutch Harbor repelled the attack with anti-aircraft guns and suffered but minor damage. In the following days the Japanese did succeed in overrunning the Aleut settlement on Attu and a temporary U.S. weather station on Kiska, but the Aleutian campaign was nevertheless a failure. Postwar studies reveal that its primary intention had been to divert American naval forces from the June 4, 1942, battle at Midway Island—a pivotal battle in the Pacific campaign that might have gone the Japanese way had the invaders succeeded in their shelling of Dutch Harbor.

Stung by the Japanese attack, the Americans moved quickly to drive them off Alaskan soil. The confrontation climaxed in May 1943 with 2½ weeks of bitter fighting on Attu, a stark, mountainous island 35 miles long and 15 miles wide. By the time it ended on May 29, of an initial force of some 2,600 Japanese, only 28 survived. Most of those who had not died in the fighting committed suicide rather than be captured. The Americans lost 549 men and suffered an additional 3,280 casualties. In proportion to the number of troops involved, it was the second-costliest battle (Iwo Jima was the costliest) of the Pacific campaign.

The retaking of Kiska was an anticlimax. For 2½ months, until mid-August, American planes and naval vessels bombarded the island almost mercilessly. When a landing force attacked on August 14, it found that the base and its complement of more than 5,000 officers, enlisted men, and civilians had been completely evacuated under the cover of fog over two weeks previously.

With the Aleutians secured, America cut back sharply on its troops in Alaska. From a high of 152,000 in 1943 the numbers were reduced to 60,000 by 1945 and only 19,000 a year later. (Today about 22,000 active-duty military personnel are stationed in Alaska.)

The impact of World War II on Alaska, like the gold rush before it, far outpaced the actual events. Between 1941 and 1945 the federal government pumped more than $1 billion into the state, much of it to develop transportation systems—the railroad, highways, airfields, docks, and breakwaters. Thousands of soldiers and construction workers who came north decided to remain when the war ended: The 1950 census indicated a territorial population of 112,000, a full 50% greater than in 1940. And while federal interest in Alaska waned slightly in the years immediately following the war, defense spending was quickly revived with the outbreak of the Cold War between the United States and the Soviet Union in the late 1940s.

STATEHOOD

As the Pentagon bolstered the Alaskan economy, the residents of the territory were looking toward its rich natural resources to do the same for their personal bank accounts. They saw statehood as a panacea for developing their ailing and seasonal commercial fishing industry, a fledgling timber industry, and a mining industry that had long since outgrown its profitability.

In fact, Alaskan statehood had been discussed in seven separate hearings in Washington and three in Alaska between 1947 and 1956. But partisanship was a stumbling block. Alaska's ambitions were closely intertwined with those of Hawaii: Alaska was envisioned as a Democratic state, Hawaii as a Republican one, and neither political party was anxious to give the other an inch toward control of the U.S. House of Representatives or Senate. The American public, on the other hand, was overwhelmingly in favor of admitting both to the Union.

Dreams finally became reality on June 30, 1958, when the U.S. Senate passed a bill approved by the House the previous August. Alaska became the 49th state of the Union on January 3, 1959, after President Dwight D. Eisenhower signed the proclamation. Democrat William A. Egan was elected Alaska's first state governor.

✪ Alaska became the 49th state of the Union in 1959.

As part of its statehood, Alaska received from the federal government a grant of 103,500,000 acres of public lands. But land alone would not solve the economic, social, and environmental problems that loomed in Alaska's future. Not only were the state's coffers dry, but the Native population was clamoring for compensation for lands taken from them by white settlers and a major confrontation was brewing between environmentalists who would protect natural resources and entrepreneurs who would exploit them for economic gains.

The brightest hopes for an economic boom were tourism, with its considerable potential, and the oil and gas industry. In 1957, in the Cook Inlet near Kenai, a modest oil strike was made and geologists indicated that greater reserves might be found in Alaskan waters.

Nature appeared to be testing Alaska's mettle when, on March 27, 1964, one of the most powerful earthquakes in history struck the state's most populous region. Measuring 8.4 on the Richter scale, the Good Friday tremor wreaked almost unimaginable devastation on Anchorage, Prince William Sound, the Kenai Peninsula, Kodiak Island, and surrounding areas. When the last shock wave had ceased, 131 people had lost their lives and property damage was estimated at between $380 million and $500 million. The force of the quake was estimated at 10 million times that of an atomic bomb. Alaskans' emotions and finances were taxed to the limit, but thanks to the support of industry and the federal government the state rebounded with astonishing speed.

Then came the announcement in early 1968 that the Atlantic Richfield Oil Company (ARCO) had discovered a gigantic oilfield in the Arctic. Suddenly Alaskans were looking at the world through rose-colored glasses.

THE PIPELINE

The turn-of-the-century gold rushes in the Klondike and in Nome were mere footnotes to Alaskan history compared with the impact of the oil discovery at Prudhoe Bay. ARCO's find was verified at approximately 9.6 billion barrels of oil, making it one of the greatest oilfields on earth.

It can be argued that Alaska came of age on September 10, 1969. On that date, possibly the biggest auction in the history of mankind was held in Anchorage as oil companies and consortiums gathered for the sale of leases on some 450,000 acres of North Slope oil lands by the state of Alaska. ARCO, British Petroleum, Colorado Oil and Gas, Sinclair, and Union Oil sought to add to leases they already held, while North Slope newcomers wanted a foothold. In the decade since statehood Alaska had held 22 previous lease sales netting less than $100 million. On this day, after fewer than seven hours of bidding, the state collected a 20% down payment on more than $900 million in lease payments for less than .001% of its landmass.

Almost immediately, talk began of building an 800-mile-long pipeline to transport the oil from the North Slope, where Arctic Ocean ice prevented shipping for all but two months of the year, to the deep-water port of Valdez on the Gulf of Alaska. Eight oil companies set up the Alyeska Pipeline Service Company to construct and maintain the Trans Alaska Pipeline. But suits filed in 1970 by environmental groups, concerned with the potential negative ramifications of a pipeline on the natural environment, and by Native villages, angered that there were no plans to compensate them for use of land through which the pipeline was to pass, prevented the start of construction pending 3½ years of legal and legislative actions. The original plan to build a conventional buried pipeline had to be shelved when it was demonstrated that oil moving at 160°F would have a disastrous effect on the Arctic permafrost. As finally built, more than half of the 48-inch-diameter pipeline is elevated above ground.

Pipeline legislation was signed on November 16, 1973, by President Richard M. Nixon. That winter, huge amounts of equipment and supplies were shuttled to temporary camps north of the Yukon River, and when spring arrived the construction effort got under way.

Over the next three years, 21,600 workers operated out of 31 construction camps along the pipeline route. The working conditions were treacherous, but the men and women who tackled the pipeline were fed and paid like royalty—wages averaged $1,200 a week. They were followed to the north by fast-buck specialists: fly-by-night entrepreneurs, flimflam artists, and prostitutes. Fairbanks became their capital, more than doubling in size from about 15,000 to some 35,000 between 1973 and 1976.

Many pipeline workers made a sizable nest egg, returned to the Lower 48, and invested wisely. Others lost their money as quickly as they made it. All contributed to the boom that saw Alaska's gross product double to $5.8 billion between 1973 and 1975, and its population grow 32.4% between 1970 and 1980.

The Trans Alaska Pipeline was completed in 1977. Oil entered Pump Station No. 1 at Prudhoe Bay on June 20, reached the Marine Terminal at Valdez on July 28, and was headed for Puget Sound aboard a supertanker on August 1. The flow started at somewhat less than capacity but increased, so that today 1.9 million barrels of oil are pumped through the line daily.

○ The Trans Alaska Pipeline pumps 1.9 million barrels of oil a day from Prudhoe Bay to Valdez.

Every resident of Alaska benefited when, in 1980, the state legislature repealed the state income tax, refunded all 1979 taxes, and established a Permanent Fund—wherein one-fourth of all royalty oil and mineral revenues were shared with the state's citizens in annual dividend checks constituting about 30% of the interest earnings. In 1982, with oil revenues decreasing, the legislature called for a constitutional amendment limiting runaway state spending. Since 1988 the rate of return to Alaska residents has been only about 5%, but that still results in dividend checks of about $900 to every man, woman, and child.

An intense national search for oil and gas on the outer continental shelf of Alaska's

North Slope was initiated in 1981 by Secretary of the Interior James Watt. Three separate competitive-bid lease sales on nearly one-third of the 23-million-acre National Petroleum Reserve were held in subsequent years. It is estimated that the original Prudhoe Bay oilfield was half depleted by 1986 and will be completely drained before the end of the current decade.

NATIVE LAND CLAIMS

A side issue of the pipeline boom, but one that has a long-reaching effect on Alaska, was the question of Native land claims. The state's Native peoples—Eskimos, Aleuts, Athabaskans, and Southeast Indians—sought assurance that they, too, would have an equal voice (and assume an equal share of the revenues) in Alaska's development. Through the long years of Alaska's exploitation by Russians and Americans alike, they had never received a kopeck or a penny of compensation.

After years of lobbying, Congress was shaken into action by a federal injunction forbidding the pipeline project to proceed until Native land claims were settled. The complex Alaska Native Claims Settlement Act was passed in 1971. In return for surrendering aboriginal claims to Alaska, the various Native groups were granted legal title to 40 million acres as well as $962.5 million, payable over a number of years. The settlement applied to all U.S. citizens with one-fourth or more Alaska Indian, Eskimo, or Aleut blood, except those for whom the Annette Island reservation had previously been established at Metlakatla.

Thirteen regional corporations were set up to administer the settlement, and each Native became the owner of 100 shares of stock in his or her particular corporation. With this new wealth, Native Alaskans quickly became influential in state politics and business. The corporations invested in hotels, real estate, natural-resource development, commercial fishing, and transportation; while some have done well, others have not.

WATCHDOGGING THE ENVIRONMENT

The early-1970s quarrels between environmentalists and developers over the potential impact of the pipeline on Alaskan wildlife and landforms were typical of the controversies that flare on many battlegrounds. The confrontation hit a peak in the late 1970s when the state of Alaska filed suit in federal court to stop President Jimmy Carter from withdrawing millions of acres of Alaskan land from economic exploitation and making them federally protected lands. The feds won: The Alaska Lands Act of 1980 placed 53 million acres into the national wildlife refuge system, 43 million acres into national parks, 3.3 million acres into national forests, and parts of 25 rivers into the national wild and scenic rivers system.

Offshore waters were also a concern. A 200-mile fishing limit went into effect in 1978, restricting foreign vessels from entering Alaskan waters without permits. The Coast Guard is still kept busy enforcing the law against ambitious Japanese, Korean, Taiwanese, and Russian vessels. A widespread system of state hatcheries was set up to replenish the fishery.

No major controversies have arisen over the development of the Red Dog lead-zinc mine northeast of Kotzebue, potentially a major revenue earner for the state as Alaska looks ahead toward the 21st century.

Environmentalists have reacted with outrage to a federal plan to open the entire 1.5-million-acre coastal plain of the Arctic National Wildlife Refuge to oil development. Conservationists insist that the delicate ecological balance would suffer permanent damage. The U.S. Fish and Wildlife Service added fuel to their fire when it reported in 1988 that environmental damage in the Arctic plain was worse than projected before exploitation. The Fish and Wildlife Service cited significant air and water pollution, as well as loss of large tracts of wildlife habitat. Some 180,000 caribou make their homes in the 18-million-acre refuge.

If some view the Arctic National Wildlife Refuge issue as a disaster waiting to happen, they can point to the well-publicized events of March 1989 as the worst legacy of the oil era. The supertanker *Exxon Valdez* ran aground on a well-marked reef a mile outside the shipping lanes, spilling more than 10 million gallons of crude oil into Prince William Sound. The resulting oil slick, when not immediately contained, spread across 3,000 square miles of coastal waters, sending its tarlike residue along once-pristine shorelines from the Kenai Fjords to Kodiak Island. The total monetary cost, not only for cleanup but in terms of lost income for fishermen and others, is still unknown; the cost to wildlife may never be tallied. Many thousands of seabirds, fish, seals, and sea otters perished as a direct result of the spill.

Today Alaskans rank second lowest in average age but eighth in per capita income of any state's residents in the Union. With oil revenues slumping, the population has leveled off at about half a million, but hopes are high that new oil or natural-gas discoveries will establish a more stable economic-growth pattern.

---

3. PEOPLE & CULTURE

The happenstance of history and climate has left Alaska only half a million independent souls spread over nearly 600,000 square miles. Their traditional isolation has tended to make the Alaskans a very independent, self-sufficient people. Half of them live in and around the only large city, Anchorage.

☼ Alaska has four major Native cultures, representing about 13% of its total population.

There are four major Native cultures: Tlingit and related Indian tribes in the southeast, Athabaskan Indians in the interior, Eskimos in the Arctic and the Bering Sea coast, and Aleuts in the southwest and Aleutian Islands. All told, they number about 64,000, or about 13% of Alaska's total population.

SOUTHEAST INDIANS

Because their homeland is in the more heavily settled Panhandle region, and because their culture is symbolized by the unmistakable totem pole, the Tlingit (pronounced "*Klin*-kit") Indians are the Natives seen most often by Alaska visitors.

About 10,000 Tlingits live along the west coast and islands of the North American continent from Prince William Sound to and beyond Ketchikan. Distantly related to the Athabaskans of the interior, they probably followed the salmon down the rivers from the mountains to the coast many centuries ago. They have much in common with other (mainly Canadian) Northwest Coast Indians like the Haida, of whom about 800 live on southern Prince of Wales Island, and the Tsimshian, whose settlement of 1,000 at Metlakatla on Annette Island is the only Indian reservation on Alaskan soil.

Unlike other Native peoples of Alaska who had to survive in a harsh environment, the Tlingit were blessed with an abundance of food and natural resources. Excellent hunters and trappers, the men hunted deer, bear, ducks, and geese with bow and arrow, and harvested the wealth of the sea. They invented ingenious traps and hooks for snaring salmon, black cod, and herring; harpooned seals and sea lions; and stalked the sea otter for its warm fur, used for clothing. Children gathered berries from the forest undergrowth, dug clams, and gathered crabs from tidal flats. Their affluence enabled the Tlingit to conduct a steady upriver trade with the Athabaskans of the interior.

Thus economically established, the Tlingit developed a complex and sophisticated society. They recognized that their lives were inextricably interwoven with those of the natural world around them, and so evolved a religion based on kinship and communication with all living things. Differences between animate beings were seen as superficial. The clans were named for legendary creatures—Raven, Eagle, and

Bear, for example—who, it was said, could appear in human form as teachers, perhaps, or heroes. Totemic symbols identified these real or imaginary animals. Because Tlingit society was matrilineal, these legends and values were passed from male to male by a maternal uncle. Marriage within the clan was forbidden. Wealth and lines of descent led to a hierarchy within the clan, and it became one of the objectives in social life to maintain the prestige of one's position, and to improve it by obtaining greater wealth or performing heroic deeds. One of the primary vehicles for so doing was the *potlatch*.

The potlatch was many things—a feast, a competition, a celebration of a marriage or a coming-of-age, a vehicle for the performing arts. Most of all it was a confirmation of status, because only a chief or clan leader could throw one. The host invited neighboring leaders of equal or greater wealth; fed, housed, and entertained them for weeks on end; then gave away much of his wealth, thereby climbing in social ranking. His wealth wasn't lost: It was an investment. Protocol demanded that his humbled guests invite him to future potlatches where he would be honored with even more riches than he doled out.

The Tlingit social system led to the development of an elaborate artistic culture to show off status and to portray the origin myths of the various clans. Most famous, of course, were the totem poles, which were carved to honor the dead, to document social events (as with the construction of a community house or holding of a potlatch), and to record history and oral tradition (for instance, to commemorate a military victory). Masks and house posts also gave wood-carvers opportunities to demonstrate their art. Ceremonial garments such as the famed Chilkat blanket (which could take a woman almost a year to weave from mountain-goat wool), spruce-root baskets, and alder bowls were other popular artistic pursuits.

ATHABASKANS

Alaska's "other" Indians, the Athabaskans, make their home in the middle and upper reaches of the vast Yukon River basin. Speakers of this family of languages include the Navajo, Apache, and Hopi, but unlike their cousins in the American Southwest, Alaska's Athabaskans are a people of subarctic scrub woodland.

Traditionally seminomadic hunters and trappers, the Athabaskans followed the caribou, moose, and bear by foot and birchbark canoe in the summer. In winter they settled in small villages, from which they fished and watched their trap lines, traveling by snowshoes or dog sled. Each family kept several well-trained dogs; from this practice the state sport of mushing evolved. With the arrival of the Europeans in the 18th and 19th centuries, the Athabaskans began to frequent trading posts and became exposed to Western culture.

The average winter village had six or fewer houses, each with a cache or storehouse. The *kashim,* or community house, was the center of the village; the settlement's prosperity was judged by the grandeur of the kashim. Here the men did their carving and tool making, and practiced singing and dancing for ceremonial occasions. Young boys slept in the kashim. Extended families were the rule, old people often living with married children. Rules of proper marriage were not as stringent as with the Tlingits.

Men and women wore identical clothing, well designed for the climate: caribou-skin trousers (with moccasins attached) and long-sleeve shirts that draped to below the knees. They also wore heavy caribou-skin gloves or mittens and a hood with a small cape attached. Women did all the tailoring and sewing, often embroidering the garments with porcupine quills and natural or dyed colors. They also made birchbark and spruce-root baskets.

Men were involved in building houses and canoes, and creating their fishing and hunting gear. Those Athabaskans who lived in the northern and western Yukon basin, bordering Eskimo lands, also carved some masks for ceremonial purposes. Festive events, held in the kashim, included the bladder feast (in which animals killed during the year were honored in masked portrayals of hunting scenes), mask and doll ceremonies, and the partner's potlatch.

ESKIMOS

Alaska's Eskimos live on the state's northern and western coasts and islands, penetrating a short distance up the valleys of major rivers like the Kuskokwim, Yukon, Kobuk, and Noatak, and as far into the Gulf of Alaska as Kodiak Island. Their population is estimated at 34,000. Members of the Eskimo race, which extends from Siberia across northern Canada to Greenland, speak numerous dialects, but in Alaska there are only two—Inupiat in the Arctic and Yupik around the Bering Sea.

Hunters on land and sea, the Eskimo traditionally derive the materials for their tools and clothing from the same animals that provide their main sources of food. They are sometimes able to supplement their diet of fish, *muktuk* (whale blubber), seal meat, walrus, polar bear, caribou, and ptarmigan with seasonal roots, bulbs, and berries.

It's a popular misconception that Alaskan Eskimos live in dome-shaped ice-block shelters called igloos. Those were strictly used as emergency bivouac shelters by the Canadian Inuit. In fact, dwellings were mainly built partially underground and covered with sod. The extended family is the primary social unit, although polyandry was common in traditional society. Rules of hospitality and alliance building called for a host to offer his wife to an unrelated visitor, with the understanding that the favor would be reciprocated. There were no chiefs or headmen, but public ridicule and fear of blood feuds helped to enforce community solidarity.

Whaling has always been an important component of the economy, and remains so in many Eskimo communities today. The popular "Eskimo blanket toss" game originated as a means of lofting a member of the tribe as high as possible above the flat terrain to look seaward to spot whales. When one of the marine behemoths was seen, open sealskin boats called *umiaks,* outfitted with paddles, bailers, and harpoons, were launched from the shore or across the icepack. It required great knowledge and skill to harpoon a whale and tow it back to shore, where the entire community participated in the job of butchering the beast.

The midsummer salute to the now highly restricted whale harvest is still the biggest event of the year in Arctic Eskimo settlements. Other elaborate ceremonies stress the Eskimo link to the supernatural. Chief among them are the bladder feast and feasts for the dead. Neighboring villages may join together for these occasions.

Masks, more common along the Bering coast than in the Arctic, are the most memorable manifestation of Eskimo art. The spread of Christianity in the 19th and early 20th centuries curtailed the staging of many traditional religious festivals and thus the use of masks, but the recent growth of tourism has revived the art of mask making.

The Eskimo apply great artistry to everything they make, from wooden kettles to finely carved ivory bow-drill handles. The women specialize in sewing and weaving everything from watertight seal-gut parkas, to walrus covers for kayaks and umiaks, to a high grade of coiled beach-grass basketry decorated with bright floral or geometric patterns.

ALEUTS

When the Russians arrived in the mid-18th century, some 20,000 Aleuts inhabited the lower Alaska Peninsula and most of the 70 islands in the 1,100-mile-long Aleutian archipelago. Unalaska Island alone had 24 Aleut villages. Fewer than 100 years later intermarriage had so reduced the number of full-blooded Aleuts that only 15 islands were inhabited, the number of villages on Unalaska had fallen to 10, and most Aleuts had adopted a European lifestyle. Today about 8,000 Natives have at least one-fourth Aleut blood; perhaps 1,300 are full-blooded. Two of the few surviving settlements are on the Pribilof Islands, where the Aleuts are under government contract to handle seal herds.

Aleut villages were typically situated on the shore near river mouths, where spawning salmon were caught seasonally. The original dwellings were large communal homes for as many as 40 interrelated families. The role of the chief was hereditary, indicating prestige rather than formal authority. Occasionally one chief might have nominal power over several villages on one island. After the arrival of the Russians, the Aleut adapted to smaller family houses called *barabara*.

The traditional Aleut lifestyle resembled that of their Eskimo cousins in many ways, with even more dependence on the sea for survival. Sea otter and seal skins served as their clothing; these and other mammals, plus fish, shellfish, and sea birds, were their sources of food. Vegetable food was sparse, although seasonal blueberries and the bulbs of the Kamchatka lily were harvested.

Clothing was typically made of seal intestines sewn with sinew, making a watertight seam. The women's finest craftsmanship was expressed in their baskets, mainly woven from a rye beach grass. The grass was collected and dried; the stems were trimmed into proper thickness by splitting with a fingernail, which the basket maker grew to a utile length. The baskets were often decorated with yarn and thread obtained in trade.

The art of Aleut males, such as the creation of stone knife blades by pecking and polishing, has not changed since the Stone Age.

The Aleut traveled between islands in one- and two-person skin boats called *bidarka* (kayaks) and large, open boats called *bidar* (umiaks).

WHITES

Alaska's white population is nearly as diverse as its indigenous population, albeit without the ancient heritage in this land. The descendants of early 19th-century Russian colonists, most of them of mixed Native blood, still worship at Orthodox churches; they can be found especially around Sitka, Kodiak Island, and the Kenai Peninsula.

"Sourdoughs," many of whose grandfathers came to Alaska during the late 19th-century gold rushes, often shun the larger cities and make their lives in the bush; their name derives from the yeasty mix that early prospectors carried to make bread and hotcakes. More recent immigrants, the largest group of whom arrived during the Trans Alaska Pipeline construction in the 1970s, have made the Alaska population the second youngest in the Union (average age: 27½) and the most affluent (average per capita income: $19,079).

If you've never spent a full winter in Alaska, by the way—if you've never hung on until "breakup," when the ice thaws on the rivers—you're a *cheechako*. If you make it, you can truly claim to be an Alaskan. If you don't, you're still an Outsider, as Alaskans call anyone from "Down South"—the Lower 48 contiguous states and Hawaii.

4. SPORTS & RECREATION

Many outdoor-oriented visitors think of fishing and hunting as being synonymous with Alaska—usually in that order.

Even if an Alaska visitor learns nothing else about fishing during his stay, a basic knowledge of different types of salmon and commercial fishing vessels will probably seep in through osmosis. This is household language in Alaska. It's just assumed that you know.

◆ **Many outdoor-oriented visitors think of fishing and hunting as being synonymous with Alaska.**

Quickly, there are five species of **salmon** in Pacific waters: chinook, sockeye, coho, humpback, and dog. To complicate matters, chinook is commonly known as king salmon, sockeye as red salmon, coho as silver salmon, humpback as pink salmon (or "humpy"), and dog as chum. The king is the largest—it must be 50 pounds to be considered "trophy class." A trophy-class silver weighs 20 pounds; chum, 15 pounds; red, 12 pounds; and pink, 9 pounds.

Three different kinds of commercial boats go after the salmon. Don't make the mistake of pointing at a purse seiner or gill-netter and calling it a troller; you'll get merely headshakes and chuckles from the locals. Purse seiners are the largest boats in the fishing fleet, running to 58 feet. The six-member crew sets a large net in a circle, tightens it with a drawstring, and hauls the works aboard, sharks and seaweed along with salmon. Only the salmon are kept; because of the indiscriminate manner in which they are caught, they are invariably canned. You can recognize a purse seiner by the boom and circular power winch that hoist the net. Gill-netters unwind their net from a spool-like reel, usually mounted on the stern of the vessel. Weights and floats drop it like a curtain in front of swimming salmon. The net's mesh is designed so that medium-sized fish are snared by their gills, while smaller fish swim through the mesh and larger ones glance off it and go around. Trollers trail baited hooks through the water from several long poles extended on both sides of the vessel. Chinook and coho salmon taken by trolling command the highest market prices; they are killed, cleaned, and placed on ice immediately after they are caught, and thus kept fresh all the way to the restaurant.

After salmon, Alaska's most popular saltwater sport fish is the **halibut,** a large, flat bottomfish that can weigh 300 pounds or more. They more typically run 20–50 pounds. Alaskan **freshwater favorites** are rainbow trout, lake trout, cutthroat, Dolly Varden, arctic char, whitefish, grayling, burbot, sheefish, and northern pike.

You have to have an Alaskan **sport-fishing license** to dip a line anywhere. Charter-boat operators usually include a $15 three-day nonresident sport-fishing license in their fee; otherwise, most sporting-goods stores are licensed as agents for the Alaska Department of Fish and Game. A 14-day nonresident license costs $30, and an annual license runs $50. Additionally, if you're a nonresident trying to hook a king salmon, you must buy a $20 stamp . . . or release the fish you've caught.

A nonresident **hunting license** will set you back $85. On top of that, you must buy a big-game locking tag (ranging in cost from $150 for Sitka black-tailed deer to $1,100 for musk oxen) for each animal you plan to take, and when hunting bear or sheep you are required to have a guide or be accompanied by a close relative Alaska resident over 19 years old. For more information on licensing regulations, contact the **Alaska Department of Fish and Game,** Division of Licensing, P.O. Box 2-5525, Juneau, AK 99802 (tel. 907/465-2376). For a complete list of registered guides and outfitters in the state, send $5 to the Alaska Department of Commerce and Economic Development, Division of Occupational Licensing, Box DLIC, Juneau, AK 99811. There are a great many special rules governing both fishing and hunting, especially the latter; obtain a current copy of "Alaska Game Regulations" from any office of the Alaska Board of Game or Alaska Department of Fish and Game.

Strict laws prohibit the taking of marine and Arctic mammals—including whales, walruses, seals, sea otters, and polar bears—by anyone but Native Alaskans traditionally dependent on them for subsistence. The restriction extends to the possession of walrus-tusk ivory, whale baleen, and sea-otter fur, until it has been crafted for sale as an authentic Native handcraft or article of clothing.

An enormous number of fishing and hunting lodges throughout the Alaskan bush entice outdoorsmen (and women) to challenge salmon with a rod or bear with a shotgun. The most popular fishing lodges are in the southwest around Bristol Bay, though those of southeast Alaska's "panhandle" are not far behind. The **Alaska Sportfishing Lodge Association,** 500 Wall St., Suite 422, Seattle, WA 98121 (tel. 206/622-3932, or toll free 800/352-2003), and **Alaska Sportfishing Packages, Inc.,** 15375 S.E. 30th Place, Suite 350, Bellevue, WA 98007 (tel. 206/644-2301, or toll free 800/426-0603), are reputable marketing agencies. Including airfare from Anchorage, you can expect to pay anywhere from $1,500 to $4,000 for a week's fishing at one of these all-inclusive lodges. Most are open only from May to September.

Alaska has more than 600 businesses catering to the adventure-travel industry, including some 250 outfitters, guides, air taxis, and boating operators registered to work in national parks and preserves. The Alaska Tourism Marketing Council's annual **"Vacation Planner"** (for a copy, write to P.O. Box 110801, Juneau, AK 99811; tel. 907/465-2010) and the current monthly issue of *Alaska* magazine (for a copy, write to 808 E St., Anchorage, AK 99501; tel. 907/272-6070) are two good places to look for the lodge or outfitter best for you. A small percentage of them are flimflam operations, so whenever possible talk to someone who has previously stayed at them.

Aside from fishing and hunting, outdoors lovers from around the world escape to the Alaskan wilderness by foot, horseback, and raft. **Backpacking** in national parks like Denali, Wrangell–St. Elias, and Gates of the Arctic is especially popular. **River rafting** is especially popular on rivers like the Chitina, the Kenai, and the Nenana. A growing number of adventure-travel companies offer organized trips. *But remember:* Whenever you venture off the main roads, you must be totally self-sufficient, and prepared for all contingencies—including bears. Heed the warning given earlier in this chapter.

Dog mushing is Alaska's state sport. If you plan to be in Alaska during the winter, it's something you can build a trip around—especially if you couple Anchorage's annual Fur Rendezvous winter festival, which incorporates the world-championship sled-dog races, with the great 1,000-mile Iditarod Trail Sled Dog Race from Anchorage to Nome less than a month later. Even summertime visitors can savor some of the flavor of mushing by watching dry-land exhibitions (with wheels on sled runners) in Fairbanks, Nome, Tok, and other locations.

For **skiing,** there are endless options for cross-country enthusiasts, limited opportunities for downhillers. Mount Alyeska, at Girdwood near Anchorage, was once a leading contender to host the Winter Olympic Games. There are other smaller areas near Anchorage, though the state's second leading ski resort is probably Eaglecrest, on Douglas Island outside Juneau. On the other hand, nordic skiers have virtually endless terrain throughout the Anchorage and Fairbanks areas. In many instances, however, they must keep alert for those out **snowmobiling.**

5. FOOD & DRINK

Gastronomically, Alaska isn't the most exciting state. For the most part the cuisine is rather ordinary and bland, unless you're a seafood lover. Then you might find yourself in seventh heaven.

۞ For the seafood lover, Alaska is seventh heaven. Probably nowhere on earth will you find better salmon or halibut, tiny Petersburg shrimp, king or tanner crab than are pulled from Alaskan waters. If you're a gourmet, you may learn the subtle taste differences between the five varieties of Alaskan salmon (many sourdoughs swear by the coho, or silver). You may also learn to love such freshwater fish as arctic char, grayling, and whitefish. Try it pan-fried, oven-baked, or alder-smoked—the way the Natives do it.

With its large Native population, of course, Alaska has a wide variety of unusual foods—though few of them ever make it onto a restaurant menu. You may occasionally find some wild game (like caribou steak) in a continental restaurant, and you'll assuredly encounter reindeer sausage on breakfast menus. But nowhere, with the possible exception of Barrow, Kotzebue, and other Eskimo towns, are you likely to see *muktuk* (whale blubber) on the menu, or *oogruk* (bearded seal meat), or even *akutak* (Eskimo ice cream, made with seal oil and snow). And you'd have to know the right places to go in Kake or Angoon to find gumboots or Chinese slippers, two varieties of chiton (a shellfish) favored by Indians of the southeast.

If the food fails to be unusual, the prices and the quantities usually are. The prices are often markedly higher than what you pay in the Lower 48, and the quantities will ordinarily be larger than what you expect in a restaurant. Blame the former on shipping costs, and credit the latter to a frontier appetite.

Eating three square meals a day—a full breakfast, lunch, and dinner—can easily cost $40 per person, even without venturing well into the bush or eating in hotel penthouses. Figure $9 for a breakfast omelet and coffee, $11 for soup, sandwich, and soft drink at lunchtime, $20 for a three-course dinner, perhaps with a single glass of wine. I try to cut costs by doing my breakfast shopping at a late-night grocery and eating my main meal of the day at lunch. Even with that, I still have to plan on $25 a day for meals.

If you're a member of a fraternal organization, such as the Eagles, Elks, or Moose, you'll find these private clubs a great place at which to get an excellent meal at reasonable cost. In many smaller towns the club becomes "the only game in town" when it comes to dining in style. Out-of-town members are welcomed with open arms; nonmembers must find a local member to sponsor them.

The drinking age in Alaska is 21. State law allows bars, restaurants, liquor stores, and other licensed establishments to operate from 8am to 5am seven days a week. Anchorage, Juneau, and many other towns have passed local ordinances reducing the hours, usually to 2am; Fairbanks is among those cities clinging to 5am closing hours.

If you're a beer drinker, be sure to try the state's own Alaskan Beer, brewed in Juneau. Alaskan Amber has twice been voted the most popular beer at the annual Great American Beer Festival in Colorado. A pale ale ("a northern light") is also manufactured.

In many bush communities, mainly because of the social misery alcohol has imposed on Alaska Natives, the sale and importation of alcoholic beverages has been banned. Barrow, Bethel, and Kotzebue have banned the sale of liquor, but allow its discreet importation.

6. PERFORMING ARTS & EVENING ENTERTAINMENT

You're not going to Alaska for its nightlife. The bawdy days of the gold rushes and the pipeline construction are now mere memories, and while most towns have their bars and every city has its dance bands, they're hardly worth a trip in themselves. Many of the performers in hotels and small clubs are musicians from the West Coast who find competition in the Lower 48 so stiff that they're forced to book a series of gigs through Alaska.

There is one true Alaskan musician: the bush balladeer. You'll occasionally find this sourdough folk singer in small clubs in out-of-the-way locations, and occasionally in bigger towns like Anchorage, Fairbanks, and Homer. Accompanied just by a guitar and a sharp wit, he is worth seeking out.

Anchorage is a city with a growing reputation for the arts. Its beautiful new Performing Arts Center stands as testimony, and its symphony and theater are highly regarded. Sitka has an acclaimed Summer Music Festival, which draws many of the world's leading classical instrumentalists, and Juneau has some fine dramatic troupes.

7. RECOMMENDED BOOKS

For general reading on modern Alaska, two of the more enjoyable books of the postpipeline era are *Going to Extremes* by Joe McGinniss (Signet, 1980) and *Coming into the Country* by John McPhee (Bantam, 1976). James Michener's epic *Alaska* (Random House, 1988) starts "about a billion years ago" and continues to modern times.

Alaska Northwest Books, 22026 20th Ave. SE, Bothell, WA 98021, publishes more books on Alaska—over 100 are in print—than any other publishing house. Among them is *The Milepost,* an annual 640-page, softcover compendium that is almost requisite if you're driving to Alaska: The book covers all highways in Alaska and Canada's Yukon Territory, plus the Alaska Highway and major access routes through British Columbia and Alberta, in mile-by-mile detail. It's best used in concert with this volume.

CHAPTER 2

PLANNING A TRIP TO ALASKA

How well you prepare for your trip will determine how smoothly it will go. A journey to Alaska, with its vast expanses of land and northerly climate, will present some problems that you probably haven't encountered on trips elsewhere. To begin with, you must contend with large distances between towns and cities, made more difficult because of the many miles of unpaved roads and the lack of a comprehensive transportation system; often you'll find that the best way of getting around—indeed, the *only* way—is by air. You must also cope with the environment, which (depending upon where you travel) can be quite forbidding during the winter months, with below-zero temperatures, heavy rainfalls or snowfalls, and/or gale-force winds. Knowing what to expect—and, perhaps as important, what *not* to expect—will enable you avoid some of the concerns that a first-time visitor to Alaska may have.

This chapter is designed to help you plan your trip with that end in view. It offers information on when to go and how to get there, as well as on how to get around once you're there. It also contains suggestions for itineraries, depending upon how many days you plan to be in Alaska and what regions of the state you intend to visit. In a step-by-step fashion, the chapter seeks to answer all the basic questions you may have as you prepare for your trip—from what clothes you should take with you, to what prices you can expect to pay, to how best to react when you suddenly come across a bear.

1. INFORMATION & MONEY

INFORMATION   There's a good variety of material available on the state of Alaska. The single best source of information (other than this book) is the **Alaska Tourism Marketing Council,** P.O. Box 110801, Dept. 901, Juneau, AK 99811 (tel. 907/465-2010). Write or give them a call and request their annual "Vacation Planner." It's free. You should also get in touch with local **visitors and convention bureaus,** mentioned in subsequent chapters of this book, for information on specific destinations.

WHAT THINGS COST IN JUNEAU*   U.S. $

Taxi from the airport to the city center	14.00
Local telephone call	.25
Double room at the Westmark Juneau (deluxe)	144.00
Double room at the Prospector Hotel (moderate)	89.00
Double room at the Alaskan Hotel (budget)	61.00
Lunch for one at the Fiddlehead (moderate)	14.00
Lunch for one at Armadillo Tex-Mex Café (budget)	7.00
Dinner for one, without wine, at the Silverbow Inn (deluxe)	30.00
Dinner for one, without wine, at the Cook House (moderate)	20.00
Dinner for one, without wine, at the City Café (budget)	10.00
Pint of beer	3.00
Coca-Cola	1.00
Cup of coffee	1.00
Gallon of gasoline	1.59
Admission to the Alaska State Museum	2.00
Movie ticket	6.00
Theater ticket (to the *Lady Lou Revue*)	14.00

*Hotel prices are peak-season (summer) rates; off-season rates are significantly lower.

WHAT THINGS COST IN ANCHORAGE*   U.S. $

Taxi from the airport to the city center	12.00
Local telephone call	.25
Double room at the Regal Alaskan Hotel (deluxe)	215.00
Double room at the Uptown (moderate)	100.00
Double room at the Midtown Lodge (budget)	40.00
Lunch for one at Simon and Seafort's (moderate)	15.00
Lunch for one at the Tundra Club (budget)	6.00
Dinner for one, without wine, at the Marx Bros. Café (deluxe)	35.00
Dinner for one, without wine, at Harry's (moderate)	20.00
Dinner for one, without wine, at Gwennie's Old Alaska Restaurant (budget)	12.00
Pint of beer	2.50
Coca-Cola	1.00
Cup of coffee	1.00
Gallon of gasoline	.97
Admission to the Alaska Zoo	3.50
Movie ticket	6.50
Theater ticket (to the Alaska Center for the Performing Arts)	20.00

*Hotel prices are peak-season (summer) rates; off-season rates are significantly lower.

MONEY As you already suspected, travel to and within Alaska is not cheap. If Frommer's decided to publish a $-a-Day guide to Alaska, we might get away with $60–$75 a day—and that's per person, if two people are traveling together, staying in budget-priced accommodations, and not traveling during the peak July–August season. If you're driving your own self-contained recreational vehicle or setting up a tent every night or staying in youth hostels whenever possible, you've greatly reduced the expense of accommodation, but you have the added expense of gasoline and vehicle maintenance. Package-tour operators can offer tempting options price-wise, so long as you don't mind having your freedom of movement somewhat abridged.

As an independent traveler planning a trip to Alaska and demanding moderate comfort, I wouldn't take less than $75 per day per person, not including my round-trip transportation expenses. Thus a couple planning a three-week Alaska vacation should figure on spending no less than $3,000 over and above the cost of getting there. It's worth it, believe me!

Now, $3,000 is an awfully large sum to be carrying as cash. And out-of-state checks are hard to cash in Alaska. I suggest purchasing traveler's checks—any kind will do—from your bank or other agent before you leave home. Remember, too, that since Alaska is the 49th state, there's no exchange rate to worry about when you use a credit card. MasterCard, VISA, and American Express are almost universally accepted in larger towns. Many off-the-beaten-track villages take only cash.

2. WHEN TO GO — CLIMATE & EVENTS

To a certain extent, the best time to visit Alaska is affected by where you plan to go and what you want to do there.

Alaska regards the visitor season as beginning on Memorial Day weekend and ending on Labor Day weekend; that's when the cruise ships and tour buses flood the state with package tourists from the Lower 48. In many instances that's the only time visitor attractions are open—as with the wildlife tours at Mount McKinley, the riverboat cruises in Fairbanks, the Russian dancers of Sitka, and almost everything in the gold rush–era city of Skagway. If you're traveling in Alaska at this time you'll have the warmest weather and the most receptive greeting committees. But you may be out of luck in finding a place to stay unless you've booked months in advance, and you'll be sharing the roads with thousands of others. July and August are the most heavily traveled months. May and June, on the other hand, are the driest months (on average) throughout the state, and temperatures are nearly as warm as later in the summer. They also offer the bonus of having less of the plague of giant mosquitoes that traditionally celebrate the Fourth of July by feasting on visitors.

Of course, Alaska's natural attractions don't go anywhere during the "off-season" for tourism. Some of them become less accessible when tourist concessions close for the season, but major roads are kept open year-round. And those hardy folks who don't mind short days or snow find plenty of places to go to in Alaska in the winter. Except in Fairbanks and other, more northerly climes, where midwinter temperatures often fall to 30° or 40° below zero Fahrenheit, the climate is a good deal warmer in Alaska than in Chicago or Minneapolis at that time of year.

CLIMATE

Alaska's image as a snow-covered wasteland is a long way from being true. In a landmass that would stretch from Lisbon to Stockholm to Istanbul if superimposed on a map of Europe, the climatic range varies from temperate rain forest to continental to arctic desert.

Most weather fronts move off the warm Japan Current, which flows through the

Alaska's Average Monthly Temperatures and Precipitation

		Jan	Feb	Mar	Apr	May	June	July	Aug	Sept	Oct	Nov	Dec
Anchorage	Temp. (°F)	15	19	25	35	47	54	58	56	48	35	22	15
	Precip. "	.8	.9	.7	.6	.6	1.0	2.0	2.3	2.5	1.9	1.1	1.1
Barrow	Temp. (°F)	−14	−19	−15	−2	19	34	38	39	31	15	−1	−12
	Precip. "	.2	.2	.2	.2	.2	.4	.9	1.0	.6	.5	.3	.2
Bethel	Temp. (°F)	7	7	12	25	40	52	55	53	45	31	17	7
	Precip. "	.8	.7	.8	.7	.8	1.3	2.2	3.6	2.6	1.5	1.0	1.0
Fairbanks	Temp. (°F)	−10	−4	10	30	48	60	62	56	45	25	4	−8
	Precip. "	.6	.4	.4	.3	.6	1.3	1.8	1.8	1.0	.8	.7	.7
Homer	Temp. (°F)	23	25	28	35	43	49	53	53	47	38	29	23
	Precip. "	2.2	1.8	1.6	1.3	1.1	1.0	1.6	2.6	3.0	3.4	2.7	2.7
Juneau	Temp. (°F)	23	28	32	39	47	53	56	55	49	42	33	27
	Precip. "	4.0	3.7	3.2	2.8	3.5	3.0	4.1	5.1	6.3	7.6	5.1	4.5
Ketchikan	Temp. (°F)	34	36	39	43	49	55	58	59	54	47	40	36
	Precip. "	14.0	12.4	12.2	11.9	9.1	7.4	7.8	10.6	13.6	22.6	17.9	15.8
Kodiak	Temp. (°F)	32	31	34	38	44	50	55	55	50	41	35	32
	Precip. "	9.5	5.7	5.2	4.5	6.7	5.7	3.8	4.0	7.2	7.9	6.9	7.4
Nome	Temp. (°F)	7	4	8	17	36	46	51	50	42	28	17	6
	Precip. "	.9	.6	.6	.7	.6	1.1	2.2	3.2	2.6	1.4	1.0	.8
Petersburg	Temp. (°F)	28	31	35	40	47	53	56	55	50	44	36	31
	Precip. "	9.3	7.9	7.2	6.9	5.9	5.0	5.4	7.6	11.2	16.8	12.0	10.7
Valdez	Temp. (°F)	23	24	30	37	45	52	55	54	47	38	29	23
	Precip. "	5.6	5.1	4.1	2.9	2.7	2.6	3.8	5.7	8.0	8.2	6.1	6.7

Gulf of Alaska. So the rainiest precincts of the state are those around the edge of the gulf. Most of southeastern Alaska and Prince William Sound are bathed in rainfall measuring 100–200 inches a year; Montague Island, at the southern entrance to the sound, recorded a North American record of 332 inches in 1976. Snowfall in this region also tends to be high—24 feet in one month and 81 feet in a winter at Thompson Pass, near Valdez—but temperatures are mild, with average summer temperatures in the 50s and average winter temperatures in the 20s. High winds (100 m.p.h. and more) whip the Aleutians with regularity, and other coastal areas frequently in fall and winter, causing waves of up to 50 feet in the Gulf of Alaska.

Anchorage, protected from most of the storms by the coastal mountains, lies in what is called the Transitional Zone. Much of the Kenai Peninsula and the Bering Sea coast also lie within this climatic belt. Precipitation averages about 15 inches a year, scattered through all months but highest in late summer. The mean daily temperature in Anchorage is 58°F in July, 13°F in January.

Interior Alaska, entirely cut off from the effect of sea breezes and at the mercy of continental weather fronts, experiences great extremes of temperature. Fort Yukon, just north of the Arctic Circle, has recorded Alaska's all-time high of 100°F, and its low of −78°F is just two degrees from the lowest ever recorded in the state. Fairbanks, the largest city in the Interior, has average July highs of 62°F but suffers through three winter months in which the average daily temperature is around −12°F. Most of the 10 inches of annual precipitation fall as summer rain.

The North Slope comprises the Arctic zone, a region marked by six months of subzero temperatures and midsummer highs that often don't exceed 40°F. Precipitation, however, is nearly as rare as a warm day. Barrow averages less than five inches of precipitation a year, though the few inches of snow that do fall stay on the ground for months.

Visitors seeking to tour the state during the time of least precipitation and warmest weather would do well to plan their trip in late May and early June. By July—in Anchorage and Fairbanks as well as Juneau—rainfall is almost double what it was a month earlier, and August is rainier still.

ALASKA
CALENDAR OF EVENTS

JANUARY

☐ **Russian Orthodox Christmas and Starring Ceremony,** Kodiak and Sitka. January 7.

☐ **Polar Bear Jump-Off,** Seward. Cold, wet high jinx in Resurrection Bay. Third weekend in January.

FEBRUARY

☐ **Tent City Days,** Wrangell. Heritage celebration, including Shady Lady Ball. First weekend in February.

☐ **Winter Carnival,** Homer. Miss Homer Pageant, parade, sporting events, exhibits. First weekend in February.

☐ **Ice Worm Festival,** Cordova. Boat and street parades, carnivals, exhibits. First full weekend in February.

○ *FUR RENDEZVOUS Anchorage's annual winter carnival, known locally as "Rondy," includes 140 different events, from snow sculpture to snowshoe softball, dog weight-pulling to hot-air ballooning, auto rallies to an Eskimo blanket toss. It kicks off with the Miners and Trappers Ball (a gigantic masquerade party) and climaxes with the Rondy Parade through downtown.*

Where: Anchorage. When: The 10 days beginning the second Friday of February. How: Make advance hotel reservations. Most events are free, but tickets are required for the Miners and Trappers Ball (limited to 4,000) and some other events. For information, contact the Anchorage Fur Rendezvous office, 327 Eagle St., Anchorage, AK 99501 (tel. 907/277-8615).

MARCH

- ☐ **Iditarod Days,** Wasilla. Costume ball, ice golf tournament. First weekend in March.
- ☐ **Month of Iditarod,** Nome. Sports events, exhibits, awards banquet for Iditarod mushers. First two to three weeks of March.

✪ *IDITAROD TRAIL SLED DOG RACE "The Last Great Race," as it is sometimes called, is the world's longest sled-dog race (officially 1,049 miles), and the richest (the jackpot is about $300,000, some $50,000 of which goes to the winner). Between 60 and 80 men and women, and more than 1,000 dogs, compete annually.*
*   **Where:** Anchorage to Nome, via McGrath and Unalakleet. **When:** Begins the first Saturday in March, and ends 11–14 days later, depending on the weather. **How:** In Anchorage, reserve your hotel room early, then join the crowd to watch the official start on Fifth Avenue. In Nome, book a room many months ahead, and call to reconfirm before you go. For information on the race itself, contact the Iditarod Trail Committee, Pouch X, Wasilla, AK 99687 (tel. 907/376-5155).*

- ☐ **Ice Festival,** Fairbanks. Parade, ice sculptures, sled-dog races, dances. Second through third full weekend of March.
- ☐ **Winterfest Winter Festival,** Skagway. Greets spring with chainsaw throwing, ore-truck pulling, other events. Mid-March.

APRIL

- ☐ **Alaska Folk Festival,** Juneau. Musical performances. First full week in April.
- ☐ **Piuraagiaqta** (spring festival), Barrow. Parade, Native competitions. Mid-April.
- ☐ **Ski-to-Sea Relay,** Juneau. Teams and individuals ski, bike, run, and paddle to the finish line. Third Saturday in April.
- ☐ **Spring Arts Festival,** Homer. Arts, crafts, music, drama, and dance by local artisans. Late April to early May.

MAY

- ☐ **Little Norway Festival,** Petersburg. Viking-style feasts, folk dances, and other folderol. Third weekend in May.
- ☐ **Kodiak Crab Festival,** Kodiak. Blessing of the fleet, Miss Kodiak pageant, parades, sporting events. Memorial Day weekend.
- ☐ **King Salmon Derby,** Ketchikan. Fishermen dip their lines for the big ones. Three weekends beginning Memorial Day weekend.
- ☐ **Halibut Derby,** Homer. Anglers compete for prizes. Memorial Day through Labor Day.

JUNE

- ☐ **Renaissance Faire,** Anchorage. Medieval merriment. Mid-June.
- ☐ **Midnight Sun Festival,** Nome. Sports and Native cultural events, including Miss Alaska Native Brotherhood pageant. June 21 and adjacent days.
- ☐ **Sunfest,** Fairbanks. Rafting, boating, midnight baseball, other events to celebrate the Summer Solstice. June 21 and adjacent days.
- ☐ **Colony Days,** Palmer. Parade, exhibits, open-air market. Third weekend in June.
- ☐ **All Alaska Logging Championships,** Sitka. Timber workers compete in 17 events for $10,000 in prize money. Late June.
- ☐ **Water Festival,** Wasilla. Land and water parades, sporting events, underwater tricycle race. Last weekend in June.

- **Summer Music Festival,** Sitka. Three weeks of performances by some of the world's leading chamber musicians. First through fourth Friday of June.
- **Nalukataq,** Barrow. Eskimo festival celebrating a successful whaling season. (*Note:* Not held every year.)

JULY

- **Independence Day celebrations,** throughout the state. July 4.
- **Mount Marathon Race,** Seward. Grueling road race up 3,000-foot mountain, parade, and carnival. July 4.
- **Soapy Smith's Wake,** Skagway. Local thespians offer a champagne toast at the grave of a 19th-century con man, Jefferson Randolph Smith. July 8.
- **Northwest Native Trade Fair,** Kotzebue. Feasting, dancing, games, and cultural demonstrations. Second week in July.
- **Moose Dropping Festival,** Talkeetna. A wilderness carnival. Second weekend in July.

✪ GOLDEN DAYS *Fairbanks citizens dress in gold rush–era attire to commemorate the 1902 gold discovery that helped found this city. Celebrations include a parade, air show, concerts, beard and mustache contests, and much more frivolity.*
    Where: *Fairbanks.* **When:** *Third through fourth weekends in July.* **How:** *Book your hotel room well ahead of time. For information, contact the Greater Fairbanks Chamber of Commerce, P.O. Box 74446, Fairbanks, AK 99707 (tel. 907/452-1105).*

- **World Eskimo-Indian Olympics,** Fairbanks. More than two dozen cultural and sporting events, including ear pulling, knuckle hopping, seal skinning, and an intertribal powwow. Late July.
- **Progress Days,** Soldotna. Rodeo, parade, air show, dances, exhibits. Last weekend in July.

AUGUST

- **Gold Rush Days,** Valdez. Parade, dance, casino night, community fish fry. Five days through the second weekend in August.
- **Silver Salmon Derby,** Seward. Alaska's largest fishing derby, held since 1956, offering more than $40,000 in prizes. Second through third weekend in August.
- **Kenai Peninsula State Fair,** Ninilchik. Parade, carnival, agricultural and arts exhibits. Third weekend in August.
- **Southeast Alaska State Fair,** Haines. Principal fair for southeast Alaska and Yukon includes a horse show, logging carnival, and outdoor entertainment. Third weekend in August.

✪ ALASKA STATE FAIR *As at any state fair, you'll find a parade, rodeo, carnival, trade show, and lots of agricultural and animal exhibits. At this 11-day event you can see how large Matanuska Valley vegetables grow under the midnight sun.*
    Where: *State Fairgrounds, Palmer.* **When:** *Fourth Friday in August through Labor Day.* **How:** *Drive up for the day from Anchorage or stay in Palmer or Wasilla (book your room well ahead).*

- **Tanana Valley Fair,** Fairbanks. Agricultural and arts exhibits, parade, carnival, outdoor entertainment. Second through third weekend in August.

SEPTEMBER

- **Great Bathtub Race,** Nome. Hilarious caper on Front Street. Labor Day.

☐ **Klondike Trail of '98 Road Relay,** Skagway. A 110-mile race to Whitehorse, Yukon. Third weekend in September.

OCTOBER

☐ **Oktoberfest,** Fairbanks. Drinking and partying in the Bavarian tradition. Early October.

⊘ *ALASKA DAY FESTIVAL* *This statewide holiday is best observed in Sitka, where possession of Alaska was formally transferred from Russia to the United States in 1867. Events include a parade, memorial service, concerts, dances, and military demonstrations. Men are fined if they don't have a beard.*
*   **Where:** *Sitka.* **When:** *Mid-October, three- to five-day weekend including October 18.* **How:** *Book your hotel room, then come to Sitka! For information, contact the Alaska Day Committee, P.O. Box 102, Sitka, AK 99835 (tel. 907/747-8814).*

☐ **Quiana Alaska,** Anchorage. A Native festival with singing, dancing, and story telling. Mid-October.

NOVEMBER

☐ **Great Alaska Shootout,** Anchorage. Leading college basketball powers from throughout the United States converge on Sullivan Arena for an eight-team tournament. Late November.

DECEMBER

☐ **Bachelor Society Ball and Wilderness Women Contest,** Talkeetna. Unmarried women haul water and firewood, then bid to drink and dance with local bachelors up for auction. First weekend in December.
☐ **Christmas Celebrations,** throughout Alaska. Parades and other events in tne spirit of the season. All month.

3. WHAT TO PACK

CLOTHING No matter what time of year you're making your Alaska trip, you should include both warm clothing and rain gear in your luggage. In the middle of summer, temperatures in Fairbanks often climb into the 80s, but they can just as easily drop into the 30s or 40s at night. A warm sweater and an overcoat should be sufficient to combat the cold, unless you're taking a side trip to Barrow or Kotzebue, in which case you'll want to add a parka or other winter coat, and perhaps some gloves and a set of long underwear. Summer daytime temperatures in those towns are commonly in the 30s. The amount and durability of the rain gear you'll need will depend on how much time you plan to spend outdoors. I have never seen an Alaskan carrying an umbrella, except in downtown Anchorage. If hiking, fishing, or other outdoor pursuits are on the agenda, get yourself a good pair of high rubber boots.

In winter you'll naturally want to bundle up in layers of wool. Any time of year, a pair of sturdy and comfortable walking shoes—not just tennis shoes—is essential.

Alaskans dress very casually. With the exception of major hotels in Anchorage, nowhere will anyone blink twice if you show up for a fancy dinner in corduroys and a plaid shirt. Men can bring along a tie for that one big night out.

It's sometimes like banging one's head against a wall to suggest it, but for your own sake, *travel as light as possible.* Except perhaps for underwear and socks, carry no more than two changes of clothing, keep your toiletries and beauty aids to a minimum, and try to avoid taking electric appliances unless you can't imagine doing without your hairdryer or electric razor for two weeks. Never carry more than you can handle by yourself without assistance: You won't find bellmen at most hotels except during the high tourist season, and you'll never see porters at smaller airports. Ideally you shouldn't have more than one suitcase and a small bag of essentials that fits neatly under your seat on the airplane.

OTHER ITEMS   There are, however, a few items you may not have considered that could prove priceless during your stay: a **travel alarm clock,** so as not to be at the mercy of your hotel for wake-up calls; a **Swiss army knife,** which has a multitude of uses, from bottle opener to screwdriver; a small **flashlight,** especially in winter when it gets dark early; a pair of **eye shades,** to help you sleep in the summer when it's still light outside; and a small **first-aid kit** (containing an antibiotic ointment, bandages, aspirin, soap, a thermometer, motion-sickness pills, and required medications) to avoid dependence on others in minor emergencies. Some travelers also appreciate: a **washcloth** in a plastic bag, on the outside chance your hotel doesn't have one; a pair of light wooden (not plastic) **shoe trees** to air out your footwear after you put in a hard day on your feet; a **magnifying glass** to read the small print on maps; and **bug spray,** to dissuade those six-legged pests so prevalent during the Alaska summer.

4. TIPS FOR THE DISABLED, SENIORS & STUDENTS

FOR THE DISABLED   The **Information Center for Individuals with Disabilities,** Fort Point Place, 27–43 Wormwood St., Boston, MA 02210 (tel. 617/727-5540), provides travel assistance and can also recommend tour operators. **Mobility International USA,** P.O. Box 3551, Eugene, OR 97403 (tel. 503/343-1284), charges a small annual fee and provides travel information for those with disabilities. A useful book for handicapped travelers is *Access to the World: A Travel Guide for the Handicapped,* by Louise Weiss; it can be ordered from Henry Holt & Co. (tel. toll free 800/247-3912).

An organized tour package can make life on the road much easier. Two well-established firms that specialize in travel for the disabled are: **Whole Person Tours,** P.O. Box 1084, Bayonne, NJ 07002 (tel. 201/858-3400); and **Evergreen Travel Service/Wings on Wheels Tours,** 4114 198th St., Suite 13, Lynnwood, WA 98036 (tel. 206/776-1184).

In Alaska, a wide range of sports and recreational activities are arranged for handicapped persons by **Challenge Alaska,** P.O. Box 110065, Anchorage, AK 99511 (tel. 907/563-2658). The annual calendar includes downhill skiing at Alyeska in winter; camping, fishing, sea kayaking, canoeing, sailing, and waterskiing in summer; and weekly social and leisure outings year-round. Write in advance for information—activities book up early.

Alaska's *Official State Travel Planner,* published by the Alaska Tourism Marketing Council, P.O. Box 110801, Dept. 901, Juneau, AK 99811 (tel. 907/465-2010), has wheelchair symbols next to businesses that offer handicapped-accessible facilities and activities.

FOR SENIORS   A first step for any senior citizen planning a trip to Alaska is to write or phone for the current edition of *Alaska's Senior Citizens' Guide,* published annually by the Anchorage Telephone Utility and distributed by the nonprofit **Older Persons Action Group,** P.O. Box 102240, Anchorage, AK 99510 (tel. 907/276-1059). This small consumer directory lists statewide services and organizations that assist seniors, as well as available discounts.

Nearly all major U.S. hotel and motel chains, and many privately owned accommodations, offer a **senior citizen discount.** Be sure to ask for the price reduction when you make your reservation, as there may be restrictions during peak periods. Then be sure to carry proof of your age (driver's license, passport) when you check in.

You can save sightseeing dollars if you are 62 or over by picking up a **Golden Age Passport** from any federally operated park, recreation area, or monument.

Elderhostel, 80 Boylston St., Boston, MA 02116 (tel. 617/426-7788 or 617/426-8056), also provides stimulating vacations at moderate prices for those over 60, with a balanced mix of learning, field trips, and free time for sightseeing. If you fancy organized tours, the **AARP Travel Service** (see below) puts together terrific packages at moderate rates, and **SAGA International Holidays,** 222 Berkeley St., Boston, MA 02116 (tel. toll free 800/343-0273), arranges tours for single travelers over 60.

Membership in two senior organizations also offers a wide variety of travel benefits: the **American Association of Retired Persons (AARP),** 1909 K St. NW, Washington, DC 20049 (tel. 202/662-4850); and the **National Council of Senior Citizens,** 1313 F St. NW, Washington, DC 20004 (tel. 202/347-8800).

Many restaurants, sightseeing attractions, and entertainment venues also offer senior discounts. Be sure to ask when you buy your ticket.

FOR STUDENTS   Before setting out, use your high school or college ID to obtain an International Student Identity Card from the **Council on International Educational Exchange (CIEE),** 205 E. 42nd St., New York, NY 10017 (tel. 212/661-1414), or 312 Sutter St., Room 407, San Francisco, CA 94108 (tel. 415/421-3473). It will entitle you to several student discounts, though not to the same extent as in many foreign countries. Remember: *Always* ask about **student discount tickets** to attractions.

For economical accommodations, as well as a great way to meet other traveling students, join **American Youth Hostels,** P.O. Box 37613, Washington, DC 20013-7613 (tel. 202/783-6161). For a small fee, they'll send a directory of all U.S. hostels, including those in Alaska.

One of the leading student travel tour operators is **Contiki Holidays,** 1432 E. Katella Ave., Anaheim, CA 92805 (tel. toll free 800/626-0611), focusing on ages 18–35. **Arista Student Travel Association, Inc.,** 11 E. 44th St., New York, NY 10017 (tel. 212/687-5121, or toll free 800/356-8861), caters to ages 15–20.

5. ALTERNATIVE/SPECIALTY TRAVEL

Twice a summer, in July and August, a refurbished school bus packed with shoestring-budget travelers takes a month-long trip from the Lower 48. Contact **Green Tortoise Alternative Travel,** P.O. Box 24459, San Francisco, CA 94124 (tel. 415/821-0803, or toll free 800/227-4766 outside California). The price runs about $1,500 for round-trip transportation—including sleeping-bag accommodation in the vehicle itself.

Escorted and independent recreational-vehicle (RV) tours are organized by **Alaska Caravan Adventures,** 2506 Glenkerry Dr., Anchorage, AK 99504 (tel. 907/338-1439, or toll free 800/288-5840 outside Alaska); **Alaska-Yukon RV Caravans,** 322 Concrete St., Anchorage, AK 99501 (tel. 907/277-7575, or toll free 800/426-9865 outside Alaska); and **Point South RV Tours,** 11313 Edmonson Ave., Moreno Valley, CA 92560-5232 (tel. 714/247-1222, or toll free 800/421-1394).

Adventure travelers and nature lovers can consult these groups for information on specialty tours and expeditions: **Alaska Wilderness Guides Association,** P.O. Box 111241, Anchorage, AK 99511 (tel. 907/276-6634); **Alaska Wildland Adventures,** P.O. Box 389, Girdwood, AK 99587 (tel. toll free 800/334-8730, 800/478-4100 in Alaska); **CampAlaska Tours,** P.O. Box 872247, Wasilla, AK 99687 (tel.

907/376-9438; fax 907/376-2353); or **Earth Tours, Inc.,** 705 W. Sixth Ave., Suite 205, Anchorage, AK 99501 (tel. 907/279-9907; fax 907/279-9862).

6. GETTING THERE

The fastest, most direct way to reach Alaska is by air. The slower, more scenic way is by sea or by road. Your means of travel should depend on your time frame and the purpose of your trip. There are numerous options in all categories.

BY PLANE

There's a reason Anchorage has become known as the "Air Crossroads of the World." Located roughly equidistant (via the polar great circle routes) from New York and Tokyo, and only slightly farther from London, Alaska's biggest city is a port of call for carriers from three continents and a midway stopover on numerous intercontinental flights.

From the Lower 48 and Canada, flights arrive not only in Anchorage, but also in Fairbanks (via Anchorage), in many of the cities of the southeast (via Juneau, Sitka, or Ketchikan), and in Yakutat and Cordova (via Juneau).

THE MAJOR AIRLINES   The star of the skies, as far as travel to and from Alaska is concerned, is **Alaska Airlines** (tel. toll free 800/426-0333). Every year since 1975 Alaska Airlines has carried more passengers between Alaska and the Lower 48 than any other airline. And with good reason: Its efficient service, frequency of flights, and network of routes around the state make it my preferred airline for travel to Alaska. The airline serves 14 cities in Alaska; 4 cities in Mexico; 17 cities in Washington, Oregon, California, Arizona, and Idaho; and Toronto, Canada. Connections from other cities are easily made at major airports. Principal offices are in Seattle. The airline also flies between Anchorage and the cities of Magadan and Khabarovsk in Russian Siberia three times weekly in summer. Vladivostok was added to the schedule in 1993.

Alaska Airlines offers a special "Buy Alaska" fare that enables travelers to make one-way stops at any Alaskan cities along their routes for just $40 each. Passengers 62 or older and children under 12 receive additional discounts on coach fares.

 FROMMER'S SMART TRAVELER: AIRFARES

1. Shop all the airlines that fly to your destination.
2. Always ask for the lowest fare, not just a discount fare.
3. Keep calling the airline—availability of cheap seats changes daily. Airline managers would rather sell a seat than have it fly empty. As the departure date nears, additional low-cost seats become available.
4. Ask about frequent-flyer programs to gain bonus miles when you book a flight.
5. Check "bucket shops" for last-minute discount fares that are even cheaper than their advertised slashed fares.
6. Ask about air/land packages. Land arrangements are often cheaper when booked with an air ticket.
7. Fly free or at a heavy discount as a "courier."
8. Look for special promotions offered by airlines such as MarkAir, which is flying new routes and struggling to gain a foothold in the market.

Three other domestic airlines—**Delta** (tel. toll free 800/221-1212), **Northwest** (tel. toll free 800/225-2525), and **United** (tel. toll free 800/241-6522)—have nonstop flights to Anchorage from Chicago, Denver, Honolulu, Los Angeles, Minneapolis, Portland, Salt Lake City, San Francisco, and Seattle; direct flights from Boston, Buffalo, Dallas/Fort Worth, Little Rock, New York, Oklahoma City, San Diego, and Washington, D.C.; and connections to almost every other town with an airport. United and Delta also have commuter flights between Anchorage and Fairbanks, and Delta makes stops in Juneau between Seattle and Fairbanks. **Hawaiian Airlines** (tel. toll free 800/367-5320) flies weekly between Honolulu and Anchorage.

Anchorage-based **MarkAir** (tel. toll free 800/426-6784, 800/478-0800 in Alaska) since 1991 has flown from Anchorage to Seattle, and during 1992 expanded its network to serve seven other mainland U.S. cities—Chicago, Denver, Las Vegas, Los Angeles, Phoenix, Portland (Ore.), and Phoenix—from Seattle. The direct Anchorage–Seattle connection is the only one between Alaska and "south," however; an attempt to route flights via Ketchikan, Sitka, and Juneau faltered.

From Canada, Yukon-based **Air North Canada** (tel. 403/668-2228, or toll free 800/764-0407 in Alaska) connects Fairbanks and Juneau with Whitehorse and Dawson City, while **Trans Provincial Airlines** (tel. 604/627-1341) connects Prince Rupert, B.C., with Ketchikan.

Three foreign carriers visit Anchorage: **British Airways, China Airlines,** and **Korean Airlines.** Northwest connects Anchorage to Tokyo with nonstop flights, while Delta has nonstops to Hong Kong.

REGULAR FARES Airfares to Alaska vary wildly, depending especially upon when you buy your ticket. You can save a lot of money by buying one of the special excursion fares that the airlines have available. These fares—which have varying advance-purchase and minimum/maximum-stay requirements—may offer discounts of 50% or more on regular economy fares. In May 1993, for example, standard round-trip coach fare on Alaska Airlines from Seattle to Anchorage was $1,012 and first-class fare was $1,332. But a typical 14-day advance-purchase fare, with a maximum stay of 21 days in Alaska, was $430; a rare budget fare of $242 was temporarily available at the same time. Discount offers such as this come and go, so be sure to inquire before you buy.

OTHER CHOICES There aren't a lot of other good-value choices in terms of airfares to Alaska. Several charter airlines, including Seattle-based **Morris Air** (tel. toll free 800/444-5660), fly to Anchorage during graveyard-shift hours; there are also charters from overseas, including Swissair subsidiary **Balair Ltd.** (tel. toll free 800/322-5247).

BY BUS

There are no direct bus routes from the Lower 48 to Alaska, save those operated by tour companies or on an irregular charter basis. It is possible, however, to travel in Canada by public transport to the Yukon and there transfer to a tour line in Alaska.

The most reliable means to reach Whitehorse from the south is with **Greyhound.** There is scheduled service to Dawson Creek from Vancouver and Calgary, thence to the Yukon. Service is available most of the year, but is considerably reduced in winter. The fare to Whitehorse from Seattle is $182 U.S. each way. It's a 58-hour journey, including three transfers in Canada: in Vancouver, Edmonton, and Dawson Creek. For information, call Greyhound (tel. 206/624-3456 in Seattle or 604/662-3222 in Vancouver, or toll free 800/661-8747 in Canada).

Three companies—two American, one Canadian—have regular summer-only service between Whitehorse, the Alaska Marine Highway ferry terminuses of Skagway and Haines, and Anchorage and Fairbanks. For schedule information on

Alaskon Express, contact Gray Line of Alaska, 300 Elliott Ave. W., Seattle, WA 98119 (tel. toll free 800/544-2206). To find out more on **Alaska-Yukon Motorcoaches,** write Alaska Sightseeing Co., 349 Wrangell St., Anchorage, AK 99501 (tel. 907/276-1305). Contact **Atlas Tours** at 609 W. Hastings St., Dept. 104, 5th Floor, Vancouver, BC V6B 4W4 (tel. 604/669-1332).

Visitors planning travel primarily by bus, rail, and ferry would be wise to consider **AlaskaPass,** the state's only all-inclusive surface transportation pass. For a set price, which varies according to length of use, the pass offers unlimited travel from Washington and British Columbia gateways throughout Alaska and the Yukon Territory. Among the transportation providers honoring the pass are the Alaska Marine Highway, Alaska Railroad, and Alaskon Express. Cost varies from $449 for an 8-day pass to $599 for a 15-day pass and $849 for a 30-day pass; children 3–11 are charged approximately two-thirds of the adult price. The pass can be purchased directly from AlaskaPass Inc., P.O. Box 897, Haines, AK 99827 (tel. 907/766-3145, or toll free 800/248-7598; fax 907/766-3245), or from Gray Line of Alaska (tel. toll free 800/544-2206).

BY CAR

The **Alaska Highway** may be the most famous road in North America, although it's not among the most traveled. Built in 1942 as a military supply route for U.S. bases in Alaska, it has outgrown its legend as a road guaranteed to ruin even the strongest vehicle.

The two-lane highway officially begins at Dawson Creek, in northern British Columbia, and ends 1,520 miles later in Fairbanks (though Delta Junction, 97 miles east of Fairbanks, also claims to be the end). Most of the road is now surfaced with asphalt. Segments of the highway (mainly in Canada) are unquestionably in poor condition, laced with loose gravel, potholes, and buckled pavement. But considering the effect that the freezing and thawing of permafrost has on any construction, it's a minor wonder that road crews are able to keep the highway open year-round at all.

The Milepost, the bible of road travel to and within Alaska, recommends that drivers take their time and drive with their headlights on at all times. Watch out for wildlife on the road, road-repair crews, flying gravel, and slippery stretches of ice or mud anytime of year. The highway is treated with calcium chloride, which keeps the dust down but corrodes paint and metal, so be sure to wash your vehicle as soon as it's practical to do so. Caulking and duct tape can help keep the dust out. If you're traveling in winter, include extra blankets and a survival kit. Last but not least, give your vehicle and tires a good mechanical checkup before you start on your journey, and carry good spare tires, plastic headlight protectors, and wrenches to tighten bolts loosened from constant vibration.

Services—gas, food, and lodging—are found along the highway at regular intervals rarely exceeding 50 miles (though there's one stretch of 100 miles without services). Not all facilities are open year-round or 24 hours a day, so try not to let your tank run down to its last gallon. Gas prices in Canada and most of Alaska (except the Anchorage area) are markedly higher than in the continental United States. Auto shops are generally well stocked, but it's wise to carry your own emergency supplies: flares, essential tools, bumper jack with lug wrench, spare fan belts, one or two spare tires, and a first-aid kit.

For highway information, contact the **Great Alaska Highways Society,** P.O. Box 74250, Fairbanks, AK 99707 (tel. 907/452-8000).

BY FERRY

The Alaska state ferry system, formally known as the **Alaska Marine Highway,** is among North America's best travel bargains. You can board the M/V *Columbia* (or occasionally another ferry) in Bellingham, Wash., and enjoy a 3½-day cruise through the beautiful Inside Passage to Skagway for as little as $432 ($380 between October and April), including overnight accommodations. Ferries depart every Friday, more frequently in summer. The price is considerably lower if you bring a sleeping bag and stretch out on the floor or in the solarium. For slight additional charges you can stop off at any cities on the southeastern route—Ketchikan, Wrangell, Petersburg, Sitka, Juneau, Haines, and smaller communities—and reboard on the ferry's next visit a few days or hours later. You can also board an Alaska Marine Highway vessel in Prince Rupert, B.C., en route to Alaska. The food served in the cafeteria is generally excellent, and boats also have cocktail lounges and gift shops.

Passenger fares are about 30% higher between May and September than in the off-season, and staterooms are also priced higher. The schedule works like this: Everyone must pay a basic deck fare with a graduated scale based on distance of travel ($236 between Bellingham and Skagway in summer, $154 between Bellingham and Ketchikan). Children 6–11 pay half price; younger kids go for free. Round-trip fares are twice the one-way price. Several types of staterooms are available on the major boats, ranging from two-berth inside cabins to four-berth cabin suites with complete toilet facilities. The fare for the latter is much more than that for the inside cabin ($339 vs. $196, summer rates).

If you're bringing a vehicle—perhaps with plans to ferry up to Skagway and return home via Whitehorse and the Alaska Highway—you'll be charged according to its overall length. You can take a 15-foot car from Bellingham to Skagway for $564, but a standard-width 50-foot RV will run you all of $2,685. Except for the largest vehicles, it appears to cost more to ship your car to Alaska in winter than in summer; in fact it's cheaper, because drivers travel free with vehicles in winter.

Anytime is a good time to take the ferry, but if you're traveling in summer be sure to book well in advance. During the off-season months you'll not only get the best fares, but you're less likely to have any trouble getting a stateroom and far more likely to meet "real" Alaskans. During one December trip I had a chance to visit with the manager of an Alaska Peninsula fishing lodge, a gold-nugget jewelry maker from Juneau, and three-quarters of the student body from tiny (about 20 students) Hydaburg High School on Prince of Wales Island.

From October through April, senior citizens travel at 50% discount off standard fares in Alaskan waters, and for just $5 if they travel standby on the commuter vessels *LeConte* and *Aurora*. But they must still pay the full Bellingham–Ketchikan winter fare ($136 in 1993). For information or reservations, contact the Alaska Marine Highway, P.O. Box R, Juneau, AK 99811 (tel. 907/465-3941, or toll free 800/642-0066). For information on accommodations and other facilities in Bellingham, contact the Bellingham/Whatcom County Visitors & Convention Bureau, 900 Potter St., Bellingham, WA 98226 (tel. 206/671-3990).

Alaska Marine Highway ferries departing from Bellingham don't make any stops in Canadian ports as they ply the waters of the Inside Passage, thus avoiding any need for Customs and Immigration inspection. If you'd like to dawdle along the British Columbia coast, look into **B.C. Ferries,** 1112 Fort St., Victoria, BC V8V 4V2, Canada (tel. 604/386-3431). The *Queen of the North* and *Queen of Prince Rupert* operate an every-other-day, 15-hour shuttle in summer between Port Hardy (at the northern tip of Vancouver Island, by the U.S.–Canadian border), via the Queen Charlotte Islands or the Indian village of Bella Bella, and Prince Rupert, where ferry connections can be made to Ketchikan. From October through May one or the other ferry operates a twice-weekly shuttle over the same route via the Queen Charlottes.

BY CRUISE SHIP

It's easy to say you want to take a cruise to Alaska. Why not? Sit back, let someone else take the worry out of travel, and just enjoy the scenery. But there is a wide variety of different cruise options available, and not all are right for you. For example, are you looking for a small, informal boat that cuts down on the frills but maximizes the scenic opportunities? Or would you be more comfortable aboard a major cruise liner with a casino, nightly cabaret entertainment, and black-tie dinners? Both options, and many others, are available in Alaskan waters.

As a first step, get hold of a copy of *Frommer's Cruises,* a 400-page compendium of everything you need to know about travel on the high seas. And don't make a choice about which ship you want to take until you've consulted your travel agent.

Annie Scrivanich of Cruise Advisors, Inc., recommends that travelers plan their trips to Alaska as if they were going only once: "They should first select the itinerary that interests them most, then the ship," she says. "They should plan well in advance. I suggest making reservations in November or December for travel in the next year. This affords the best selection of cabins and sailings. Plus, most cruise lines offer substantial discounts to those who reserve early."

Cruise Advisors, Inc., 2442 N.W. Market St., Suite 367, Seattle, WA 98107 (tel. 206/784-9852, or toll free 800/544-9361), has an annual "Alaska Discount Cruise Guide" listing a wide range of the lowest cruise fares available.

CHOOSING A CRUISE LINER Marylyn Springer and Donald Schultz, the authors of *Frommer's Cruises,* advise that a ship's personality is all-important in choosing your cruise. And ships "really do have personalities," they insist. "To be perhaps a bit more accurate about that, it's really the crew, the officers, and the philosophy of the ship's owners that impart 'personality' to the vessel. Food, entertainment, crew nationality, crew-to-passenger ratio, cruise length, and even historical factors all play a part [in establishing an] informal or formal atmosphere on board. That formality, or lack of it, is reflected in luxuriousness of accommodations, cruise price, on-board entertainment, and often in crew-to-passenger ratio."

The more you are willing to pay, in other words, the higher will be the standard of stateroom and entertainment you'll get, the more crew members will be available to serve your every need, and the more you can expect older and more affluent and sophisticated fellow passengers. The inverse also follows: Shorter, lower-cost cruises have comfortable but not ritzy quarters, on-deck parties instead of string quartets, and a younger group of passengers.

Don't forget to consider ports of call when making your choice of vessel. Is there a particular place you want to visit? Or is the cruise experience enough in itself? Many Alaska cruise lines offer package tours that enable you to combine a sea cruise with a land tour.

Every cruise ship has a range of prices. Normally the upper and lower figures indicate the luxury and location of your stateroom. Outside (ocean-view) cabins cost more than inside (no-view) cabins, and suites with separate sitting rooms and bedrooms are at the top end of the price spectrum. If you travel in the "value season," before mid-June or after Labor Day, you'll save about 10%. Meals and entertainment on board are included in the price you pay, but drinks, casino charges, tips, shopping, shore excursions, and land transportation are not.

Several cruise lines are becoming responsive to the needs of physically handi-capped travelers. Holland America's *Westerdam* and Princess's *Regal Princess* have cabins specially designed for the wheelchair traveler.

THE CRUISE SHIP ROSTER There are always new ships and cruise lines plying Alaskan waters and older ones placed in drydock, so don't regard the following list as definitive. Your travel agent should have the most recent information on cruise ships and schedules.

Alaska Sightseeing/Cruise West The *Spirit of Alaska* and *Spirit of Discovery* leave Seattle every other Saturday, mid-May to mid-September, on seven-day Inside Passage cruises to Juneau, with stops in Victoria, Ketchikan, Misty Fjords, Petersburg, LeConte Glacier, Sitka, and Glacier Bay. Itineraries are reversed on alternate weeks. Fares are $1,495–$2,895. The *Sheltered Seas,* a 90-foot charter yacht, leaves Ketchikan on Wednesday and Juneau on Saturday, mid-May to mid-September, on five-day cruises through the Inside Passage. The cost is $899–$1,299, including overnight accommodation in on-shore hotels at Petersburg, Juneau, and Ketchikan. These are intimate, casual means of touring, with a maximum of 80 passengers on a trip. Contact Alaska Sightseeing/Cruise West, Fourth and

Battery Building, Suite 700, Seattle, WA 98121 (tel. 206/441-8687, or toll free 800/426-7702).

Clipper Cruise Line The 98-passenger *Society Explorer* operates an eight-day June itinerary between Prince Rupert (B.C.) and Juneau, and an 11-day July-August voyage between Prince Rupert and Kodiak Island. The Juneau cruise, priced at $1,950–$2,850, includes Misty Fjords, Wrangell, Admiralty Island, Tracy Arm, Skagway, Haines, Glacier Bay, and Sitka. The Kodiak Island trip, with fares of $2,750–$3,650, omits Skagway, Haines, and Sitka, but includes Prince William Sound (with the Columbia Glacier), Seward, and Kenai Fjords National Park. This vessel is an ocean-going exploration ship with comfortable cabins, excellent service, and good food. Contact Clipper Cruise Line, 7711 Bonhomme Ave., St. Louis, MO 63105 (tel. 314/727-2929).

Costa Cruises The *Daphne* leaves Vancouver every Friday, mid-May to mid-September, on seven-day cruises to Wrangell, Endicott Arm, Juneau, Skagway, Davidson and Rainbow Glaciers, and Ketchikan. The cost is $1,380–$5,245. This spacious, 450-passenger luxury yacht—with a casino, gymnasium, swimming pool, library, shopping arcade, theater, cabaret lounge, and discotheque—has Italian officers and a generally casual atmosphere. Contact Costa Cruises, World Trade Center, 80 S.W. 8th St., Miami, FL 33130 (tel. 305/358-7330, or toll free 800/462-6782).

Cunard/Norwegian American Cruises The *Sagafjord* leaves Vancouver or Anchorage, June through late August, on 10- and 11-day cruises to Ketchikan, Endicott Arm, Skagway, Sitka, Yakutat, Hubbard Glacier, Valdez, College Fjord, Seward, Kenai Fjords, Homer, and Cook Inlet. The *Sagafjord* is the only ship to sail into Anchorage. The cost is $3,180–$7,140, including round-trip airfare to port. This is one of the top cruise ships in the world, with a rich wood-and-copper interior design. Handling 589 passengers, it has a complete health and exercise spa, swimming pool, shopping mall, ballroom and nightclub, and many other elegant touches. Contact Cunard Lines, 555 Fifth Ave., New York, NY 10017 (tel. 212/661-7505, or toll free 800/880-7500 or 800/221-4800, 800/221-4444 in the Northeast, 800/522-7520 in New York State).

Holland America Line/Westours The *Noordam, Westerdam,* and *Nieuw Amsterdam* leave Vancouver every Tuesday, Thursday, and Saturday, respectively, late May to mid-September, on three-, four-, and seven-day cruises to Ketchikan, Juneau, Glacier Bay, and Sitka. The cost is $1,195–$3,795. The company's flagship, the *Rotterdam,* departs every other Sunday from Vancouver, B.C., for Seward on a seven-glacier route. The fare is $1,895–$3,445. All four ships have Dutch officers, an Indonesian/Filipino crew, and a no-tipping policy. All have casinos, gymnasiums and weight rooms, swimming pools, tennis courts, libraries, shopping arcades, theaters, and several lounges and discotheques, with evening entertainment ranging from cabaret shows to sedate string quartets to disco music. The *Nieuw Amsterdam* and its twin, the *Noordam,* are floating museums of historic art. They accommodate 1,214 passengers. The recently refurbished *Rotterdam,* 10 decks high and three-quarters as long as the Empire State Building is tall, has cabins for 1,114. The *Westerdam,* with a capacity of 1,300 passengers, is the Holland America Line's largest ship. (It was built in 1986 as the *Homeric.*) Contact Holland America Line/Westours, 300 Elliott Ave. W., Seattle, WA 98119 (tel. 206/281-3535 or 281-1970, or toll free 800/426-0327).

Princess Cruises Six ships are in Alaska service during the summer season. Four of them—the *Pacific Princess, Island Princess, Dawn Princess,* and *Fair Princess*—leave Vancouver every other Thursday and Saturday, mid-May to mid-September, on seven-day Gulf of Alaska cruises to Whittier, with stops in Ketchikan, Juneau, Skagway, Glacier Bay, and Columbia Glacier. Itineraries are reversed on alternate weeks. Fares run $999–$3,609. The *Regal Princess* sails every Saturday from Vancouver on three-, four-, and seven-day cruises to Southeast Alaska, visiting Juneau, Skagway, Glacier Bay, and Ketchikan. Fares are $1,199–$3,849. The *Sky Princess* sails round-trip from San Francisco on a 10-day itinerary that features Ketchikan, Juneau, Skagway, Glacier Bay, Sitka, and Victoria. Fares are $1,799–$5,099. All ships have British officers and staff, Italian dining room personnel, and an international crew. All have casinos, workout facilities, swimming pools, libraries, shopping arcades, and theaters. Contact Princess Cruises, 10100 Santa Monica Blvd., Los Angeles, CA 90067 (tel. 213/553-1770, or toll free 800/421-0522, 800/252-0158 in California).

Regency Cruises   The *Regent Sea* and *Regent Sun* leave Vancouver every other Friday and Sunday, mid-May to mid-September, on seven-day cruises to Whittier via Ketchikan, Juneau, Skagway, Sitka, and Prince William Sound (Columbia Glacier). The 725-passenger vessels return to Vancouver from Anchorage on alternate weeks. The cost is $1,195–$2,695. The Panamanian-registered ships have seven passenger decks, a casino, sports deck and gymnasium, indoor and outdoor pools, library, shopping arcade, theater, and several lounges including a cabaret and discotheque. Contact Regency Cruises, 260 Madison Ave., New York, NY 10016 (tel. 212/972-4774, or toll free 800/388-5500).

Royal Caribbean Cruise Line   The *Sun Viking* leaves Vancouver every Sunday, mid-May to mid-September, on seven-day cruises to Skagway via Misty Fjords, Ketchikan, Tracy Arm, Juneau, and Haines. The cost is $1,095–$3,445. This 725-passenger vessel, with an international crew, has a casino, library, and several lounges with live entertainment. Contact the Royal Caribbean Cruise Line, 1050 Caribbean Way, Miami, FL 33132 (tel. toll free 800/327-6700).

Royal Cruise Line   The *Royal Odyssey* leaves Vancouver every other Wednesday, mid-May to mid-July, on seven-day Gulf of Alaska cruises to Whittier with stops in Ketchikan, Juneau, and Skagway. Scenic highlights include Tracy Arm, Hubbard Glacier, Columbia Glacier, and College Fjord. Itineraries are reversed on alternate weeks. Fares range from $1,498 to $5,568. This 765-passenger vessel has a theater, library, boutique, discotheque, and several lounges with live entertainment. Officers and staff are Greek. This is a great trip for singles: There are 55 single-berth cabins, and ladies may be charmed by the gentlemen hosts who are willing companions for dining, dancing, card games, and shore excursions. Contact Royal Cruise Line, 1 Maritime Plaza, San Francisco, CA 94111 (tel. toll free 800/227-4534).

Seven Seas Cruise Line   The *Song of Flower* departs Vancouver every other Saturday, mid-June to mid-September, on seven-day Gulf of Alaska cruises to Whittier via Ketchikan, Tracy Arm, Juneau, Skagway, Haines, Sitka, and Hubbard Glacier. Itineraries are reversed on alternate weeks. Fares run $2,350–$3,995. The ultra-deluxe vessel carries only 172 guests, enabling it to offer a high level of personalized service. Activities and facilities include fitness and sports programs, a well-stocked library, a video library (every cabin has a VCR), a discotheque, and a casino. The ship has Norwegian officers, Scandinavian cabin stewards, and a European dining staff. Contact Seven Seas Cruise Line, 2300-55 W. Hastings St., Vancouver, BC V6N 4N5, Canada (tel. toll free 800/661-5541).

Special Expeditions   Sven-Olof Lindblad's M.V. *Sea Lion* and *Sea Bird* are one-class ships, carrying 74 passengers in 39 outside cabins. Their 11-day cruises, with three departures a month, June to September, begin in Prince Rupert, B.C., and include Agate Beach, Sumner Strait, Admiralty Island, Seymour Canal, Tracy Arm, Glacier Bay, Elfin Cove, LeConte Glacier, and Misty Fjords. Ports of call are Sitka and Petersburg. The fare is $2,850–$3,930. The ships' shallow draft of eight feet allows them access to waterways inaccessible by other vessels. These cruises, therefore, focus on Alaska's natural habitat. Each voyage carries a staff of naturalists who conduct informal lectures on natural history. Contact Special Expeditions, Inc., 720 Fifth Ave., New York, NY 10019 (tel. 212/765-7740, or toll free 800/762-0003).

World Explorer Cruises   The *Universe* leaves Vancouver every other Sunday, May through early September, on 14-day cruises to Juneau, Skagway, Glacier Bay, Valdez, Columbia Glacier, Seward, Wrangell, Sitka, Ketchikan, and Victoria. The cost is $1,995–$3,895. This 550-passenger ship is a floating university for half the year, chartered to the University of Pittsburgh's semester-at-sea program, so it has one of the largest libraries afloat: 11,000 volumes! Academic lecturers and quality musicians make this a favorite cruise for professional people and educators. The *Universe* also has a swimming pool, shops, a theater, five lounges, and a nightclub. The ship has an

American staff and a Chinese crew. Contact World Explorer Cruises, 555 Montgomery St., San Francisco, CA 94111 (tel. 415/391-9262, or toll free 800/854-3835, 800/222-2255 in California).

PACKAGE TOURS

Many travelers find it most convenient, and often (depending on their desired level of travel) less expensive, to leave their Alaskan visit in the hands of tour experts. Travel packagers handle a large percentage of Alaska tourists each year, most often through "cruise/tour" packages that combine a week's cruise up the Inside Passage with bus and rail travel through the Yukon to Anchorage, Denali National Park, Fairbanks, and Prince William Sound. Tour options like Arctic excursions (to Barrow, Kotzebue, and Nome) may be thrown in. A few companies offer trips to the Kenai Peninsula, Kodiak Island, the Pribilofs, the Aleutians . . . even Russian Siberia. Shop around (or have your travel agent do it for you) and determine which itinerary and price range best suit you. These are some of the major tour operators:

Alaska Sightseeing/Cruise West, Fourth and Battery Building, Suite 700, Seattle, WA 98121 (tel. 206/441-8687, or toll free 800/426-7702; fax 206/441-4757), or 543 W. Fourth Ave., Anchorage, AK 99501 (tel. 907/276-1305).

Alaska Travel Adventures, 9085 Glacier Hwy., Juneau, AK 99801 (tel. 907/789-0052).

Alaska Travel Bureau/Cruise Alaska Tours, 15385 S.E. 30th Place, Suite 350, Bellevue, WA 98007 (tel. 206/641-0508, or toll free 800/426-2134; fax 206/562-9608).

Atlas Tours, 609 W. Hastings St., Dept. 104, 5th Floor, Vancouver, BC V6B 4W4, Canada (tel. 604/669-1332; fax 604/687-6113).

Holland America Line/Westours-Gray Line of Alaska, 300 Elliott Ave. W., Seattle, WA 98119 (tel. 206/281-3535, or toll free 800/426-0327; fax 206/283-2687), or 547 W. Fourth Ave., Anchorage, AK 99501 (tel. 206/277-5581, or toll free 800/544-2206).

Knightly Tours, P.O. Box 16366, Seattle, WA 98116 (tel. toll free 800/426-2123).

MarkTours, P.O. Box 196769, Anchorage, AK 99519 (tel. 907/243-6275, or toll free 800/426-6784, 800/478-0800 in Alaska; fax 907/248-4969).

Princess Tours, 2815 Second Ave., Suite 400, Seattle, WA 98121 (tel. 206/728-4202, or toll free 800/647-7750; fax 206/443-1979).

Among agencies that design custom itineraries statewide for clients are these:

Homer Vacations & Conventions, P.O. Box 1050, Homer, AK 99603 (tel. 907/235-2575).

The Travel Connection, P.O. Box 645, Haines, AK 99827 (tel. 907/766-2681; fax 907/766-2585).

World Express Tours, 200 W. 34th Ave., Suite 393, Anchorage, AK 99503 (tel. toll free 800/544-2235).

7. GETTING AROUND

Unlike most other parts of the United States, you can't drive everywhere in Alaska. But between the road, rail, sea, and air networks, no area of the state is entirely inaccessible.

BY PLANE

Alaskans fly more private planes than do citizens of any other state—and perhaps any other nation as well. Statistics in 1990 showed that there were some 10,000 registered pilots in Alaska, one for every 55 residents, and about 9,400 registered aircraft. Compare those numbers with statistics for the entire United States: one pilot for every

400 Americans, one aircraft for every 850. There are more than 600 airports in Alaska, including seaplane landing sites and heliports.

Certainly Alaska is so vast in area, and has so few roads, that the only practical way to reach most communities is by small plane. Indeed the exploits of many of Alaska's pioneer bush pilots are legendary. Twin-engine planes, which often must cope with notoriously poor runways, are frequently outfitted with floats for water landings or skis for snow landings.

Statewide service aboard larger aircraft is provided by **Alaska Airlines** (tel. toll free 800/426-0333) to Anchorage, Bethel, Cordova, Fairbanks, Glacier Bay, Juneau, Ketchikan, Kotzebue, Nome, Petersburg, Prudhoe Bay, Sitka, Wrangell, and Yakutat. Through subcontract agreements with other air carriers, Alaska Airlines also serves 60 bush villages.

MarkAir (tel. toll free 800/426-6784, 800/478-0800 in Alaska) is the state's largest home-based carrier, with extensive passenger service throughout the state. Its fleet of Boeing 737s and smaller DeHavillands serves Anchorage, Adak, Aniak, Barrow, Bethel, Cold Bay, Cordova, Dillingham, Dutch Harbor, Fairbanks, Galena, Homer, Kenai, King Salmon, Kodiak, Kotzebue, McGrath, Nome, the Pribilofs, Prudhoe Bay, St. Mary's, Sandpoint, Unalakleet, and Valdez. **MarkAir Express** serves 100 more small rural communities from hub towns.

Reeve Aleutian Airways (tel. 907/243-4700 in Anchorage, or toll free 800/544-2248) is Alaska's oldest airline, founded in 1932 by a Kansas barnstormer named Bob Reeve. It provides regular service on Boeing 727s from Anchorage to the weather-battered, 3,000-mile-long Aleutian chain, including Adak, Cold Bay, King Cove, Port Heiden, St. Paul (Pribilofs), Sand Point, Unalaska (Dutch Harbor), and smaller communities.

Commuter service is provided by a plethora of small commuter airlines and air-taxi services. Among those exclusively serving the southeast are **Ketchikan Air Service** (tel. 907/225-6608 in Ketchikan), **L.A.B. Flying Service** (tel. 907/766-2222 in Haines), and **Wings of Alaska** (tel. 907/789-0790 in Juneau, or toll free 800/478-WING in Alaska).

In south-central Alaska, **Era Aviation** (tel. 907/248-4422, or toll free 800/843-1947 outside Alaska), the Alaska Airlines commuter line, flies from Anchorage to Barrow, Homer, Iliamna, Kenai, Kodiak, and Valdez, and from Bethel to 17 bush communities in southwestern Alaska. **Southcentral Air** (tel. 907/283-7064 in Anchorage), a United associate, serves Homer, Kenai, and Kodiak from Anchorage.

In interior and arctic Alaska, look for **Bering Air** (tel. 907/443-5464 in Nome), with service throughout western Alaska and into the adjacent Russian Far East; **Cape Smythe Air Service** (tel. 907/852-8333 in Barrow or 907/443-2414 in Nome), flying between Barrow, Kotzebue, Nome, Point Hope, Prudhoe Bay, and many other arctic and northwestern Alaska communities; and **Larry's Flying Service** (tel. 907/474-9169 in Fairbanks), which flies between Fairbanks and Anaktuvuk Pass, Bettles, Fort Yukon, and other points.

Each community has its own local air-taxi services, and frequently helicopter service as well. At least once on your Alaskan trip, plan to invest $100 or so in a flightseeing excursion—it may be the highlight of your trip.

BY TRAIN

First opened in 1923, the Alaska Railroad runs 470 miles from Seward and Whittier, the deep-water ports of south-central Alaska, through Anchorage to Denali National Park and Fairbanks.

The railroad now operates four basic routes: a daily express schedule between Anchorage and Fairbanks via Wasilla, Talkeetna, and Denali National Park; a twice-weekly Anchorage–Fairbanks "dayliner" service, stopping at every small station (including flag stops) on the route; a Thursday-through-Sunday summer run between Anchorage and Seward; and a shuttle service several times daily between Portage station (near Girdwood, east of Anchorage) and the Prince William Sound port of

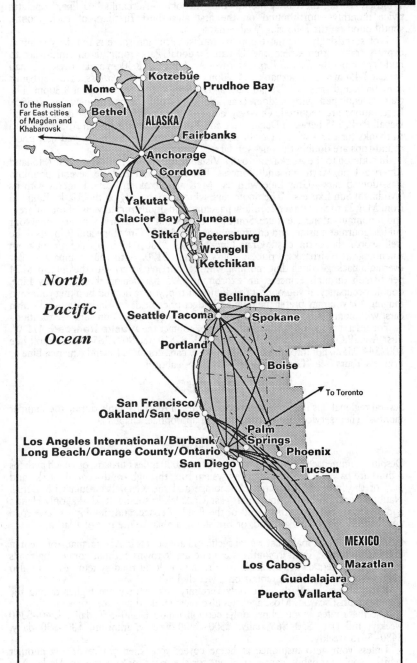

ALASKA AIRLINES ROUTES

500 mi
0
805 km

N

ALASKA

Nome
Kotzebue
Prudhoe Bay
To the Russian Far East cities of Magdan and Khabarovsk
Bethel
Fairbanks
Anchorage
Cordova
Yakutat
Glacier Bay
Juneau
Sitka
Petersburg
Wrangell
Ketchikan

North Pacific Ocean

Bellingham
Seattle/Tacoma
Spokane
Portland
Boise

To Toronto

San Francisco/Oakland/San Jose
Palm Springs
Los Angeles International/Burbank/Long Beach/Orange County/Ontario
Phoenix
San Diego
Tucson

MEXICO

Los Cabos
Mazatlan
Guadalajara
Puerto Vallarta

5575

Whittier. During the winter months the Anchorage–Fairbanks "dayliner" operates twice monthly—northbound on the first and third Tuesdays of each month, southbound on the following Wednesdays.

Not surprisingly, the most popular tourist excursion route is the daily summer express train, often called the Denali National Park route. From mid-May to mid-September the *Denali Express* leaves Anchorage at 8:30am and arrives in Denali Park at 3:45pm and in Fairbanks at 8:30pm. The *Anchorage Express* leaves Fairbanks at 8:30am, and arrives in Denali Park at 12:15pm and in Anchorage at 8:30pm. The train is equipped with a dome car and offers full dining-and-beverage service. Reservations are required. One-way adult fares are $85 between Anchorage and Denali Park, $45 between Denali Park and Fairbanks, $120 between Anchorage and Fairbanks (or $130 with a Denali stopover). Children 2–11 are charged half price; round-trips are double the one-way fares.

In addition to the Alaska Railroad's Vistaliner dome car, both Gray Line (Holland America Line/Westours) and Princess Tours own and operate several premium glass-domed cars—Gray Line with its "McKinley Explorer" cars, Princess with its "Midnight Sun Express." The dome cars, which depart daily on the Alaska Railroad from May 21 to September 20, allow passengers an unobstructed view of the tall trees and mountains along the route. Some passengers find the luxury of professional tour guides, gourmet cuisine, and entertainment provided by Gray Line and Princess to be well worth the extra cost. Gray Line charges $180 (children, half price) from Anchorage to Fairbanks; Princess Tours charges $170. Both tour companies offer overnight packages (including morning wildlife tour) in concert with the rail trip: $274 per person through Princess, an exorbitant $395 per person through Gray Line, double occupancy. If you opt for the dome-car trip, you're best off booking your own lodging. Or you may prefer the quieter, budget-priced ride in Alaska Railroad's own cars, with commentary and guitar playing by college students on summer vacation.

For reservations and further information, contact the **Alaska Railroad,** 411 W. First Ave. (P.O. Box 107500), Anchorage, AK 99510 (tel. 907/265-2623, or toll free 800/544-0552). For information on the luxury cars, contact Holland America Line or Princess Tours (see "Getting There" "By Ship," above).

BY BUS

Several regional bus lines operate specific routes in Alaska, mainly during the summer months. Their services are discussed in the appropriate chapters.

BY CAR

Despite its immense size, Alaska has less than 16,000 miles of roads, of which perhaps a third are paved. The main highway system runs through south-central Alaska and part of the Interior, connecting Anchorage and the Kenai Peninsula with Denali National Park, Fairbanks, and points east (Canada). In southeast Alaska, only Haines and Skagway, at the northern end of the Inside Passage, and tiny Hyder have road connections (via the Yukon and/or British Columbia) to the rest of Alaska.

RENTALS   Most major car-rental agencies have outlets in Alaska, many of them in every town of size. Even in southeastern and arctic towns without connecting roads from outside, rentals are available for driving the local road system. You can also obtain recreational vehicle rentals on a weekly basis.

Rates change regularly. The only certainty is that they are higher during the summer tourist season. Most agencies also have reduced rates on weekends.

Use these rates as guidelines only: economy model, $40–$50 daily, $240–$300 weekly; full size, $50–$65 daily, $300–$400 weekly; minivan, $80–$90 daily, $480–$615 weekly.

Unless your auto insurance at home covers you when you're driving another vehicle, you'll probably want to pay out for the extra for coverage in Alaska. You might encounter hazards like rock slides and renegade moose on the open road; and if you're in Alaska in the winter, snow driving can be extremely treacherous.

GASOLINE   The price of gas in Anchorage is comparable to prices in the Lower 48, but elsewhere in Alaska it's considerably higher. As a general rule, the farther you get from major cities, the more you'll have to pay for gas. Sometimes it's hard to accept that you can be virtually straddling the pipeline but paying upward of $1.60 a gallon to fill your tank.

The frigid winter weather in many parts of Alaska, particularly the Interior, creates some unusual maintenance problems for motor vehicles. Throughout the state you'll see what appear to be electric plugs protruding through the front grills of cars. Outside hotels in Fairbanks and other inland towns, you'll see a line of what appear to be electric sockets in the parking lots. As you may have guessed, the plugs fit in the sockets. How else are you going to keep your vehicle charged in −40°F weather?

DRIVING RULES   Driving age in Alaska is 16 with parental consent, or 18 for a full operator's license. The mandated speed limit on all highways, unless otherwise posted, is 55 m.p.h. Seatbelts are required, and all children age 4 and younger must ride in a federally approved child-safety seat. You should drive defensively at all times.

Drunk-driving laws are tough. First offenders are subject to a mandatory 72-hour jail sentence and the 30-day loss of all driving privileges. Additional offenses bring increasingly stiffer penalties. There are also fines for littering.

ROAD MAPS   The single-best detailed map book is the 156-page *Alaska Atlas & Gazeteer* ($19.95), first published in 1992 by DeLorme Mapping (tel. toll free 800/227-1656).

One of the better planning maps for Alaska trips is included in *The Milepost* ($16.95), an annual 530-page, soft-cover compendium that is almost requisite if you're driving to Alaska. Published by the Alaska Northwest Publishing Co., 130 Second Ave. S., Edmonds, WA 98020, the book covers all highways in Alaska and Canada's Yukon Territory, plus the Alaska Highway and major access routes through British Columbia and Alberta, in mile-by-mile detail. Its major weakness is that hotels and restaurants are listed only if they buy advertising, so it's best used *in concert with this volume.*

Other good maps are published by oil companies—I especially like the one distributed by the Alaska-owned Tesoro stations—and by the Alaska Division of Tourism.

BREAKDOWNS/ASSISTANCE   Members of the American Automobile Association can get free emergency road service wherever they are, 24 hours, by calling AAA's emergency number (tel. toll free 800/336-4357).

BY FERRY

The **Alaska Marine Highway** (tel. 907/465-3941, or toll free 800/642-0066) has two ferry systems with eight boats in continual operation. The Southeast System serves 15 towns in Alaska's Panhandle, while the Southwest System stops in 12 towns in Prince William Sound, the Kenai Peninsula, and Kodiak Island, with seven trips a year to the Alaska Peninsula and the Aleutians.

The five boats that cover longer distances—the *Columbia, Malaspina, Matanuska, Taku,* and *Tustumena*—have staterooms for overnight guests. The three smaller boats—the *Aurora, Bartlett,* and *LeConte*—ply shorter routes and have no staterooms, so those on overnight excursions must spread blankets or sleeping bags across lounge seats or on the floors. All boats have food service and a solarium; all but the *Bartlett* (the Prince William Sound commuter) have a cocktail lounge.

Sample fares in summer 1993 (not including stateroom): Juneau to Ketchikan, $72; Juneau to Skagway, $24; Juneau to Sitka, $24; Valdez to Homer, $136; and Homer to Kodiak, $46. Rates are 20%–30% less from October to May.

HITCHHIKING

You may find some folks by the side of the road with their thumbs out, but because of the great distances involved in driving in Alaska, it's not widely practiced.

SUGGESTED ITINERARIES

Alaska is so vast, it's virtually impossible to see with limited time and money. Roads are few, ferries are slow, and airfares are high. If you have only a week or two at your disposal, it's best to focus on specific parts of the state.

In the following itineraries, I offer three separate one-week suggestions. Two of them feature southeastern Alaska: The first itinerary combines air travel to and from Alaska with in-state transportation on the Alaska Marine Highway, the state ferry system (you'll need to consult current ferry schedules). This tour is most conveniently done if your "Day 1" is a Wednesday. The second itinerary involves only air links and can be started any day. The third one-week suggestion is for an Anchorage–Denali National Park–Fairbanks trip.

If you have more than one week, consider either of the following suggestions: a two-week itinerary that combines a tour of Southeast Alaska with a tour of Anchorage and Fairbanks; or a three-week itinerary that expands on the two-week program.

IF YOU HAVE ONE WEEK: SOUTHEAST ALASKA

Alternative 1 — By Ferry

Day 1: Take a morning flight from Seattle to Ketchikan. Explore Alaska's southern gateway, including the Creek Street Historic District, the Totem Heritage Center, and Saxman Native Village.

Day 2: Morning ferry from Ketchikan. Spend all day cruising the Inside Passage, with stops in Wrangell (midafternoon) and Petersburg (early evening). Sleep aboard the boat.

Day 3: Arrive in Sitka midmorning. You have eight hours to explore the former Russian capital of Alaska, including Sitka National Historical Park, the Sheldon Jackson Museum, and St. Michael's Cathedral. Early-evening ferry departure for Juneau; sleep aboard ship.

Day 4: Arrive in Juneau late morning after stops in Angoon, Tenakee, and Hoonah. In the afternoon, see the Mendenhall Glacier or the Alaska State Museum.

Day 5: Take a late-morning ferry to Skagway, cruising the spectacular Lynn Canal and arriving in time for dinner. See the *Skaguay in the Days of '98* show in the evening.

Day 6: Spend the day seeing the gold-rush town of Skagway and ride on the White Pass & Yukon Route railway. About midnight, board a southbound ferry and sleep en route to Juneau.

Day 7: You'll arrive in Juneau for breakfast. Treat yourself to a flightseeing trip over Glacier Bay before catching your flight back to Seattle and home.

Alternative 2 — By Air

Day 1: Take a morning flight from Seattle to Ketchikan. Explore the Creek Street Historic District, the Totem Heritage Center, and Saxman Native Village.

Day 2: Take a morning flight to Sitka. See Sitka National Historical Park, the Sheldon Jackson Museum, and St. Michael's Cathedral.

Day 3: In the morning, fly to Juneau. See the Mendenhall Glacier, the Alaska State Museum, and other sights.

Day 4: Take a morning flight to Gustavus (Glacier Bay). Transfer to Glacier Bay National Park and enjoy an afternoon nature walk.

Day 5: See Glacier Bay on an eight-hour cruise aboard the *Spirit of Adventure*. In late afternoon or early evening, fly to Skagway.

Day 6: Spend a full day in Skagway. Ride the White Pass & Yukon Route railway and explore the century-old downtown, now comprised in Klondike Gold Rush National Historical Park. Don't miss the *Skaguay in the Days of '98* stage show.

Day 7: Fly to Juneau, where you can opt to stay an extra day or longer, continue on to Anchorage, or return home via Seattle.

IF YOU HAVE ONE WEEK: ANCHORAGE-FAIRBANKS

Day 1: Take a morning flight into Anchorage. Rent a car for two days to see the state's largest city, including the Anchorage Museum of History and Art.

Day 2: Drive out Turnagain Arm to the Portage Glacier. Stop for lunch in Girdwood, where you can see the Mount Alyeska resort and explore the Crow Creek Mine. Return your car at the end of the day.

Day 3: Depart on the Alaska Railroad at 8:30am (May to September) for Denali National Park and Fairbanks. Disembark at Denali at 3:45pm, with enough daylight left to explore the community surrounding park headquarters.

Day 4: Take an all-day bus tour of the national park, either on the park's free shuttle buses or as part of the concessionaires' narrated wildlife tours. The earlier you leave, the better your chance of seeing a cloudless Mount McKinley.

Day 5: You'll have time for river rafting or day hiking before getting back on the train at 4:15pm to continue to Fairbanks. You'll arrive 8:30pm, in time for a late dinner.

Day 6: There's a lot to see in and around Fairbanks, so you may want to rent a car. Check out the University of Alaska's museums and research facilities, one of the area's restored gold camps, or the Alaskaland theme park.

Day 7: Enjoy a morning riverboat cruise down the Chena and Tanana Rivers. Then head for the airport for your long flight home.

IF YOU HAVE TWO WEEKS

Day 1: Take a morning flight from Seattle to Ketchikan. Explore the Creek Street Historic District, the Totem Heritage Center, and Saxman Native Village.

Day 2: In the morning, fly to Sitka. See Sitka National Historical Park, the Sheldon Jackson Museum, and St. Michael's Cathedral.

Day 3: Take a morning flight to Juneau. See the Mendenhall Glacier, the Alaska State Museum, and other sights.

Day 4: In the morning, fly to Gustavus (Glacier Bay). Transfer to Glacier Bay National Park and enjoy an afternoon nature walk.

Day 5: See Glacier Bay on an eight-hour cruise aboard the *Spirit of Adventure*. In late afternoon or early evening, fly to Skagway.

Day 6: Spend the full day in Skagway. Ride the White Pass & Yukon Route railway and explore the century-old downtown, now comprised in Klondike Gold Rush National Historical Park. Don't miss the *Skaguay in the Days of '98* stage show.

Day 7: Fly to Juneau, connecting there to an onward flight to Anchorage. Spend the afternoon sightseeing around Anchorage.

Day 8: Join a two-day tour of Prince William Sound. You'll bus to Portage, make a short rail connection to Whittier, then board a cruise boat for a tour of College Fjord and the great Columbia Glacier en route to Valdez, where you spend the night.

Day 9: Return to Anchorage via Thompson Pass and the Copper River Valley.

Day 10: Take the Alaska Railroad to Denali National Park, arriving midafternoon with enough daylight left to explore the community surrounding park headquarters.

Day 11: Take an all-day bus tour of the national park, either on the park's free shuttle buses or as part of the concessionaires' narrated wildlife tours. The earlier you leave, the better your chance of seeing a cloudless Mount McKinley.

Day 12: You'll have time for river rafting or day hiking before getting back on the train to continue to Fairbanks. You'll arrive in time for a late dinner.

Day 13: There's lots to see in and around Fairbanks, so you may want to rent a car. Check out the University of Alaska's museums and research facilities, one of the area's restored gold camps, or the Alaskaland theme park.

Day 14: Enjoy a morning riverboat cruise down the Chena and Tanana Rivers. Then head for the airport for your long flight home.

IF YOU HAVE THREE WEEKS

Days 1-9: Follow the suggestions for the first nine days of the two-week itinerary, above.

Day 10: Rent a car and drive via Mount Alyeska and Portage Glacier to Seward. Take time to enjoy the spectacular drive.

Day 11: Enjoy a half-day cruise along the coast of Kenai Fjords National Park. Then continue your drive out the Sterling Highway, rounding the last turn to Kachemak Bay by late afternoon.

Day 12: Spend all day in beautiful Homer. Go halibut fishing, take a boat tour to the Center for Alaskan Coastal Studies, wander the Spit, or explore the Pratt Museum and other highlights of downtown Homer.

Day 13: Drive back to Anchorage via the Kenai National Wildlife Refuge, keeping your eyes open for moose in the meadows, Dall sheep on the rocky hillsides, and bald eagles perched above the Kenai River. Return your car at the end of the day.

Day 14: Take the Alaska Railroad to Denali National Park, arriving midafternoon.

Day 15: Take an all-day wildlife tour of the national park by bus, leaving early enough to see Mount McKinley without a cloudcap.

Day 16: Spend the morning and early afternoon in the park, then continue north on the Alaska Railroad to Fairbanks.

Day 17: Rent a car for the day to see Fairbanks, including the University of Alaska, the area's resurrected gold camps, and the Alaskaland theme park. Consider a morning or afternoon riverboat cruise down the Chena and Tanana Rivers.

Days 18–20: Join a three-day tour either to Barrow and Prudhoe Bay or to Nome and Kotzebue. Barrow and Kotzebue are Eskimo towns, fascinating for their preservation of Native culture. Prudhoe Bay is North America's leading oil-production center; Nome is famous as the goal of the annual Iditarod sled-dog race and a turn-of-the-century gold-mining mecca.

Day 21: Catch a flight home. Your three-week Alaska experience has regretfully come to an end. But you'll be back.

8. WHERE TO STAY

Alaskan accommodations are, as a rule, excellent. Lodging in major cities, including Anchorage, Fairbanks, and Juneau, is on a par with that found in similarly sized communities in the Lower 48. The farther from population centers you travel, the more rustic your lodging is likely to be.

During most of the year you'll have no problem arriving without reservations and walking into the room of your choice. That is decidedly *not* true during the peak summer season, when advance reservations are essential. It's important also that you check the local calendar: During festival periods rooms are also snapped up in a hurry.

Seasonal rates are the rule rather than the exception in most of Alaska. In some areas, like Anchorage, the difference between winter and summer rates may be only 10%–20%. In other parts of the state, including Fairbanks, summer rates can be 50% or more above winter rates. The explanation is that if the hotel or motel operators don't make their money during the brief visitor season, they might go hungry all year.

Virtually every Alaskan community, no matter what size, has a **city or borough bed tax,** which may range from 2% to 8%. This is *not* included in the rates quoted in this book; the local tax is noted separately at the beginning of each "Where to Stay" section. Specific information about arranging for the various types of accommodations outlined below is also provided in the individual chapters.

HOTELS With the exception of some of those in Anchorage, major hotels are not of international standard, though many deserve a "first-class" label. They cater primarily to house guests, running their restaurants and bars as adjuncts. Bathrooms are excellent, containing not only ample towels and soap, but often an array of complimentary amenities—shampoo, hand lotion, and shoeshine and sewing kits among them. Room telephones and televisions are standard equipment in better hotels. Rates commonly run $80 a night and upward to the $200 range.

The second tier of hotel accommodation falls into the budget category, often in the $30- to $60-a-night range. Rooms here tend to be secondary to the bar and restaurant on the ground floor: They're frequently up a side stairs, with a shared bathroom down the hall. A few of the more respectable entries in this classification may be listed in this book as budget alternatives.

MOTELS These are mainly located in cities and towns, with a rare few along the state's highways. Don't plan on driving on ahead with the intention of finding a vacant motel room en route to your final destination. You may have a long drive.

Most motels are moderately priced, in the $60–$90 range.

ROADHOUSES First built along the routes that took turn-of-the-century fortune hunters from the seaports to the goldfields, these wayside lodges usually incorporate a good restaurant and small bar with a handful of rustic rooms. They normally have a sink in the room but a shared bath. Prices are reasonable. Though rarely modern, these take the place of motels along Alaska's highways.

YOUTH HOSTELS Alaska has 12 youth hostels, all of them easily reached by road or ferry. Charges are typically $7–$22 a night, depending in part on whether you're a member of the International Youth Hostel Federation. All have separate men's and women's dormitories and bathrooms, communal kitchens, and common rooms. Some have a family room set aside. Blankets and cooking utensils are provided; you must bring a sheet sack or sleeping bag, and food. To help keep maintenance costs to a minimum, you'll normally be assigned a cleanup chore.

Alaskan hostels are in or near Anchorage, Delta Junction, Fairbanks, Girdwood, Haines, Juneau, Ketchikan, Palmer, Seward, Sitka, Soldotna, and Tok. The Delta Junction, Fairbanks, Ketchikan, Palmer, Sitka, and Tok hostels are open summer only.

Annual adult membership costs $20; individuals under 18 or over 55 pay $10. For information, contact the **Alaska Council, American Youth Hostels,** 700 H St., Anchorage, AK 99501 (tel. 907/276-3635).

BED & BREAKFASTS This option allows you to stay in a private home, relax with hosts anxious to share their knowledge about Alaska, and enjoy a breakfast that may range from bran muffins and coffee to hearty sourdough pancakes. Most B&Bs have no more than three or four guest rooms available for rent. Prices are typically $50–$80 a night per couple.

SERVICED APARTMENTS There aren't many serviced apartments around, although their numbers are increasing. They can be a great bargain for families, who get a two- or three-bedroom apartment with all bedding and cooking utensils provided, and maid service once or twice weekly. Long-term rentals are considerably cheaper than one- or two-night stays.

CAMPING GROUNDS There are plenty of campgrounds along the highways all over the state. Most accommodate recreational vehicles as well as tent-campers. In the southeastern and south-central regions, most are operated by the Forest Service and have a nominal usage fee of $5 or so. Facilities in state and national parks are likewise low priced. Private campgrounds, especially those providing electric hookups for RVs, may cost up to $20.

FISHING & HUNTING LODGES With few exceptions, these are off the beaten path and must be reached by small plane or, in some instances, chartered boat. You normally visit the lodge on a three- to seven-day package, which includes round-trip transportation, lodging (which can be rustic to contemporary), all meals, sporting equipment, and guide service. Prices run in the thousands of dollars. Look at the advertisements in *Alaska* magazine or any magazine catering to hunters or fishermen if you think you might be interested.

FOREST SERVICE CABINS One of Alaska's unique travel bargains is its system of 180 primitive cabins scattered throughout Tongass and Chugach National Forests. At $20 a night per cabin (not per person), they offer an opportunity for a cheap vacation. A few can be reached by trail off a main road, but most are in isolated locations requiring a fly-in or boat drop. Most have sleeping lofts for six people, wood stoves, tables, pit toilets, and a firewood cache. You must provide your own bedding and food, as well as all other requirements.

Cabin permits are issued either on a first-come, first-served basis or by drawing, with applications taken six months in advance. Cabins are open for use year-round, but fill up quickly during fishing and hunting seasons and in the summer. For information and reservations, write to **Tongass National Forest,** P.O. Box 1628, Juneau, AK 99802; or **Chugach National Forest,** 201 E. Ninth Ave., Anchorage, AK 99501.

FAST FACTS: **ALASKA**

American Express In Anchorage, travel services are available through Global Travel, 2522 Arctic Blvd., Suite 100 (tel. 907/276-2310), open Monday through Friday from 7:30am to 6pm. In Juneau, see Alaska Travel, 101 N. Franklin St. (tel. 907/586-1235), open Monday through Friday from 8am to 5:30pm and on Saturday from 9am to 4pm. To talk to an agent or to report a lost or stolen charge card, call toll free 800/528-4800.

Business Hours Hours vary, but most city stores are open by 10am weekdays and remain open until 5 or 6pm. Many also open on Saturday as well. During the height of the summer tourist season, you'll find many stores open seven days a week until 9 at night. And businesses in communities on cruise-ship routes will often open especially for short-time visitors, no matter how inconvenient the hour.

Camera/Film See "Photographic Needs," below.

Climate See "When to Go," in this chapter.

Consulates Most consular and other business with foreign governments is handled through their nearest consulates, in Seattle and San Francisco, or through their embassies in Washington, D.C. To contact the consulates of the nations nearest Alaska, call: for Canada, 206/443-1777 in Seattle; for Russia 415/202-9800 in San Francisco.

Crime See "Safety," below.

Driving Rules See "Getting Around" "By Car," in this chapter.

Drugstores All cities and major towns have late-night pharmacies. If you're having trouble getting a prescription filled, call the local hospital or medical center. Telephone numbers are listed in specific chapters.

Embassies See "Consulates," above.

Emergencies In major communities, dial **911** for police, fire, or ambulance. In small bush settlements, dial **0** for the operator.

Guides Cities and towns throughout the state offer a variety of options. Contact local convention and visitor bureaus or the state Division of Tourism (tel. 907/465-2010) for lists of qualified guides. If you plan to get off the roads and explore Alaska's bountiful wilderness, you'll want a list of registered guides and outfitters. To obtain such a list, write and send $5 to the Alaska Department of Commerce and Economic Development, Division of Occupational Licensing, Box DLIC, Juneau, AK 99811.

Holidays

New Year's Day January 1
Martin Luther King Day Third Monday in January
Presidents Day Third Monday in February
Memorial Day Last Monday in May
Independence Day July 4
Labor Day First Monday in September
Columbus Day Second Monday in October
Veterans (Armistice) Day November 11
Thanksgiving Day Last Thursday in November
Christmas Day December 25

Hotlines Major cities have a variety of hotlines open 24 hours, including crisis and poison-control lines. Anchorage, as the state's largest city, has many other services, including relief for rape victims and battered women. See the city chapters for local numbers, including those for road conditions, weather forecasts, and events calendars.

Information See "Information and Money" in this chapter, and specific city chapters for local information offices.

Pets It may be wise to leave Marmaduke or Garfield home when you undertake this trip, even if you're taking an RV. The most important reason is the potential of confrontation with Alaska's abundant—and often dangerous—wildlife. Should your pet wander away from your campsite, your hope of finding it again would be slim at best. Even if you're planning to stay in cities, you'll have a hard time finding an accommodation that will accept a pet.

Photographic Needs All sizable communities—including Anchorage, Fairbanks, Juneau, and Ketchikan—have reputable camera stores to assist with all photographic needs. Film is widely available at tourist attractions as well.

Police City police and state troopers react quickly to calls. Dial 911 for emergency response.

Radio and Television Alaska has 82 commercial and public radio stations, divided equally between AM and FM frequencies. There are also five FM stations in the Alaska Forces Radio Network. Because of the isolation of many of the state's communities, radio plays a vital communication role. More than 20 stations in 18 communities have "clear channel" status to allow personal messages to be transmitted without interference.

The state also has 11 commercial and four public television stations. Five of the commercial stations are in Anchorage; there are two in Fairbanks and one each in Juneau, Kenai, North Pole (suburban Fairbanks), and Sitka. Public TV stations are in Anchorage, Bethel, Fairbanks, and Juneau. Regular network programs from ABC (American Broadcasting Company), CBS (Columbia Broadcasting System), and NBC (National Broadcasting Company), as well as PBS (Public Broadcasting System), reach Alaska on a time-delayed basis. Satellite and cable television, such as CNN (Cable News Network), is available in most large communities.

Restrooms There are restroom facilities in most public buildings. Restaurants will let you use their restrooms if you order something, even if it's just a cup of coffee.

Safety Follow the same commonsense precautions when traveling in Alaska as you would anywhere else. Stay alert at all times and avoid isolated areas, particularly after dark. Wear a moneybelt and keep a close eye on your possessions, especially those that are easy targets for thieves and pickpockets—cameras, purses, and wallets.

More specific to Alaska is the importance of safety in the natural environment. If you're traveling in a car or bus and encounter a bear, moose, or other wild animal on or near the road, *stay in your vehicle!* A bear can be dangerous when spooked or threatened. If you're camping or hiking in the wild, observe the rules of dealing with wildlife: For instance, don't turn your back to a bear and run; doing so can invite pursuit. If you're planning a camping or backpacking trip, be sure to get the pamphlet "The Bears and You" from any office of the U.S. Forest Service or the Alaska Department of Fish and Game.

If you're on a small boat, wear a lifejacket at all times, no matter how good a swimmer you may be. The waters of Alaska are frigid, even in summer; if your vessel capsizes, you can quickly become hypothermic. The lifejacket will keep you afloat, even if you're too cold to keep swimming, until rescuers arrive.

State Symbols Alaska's flag, consisting of eight stars of gold on a field of blue, was designed in 1926 by a 13-year-old orphan, Benny Benson, in a territory-wide school contest. Simple in concept, it shows the constellation known as the Big Dipper pointing at the North Star. Explained Benson: "The blue field is for the Alaska sky and the forget-me-not, an Alaska flower. The North Star is for the future state of Alaska, the most northerly in the Union. The dipper is for the Great Bear—symbolizing strength." The state's motto, appropriately, is "North to the Future."

The state fish and state bird are the king salmon and the willow ptarmigan, a small arctic grouse that changes its plumage from brown in summer to white in winter. The state tree is the Sitka spruce, which grows to some 160 feet in height and 3–5 feet in diameter.

Taxes   Alaska has no state income tax, but many cities and boroughs impose sales and hotel taxes. See chapters on specific destinations.

Telephone/Telex/Fax   Long-distance telephone service is available to every community with 25 or more residents. Alascom, Inc., which provides service throughout the state, has had its own telecommunications satellite (*Aurora*) since 1982. Telex and fax service is widely available.

Television   See "Radio and Television," above.

Time   Alaska standard time is one hour earlier than Pacific standard time and four hours behind eastern standard time. When it's noon in New York and 9am in San Francisco, it's 8am in Sitka, Anchorage, and Dutch Harbor. The western Aleutians and some Bering Sea islands are on Hawaii time, which is an hour earlier than Alaska time; when it's 8am in Dutch Harbor, it's 7am in Adak.

Tourist Offices   See "Information and Money," in this chapter, and also specific city chapters.

Water   Anything from a tap is safe. If you're in the wilderness, you can't be as sure—giardia parasites may inhabit the stream or lake water that seems so pure. It's safest to practice water purification, either by treating the water with tablets or iodine or by boiling it.

Weather   See "When to Go," in this chapter. Beware of the wind-chill factor, which can lower the effective air temperature many degrees.

CHAPTER 3

FOR FOREIGN VISITORS

1. PREPARING FOR YOUR TRIP

2. GETTING TO & AROUND THE U.S.

• **FAST FACTS: FOR THE FOREIGN TRAVELER**

• **THE AMERICAN SYSTEM OF MEASUREMENTS**

Before undertaking a trip to Alaska, foreign travelers must make sure that they have satisfied the basic entrance requirements for a visit to the United States. This chapter discusses those requirements, as well as all other matters, such as travel insurance and means of transportation once you arrive, that you should know in order to make your trip as smooth and uncomplicated as possible. A list of fast facts at the end, followed by the American system of measurements, is intended to acquaint the foreign traveler with some of the customs and practices in the United States as well as provide him or her with essential information.

1. PREPARING FOR YOUR TRIP

NECESSARY DOCUMENTS Most foreigners entering the United States must carry two documents: a valid **passport,** expiring not less than six months prior to the scheduled end of their visit to the U.S.; and a **tourist visa,** which can be obtained without charge at any American consulate.

Exceptions are Canadian nationals, who merely have to carry proof of residence, and British and Japanese nationals, who require a passport but no visa.

To obtain a visa, you merely complete a form and submit a passport photo. At most consulates, it's an overnight process, though it can take longer during the busy summer period of June, July, and August. Those who apply by mail should enclose a large self-addressed, stamped envelope, and can expect a response in about two weeks. Besides at consulates, visa application forms can be obtained from airline offices and leading travel agencies.

In theory, a tourist visa (Visa B) is valid for single or multiple entries for a period of one year. In practice, the consulate that issues the visa uses its own discretion in granting length of stay. Applicants of good appearance, who can supply the address of a relative, friend, or business acquaintance in the United States, are most likely to be granted longer stays. (American resident contacts are also useful in passing through Customs quickly and for numerous other details.)

MEDICAL REQUIREMENTS New arrivals in the United States do not need inoculations unless they are coming from, or have stopped over in, an area known to be suffering from an epidemic, especially cholera or yellow fever.

Anyone applying for an immigrant's visa must undergo a screening test for the

AIDS-associated HIV virus, under a law passed in 1987. This test does not apply to tourists.

Any visitor with a medical condition that requires treatment with narcotics or other drugs, or with paraphernalia such as syringes, must carry a valid, signed prescription from a physician. This allays suspicions of drug smuggling by Customs or other officials.

TRAVEL INSURANCE All such insurance is optional in the United States. Medical care here is very costly and there is no free medical care for visitors, however, and every traveler is strongly advised to secure full insurance coverage before starting a trip.

For a relatively low premium, numerous specialized insurance companies will cover loss or theft of baggage, costs of trip cancellation, guaranteed bail in the event of a lawsuit or other legal difficulties, the cost of medical assistance (including surgery and hospitalization) in the event of sickness or injury, and the cost of an accident, death, or repatriation. Travel agencies, automobile clubs, and banks are among those selling travel insurance packages at attractive rates.

SAFETY

GENERAL While tourist areas are generally safe, crime is on the increase everywhere, and U.S. urban areas tend to be less safe than those in Europe or Japan. Visitors should always stay alert. This is particularly true of large U.S. cities. It is wise to ask the city or area's tourist office if you are in doubt about which neighborhoods are safe. Avoid deserted areas, especially at night. Don't go into any city park at night unless there is an occasion that attracts crowds—for example, New York City's concerts in the parks. Generally speaking, you can feel safe in areas where there are many people, and many open establishments.

Avoid carrying valuables with you on the street, and don't display expensive cameras or electronic equipment. Hold on to your pocketbook, and place your billfold in an inside pocket. In restaurants, theaters, and other public places, keep your possessions in sight.

Remember also that hotels are open to the public, and in a large hotel, security may not be able to screen everyone entering. Always lock your room door; don't assume that once inside your hotel you are automatically safe and need no longer be aware of your surroundings.

DRIVING Safety while driving is particularly important. Question your rental agency about personal safety, or ask for a traveler safety tips brochure when you pick up your car. Obtain written directions, or a map with the route marked in red, from the agency showing how to get to your destination. And, if possible, arrive and depart during daylight hours.

Recently more and more crime has involved cars and drivers. If you drive off a highway into a doubtful neighborhood, leave the area as quickly as possible. If you have an accident, even on the highway, stay in your car with the doors locked until you assess the situation, or until the police arrive. If you are bumped from behind on the street or are involved in a minor accident with no injuries and the situation appears to be suspicious, motion to the other driver to follow you. *Never* get out of your car in such situations. You can also keep a pre-made sign in your car which reads: "PLEASE FOLLOW THIS VEHICLE TO REPORT THE ACCIDENT." Show the sign to the other driver and go directly to the nearest police precinct, well-lighted service station, or all night store.

If you see someone on the road who indicates a need for help, do not stop. Take note of the location, drive on to a well-lighted area, and telephone the police by dialing 911.

Park in well-lighted, well-traveled areas if possible. Always keep your car doors locked, whether attended or unattended. Look around you before you get out of your car, and never leave any packages or valuables in sight. If someone attempts to rob you or steal your car—do not try to resist the thief/carjacker—report the incident to the Police Department immediately.

The Crime Prevention Division of the Police Department, City of New York, publishes a "Safety Tips for Visitors" brochure. It is translated into French, Spanish, Hebrew, German, Japanese, Dutch, Italian, Russian, Chinese, Portuguese, and Swedish and contains general safety information. For a copy write to: Crime Prevention Division Office of D.C.C.A., 80-45 Winchester Blvd., Queens Village, NY 11427.

2. GETTING TO & AROUND THE U.S.

Nearly all major airlines, including those of the United States, Europe, Asia, Australia, and New Zealand, offer APEX (advance purchase excursion) fares that significantly reduce the cost of transoceanic air travel. This enables travelers to pick their dates and ports, but requires that they prepurchase their ticket and meet minimum- and maximum-stay requirements—often 15–90 days. Season of travel and individual airline discounts also affect fares, but this is the most widely acknowledged means of cheap, flexible travel.

Some large airlines, including Delta, Northwest, TWA, and United, have in the past offered foreign travelers special add-on discount fares under the name "Visit USA." Though not currently available, they may be repeated in the future, and are worth asking a travel agent about. These tickets (which could be purchased overseas only) allowed unlimited travel between U.S. destinations at minimum rates for specified time periods, such as 21, 30, or 60 days. Short of bus or train travel, which can be inconvenient and time-consuming, this was the best way of traveling around the country at low cost.

AMTRAK, the American rail system, offers a USA Railpass to non–U.S. citizens. Available only overseas, it allows unlimited stopovers during a 45-day period of validity. Fares vary according to the size of the region being traveled. There are no AMTRAK connections to Alaska; however, it is possible to travel by rail as far as Prince Rupert, B.C. and ferry north or to Dawson Creek, B.C. and bus it up the Alaska Highway.

Foreign students can obtain the International Ameripass for unlimited bus travel on Greyhound/Trailways throughout the U.S. and Canada. Available for 7–30 days, it can be purchased with a student ID and a passport in New York, Orlando, Miami, San Francisco, and Los Angeles.

Foreign visitors who plan to rent a car can visit an American Automobile Association (AAA) office to obtain a "touring permit," which validates a foreign driver's license.

For detailed information on travel by car, train, and bus, see "Getting Around" in Chapter 2.

 FAST FACTS **FOR THE FOREIGN TRAVELER**

Area Code   See "Telephone and Fax," below.
Business Hours   See "Business Hours" in "Fast Facts: Alaska," in Chapter 2.
Currency and Exchange   In the American monetary system, one **dollar** ($1) is made up of 100 **cents** (100¢). Foreign visitors accustomed to paper money of varied colors and sizes should look carefully at the U.S. "greenbacks"—all **bills** are

green, and all are the same size regardless of value. Aside from the numbers, Americans often differentiate them by the portrait they bear: The $1 bill ("a buck") depicts George Washington; the seldom-seen $2, Thomas Jefferson; the $5, Abraham Lincoln; the $10, Alexander Hamilton; the $20, Andrew Jackson. Larger bills, including the $50 (Ulysses S. Grant) and the $100 (William McKinley), are not welcome in payment for small purchases.

There are six **coins,** four of them widely used: 1 cent (1¢, or a "penny"), which is brown copper; 5 cents (5¢, or a "nickel"); 10 cents (10¢, or a "dime"); and 25 cents (25¢, or a "quarter"). The 50-cent piece (50¢, or a "half dollar") is less widely circulated and $1 coins (including the older, large silver dollar and the newer, small Susan B. Anthony coin) are rare.

If they're denominated in U.S. dollars, you can easily cash **traveler's checks** in payment for goods or services at most hotels, motels, restaurants, and large stores. A major bank is the only place where you can confidently cash traveler's checks in any currency other than U.S. dollars. In fact, don't plan on changing any foreign currency here; the foreign-exchange bureaus common in other countries are largely absent from U.S. cities.

You'll find **credit and charge cards** the most widely used method of payment by travelers in the United States. In Alaska, VISA (BarclayCard in the United Kingdom, Chargex in Canada) and MasterCard (EuroCard in Europe, Access in Britain, Diamond in Japan) are accepted almost everywhere. American Express is taken by most establishments; Diners Club and Carte Blanche, by a large number; Discover, EnRoute, and JCB (the Japanese Credit Bank card), by an increasing number. Use of this "plastic money" reduces the necessity to carry large sums of cash or traveler's checks. It is accepted almost everywhere, except in food stores selling groceries and liquor. Credit cards can be recorded as a deposit for car rental, as proof of identity (often preferred to a passport) when cashing a check, or as a "cash card" for withdrawing money from banks that accept them.

Customs and Immigration U.S. Customs allows each adult visitor to import, duty free, one liter of wine or hard liquor, 1,000 cigarettes or 100 cigars (*not* from Cuba) or three pounds of smoking tobacco, and $400 worth of gifts. The only restrictions are that the visitor must spend at least 72 hours in the U.S., and must not have claimed these exemptions within the preceding six months. Food and plants are forbidden from import.

Foreign visitors may import or export up to $5,000 in U.S. or foreign currency, with no formalities. Larger amounts of money must be declared to Customs.

Visitors arriving by air, no matter what the port of entry, are well advised to be exceedingly patient and to resign themselves to a wait in the Customs and Immigration line. At busy times, especially when several overseas flights arrive within a few minutes of each other, it can take two or three hours just to get a passport stamped for arrival. Allot *plenty* of time for connections between international and domestic flights!

Border formalities by road or rail from Canada are relatively quick and easy.

Drinking Laws The legal age for the purchase and consumption of alcoholic beverages is 21; proof of age is required. Alcoholic beverages are sold or served in liquor stores, restaurants, and bars licensed by the state.

Note, however, that several rural communities in Alaska have banned the sale and consumption—as well as the *importation*—of alcoholic beverages. You could be arrested, fined, jailed, or deported for violating these local ordinances. So, before traveling to a remote destination, be sure to inquire about the local drinking laws.

Electricity Electrical service in the United States is 110 volts A.C., 60 cycles. If you're bringing hairdryers or other electrical appliances, you may need a transformer and/or adapter plugs.

Embassies and Consulates All embassies are in the U.S. national capital, Washington, D.C., and most nations have as well a mission to the United Nations in New York City. Consular representatives are located in various cities around the country.

Listed here are the embassies and some consulates of the major English-speaking countries, none of which, however, has a consulate in Alaska. Travelers from other countries can obtain telephone numbers for their embassies and consulates by calling "Information" in Washington, D.C. (tel. 202/555-1212).

The embassy of **Australia** is at 1601 Massachusetts Ave. NW, Washington, DC 20036 (tel. 202/797-3000). The Australian consulate in Hawaii is at 1000 Bishop St., Penthouse, Honolulu, HI 96813 (tel. 808/524-5050). There are consulates on the mainland West Coast at 611 N. Larchmont Blvd., Los Angeles, CA 90004 (tel. 213/469-4300), and at 360 Post St., San Francisco, CA 94108 (tel. 415/362-6160); and on the East Coast in the International Bldg., 636 Fifth Ave., Suite 420, New York, NY 10111 (tel. 212/245-4000). Other Australian consulates are in Chicago and Houston.

The embassy of **Canada** is at 1746 Massachusetts Ave. NW, Washington, DC 20036 (tel. 202/785-1400). There are Canadian consulates on the mainland West Coast at 300 S. Grand Ave., Suite 1000, Los Angeles, CA 90071 (tel. 213/687-7432); One Maritime Plaza, Golden Gateway Center, San Francisco, CA 94111 (tel. 415/981-8541); and 412 Plaza 600, Sixth and Stewart, Seattle, WA 98101 (tel. 206/443-1777). On the East Coast, there's a consulate at 1251 Ave. of the Americas, New York, NY 10020 (tel. 212/768-2400). Other Canadian consulates are in Atlanta, Buffalo (N.Y.), Chicago, Cleveland, Dallas, Detroit, and Minneapolis.

The embassy of the **Republic of Ireland** is at 2234 Massachusetts Ave. NW, Washington, DC 20008 (tel. 202/462-3939). There are Irish consulates on the mainland West Coast at 655 Montgomery St., Suite 930, San Francisco, CA 94111 (tel. 415/392-4214); and on the East Coast in the Chase Bldg., 535 Boylston St., Boston, MA 02116 (tel. 617/267-9330); and 515 Madison Ave., New York, NY 10022 (tel. 212/319-2555). There's another Irish consulate in Chicago.

The embassy of **New Zealand** is at 37 Observatory Circle NW, Washington, DC 20008 (tel. 202/328-4800). The only New Zealand consulate in the U.S. is at 10960 Wilshire Blvd., Suite 1530, Los Angeles, CA 90024 (tel. 213/477-8241).

The embassy of the **United Kingdom** is at 3100 Massachusetts Ave. NW, Washington, DC 20008 (tel. 202/462-1340). There's a consulate on the mainland West Coast at 1766 Wilshire Blvd., Suite 400, Los Angeles, CA 90025 (tel. 310/477-3322); and on the East Coast at 845 Third Ave., New York, NY 10022 (tel. 212/745-0200). Other British consulates are in Atlanta, Chicago, Houston, and Miami.

Emergencies A single emergency telephone number, **911,** will put you in touch with the police, an ambulance, or the fire department in most of Alaska. You can also obtain emergency assistance by dialing **0** (zero) for an operator.

Gasoline Gasoline is sold by the gallon (see "The American System of Measurements," below). For specific information about gassing up in Alaska, see "Getting Around" "By Car" in Chapter 2.

Holidays

New Year's Day January 1
Martin Luther King Day Third Monday in January
Presidents Day Third Monday in February
Memorial Day Last Monday in May
Independence Day July 4
Labor Day First Monday in September
Columbus Day Second Monday in October
Veterans (Armistice) Day November 11
Thanksgiving Day Last Thursday in November
Christmas Day December 25

Information See "Information and Money," in Chapter 2, for general information about the state of Alaska. For more detailed information about specific areas, see the individual cities in the regional chapters.

Legal Aid Those accused of serious offenses are advised to say and do nothing before consulting an attorney. Under U.S. law, a person who is arrested is permitted one telephone call to a party of his or her choice: Call your embassy or consulate! If you are pulled up for a minor infraction, such as a traffic offense, do *not* attempt to pay the fine directly to a police officer—you may wind up arrested on the much more serious charge of attempted bribery. Pay fines by mail, or directly to the clerk of a court.

Mail If you have made accommodations reservations well in advance, you can receive mail in Alaska at your hotel; all accommodations listed in this guide have complete mailing addresses included. Otherwise, your mail should be directed to you, "c/o General Delivery" (American for "Poste Restante"), at the central post office of the city or town you will be in. You will need your passport or other photo ID in order to pick up "General Delivery" mail.

Postage on letters sent within the United States is 29¢ for the first half ounce (about 14 grams), and 23¢ for each additional half ounce. Postcards are 19¢. Airmail postage to foreign destinations costs 50¢ for the first half ounce, 95¢ for the first ounce, and 39¢ for each additional half ounce.

Medical Emergencies See "Emergencies," above. In addition, medical facilities in the larger cities are listed in the regional chapters.

Newspapers and Magazines Foreign publications may be hard to find in Alaska except at a few rare newsstands in Anchorage. Your best bet for staying abreast of foreign news is to pick up a copy of the *New York Times* or an American weekly newsmagazine, such as *Time* or *Newsweek*.

Post See "Mail," above.

Radio and Television See "Fast Facts: Alaska" in Chapter 2. Audiovisual media, with three coast-to-coast networks, ABC, CBS, and NBC, joined in recent years by Fox, PBS, and CNN, play a major part in American life. Few accommodations in Alaskan cities and towns do not include a TV as a standard furnishing.

Restrooms See "Toilets," below.

Taxes In the United States, there is no VAT (value-added tax) or other indirect tax at a national level. Alaska has no state sales tax, but many cities and boroughs impose taxes of varying amounts on gross receipts, including hotel and restaurant bills and shop purchases. See chapters on specific destinations for more information.

Telephone and Fax Public telephone booths are easily seen in cities like Anchorage and Fairbanks, but may be more difficult to find in smaller towns. Stores and gas stations are your best bets. Hotels often add a per-call surcharge to your room bill of up to 75¢, although the standard charge for **local calls** is but 25¢.

Each local region in the country has been assigned an **area code,** some covering only part of a metropolitan area (Greater Los Angeles, for example, has six area codes) while some cover a large area. All of Alaska has a single area code: 907. Do not use the area code to call local numbers (within the same area code).

To make **long-distance calls** within the United States and to Canada or the Caribbean, dial 1 followed by the area code and the number you want. For reversed-charge, collect, and/or person-to-person calls, dial 0 (zero) instead of 1; then follow the same procedure as above and an operator will come on the line. For long-distance directory assistance, dial 1, the area code you need, and then 555-1212.

For direct **overseas calls,** dial 011, followed by the country code (Australia is 61; Ireland, 353; New Zealand, 64; United Kingdom, 44) and then by the city code and the number of the person you are calling.

Instant facsimile transmission or **fax service** can be provided by major hotels at a nominal charge, or by business service centers in most towns and cities.

Time The United States is divided into six time zones. From east to west, they are: eastern standard time (EST), central standard time (CST), mountain standard time (MST), Pacific standard time (PST), Alaska standard time (AST), and Hawaii standard time (HST). Keep time zones in mind when traveling or telephoning long distances in the United States. For example, noon in New York City (EST) is 11am in Chicago (CST), 10am in Denver (MST), 9am in Los Angeles (PST), 8am in Anchorage (AST), and 7am in Honolulu (HST). Daylight saving time is in effect from the last Sunday in April through the last Saturday in October; this alters the clock so that sunrise and sunset are an hour later.

Tipping Service in America is some of the best in the world, and tipping is the reason why. The amount you tip should depend on the service you have received. Good service warrants the following tips: bartenders, 15%; bellhops, $2 to $4; cab drivers, 15%; cafeterias and fast-food restaurants, no tip; chambermaids, $1 per person per day; cinemas, no tip; checkroom attendants, 50¢ to $1 (unless there is a charge, then no tip); gas-station attendants, no tip; hairdressers, 15% to 20%; parking valets, $1; redcaps (in airports and railroad stations), $2 to $4; restaurants and nightclubs, 15%.

Toilets Some foreign visitors complain that public "johns" are hard to find in the States. There are none on the streets, but most hotels, restaurants, bars, department stores, gasoline stations, museums, and other tourist attractions have them available. In a restaurant or bar, it's usually appropriate to order at least a cup of coffee or a soft drink before using the restrooms.

Visas See "Preparing for Your Trip," in this chapter.

Yellow Pages There are two kinds of telephone directory available. The general directory is called *White Pages,* and includes individuals and businesses alphabetically by name. The second directory, called the *Yellow Pages,* lists all local services, businesses, and industries alphabetically by category, with an index in the back. Listings include not only the obvious, such as automobile repairs and drugstores (pharmacies), but also restaurants by cuisine and location, places of worship by religious denomination, and other information that a tourist might **not** otherwise readily find. The *Yellow Pages* also include city plans or detailed area maps and often show postal ZIP Codes and public transportation routes.

THE AMERICAN SYSTEM OF MEASUREMENTS

LENGTH

1 inch (in.)			=	2.54cm			
1 foot (ft.)	=	12 in.	=	30.48cm	=	.305m	
1 yard (yd.)	=	3 ft.			=	.915m	
1 mile (m)	=	5,280 ft.					= 1.609km

To convert miles to kilometers, multiply the number of miles by 1.61. Also use to convert speeds from miles per hour (m.p.h.) to kilometers per hour (kmph).

To convert kilometers to miles, multiply the number of kilometers by .62. Also use to convert kmph to m.p.h.

CAPACITY

1 fluid ounce (fl. oz.)			=	.03 liters		
1 pint (pt.)	=	16 fl. oz.	=	.47 liters		
1 quart (qt.)	=	2 pints	=	.94 liters		
1 gallon (gal.)	=	4 quarts	=	3.79 liters	=	.83 Imperial gal.

To convert U.S. gallons to liters, multiply the number of gallons by 3.79.

To convert liters to U.S. gallons, multiply the number of liters by .26.

To convert U.S. gallons to Imperial gallons, multiply the number of U.S. gallons by .83.

To convert Imperial gallons to U.S. gallons, multiply the number of Imperial gallons by 1.2.

WEIGHT

1 ounce (oz.)			=	28.35g			
1 pound (lb.)	=	16 oz.	=	453.6g	=	.45 kg	
1 ton			=	2,000 lb.	=	907kg	= .91 metric tons

To convert pounds to kilograms, multiply the number of pounds by .45.
To convert kilograms to pounds, multiply the number of kilograms by 2.2.

AREA

1 acre				=	.41ha		
1 square mile	=	640 acres	=	259ha	=	2.6km²	

To convert acres to hectares, multiply the number of acres by .41.
To convert hectares to acres, multiply the number of hectares by 2.47.
To convert square miles to square kilometers, multiply the number of square miles by 2.6.
To convert square kilometers to square miles, multiply the number of square kilometers by .39.

TEMPERATURE

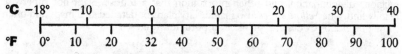

To convert degrees Fahrenheit to degrees Celsius, subtract 32 from °F, multiply by 5, then divide by 9 (example: 85°F − 32 × 5/9 = 29.4°C).
To convert degrees Celsius to degrees Fahrenheit, multiply °C by 9, divide by 5, and add 32 (example: 20°C × 9/5 + 32 = 68°F).

CHAPTER 4
SOUTHEAST ALASKA

Alaska's Panhandle stretches some 600 miles along the eastern shore of the Pacific Ocean from Mount St. Elias to Dixon Entrance, near Prince Rupert, B.C. Over 90% of its land area—comprising the 1,000 islands of the Alexander Archipelago and the adjacent North American mainland—is federal land. Tongass National Forest, with 16.9 million acres, is the country's largest. Two national parks (Glacier Bay and Wrangell–St. Elias) and two national monuments (Misty Fjords and Admiralty Island) occupy most of the rest of the territory.

The most remarkable feature of "Southeast," as it prefers to be known, is its waterways. The region has more than 10,000 miles of shoreline. Nearly all the major towns are located on sheltered straits and bays miles from open water. The state ferry system and most cruise ships take advantage of the calm waters of this Inside Passage. Some of the passages are of striking beauty, such as the Lynn Canal between Juneau and Skagway, and the Behm Canal ("Misty Fjords") near Ketchikan. Snow-clad mountains tower as much as 15,000 feet above these waterways, and dozens of glaciers pour their centuries-old rivers of ice directly into bays and inlets.

Only about 70,000 permanent residents inhabit this natural wonderland. The vast majority live in a handful of settlements that sprinkle the densely forested coastline. The state capital of Juneau, with a population of around 30,000, is the "yuppiest" Alaskan city; its economy is built around government and service industries. But every town in the southeast has a distinct character. Ketchikan (pop. about 14,000), Alaska's rainy southern gateway, is a fishing and lumber town with a rich Indian heritage. Sitka (pop. 8,500) is proud of its Russian history. Wrangell (pop. 2,600) has a frontier atmosphere, while Petersburg (pop. 3,600), founded by Norwegians, still has an affluent Scandinavian flavor. Haines (pop. 2,000), built in part around an old military barracks, boasts the largest concentration of bald eagles in the world. Skagway (pop. 700), jumping-off point for the Klondike gold rush, feeds on summer tourists who disembark from cruise ships to explore its turn-of-the-century community.

There's one drawback: It rains a lot here. Late spring and early summer are the driest times, but that's relative. Juneau gets an average annual precipitation of 56 inches, Petersburg gets 105 inches, and Ketchikan gets a whopping 155 inches. Seattle, which has a reputation for wetness, by contrast averages only 34 inches a year. If you're going to southeast Alaska, don't forget your raincoat and boots! On the plus side, temperatures are mild, with July averages of 56°F in Juneau, 58°F in Ketchikan, and January averages of 23°F in Juneau, 34°F in Ketchikan.

WHAT'S SPECIAL ABOUT SOUTHEAST ALASKA

Heritage
- ☐ Sitka, the 19th-century capital of Russian Alaska.
- ☐ Skagway, launching pad for the Klondike Gold Rush.
- ☐ Petersburg, where "Little Norway" lives on.

Scenery
- ☐ Glacier Bay, a geologists' and naturalists' dream.
- ☐ Mendenhall Glacier, Alaska's most accessible river of ice.
- ☐ Misty Fjords, where half-mile-high granite cliffs flank a narrow waterway.

Wildlife
- ☐ Grizzly bears—in particular, those of Kootznoowoo Wilderness on Admiralty Island, where bears outnumber humans.
- ☐ Bald eagles, especially the thousands that visit the Chilkat River beginning in November each year.

- ☐ Whales, including the humpback whales that migrate each year to Glacier Bay.

Native Culture
- ☐ The Tlingit totem-pole carvers of Ketchikan, Wrangell, and other towns.
- ☐ The Chilkat blanket makers of the Haines area.
- ☐ The traditional Haida villages on Prince of Wales Island and the Tsimshians of Metlakatla.

Outdoor Sports
- ☐ Fishing for salmon and halibut from one of the region's many wilderness lodges.
- ☐ Kayaking through the primeval passages of Glacier Bay or the Misty Fjords.
- ☐ Skiing at Eaglecrest, high atop Douglas Island overlooking Juneau.

For tourist information, contact the **Southeast Alaska Tourism Council,** P.O. Box 20710, Juneau, AK 99802 (tel. 907/586-2989). Each major town has its own visitors' bureau or chamber of commerce to assist you in finding lodging and to provide other information.

SEEING SOUTHEAST ALASKA

GETTING THERE

There are only two practical ways to get to southeast Alaska—by air and by sea. There are highway connections only to Haines and Skagway. But even though schedules will place a few limitations on your travel plans, you'll have no problem getting around.

BY PLANE   From Seattle, **Alaska Airlines** has daily nonstop flights to and from Juneau and Ketchikan; direct flights to Sitka, Wrangell, Petersburg, and Yakutat; and thrice-weekly connections to Gustavus for Glacier Bay (daily in summer). All points connect with the rest of Alaska via three daily Juneau–Anchorage flights. Call for reservations and information (tel. 907/789-0600 in Juneau, 907/225-2141 in Ketchikan, 907/874-3308 in Wrangell, 907/772-4255 in Petersburg, 907/966-2266 in Sitka, 907/784-3366 in Yakutat, or toll free 800/426-0333).

Once you're in a gateway city, numerous local air-taxi services will carry you to any settlement or isolated bay. These include **Ketchikan Air Service** (tel. 907/225-6608) in Ketchikan, **Wings of Alaska** (tel. 800/478-WING) in Juneau, and **L.A.B. Flying Service** (tel. 907/766-2222) in Haines.

SOUTHEAST ALASKA

0 |===| 40 mi
0 |===| 64 km

To Bellingham and Seattle →

--- Alaska Marine Highway System (Ferry Routes)

BRITISH COLUMBIA

UNITED STATES

Dixon Entrance

Prince Rupert

Portland Canal

Hyder

Misty Fjords National Monument

Behm Canal

Revillagigedo Island

Ketchikan

Annette Island

Metlakatla

Clarence Strait

Thorne Bay

Prince of Wales Island

Hollis

Hydaburg

Wrangell Island

Etolin Island

Klawock

Craig

Edna Bay

Zarembo Island

Wrangell

Mitkof Island

Kupreanof Island

Petersburg

Sumner Strait

Port Alexander

Kuiu Island

Chatham Strait

Stikine River

CANADA

UNITED STATES

National Forest

Kake

Frederick Sound

Entrance Island

Stephens Passage

Admiralty Island

Tongass

Admiralty Island National Monument

Angoon

Baranof Island

Sitka

Tenakee Springs

Chichagof Island

Hoonah

Pelican

Chichagof

Alexander Archipelago

Gulf of Alaska

Taku Inlet

Juneau

Mendenhall Glacier

Lynn Canal

Icy Strait

Gustavus

Glacier Bay

Elfin Cove

Cross Sound

Glacier Bay National Park and Preserve

Muir Glacier

Haines

Haines Highway

Skagway

98

BRITISH COLUMBIA

← To Tok, Fairbanks and Alaska Highway North

To Anchorage

6576

BY BUS   Haines and Skagway—both on the Alaska Marine Highway—are served by **Alaskon Express** buses (tel. toll free 800/544-2206), with twice-weekly service to Whitehorse, Fairbanks, and Anchorage. For information, call the toll-free number or contact Gray Line of Alaska, 300 Elliott Ave. W., Seattle, WA 98119 (tel. 907/983-2241 in Skagway, 907/766-2468 in Haines). **Alaska-Yukon Motorcoaches**, 349 Wrangell St., Anchorage, AK 95501 (tel. 907/276-1305, or toll free 800/637-3334), provides similar service.

BY CAR   Yes, you can reach the southeast by paved highway . . . but your choice of destination is limited to Skagway or Haines.

Main access to Skagway is provided by Klondike Hwy. 2, which branches off the Alaska Hwy. at Mile 905, just south of the city of Whitehorse. The road climbs 98 miles over magnificent White Pass (3,290 feet) before dropping sharply to Skagway. This pass has been kept open through the winter snow since 1986–87. Heading north on the Alaska Hwy. through the Yukon, you can turn off at Mile 866, Jake's Corner, onto gravel Yukon Hwy. 8, which connects with fully paved Klondike Hwy. 2 at Carcross.

To reach Haines, continue on the Alaska Hwy. about 100 miles west from Whitehorse to the village of Haines Junction at Mile 1,016. Here the spectacular Haines Hwy. turns south for 151 miles, skirting Canada's Kluane National Park and climbing over Chilkat Pass (3,493 feet). The road enters the United States 41 miles northwest of Haines. A little less than half of the highway is gravel.

For many years there has been talk about giving Juneau a road connection to "outside"—either to Haines (with a short ferry connection across the Lynn Canal) or to Atlin, B.C.—but so far these plans remain pipe dreams. There also are occasional mutters about connecting Wrangell by road with British Columbia's Cassiar Hwy. up the Stikine River. Tiny Hyder, alone in its isolation across the Portland Canal from Stewart, B.C., already is joined to Canada by highway bridge; its only connection to the rest of Alaska is a weekly ferry to Ketchikan.

BY FERRY   With no highways connecting the major settlements of the southeast, the state ferry system—properly called the **Alaska Marine Highway**—is the link on which most of the region's residents depend. Since becoming fully operational in 1963, the system has provided efficient and punctual service from Skagway to Ketchikan and all the way to Washington state. The southern terminus has been in Bellingham, Wash., since 1989, when it was moved from Seattle.

The *Matanuska* and *Columbia* each provide sailings from Bellingham every Tuesday and Friday in summer for Ketchikan, Wrangell, Petersburg, Sitka, Juneau, Haines, and Skagway. (There's one boat a week, on Friday, in winter.) The *Malaspina* and *Taku* provide similar twice-weekly service from Prince Rupert, B.C. The marine "milk run" operator is the *LeConte,* which stops at least once a week (and sometimes as often as three times a week) in Petersburg, Kake, Sitka, Angoon, Tenakee Springs, Hoonah, Juneau, Haines, and Skagway. The *Aurora* operates continually between Prince Rupert, Ketchikan, Metlakatla, and Hollis (Prince of Wales Island), with a weekly side trip to Hyder.

Everyone pays a standard walk-on fare, not including meals or berths; children 6–11 pay half fare, and those under 5 sail free. If you take a cabin, you pay extra for that; prices are per cabin, not per person, and vary according to the cabin's size and location on the ship. If you're bringing a car, you'll also pay for its passage; costs vary with vehicle length.

The sample fares in the accompanying table are for adult walk-on passage, a two-berth cabin with ocean view and complete facilities, and a vehicle 10–15 feet in length. Thus a couple traveling from Bellingham to Skagway with their compact car and staying in a two-berth cabin would pay $1,264 for the four-day, one-way journey—$228 less if they brought their sleeping bags and stretched out in the solarium at night. But unless you're continuing to the Interior or returning home via the Alaska Highway through Canada, there's little reason to bring your car.

STANDARD FARES

	Walk-on Passage	Two-Berth Cabin	Vehicle [10-15 ft.]
From Bellingham to:			
Ketchikan	$154	$153	$363
Juneau	$216	$210	$518
Skagway	$236	$228	$564
From Prince Rupert to:			
Skagway	$118	$108	$278

The ferry system used to allow free stopovers en route, but no more. To stop in Ketchikan, Sitka, and Juneau en route to Skagway, you'll have to pay $154 (Bellingham-Ketchikan), $52 (Ketchikan-Sitka), $24 (Sitka-Juneau), plus $24 (Juneau-Skagway)—a total of $254 or $18 over the straight Bellingham-Skagway fare.

I've covered details of Alaska ferry service in "Getting Around" "By Ferry," in Chapter 2. For schedules, reservations, and other information, contact the Alaska Marine Highway, P.O. Box R, Juneau, AK 99811 (tel. toll free 800/642-0066). Local offices are in Juneau (tel. 907/465-3941), Ketchikan (tel. 907/225-6181), Wrangell (tel. 907/874-3711), Petersburg (tel. 907/772-3855), Sitka (tel. 907/747-3300), Haines (tel. 907/766-2113), Skagway (tel. 907/983-2229), Prince Rupert (tel. 604/627-1744), and Bellingham (tel. 206/626-8445 days or 206/676-0212 for 24-hour recorded information).

BY CRUISE SHIP Twelve different cruise lines operate 21 separate ships on voyages through the Inside Passage. Some of these ships are small, carrying as few as 90 passengers; others are ocean-going behemoths that take upward of 1,000 passengers. Peruse the section on "Getting There" "By Cruise Ship," in Chapter 2, before deciding on which ship, if any, is most appropriate for you. All cruise ships stop in Juneau, most also pause in Ketchikan and/or Sitka, and many make additional stops at southeast Alaska's other ports.

A SUGGESTED ROUTE

It makes most sense either to begin your journey at Ketchikan and work your way north or to conclude your trip in Ketchikan and continue south. Ferry schedules and available time will determine how long you can tarry at each stop. If you've got two weeks, I'd suggest working north in this order: two nights in Ketchikan, a night each in Wrangell and Petersburg, two nights in Sitka, two to three nights each in Juneau and Glacier Bay, a night in Haines, and two to three nights in Skagway.

---

1. KETCHIKAN

650 miles N of Seattle, 285 miles S of Juneau

GETTING THERE   By Plane   Alaska Airlines (tel. 907/225-2141 or 225-3138) has direct connections to Ketchikan from Seattle and Juneau, as well as Sitka, Petersburg, and Wrangell. Ketchikan Air Service (tel. 907/225-6608) flies to local destinations, including Prince of Wales Island and Metlakatla. Trans Provincial Airlines (tel. 604/627-1351) flies between Ketchikan and Prince Rupert, B.C., making this truly an international airport.

By Ferry There are 13 northbound and 16 southbound arrivals weekly during the peak summer season, including Thursday and Sunday mornings from Bellingham, Wash. (the *Columbia*), and six times weekly from Juneau. The schedule is reduced in winter, but weekly connections from Bellingham remain constant. The terminal is at 3501 N. Tongass Ave. (tel. 907/225-6181), about two miles north of downtown.

DEPARTING The Ketchikan Airport Shuttle (tel. 225-5429) will pick you up at your hotel, drive right onto the airport ferry, and deliver you and your luggage to the "departing passengers" door for $11–$12. Company vans will also deliver you to the Alaska Marine Highway ferry dock.

SPECIAL EVENTS Festival of the North, music and arts, three weekends in February; King Salmon Derby, three weekends starting Memorial Day; Fourth of July weekend, featuring a logging carnival and parade; Blueberry Festival, music and arts, second weekend in August.

Long, skinny Ketchikan snakes for several miles along the southwestern shore of Revillagigedo Island, facing Tongass Narrows. Built partly on a steep hillside and partly on pilings driven into the narrows, it's the first town that travelers reach when ferrying northward—thus its moniker, "Alaska's First City." In fact it's the state's fourth-largest community (after Anchorage, Fairbanks, and Juneau). Half the 14,000 inhabitants live in the city proper, the others within commuting distance. In terms of economy and climate Ketchikan has more in common with Seattle than it does with Anchorage, 750 miles north.

Don't come to Ketchikan expecting clear skies. With an average annual rainfall of 155 inches, it's unlikely you'll get them. Even in the "dry" season (May, June, and July), Ketchikan averages 8 inches of rain per month. October through December are the rainiest times—average October precipitation is 25 inches, and a record 43 inches once fell in November. Ketchikan also gets about 52 inches of snow a year, but it doesn't last long. The average January temperature is 34°F, so rain quickly washes the white stuff away . . . then freezes overnight, sometimes playing havoc with city plumbing. The steep stairs that climb many hillsides in place of streets were built by residents who didn't want to fight ice and mud to get home.

Ketchikan got its name from a Tlingit settlement, Kitschk-hin—*hin* meaning "creek" and *kitschk* meaning "thundering wings of an eagle." The town was established in 1887 with the construction of a salmon cannery at the mouth of Ketchikan Creek, which even today, citizens say, is so thick with spawning salmon in the fall that "you can walk across on their backs." Gold was discovered in the area in 1898, followed soon thereafter by silver and copper, and Ketchikan found its niche as a supply center. Though mining faded in importance, the fishing industry continued to boom. In the 1930s Ketchikan had a dozen canneries and was called the "Salmon Capital of the World." Overfishing eventually caused a drastic decline in fishing income, but the economy diversified so that today the timber industry is on an almost equal footing with the fleet (the timber industry's most visible sign is the $80-million Louisiana-Pacific Corp. pulp mill at Ward Cove, north of the city).

Today Ketchikan is proud to show off its Native heritage. Situated at the conjunction of three cultures—Tlingit, Haida, and Tsimshian—Ketchikan features the Totem Heritage Cultural Center, the Totem Bight State Park, and the Saxman Native Village and Totem Pole Park.

There are about 35 miles of roads extending north and south of Ketchikan along the west coast of Revillagigedo Island. (The island was named by Capt. George Vancouver for an 18th-century Spanish viceroy; locals just pronounce it "Ruhvilla.") There are sportfishing lodges and resorts at both ends of the road, although most wilderness camps are "fly-in" getaways.

Ketchikan is the gateway to Misty Fjords National Monument; to the numerous settlements on Prince of Wales Island, southeast Alaska's largest island; and to the Tsimshian town of Metlakatla on Annette Island, the only Indian reservation in the state of Alaska.

You'll find the flavor of Ketchikan decidedly blue collar, especially around the colorful waterfront. Fishermen and loggers contribute to a rowdy atmosphere in the cafés and bars along Front Street and out Tongass Avenue. During the summer months, when gift shops brighten their showcase windows for the cruise-ship throngs, this isn't quite as evident. But drop into town any other time of year and if you're not wearing a wool hat and "Ketchikan sneakers" (rubber mud boots), you'll feel out of place.

ORIENTATION

ARRIVING The **Ketchikan International Airport** stands apart from the rest of the city on Gravina Island, across Tongass Narrows; until a bridge is built (still a hot topic of discussion), it must be reached by ferry shuttle. The ferry crossing takes seven minutes and costs $2.50 (including a return trip the same day). A boat leaves the Ketchikan mainland at 15 and 45 minutes past the hour, and departs Gravina Island on the hour and half hour. It carries nine cars (at $5 per vehicle) and a couple of dozen foot passengers. Note: There's no baggage storage available at the Ketchikan airport. The Alaska Marine Highway **ferry terminal** is a couple of miles north of the airport ferry dock.

INFORMATION The **Ketchikan Visitors Bureau** is opposite the cruise-ship landing dock at 131 Front St., Ketchikan, AK 99901 (tel. 907/225-6166; fax 907/225-4250). If you plan to do any fishing, hunting, hiking, or boating in the Ketchikan area, you may want to visit or call the **U.S. Forest Service Information Center,** in the Federal Building at Mill and Stedman Streets (tel. 907/225-3101). Open Monday through Friday from 8am to 4:30pm plus summer weekends and during cruise-ship arrivals, the information center has displays and slide programs on local forest and wildlife management, plus a variety of free maps and pamphlets.

CITY LAYOUT Ketchikan spreads northwest to southeast along the riverine Tongass Narrows. The ferry terminals—both for the Marine Highway System and for the Ketchikan International Airport—are at the north end of town, along with the post office; most city buildings, as well as the Totem Heritage Center and historic district, are 2½ miles south. Often congested with traffic, Tongass Avenue connects the two halves of town. The Plaza Port West shopping mall is situated about halfway between, in the Westend Commercial District.

GETTING AROUND

An efficient **borough bus** service (tel. 228-6625) runs between Ketchikan's main post office, near the ferry terminal at the north end of town, and the Robertson Building, at the south end, at half-hourly intervals from 6:45am to 6:45pm Monday through Saturday. The fare is $1.

Taxis are $2 at flagfall and cost about $8 from downtown to the ferry terminal; call **Alaska Cab** (tel. 225-2133), **Yellow Taxi** (tel. 225-5555), or **Sourdough Cab** (tel. 225-5544).

Alaska Car Rental (tel. 907/225-5000, or toll free 800/478-0007) and **Avis** (tel. 907/225-4515, or toll free 800/331-1212) have outlets at the airport.

FAST FACTS

Area Code The telephone area code is 907.

Emergencies In a life-threatening emergency, phone 911. For less serious problems, call the city police (tel. 225-6631), the state troopers (tel. 225-5118), the fire department (tel. 225-9616), the Coast Guard (tel. 225-5666), or the Ketchikan Volunteer Rescue Squad (tel. 225-9616). For medical assistance, visit Ketchikan General Hospital, 3100 Tongass Ave. (tel. 225-5171).

Newspaper Read the *Ketchikan Daily News,* published Monday through Saturday, for information regarding local events and activities.

Telecommunications The Alascom Teleservices Center, 315 Mill St., provides a long-distance call station and free fax and computer services—you just pay the long-distance charges.

WHAT TO SEE & DO

SIGHTS & ATTRACTIONS

Many visitors' first stop is the ✪ **Creek Street Historic District,** formerly known as "The Line"—from 1902 to 1954 southeast Alaska's most notorious red-light district.

This zigzagging boardwalk on pilings above Ketchikan Creek supported at least 30 "sporting houses" in its heyday. "It was the only place in Alaska where both fish and fishermen went upstream to spawn," one old-timer told me.

Territorial law said that no more than two women could live in a house or it could be considered an illegal brothel—so women like Frenchie and Black Mary merely lived alone and carried on. They observed a 4am curfew, had weekly health checkups, and agreed to shop downtown only on Wednesday.

But not everything was above board: In Prohibition times Creek Street was the one place in Ketchikan where liquor was easily obtained, smuggled from Canada by boats that unloaded their cargoes through trap doors.

Today the old houses are being spruced up and converted into small shops and businesses.

Several wooden platforms for viewing spawning salmon between June and August have recently been built as extensions of Creek Street. As many as 1,500 king salmon, weighing up to 50 pounds, return up Ketchikan Creek each year to deposit their roe. Ten times that many pink salmon, usually weighing no more than five pounds, also make the journey. Fishing is not allowed in the creek.

Perhaps the best reason to spend time in Ketchikan is to absorb its Native Indian culture. This area is unique in Alaska because three separate tribes lived in close proximity. While Tlingit are predominant on Revillagigedo Island and throughout southeast Alaska, the southern half of Prince of Wales Island is principally Haida, and nearby Annette Island is a Tsimshian reservation.

Totem carvers today teach their craft at the ✪ **Saxman Totem Park,** billed as "the world's largest collection of totem poles." It's three miles south of downtown Ketchikan in the Tlingit village of Saxman, founded in the late 1800s by Natives who migrated from outlying villages, then returned to their original homes in the 1930s to recover 25 totems. Some poles were repaired, restored, and brightly painted; replicas were made of others. The spectacular totem pole at the entrance to the park is called the "Sun and Raven"; a native guide will tell you the story behind this and other poles. But you might recognize Abraham Lincoln immediately by his stovepipe hat.

While you're in Saxman, enjoy the Cape Fox Dancers and Naa Kahidi Theater, take in the craft demonstrations and village museum, and sample some Native cooking. Artisans will be happy to accept a commission to carve you a personal totem pole, by the way—at $5,000 a foot! Call 225-9038 for general information about Saxman tours and events.

Another significant monument to Native culture in the area, on the site of a former Tlingit summer camp, is **Totem Bight State Historical Park,** 10 miles north of the city on the Tongass Highway. You'll find replicas of a 19th-century clan house and 14 Tlingit and Haida totem poles. The setting is lovely: You must park your vehicle and walk a couple of hundred yards through rain forest (complete with interpretive signs) to reach the park clearing on a small coastal cove. A brochure identifies each pole. Bald eagles can often be seen atop trees and totem poles in this vicinity.

DOLLY'S HOUSE, 24 Creek St. Tel. 225-6329.

This two-story green structure has been preserved just as it was when the Line was

done away with in 1954. Its colorful madam, Dolly Copeland Arthur, lived in the house from 1919 to 1970; she died in 1975 in a local nursing home. Her house is now a period museum. In its five-room world of brass beds and floral wallpaper, with secret wall panels for bootleg whisky, you'll get a glimpse of the old times.
Admission: $2.
Open: Mid-May to Sept, daily 9am–5pm. **Closed:** Oct to mid-May.

TOTEM HERITAGE CENTER, 601 Deermount Ave. Tel. 225-5900.

✪ This fine museum was built by the city in 1976 to preserve and exhibit a unique collection of 33 original totem poles and house posts from nearby Tlingit and Haida villages, all abandoned around the turn of the century. Totem poles were never built to last; as they weathered away, new poles were carved and erected to honor the dead, to record history and oral tradition, and to document social events. The poles on display, carved from cedar between 1850 and 1900, were saved for posterity as examples of the work of master carvers.

Between October and May, classes in Native arts, crafts, and culture are taught by tribal elders of the Alaska Native Brotherhood/Sisterhood and the Southeast Alaska Indian Arts Council. Some of the classes' work is on sale in the center's small gift shop.
Admission: $2 adults, free for children under 18; free for all visitors on Sun and during the off-season.
Open: June–Sept, Mon–Sat 8am–5pm, Sun 9am–5pm; Oct–May, Tues 1–5pm and 6–9pm, Wed–Fri 1–5pm. Times may be extended when cruise ships are in port.
Directions: Turn left off Stedman Street onto Deermount Avenue, about three blocks east of Creek Street.

TONGASS HISTORICAL MUSEUM, 629 Dock St. Tel. 225-5600.

The Totem Heritage Center is administered by this museum, which overlooks Ketchikan Creek from the Centennial building it shares with the public library. The Tongass museum documents Ketchikan's Native and white history with photos and artifacts, including a renowned collection of Indian basketry and steamed bentwood boxes. Look for the work of local Tlingit artist Nathan Jackson. A short distance outside the building is a 1983 totem pole, carved by Dempsey Bob, that depicts the tale of "The Raven Stealing the Sun."
Admission: $1 adults, free for children; free for everyone Sun.
Open: June–Sept, Mon–Sat 8:30am–5pm, Sun 1–5pm; Oct–May, Wed–Fri 1–5pm, Sat–Sun 1–4pm.

WALKING TOUR — KETCHIKAN

Start: Ketchikan Visitors Bureau.
End: Ketchikan Visitors Bureau.
Time: Approximately two hours.
Best Times: Any dry day in June or July.
Worst Times: When it rains, which is often.

Start at the:

1. **Ketchikan Visitors Bureau,** at 131 Front St., where you can pick up a brochure with a map recommending walking tours of Ketchikan (this tour combines the city's high points). From the bureau's waterfront headquarters, head east on Mission Street. A block and a half ahead on your left is:
2. **St. John's Episcopal Church.** The town's oldest church was built in 1903 as part of a complex that included a hospital and a school. Its interior paneling is red cedar provided by early Saxman Indians. The hospital is now a center for those

who live and work on the sea. Turn right here, at Bawden Street, and left again at Mill Street. At Mill and Stedman Streets, is the:

3. **U.S. Forest Service headquarters,** with public displays and information about the surrounding Tongass National Forest.

Opposite the Forest Service building, at Stedman and Dock Streets, is the:

4. **Chief Johnson Totem Pole,** an exact replica of a 1901 pole that was moved to the Totem Heritage Center in 1982. Created by hand in 1989 by Tlingit carver Israel Shotridge, it tells the story of the Raven clan and the world's first salmon. Just ahead on Dock Street is the:

5. **Tongass Historical Museum** (see above). Turn right here and cross Ketchikan Creek on the footbridge to:

6. **Creek Street,** and turn right down the boardwalk. This historical district includes:

7. **Dolly's House** (see above), one of Ketchikan's most popular attractions today. From the boardwalk behind the Eagles Hall, a free tramway climbs the steep hill to the:

8. **Westmark Cape Fox Lodge.** The view from the hotel lobby is impressive (see "Where to Stay," below).

Creek Street rejoins Stedman Street opposite:

9. **Thomas Basin,** one of the city's three major harbors and possibly the most picturesque. Before it was dredged in 1931 this was a broad, sandy tidal flat where young Ketchikan folk had a baseball field. As the tide came in, old-timers report, outfielders chased fly balls in a skiff! Today you can watch fishermen repair their nets and trawlers return with their catch.

Along the south shore of the harbor is:

10. **Thomas Street,** one of the few remaining wood-plank streets in Ketchikan. Canneries and fish-processing firms can be found out this lane. Farther south on Stedman Street, on your right, is the:

11. ***Return of the Eagle*** mural, a 70- by 120-foot work by artist Don Barrie, assisted by 25 Native youth, that depicts ancient legends. Just past the mural, turn left on Deermount Street, past the Ketchikan Indian Corporation headquarters, and proceed to the city's outstanding:

12. **Totem Heritage Center** (see description, above). Across Ketchikan Creek from the Heritage Center is the:

13. **Deer Mountain Fish Hatchery,** open for public observation in the summer daily from 9am to 12:30pm and 1:30 to 5:30pm. Biologists from the Alaska Department of Fish and Game raise 300,000 coho and chinook salmon for release into the creek each year. There's a short trail to:

14. **City Park,** where picnic tables now surround the ponds used as holding tanks for Ketchikan's first hatchery in the early 1900s.

If you follow Park Avenue back down Ketchikan Creek toward downtown, you'll have an opportunity to watch spawning salmon fighting their way upstream from numerous viewpoints. There's a:

15. **fish ladder** where Park Avenue crosses the creek at Harris Street; this gives the spawners an easy route around a set of falls. Where Park meets Bawden Street, look uphill to see the:

16. **Grant Street Trestle,** the last surviving turn-of-the-century walkway that pioneers built to cope with Ketchikan's steep, rocky terrain. Another testament to architectural ingenuity is:

17. **Edmond Street,** which heads uphill from Dock Street just around the corner from Bawden. The "street" is actually a long set of stairs, leading to a great view from the top. Plenty of houses have an Edmond Street address—but none has on-street parking!

From here, you can follow Dock Street to the waterfront at Front Street, and return to the Ketchikan Visitors Bureau, one block south.

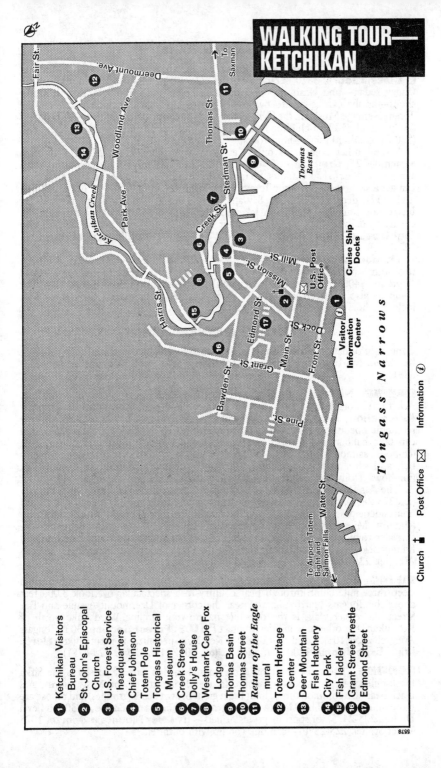

WALKING TOUR—KETCHIKAN

Tongass Narrows

Church ✝ Post Office ✉ Information ⓘ

1. Ketchikan Visitors Bureau
2. St. John's Episcopal Church
3. U.S. Forest Service headquarters
4. Chief Johnson Totem Pole
5. Tongass Historical Museum
6. Creek Street
7. Dolly's House
8. Westmark Cape Fox Lodge
9. Thomas Basin
10. Thomas Street
11. *Return of the Eagle* mural
12. Totem Heritage Center
13. Deer Mountain Fish Hatchery
14. City Park
15. Fish ladder
16. Grant Street Trestle
17. Edmond Street

5578

ORGANIZED TOURS

Undoubtedly the most fun way to tour Ketchikan is with Lois Munch and her ✪ **Classic Tours,** 3820 Baranof Ave. (tel. 225-3091). Munch drives a restored '55 Chevy sedan—and wears a period outfit complete with poodle skirt and saddle shoes—as she carries one to five passengers to city sights, including Saxman, the Totem Heritage Museum, the fish hatchery, and a remote bald eagle's nest. The fare is $35 per adult ($20 for children 6–12; under 6, free) for 1½-hour tours; $50 per adult ($30 for children) for 2½-hour tours.

Several other companies offer Ketchikan city tours. From May 15 through September 25, **Gray Line of Alaska** (tel. 225-5930) takes ferry passengers for a 1-hour city tour ($12 for adults, $6 for children under 12), and those with more time can get a seat on the 2½-hour Totem Bight Tour ($29 for adults, $14.50 for children under 12), departing daily at 8:30am. Gray Line also offers a unique half-day bus/canoe tour to a mountain lake ($59 for adults, $35 for children under 12), departing daily at 9am and 3pm. Other seasonal tour operators include **Alaska Sightseeing Tours** (tel. toll free 800/621-5557) and **Ketchikan Local Tours** (tel. 225-1989).

Outdoor Alaska, 215 Main St., Suite 211 (tel. 225-6044), offers a unique two-hour historical harbor tour aboard the *Misty Fjord, Crystal Fjord,* or *Emerald Fjord* for $40 per person from Memorial Day weekend through Labor Day. The company also offers cocktail cruises every Saturday night from 7 to 9pm for $15, including hors d'oeuvres and a no-host bar.

SPORTS & RECREATION

General information on swimming, tennis, aerobics, and other athletic pursuits in Ketchikan can be obtained from **Ketchikan Parks and Recreation** (tel. 225-3881).

FISHING No fewer than 19 charter-boat operators are registered in Ketchikan. Ask the visitors bureau for a list, or contact the **Ketchikan Marine Charter Association,** P.O. Box 7896, Ketchikan, AK 99901 (tel. 907/225-2628). One reputable operator is **Ketchikan Sportfishing** (tel. toll free 800/488-8254). You can take halibut, red snapper, sea bass, or cod through most of the year, king (chinook) salmon May through July, pink (humpback) salmon June through September, and silver (coho) salmon July through September. There's also trout fishing (rainbows, Dolly Vardens, and cutthroat) in inland lakes and streams.

The **Alaska Department of Fish and Game,** 2030 Sea Level Dr., Suite 205 (tel. 225-2859), can provide plenty of details. Don't forget to buy a license (a 10-day nonresident pass costs $15). If you're planning to rent a boat—**Knudson Cove Marina,** Mile 14.8 on North Tongass Highway (tel. 247-8500), can help you—be sure also to pick up a tide table. Respect the weather and the very cold water. A good fishing-tackle dealer is **Plaza Sports,** in the Plaza Shopping Center, 2417 Tongass Ave. (tel. 225-1587).

HIKING There is no shortage of opportunities here. The Deer Mountain Trail, a steep three-mile climb through bear country to a spectacular overlook 3,000 feet above the Tongass Narrows, starts near the corner of Deermount Avenue and Fair Street. An easier walk is the one-mile nature trail circling Ward Lake north of Ketchikan. For other possibilities, contact the **U.S. Forest Service,** 3031 Tongass Ave. (tel. 225-3101). Local tour operator Ken Mix specializes in nature hikes: **North Wind Expeditions,** 1200 Woodside St. (tel. 907/247-2270 or 225-4751).

HUNTING The most common game animal in this part of Alaska is the Sitka black-tailed deer. Mountain goats are frequently spotted in the Misty Fjords, and black bears are common throughout the region. Brown bears (grizzlies) and moose are more unusual here. The **Alaska Department of Fish and Game,** 2030 Sea Level Dr. (tel. 225-2475), or sporting goods dealers—try **Deer Mountain Sports,** 1025 Water St. (tel. 225-2890)—can line you up with outfitters.

KAYAKING & CANOEING **Outdoor Alaska,** 215 Main St. (P.O. Box 7814), Ketchikan, AK 99901 (tel. 907/225-6044), rents kayaks and organizes sea-kayaking expeditions for those with time and adventurous spirit. The cost for three days and two nights runs about $180. **Kayak Alaska,** which runs the Kayak Shop at 407 Stedman St. (tel. 225-1736) in the "Once in a Blue Moose" gift shop, offers sales, rentals, and instruction. Tours of the waterfront and Saxman Village cost $40–$50 for 2½–4 hours. Guided sea-kayaking trips are also operated by **Southeast Exposure,** 507 Stedman St. (tel. 225-8829).

Canoes can be rented from the **City Parks and Recreation Department** (tel. 225-3881).

WINTER SPORTS On almost any winter weekend you'll find a couple of hundred **ice skaters** on family outings at Ward Lake, eight miles north of Ketchikan. The U.S. Forest Service maintains picnic and barbecue shelters year-round. Another eight miles inland up Ward Lake Road is Harriet Hunt Lake, where the **Ketchikan Ski Club** has a pair of rope tows operating on weekends when there's sufficient snow. There's also cross-country skiing, snowmobiling, and ice skating at the **Harriet Hunt recreation area.** Contact the Ketchikan Visitors Bureau for details.

SHOPPING

There are some excellent local artists and craftspeople, who, in many of their works, employ Indian motifs. Look for their work at **Morning Raven,** 20 Creek St. (tel. 225-5060). **Alaska Eagle Arts,** Creek Street (tel. 225-8365), and the **Scanlon Gallery,** 310 Mission St. (tel. 225-4730), have fine collections of paintings, sculptures, and jewelry by Alaskan artists.

Among the numerous gift shops near the cruise ship dock are **Tom Sawyer's Jewelry and Curios,** 304-306 Mission St. (tel. 225-4220); **Authentic Alaska Craft,** 318 Dock St. (tel. 225-6925); and **Denise's Arctic Gold,** 224 Front St. (tel. 225-3267).

Need film? Try **Schallerer's Photo and Gift,** 218 Front St. (tel. 225-4210). A book? Among the most interesting bookstores in Ketchikan is the **Voyageur Book Store,** 405 Dock St. (tel. 225-5011), the place for new releases and gift books; I have a soft spot for **Parnassus,** upstairs at 28 Creek St. (tel. 225-7690), where you can browse through used books while listening to classical music and sipping espresso. In addition to the independent bookstores, the nationwide chain store **Waldenbooks** is represented in Ketchikan at 103 Plaza Port (tel. 225-8120).

You can't tour **Silver Lining Seafoods,** 1705 Tongass Ave. (tel. 225-6664 or 225-9865), on your own, but you can visit the shop to sample and purchase fresh seafood, smoked salmon, or gift packs for shipment home at wholesale prices. Don't miss the large aquarium of native Alaskan marine life.

WHERE TO STAY

A dearth of first-class hotel rooms in Ketchikan was amended when Westmark Hotels opened their new Cape Fox Lodge in late 1990. There are now ample rooms in all price categories.

Tax Add 9% tax (4% city bed tax, 5% sales tax) to all room prices quoted. Outside Ketchikan city, a 1½% sales tax applies at wilderness lodges within the borough.

EXPENSIVE

SALMON FALLS RESORT, Mile 17, N. Tongass Hwy. (P.O. Box 5420), Ketchikan, AK 99901. Tel. 907/225-2752, or toll free 800/247-9059. Fax 907/225-2710. 68 rms (all with bath). TEL

$ Rates: Year-round, $139 single or double. Guided charter-boat fishing package, $1,695 double (four days, three nights); self-guided packages from $1,295. AE, MC, V.

An impressive, new luxury fishing resort (it opened in 1988), Salmon Falls has the advantage of road accessibility from Ketchikan: Guests needn't pay an added fly-in/fly-out tab. All-inclusive fishing packages are available aboard 25-foot cabin cruisers; self-guided tours include a 19-foot skiff and gear.

Units appear rustic, with peeled pine-log construction, but they all have two double beds and other modern furnishings and amenities.

Dining/Entertainment: Meals are served in the Hospitality Center, an octagonal, beamed lodge with a 40-foot section of the Alaska Pipeline as its center support! Excellent dinners are priced in the $15–$22 range from 5 to 10pm daily; breakfast is served from 6 to 8am, and lunch from noon to 2pm.

Services: Room service, valet laundry, courtesy yacht shuttle from Ketchikan airport.

Facilities: Coin-operated laundry, fishing-gear shop, conference center for 100 guests.

WESTMARK CAPE FOX LODGE, 800 Venetia Way, Ketchikan, AK 99901. Tel. 907/225-8001, or toll free 800/544-0970. Fax 907/225-8286. 70 rms, 2 suites. TV TEL **Transportation:** Take a courtesy car from the airport or ferry terminal, or board the tramway from Creek Street.

$ Rates: May 15–Sept 15, $134–$140 single; $144–$150 double; $200 suite. Sept 16–May 14, $92–$98 single; $102–$106 double; $79 single or double Fri–Sun, $200 suite. AE, CB, DC, DISC, MC, V.

Built like a Tlingit clan house atop a bluff overlooking downtown Ketchikan, this new hotel—owned by the Tlingits' Cape Fox Corporation—is the finest accommodation in southeast Alaska. Outside its front door, six totem poles welcome newcomers into a central meeting area. From the rear, Alaska's only funicular tramway climbs a steep hill from Creek Street. No matter which way you arrive, there's a spectacular view across the Tongass Narrows from the lobby, with its stone fireplace and library. A totemic screen, *Gathering of the Clans,* by noted Native artist Nathan Jackson, is mounted at the top of the staircase landing above the lobby.

There are 36 guest rooms in the main lodge and three dozen more in three hillside lodges named for the Raven, Bear, and Eagle clans. Standard rooms have a king-size bed or two double beds, knotty-pine furnishings, a TV hidden in an armoire, a working desk and easy chair, reading lamps, spacious tiled baths, and charcoal carpeting. Only 12 rooms do not have water views. The two suites have living rooms, Jacuzzi tubs, and small refrigerators.

Dining/Entertainment: The Heen Kahidi Dining Room and Lounge offers traditional American cuisine with a focus on seafood and "healthwise" meals. Main courses are priced $15.95–$32.95. Huge picture windows face into the tops of Douglas fir trees, where bald eagles nest, giving diners a unique perspective. Meals are served daily from 6am to 11pm from May 15 to September 15, 7am to 10pm off-season.

Services: Room service, valet laundry, courtesy shuttle, rooms for nonsmokers, and disabled guests.

Facilities: Gift shop with Native crafts and clothing, meeting room accommodating 200 people.

MODERATE

BEST WESTERN LANDING HOTEL, 3434 Tongass Ave., Ketchikan, AK 99901. Tel. 907/225-5166. Fax 907/225-6900. 46 rms, 1 suite. TV TEL
$ Rates: May–Oct 15, $85–$98 single or double; $160 suite. Oct 16–Apr, $68–$80 single or double; $130 suite. AE, CB, DC, DISC, MC, V.

Set against the hills at the northern end of town, this horseshoe-shaped motel has rooms simply but tastefully furnished with queen-size or double beds and combination desk-dressers. A handful of upgraded minisuites have refrigerators and microwave ovens. Books and postcards are sold in the cozy lobby. An adjoining café (open daily from 6am to 10pm) has lunches for about $6 and dinners in the $11–$13 range, and Jeremiah's Lounge, on the second floor, features live entertainment. The hotel offers courtesy van service and an exercise room.

INGERSOLL HOTEL, 303 Mission St. (P.O. Box 6440), Ketchikan, AK 99901. Tel. 907/225-2124, or toll free 800/478-2124 in Alaska. Fax 907/225-8530. 60 rms. TV TEL
$ Rates (including continental breakfast): Apr–Sept, $85 single; $95 double. Oct–Mar, $59 single; $64 double. AE, CB, DC, DISC, MC, V.

The three-story Ingersoll, built of reinforced concrete in 1924 on the site of a fire-ravaged 1899 inn, has fully renovated rooms decorated in soft pastels with oak trim. A typical room has two double beds, a large dresser and desk, and Alaskan art prints on the walls. Many of the rooms have views over the Tongass Narrows. Local calls from the rooms are 25¢, and cable television features 26 channels. Rooms for nonsmokers and disabled guests are available; the hotel also offers valet laundry service and a courtesy shuttle to and from the airport and ferry terminal.

ROYAL EXECUTIVE SUITES, 1471 Tongass Ave., Ketchikan, AK 99901. Tel. 907/225-1900. Fax 907/225-1795. 14 rms, 6 suites. TV TEL
$ Rates (for one or two guests): Apr–Sept, $90 studio; $115 deluxe studio; $160 suite. Oct–Mar, $75 studio; $95 deluxe studio; $125 suite. AE, CB, DC, DISC, MC, V.

This small luxury hotel, designed by owner Kirk Thomas, a former bush pilot, is built on pilings that extend into the Tongass Narrows. The rooms, all with refrigerators, have a pastel color scheme—slate-blue carpeting, lilac upholstery, natural-wood trim—and rheostatic lighting. The deluxe studios have in-room Jacuzzis. Each two-room suite contains a full kitchen, living room with telephone (local calls are 40¢) and 23-channel cable television, a spacious bedroom with clock radio, and in-room Jacuzzi. Full-wall windows with blinds overlook the harbor; on the top floor, they extend to the ceiling. The hotel has a private "spa" with sauna and hot tub (available by appointment) and a laundry free to guests. Room service is provided by a local caterer.

INEXPENSIVE

GILMORE HOTEL, 326 Front St., Ketchikan, AK 99901. Tel. 907/225-9423. Fax 907/225-6900. 42 rms (all with bath). TV TEL
$ Rates: May–Oct 15, $64–$74 single; $72–$88 double. Oct 16–Apr, $52–$62 single; $56–$76 double. AE, CB, DC, DISC, MC, V.

Recently refurbished, this Roaring '20s period hotel—listed on the National Register of Historic Places—now has a bright, floral charm it once lacked. The restoration gave every room a private bath, direct-dial phones, Home Box Office, and modern wood furnishings. Room service is available from Annabelle's, one of Ketchikan's finest restaurants, on the ground floor. Valet laundry and courtesy van service are also offered, and coffee is always on in the lobby.

NEW YORK HOTEL, 207 Stedman St. (P.O. Box 9112), Ketchikan, AK 99901. Tel. 907/225-0246. 8 rms (all with bath). TV TEL
$ Rates (including continental breakfast): May–Sept, $79 single or double. Oct–Apr, $59 single or double. MC, V.

Five years of money, labor, and love went into this vintage-1925 hotel before Fred Oschner reopened in September 1991. Now, guests can look through the lace curtains of the small lobby, with its original player piano, to the yachts and fishing vessels of Thomas Basin. A steep staircase leads to the cozy rooms, all with antique furnishings, queen-size beds, and tiled full bathrooms. Downstairs, the New York Café serves light sandwiches, desserts, and espresso.

SUPER 8 MOTEL, 2151 Sea Level Dr. (P.O. Box 8818), Ketchikan, AK 99901. Tel. 907/225-9088, or toll free 800/843-1991. 82 rms (all with bath). TV TEL
$ Rates: Apr–Sept, $75.90 single; $85.90 double; $88.90 twin. Oct–Mar, $65.90 single; $75.90 double; $78.90 twin. AE, CB, DC, DISC, MC, V.

This franchise property has spacious rooms with queen-size beds and double-insulated walls. The motel has special no-smoking rooms and a conference room that holds up to 35 people. Other facilities include a guest laundry, video-game room, complimentary freezers for successful fishermen, a courtesy van, and coffee 24 hours a day.

BUDGET

KETCHIKAN YOUTH HOSTEL, Grant and Main Sts. (P.O. Box 8515), Ketchikan, AK 99901. Tel. 907/225-3780. 2 dorm rms (each with shared bath)

$ Rates: $5 per bed for American Youth Hostels members, $8 for nonmembers. AYH memberships $20 extra. No credit cards.

Located in the Methodist church, this hostel will put you in a gender-separated dorm room if you've brought your own sleeping bag. The hostel opens Memorial Day and closes Labor Day; hours are strict—you may come and go as you please only from 6 to 8:30am and 7 to 11pm. Concessions are made for late ferry arrivals, but you should call the hostel when you arrive to let the people there know you're on your way.

RAIN FOREST INN, 2311 Hemlock St. (P.O. Box 3211), Ketchikan, AK 99901. Tel. 907/225-9500; TTD 907/225-6302 for the hearing impaired. 8 rms (all with shared bath).

$ Rates: $21 per bed; $45 double or twin; $56 for four. MC, V.

This dormitory-style property gives guests a choice of renting by the bed or by the room; each room holds two to four people. Visitors staying more than a night or two get kitchen privileges. Showers and coin-operated laundry facilities are available, along with complimentary morning coffee. There's also a gift shop here.

BED & BREAKFAST

KETCHIKAN BED & BREAKFAST, P.O. Box 3213, Ketchikan, AK 99901. Tel. 907/225-8550 or 225-4232. 20 rms.

$ Rates (including breakfast): May–Sept, $50–$65 single; $60–$75 double. Oct–Apr, $40–$55 single; $50–$65 double. CB, DC, MC, V.

This reservation service is designed for travelers who wish to stay in private homes, many of them within easy walking distance of downtown. Rooms are available in typical homes like Bowey's B&B, 2021 First Ave. (tel. 907/225-3494), and Main Street B&B, P.O. Box 7473, Ketchikan, AK 99901 (tel. 907/225-8484); in country-style private cottages, like those of the Great Alaska Cedar Works, 1527 Pond Reef Rd. (tel. 907/247-8287); or in a beachfront apartment 10 miles from town at North Tongass B&B, P.O. Box 684, Ward Cove, AK 99928 (tel. 907/247-2467).

FISHING RESORTS

The **Salmon Falls Resort,** noted above, is probably the best of several fishing resorts accessible from downtown Ketchikan by road. Others include the **Clover Pass Resort,** Mile 15, N. Tongass Hwy. (P.O. Box 7322), Ketchikan, AK 99901 (tel. 907/247-2234), open April through September, with 26 rooms priced at $70 single or double and a half dozen cabins at $100 flat rate; and the **Alaskan Home Fishing Lodge,** 11380 Alderwood St. N., Ketchikan, AK 99901 (tel. 907/225-6919), 11 miles north of town, with five luxurious rooms priced at $75–$125 double from May 15 to September 20, and $65–$105 double from September 21 to May 14. (Prices include breakfast and dinner, TV and Jacuzzi; guided fishing from cabin cruisers costs extra.)

Among the deluxe fly-in wilderness lodges in the Ketchikan area are the **Yes Bay Lodge,** Yes Bay, AK 99950 (tel. 907/247-1575), 50 miles north of Ketchikan at the mouth of the McDonald River; and the **Meyers Chuck Lodge,** P.O. Box 6141, Ketchikan, AK 99901, in winter, or Meyers Chuck, AK 99903, in summer (tel. 907/225-4608). Both offer full-board packages, with three nights at Yes Bay around

$1,500 per person and three nights at Meyers Chuck around $1,100. A full listing of lodges is available from the Ketchikan Visitors Bureau (see "Orientation," above).

The **U.S. Forest Service** (tel. 225-3101 for reservations) maintains numerous cabins in remote areas of Tongass National Forest for $20 a night. There are 16 on Revillagigedo Island alone. You only have to fly, boat, or walk in and supply your own food and bedding.

CAMPGROUNDS

There's camping at several locations in the Ketchikan area. Nicest are the U.S. Forest Service's **Signal Creek** campground, 7½ miles north of the city on Ward Lake Road, with eight tent and 17 RV units; **Last Chance** campground, with 23 tent spaces, two miles farther up the same road; and **Settlers Cove** state campground, 18 miles north of Ketchikan, with nine tent spaces and seven RV pads. All have tables, water, pit toilets, and a two-week camping limit. All areas charge $5 a night.

WHERE TO DINE

EXPENSIVE

ANNABELLE'S PARLOR, in the Gilmore Hotel, 326 Front St. Tel. 225-9423.
   Cuisine: CONTINENTAL/SEAFOOD. **Reservations:** Recommended.
$ Prices: Appetizers $9.95–$12.95; main courses $18.95–$28.95; brunch $13.95–$18.95; high tea $10.95. AE, CB, DC, DISC, MC, V.
   Open: Dinner daily 7–10pm; high tea Sat 2–5pm; brunch Sun 10am–4pm.
Annabelle's hearkens back to the Roaring '20s. Its plush floral carpeting, high-backed upholstered chairs, and elegant decor bring that era alive. To your left is Annabelle's Chowder House (see below).

A delicious high tea, complete with scones, is served on Saturday afternoons; champagne brunch draws throngs of townspeople on Sunday. But Annabelle's is best known for dinner. You can start with oysters à la Gino (in Newburg sauce with crab) or scallops Monaco (wrapped in bacon with mornay sauce), then move on to a main dish like halibut Olympia, grilled salmon with tarragon mayonnaise, or king crab legs. If you're a beef eater, Annabelle's serves only corn-fed Omaha choice: Choose a filet, a New York steak, or prime rib on the weekends.

MODERATE

KETCHIKAN CAFE, 314 Front St., 3rd Floor. Tel. 247-CAFE.
   Cuisine: AMERICAN. **Reservations:** Not accepted.
$ Prices: Breakfast $6.95–$11.95; lunch $6.95–$10.95; dinner $14.95–$19.95. No credit cards.
   Open: Daily 8am–9pm.
   You must climb 42 narrow steps to reach this unlikely eatery two stories above the Totem Bar, but most guests find the ascent worthwhile. Generous omelets, oversize sandwiches, and a home recipe for pan-fried trout carry the early-to-midday menu. In the evening, five-course inclusive dinners feature steak, seafood, and such house specials as Cornish game hen and chicken prosciutto.

NEW PEKING CHINESE RESTAURANT, 4 Creek St. Tel. 225-9355.
   Cuisine: CHINESE. **Reservations:** Not required.
$ Prices: Lunch $6.95–$10.95; dinner $9.95–$19.95. MC, V.
   Open: Lunch Mon–Fri 11:30am–2:30pm; dinner Mon–Fri 5–10pm, Sat–Sun 4–10pm.
"Exquisite health gourmet Chinese cuisine with European touch." That's the claim made by this two-story restaurant overlooking Ketchikan Creek, and it does well

delivering a little of everything for lovers of Oriental food. Mandarin, Szechuan, and Cantonese cuisine are the best, with combination dinners and luncheon specials; Japanese and Korean meals and Mongolian beef are also featured.

ROLLER BAY CAFE, 1287 Tongass Ave. Tel. 225-0696.
   Cuisine: AMERICAN. **Reservations:** Not accepted.
$ Prices: Appetizers $4.95–$7.95; main courses $11.95–$24.95; breakfast $3.50–$10.95; lunch $4.95–$8.95. No credit cards.
   Open: Sun–Thurs 6am–9pm, Fri–Sat 6am–10pm.

S Before the new Ketchikan airport opened in 1976, the building that houses this restaurant was the city's seaplane terminal. Today, diners can still watch planes and boats come and go from their perch on pilings that extend into the Tongass Narrows. The menu here is rightfully heavy on seafood, including local salmon and halibut, snapper and prawns. The kitchen serves up a great cioppino (a seafood chowder with lobster, three kinds of clams, halibut, shrimp, and smoked salmon), as well as giant slabs of prime rib, steak, chicken, and burgers. The restaurant is licensed for beer and wine only.

INEXPENSIVE

ANNABELLE'S FAMOUS KEG AND CHOWDER HOUSE, in the Gilmore Hotel, 326 Front St. Tel. 225-6009.
   Cuisine: INTERNATIONAL. **Reservations:** Not required.
$ Prices: All meals $4.95–$10.95. AE, CB, DC, DISC, MC, V.
   Open: Breakfast daily 7–10am; lunch/dinner 11:30am–10pm.
Adjoining the formal Annabelle's Parlor is this casual bar and grill, with hardwood floors, a pressed-copper ceiling, a long mahogany bar, and a Wurlitzer jukebox. Breakfasts are an event, with meals like the Hangtown fry (scrambled eggs with oysters) and the Gilmore's own sourdough pancakes (made with 1927 starter). Smoked salmon chowder, Oriental crab salad, and a beer-batter fish and chips are standards on the lunch and dinner menu, printed like a 1920s newspaper.

HARBOR INN, 320 Mission St. Tel. 225-2850.
   Cuisine: AMERICAN. **Reservations:** Not accepted.
$ Prices: Breakfast $4.50–$7.50; lunch $3.50–$7.50; dinner $8.50–$11.50. No credit cards.
   Open: Daily 24 hours.
A blue-collar hangout in the heart of downtown, this café advertises the largest breakfast menu in Ketchikan—with portions to match. How does three eggs, hotcakes, meat, and juice sound? There are good burgers and other sandwiches at lunchtime, filling New York steak-and-fries meals in the evening.

LATITUDE 56, 2050 Sea Level Dr. Tel. 225-9011.
   Cuisine: AMERICAN. **Reservations:** Not accepted.
$ Prices: Average meal $5.50–$10.50. No credit cards.
   Open: Daily 6am–10pm.
If you don't mind the vaguely muffled sound of tenpins being shattered by bowling balls, you can get Ketchikan's best hamburger here. The restaurant offers a wide variety of burgers, from chile burgers to mushroom burgers to everyday cheeseburgers. There are no windows, though, so this isn't a place to come for the view.

PIZZA MILL, 808 Water St. Tel. 225-6646.
   Cuisine: PIZZA/DELI. **Reservations:** Not accepted.
$ Prices: Average meal $3.50–$18.50. No credit cards.
   Open: Mon–Thurs 11am–10:30pm, Fri–Sat 11am–midnight, Sun 5–10:30pm (deliveries after 5pm only).
Pizza lovers can be happily sated by their favorite combinations—from pepperoni-and-black-olive extravaganzas to gigantic creations with everything but the kitchen sink—at this unimposing little café just north of downtown. There are more than 22 types of pizza on the menu, as well as sandwiches, salads, and homemade soups.

BUDGET

THE 5-STAR CAFE, 5 Creek St. Tel. 247-STAR.
   Cuisine: NATURAL FOODS. **Reservations:** Not accepted.
$ Prices: Average meal $2.25–$6.75. No credit cards.
   Open: Mon–Sat 9am–6pm.

⑤ Ketchikan's young, artsy population enjoys this eatery, which shares a building with the Alaska Eagle Arts gallery and a health-food store. The works of local artists on the walls, and the open kitchen, attract more attention than the simple wooden tables on a hardwood floor. Blackboard specials change daily, but they always include a hot dish (eggplant calzone, for instance), homemade soups and salads, and sandwiches like the black-bean burrito and the ever-popular P.B.T.H.B. (peanut butter, tahini, honey, and banana). Desserts are wonderful. A few meat items are on the menu, but the restaurant is health conscious: No smoking is permitted.

GRANDELI'S, 2417 Tongass Ave. Tel. 225-9880.
   Cuisine: DELI. **Reservations:** Not accepted.
$ Prices: Average meal $3–$7.50. No credit cards.
   Open: Mon–Fri 10am–9pm, Sat 10am–6pm, Sun noon–6pm.
Ketchikan's best deli is located in the city's only mall. It'll pack submarines and other sandwiches for your excursion, if you like, or serve up quick barbecued-chicken dinners.

EVENING ENTERTAINMENT

Nightlife in Ketchikan isn't as wild as it was when Creek Street was in its full glory, nor is it as brassy as when burlesque dancers from the late lamented Shamrock Club accosted tour buses on Stedman Street well into the 1970s. But it still can be lively . . . and rowdy.

The most popular spot for dancing to live music, at this writing, was the upscale **Jeremiah's Lounge,** in the Best Western Landing Hotel, 3434 Tongass Ave. (tel. 225-5166), opposite the ferry landing. But numerous sailors' and loggers' bars downtown also have action, including the **Bankshot Tavern,** 127 Main St. (tel. 225-9950), for rock, and the **Pioneer Bar,** 122 Front St. (tel. 225-3210), for country-and-western.

There are numerous other bars in the vicinity. For a drink and conversation, I'd recommend the classy **Annabelle's Famous Keg and Chowder House,** in the Gilmore Hotel, 326 Front St. (tel. 225-9423). For more local flavor, check across the street at the **Sourdough Bar,** 301 Front St. (tel. 225-2217), with a photo gallery of shipwrecks lining its walls, or next door at the **Totem Bar,** 314 Front St. (tel. 225-9521), where you can buy souvenirs and keep the Mason jar from which you drink.

The local cinema is the **Coliseum Twin Theatre,** 405 Mission St. (tel. 225-2294), with two shows nightly and weekend matinees. You can find out about local entertainment by contacting the **Ketchikan Area Arts and Humanities Council,** 338 Main St. (tel. 225-2211).

MAIN STREET THEATRE, 338 Main St. Tel. 225-4792.
   You won't want to miss *The Fish Pirate's Daughter,* a farcical melodrama staged at 7 and 8:45pm every Friday in July and August. Audiences boo villainous cannery owner Kurt Von Ohlsun, lust after Creek Street madam Violet LaRosa, and swoon for Sweet William Uprightly, the highly principled "Commissioner of Fish." The First City Players have made this a Ketchikan attraction since 1967.
   Admission: Tickets, $7.

EASY EXCURSIONS

The quickest and easiest way to travel outside Ketchikan is by plane. Several air-taxi services operating seaplanes are located along the Tongass Avenue strip. They include **Taquan Air Service,** 1007 Water St. (tel. 225-9668), and **Ketchikan Air Service,**

1719 Tongass Ave. (tel. 225-6608). Standard charter rates are $120 per person for a 90-minute flight.

⭐ **MISTY FJORDS NATIONAL MONUMENT** The most efficient ways to visit Misty Fjords National Monument—blanketing 3,570 square miles east of Ketchikan—are by air and by boat. Long fingers of water flanked by 3,000-foot granite cliffs extend east and west off long, narrow Behm Canal, a natural extension of the northeastern Pacific Ocean. Walker Cove and Rudyerd Bay are exceptionally picturesque. Active glaciers wind from 7,000-foot-plus peaks on the Canadian border, joining with the heavy southeastern Alaskan rainfall to feed the lush vegetation and myriad rivers, lakes, and streams. The area's great mineral wealth is coveted: When molybdenum was discovered a few years ago, part of the monument was set aside for mine development. There are large numbers of bears, deer, wolves, mountain goats, and bald eagles. The U.S. Forest Service has 14 rustic cabins throughout the national monument, most of them on inland lakes accessible only by floatplane or by a strenuous combination of boat and backpacking. National monument headquarters is at 1817 Tongass Ave. (P.O. Box 6137), Ketchikan, AK 99901 (tel. 907/225-2148).

Air-taxi operators offer flightseeing tours over the Misty Fjords for rates of $80–$110 per person. Alternatively, **Outdoor Alaska** (tel. 225-6044) has 11-hour cruises into the national monument aboard the *Misty Fjords* for $135 ($100 for kids 3–11), leaving at 8:30am daily except Tuesday and Thursday, Memorial Day weekend through Labor Day. Meals are included. Outdoor Alaska also offers a 7-hour cruise/fly option for $175 ($135 for children). And it has dropoff and pickup service for kayakers, canoeists, and fishermen for just $15 above the cruise price. Custom cruise tours are also offered by **Chinook Charters,** 428 Tower Rd. (tel. 225-9225); **Ken's Charters,** P.O. Box 9609, Ketchikan, AK 99901 (tel. 225-7290); and **Northern Lights Charters,** P.O. Box 793, Ward Cove, AK 99928 (tel. 907/247-8488).

PRINCE OF WALES ISLAND At 2,731 square miles, heavily forested Prince of Wales is the third-largest American island (after Kodiak Island and Hawaii's Big Island). Measuring roughly 130 miles north-south and 30 miles east-west, it has more than 700 miles of roads built for its thriving logging industry. Yet there's only one port of entry for vehicular traffic, a small one at Hollis (pop. 150), with no phones, restaurants, or visitor facilities. Passengers and vehicles can travel between Ketchikan and Hollis aboard the ferry *Aurora* nine times weekly in summer, less frequently in winter. The passenger fare is $18. From Hollis, an all-weather road leads 31 miles to the communities of Klawock and Craig, 6 miles apart.

It's more convenient, if also more expensive, to fly from Ketchikan to Prince of Wales—about $60 one way.

Craig (pop. 1,500) sits picturesquely on a tiny island connected to the Prince of Wales mainland by a short causeway. The Prince of Wales nerve center, it's home to many loggers and a purse-seine fishing fleet. Accommodation can be found at the 16-unit **Haida Way Lodge,** P.O. Box 90, Craig, AK 99921 (tel. 907/826-3268), which has television, five kitchenette units, and a licensed restaurant; rates start at $70 in summer ($60 in winter), plus 4% tax. For fine seafood, go to **Ruth Ann's Restaurant,** on the waterfront (tel. 826-3377). For general information on the town, contact Craig City Hall (tel. 826-3275) or the U.S. Forest Service (tel. 826-3271).

Klawock (pop. 900) was the location of Alaska's first salmon cannery (1878). Today a newer cannery remains important, but a 20-year-old sawmill is also a big employer. For visitors, the most impressive attraction is the totem park on the hill overlooking town. It contains 21 totem poles from the abandoned Tlingit village of Tuxekan, 25 miles north; some are replicas, others restored originals. **Fireweed Lodge,** P.O. Box 116, Klawock, AK 99925 (tel. 907/775-2930), has 20 rooms with private baths, family-style meals, complete fishing and hunting packages, and rental cars. Nightly rates range from $74 to $129, including meals. The **Log Cabin Resort,** P.O. Box 54, Klawock, AK 99925 (tel. 907/755-2205, or toll free 800/544-2205), has rustic beach cabins with kitchens and baths, tent sites, and RV hookups. Boats and canoes are available for rent. The folks who run the Log Cabin

Campground also run **Klawock Wilderness Adventure,** which takes overnight canoeing and kayaking trips from May to September.

There are few other substantial communities on Prince of Wales Island. On the east coast, **Thorne Bay** (pop. 600) is headquarters of the huge Louisiana-Pacific Corp. logging operation. You'll find a restaurant and gas station, and lodging in cabins at **McFarland's Floatel,** P.O. Box 19149, Thorne Bay, AK 99925 (tel. 907/828-3335), with rates starting at $120 a night per cabin. **Coffman Cove** (pop. 275) is a family-owned logging community; although everyone lives in a mobile home, the community has a general store, gift shop, café, and gas pump. The **Coffman Cove Wilderness Lodge,** 110 Bayview Dr., Coffman Cove, AK 99950 (tel. 907/329-2249), has bed-and-breakfast accommodations for $50 single, $65 double, year-round, with fishing and hunting add-ons available.

The fishing town of **Hydaburg** (pop. 450) is the largest Haida Indian community in Alaska. A totem park contains numerous poles from three abandoned Haida villages. A hotel-restaurant is under construction.

With excellent freshwater and saltwater fishing in Prince of Wales' waters, it isn't surprising that the 19 cabins maintained by the U.S. Forest Service here are in high demand. There are also several fishing resorts, the best of which is the **Waterfall Resort,** P.O. Box 6440, Ketchikan, AK 99901 (tel. 907/225-9461, or toll free 800/544-5125; fax 907/225-8530). It's located 13 miles southwest of Craig. With the infusion of nearly $10 million into a historic 1912 cannery, Waterfall opened in 1982 as a luxury lodge. From mid-May through mid-September the resort accommodates 84 visitors in 26 bungalows, four luxury condominiums, and 10 lodge rooms. Each room has a full bath, electric heating, wall-to-wall carpeting, and wood furnishings, plus a wet bar and refrigerator. The dining room serves family-style meals; there's also full bar service. The resort offers video movies and games in the recreation lounge, overlooking a lagoon; an exercise room and hot tub; and executive conference facilities. It also has a general store and even its own water- and sewage-treatment plant. (Remember, you're in isolation.)

There are 25 cabin cruisers in the resort's fishing fleet; your guide's fee (but not his tip) is included in your package cost. It takes 80 full-time employees to keep the operation running smoothly. The cost, for a minimum stay of three nights, is $2,125 per person, double occupancy; add $495 for each additional night, so if you remain a week, the cost is $4,105. That includes round-trip air transportation from Ketchikan, 65 miles distant.

Another excellent wilderness lodge on Prince of Wales Island—only 20 minutes from Ketchikan, in secluded Saltery Cove on the east coast—is the **Sportsman's Cove Lodge,** c/o Southeast Alaska Sportfishing Adventures, P.O. Box 2486, Olympia, WA 98507 (tel. 206/956-3333, or toll free 800/962-7889; fax 206/956-0835). The lodge accommodates 18 guests per day in large double rooms with private baths. Anglers use new 36-foot boats to pursue salmon and halibut.

For wilderness lovers of a different nature, a network of limestone caverns has recently been discovered on Prince of Wales Island. Among them is **El Capitan,** the largest cave known in Alaska (more than 9,000 feet has been mapped), and a 600-foot pit, the deepest ever found in the United States.

METLAKATLA Sawmilling and fish processing are the economic stabilizers in Metlakatla, a Tsimshian Indian town of 1,400 people some 15 miles south of Ketchikan. Metlakatla is the main community in the Annette Island Indian Reservation, the only such federal reserve in Alaska. The town was founded in 1887 when Fr. William Duncan led a migration of Tsimshians from nearby British Columbia to escape Anglican church interference with the community's affairs. At Duncan's urging, the U.S. Congress granted the Metlakatla Indians title to the entire 86,000-acre island in 1891.

The ferry *Aurora* sails between Ketchikan and Metlakatla four times a week (fare: $12), but most folks fly the short hop. Even if you go by sea, you'll probably have to walk the mile from the ferry terminal to town, as there are no buses or taxis.

The **Duncan Cottage Museum,** where the community's founder lived until his death in 1918, is a national historic site, containing, from among Fr. Duncan's possessions, a pioneer apothecary. It's open year-round, on weekdays from 9:30am to 4pm and weekends by request. You can also see the **Duncan Memorial Church,** a replica built after the original burned down in 1948. Tours of the **Annette Island Cannery** can be arranged from June 15 to September 1. The **Tribal Longhouse** is home to the colorful Metlakatla Indian Dancers.

For further information on these attractions, plus historic walking tours and a salmon barbecue, contact the **Metlakatla Division of Tourism,** P.O. Box 45, Metlakatla, AK 99926 (tel. 907/886-1216).

HYDER About 85 people still make their home in this "Friendliest Ghost Town in Alaska," which has more in common with British Columbia (including an area code) than with its own state. Located at the edge of Misty Fjords National Monument (18 miles by trail) and at the head of the beautiful Portland Canal, Hyder is connected by road and bridge with Stewart, B.C. (pop. 2,200), two miles distant. Hyder briefly boomed after gold and silver were discovered in 1919, and mining is still a popular local avocation. But the real modus operandi today is obvious: The town is without a bank, yet it has two bars, both of them open till 5am! The ferry *Aurora* visits on Monday morning from Ketchikan (fare: $36).

Accommodation is available in Hyder at the **Grand View Inn,** P.O. Box 49, Hyder, AK 99923 (tel. 604/636-9174), and the **Sealaska Inn,** Premier and Nevada Avenues (P.O. Box 91), Hyder, AK 99923 (tel. 604/636-9001; fax 907/636-9003).

---

2. WRANGELL

90 miles N of Ketchikan, 47 miles S of Petersburg

GETTING THERE   By Plane   Alaska Airlines (tel. 907/874-3308) has two flights daily with direct connections to Juneau, Ketchikan, and Seattle. **Ketchikan Air** (tel. 907/874-2369) has several scheduled flights daily to Ketchikan and Petersburg, with half-price tickets for children 12 and under. **Sunrise Aviation** (tel. 907/874-2319) offers charter air-taxi services.

By Ferry Alaska Marine Highway vessels (tel. 874-3711 for recorded information, 874-2021 for reservations) arrive and depart six times a week in summer, less frequently in winter. The fare to Wrangell is $22 from Ketchikan, $16 from Petersburg, $54 from Juneau.

SPECIAL EVENTS The **Tent City Festival,** on the first weekend in February, recalls the 19th-century "boom town" days when thousands of gold miners wintered here in tents. Everyone in town dons period clothing for the Shady Lady Ball; the other highlight is the John Muir Enduro, a race up Mount Dewey in mud or snow! The **Fourth of July** is also a major occasion, with a logging show, fireworks, a parade, and other events.

Wrangell has a frontier air about it not observed in other southeast Alaska towns. You'll notice it the moment you step off the ferry to be greeted by the colorfully costumed "Shady Ladies." You'll see it in the false facades of the old wooden buildings lining the main street. You'll feel it in the independent spirit of the townspeople.

Wrangell (pop. 2,600) is at the northern tip of 30-mile-long Wrangell Island, just 7 miles from the mouth of the Stikine River—the only portal to the Canadian interior between Skagway and Prince Rupert. That geographical anomaly has shaped the town's past, present, and future.

Wrangell is the only town in Alaska to have been under three different national flags—Russian, British, and American. It was founded in 1833 by Russian fur traders, who built Redoubt St. Dionysius to discourage intrusions by the British Hudson's Bay Company, which had navigation rights up the Stikine River to Canada. In 1840 the fort was leased to the British for other concessions and the Union Jack flew over the renamed Fort Stikine until the U.S. purchase of Alaska in 1867. The Americans named the site Fort Wrangell after Baron Ferdinand Petrovich von Wrangell, manager of the Russian-American company in the 1830s.

Furs and Canadian gold rushes nurtured the town's economy during its early decades. Bars, gambling halls, and brothels sprang up almost overnight; during the Cassiar Gold Rush of the late 1870s the population of Wrangell reached an estimated 15,000. When naturalist John Muir visited the town in 1879, he called Wrangell "the most inhospitable place at first sight I had ever seen," built with a "devil-may-care abandon." Steamship service up the Stikine began with the gold rushes and continued as far as Telegraph Creek, B.C., into the 1930s.

In the late 1880s, Wrangell's first salmon cannery and Alaska's first sawmill were built on the island, and the economy (and population) became more stable. Today the Wrangell Forest Products sawmill, rebuilt six miles south of town in 1981, ships spruce and hemlock to Pacific Rim markets, and a fleet of trollers, seiners, and gill netters make fishing a major industry.

Wrangell's climate is mild. Summer temperatures average 60°F; winter temperatures are in the 20s and 30s. Although it's only 90 miles north of Ketchikan, Wrangell gets half the rainfall of its neighbor—a "mere" 80 inches a year.

ORIENTATION

ARRIVING   The **ferry terminal** is on the north side of downtown; **Wrangell Airport** is about a mile northeast. Some accommodations provide courtesy transportation; otherwise, there are taxis.

INFORMATION   The **visitors center,** an A-frame structure on Outer Drive facing the harbor, is the main source of local information. Open weekdays from 10am to 4pm in summer and when cruise ships are in port, it's operated by the **Wrangell Chamber of Commerce,** P.O. Box 49, Wrangell, AK 99929 (tel. 907/874-3901; fax 907/874-3104). For information on outdoor activities, visit or write the offices of the **Wrangell Ranger District,** U.S. Forest Service, 525 Bennett St. (P.O. Box 51), Wrangell, AK 99929 (tel. 907/874-2323).

CITY LAYOUT   The town curves around a small harbor at the northern tip of Wrangell Island. Most businesses and points of interest are found in a one-mile stretch from the ferry dock to Shakes Island (in the Inner Harbor). **Front Street** is the main thoroughfare; its eastern side retains a false-fronted frontier feeling, though its shoreward face was rebuilt twice after fires in 1906 and 1952. The **Zimovia Highway,** extending from the ferry dock (via Second Street and Church Street) south for 11 miles, is the chief artery on 15- by 30-mile Wrangell Island.

GETTING AROUND

There are two taxi companies, **Star Cab** (tel. 874-3622 or 874-3511) and **Porky's Cab** (tel. 874-3603). You can rent cars from **All Star,** at the Thunderbird Hotel on Front Street (tel. 874-3322). Wrangell has no public transportation system.

FAST FACTS

Banks   The town has two full-service banks.

Emergencies   In case of emergency, call 874-3304 for the police, 874-2000 to report a fire or get an ambulance. For medical help, a physician is always on call at Wrangell General Hospital, 310 Bennett St. (tel. 874-3356).

Newspaper The weekly *Wrangell Sentinel,* begun in 1902, is the oldest continuous publication in Alaska.

WHAT TO SEE & DO
SIGHTS & ATTRACTIONS

For ancient history, see the fascinating **petroglyphs** on a beach 20 minutes' walk (about half a mile) north of the ferry terminal. Visit at low tide—these mysterious prehistoric rock carvings are just above the 12-foot tide level. (Be sure to get a tide table, available locally.) A slippery boardwalk leads from the highway to the gravel beach. Turn right at the foot of the boardwalk and begin looking immediately for strange faces and spiral symbols on the larger rocks. Some scholars think these carvings may date back 8,000 years! Their creators are completely unknown. Their purpose is likewise baffling; the only clue is that all but three of the 40 or so known petroglyphs face out to sea. Local shops will sell you rice paper and other supplies to make rubbings. Ferns, crushed into balls, are better coloring agents than crayons or charcoal.

Five miles northeast of Wrangell, opposite the mouth of the Stikine River, is a rock phenomenon to match the petroglyphs. This one, however, is natural. The **Garnet Ledge** is the property of the Boy Scouts of America and is shared by all of Wrangell's children. You might meet kids peddling garnets at the ferry or cruise-ship dock, or you can buy the stones at the museum. Wrangell's garnets are said to have a unique crystalline structure. Though adults are forbidden from exploiting the semiprecious gems for commercial use, you can get a permit to work the ledge with hand tools only. Inquire at the Wrangell museum. Access is by boat or floatplane.

You can drive five miles south of Wrangell down the Zimovia Highway for a look at the **Wrangell Institute,** an enormous Native boarding school on 140 acres of land facing Shoemaker Harbor. Formerly operated by the federal Bureau of Indian Affairs, it was closed in 1975 when the oil boom provided money for schools all over the state. Today the Cook Inlet Native Corporation has the long-vacant institute on the sales block. Aspiring resort developers can contact the City of Wrangell's Office of Economic Development for details.

Most of the city's sights, including several 19th- and early 20th-century churches, are included in the **Wrangell Walking Tour,** described in the annual "Wrangell Guide," published by the *Wrangell Sentinel* and distributed by the Visitors Center.

CHIEF SHAKES ISLAND, off Shakes St. Tel. 874-3505 or 874-3747.

✪ Tiny Chief Shakes Island, which divides the Inner and Outer Harbors, is a restored Tlingit settlement connected to Wrangell Island by a wooden footbridge off Shakes Street. Its centerpiece is the Tribal House of the Bear, an Indian community center originally built about 1800 and reconstructed in 1939 by the Civilian Conservation Corps. Inside you'll find a central firepit, two tiers of wooden platforms where tribe members slept, and the chief's private quarters. Six house totems, two of them a century old, relate clan legends. Numerous totem poles stand outside the house; some are original to the site, some were moved from other locations, and some are replicas. The most popular seems to be the "Three Frogs Totem," constructed to ridicule three women of the Kiksadi clan who married three Shakes clan slaves. It has been restored after having been badly vandalized in 1985.

You can also visit the **grave of Chief Shakes V,** two blocks away on the hillside across from Hansen's Boat Shop on Case Avenue. The plot, surrounded by a picket fence, is marked by two killer whale totems in ill repair. Shakes V was ruler from the 1830s to 1850s. (In all, there were eight chiefs named Shakes.)

Admission: $1.

Open: Tribal house, mid-May to mid-Sept, during cruise-ship arrivals and by appointment; contact the Wrangell Cooperative Association at the numbers listed above. Totems can be visited anytime, day or night.

OUR COLLECTIONS, Evergreen Ave. Tel. 874-3646.

If you like to spend Sunday afternoons at garage sales and antiques stores, then this

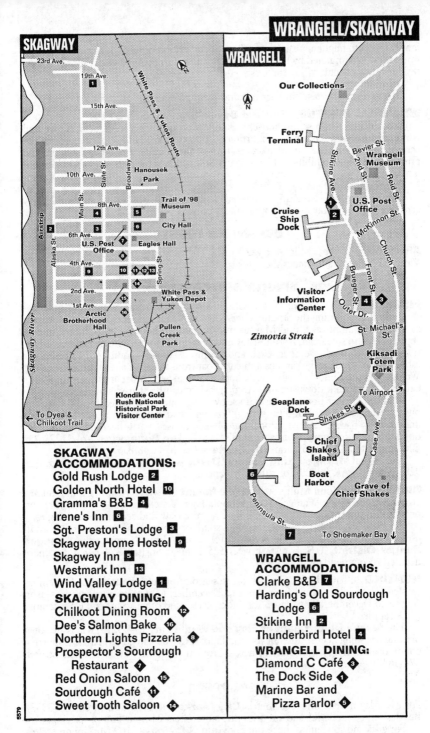

WRANGELL/SKAGWAY

SKAGWAY

23rd Ave.
19th Ave. **1**
15th Ave.
12th Ave.
White Pass & Yukon Route
10th Ave.
State St.
Broadway
Hanousek Park
8th Ave. **4** **5**
Trail of '98 Museum
Main St.
2 **3** **6**
City Hall
6th Ave.
Alaska St.
U.S. Post Office **7**
Eagles Hall
Spring St.
4th Ave.
9 **10** **11** **12** **13**
14
2nd Ave.
15
White Pass & Yukon Depot
1st Ave.
Arctic Brotherhood Hall **16**
Pullen Creek Park
Airstrip
Skagway River
← To Dyea & Chilkoot Trail
Klondike Gold Rush National Historical Park Visitor Center

WRANGELL

Our Collections
Ferry Terminal
Stikine Ave.
Bevier St.
2nd St.
Wrangell Museum
Reid St.
U.S. Post Office
1
2
McKinnon St.
Cruise Ship Dock
Church St.
Brueger St.
Front St.
Visitor Information Center
Outer Dr.
4 **3**
St. Michael's St.
Zimovia Strait
Kiksadi Totem Park
To Airport →
Seaplane Dock
Shakes St.
Case Ave.
5
Chief Shakes Island
6
Boat Harbor
Grave of Chief Shakes
Peninsula St.
7
To Shoemaker Bay ↓

SKAGWAY ACCOMMODATIONS:
Gold Rush Lodge **2**
Golden North Hotel **10**
Gramma's B&B **4**
Irene's Inn **6**
Sgt. Preston's Lodge **3**
Skagway Home Hostel **9**
Skagway Inn **5**
Westmark Inn **13**
Wind Valley Lodge **1**

SKAGWAY DINING:
Chilkoot Dining Room **12**
Dee's Salmon Bake **16**
Northern Lights Pizzeria **8**
Prospector's Sourdough Restaurant **7**
Red Onion Saloon **15**
Sourdough Café **11**
Sweet Tooth Saloon **14**

WRANGELL ACCOMMODATIONS:
Clarke B&B **7**
Harding's Old Sourdough Lodge **6**
Stikine Inn **2**
Thunderbird Hotel **4**

WRANGELL DINING:
Diamond C Café **3**
The Dock Side **1**
Marine Bar and Pizza Parlor **5**

5579

family museum might appeal to you. The eclectic exhibit of tools, furniture, and other bric-a-brac accumulated by Bolly and Elva Bigelow during their five decades of Alaska residency is unusual, to say the least.

Admission: Donation.

Open: During cruise-ship arrivals and by appointment.

WRANGELL MUSEUM, 2nd and Bevier Sts. Tel. 874-3770.

Situated in a 1906 schoolhouse, the collection here interprets local Native and white history and culture with artifacts, photographs, and tape recordings. A ceremonial Tlingit dance blanket, a turn-of-the-century linotype machine and printing press, and exhibits of 19th-century Stikine River fur trapping will tickle your fancy.

Admission: $1.

Open: May 15–Sept 15, Mon–Sat 1–4pm (daily for cruise-ship and ferry arrivals); Sept 16–May 14, by appointment only.

ORGANIZED TOURS

Allweather Tours, Mile 4 on Zimovia Highway (tel. 874-2335), will escort Wrangell area tours. Contact them for specific routes and rates.

SPORTS & RECREATION

FISHING There are five major salmon-spawning streams within 20 miles of Wrangell, not counting the Stikine River. Kings run May to December; coho, August to October; humpbacks, mid-May to mid-September; sockeye and chum, June to September; and steelhead, April to May and September to December. Halibut season runs March through October. Crab and shrimp fishermen require pots. Freshwater fishermen will find Dolly Vardens and cutthroat trout at Pat's Lake, 11 miles south of Wrangell off the Zimovia Highway. (Salmon spawn in September at the mouth of Pat's Creek, a short walk downstream.) Arctic grayling can be snared at Tyee Lake.

Wrangell charter boats are fast and seaworthy, built scow-nosed for the treacherous currents, sand bars, and (in spring) floating ice at the mouth of the Stikine. It's important to have local navigational knowledge. Coast Guard–licensed charter-boat operators include **Terry Buness** (tel. 874-3061), **Tim Buness** (tel. 874-3122), **TH Charters** (tel. 874-3455), and **TK Charters** (tel. 874-2488).

The annual **Wrangell King Salmon Derby** is held in May. Write to P.O. Box 928, Wrangell, AK 99929, for full information.

HIKING Trace John Muir's steps up the **Mount Dewey Trail,** beginning on 3rd Street a block above Wrangell High School. There's a clearing at the top where an observation tower once stood. You'll have a great view and see many bald eagles.

Opposite Shoemaker Harbor, five miles south of Wrangell, a one-mile trail leads to pretty **Rainbow Falls.** Come prepared for mud and rain. Contact the **Wrangell Ranger District,** U.S. Forest Service, 525 Bennett St. (tel. 874-2323), for more detailed recommendations.

HUNTING Brown bears (grizzlies) are in season April to June and again September to December; black bears, from April to December. Mountain goats are in season August to December. The season for ducks, geese, and other waterfowl is September to December.

The **Alaska Department of Fish and Wildlife** (tel. 874-3215) will issue you a hunting or fishing license and tell you regulations. Or you can go directly to a sporting goods dealer. Try **Angerman's,** across from the Stikine Inn, at 6 Front St. (tel. 874-3640).

SHOPPING

For everyday needs, your best bet is **City Market,** 435 Front St. (tel. 874-3333). Besides selling groceries and sundries, the store offers 24-hour film processing.

For gifts and souvenirs, check out **Sylvia's Gift House,** 109 McKinnon St. (tel.

874-3852); **Norris Gifts,** 124 Front St. (tel. 874-3810); or **Mardina Dolls,** 715 Case Ave. (tel. 874-3854).

You can buy fresh or frozen local salmon, halibut, shrimp, and Dungeness crab at **Sea Level Seafoods,** on the waterfront at the south edge of town (tel. 874-2401), or **Alaska Crown Seafoods,** next to the ferry terminal on Stikine Avenue (tel. 874-3351). While you're there, inquire about an informal tour.

WHERE TO STAY

Tax A 7% city sales tax applies to all hotel and restaurant bills.

CLARKE B&B, 732 Case Ave. (P.O. Box 1020), Wrangell, AK 99929. Tel. 907/874-2125 or 874-3863. 3 rms (1 with bath).
$ Rates (including breakfast): $40 single; $50 double. MC, V.
Marlene Clarke's A-frame home overlooking the Inner Harbor stands out among several Wrangell B&Bs. One of her units, an efficiency apartment, even has a small kitchen with a refrigerator. Clarke's sourdough waffles make a great breakfast. For a full list of another half dozen B&Bs in town, contact the visitors center.

HARDING'S OLD SOURDOUGH LODGE, 1104 Peninsula St. (P.O. Box 1062), Wrangell, AK 99929. Tel. 907/874-3613 or 874-3455. 20 rms (none with bath).
$ Rates (including breakfast): $71 single; $91 double. DC, MC, V.
Across the Inner Harbor from Shakes Island, on Shustack Point, Harding's is a fishing lodge in a semi-urban setting. Lloyd and Dolores Harding, longtime Wrangellites, have instilled the cozy rooms, each individually decorated, with a real family feeling. Toilets, showers, and a guest laundry—as well as a recreation room, television, and a sauna and steambath—are down the hall. Transportation is provided to the ferry dock and airport. All dining is family style, and Dolores's cooking is famous. Charters extra.

ROADHOUSE LODGE, Mile 4.4, Zimovia Hwy. (P.O. Box 1199), Wrangell, AK 99929. Tel. 907/874-2335. 10 rms, 1 suite (all with bath). TV
Transportation: Airport and ferry pickup service is provided.
$ Rates: $58 single; $64 double. MC, V.
The rustic Roadhouse Lodge overlooks Shoemaker Harbor, where humpback whales and sea lions can often be seen at play. All rooms have queen-size or twin beds and rocking chairs. Dinners, served in the restaurant from 6pm, include salad bar, potato, and dessert; try the shrimp sautéed in seasoned butter, for $18. Salmon and halibut bakes are held for groups of 10 or more. Guests can join hosts Dick and Dottie Olson on their city tours (offered to cruise-ship arrivals) at no charge.

STIKINE INN, 107 Front St. (P.O. Box 990), Wrangell, AK 99929. Tel. 907/874-3388. Fax 907/874-3923. 34 rms, 2 suites (all with bath). TV TEL
$ Rates: May–Sept, $60 single; $65 double; $72 twin; $90 suite. Oct–Apr, $50 single; $55 double; $62 twin; $70 suite. AE, CB, DC, MC, V.
The most popular choice in town is the Stikine Inn, overlooking the waterfront. Request a room in the "new" (1982) addition, where you'll get a larger bed and won't have to cope with the live rock music booming from the Stikine Bar cocktail lounge directly below. The rooms are nicely appointed in an autumnal color scheme, with wall-to-wall carpeting, desk/dresser, and electric baseboard heating. The Dock Side Restaurant offers full meal service daily; the hotel also has a hair salon, a travel agency, and a 24-hour desk.

THUNDERBIRD HOTEL, 223 Front St. (P.O. Box 110), Wrangell, AK 99929. Tel. 907/874-3322. 14 rms (all with bath). TV TEL
$ Rates: $45 single; $52 double; $59 twin. Rental-car/room packages available. MC, V.

The older Thunderbird looks somewhat depressing when seen from the outside. But this one-story hotel has spacious rooms with clock radios, desks, and other amenities. Soda and ice machines are in the corridor, and Wrangell's only coin-op laundry (open from 7am to 8pm) is next door to the hotel.

CAMPING

There's no charge for campers to erect their tents or park their RVs at **Shoemaker Bay** boat harbor, 5 miles south of Wrangell on the Zimovia Highway. The undeveloped **Pat's Lake Campground,** 11 miles south of Wrangell, is popular with those who prefer a more rustic setting.

WHERE TO DINE

Wrangell grocery prices are the lowest in southeast Alaska. However, if you want to eat out or have no place to cook, here are a few of the options:

DIAMOND C CAFE, 215 Front St. Tel. 874-3677.
   Cuisine: DELI. **Reservations:** Not accepted.
   $ Prices: $2.50–$7.50. No credit cards.
   Open: Breakfast/lunch only, Mon–Sat 7am–3pm.
A popular delicatessen in the Kadin Building on Wrangell's main street, the Diamond C is open for breakfast and lunch only. Homemade quiches, soups, and desserts highlight its menu.

THE DOCK SIDE, in the Stikine Inn, 107 Front St. Tel. 874-3737.
   Cuisine: STEAK/SEAFOOD. **Reservations:** Recommended.
   $ Prices: Appetizers $4.50–$7.50; main courses $10–$22; breakfast $3.25–$8.50; lunch $3.50–$9.50. AE, CB, DC, MC, V.
   Open: Mon–Sat 6am–10pm, Sun 7am–10pm.
A coffee shop for breakfast and lunch, a comfortable restaurant with windows on the Zimovia Strait for dinner, the Dock Side occupies much of the ground floor of the Stikine Inn, Wrangell's best-known hotel. The menu focuses on hearty steaks and local seafood.

MARINE BAR AND PIZZA PARLOR, 274 Shakes St. Tel. 874-3005.
   Cuisine: PIZZA. **Reservations:** Not required.
   $ Prices: Pizzas $11–$20. MC, V.
   Open: Daily 5–10pm.
Located on the original site of Russian Redoubt St. Dionysius, this popular local hangout features a variety of pizzas.

EVENING ENTERTAINMENT

Live music, provided by young rock bands from the Lower 48, blares most nights at the **Stikine Bar,** in the Stikine Inn, 107 Front St. (tel. 874-3511). The **Totem Bar,** on Front Street (tel. 874-3533), is a local favorite, with a waiting line at the pool tables. The **Shady Lady Brig Bar,** on Front Street near Shakes Street (tel. 874-3442), is popular with commercial fishermen. The real action in town is at the **Elks Lodge,** on Front Street next door to the Stikine Inn (tel. 874-3716)—but you have to be a member, as most of the townsfolk are.
   The best entertainment is provided by the several local dance and theater groups. They perform at festivals and frequently meet cruise ships, but other performances must be arranged in advance. Look for the **Shady Ladies** (tel. 874-3751), elegantly costumed like 19th-century saloon girls; the **Tent City Players** (tel. 874-2316); and the **Native Dancers** (tel. 874-3575). The **Wrangell Arts Council** (tel. 874-2027) can provide information about other activities.

EASY EXCURSIONS

Air charter is the most efficient way to see the wilderness around Wrangell. **Sunrise Aviation** (tel. 874-2319) offers combination tours of the lower Stikine River and the LeConte Glacier (see the "Petersburg" section in this chapter) for $120 an hour. **Ketchikan Air** (tel. 874-2369) has river-glacier tours for $180 in a six-passenger Cessna 207; fill up the plane and the cost is minimal. Charter services are provided to other destinations by both carriers for about $190 an hour.

For boat travel, contact the **Wrangell Chamber of Commerce** (tel. 874-3901).

THE STIKINE RIVER The 330-mile-long Stikine (pronounced "Stick-*een*") is the fastest navigable river on the North American continent. Only 30 miles of it are in the United States, and these are preserved in the Stikine-LeConte Wilderness Area. No trails penetrate this wilderness, so boat and floatplane provide the only access. **Chief Shakes Hot Springs,** 22 miles from Wrangell, and the **Garnet Ledge,** five miles from town, are the two most popular local destinations.

Adventurers who make the 150-mile trip upstream to **Telegraph Creek,** B. C. (pop. 300), will be awed by the variety of landforms flanking the river: lava flows and cinder cones, 10,000-foot mountains, glaciers hanging from alpine valleys. Above Telegraph Creek the surging waters have carved the impenetrable 55-mile-long Grand Canyon of the Stikine through 1,000-foot canyon walls. Below the town, kayakers, canoeists, and rafters can travel all the way to Wrangell, enjoying prolific wildlife.

Although the Stikine is a designated wilderness river, it is heavily used by Canada for commercial purposes. Even in the most pristine stretch, kayakers might encounter barges or log rafts. Canadian Customs operates part-time at a border house on the riverbank; visitors clear there before proceeding upstream. River travelers returning to Alaska report to U.S. Customs at Wrangell.

Tim and Terry Buness, who operate **Buness Bros.** sporting-goods store at 64 Front St. (tel. 874-3811), offer motorized charter tours up the Stikine and to other wilderness destinations.

The U.S. Forest Service maintains 13 primitive **cabins** along the lower river and near its mouth; they can be reserved for $20 a day. Contact the Wrangell Ranger District, P.O. Box 51, Wrangell, AK 99929 (tel. 907/874-2323). The U.S. Forest Service also has $3 maps of Stikine River canoe/kayak trails.

ANAN CREEK About 30 miles south of Wrangell, opposite the south end of Wrangell Island, Anan Creek flows from Anan Lake into Ernest Sound. In July and August some 200,000 spawning humpback salmon return to this creek, attracting huge numbers of seals, eagles, and bears. For these two months the Forest Service maintains a day-use **bear observatory** for photography buffs one mile upstream from its Anan Bay cabin. Bear watchers are advised to make plenty of noise until they reach the observatory, and to arm themselves in case of bear emergencies. The grizzly, one longtime observer told me, "is the *ursus* equivalent of a sumo wrestler. Black bears are basically more docile, but they're just as unpredictable."

You can reserve the Anan Bay cabin, or any of nine other cabins in the southern part of the Wrangell Ranger District, for $20 a day. Eagle Lake and Marten Lake are favorites. Contact **Sunrise Aviation** or **Ketchikan Air** for air transportation; **TH Charters,** P.O. Box 934, Wrangell, AK 99929 (tel. 907/874-3455), for boat charters.

---

3. PETERSBURG
137 miles N of Ketchikan; 148 miles S of Juneau

GETTING THERE By Plane Petersburg Airport, built in 1969 on the muskeg east of town, is served by **Alaska Airlines** (tel. 907/772-4255), with direct connections daily to Juneau, Ketchikan, and Seattle, and nonstop flights to Sitka and Wrangell. **Wings of Alaska** (tel. 907/772-3536) has daily year-round service to Juneau and Kake; **Ketchikan Air** (tel. 907/874-2369) has regularly scheduled commuter flights to Wrangell and Ketchikan. **Kupreanof Flying Service** (tel. 907/772-3396), **Nordic Air** (tel. 907/772-3535), and **Pacific Wing** (tel. 907/772-4258) have air-taxi and charter service.

By Ferry   Alaska Marine Highway vessels (tel. 772-3855) arrive and depart seven times a week in summer, less frequently in winter. The fare to Petersburg is $71 from Ketchikan, $78 from Juneau.

SPECIAL EVENTS   The ✪ **Little Norway Festival** is held annually on the weekend closest to Norwegian Independence Day, May 17. There's folk dancing in national costume, "raids" from the Viking ship *Valhalla,* and feasting on typically Norse dishes.

Other major annual events: **Petersburg Salmon Derby,** four days over Memorial Day weekend; **Fourth of July** parade and fireworks; **October Arts Festival** with the Shakespearean Mitkof Dessert Theater; and **Julebukking,** on Christmas Eve, when local merchants and shopkeepers invite patrons into the "back room" to partake of Norwegian holiday punch and other delicacies.

———

Alaska's Little Norway tries hard to perpetuate its reputation as a Scandinavian enclave on the Inside Passage. Colorful *rosemaling* designs decorate many of the houses and the venerable Sons of Norway Hall, and the Little Norway Festival in May is the highlight of the social calendar. Not as immediately evident is a clannishness and Scandinavian reserve among the residents of this town of 3,600. A large halibut and salmon fleet and related fish-processing industries are the economic mainstays.

Located on the beautiful Wrangell Narrows at the northern end of Mitkof Island, halfway between Ketchikan and Juneau, Petersburg was founded in 1897 by Peter Buschmann, a Norseman (of course). Buschmann found a natural harbor, lumber for building, ice from the nearby LeConte Glacier, and rich fishing grounds in easy reach, so he settled with his family and built a salmon cannery (now Petersburg Fisheries/ Icicle Seafoods) and a sawmill. With Scandinavian practicality, Buschmann realized that slow, steady economic growth was healthier than the boom-and-bust cycle promised by gold rushes. So he began enticing Seattleites to work in his cannery for $35 a month. By 1925 the town was making more money from the seas than any other Alaskan town was making from gold mines. That affluence has continued to the present day. A drive north from downtown along Nordic Drive and Sandy Beach Drive reveals an unusually large number of fine homes.

Petersburg averages 105 inches of rain annually, considerably more than Juneau but far less than Ketchikan. Average temperatures range from the 60s in summer to the 30s in winter.

ORIENTATION

ARRIVING   The **ferry terminal** is south of downtown at Mile 0.9 on the Mitkof Highway. **Wrangell Airport** is less than a mile east via Haugen Drive. Some accommodations provide courtesy transportation; otherwise, there are taxis.

INFORMATION   You can get free maps, literature, and an answer to almost any question Monday through Friday from 8am to 5pm at the **Petersburg Chamber of Commerce** information center, on the corner of First and Fram Streets (P.O. Box 649), Petersburg, AK 99833 (tel. 907/772-3646). Another prime source of information is the **Petersburg Ranger District,** U.S. Forest Service, in the Federal Building at Nordic Way and Gjoa Street (P.O. Box 1328), Petersburg, AK 99833 (tel. 907/772-3871).

CITY LAYOUT   **Nordic Drive** is the town's main road; it becomes the **Mitkof Highway** as it approaches the ferry dock. Numbered streets (1st through 8th) parallel

Nordic to the east, while lettered streets (Balder, Charles, Dolphin, Excel) intersect it at right angles from north to south. Harbor Way, Sing Lee Alley, and a couple of other lanes that don't fit the pattern are west of Nordic Drive, facing the harbor.

GETTING AROUND

City Cab (tel. 772-3003) handles most ground transportation. **All Star Rent-a-Car** (tel. 772-4281) has an outlet at Scandia House, and **Avis** (tel. 772-4716) can be found at the Tides Inn. Petersburg has no public transportation system.

The Tides Inn, 1st and Dolphin Streets (tel. 772-4288), rents **bicycles** at $5 an hour, $20 for eight hours.

FAST FACTS

Banks   The town has two full-service banks.

Emergencies   In an emergency, dial 911, or call 772-3838 for the police, to report a fire, to request an ambulance, or to reach the poison-control center. For medical assistance, visit Petersburg General Hospital, 201 Fram St. (tel. 772-4291).

Newspaper   The *Petersburg Pilot* is published weekly.

WHAT TO SEE & DO

SIGHTS & ATTRACTIONS

The famous **Sons of Norway Hall,** on Sing Lee Alley (tel. 772-4575)—declared a National Historic Site in 1979—was built in 1912 on pilings over picturesque Hammer Slough. It houses Fedrelandet No. 23 of the Sons of Norway, an international fraternal organization to preserve the Norwegian ethnic heritage, and was the home of all community gatherings in early Petersburg. Visit the **Husfliden** ("cottage industry") gift and handcraft shop on its second floor, especially if you'd like to know more about the *rosemaling* style of decorative house painting.

Nearby, **Petersburg Boat Harbor** has 489 stalls for Alaska's largest commercial halibut fleet and other fishing and pleasure boats. A boardwalk enables you to walk from end to end. It's one of many stops on a walking tour described in the annual "Viking Visitor Guide"—published by the *Petersburg Pilot* and distributed by the chamber of commerce—that will introduce you to a variety of fascinating nooks and crannies.

South on the Mitkof Highway, you can watch salmon climb the **Falls Creek Fish Ladder** (Mile 10.8) en route to the $2.2-million **Crystal Lake Hatchery** on Blind Slough at Mile 17 (tel. 772-4772), which welcomes the public for guided tours of its salmon and steelhead hatching and rearing facilities (open from 8am to 4pm daily). Nearby is a Forest Service **observatory** for watching 60–80 trumpeter swans that winter at Blind Slough. All the while, look out on the Wrangell Narrows, the strait that separates Mitkof from Kupreanof island, for bald eagles, sea otters, porpoises, seals, and perhaps whales.

CLAUSEN MEMORIAL MUSEUM, 2nd and Fram Sts. Tel. 772-3598.

The collection here stresses Petersburg's historic ties to the sea. Among the exhibits are two mounted world-record salmon (a 126½-pound king and a 36-pound chum), a re-created cannery office, displays of past and present fishing methods, and pioneer artifacts (including some brought by town founder Peter Buschmann). On the lawn is Carson Boysen's 11-foot bronze sculpture and fountain, *Fisk* (Norwegian for "fish").

Admission: $1.

Open: May–Sept, Sat–Thurs 12:30–5pm; Oct–Apr, Wed–Thurs and Sun 12:30–5pm, or by appointment. **Closed:** New Year's and Christmas Days.

ORGANIZED TOURS

Any land and sea arrangements can be handled by **Viking Travel,** P.O. Box 787, Petersburg, AK 99833 (tel. 772-3818). Popular but expensive is Viking's half-day harbor tour aboard the F/V *Chan IV.* Syd Wright, former principal of Petersburg High School, visits various types of fishing vessels and explains their functions, then pulls shrimp pots through Frederick Sound and provides wine with which to sample the fisherman's bounty. The price is a flat $320 for four to six people.

Patty Norheim's **Tongass Traveller** (tel. 772-4837) offers a tour of Mitkof Island that includes a cannery tour and shrimp cocktail.

SPORTS & RECREATION

The new city **swimming pool** is at the elementary school on Dolphin Street between 3rd and 4th Streets (tel. 772-3304). Call for hours; admission is $1.50 for adults, 75¢ for children and seniors. There are exercise and weight machines in the high school's **gym,** at the west end of 2nd Street, at Charles Street (tel. 772-4434), open weekday evenings. This facility also has limited times scheduled for basketball and volleyball. Contact the city Parks and Recreation office (tel. 772-3392) for full information. **The Spa,** in Scandia House (tel. 772-4266), charges $7.50 per person for a private room with a hot tub. There are also saunas and tanning booths.

Complete information on all recreational pursuits can be obtained from the chamber of commerce (tel. 772-3646).

FISHING All waters, both fresh and salt, are open year-round to sport fishing except near fish ladders and hatcheries. You can go after king salmon from May to July, silvers in August and September, pinks from mid-July through August, chum from July to September. Steelhead run in May and June. Rainbow, Dolly Varden, and cutthroat trout are best between May and October. The best time for halibut is June to October. You can also find cod, red snapper, flounder, herring, and tanner crab year-round.

Charter operators—there are at least a dozen—include Dan O'Neil's **Secret Cove Charters** (tel. 772-3081), **Dick Hindman Charters** (tel. 772-4478), and Charlie Casey's **Agapé Charters** (tel. 772-3551). Skiffs with outboard motors can be rented from **Tongass Marine** (tel. 772-3905). Consult the U.S. Coast Guard near the ferry terminal for information on tides and currents. Petersburg shops sell marine charts, topographic maps, and tide charts. The **Petersburg Salmon Derby** is held Memorial Day weekend.

HIKING Raven Trail, a 3½-mile walk beginning behind the airport, is the most popular trail on Mitkof Island. It leads to the Forest Service's Raven's Roost Cabin at 1,745 feet elevation, which has outstanding views of Petersburg and the Wrangell Narrows. About half the trail is boardwalk, but there are some very steep sections. A quarter-mile planked trail leads off the Mitkof Highway at Mile 16 to Blind River Rapids. Check with the U.S. Forest Service (tel. 772-3871) for current conditions and other trail information.

HUNTING Black bear are in season from September 1 to June 15. You can hunt mountain goat in August and September, and moose from September 15 to October 15. Go after waterfowl from September 1 to December 16, ptarmigan in August and September, and grouse from August 1 to May 15. The **Alaska Department of Fish and Game,** in the State Office Building, Sing Lee Alley (tel. 772-3801), can give you full information on licenses and game regulations. The **Trading Union,** Nordic Drive at Dolphin Street (tel. 772-3881), and **Hammer & Wikan,** Nordic Drive at Excel Street (tel. 772-4246), have complete sporting-goods departments for hunting and fishing.

WINTER SPORTS Travel by cross-country skis or snowshoes into Raven's Roost, where you can reserve the Forest Service cabin for $20 a night. Some alpine diehards have hired helicopters to ski the slopes in this area. Cross-country skiing and snowmobiling are also popular along the Three Lakes Loop Road, a logging road in the southeastern part of Mitkof Island. Icefishing is popular here (at Sand, Hill, and Crane Lakes) and at Petersburg Lake, on Kupreanof Island, nine air miles from Petersburg.

SHOPPING

Hammer & Wikan, Nordic Drive at Excel Street (tel. 772-4246), and the **Trading Union,** Nordic Drive at Dolphin Street (tel. 772-3881), stock many Norwegian gift items, including pewter, crystal, and baking ware. Here you can also buy the *Norwegian Book of Knowledge*—40 pages, all of them blank. **Lee's,** 212 Nordic Dr. (tel. 772-4229), specializes in Norwegian knit sweaters and other outdoor wear. **Diamanté,** Nordic Drive at Fram Street (tel. 772-4858), has an excellent selection of both Alaskan and Norwegian gifts. **Jewell's by the Sea,** 806 S. Nordic Dr. (tel. 772-3620), three blocks north of the ferry dock, is the best place to check out local artists.

WHERE TO STAY

Tax The local tax on hotel rooms is 9%.

BEACHCOMBER INN, 384 Mitkof Hwy. (P.O. Box 570), Petersburg, AK 99833. Tel. 907/772-3888. 8 rms (4 with bath). TV **Transportation:** Courtesy van from the ferry or airport.
$ Rates: $45–$55 single; $55–$65 double. AE, CB, DC, DISC, MC, V.
A cannery from 1912 to 1949, the Beachcomber now offers salmon- and halibut-fishing packages; nonfishing guests can watch eagles dive for fish. The guest rooms, all upstairs, are cozy and comfortable, but this is more a place for outdoors lovers than folks who plan to camp out in their rooms. The outstanding restaurant (see "Where to Dine," below) draws throngs from town.

JEWELL'S BY THE SEA, 806 S. Nordic Dr. (P.O. Box 1662), Petersburg, AK 99833. Tel. 907/772-3620. 2 rms (with shared bath).
$ Rates (including full breakfast): May–Sept, $50 single; $60 double. Oct–Apr, $45 single; $55 double. AE, DISC, MC, V.
This beachfront home is not only Petersburg's only bed-and-breakfast, it's also the town's most notable gallery of locally produced arts and crafts. Rooms are comfortable and homey. Guests share a bathroom, a sitting room, and a TV room. No smoking or alcoholic beverages are permitted. Free pickup and delivery from the ferry terminal and airport are offered year-round.

SCANDIA HOUSE, 110 N. Nordic Dr. (P.O. Box 689), Petersburg, AK 99833. Tel. 907/772-4281. 24 rms (16 with bath), 6 suites. TV TEL
$ Rates (including continental breakfast): $55–$60 single or double, without bath; $70–$75 single or double with bath; $78–$83 suite for two. Additional person $10 extra. AE, CB, DC, DISC, MC, V.
Original oil paintings of townspeople in Norwegian costume decorate the rooms and lobby of this main-street landmark. The rooms of the former Mitkof Hotel, built in 1910 by immigrants, have been completely renovated with the local touch. A rose-color theme was given to second-floor rooms, evergreen to those on the third. All rooms have built-in clock radios, and suites have a kitchen. A spa and saunas are on the premises. The hotel also offers complete sport-fishing packages, from skiff rentals to charter trips, plus freezer space and shipment of your catch.

TIDES INN, 1st and Dolphin Sts. (P.O. Box 1048), Petersburg, AK 99833, Tel. 907/772-4288. Fax 907/772-4286. 47 rms (all with bath). TV TEL
$ Rates (including continental breakfast): Apr–Sept, $70 single; $75 double. Oct–Mar, $65 single; $70 double. AE, CB, DC, DISC, MC, V.
The Tides has two wings of rooms. Those in the newer (1984) wing are far the superior: They have harbor views, fresher decor, and baseboard heating, a step above the electric heaters in the older wing during the winter cold. One of the nicest features

is a large lobby area with newspapers, magazines, and notebooks chock full of tourist information about all corners of southeast Alaska. Car and bicycle rentals are also available. The motel is accessible to disabled guests.

CAMPGROUNDS

There are two recreational-vehicle parks in Petersburg. **LeConte RV Park** has 10 full-service hookups and four open spaces near downtown at 4th Street and Haugen Drive (tel. 772-4680). **Twin Creek RV Park,** 7½ miles south on the Mitkof Highway (tel. 772-3282 or 772-3244), has 20 spaces with electricity and water. Both have restrooms, showers, and dump stations, and both charge upward of $10 a night.

Tent campers can trek out to **Tent City,** the city campground, near the airport on Haugen Drive (tel. 772-3003), with 36 tent platforms, a central cooking area, and restrooms. The charge is $5 a night, with weekly reservations accepted. If Tent City is already full with summer cannery workers, there are two free but unimproved campgrounds south of Petersburg on the Mitkof Highway: **Ohmer Creek** (21 miles) and **Summer Strait** (26 miles). Bring water.

WHERE TO DINE

BEACHCOMBER INN, 384 Mitkof Hwy. Tel. 772-3888.
   Cuisine: STEAK/SEAFOOD. **Reservations:** Recommended.
$ **Prices:** Appetizers $6–$10; main courses $13–$24. AE, CB, DC, DISC, MC, V.
   Open: Dinner only, daily 6–10pm.

Petersburg's finest restaurant overlooks the Wrangell Narrows from big picture windows on Scow Bay, four miles south of town. Housed in a former cannery, it's best known for its steaks and seafood. This is the place to sample those tiny, tasty Petersburg shrimp. (A full dinner runs about $17.) There's live entertainment in the Cannery Lounge Wednesday through Sunday in summer.

HARBOR LIGHTS PIZZA, 16 Sing Lee Alley. Tel. 772-3424.
   Cuisine: ITALIAN. **Reservations:** Not accepted.
$ **Prices:** Average meal $4.50–$18.50. DC, MC, V.
   Open: Sun–Thurs 11am–11pm, Fri–Sat, 11am–midnight.

Located on a pier at the mouth of Hammer Slough, Harbor Lights is more than a pizza parlor. While you can get a Viking Special (pepperoni, green pepper, and sausage) or even an oyster pizza, you'll also find sandwiches, a full salad bar, a beer garden, and luncheon specials. Historic Petersburg photos decorate the walls.

HELSE, Sing Lee Alley and Harbor Way. Tel. 772-3444.
   Cuisine: NATURAL FOODS. **Reservations:** Not accepted.
$ **Prices:** Average meal $3–$7.50. No credit cards.
   Open: Tues–Sat 9am–5pm.

This health-food deli serves hearty homemade soups with bread, and frequent Mexican specials. Try the King Neptune sandwich: shrimp, avocado, sprouts, and tomatoes.

HOMESTEAD CAFE, 206 N. Nordic Dr. Tel. 772-3900.
   Cuisine: AMERICAN. **Reservations:** Not accepted.
$ **Prices:** Breakfast/lunch $4–$10; dinner $11–$19. AE, CB, DC, MC, V.
   Open: May–Sept, Mon 6am–Sat 10pm (24 hours daily; closed Sun); Oct–Apr, Mon–Sat 6am–10pm.

If you want to sit with the locals, look no farther than the Homestead Café. Local fishermen have a twice-a-day ritual at this 24-hour restaurant: They roll the dice to see who buys coffee for the house. More gossip passes from mouth to ear at the Homestead's counter and booths than anywhere else in Petersburg. Sourdough pancakes are a great way to start your day; in the evening, a generous salad bar precedes hearty steak and seafood meals.

JOAN MEI, 300 N. Nordic Dr. Tel. 772-3456.
   Cuisine: CHINESE/AMERICAN. **Reservations:** Not accepted.

$ Prices: Average meal $3–$7. No credit cards.
Open: Daily 8am–10pm.

Joan Mei may look like no more than a glorified hamburger stand—but it offers greater variety than any McDonald's or Dairy Queen. Come for cheeseburgers or tacos, Chinese or Vietnamese fast food.

PELLERITO'S PIZZERIA, 1105 S. Nordic Dr. Tel. 772-3727.
   Cuisine: ITALIAN. **Reservations:** Not accepted.
$ Prices: Average meal $3–$17. No credit cards.
   Open: Daily 7am–11pm.

Come for breakfast, when you can enjoy Pellerito's homemade sweet rolls: cinnamon, blueberry, blackberry, or brandied peach. Come for lunch—for submarines and other tasty sandwiches. Better yet, come for hand-thrown pizza or calzone dinners. The restaurant makes its own pasta and pizza dough, and has gelato (Italian ice cream), too. You can bring your pizza upstairs to the popular Skoal Pub, if you like.

THE QUAY, 1103 S. Nordic Dr. Tel. 772-4600.
   Cuisine: STEAK/SEAFOOD. **Reservations:** Recommended for dinner.
$ Prices: Appetizers $6–$10; main courses $11–$23; breakfast $3.50–$8.50; lunch $4.50–$9. AE, CB, DC, MC, V.
   Open: Daily 6am–10pm.

There's a Norwegian nautical flavor to the Quay (pronounced "key"), right down to the dinner appetizers of pickled herring and flatbread. Full as well as continental breakfasts are served, and a variety of sandwiches are offered up at lunch. For dinner, enjoy prime rib or halibut, or go the light route with a salad bar and oyster stew. There are always daily specials; a big brunch is served on Sunday from 10am to 2pm.

EVENING ENTERTAINMENT

The action is at **Kito's Kave,** an otherwise nondescript red building at the decidedly un-Norwegian intersection of Sing Lee Alley and Chief John Lott Street (tel. 772-3207). A live band plays Tuesday through Sunday from 9pm to 2am, unless preempted by special visitors—such as the Chippendale male strippers. Thursday night is Ladies' Night; Monday night there's a local jam session. The **Skoal Pub,** 1105 S. Nordic Dr. (tel. 772-3727), across from the ferry terminal, is equally popular. If you just want a quiet drink, your best bet may be the **Harbor Bar,** Nordic Drive near Dolphin Street (tel. 775-4526).

The **Viking Theater,** downtown on Nordic Drive (tel. 772-4204), has shows Thursday through Sunday nights. Look also for a community theater group known as the **Mitkof Mummers** (tel. 772-4859). The traditional **Leikaring dancers** sometimes perform for cruise ships at the Sons of Norway Hall. For information on these and other activities, contact the **Petersburg Arts Council** (tel. 772-4573).

EASY EXCURSIONS

The spectacular ✪ **LeConte Glacier,** 20 air miles east of Petersburg, is the southernmost active tidewater glacier in North America. As the glacier advances, large chunks of ice break off and tumble into LeConte Bay with a roar, creating icebergs such as those that once provided refrigeration for Petersburg's seafood shipments. One of a dozen glaciers that make up the huge Stikine Icefield surrounding 9,077-foot Devil's Thumb, the LeConte is believed to have retreated slightly in recent years. It was first observed by John Muir in 1879 and charted eight years later.

Local air services and charter boats offer excursions to the glacier. Check with air-taxi services listed under "Orientation" and charter operators listed under "Fishing" in "Sports and Recreation," in "What to See and Do," above, in this section.

Kake, a Tlingit community 40 miles from Petersburg on the northwest shore of huge (1,084 square miles) Kupreanof Island, is best known as the home of the "world's tallest totem pole" (132 feet), featured at the Expo 1970 world's fair in Osaka, Japan. As is characteristic in southeast Alaska, the town's economy is based on fishing and logging. Kake's 680 people are served by the ferry *LeConte* every Monday (southbound) and Tuesday (northbound). You can stay at the **New Town Inn,** P.O. Box 222, Kake, AK 99830 (tel. 907/785-3472 or 785-3885), where singles cost $71 and doubles are $79, including three meals. Tax is 5%. The inn is open year-round.

There are 21 public-use U.S. Forest Service **cabins** in the Petersburg Ranger District. Only one of them (Raven's Roost) is on Mitkof Island. There are 12 cabins on Kupreanof Island, four around Thomas Bay on the North American mainland, and two each on Kuiu and Woewodski Islands. They can be reserved for $20 a day; you must provide your own transportation, food, and survival equipment. Contact the Petersburg Ranger District, P.O. Box 1328, Petersburg, AK 99833 (tel. 907/772-3871).

There are no cabins in the **Tebenkof Bay Wilderness,** on the west side of Kuiu Island, 50 miles southwest of Petersburg. But wildlife abounds in this 66,800-acre expanse encompassing numerous broad bays and small islets. This is strictly for the adventurous—approach is by floatplane or boat only. Amateur archeologists will find several historic Tlingit sites.

---

4. SITKA

136 miles SW of Juneau, 156 miles NW of Petersburg

GETTING THERE   By Plane   Sitka is served by nonstop daily **Alaska Airlines** (tel. 907/966-2266, or 966-2261 for information) flights to and from Juneau and Ketchikan, and direct flights to Anchorage, Seattle, and San Jose and Long Beach, California. Local air-taxi services include **Bellair, Inc.** (tel. 747-8636), and **Mountain Aviation** (tel. 966-2288).

By Ferry   Alaska Marine Highway vessels (tel. 747-8737, or 747-3300 for recorded information) arrive and depart eight times a week in summer, less frequently in winter. The fare to Sitka is $52 from Ketchikan, $24 from Juneau or Petersburg.

SPECIAL EVENTS   Alaska Day, October 18, is Sitka's big day. Each year a three- to five-day festival is woven around this date to commemorate the 1867 transfer of Russian Alaska to the United States. Events include a memorial service, parade, military demonstrations, Native and Russian dancing, concerts, fun races, and the Lord Baranof Ball. You can get fined ($1) if you're male and not wearing a beard.

Since 1972 the ✪ **Sitka Summer Music Festival** has attracted some of the world's leading chamber musicians for three weeks in June. The musicians play to sell-out crowds of 500 in the Centennial Building. Individual-performance tickets are $7 for adults, $4 for students and seniors. A summer writers' symposium is scheduled at the same time. For information, contact P.O. Box 907, Sitka, AK 99835 (tel. 907/747-6774).

Other events include **Russian Christmas,** January 7, the biggest day of the Orthodox religious calendar; and the **All-Alaska Logging Championships,** in late June.

Alaska's most historic city, and one of its most beautiful, looks out on the Gulf of Alaska and the Pacific Ocean, gazing westward toward the Russian behemoth that founded it nearly two centuries ago. Many of the sights of modern Sitka—St. Michael's Russian Orthodox Cathedral, the bishop's house, the old cemetery—harken to the days when Alexander Baranov (Baranof) and his men held sway from Castle Hill. But Sitka also has a rich Tlingit heritage, as evidenced by the exhibits in the Southeast Alaska Indian Cultural Center. And its cultural orientation is praiseworthy: The annual Summer Music Festival attracts some of the world's finest classical musicians, and the Sheldon Jackson Museum of Native artifacts is renowned.

Magnificent Mount Edgecumbe looms mysteriously across Sitka Sound from the town, which nestles along the sound's islet-filled eastern shore. About 8,500 people live here, making Sitka Alaska's fifth-largest city and the third largest in the southeast. It's the only sizable community on 1,636-square-mile Baranof Island.

Sitka's location on the mild Japan Current has given it a climate that has been described as "perpetually autumn." Sitkans get used to morning fog. They expect about a month and a half of clear, crisp weather over the course of the year—the mean temperature in July is a scorching 54°F—and about eight months' worth of rain or snow. Average annual rainfall is 95 inches (October is the wettest month, June the driest), and average snowfall is about 70 inches—though it melts quickly in January's 35°F heat.

The history of Sitka is the chronicle of early Alaska. A small fort called Redoubt Arkhangelsk Mikhailovsk was established in 1799 about six miles north of the modern town (the site is commemorated by Old Sitka State Park). The fort was burned to the ground, and most of its occupants slain, by hostile Tlingits in 1802; but two years later the Russians retaliated, bombarding the Native stronghold (on the site of modern Sitka National Historical Park) with cannons until the Tlingits fled. They didn't return to Sitka until 1821, and thereafter lived in an uneasy truce with the Russians. The colonists reconstructed the town, now called Novoarkhangelsk (New Archangel), on its present site in 1804 and made it the capital of Russian Alaska until sovereignty passed to the United States in 1867.

Sitka (from its Tlingit name Shee-atika, meaning "by the sea") remained the Alaskan capital until mining income convinced the U.S. government to transfer administrative headquarters to Juneau in 1906. Gold was never found in large quantities on Baranof Island, but fishing became important after a salmon cannery was built there in 1878. A Presbyterian mission school opened in Sitka the same year; it eventually became a Native vocational school, which today is Sheldon Jackson College.

Several thousand military personnel and civilian workers moved to Sitka just before and during World War II, occupying the army's Fort Ray and a naval air station on adjacent Japonski Island. When the troops pulled out after the war, commercial fishing once again took first place in the economy. Today it's supported by summer tourism and timber—especially the $70-million, Japanese-owned Alaska Pulp Corp. mill at Silver Bay, six miles east of town.

ORIENTATION

ARRIVING If you arrive by air, you'll land at the former naval air station on Japonski Island, 1.7 miles from downtown Sitka. **Sitka Airport** is connected with the town by the John O'Connell Memorial Bridge, built in 1972. The Alaska Marine Highway **ferry terminal** (tel. 747-8737, or 747-3300 for information) is seven miles north of town on Halibut Point Road.

The **Prewitt Enterprises school bus** (tel. 747-8443) will pick you up at either the airport or the ferry and will drop you off at your hotel for $10 round-trip. Taxi fare from the ferry dock to town runs about $12. There is no public bus system in Sitka.

INFORMATION The **Sitka Convention and Visitors Bureau** is in the Centennial Building, 330 Harbor Dr. (P.O. Box 1226), Sitka, AK 99835 (tel. 907/747-5940; fax 907/747-3739). Also in the building are the **Greater Sitka Chamber of Commerce**, P.O. Box 638, Sitka, AK 99835 (tel. 907/747-8604); the Isabel Miller Museum; and an auditorium, where the New Archangel Dancers and the maestros of the Sitka Summer Music Festival perform.

For information on outdoor activities, contact the **Sitka Ranger District,** U.S. Forest Service, 204 Siginaka Way, Sitka, AK 99835 (tel. 907/747-6671); the **National Park Service,** P.O. Box 738, Sitka, AK 99835 (tel. 907/747-6281); **Alaska State Parks,** P.O. Box 142, Sitka, AK 99835 (tel. 907/747-6249); and the **Alaska**

Department of Fish and Game, P.O. Box 510, Sitka, AK 99835 (tel. 907/747-6688).

CITY LAYOUT Sitka doesn't have the neat street layout of other southeast towns. It's easiest to think of the center of town as being the unmistakable onion spires of St. Michael's Cathedral. The cathedral is an island in the middle of **Lincoln Street,** which runs from the foot of Castle Hill (about three blocks west of St. Michael's) all the way to Sitka National Historical Site (a good mile southeast of the cathedral). Its main intersection is near **Crescent Harbor,** where Harbor Drive and Lake Street join. Here, within a block of the cruise-ship dock, you'll find the Centennial Building and visitors bureau offices, Westmark Shee Atika, and the Russian Bishop's House. Sheldon Jackson College is half a mile away.

GETTING AROUND

Arrowhead Taxi (tel. 747-8888) and **Sitka Taxi** (tel. 747-5001) don't have meters but charge set fares based on mileage.

For car rentals, check **Avis** (tel. 966-2404) or **All Star Rent-a-Car** (tel. 966-2552) at the airport; **AAA Auto Rental** at 2033 Halibut Point Rd. (tel. 747-8228); or **Advantage** at 713 Katlian St. (tel. 747-7557).

FAST FACTS

Emergencies In an emergency, dial 911, or call 747-3245 for the city police or 747-3233 to report a fire. For medical assistance, the Sitka Community Hospital is at 209 Moller Dr. (tel. 747-3241), at the north end of town.

Newspaper The *Daily Sitka Sentinel* is published five days a week.

WHAT TO SEE & DO

SIGHTS & ATTRACTIONS IN TOWN

SITKA NATIONAL HISTORICAL PARK, Metlakatla St. (P.O. Box 738), Sitka, AK 99835. Tel. 907/747-6281.

✪ You can relive history at the site where Russians overran a Tlingit Indian stronghold and captured Sitka in 1804. A short trail winds past numerous totem poles to the actual battleground. The visitors center contains museum exhibits of southeast Alaska Indian culture and offers an audiovisual presentation on Sitka's Russian history. You get an impressive sense of the continuity of Native culture when you visit the adjoining Southeast Alaska Indian Cultural Center, where craftspeople are at work on wood carving, silver engraving, and beading projects. Here you can learn firsthand the legends behind the Indians' art. Native crafts are scheduled daily in summer only.

Admission: Free.

Open: June–Sept, daily 8am–6pm; Oct–May, Mon–Fri 8am–5pm. **Closed:** New Year's, Thanksgiving, and Christmas Days.

RUSSIAN BISHOP'S HOUSE, Lincoln St. at Monastery St. Tel. 747-6281.

✪ The Russian Bishop's House is also administered by the National Park Service. Built in 1842, it was the seat of power and authority for the Russian Orthodox church in Alaska until long after political sovereignty had passed to the United States. Its principal occupant, Bishop (now Saint) Innocent Veniaminov, was appointed metropolitan of Moscow in 1868. Restoration work, based on the original plans and inventories, has returned this building—the only complete Russian colonial structure standing in the western hemisphere—close to its original appearance. Ground-floor classrooms and priests' quarters hold museum displays of Russian history, while upstairs, in the bishop's residence, National Park Service employees interpret the ecclesiastical lifestyle amid original furnishings. The old chapel was reconsecrated in 1988.

Admission: Free (donations accepted).

Open: June–Sept, daily 9am–5pm; Oct–May, by appointment (usually Tues, Thurs, and Sat).

ST. MICHAEL'S CATHEDRAL, Lincoln St. at Observatory St. Tel. 747-8120.

✪ The gray-and-white frame building that you see today isn't the same one that stood on this spot during the Russian era. A downtown fire destroyed the original in 1966, but the tragedy could have been much worse if townspeople hadn't carried to safety many priceless icons and other art treasures. These works are now showcased on the inner walls of the new cathedral.

An exact replica of the earlier building, the cathedral was completed in 1976 at a cost of $600,000. Take special note of Vladimir Borovikovsky's 18th-century painting of *Our Lady of Sitka,* to the left of the ornate altar screen. Thousands who pray to this "Sitka Madonna" regard her as a miracle healer. The image of St. Michael the Archangel, carried from Russia in 1816, represents the cathedral's patron saint.

Services are held at 9:30am every Sunday and at 6:30pm on Wednesday throughout the year. Visitors are welcome, but must be prepared to stand through the service (there are no pews).

Admission: $1 donation requested.

Open: June–Sept, Mon–Sat 11am–3pm, Sun 11am–noon, (cruise-ship days, 9am–3pm); Oct–May, by appointment.

SHELDON JACKSON MUSEUM, 104 College Dr. Tel. 747-8981.

✪ This red octagonal building just off Lincoln Street houses Alaska's oldest and one of its finest collections of Native artifacts. Jackson, a Presbyterian missionary who founded the school in 1878 and built this concrete museum in 1895, gathered most of the articles in the late 1800s during his travels through the Alaska territory and along the coast of Siberia. There is a fascinating display of Native vehicles: boats like the Eskimo umiak, Aleut bidarka, Athabaskan bark canoe, and Tlingit dugout, plus a reindeer sled and various dog sleds; several vehicles are suspended from the ceiling. There are also excellent miniatures of fish traps and game snares, as well as weapons, ceremonial masks, and hundreds of other items representing Alaska's four main ethnic divisions.

Admission: $2 adults, free for children under 18.

Open: Mid-May to mid-Sept, daily 8am–5pm; mid-Sept to mid-May, Tues–Sat 10am–4pm.

ISABEL MILLER MUSEUM, 330 Harbor Dr. Tel. 747-6455.

This little museum's varied collection includes a full-scale model of Sitka under the Russians, ice saws used in the 1850s to cut ice blocks for shipment to San Francisco, a facsimile of the $7.2-million purchase agreement for Alaska signed in 1867 by Secretary of State William Seward (the original is in the Smithsonian Institution), and one of the original copies of the Alaska State Constitution. The museum is named after former Sitka Historical Society director Isabel Miller, who celebrated her 89th birthday in 1993.

Admission: Free (donations accepted).

Open: May–Sept, Mon–Sat 8am–5pm, Sun and cruise-ship days 8am–1pm; Oct–Apr, Tues–Sat 10am–4pm.

ALASKA RAPTOR REHABILITATION CENTER, 1101 Sawmill Creek Rd. Tel. 747-8662.

Injured and ailing eagles, hawks, owls, and other birds of prey are brought to this facility for treatment. Birds whose injuries are too severe for release are trained for public education or captive-breeding programs. Visitors to the volunteer-run center can see bald eagles and other raptors being treated and exercised.

Admission: Guided tours $10; self-guided tours free (donations accepted).

Open: Open houses and tours are held frequently in summer, less often in winter. There's no set schedule; call ahead for times or for an appointment.

NEARBY ATTRACTIONS

Baranof Island doesn't have many miles of road—fewer than 30, in fact. But there are several points of interest you can get to by car. One is **Old Sitka State Historic Site,** administered by the state parks system (tel. 747-6249). About 7½ miles north of modern Sitka on Halibut Point Road just past the ferry terminal, it was the location of the original 1799 Russian settlement routed by the Tlingits. There's a small nature-and-history trail, and a 24-hour interpretive center. Evening programs are often presented. Starrigavan campground is a quarter mile farther north.

You can turn off Halibut Point Road onto **Harbor Mountain Road** four miles north of Sitka and wind your way three miles up a narrow gravel road to a spectacular view at 2,100 feet elevation. A short, steep trail climbs another 1,000 feet from a picnic area to a mountaintop lookout.

Heading south, **Sawmill Creek Road** runs 13 miles to the Green Lake hydroelectric plant (public access is not permitted). En route, 5¼ miles southeast of the city, you'll pass the Alaska Pulp Corp. mill.

World War II buffs can find gun emplacements and lookout stations on **Japonski Island,** site of the airport, the U.S. Coast Guard station, and Mount Edgecumbe High School.

WALKING TOUR — SITKA

Start: Centennial Building, 330 Harbor Dr.
End: Sitka National Historical Park, or for a longer walk, the Alaska Raptor Rehabilitation Center.
Time: One to six hours, depending on the time spent at attractions en route.
Best Times: Any summer weekday after 11am.
Worst Times: Sunday or Monday in other seasons.

Start at the:

1. **Centennial Building,** on Crescent Harbor, where the visitors bureau and chamber of commerce offices, as well as the Isabel Miller Museum (see above) and the performing arts auditorium, are located. There's a wildlife display in the lobby (in summer the Baranof Arts and Crafts Association has a sale here). Pick up a copy of the walking-tour map from the convention and visitors bureau to help guide you on your way.

   Notice a large home dominating a small island in the sound just behind the Centennial Building. Connected to Maksoutoff Street by a causeway, this private residence was built in 1915 on the foundation of a Russian saltery. Its basement walls are 8–10 feet thick.

   Walk down Harbor Drive to Observatory Street, then turn right a block to Lincoln Street. You're in the heart of downtown, dominated by:

2. **St. Michael's Cathedral** (see above). At 224 Lincoln St., stop to look into the:

3. **Sitka Lutheran Church** (tel. 747-3338), facing St. Michael's. A tiny museum here explains that this was the first organized Lutheran congregation west of the Rocky Mountains, founded in 1840 by Finns working for the Russian-American Company. Still in use, the pipe organ is the first on the continent's west coast.

   Walk down Lincoln Street away from the cathedral toward Katlian Street. At the corner of Lincoln and Katlian Streets is the:

4. **Pioneer Home** (tel. 747-3213), which would be Sitka's dominant building were it not for St. Michael's. A huge red-roofed structure built of yellow brick in 1934, it was the first state-supported long-term residence for "sourdoughs" requiring

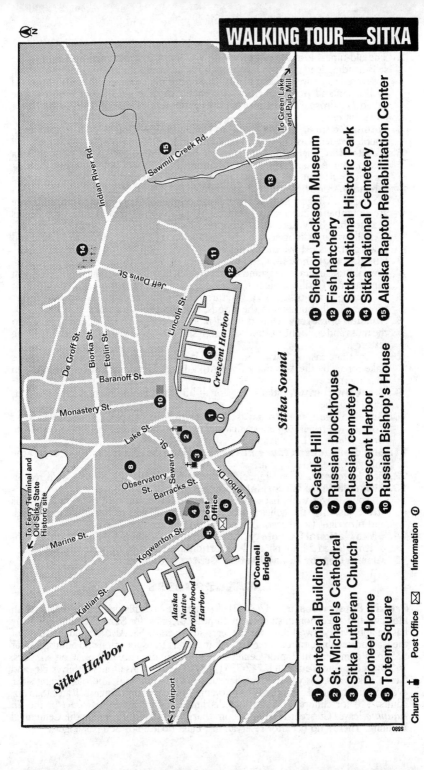

WALKING TOUR—SITKA

① Centennial Building
② St. Michael's Cathedral
③ Sitka Lutheran Church
④ Pioneer Home
⑤ Totem Square
⑥ Castle Hill
⑦ Russian blockhouse
⑧ Russian cemetery
⑨ Crescent Harbor
⑩ Russian Bishop's House
⑪ Sheldon Jackson Museum
⑫ Fish hatchery
⑬ Sitka National Historic Park
⑭ Sitka National Cemetery
⑮ Alaska Raptor Rehabilitation Center

Church ✝ ■   Post Office ⊠   Information ⑦

Sitka Sound

Sitka Harbor

Crescent Harbor

Alaska Native Brotherhood Harbor

O'Connell Bridge

Post Office

Indian River Rd.
Sawmill Creek Rd.
Jeff Davis St.
Lincoln St.
De Groff St.
Biorka St.
Etolin St.
Baranoff St.
Monastery St.
Lake St.
Seward St.
Observatory St.
Barracks St.
Kogwanton St.
Marine St.
Katlian St.
Harbor Dr.

To Green Lake and Pulp Mill →
To Ferry Terminal and Old Sitka State Historic site →
To Airport →

5580

some degree of medical care. There are now several such homes around the state. The old-timers love to reminisce with visitors. A basement arts-and-crafts shop sells handmade items Monday through Friday from 8am to 4pm, and the garden is devoted to native Alaskan plants. In front of the home, on grounds once used by Russian and American troops for parade drills, is a 13½-foot bronze statue called *The Prospector,* sculpted in 1949 by Alonzo Victor Lewis. The Pioneer Home looks out on:

5. **Totem Square,** a park block containing a 1940 totem pole topped by a double-headed Russian eagle. Just south of Totem Square is:
6. **Castle Hill.** There's not much to see here anymore except the view of Sitka Sound. But Alexander Baranov's mansion ("Baranov Castle"), where the first American flag in Alaska was raised in 1867 during the transfer-of-power ceremony, stood here until it burned down in 1894. Before that the hill had been the site of a Tlingit village. A few Russian cannons still point out to sea, and there are a number of interpretive historical plaques. A short trail to the hilltop begins next to the Harry Race Drug Store on Lincoln Street.

   Follow Barracks Street a block north from the Pioneer Home to Marine and Seward Streets. Above the corner is a:
7. **Russian blockhouse,** a solid-log replica of one of three 1805-era structures. Several Russian gravesites stand nearby, which may be of particular interest if you can read the Cyrillic alphabet.

   A couple of blocks east, if you turn off Seward and climb Observatory Street to where it disappears into the woods, you can explore an old:
8. **Russian cemetery,** with its wooden double crosses slowly decaying back into the moss and soil. The Orthodox church still uses these grounds, which are being restored.

   Continue east on Seward Street until it rejoins Lincoln Street where it crosses Lake Street by the Westmark Shee Atika hotel. Continue east on Lincoln. On your right is:
9. **Crescent Harbor,** Sitka's busy small-boat and fishing harbor. On your left, you'll pass the:
10. **Russian Bishop's House** (see above) and the campus of Sheldon Jackson College, where author James Michener made his home base in 1984–87 while he wrote *Alaska.* The acclaimed:
11. **Sheldon Jackson Museum** (see above) is on the edge of campus. Just past the college, on your right, is a:
12. **fish hatchery.** Where Lincoln Street ends at Metlakatla Street, you'll reach:
13. **Sitka National Historical Park** (see above).

    For a longer walk, backtrack on Lincoln Street and turn right on Jeff Davis Street, just after the college; proceed two long blocks to Sawmill Creek Road, and turn right (southeast). Behind Sheldon Jackson College is:
14. **Sitka National Cemetery,** the oldest national cemetery west of the Mississippi River (open 24 hours). And a short distance farther, on your left, is the:
15. **Alaska Raptor Rehabilitation Center** (see above).

ORGANIZED TOURS

Prewitt Enterprises (tel. 747-8443) offers a three-hour historical tour of Sitka each morning and afternoon in summer, with hotel pickups, for $22. The same company has an abbreviated two-hour tour for ferry stopovers at $8. Also offered are tours of the Raptor Rehabilitation Center for $18 (including transportation and admission), or $35 for a combination Raptor Center–city tour. Children are half price on all tours.

Allen Marine Tours (tel. 747-8941) has 2½-hour cruise tours to Silver Bay and Green Lake Falls, for views of the harbor, wildlife, pulp mill, and old mining sites, every Saturday, Sunday, and Monday evening June through August. Rates ($25 for adults, $10 for children) do not include dinner. Either the *St. Michael* or the *St. Aquilina* leaves Crescent Harbor at 6pm sharp from the dock beside the Centennial Building. There's no need for reservations: Each boat holds 300 passengers.

Sitka Wildlife Tours (tel. 747-5576), operated by Alaska Travel Adventures of Juneau, scours Sitka Sound by catamaran yacht and inflatable raft in a 3½-hour search for marine life, including whales. The fare is $79 for adults, $50 for children.

SPORTS & RECREATION

Sitka has two indoor **swimming pools,** one of which is at Blatchley Middle School, Halibut Point Road (tel. 747-5677); call for hours and regulations. There are also tennis courts, basketball and volleyball courts, softball fields, and a running track at various public schools. The visitors bureau can direct you.

FISHING   Some of Alaska's best fishing for salmon, halibut, and trout can be found in the waters around Sitka. Some 22 charter operators can arrange a trip appropriate to your purpose; the convention and visitors bureau can provide a comprehensive list. Typical rates are $90–$150 per person for a full day of ocean fishing, $75–$100 for half a day.

Several state fishing records have been set in Sitka—including a 440-pound halibut, a 93-pound king salmon, a 26-pound coho, a 47-pound lake trout, a 17-pound Dolly Varden, and an 8-pound cutthroat trout. Before you can catch them, though, you must have a license. If your charter operator doesn't make the appropriate arrangements for you, drop by **Murray Pacific Supply Corp.,** 475 Katlian St. (tel. 747-3171). Small skiffs are available for rent from **Baranof Sportsman's Vacations,** 325 Seward St. (tel. 747-4937). The Sport Fish Division of the **Alaska Department of Fish and Game,** 304 Lake St. (tel. 747-5355), will answer any questions you may have about regulations.

If you prefer freshwater fishing, you can drive to Blue Lake, 7½ miles east of Sitka near the pulp mill; it's populated by rainbow trout two feet in length and larger. The big lake trout are in landlocked fjords like Redoubt Lake, only about 15 miles south of Sitka as the eagle flies, but a floatplane trip away or a rugged hike from the Green Lake Power Plant. Salmon runs on the Indian River and Starrigavan Creek are spectacular: It's hard to see the bottom of the foot-deep streams for the fish!

The **Sitka Salmon Derby** is held annually over the three-day Memorial Day weekend and the following weekend in early June. A $5,000 grand prize is at stake. For entry information and rules, write to the Sitka Sportsman's Association, P.O. Box 1200, Sitka, AK 99835.

HIKING   The **Sitka Ranger District,** U.S. Forest Service, P.O. Box 1980, Sitka, AK 99835 (tel. 907/747-6671), has published a superb "Recreational Opportunity Guide" that details 33 hikes in its quadrant of the Tongass National Forest. Ten of the hikes are accessible from the Sitka road system, including a stroll through Sitka National Historical Park and the easy **Indian River Trail,** 5½ miles from its trailhead off Sawmill Creek Road to Indian River Falls. Deer are frequently seen in the rain forest, and bear are often spotted as well. Plan accordingly.

The three-quarter-mile **Beaver Lake Trail,** just above the pulp mill near Blue Lake, is steep but beautiful. If you take a skiff 10 miles across Sitka Sound to Fred's Creek Cabin on the southeastern shore of Kruzof Island, you'll find the trail to the summit crater of dormant 3,201-foot **Mount Edgecumbe.** The 6.7-mile (one-way) trail is in good condition but frequently muddy. Above 2,000 feet the ground is covered by a thick layer of red volcanic ash. On any of these hikes, insect repellent and rubber footwear are essential.

HUNTING   Sitka black-tailed deer are the favorite target of hunters in this region, but you can also go after brown bear, mountain goats, and a rich variety of waterfowl. Contact the Game Division of the **Alaska Department of Fish and Game,** 304 Lake St. (tel. 747-5449), for specific regulations and other information; and get your license from a good outfitter like **Mac's Sporting Goods,** 213 Harbor Dr. (tel. 747-6970).

KAYAKING   **Baidarka Boats,** P.O. Box 2158, Sitka, AK 99835 (tel. 907/747-8996), has year-round rentals of ocean kayaks and will custom-organize a trip for you.

SAILING **Wyldewind Sail Charters,** P.O. Box 2264, Sitka, AK 99835 (tel. 907/747-3287 or 747-5734), will take up to six guests on short or extended sailing trips aboard a 37-foot yacht through southeast Alaska. Wilderness tours, wildlife photography, and whale-watching are specialties. Rates are $65 per person per day, with a three-person minimum. **Waltzing Bear Charters,** 4600 Halibut Point Rd. (tel. 747-3608), charges $850 per week for longer sailing excursions.

SCUBA DIVING You can go out for the day with a certified dive instructor as your guide for $75 per person, gear rentals not included. Contact **Seafood Safaris,** P.O. Box 2585, Sitka, AK 99835 (tel. 907/747-5970), or **Myriad Adventures,** 203 Lincoln St. (tel. 747-8279).

SHOPPING

Businesses in Sitka open between 8 and 10am weekdays and remain open until 5pm or later.

The things to shop for are Russian as well as Native items. Seek out hand-painted lacquer boxes and eggs, religious icons and etched plaques, Matrushka dolls, even antique brass samovars (tea urns). A good place to start your search is the **Russian-American Company** in MacDonald's Bayview Trading Company mall, 407 Lincoln St. (tel. 747-6228), where you may be greeted by a store manager in a Russian hat and greatcoat. **Taranoff's Sitkakwan Gifts,** 208 Katlian St. (tel. 747-8667), has some remarkable antique Russian jewelry, as well as some beautiful Tlingit silver and other artifacts. A wider selection of quality Native arts and crafts can be found at **Baranof Indian & Eskimo Arts,** across from St. Michael's at 237 Lincoln St. (tel. 747-6556). Art collectors should visit the **Impressions Gallery,** 233 Lincoln St. (tel. 747-5502), for an extensive assortment of southeast Alaska art. **Old Harbor Books,** 201 Lincoln St. (tel. 747-8808), has a selection of new books, topographical maps, and nautical charts.

WHERE TO STAY

As elsewhere in Alaska, Sitka's hotel prices tend to vary seasonally, though perhaps not in so marked a degree.

Taxes There's a 4% city tax, and an additional 4% local bed tax on all room rates.

EXPENSIVE

WESTMARK SHEE ATIKA, 330 Seward St. (P.O. Box 78), Sitka, AK 99835. Tel. 907/747-6241, or toll free 800/544-0970. Fax 907/747-5846. 96 rms. TV TEL

$ Rates: May 15–Sept 15, $110 single; $118 double. Sept 16–May 14, $94 single; $100 double. AE, CB, DC, MC, V.

Built in 1978 by the Native-owned Shee Atika Corporation, this is one of southeast Alaska's finest hotels. A Native art motif in stained wood runs throughout. Full wall murals depicting local Tlingit history and a grand piano add atmosphere to a sunken seating area that surrounds a lobby fireplace.

The clean and spacious rooms feature wood decor, rust-colored carpeting, and a Native wall mural. Each has individually controlled baseboard heating, a desk-dresser, table and chairs, and queen-size or double beds. Some third-floor rooms have magnificent views of the harbor; others look out at the mountains backing Sitka. Vending machines are on each floor and in the lobby.

Dining/Entertainment: The hotel's Raven Room and Kadataan Lounge, with their log beams and house poles, give you the feeling of being inside a modern Tlingit community house. The excellent restaurant, with seafood, pasta, and continental specialties in the $12–$18 range, is open Monday through Saturday from 7am to 2pm and 5 to 10pm, and on Sunday from 7am to 2pm and 5 to 9pm. A guest band plays light rock music for dancing in the lounge Monday through Saturday from 9pm.

Services: Room service (daily 7am–10pm), valet laundry, rooms for nonsmokers and disabled guests.

Facilities: Conference rooms.

MODERATE

POTLATCH HOUSE, 713 Katlian St. (P.O. Box 58), Sitka, AK 99835. Tel. 907/747-8611. Fax 907/747-5810. 24 rms (all with bath). TV TEL

$ Rates: May–Sept, $67 single; $71 double. Oct–Apr, $57 single; $61 double. Children under 12 stay free in parents' room. AE, MC, V.

The remodeled motel-style units in the Potlatch House, six blocks north of downtown, are pleasant; all are wood paneled and carpeted and have baseboard heating. Four kitchenettes are offered for no additional charge. There are guest laundry facilities, rental-car-and-room packages are available, and courtesy pickup is provided from the airport or ferry. The Canoe Club restaurant and lounge is open for three meals daily.

SUPER 8 MOTEL, 404 Sawmill Creek Blvd., Sitka, AK 99835. Tel. 907/747-8804. Fax 907/747-8804, ext. 103. 35 rms (all with bath), 1 suite. TV TEL

$ Rates: $71 single; $78 double. Additional person $5 extra. AE, CB, DC, DISC, MC, V.

An imitation Tudor-style structure near downtown, the Super 8 offers double or queen-size beds and recliners in all rooms. No-smoking rooms and a waterbed room are available, and pets are permitted. Free coffee is served in the lobby every morning. But unlike many other Super 8s, this one does not provide a courtesy van or guest laundry.

INEXPENSIVE

There are numerous bed-and-breakfast homes in this price range. Besides the pair listed below, they include the **Biorka B&B,** 611 Biorka St., Sitka, AK 99835 (tel. 907/747-3111), $50 single, $55 double; the **Creek's Edge Guest House,** 109 Cascade Creek Rd., Sitka, AK 99835 (tel. 907/747-6484), $45 single, $55 double, $75 suite; **Hannah's B&B,** 504 Monastery St., Sitka, AK 99835 (tel. 907/747-8309), $40 single, $50 double; and the **Mountain View B&B,** 201 Cascade Creek Rd., Sitka, AK 99835 (tel. 907/747-8966), $50 single, $60 double.

HELGA'S B&B, 2821 Halibut Point Rd. (P.O. Box 1885), Sitka, AK 99835. Tel. 907/747-5497. 5 rms (all with bath).

$ Rates (including breakfast and room tax): $50 single; $60 double. Children stay free in parents' room. MC, V.

On the shore of Sitka Sound, about three miles north of the city toward the ferry dock, this bed-and-breakfast is an ideal choice for a family with a car or RV unit. One of the five rooms is a large family room with kitchenette, and Helga has two college-age daughters available for babysitting. A full breakfast is served from 6:30 to 9am. Half a block away is the Channel Club, Sitka's best-known restaurant.

KARRAS B&B, 230 Kogwanton St., Sitka, AK 99835. Tel. 907/747-3978. 4 rms (all with shared bath).

$ Rates (including breakfast): $43.20 single; $54–$59.40 double. MC, V.

Operated by a Greek man and his Tlingit wife, well versed in Native legends, this bed-and-breakfast has a lovely view toward Mount Edgecumbe. A full breakfast is served from 7:30 to 8:30am. The family has a small library of Christian books, with reading space around a wood stove. No smoking, alcohol, pets, or unmarried couples allowed.

SITKA HOTEL, 118 Lincoln St., Sitka, AK 99835. Tel. 907/747-3288. 60 rms (28 with bath). TEL

$ Rates: $45 single without bath, $50 single with bath; $50 double without bath, $55 double with bath. No credit cards.

This hotel will appeal to travelers who want a convenient location at low cost. The spartan inn's rooms have single or twin beds and hot-water radiator heating.

BUDGET

SITKA YOUTH HOSTEL, 303 Kimshan St. (P.O. Box 2645), Sitka, AK 99835. Tel. 907/747-8356. 20 beds.

$ Rates: June–Aug, $5 for AYH members, $8 for nonmembers. American Youth Hostel memberships $20 extra. **Closed:** Sept–May.

Located in the basement of the United Methodist church, Sitka's hostel is a stiff walk north of downtown. It has 20 beds in men's and women's dormitories (bring your own sleeping bag) and showers. But there are no cooking facilities. You can check in, and come and go freely, only between 8 and 9:30am and between 6 and 11pm.

CAMPGROUNDS

There's overnight camping at the **Starrigavan Campground,** three-quarters of a mile north of the ferry dock, with 30 units; and the **Sawmill Creek Campground,** six miles east of Sitka on Blue Lake Road, with nine units. Both sites have picnic tables, fireplaces, and toilets, but no water: Creek water should be boiled. Both are managed by the Sitka Ranger District, U.S. Forest Service, and welcome RVs and tent campers. The overnight fee is $5 at Starrigavan, but free at Sawmill Creek.

RVs can choose to stay closer to Sitka at **Sealing Cove,** across O'Connell Bridge on Japonski Island. The fee there is $5, and there's a 15-day limit.

WHERE TO DINE

For a not particularly cosmopolitan town of its size, Sitka has a surprising variety of cuisines. In addition to fine seafood restaurants and good hotel dining, Chinese, Filipino, Russian, Mexican, and Italian menus can all be found within a few short blocks of one another.

EXPENSIVE

CHANNEL CLUB, 2906 Halibut Point Rd. Tel. 747-9916.
   Cuisine: STEAK/SEAFOOD. **Reservations:** Recommended.
$ Prices: Appetizers $5–$9; main courses $12–$19. AE, CB, DC, MC, V.
   Open: Dinner only, Sun–Thurs 5–10pm, Fri–Sat 5–11pm.

Start with the 30-item salad bar, a meal in itself or included with your dinner. Then order from the items posted on the wall. The steaks are legendary—12-, 16-, and 20-ounce cuts. If the nautical decor puts you in the mood for seafood, go for the halibut cheeks. Fully licensed, with a good domestic wine selection, the Channel Club has won the prestigious Silver Spoon Award from the Gourmet Club of America on three separate occasions. It's located about halfway between downtown and the ferry terminal.

STATON'S STEAK HOUSE, 228 Harbor Dr. Tel. 747-3396.
   Cuisine: STEAK/SEAFOOD. **Reservations:** Recommended.
$ Prices: Appetizers $5-$10; main courses $12-$18; lunch $6-$10.50. AE, CB, DC, MC, V.
   Open: Lunch Mon–Sat 11:30am–2pm; dinner Tues–Sat 5–10pm.

Dimly lit in tones of orange and red, with miniature Native masks and totem poles on one wall and a giant king crab on another, Staton's is a steak-and-seafood house with a local following. Dinners include soup, salad, potato, and vegetable. Try the pepper steak or the gourmet halibut and chips. Gold-nugget jewelry and other glittery delights are sold at the cashier's counter. Prime rib is offered on Wednesday and Saturday.

MODERATE

MARINA RESTAURANT, 205 Harbor Dr. Tel. 747-8840.
  Cuisine: ITALIAN/MEXICAN. **Reservations:** Not required.
$ Prices: Lunch/dinner $8–$16. AE, CB, DC, DISC, MC, V.
  Open: Mon–Thurs 11am–11pm, Fri–Sat 11am–midnight, Sun 4–11pm.

⑤ Formerly a Lincoln Street pizzeria, the Marina enlarged its seafood menu when it moved into the second floor of a new building. The wrought-iron railings and checkered tablecloths have been replaced by a pink-toned decor. But the menu still emphasizes Italian and Mexican cuisine, including a wide range of pizzas. If you don't feel like chicken cacciatore or linguine with clam sauce, consider a chimichanga. The Marina is licensed for wine and beer, and has well-separated smoking and nonsmoking sections.

TWIN DRAGON CHINESE RESTAURANT, 210 Katlian St. Tel. 747-5711.
  Cuisine: CHINESE. **Reservations:** Not required.
$ Prices: Lunch $7–$12; dinner $11–$20. AE, MC, V.
  Open: Lunch Mon–Sat 11:30am–3pm; dinner Mon–Sat 5–10pm.
The Twin Dragon has good Mandarin, Szechuan, and Cantonese food. The atmosphere is as Chinese as the immigrant management. Try the scallops in black-bean sauce or the spicy Kung Pao chicken.

INEXPENSIVE

BAYVIEW RESTAURANT, 407 Lincoln St. Tel. 747-5440.
  Cuisine: AMERICAN/RUSSIAN. **Reservations:** Not required.
$ Prices: $4.25–$9.50. AE, CB, DC, MC, V.
  Open: Mon–Sat 6am–9pm, Sun 8am–2pm.

⑤ Large picture windows look across Crescent Harbor from this café upstairs in the Bayview Trading Company mall. Locally famous for its 25 varieties of burgers, it also has homemade soups, deli sandwiches, and desserts, plus borscht, pirozhkis, and other Russian dishes that would have made Alexander Baranov feel right at home.

EL DORADO, 714 Katlian St. Tel. 747-5070.
  Cuisine: MEXICAN/SOUTH AMERICAN. **Reservations:** Not required.
$ Prices: Lunch $4.50–$7; dinner $8–$13. MC, V.
  Open: Daily 10am–11pm.

✪ The El Dorado, which is situated opposite the Potlatch House motel, is a "must" for south-of-the-border fanatics.
  Its owners, Antonio and Dora Vasquez, specialize in Mexican and South American cuisine. Try the delicious and zesty chili verde con nopales (pork
⑤ simmered in tomatilla sauce with cactus).
  A variety of pizzas are also on the menu.

BUDGET

THE BACKDOOR CAFE, 203 Lincoln St. Tel. 747-8856.
  Cuisine: DELI. **Reservations:** Not accepted.
$ Prices: Average meal $1.50–$4.50. No credit cards.
  Open: Mon–Fri 9am–5pm, Sat 10am–4pm.
A center for Sitka's creative community, the Backdoor—so named because it's in the

rear of the city's leading bookstore—offers frequent art shows, poetry readings, and other such evening activities. Baked goods, sandwiches, and finger food are the fare here, along with home-brewed coffee and soft drinks.

EVENING ENTERTAINMENT

Every Sitka visitor should see the world-famous ✪ **New Archangel Dancers,** an all-woman troupe that performs whenever there's a cruise ship in town. Dressed in colorful folk costumes, these dancers have researched and choreographed their Russian leaps and twirls since 1969. All performances are at the Centennial Building auditorium; check with the visitors bureau for the dance schedule. Admission is $4. To find out about off-season performances, contact the dancers at P.O. Box 1687, Sitka, AK 99835 (tel. 747-5940).

Other Sitka performing-arts groups include the **Gajaa Heen** and **Noow Tlein** Tlingit dancers, who stage their shows at the Alaska Native Brotherhood Hall on Katlian Street.

Sitka's best spot for loud rock 'n' roll is the **Kiksadi Club,** two miles south of downtown at 1516 Sawmill Creek Rd. (tel. 747-3285). There's a good dance floor in front of a well-positioned stage, which frequently attracts California-based new wave bands. Music starts at 9pm nightly except Monday. Nondancers can play pool or video games.

Back in town, you can stroll down the road to **Ernie's Old Time Saloon,** 130 Lincoln St. (tel. 747-3334), a popular local watering hole whose interior walls are cloaked with mounted fish and game. The clientele is a bit crustier, but no less interesting, at the **Pioneer Bar,** 212 Katlian St. (tel. 747-3456).

The **Coliseum Twin Theater,** 315 Lincoln St. (tel. 747-6920), has first-run films Thursday through Sunday nights, plus a Sunday matinee.

EASY EXCURSIONS

As the only sizable community for nearly 100 miles in any direction (Juneau and Petersburg are both over 90 miles away by air), Sitka is understandably a major jumping-off point for wilderness excursions. Fewer than 500 people live in the tiny scattered settlements beyond Sitka on 1,636-square-mile Baranof Island. Even less populated is the west coast of 2,062-square-mile Chichagof Island, separated from Baranof by narrow Peril Strait. There are only two practical forms of transportation—charter boat and air taxi.

The U.S. Forest Service maintains 18 public-use **cabins** in the Sitka Ranger District. Six are on high lakes in the rugged, heavily glaciated **South Baranof Wilderness;** another four are in the forested lowlands of **West Chichagof–Yakobi Wilderness** north of Sitka. Three cabins are on Baranof Island, three on Kruzof Island around the base of Mount Edgecumbe, and two on the east side of Chicagof Island. The Lake Eva cabin on the northeast shore of Baranof Island has even been equipped with ramps to be accessible to the disabled. These primitive cabins, which sleep four to six, can be reserved for $20 a night; book well ahead and supply all your own food and equipment. Contact the U.S. Forest Service, 204 Siginaka Way, Sitka, AK 99835 (tel. 907/747-6671).

Local air charters include **Bellair, Inc.,** P.O. Box 371, Sitka, AK 99835 (tel. 907/747-8636), with rates from $219 per hour for a three-passenger Cessna 185 and $365 per hour for a seven-passenger Beaver; and **Mountain Aviation,** P.O. Box 875, Sitka, AK 99835 (tel. 907/966-2288), charges $200 per hour for a Cessna or $310 for a five-passenger Beaver.

Many of Sitka's charter operators offer overnight trips to wilderness areas and provide cabin and trail dropoff service. Try **Bluewater Charters,** P.O. Box 3107, Sitka, AK 99835 (tel. 907/747-5576); **Jolly Roger Charters,** P.O. Box 1801, Sitka, AK 99835 (tel. 907/747-3530); or **Baranof Sportsman's Vacations,** 325 Seward St. (tel. 907/747-4937).

Steller Charters, 2810 Sawmill Creek Rd., Sitka, AK 99835 (tel. 907/747-6711 or 747-5576), specializes in natural history cruises. A "must" sight is the ✪ **St.**

Lazaria Island National Wildlife Refuge, a 65-acre sanctuary 15 miles south-west of Sitka, just off the foot of Mount Edgecumbe. The island, shaped like a dumbbell with its long tidal flat connecting two steep forested bluffs, provides ideal breeding grounds for thousands of sea birds, including puffins, petrels, auklets, murres, guillemots, cormorants, and gulls.

Many visitors are surprised to find this stretch of southeast Alaska sprinkled with hot springs. About 20 miles south of Sitka, right on the coast, are the **Goddard Hot Springs.** There was a resort here once, but today bathhouses are the only facilities. Halfway up the east coast of Baranof Island, about 20 miles due east of Sitka (but a 120-mile boat trip), the community of Baranof lies on Warm Springs Bay. The **Baranof Warm Springs Lodge** (mail address: 9720 Trappers Lane, Juneau, AK 99801; tel. 907/789-5070 or 789-9345) is open May through September, with individual cabins built around 110°F springs and family-style meals served in a central lodge. A third set of hot springs, on the west coast of Chichagof Island some 65 air miles northwest of Sitka, are the **White Sulphur Springs.** There's a coveted U.S. Forest Service cabin here with a hot tub looking out on the Pacific Ocean.

If you make it all the way to White Sulphur, you may decide to continue through the Lisianski Strait and Lisianski Inlet to **Pelican,** a commercial fishing and crabbing village with a population of about 200. The ferry *LeConte* makes a stop in Pelican—for two hours every other Thursday. The main road is no more than a boardwalk built on pilings. The **Harbor Bed and Breakfast,** P.O. Box 717, Pelican, AK 99832 (no phone), has a TV, laundry, and open kitchen for $65 double. **Rosie's Bar and Grill,** P.O. Box 754, Pelican, AK 99832 (no phone), has four rooms available for overnights ($65 single or double) and a reputation for ribaldry known throughout Alaska. There are no pelicans in Pelican, by the way; it was named after a Finnish fish packer's boat in 1938.

The **Lisianski Fishing Lodge,** P.O. Box 776, Pelican, AK 99832 (tel. 907/735-2266), has a guest cabin that sleeps five for $240 apiece per day, with full board. It's operated by Paul and Gail Corbin, who also operate fishing and sightseeing charters between Pelican and Sitka on the 53-foot ketch *Demijohn*. From September to May, contact 617 Katlian St., A-3, Sitka, AK 99835 (tel. 907/747-6273).

At the southern tip of Baranof Island, **Port Alexander** is an abandoned whaling port that only half a dozen fishing families still call home. The only real distinction this remote area now has is its weather—it's laced by 100-m.p.h. winds in the fall, and a weather station at **Little Port Walter** records an average annual rainfall of 221 inches, the most in southeast Alaska.

---

5. JUNEAU

285 miles N of Ketchikan, 105 miles S of Skagway,
650 miles SE of Anchorage

GETTING THERE By Plane Alaska Airlines (tel. 907/789-0600, or toll free 800/426-0333) flies directly from Seattle nine times daily in summer, five times daily the rest of the year. The airline also has four daily flights from Anchorage and Ketchikan, three from Sitka, one each from Petersburg, Wrangell, Cordova, and Yakutat, and a daily summer flight to and from Gustavus (Glacier Bay). **Delta Airlines** (tel. toll free 800/241-4141) serves Juneau during the summer season with a daily nonstop flight from Fairbanks and another from Los Angeles via Seattle. **Air North Canada** (tel. toll free 800/764-0407) flies from Fairbanks as well as Whitehorse, Dawson, and other communities in the Yukon and Northwest Territories.

Numerous smaller air-taxi lines serving southeast Alaska are based at the Juneau Airport. I have enjoyed trips with **L.A.B. Flying Service** (tel. 789-9160) to Skagway, Haines, and Glacier Bay. Others include **Alaska Coastal Airlines** (tel. 789-7818), **Glacier Bay Airways** (tel. 789-9009), **Haines Airways** (tel. 789-2336), **Skagway Air Service** (tel. 789-2006), and **Wings of Alaska** (tel. 789-0790).

Be prepared for surprises in Juneau's air space. In early 1987, believe it or not, an Alaska Airlines Boeing 737 collided with a salmon in mid-air shortly after takeoff! This is no tall tale: The pilot reported that he had startled a bald eagle with the finny fellow in its talons, and the fish was dropped onto the cockpit. The only apparent casualty was the salmon.

By Ferry Eighteen ferries a week—nine northbound, nine southbound—stop during summer at the Auke Bay terminal of the Alaska Marine Highway System (tel. 907/465-3941, or toll free 800/642-0066). The schedule is cut back somewhat during the winter months. The *Columbia* or *Matanuska* ferry connects Juneau with Bellingham, Wash., once a week (twice during the peak summer season), and the twice-weekly *Taku* and *Malaspina* go as far as Prince Rupert. The *LeConte* stops at every small port between Petersburg and Juneau three times a week. The terminal is 14 miles northwest of downtown, but there's a city ticket office at 1591 Glacier Ave.

By Cruise Ship The Juneau terminal is on the south side of downtown, in the 400 block of South Franklin Street, within easy walking distance of major historic sites. For specific cruise-ship information, see "Getting There" "By Cruise Ship" in Chapter 2.

SPECIAL EVENTS The **Fourth of July** agenda occupies a couple of weeks, beginning with the summer solstice: It includes a variety of sports and athletic events, navy air and sea shows, and contests such as watermelon-eating, pie-throwing, and sand-castle-building. The big day itself is highlighted by parades through downtown Juneau and Douglas, followed by carnivals and barbecues. For more information, contact the Juneau Festival Association (tel. 364-3346).

Other festive occasions include the **Ski-to-Sea Relay,** on the first weekend of April; the **Alaska Folk Festival,** in the second week of April; the **Golden North Salmon Derby,** in mid-August; the University of Alaska–Juneau's **Tuxedo Junction,** a formal "Monte Carlo" night at Centennial Hall in early November; and **Open House at the Governor's Mansion,** one weekday evening in the first or second week of December.

Steep cliffs and mighty glaciers provide a startling backdrop for what may be the most beautiful state capital in America.

Waterfalls tumble down the walls of the near-vertical slopes. Residents of houses reached only by stairways can feel their summer spray—and in winter, they know the threat of avalanches. Turn-of-the-century gold mines, bored deep into the mountain rock, impart a sense of history and sudden wealth.

The whisker-thin Gastineau Channel separates Juneau, on the North American mainland, from mountainous Douglas Island. The two are connected by bridge. Cruise boats anchor only a few hundred yards south, allowing their passengers to disembark and wander through the city's historic South Franklin district.

For all its natural beauty and tourist appeal, Juneau is first and foremost a government town. Most of its 30,000 citizens are directly or indirectly involved with state administration or supportive services. The people of Juneau, in fact, speak of three distinct "seasons." From January to April the state legislature is in session and several thousand temporary residents—lawmakers' staffs, lobbyists, and so forth—move into the city. From May through mid-September it's the tourist season, when thousands of visitors disembark from cruise boats in a single day. But from mid-September to December the city is suddenly quiet and townspeople go about their lives in a sort of hush.

Juneau hasn't always been a political percolator. Mining provided the early economic base. On October 4, 1880, a pair of struggling prospectors, Richard Harris and Joe Juneau, guided by Chief Kowee of the Tlingit Auk clan, discovered quartz outcroppings heavily streaked with gold along upper Gold Creek. Within 15 days they had written a code of laws for the newly created Harris Mining District and staked a 160-acre townsite along the channel. First called Harrisburgh, the town's name was changed the following May to Rockwell, after a U.S. naval commander, and a few months later to Juneau City. Many turn-of-the-century buildings still stand today along South Franklin Street.

By the spring of 1881, Gold Creek was crawling with prospectors—some exultant, all expectant. But even more lucrative was Douglas Island, across the channel. A San Francisco carpenter named John Treadwell made a lucky strike near Ready Bullion Creek and established a company that produced more than $70 million in gold over the next four decades. Indeed, consolidated companies that could afford large-scale hard-rock mining were the ones that achieved success here; the solo shovel-and-sluice-box technique was more suited for Nome or the Klondike than for Juneau. But the two biggest companies—Treadwell and Alaska-Gastineau—closed down within a few years of each other (in 1917 and 1922), and their heir apparent, Alaska-Juneau, constructed in 1916, had its finale written by the war in 1944.

By this time Juneau's economy had diversified. The capital was transferred here from Sitka in 1906 because of Juneau's growth and location on the Inside Passage, and because of Sitka's decline after the departure of the Russian fur traders and whalers.

When gold's tides ebbed, those of commercial fishing were on the rise. A salmon and halibut fleet, canneries, and cold-storage facilities boomed in the 1930s. The fleet remains, but the canneries have disappeared, to be replaced today by a few small-scale fish-processing operations.

Since statehood in 1959, the city's administrative role has increased manyfold. Government directly employs every other Juneau resident. In the mid-1970s and early 1980s, there were attempts by upstate Alaskans to move the state capital to Willow, a small town in the Susitna Valley, north of Anchorage. But the state's voters repeatedly turned down the move, and Alaska's political heartbeat remains in Juneau.

Without question, Juneau has become the most highbrow community in southeast Alaska. Conversations in fern-endowed restaurants tend toward music and literature rather than hunting or logging. The state university has a branch here (Alaska–Southeast), and there's a symphony, a professional theater group, and a world affairs council that sponsors lectures by a variety of internationally known speakers. Even the sawdust floor of the venerable Red Dog Saloon is sometimes the venue for performances by artists from "down south."

But Juneau folk don't forget their ties to wilderness. How could they, wedged as they are between mountains and sea? Spectacular cliff-constricted waterways like the Taku Inlet and Lynn Canal are barely a stone's throw away, and Admiralty Island National Monument, home of one of the last great concentrations of Alaskan brown bear, is barely 10 air miles from downtown Juneau.

When the clouds separate, there are few cities more striking than Juneau. Unfortunately, they rarely separate—especially over downtown, which gets 92 inches of precipitation a year (compared with 56 inches at the airport, nine miles northwest). More than 100 inches of snow fall between November and April. (Note: Depending on the wetness of the snow, 10–12 inches of the white stuff equals one inch of rainfall in the precipitation count.) The average July high is 63°F; the average January low is 20°F.

ORIENTATION

ARRIVING   Juneau International Airport (yes, there are flights into Canada) is frequently maligned. There's nothing wrong with its facilities—it's just that thick fog banks, crushing down the Gastineau Channel, may cause some late fall and winter flights to be shelved for hours. If you do get stuck, the Glacier Restaurant and Lounge (tel. 789-9538), open from 6am to 11pm daily, plus a well-stocked gift shop and newsstand, will keep you entertained.

INFORMATION   The **Davis Log Cabin Information Center,** 134 3rd St., at Seward Street, Juneau, AK 99801 (tel. 907/586-2284), can tell you everything you'd ever want to know about Juneau, and then some. The cabin is an attraction in its own right—it's a Juneau centennial re-creation of an 1881 cabin that was the city's first church and later a school, carpentry shop, and brewery office. Operated by the Juneau

Convention and Visitors Bureau, the Log Cabin provides brochures, maps, tour schedules, events listings, and information on foreign-language interpreters for those who require them. There are also information centers at the airport terminal and, in summer only, on the waterfront at the Marine Park kiosk; at the cruise-ship terminal, 470 S. Franklin St.; and at the Auke Bay ferry terminal. There are plans to build a major new information center closer to the waterfront. A 24-hour recorded schedule of events and activities is on the telephone line: 586-JUNO.

The **Juneau Convention and Visitors Bureau,** 369 S. Franklin St., Suite 201, Juneau, AK 99801 (tel. 907/586-1737), provides assistance to organizations planning trade shows, conventions, seminars, or group tours. Its main facility is the Centennial Hall Convention Center, 101 Egan Dr. (tel. 586-5283).

Within Centennial Hall is the **U.S. Forest Service Information Center** (tel. 586-8751), open from 8am to 5pm weekdays and summer weekends. The Forest Service has more than a dozen films, videotapes, and slide programs on wildlife, history, and lifestyles in Tongass National Forest, that it will show upon request. Native craftspeople, including wood-carvers and weavers, often demonstrate their arts here. This is also the place to find out about backcountry travel and wilderness-cabin rental.

Other helpful contacts include the **Juneau Chamber of Commerce,** 124 W. 5th St., Juneau, AK 99801 (tel. 907/586-6420); the **Alaska Division of Tourism,** P.O. Box E, Juneau, AK 99811 (tel. 907/465-2010); and the **National Park Service,** P.O. Box 1089, Juneau, AK 99802 (tel. 907/586-7937).

CITY LAYOUT Juneau is divided into three distinct parts. **Downtown,** where the government complex, historical district, and cruise-ship docks are located, clings to the foot of 3,819-foot Mount Roberts. **Douglas Island,** site of the old Treadwell mine, is now a pleasant suburb across the Gastineau Channel. And fully half of Juneau's citizens live in the **Mendenhall Valley/Auke Bay** district, nestled in the broad delta below spectacular Mendenhall Glacier, 13 miles northwest of downtown. The airport and big shopping malls are in the valley; the ferry terminal and university are at Auke Bay. There are a few homes and businesses at Salmon Creek, three miles northwest of downtown, and at Lemon Creek, five miles northwest. Egan Drive, which turns into the Glacier Highway, is the sole artery connecting Auke Bay to downtown Juneau.

GETTING AROUND

BY BUS As befits a capital city of nearly 30,000, Juneau has an excellent municipal bus system, **Capitol Transit.** Visitors may be interested in the hourly service connecting downtown Juneau with the valley and Auke Bay (7:05am to 11:45pm) and with Douglas (7am to 11:30pm) for only $1.25. The Mendenhall Valley and Auke Bay routes stop 1¾ miles short of the ferry dock. Sunday service is limited, but there are express buses during weekday rush hours. There's also a downtown–Auke Bay express bus, operating 7:30am to 6pm weekdays only, which makes an airport stop. For complete schedule information, visit 155 S. Seward St. (tel. 789-6901).

Airport shuttle service is provided by **Gray Line** (tel. 586-3773 in summer, 586-9625 in winter) for $6 per person. At this writing, there is no shuttle to and from the ferry terminal; call the visitor center to inquire or be prepared to hire a taxi to downtown—at a fare of about $21.

BY TAXI The two cab companies have similar rates. **Taku Taxi** (tel. 586-2121) and **Capital Cab** (tel. 586-2772) both charge about $14 between the airport and downtown ($2 at flagfall and 75¢ a mile).

BY CAR Although Juneau isn't endowed with road connections to other cities on the North American mainland, there are about 100 miles of paved road in the area, so a vehicle is useful. The Glacier Highway, in fact, runs for 40 miles, from downtown

Juneau past Auke Bay to Echo Cove on the Lynn Canal. (A proposed Juneau–Haines road-and-ferry link remains mere rumor.)

Several major American car-rental firms have Juneau airport counters: **Avis** (tel. 907/789-9450, or toll free 800/331-1212), **Budget** (tel. 907/789-5186, or toll free 800/527-7000), **Hertz** (tel. 907/789-9494, or toll free 800/654-8200), and **National** (tel. 907/789-9814, or toll free 800/227-7368). If price is more important than convenience, check these other agencies: **Evergreen Ford,** 8895 Mallard St. (tel. 907/789-9386); **Payless,** 5454 Jenkins Dr., Lemon Creek (tel. 907/780-4144, or toll free 800/792-7219); **All Star Rent-a-Car,** Airport Mall, Auke Bay (tel. 907/790-2414, or toll free 800/722-0741); and **Rent-a-Wreck,** 8600 Airport Blvd., Juneau (tel. 907/789-4111, or toll free 800/421-7253 outside Alaska). It's wise to book ahead during the summer. There are no rental cars in downtown Juneau, though most firms are happy to pick up clients at downtown hotels.

BY BICYCLE   Mountain bikes are available for rent from **Outward Mobility ("O.M.") Cycle Rentals,** on Seward Street between Front and 2nd Streets (tel. 586-2277). The rate is $5 per hour, $15 for a half day (four hours), or $25 for the whole day. Bicycle paths or lanes parallel the Glacier Highway, Mendenhall Loop Road, Douglas Highway, and several other main arteries.

FAST FACTS

Banks   Several banks have branches both downtown and in the valley.

Emergencies   In a life-threatening emergency, dial 911. You can also call the city police (tel. 586-2780), the Alaska State Police (tel. 789-2161), the Coast Guard (tel. 586-2680), the crime line (tel. 586-4243), the drug and alcohol crisis line (tel. 586-9508), maritime search and rescue (tel. toll free 800/478-5555), the poison control center (tel. 586-2627), the pollution hotline (tel. 586-2680), the rape and abuse hotline (tel. 586-1090), and the suicide prevention hotline (tel. 586-4357).

For medical assistance, the Bartlett Memorial Hospital, at Mile 3.5 on the Glacier Highway (tel. 586-2611), provides complete medical services.

Newspapers   The local newspaper is the *Juneau Empire,* published daily except Saturday. You can usually find a copy of *USA Today,* the *Anchorage Daily News,* or the *Seattle Post-Intelligencer* at a premium price.

Post Office   The post office is in the Federal Building, on Glacier Avenue at 9th Street, although a branch office at 111 S. Seward St. is more convenient for most visitors.

Telecommunications   There are public phones and restrooms in the Municipal Building, across Egan Drive from Marine Park, open Monday through Friday from 8am to 6pm and on Saturday and Sunday from 7am to 6pm. During summer only, the Alascom Teleservices Center, 245 Marine Way, provides a long-distance call station and free fax and computer services—you just pay the long-distance charges.

WHAT TO SEE & DO

SIGHTS & ATTRACTIONS

Juneau's attractions can be divided into two categories—architectural and natural. The former consist mainly of government and other public buildings, concentrated in the downtown area; the latter include sights of extraordinary scenic beauty, among them the great Mendenhall Glacier.

Public Buildings and Museums

Just as government and bureaucracy command Juneau's lifestyle and economy, government buildings dominate its skyline.

GOVERNOR'S MANSION, 716 Calhoun Ave.

This impressive white colonial-style structure, seen high on a hill from most locations in downtown Juneau, can be visited by drop-in individuals only during an annual one-day open house in early December. If you happen to be around, you'll be impressed by the well-kept original period furnishings dating from the time of the house's construction in 1912.

Admission: Free.

Open: Only during open house in December.

HOUSE OF WICKERSHAM, 213 7th St. Tel. 586-9001.

Perhaps the greatest statesman of Alaska's territorial era was James Wickersham. Historian and anthropologist, mountaineer and environmentalist, congressman and federal judge, he did much to establish the credibility of rough-and-ready Alaska in the eyes of Washington, D.C., 5,000 miles away. Wickersham died in 1939, and today his Juneau home is a state historic site. Operated by the State Division of Parks and a volunteer staff, it holds a remarkable private collection of Native, Russian, and pioneer artifacts, books, and documents, including the judge's 47-volume handwritten diary.

Admission: $1 donation requested.

Open: June–Aug, Sun–Fri noon–5pm, Sat 10am–2pm, and by appointment. *Note:* The House of Wickersham has been closed for renovation; a reopening date has not been set.

STATE CAPITOL BUILDING, 4th and Main Sts. Tel. 465-3854.

The governor and members of the legislature have their offices in this unpretentious State Capitol building. When the legislature is in session (from the second week of January to the first week of May), you may take a seat in the second-floor visitor's galleries of the Senate or House of Representatives.

Built in 1931 as the Federal and Territorial Building, the Capitol's most notable architectural features are the four columns at its entrance, fashioned of marble from Prince of Wales Island. The corridors of the second and fifth floors contain historic photos of early Juneau; the governor's office is on the third floor.

Admission: Free.

Open: Tours, daily 9am–4:30pm in summer.

STATE OFFICE BUILDING, 4th St. and Calhoun Ave. Tel. 465-2111.

Most Juneau visitors doing government business spend at least some time in the State Office Building, indecorously known by some as the "S.O.B." Because of its hillside location, the building has two main entrances. One, the less conspicuous of the two, leads from a Willoughby Avenue parking lot to ground-floor elevators; the other, off 4th Street opposite the Capitol Building, provides direct access to the eighth floor. Casual visitors should head straight for the eighth-floor Grand Court, where brown-bag lunch concerts are presented at noon every Friday on a fully restored 548-pipe theater organ. A century-old Haida totem pole, called the "Old Witch," towers above. Bibliophiles will find the State Library and Alaska Historical Library on this floor.

Admission: Free.

Open: Mon–Fri 8am–5pm.

ALASKA STATE MUSEUM, 395 Whittier St. Tel. 465-2901.

Here you can develop an understanding of Alaskan history, from ancient to modern. On the first floor you'll find extensive displays of Native artifacts and lifestyles. As you climb a spiral ramp to the second floor, you'll circle a museum highlight, complete with sound effects: a family of eagles in their aerie high atop a tree, with brown bears resting at its foot. On the upper floor you'll find the following subjects featured: the purchase and exploration of Alaska, the state's Russian heritage, Alaska's maritime history, gold mining, and the Alaska pipeline.

There's also a gift shop, as well as rooms for temporary exhibitions. Only about

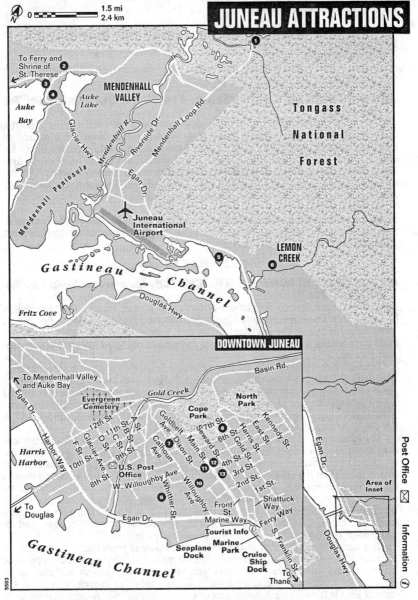

JUNEAU ATTRACTIONS

0   1.5 mi / 2.4 km

Tongass National Forest

MENDENHALL VALLEY

Auke Lake
Auke Bay
Fritz Cove

To Ferry and Shrine of St. Therese

Mendenhall Peninsula

Glacier Hwy
Mendenhall R.
Riverside Dr.
Mendenhall Loop Rd.
Egan Dr.

Juneau International Airport

LEMON CREEK

Gastineau Channel

Douglas Hwy.

DOWNTOWN JUNEAU

To Mendenhall Valley and Auke Bay

Basin Rd.
Gold Creek

Evergreen Cemetery

Cope Park
North Park

Harris Harbor

Egan Dr.
Harbor Way

12th St.
11th St.
10th St.
9th St.
8th St.
F St.
Glacier Ave.
D St.
C St.
B St.
A St.

Goldbelt Ave.
Calhoun Ave.
Dixon St.
Main St.
Seward St.
7th St.
6th St.
5th St.
4th St.
3rd St.
2nd St.
1st St.
Gold St.
Harris St.
East St.
Kennedy St.

U.S. Post Office
W. Willoughby Ave.
Willoughby Ave.
Whittier St.
Egan Dr.

To Douglas

Front St.
Marine Way
Tourist Info
Marine Park
Seaplane Dock
Cruise Ship Dock
To Thane

Shattuck Way
Ferry Way
S. Franklin St.

Egan Dr.
Douglas Hwy.

Area of Inset

Post Office ⊠
Information ⓘ

Gastineau Channel

5583

Alaskan Brewing Company ❻	Juneau-Douglas City Museum ⑪	
Alaska State Museum ❾	Mendenhall Glacier Visitor Center ❶	
Auke Bay Fisheries Laboratory ❹	Mendenhall Wetlands Refuge ❺	
Chapel by the Lake ❷	State Capitol Building ⑫	
Davis Log Cabin ⑬	State Office Building ⑩	
Governor's Mansion ❼	University of Alaska—Southeast ❸	
House of Wickersham ❽		

10% of the museum's collection is displayed at any one time; the balance can be seen by appointment.
Admission: $2.
Open: Mid-May to mid-Sept, Mon–Fri 9am–6pm, Sat–Sun 10am–6pm; mid-Sept to mid-May, Tues–Sat 10am–4pm.

JUNEAU-DOUGLAS CITY MUSEUM, 114 W. 4th St., at Main St. Tel. 586-3572.
This museum has historical exhibits that emphasize the local mining industry, including lifestyles and working conditions. The museum also has a gallery of changing community exhibits from all over Alaska, a hands-on Discovery Room for children, and a re-created turn-of-the-century general store and homestead. Brochures will start you on self-guided walking tours of the Juneau Historic District, totem poles, the Treadwell Mine, and Last Chance Basin. The museum has a small research library and video theater, as well as a gift shop.
Admission: $1.
Open: Mid-May to mid-Sept, Mon–Fri 9am–5pm, Sat–Sun 11am–5pm; mid-Sept to Dec and Mar to mid-May, Thurs–Sat noon–4:30pm, or by appointment.
Closed: Jan–Feb.

Mendenhall Valley

MENDENHALL GLACIER VISITOR CENTER, Mendenhall Loop Rd. Tel. 907/789-0097.
⭐ If you have time to see just one attraction in Juneau, make it the Mendenhall Glacier. There are certainly bigger, more majestic glaciers in Alaska, but none is as accessible as the Mendenhall. In fact, thousands of Juneau residents have built their houses in the broad valley that this glacier occupied little more than two centuries ago.
The visitor center overlooks the foot of the glacier, where it drops 100 feet into icy Mendenhall Lake. Here you can observe what makes this and other glaciers what they are—perpetually moving rivers of ice, flowing from alpine terrain where they are fed by a continual supply of snow. Conditions of high overcast are ideal for glacier-watching because they bring out the cobalt blues of recently exposed, condensed ice, but the sight can be fascinating anytime.
The glacier is located about five miles inland from Juneau Airport. In 1750 it was only about 2½ miles from the coast of the Gastineau Channel. But long-term climatic trends and other factors create cycles of glacial advance and retreat. The half mile of bedrock between the visitor center and the glacial face, in fact, has all been exposed since 1940. Several well-marked trails provide a rare opportunity to study natural transition in an unusual ecological habitat. Tongass National Forest naturalists regularly lead interpretive walks on these trails in summer. The visitor center's facilities include scale models of the glacier, one of them a cross-section, and an audiovisual room where films and slide shows are presented.
You can only see the foot of the Mendenhall Glacier from the visitor center. To fully appreciate its 12-mile length and 1½-mile girth, you'll have to board a plane or helicopter and hover over—or better yet, land on—the Juneau Icefield. At an elevation of 5,000–6,000 feet, it's about 1,500 square miles in area, larger than the state of Rhode Island. One hundred feet of snow falls each year, enough to nourish 36 glaciers. **Temsco Helicopters,** 1650 Maplesden Way, Juneau, AK 99801 (tel. 907/789-9501), has exclusive access to Mendenhall Glacier and offers a variety of tours departing from Juneau. The price ranges from $129 to $189 and flying times range from 50 minutes to one hour and 20 minutes.
Another way to experience the glacier's output is to take a river-rafting trip, dodging small icebergs in Mendenhall Lake and floating down the Mendenhall River toward the sea. Exciting but certainly not perilous, these 3½-hour trips are operated daily, May through September, by **Alaska Travel Adventures,** 9085 Glacier Hwy. (tel. 789-0052). The price is $75 for adults, $48 for children 12 and under.
Admission: Free.

Open: May–Sept, daily 9am–6:30pm; Oct–Apr, Sat–Sun 9am–4pm.

GASTINEAU SALMON HATCHERY VISITOR CENTER, 2697 Channel Dr. Tel. 463-4810.

★ This $7-million facility, located en route to the Mendenhall Valley, is more than just another fish hatchery. Granted, it's already a major producer of king, silver, pink, and chum salmon for the region. But it has been designed for the visitor, to showcase southeast Alaska's commercial fishing industry. During spawning seasons, through the underwater-viewing window, you can see adult salmon fighting their way up the 450-foot fish ladder, Alaska's largest. Many are collected for their eggs and milt, and their progeny are held in incubators. Also here, you can see more than 100 saltwater species from Alaskan waters in floor-to-ceiling aquarium tanks; study modern marine electronics and commercial fishing techniques in visitor-center displays; visit a small marketplace selling everything from canned smoked salmon to salmon leather wallets; and dip a line from an adjacent fishing pier with rental rods and reels and fish-cleaning stations.

Admission: $2.25 adults, $1 children under 12.

Open: Mid-May to mid-Sept, Sun–Fri 10am–6pm, Sat noon–5pm; mid-Sept to mid-May, by appointment.

MENDENHALL WETLANDS REFUGE, flanking Gastineau Channel. Tel. 465-4270.

The tidal lands and estuaries at the end of the glacial valley, surrounding the airport and on both sides of the Gastineau Channel, have been designated as a nature preserve. Principally a habitat for waterfowl and migratory birds, they also attract numerous small mammals, such as muskrats. Bald eagles and bears are common visitors during salmon-spawning season. The refuge is administered by the Alaska Department of Fish and Game. Wear rubber boots if you visit.

Admission: Free.

Open: Daily 24 hours.

ALASKAN BREWING COMPANY, 5429 Shaune Dr., Lemon Creek. Tel. 780-5866.

Only two years after this brewery was established in 1986, its Alaskan Amber was acclaimed as the "best beer in the nation" at the Great American Beer Festival in Colorado. The making of this beer and the light Alaskan Pale Ale—both prepared without pasteurization or preservatives—is shared with brewery visitors. There's also a gift shop at the brewery.

Admission: Free.

Open: May–Sept, Tues–Sat 11am–5pm; Oct–Apr, Thurs–Sat, 11am–4:30pm. Tours on the half hour. **Directions:** Turn right onto Glacier Highway off Egan Drive, four miles north of downtown; about two miles farther, turn right again on Anka Drive and immediately right on Shaune Drive.

Auke Bay

The Auke Bay neighborhood, just northwest of the Mendenhall Valley and north of Douglas Island, is built around a busy public boat harbor and serene Auke Lake. The small **University of Alaska–Southeast** (tel. 789-4458), a branch of the state institution (with headquarters in Fairbanks), opened its lakefront campus in 1971. Nearby, the United Presbyterian church's **Chapel by the Lake** (tel. 789-7592), constructed of spruce logs in 1958, has a picture window with a stunning view across Auke Lake to Mendenhall Glacier. Volunteers will show you around during the summer; you're welcome to attend Sunday services, at 8:30 and 10am in summer, 9:30 and 11am the rest of the year. The **Auke Bay Fisheries Laboratory** (tel. 789-7231), a joint venture of UAS and the National Marine Fisheries Service, is on the bay at Mile 12 on Glacier Highway; visitors enjoy its saltwater aquarium.

The Alaska Marine Highway ferry terminal is on the north side of Auke Bay, at

Mile 14 on Glacier Highway. A mile farther, the **Auke Village Recreation Area** marks the original site of the Auk Tlingit winter village with a beach, picnic area, and campground. The unusual Yax-te totem pole with its raven crest was a 1941 gift to the Auk clan from Tlingits on Prince of Wales Island. Don't return to town until you've driven out to Mile 23, where the memorable Roman Catholic **Shrine of St. Therese** sits among trees on an island connected to the mainland by a quarter-mile causeway. Hand-hewn from rock by a Jesuit priest in 1938, the picturesque chapel, open daily, is a popular location for weddings. Sunday Mass is said at 1pm during the summer months.

Douglas Island

There are only about 21 miles of road on Douglas Island, and they are without the attractions of the mainland. The town of Douglas is pleasant but unremarkable, with few surviving remnants of the great Treadwell mine. From the North Douglas Highway, 9½ miles north of the Douglas Bridge, there's a scenic overlook offering a fine view of the Mendenhall Glacier across Gastineau Channel.

The best reason to go to Douglas Island in summer used to be a visit to Eaglecrest, a winter ski resort that once offered daily trips up its mile-long chair lift to spectacular views and a self-guiding nature trail through alpine meadows at 3,000 feet. Summer trips have been halted, and as of this writing there are no plans to start them again.

WALKING TOUR — DOWNTOWN JUNEAU

Start: Cruise-ship terminal, 470 S. Franklin St.
End: Centennial Hall, 101 Egan Dr.
Time: Approximately 1½ hours.
Best Times: Weekdays, May to July.
Worst Times: Inclement fall and winter days.

HISTORIC JUNEAU Juneau greets well over 100 cruise ships during the May-to-September season. They unload at a new cruise-ship terminal near the south end of the **People's Wharf** neighborhood, Juneau's most historic district, which extends along South Franklin Street. Through the first half of this century it was the focus of commerce, with its municipal wharf, sawmill, and gold mill, and its entertainment, including bars, pool halls, and a red-light district. Many turn-of-the-century buildings remain. In 1986 their proud tenants launched a long-term project aimed at full renovation of the district as a tourist attraction. Beginning at the:

1. **cruise-ship terminal,** as you wander north along South Franklin Street, you'll see building plaques that have been designed to explain how ladies of the evening between the 1920s and the 1950s flaunted their wares from "cigar store" display windows; and how police visited such dens of iniquity as the Occidental Bar, known to locals as the "Bucket of Blood," to hand unruly patrons one-way "blue tickets" to the next boat out of town. The new:
2. **Juneau City Library** opened in 1989 atop a five-story parking garage at South Franklin Street and Admiralty Way. From the top there's a panoramic view across the Gastineau Channel to Douglas Island. Facing it is the century-old:
3. **Red Dog Saloon,** 278 S. Franklin St., southeast Alaska's best-known bacchanalian landmark. Just to the west is the relaxed waterfront atmosphere of:
4. **Marine Park.** Across Egan Drive from the park is the:
5. **Municipal Building,** whose assembly chambers contain an 8- by 50-foot photomural of the Mendenhall Glacier.
    From the Red Dog Saloon, proceed north on Franklin Street, passing such well-known buildings as the:
6. **Alaskan Hotel,** 167 S. Franklin St., and the:

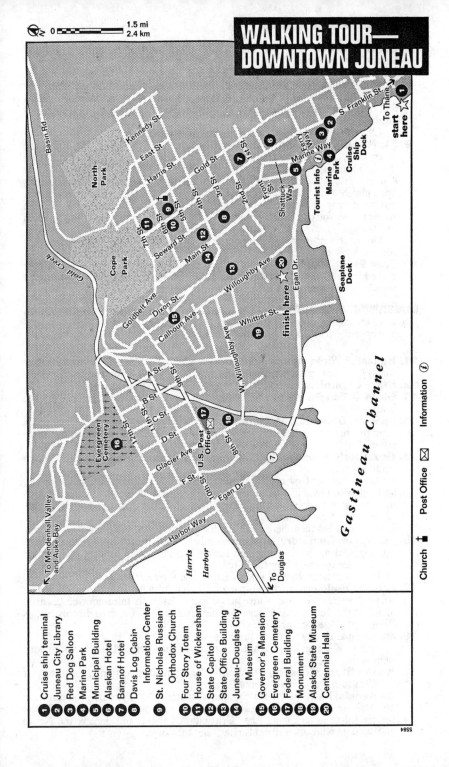

   7. Baranof Hotel, 127 N. Franklin St. A block west of Franklin, at 3rd and Seward Streets, is the:
   8. Davis Log Cabin Information Center, a re-created 1881 cabin that was the city's first church and later a school, carpentry shop, and brewery office (see "Orientation," above). If you're here during Alaska's off-peak season and didn't find the visitor center at the cruise-ship terminal open, this is your best source of information.
      Climb two blocks north from the Davis Log Cabin to:
   9. St. Nicholas Russian Orthodox Church, 326 5th St. (tel. 586-1023), the oldest original Orthodox church building in southeast Alaska. Erected in 1894, the octagonal structure is tiny, only 20 feet in diameter. Priceless icons and church treasures, some of which date from the 18th century, adorn the walls. It's open mid-May through September, daily from 9am to 6pm; at other times, you can make an appointment. If you're interested in standing through services (there are no pews), you can attend vespers at 7pm on Saturday or divine liturgy at 10am on Sunday.
      One of the most impressive of the city's several totem poles is visible from the church. Walk up to the park block at 6th and Seward Streets to the:
   10. Four Story Totem. If you can "read" this 45-foot totem pole, a Haida pole carved in 1940, it will tell you about a monster frog, a bear with a fish trap, a shaman who captured an otter, and an octopus and halibut.

GOVERNMENTAL JUNEAU   The second part of this tour will take you through Juneau as the capital of a vital state.
   Just above the park block is the:

   11. House of Wickersham, a state historic site at 213 7th St. Now retrace your steps down Seward to 4th Street, and turn west; you'll come first to the:
   12. State Capitol, at 4th and Main Streets. Catercorner is the:
   13. State Office Building, which houses the State Historical Library. Opposite both is the:
   14. Juneau–Douglas City Museum, at 114 W. 4th St. A short distance uphill from this busy corner, where 4th Street turns into Calhoun Avenue, is the white colonial-style:
   15. Governor's Mansion, 716 Calhoun Ave. All these buildings are discussed in detail above.
      Just before the Governor's Mansion, turn left off Calhoun onto Indian Street, and follow it downhill as it curves left and becomes 9th Street. History diehards may want to turn right (north) again on B Street, across Gold Creek, to the graves of city founders Joe Juneau and Richard Harris, as well as the Tlingit chief Kowee, who led them here to search for gold. All are buried in:
   16. Evergreen Cemetery, on the west side of 12th Street near B Street. Juneau actually died in the Klondike and Harris in a sanitarium in Oregon, but their bodies were returned here for burial.
      If you continue west down 9th Street, you'll reach the:
   17. Federal Building, at the corner of Glacier Avenue. The Bureau of Indian Affairs has created a fine Native arts display outside its third-floor offices here. South of the Fed, where Glacier Avenue crosses Gold Creek and turns east as Willoughby Avenue, there's a:
   18. monument to city founders Juneau and Harris.
      Follow Willoughby to Whittier Street and turn right. Half a block to your right is the:
   19. Alaska State Museum, 395 Whittier St., a fine introduction to the history of the 49th state (see above). Opposite is:
   20. Centennial Hall, the Juneau convention center at 101 Egan Dr.; you can enter off Whittier and walk through the building, pausing to visit the U.S. Forest Service Information Center (see "Orientation," above) and observe the Native craftspeople who often demonstrate their work here.

To return to your starting point, if you wish, follow Egan Drive east to Marine Park, then proceed south along the water to the cruise-ship terminal.

ORGANIZED TOURS

Packages are offered from mid-May through September by **Gray Line of Alaska,** 127 N. Franklin St., in the Westmark-Baranof Hotel (tel. 586-3773 or 586-9625). Especially popular is a 2½- to 3-hour Mendenhall Glacier–Auke Bay tour priced at $29 ($14.50 for children under 12). Times may vary slightly, but there are always morning and afternoon departures. Gray Line also has a two-hour city tour for $20 ($10 for children).

The itineraries and prices of locally owned tour companies may be more appealing. **Eagle Express** (tel. 789-5720), **Mendenhall Glacier Transport** (tel. 789-5460), and **Ptarmigan Ptours** (tel. 789-5427) all offer city tours of two to three hours, including the historic downtown, Auke Bay, and Mendenhall Glacier, for fares of $9–$10 per head, with discounts for children.

Alaska Travel Adventures, 9085 Glacier Hwy. (tel. 789-0052), offers a 90-minute historic tour hearkening back to the gold-rush era for $24 (children pay $16). A prospector-guide leads the trip through the historic district to the Alaska-Juneau Mine site, where participants are given gold-panning lessons in Gold Creek.

Alaska Rainforest Tours, 369 S. Franklin St., Suite 200 (tel. 463-3466), features a variety of all-day hiking, cruising, and adventure cruise trips, as well as birding tours and kayaking excursions.

Outstanding air tours of Mendenhall Glacier and the Juneau Icefield are offered by **✪ Temsco Helicopters,** 1650 Maplesden Way (tel. 789-9501). The 50-minute, $129 Mendenhall Glacier Tour and the 90-minute, $189 Glacier Explorer both provide passengers with an opportunity to disembark onto the glacial ice. There you'll be met by professional glaciologists who will warn you that glacial crevasses are akin to river rapids and many times more dangerous: Don't go leap-frogging. Heli-tours, priced at $155 per hour, are also offered by **ERA Helicopters,** 6160 S. Airpark Dr. (tel. 586-2030). **Wings of Alaska,** 1873 Shell Simmons Dr. (tel. 789-0790), and other operators take floatplanes over the icefield. Seeing a glacier in this way is a humbling experience, an unforgettable memory. I highly recommend it.

SPORTS & RECREATION

The **Juneau Parks and Recreation Department,** 155 S. Seward St. (tel. 586-5226), has an outstanding variety of programs for Juneau residents and visitors. You can go **swimming** every day of the week at the Augustus Brown Pool, 1619 Glacier Ave., next to Juneau Douglas High School (tel. 586-5359). Open times vary, but the pool is normally open for public lap swimming daily from noon to 1:30pm and weekdays from 5:30 to 6:30pm. Adult fees are $3 an hour.

The **Juneau Racquet Club,** 2841 Riverside Dr., near the Mendenhall Shopping Center (tel. 789-2181), has racquetball courts, four full-size tennis courts, basketball and badminton courts, an aerobics room, saunas, and whirlpools. By paying a guest fee, out-of-town visitors are entitled to use club facilities. There are outdoor **tennis courts** at Cope Park near downtown, at Adair-Kennedy Park in the valley, and at Robert Savikko Recreation Area in Douglas. The last also has a jogging track and an unusual (for southeast Alaska) sandy beach.

Mountain bikes can be rented from **O.M. Cycle Rentals,** 317 S. Franklin St. (tel. 586-2277), for $5 an hour or $25 a day. A 15-mile bike path running all the way to the Mendenhall Glacier begins near the Federal Building at 12th Street and Glacier Avenue.

Some contacts for other sports: body-building, **Southeast Body Building Gym,** 5720 Glacier Hwy. (tel. 780-4800); bowling, **Channel Bowl,** 608 Willoughby Ave. W. (tel. 586-1165); diving, **Scuba Crafts,** 4485 N. Douglas Hwy. (tel. 586-2341); golf, **Mendenhall Golf** (nine holes, par 3), 2101 Industrial Dr. (tel. 789-7323); and shooting, **Hank Harmon Memorial Rifle Range,** 6200 Montana Creek Rd. (tel. 789-5920).

FISHING Dozens of sport-fishing charters operate out of Juneau. The **Juneau Sportfishing Association** (tel. 907/586-1887, or toll free 800/544-2244) can make all arrangements for you. Or ask the folks at the Davis Log Cabin (see "Orientation," above) to provide you a list of local charter operators. Expect to pay $110 per person for a half-day, $185 for a full-day (eight-hour) charter. The best fishing coincides with the May-through-September tourist season, when all five salmon species plus halibut, cutthroat, steelhead, and Dolly Varden trout thrive. Most freshwater lakes and streams are fertile grounds for salmon and trout, the latter even in winter when ice fishing is popular.

The **Alaska Department of Fish and Game,** 802 3rd St., Douglas (tel. 907/465-4270), has a weekly fishing report line: Call 465-4116. You can obtain a license from most charter operators, from the Davis Log Cabin, or from sporting-goods dealers like **Orsi's Custom Rods & Tackle,** 4445 Mendenhall Rd. (tel. 789-3537). If you prefer not to book with a charter operator but to rent a skiff and motor instead, check **Auke Bay Marine** at the Auke Bay Boat Harbor (tel. 789-2913, or 586-1402 off-season).

The **Golden North Salmon Derby,** held over three days in early or mid-August, has been staged annually since 1947. Over $100,000 in prizes is awarded each year! The biggest-ever winner weighed in at more than 59 pounds; the smallest, barely under 30 pounds.

Among the many wilderness hunting and fishing lodges in the Juneau area is the **Taku Glacier Lodge** (mailing address: 2 Marine Way, Suite 228, Juneau, AK 99801; tel. 907/586-1362), 30 air miles east near the top end of the Taku Inlet. The lodge, open May 15 to October 1, has six units with private baths, and holds a daily salmon bake. Three-hour flight tours over the Juneau Icefield, which include a salmon bake at the Taku Lodge, can also be arranged. **Adlersheim Lodge,** on the Lynn Canal 35 miles north of Juneau, is directly accessible by road via the Glacier Highway. Contact P.O. Box 210447, Auke Bay, AK 99821 (tel. 907/780-4778). Other lodges on Admiralty and Chichagof Islands are mentioned later in this chapter. There are 36 primitive U.S. Forest Service **cabins** in the Juneau Ranger District of Tongass National Forest, available by reservation for $20 a night. Visit the Forest Service at the Centennial Building or call 586-8751 for information.

HIKING Every hiker's first step should be through the doors of the Centennial Building to the U.S. Forest Service information office. There, ask to purchase the 61-page "Juneau Trails" guide, a bargain at $3. If you're in reasonably good shape, a popular hike is the steep climb up 3,665-foot **Gastineau Peak** (2¾ miles), continuing to 3,820-foot **Mount Roberts** (4½ miles). It begins up a wooden stairway at the end of 6th Street in downtown Juneau. At the end of Gold Creek Basin, you can retrace the steps of Joe Juneau and Richard Harris up the 3½-mile ✪ **Perseverance Trail** to several old mining excavations. Another 25 trails are detailed in "Juneau Trails." Remember that the weather can change quickly, and bears can be encountered on any trail. Be prepared.

Guided all-day hikes for groups of six or fewer are offered by **Alaska Rainforest Tours,** 369 S. Franklin St., Suite 200 (tel. 463-HIKE). Cost, including lunch and transportation, is $80–$100 per person. The ✪ **Juneau Parks and Recreation Department,** 155 S. Seward St. (tel. 586-5226), conducts free day hikes on Wednesday and Saturday, April through October. Adult visitors are welcome to join.

HUNTING Sitka black-tailed deer and waterfowl are the most highly sought species. Black and brown bears, mountain goats, moose, and wolves are also tracked. Many charter boats and air services serve the needs of hunters. Check regulations with the **Alaska Department of Fish and Game,** Game Division, P.O. Box 3-2000, Juneau, AK 99802 (tel. 907/465-4190). A professional guide must accompany nonresidents on bear hunts. You can obtain a list of registered guides for $5 from the **Division of Occupational Licensing,** Guide Licensing and Control Board, P.O. Box D, Juneau, AK 99811 (tel. 907/465-2542).

KAYAKING Alaska Discovery, 234 Gold St. (tel. 463-5500), offers rentals of single kayaks for $40 a day, double kayaks for $50 a day, with discounts for weekends or rentals of five days or longer. One-day kayak trips in the Juneau area—offered daily, May through September—run $95 per person, all-inclusive. Advance reservations are recommended.

Guides lead longer trips of 5–12 days for $1,200–$3,000, including all meals, equipment, insurance, guide service, and plane or boat charter costs. Admiralty Island, Glacier Bay, and Tracy Arm are the most popular destinations for trips from Juneau. Write or call for brochures.

SAILING   Guided or bare-boat cruises of 2–14 days are offered by **58°22′ North Sailing Charters,** Aurora Basin H-6 (tel. 789-7301), from May through August. Sailors travel aboard the 30-foot *Whisper* ($320 a day plus $20 per person) or the 36-foot *Commitment* ($400 a day plus $20 per person). American Sailing Association courses, from a basic introduction to bareboat charter, are also offered by 58°22′ North.

The highlight of southeast Alaska's sailing season is a June race from Juneau, around Admiralty Island and return. It takes five days, including a mandatory 18-hour layover at Baranof Hot Springs.

SKIING   Alaska's no. 2 winter resort is the **Eaglecrest** ski area on Douglas Island; only Mount Alyeska near Anchorage has more facilities. Eaglecrest has a 1,400-foot vertical drop from its 3,000-foot summit and 640 acres of open bowl, glade, and trail skiing. Two chair lifts (one a mile long) and a platter pull serve 29 trails, marked beginner to expert. The day lodge houses a professional ski school and ski patrol, a rental and repair shop, and a snack bar. Depending on snow conditions, the area operates from Thanksgiving to mid-April, Wednesday through Sunday from 9am to 4pm, with night skiing on Thursday until 9pm. Full-day, all-lift tickets cost $23 for adults, $16 for youth (grades 7–12) and seniors, $11 for children. Eaglecrest has a city office at 155 S. Seward St., Juneau, AK 99801 (tel. 907/586-5284), and recorded up-to-date snow reports on a message phone (tel. 586-5330).

Eaglecrest has six miles of cross-country trails track-set for Nordic skiers as conditions warrant. Tickets are $7. Other popular no-cost, cross-country trails are on Forest Service land. The **Dan Moller Trail** on Douglas Island leads 3⅓ miles from West Juneau up Kowee Creek to the Douglas Ski Bowl, where skiers schussed before Eaglecrest opened in 1976. The 3-mile **Spaulding Meadows Trail** at Auke Bay is closed to snowmobiles, while the 3½-mile **Windfall Lake Trail,** beginning at Mile 27 of the Glacier Highway, leads to a lake that attracts ice-fishermen for cutthroat and Dolly Varden. You can rent ski equipment at the **Foggy Mountain Shop,** 134 Franklin St. (tel. 586-6780), or at Eaglecrest.

If you prefer company, you can join a free **Juneau Parks and Recreation Department** cross-country hike on Wednesday or Saturday in winter (tel. 586-5226 for information).

SHOPPING

It seems as though half the storefronts on historic South Franklin Street are gift shops selling Alaskan souvenirs made in Taiwan. Take time to browse, and spend your money cautiously. One outstanding shop in this area is **✪ Objects of Bright Pride,** 165 S. Franklin St. (tel. 586-4969), which displays exclusive museum-quality works by Native and non-Native artisans—and prices them accordingly. **Latitude 58,** 170 S. Franklin St. (tel. 586-1770); the **Mt. Juneau Trading Post,** 151 S. Franklin St. (tel. 586-3426); the **Juneau General Store,** Ferry Way and South Franklin Street (tel. 463-3626); and **George's Gift Shop,** 194 S. Franklin St. (tel. 586-1810), have a good selection of standard gift items at reasonable prices.

Many fine artists make their homes in the Juneau area. Among the best known is Rie Muñoz, whose colorful paintings and murals with Native Alaskan themes can be found in galleries, museums, and commercial establishments all over the southeast and elsewhere around the state. The **✪ Rie Muñoz Gallery** is at 233 S. Franklin St. (tel. 586-1212). **Annie Kaill's,** 244 Front St., has an especially fine collection of limited-edition prints by Alaskan artists John Fehringer and Byron Birdsall. **Artists' Cove Gallery,** 291 S. Franklin St. (tel. 463-3771), and **Deroux Terzis** in Merchant's Wharf, 14 Marine Way (tel. 463-3349), have outstanding contemporary collections. **Gallery of the North,** 149 S. Franklin St., is the best place to find traditional and modern Native arts and crafts.

If your plans don't take you to Sitka, you can get a taste of Russia at the **Russian Shop,** on the second floor of the Senate Building at 175 S. Franklin St. (tel. 586-2778). Here you can find a wide selection of Orthodox religious icons, lacquer boxes, samovars, stacking Matrushka dolls, and other items. In the same building, on the first floor, is the **Christmas Store** (tel. 586-5770), merchandiser of specialty Alaskan ornaments and other gifts.

If you need film or camera repair, visit **Southeast Exposure,** at 216 2nd St. (tel. 586-1055). **Big City Books,** 100 N. Franklin St., across from the Baranof Hotel (tel. 586-1772), and **Hearthside Books,** with shops at 254 Front St. (tel. 586-1726) and in the Nugget Mall, Mendenhall Valley (tel. 789-2750), are Juneau's leading bookstores. An antiquarian dealer is the **Alaska Heritage Bookshop,** 174 S. Franklin St. (tel. 586-6748).

A unique Alaskan gift is fresh or smoked salmon. Several firms can ship it home for you, including **Taku Smokeries,** 230 S. Franklin St. (tel. 463-3474). Check at the Davis Log Cabin (see "Orientation," above) for other suggestions.

WHERE TO STAY

There are more than a dozen tourist-class hotels in Juneau, ranging from plush new accommodations to turn-of-the-century classics. Most of them are in the downtown area, but several of the newer motels are near the airport at the foot of the Mendenhall Valley.

Taxes   There's a whopping 11% tax: 4% city tax plus 7% bed tax.

EXPENSIVE

BARANOF HOTEL, 127 N. Franklin St., Juneau, AK 99801. Tel. 907/ 586-2660, or toll free 800/544-0970. Fax 907/463-3567. 176 rms, 24 suites. TV TEL

$ Rates: May 16–Sept 15, $111–$119 single; $115–$123 double. Sept 16–May 15, $96–$104 single; $100–$108 double; to $190 suite. AE, CB, DC, DISC, MC, V.

This classically elegant, nine-story Westmark hotel, which celebrated its 50th anniversary in 1989, is convenient to all Juneau attractions yet enough removed from the busiest streets to be relatively quiet. On the walls of the subtly lit lobby—redone after a devastating 1984 fire that began in a hotel restaurant—are original oil paintings by Sydney Lawrence, Fred Machetanz, and other noted Alaskan artists.

The hotel's rooms include 14 efficiency units and 10 one-bedroom suites. One of the Baranof's eccentric charms is that each floor and every unit is different, both in layout and decor. But all rooms have modern furnishings, in-room movies, baseboard steam heating, and such amenities as shampoo and sewing kit. The uppermost have double-paned windows and fine views. Most of the larger units have queen-size beds, large mirrors, walk-in closets, and desks. Try to avoid the small rooms in the rear of the hotel.

Dining/Entertainment: The sophisticated Gold Room, skylit and dominated by a Ziegler oil painting, is famous for its exclusive dinners and attentive service. If you start with vichyssoise or wilted-spinach flambé, then feast on chateaubriand complemented by a bottle of fine French burgundy, you can expect to pay about $70 for two. It's open from 5 to 10pm nightly. The Bubble Room piano bar, which opens directly on to the lobby, is *the* place for after-work "work" in Juneau—some claim that more legislation has been determined in this lounge than at any other place in Alaska. The Capital Café is open for three meals, seven days a week.

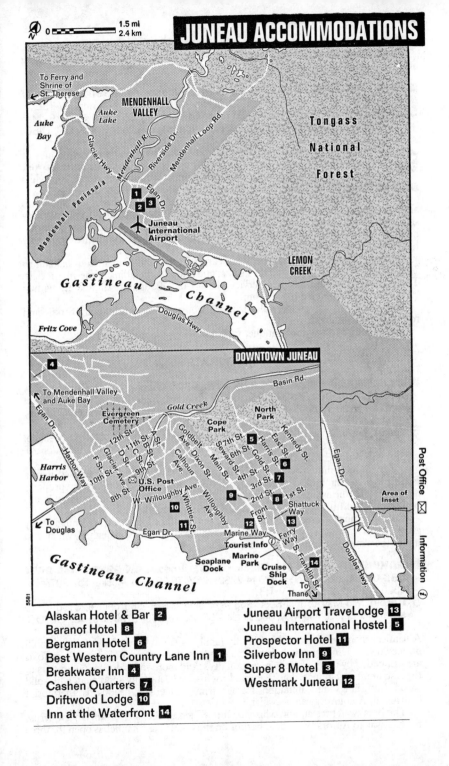

JUNEAU ACCOMMODATIONS

0 1.5 mi / 2.4 km

To Ferry and Shrine of St. Therese

MENDENHALL VALLEY

Auke Lake

Auke Bay

Mendenhall Peninsula

Glacier Hwy.

Mendenhall R.

Riverside Dr.

Mendenhall Loop Rd.

Egan Dr.

1
2 **3**

✈ Juneau International Airport

Tongass National Forest

LEMON CREEK

Gastineau Channel

Fritz Cove

Douglas Hwy.

Post Office ⊠

Information ⓘ

DOWNTOWN JUNEAU

4

To Mendenhall Valley and Auke Bay

Egan Dr.

Gold Creek

Basin Rd.

Evergreen Cemetery

12th St.
11th St.
10th St.
9th St.
8th St.

A St.
B St.
C St.
D St.
F St.
Glacier Ave.

Harris Harbor

Harbor Way

U.S. Post Office ⊠

W. Willoughby Ave.

To Douglas

Goldbelt Ave.
Calhoun Ave.
Dixon St.
Main St.

Cope Park

North Park

7th St.
6th St.
5th St.
4th St.
3rd St.
2nd St.
1st St.

Seward St.
Gold St.

Kennedy St.
East St.
Harris St.

5

6

7

9

8

Shattuck Way

Whittier St.
Willoughby Ave.

10

11

12

Front St.

13

Egan Dr.

Marine Way

Tourist Info

Seaplane Dock

Marine Park

Cruise Ship Dock

Ferry Way

S. Franklin St.

14

To Thane

Egan Dr.

Douglas Hwy.

Area of Inset

Gastineau Channel

5581

Alaskan Hotel & Bar **2**
Baranof Hotel **8**
Bergmann Hotel **6**
Best Western Country Lane Inn **1**
Breakwater Inn **4**
Cashen Quarters **7**
Driftwood Lodge **10**
Inn at the Waterfront **14**

Juneau Airport TraveLodge **13**
Juneau International Hostel **5**
Prospector Hotel **11**
Silverbow Inn **9**
Super 8 Motel **3**
Westmark Juneau **12**

Services: Room service, valet laundry, courtesy van, no-smoking rooms.
Facilities: Gift shop, beauty parlor, travel agency, Alaska Airlines office, banquet and meeting facilities.

WESTMARK JUNEAU, 51 W. Egan Dr., Juneau, AK 99801. Tel. 907/586-6900, or toll free 800/544-0970. Fax 907/258-0560. 105 rms. TV TEL
$ Rates: May 16–Sept 15, $144–$148 double; $132–$136 single. Sept 16–May 15, $98–$104 single; $102–$108 double; from $160 suite. AE, CB, DC, DISC, MC, V.

★ A huge eagle, painstakingly carved from wood by the newest techniques of laser art, greets you as you enter the Westmark's lobby. More such artwork adorns the walls overlooking the aptly named Woodcarver restaurant, while green carpeting and standing plants lend a foresty feeling to the lobby.

The hotel's rooms are decorated in green and mauve or shades of blue, with all-modern furnishings and thermostat-controlled forced-air heating. Complimentary shampoo and a sewing kit are provided in the bathrooms. As you might expect of a hotel so near the convention center and State Office Building, the clientele is heavily business and government oriented.

Dining/Entertainment: The Woodcarver Restaurant is open from 6:30am to 2pm and 5 to 9:30pm. It's noted for its beef and seafood, including prime-rib specials. The adjoining lounge has bar service daily from 4:30pm to midnight, with a "Munchie Bar" open from 5 to 7pm.

Services: Room service, valet laundry, courtesy van, no-smoking rooms and rooms for the disabled.

Facilities: Meeting and banquet facilities.

MODERATE

BEST WESTERN COUNTRY LANE INN, 9300 Glacier Hwy., Juneau, AK **99801. Tel. 907/789-5005,** or toll free 800/528-1234, 800/334-9401 in Alaska. Fax 907/789-9585. 53 rms, 5 suites. TV TEL **Transportation:** Courtesy service provided to the airport and ferry terminal.
$ Rates (including continental breakfast): Mid-May to mid-Sept, $74.95 single; $84.95 double; $94.95 suite. Mid-Sept to mid-May, $69.95 single; $79.95 double; $89.95 suite. AE, CB, DC, DISC, ER, MC, V.

Yes, they do have motels with swimming pools in Alaska. Here, it's housed with a Jacuzzi in a solarium adjacent to the small lobby. Rooms in this two-story property have standard furnishings (including two queen-size beds), with country-style appointments and full baths. Local calls are free. Pets are allowed.

Complimentary coffee, tea, and fruit are served in the lobby each morning. Many guests visit Grandma's Farmhouse Restaurant—also in the Mendenhall Valley and under the same ownership—for other meals.

BREAKWATER INN, 1711 Glacier Ave., Juneau, AK 99801. Tel. 907/586-6303, or toll free 800/544-2250, 800/478-2250 in Alaska. Fax 907/463-4820. 39 rms, 2 suites. TV TEL
$ Rates: Mid-May to mid-Sept, $65–$75 single; $75–$85 double; $100–$110 suite. Mid-Sept to mid-May, $55 single; $65 double; $90–$100 suite. AE, CB, DC, DISC, MC, V.

A nautical theme dominates this friendly family-oriented hotel. As you enter, you'll notice on your left a large woodcut depicting the achievements of sailors. Glass floats are suspended by ropes over the reception desk, and more ropes direct you upstairs to the restaurant and lounge. The renovated rooms are beautifully appointed, with solid wood furnishings and imitation leather trim. Forced-air heating is thermostat controlled. A courtesy van is available.

The Breakwater restaurant, whose picture windows offer a wide-angle view across the highway to Aurora Basin boat harbor on the Gastineau Channel, is open for three meals a day from 7am to 10pm. Lunches run about $7–$10; steak and seafood dinners, $16–$20. The lounge has a big-screen TV for satellite-relayed sports events.

DRIFTWOOD LODGE, 435 Willoughby Ave. W., Juneau, AK 99801. Tel. 907/586-2280, or toll free 800/544-2239. Fax 907/586-1034. 42 rms, 20 suites. TV TEL

$ Rates: Mid-May to mid-Sept, $55–$65 single; $68–$72 double; $78 one-bedroom suite; $95 two-bedroom suite. Mid-Sept to mid-May, $49–$59 single; $62–$66 double; $72 one-bedroom suite; $89 two-bedroom suite. AE, CB, DC, DISC, ER, MC, V.

Located near the Alaska State Museum and government complex, adjoining an excellent restaurant (the Fiddlehead), and sharing a parking lot with a grocery and liquor store, the Driftwood gets points for its central location. It's a three-story, private-entrance facility with no elevators but lots of staircases. The higher rates are for the 21 units and 20 suites with kitchens, stocked with pots, plates, and silverware. All rooms have electric baseboard heating. A guest laundry is open from 7am to 10pm, but irons are hard to come by. A courtesy van is available and the lodge is located on a city bus route. Rooms equipped for the disabled are available.

JUNEAU AIRPORT TRAVELODGE, 9200 Glacier Hwy., Mendenhall Valley (P.O. Box 2240), Juneau, AK 99803. Tel. 907/789-9700, or toll free 800/255-3050. Fax 907/789-1969. 86 rms. TV TEL **Transportation:** Courtesy service provided to the airport and ferry terminal.

$ Rates: Mid-May to mid-Sept, $110 single; $120 double. Mid-Sept to mid-May, $80 single; $90 double. AE, CB, DC, DISC, ER, MC, V.

⭐ The spacious rooms at this three-story motel have been rated the highest in the national TraveLodge system for cleanliness. All boast pastel blue or mauve decor, two queen-size beds, and private baths. The motel has a no-smoking floor, as well as rooms for the disabled. It also has an indoor swimming pool and spa, a gift shop, and a beauty parlor.

Fernando's, a popular Mexican restaurant and lounge, is attached to the motel (see "Where to Dine," below).

PROSPECTOR HOTEL, 375 Whittier St., Juneau, AK 99801. Tel. 907/586-3737, or toll free 800/331-2711. Fax 907/586-1204. 49 rms, 10 suites. TV TEL

$ Rates: Mid-May to mid-Sept, $75–$89 single or double; $100–$200 suite. Mid-Sept to mid-May, $62–$72 single or double; $85–$200 suite. AE, CB, DC, DISC, MC, V.

Ⓢ Don't be deceived by the Prospector's cozy lobby: The rooms are huge. Each one is decorated in pastel shades of purple and gray with rust- or charcoal-colored carpeting. Newly renovated, the rooms include a walk-in closet, electric baseboard heating, and remote-control TV. Seaside rooms look across Egan Drive to the Gastineau Channel. All rooms, in fact, have mountain or water views, except for the cheaper basement rooms. Ten suites have full kitchens; 20 other efficiency units have small kitchens without utensils.

The Diggings restaurant/lounge is open Monday through Saturday from 7am to 10pm, and on Sunday for brunch from 9am to 3pm and dinner from 5 to 10pm. Roast prime rib, cooked 4½ hours in rock salt, is the specialty of the house; Alaskan seafood is also featured. Lunches run $6–$11, dinner entrees, $12–$22. A live band plays light pop music for dancing Tuesday through Saturday nights.

SILVERBOW INN, 120 2nd St., Juneau, AK 99801. Tel. 907/586-4146. 6 rms. TEL

$ Rates (including continental breakfast): Summer, $95 single; $105 double. Winter, $65 single; $75 double. AE, CB, DC, DISC, MC, V.

One of southeast Alaska's finest restaurants (see "Where to Dine," below) also has accommodations on its second and third floors. Each cozy room has a private bath but a European feel; owner Richard Lee may eventually add more rooms. All are no-smoking. Each has an antique desk and wardrobe, double bed, electric heating, and clock radio. There are no TVs, but light jazz is sometimes played downstairs.

SUPER 8 MOTEL, 2295 Trout St., Juneau, AK 99801. Tel. 907/789-4858, or toll free 800/843-1991. Fax 907/789-5819. 72 rms, 3 suites. TV TEL
Transportation: Courtesy service provided to the airport and ferry terminal.
$ Rates: Mid-May to mid-Sept, $81 single; $94 double; $109 suite. Winter, $60 single or double; $89 suite. AE, CB, DC, MC, V.

Super 8 gives you a lot for your money. Though a bit spartan in atmosphere, with nothing but a mirror and a print on the cream-colored walls, each room contains everything you need to be comfortable: queen-size bed, built-in desk/dresser/luggage rack, ample lighting, and electric baseboard heating. There are vending machines on the second floor, a guest laundry, and a computerized elevator. The motel is accessible to the disabled. A courtesy van leaves for downtown at 7:30am and 4:30pm. The lobby coffee is complimentary; a McDonald's restaurant is next door.

BUDGET

ALASKAN HOTEL & BAR, 167 S. Franklin St., Juneau, AK 99801. Tel. 907/586-1000, or toll free 800/327-9347. Fax 907/463-3775. 40 rms (10 with bath). TV
$ Rates: $40 single without bath, $55–$60 single with bath; $46 double without bath, $61–$66 double with bath. 11% tax included off-season only (mid-Sept to mid-May). AE, DISC, MC, V.

There may be no better place to stay in Alaska to get a feeling for the gold-rush era. From the moment you step through the hotel's swinging doors, you'll feel as though you've been transported back to Victorian times. Built in 1913, the Alaskan Hotel is on the National Register of Historic Places. Its small rooms are on two upstairs floors (no elevators) whose corridors are lined with old photos of historic Juneau. Each is decorated in turn-of-the-century bordello style, with an antique oak headboard, desk, and chair and a combination wardrobe/dresser. Even the toilets and sinks are antique, whether you opt for a room with a private bath or share a facility in the hall. The hotel has hot-water radiator heating, a guest laundry, and antique-style oak wall phones in the corridors. Some kitchenettes are available. A hot tub and sauna are in the basement; you may rent either one for $20 an hour.

BERGMANN HOTEL, 434 3rd St., Juneau, AK 99801. Tel. 907/586-1690. Fax 907/463-2678. 24 rms (none with bath), 6 suites. TV TEL
$ Rates: Mid-May to mid-Sept, $55 single; $65 double. Mid-Sept to mid-May, $39 single; $45 double. AE, DISC, MC, V.

Built in 1913 by an immigrant German widow named Marie Bergmann, this hotel—listed on the National Register of Historic Places—was once considered Juneau's finest. It underwent a major renovation in the late 1980s; now each room is adorned differently, with modern furnishings, antique photographs, and flowers. The rooms are quiet, with wall-to-wall carpeting; all have sinks. Guests share bathrooms and a laundry. The hotel's Grubstake restaurant (tel. 463-5669) is noted for its steaks, seafood, and homemade salads; it's open weekdays for lunch, nightly for dinner. A little pub with a dedicated following is in the basement.

CASHEN QUARTERS, 315 Gold St., Juneau, AK 99801. Tel. 907/586-9863. 5 rms (all with bath).
$ Rates (including continental breakfast): May–Sept, $55 single; $65 double. Oct–Apr, $45 single or double. No credit cards.

These recently redecorated housekeeping units are part of a refurbished home at 303 Gold St., on the corner of 3rd Street. Clean and spacious, with stoves and refrigerators, forced-air heating, double beds, and easy chairs, they appeal mainly to families and older visitors. Televisions and phones are available.

INN AT THE WATERFRONT, 455 S. Franklin St., Juneau, AK 99801. Tel. 907/586-2050. 15 rms, 6 suites (17 with bath). TV TEL
$ Rates: Mid-May to mid-Sept, $35 single without bath, $59 single with bath; $39 double without bath, $68 double with bath; $76–$115 suite. Mid-Sept to mid-May, $25 single without bath, $40 single with bath; $29 double without bath, $50 double with bath; $57–$83 suite. AE, CB, DC, MC, V.

In 1986, Bill Cullinane and Ann House bought an 1898 brothel-turned-flophouse hotel across from the cruise-ship terminal. Two years later they opened with intimate rooms and suites, all furnished with antique wardrobes (some also with desks), modern beds, and a soothing color scheme of taupe carpets and blue bedspreads and curtains. The restoration introduced all-new heating, electrical, and plumbing systems, insulation, and siding, and it enabled the hotel to reopen the long-lost Crystal Baths, where up to eight people at a time can bask in steam for $10 an hour. The inn's Summit Restaurant and Lounge (see "Where to Dine," below) has long been considered one of Juneau's premier steakhouses.

BED-&-BREAKFAST

The **Alaska Bed & Breakfast Association,** Southeastern Alaska, P.O. Box 21890, Juneau, AK 99802 (tel. 907/586-2959), is a central booking agency for many of the B&Bs in the Juneau area. An effort is made to place visitors with compatible families—smokers, pet lovers, and so forth. Most rooms run $50–$90 double.

Among the B&Bs represented are:

Blueberry Lodge, 9436 N. Douglas Hwy., Douglas, AK 99824 (tel. 907/463-5886), a handcrafted-log lodge near the entrance to Eaglecrest Ski Area.

Crondahl's, 626 5th St., Juneau, AK 99801 (tel. 907/586-1464), located five blocks from the Capitol.

Dawson's, 1941 Glacier Hwy., Juneau, AK 99801 (tel. 907/586-9708), near the airport.

Grandma's Feather Bed, 2358 Mendenhall Loop Rd., Juneau, AK 99803 (tel. 907/789-5566; fax 907/789-2818), with seven Jacuzzi suites (priced over $100 in summer) on the upper floor of a popular country-style restaurant.

Lost Chord, 2200 Fritz Cove Rd., Juneau, AK 99801 (tel. 907/789-7296), in a secluded cove 14 miles from downtown near Auke Bay.

Windsock Inn, 410 D St. (P.O. Box 223), Douglas, AK 99824 (tel. 907/364-2431), in Juneau's sister city across the Gastineau Channel.

A YOUTH HOSTEL

JUNEAU INTERNATIONAL HOSTEL, 614 Harris St., Juneau, AK 99801. Tel. 907/586-9559. 32 beds.
$ Rates: $8 for American Youth Hostels members, $11 for nonmembers. Annual membership $20 extra. No credit cards.

All ages are welcome to stay at this three-story yellow "youth" hostel, provided they conform willingly to the hostel's somewhat restrictive rules. It's open from 7 to 9am and 5 to 10:30pm. Smoking and alcohol are taboo. You share eight-bed dormitory rooms and common bathrooms (segregated by sex), pay 50¢ if you want a shower, and limit your stay to three days. Blankets are supplied, but you must have your own "sheet sleeping sack" or buy one for 75¢. A community kitchen, laundry, and common room (for reading and conversation) make this easier to take. Reservations are accepted.

CAMPGROUNDS

There are two Forest Service campgrounds near Auke Bay. The **Auke Village Campground,** Mile 15.8 on the Glacier Highway, has 11 sites; the **Mendenhall Lake Campground,** off Montana Creek Road five miles from the ferry terminal, has 60, including 10 for trailers and 7 specifically for backpackers. Both have wood and water, but Auke Village has flush toilets while Mendenhall Lake has mere pit facilities. Units cost $5 per night. No reservations are taken. Contact the Juneau Ranger District, U.S. Forest Service, P.O. Box 2097, Juneau, AK 99803 (tel. 907/586-8800), for more information.

Recreational vehicles are best served at the **Auke Bay RV Park,** 11930 Glacier Hwy. (P.O. Box 210215), Auke Bay, AK 99821 (tel. 907/789-9467), which takes reservations for its 25 spaces with electric, water, and sewer hookups.

WHERE TO DINE

Probably because of its role as Alaska's governmental center, Juneau has as much variety in restaurants as any other city in the state, with the exception of Anchorage. It also has a heavy business turnover. New restaurants continue to open and close, so there's no guarantee the ones mentioned here will still be operating when you visit. But hotel restaurants such as the Baranof Hotel's Gold Room, the Westmark's Woodcarver, the Prospector's Diggings, and the Breakwater, described in the "Where to Stay," above, offer consistently excellent food and service, for rather high prices.

EXPENSIVE

THE FIDDLEHEAD, 429 Willoughby Ave. W., downtown. Tel. 586-3150.
   Cuisine: INTERNATIONAL. **Reservations:** Recommended.
$ **Prices:** Appetizers $5.95–$10.95; main courses $16.95–$22.95; breakfast $4.50–$8.95; lunch $7.95–$13.95. AE, CB, DC, MC, V.
   Open: Mon–Fri 6:30am–10pm, Sat–Sun 7am–10pm.

The Fiddlehead is one of my two favorite restaurants in Juneau (the other is the Silverbow Inn). Live jazz and classical piano weekends, handcrafted stained-glass windows, and the work of local artists and photographers on the walls create an artsy atmosphere in this local standby, now in its second decade in business. A recent upstairs addition enables the restaurant to split its dinner business between fine dining (in the elegant new Fireweed Room) and casual meals (downstairs, where the lunch menu is served until 10pm).

The emphasis is on wholesome foods. You might opt for a breakfast of granola with yogurt or, for a heartier appetite, huevos Havana—fried eggs and salsa on black beans and brown rice with sour cream and tortillas. Homemade soups, salads, and burgers, plus light dishes like chicken Tadziks or pasta in peanut sauce, are offered at lunch. The Fireweed Room's international dinner entrees include penne Amatriciana (Italian), gai yang (a Thai chicken dish), and grilled New York steak with onions and mushrooms. As might be expected of a restaurant with its own bakery, desserts are superb: chocolate cake, ice cream pie and crème brûlée, for instance, accompanied by espresso coffee. There's a menu of domestic and imported wines and beers.

MIKE'S, 1120 2nd St., Douglas. Tel. 364-3271.
   Cuisine: STEAK/SEAFOOD. **Reservations:** Recommended.
$ **Prices:** Appetizers $5–$8; main courses $14–$18. AE, MC, V.
   Open: Lunch Tues–Sun 11:30am–1:30pm; dinner Tues–Sun 5–10pm.

No restaurant in Juneau has survived longer than this one. Mike Pusich opened his original Douglas saloon in 1914 and it has been going strong ever since (except for the years of Prohibition, when he survived by selling clothes and groceries). A 1937 fire destroyed the Dreamland nightclub, as it was known; but Mike's Place soon reappeared on the site. That was well over 50 years ago. Mike's eldest son, Rudy Pusich, took over upon his father's death in 1953 and still holds forth.

As you enter the restaurant, you'll have a chance to study several photos of the early 20th-century boom times of the Treadwell Mine here in Douglas. Then you'll descend the stairs to an elegant room on a hill above the Gastineau Channel. It's quiet during the week, but on weekends a band plays light rock and contemporary standards to dance to. Dinners with seafood—especially halibut and Petersburg shrimp—rank high on the list of suggestions. Lunch specials are available.

SILVERBOW INN, 120 2nd St., downtown. Tel. 586-4146.

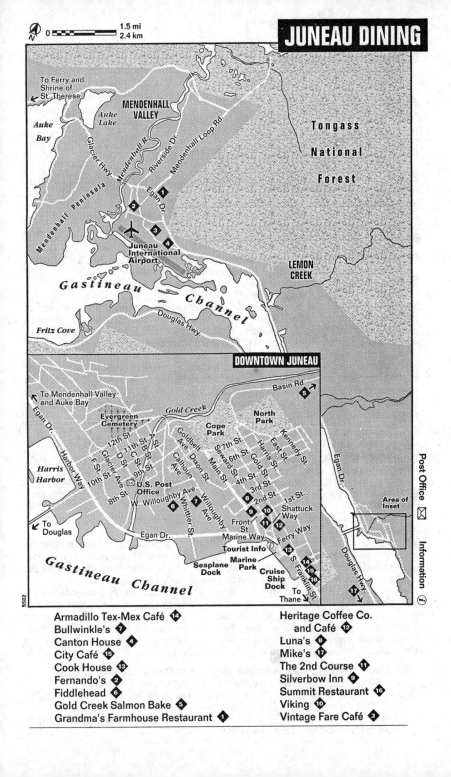

JUNEAU DINING

0 |▭▭▭▭▭| 1.5 mi
2.4 km

To Ferry and
Shrine of
St. Therese

**MENDENHALL
VALLEY**

Auke
Bay

Auke
Lake

Tongass

National

Forest

Glacier Hwy.

Mendenhall R.

Riverside Dr.

Mendenhall Loop Rd.

Egan Dr.

Mendenhall Peninsula

1

2

3

4

**Juneau
International
Airport**

**LEMON
CREEK**

Gastineau

Channel

Fritz Cove

Douglas Hwy.

DOWNTOWN JUNEAU

To Mendenhall Valley
and Auke Bay

Egan Dr.

Gold Creek

**Evergreen
Cemetery**

**North
Park**

**Cope
Park**

12th St.

11th St.

Glacier Ave.

F St.

D St.

C St.

B St.

A St.

10th St.

9th St.

8th St.

Goldbelt Ave.

Dixon Ave.

Calhoun Ave.

Main St.

Seward St.

7th St.

6th St.

Gold St.

Harris St.

East St.

Kennedy St.

4th St.

3rd St.

2nd St.

1st St.

*Harris
Harbor*

Harbor Way

U.S. Post
Office

W. Willoughby Ave.

Willoughby Ave.

Whittier St.

To
Douglas

Egan Dr.

Shattuck
Way

Ferry Way

S. Franklin St.

Front
St.

Marine Way

Tourist Info

**Marine
Park**

Egan Dr.

Douglas Hwy.

**Seaplane
Dock**

**Cruise
Ship
Dock**

To
Thane

Basin Rd.

5

6

7

8

9

10

11

12

13

14

15

16

17

**Area of
Inset**

Post Office ⊠

Information ⓘ

5582

Armadillo Tex-Mex Café **14**	Heritage Coffee Co. and Café **12**
Bullwinkle's **7**	Luna's **8**
Canton House **4**	Mike's **17**
City Café **15**	The 2nd Course **11**
Cook House **13**	Silverbow Inn **9**
Fernando's **2**	Summit Restaurant **16**
Fiddlehead **6**	Viking **10**
Gold Creek Salmon Bake **5**	Vintage Fare Café **3**
Grandma's Farmhouse Restaurant **1**	

Cuisine: CREATIVE CONTINENTAL. **Reservations:** Recommended.
$ **Prices:** Appetizers $6.95–$7.95; main courses $12.95–$24.95. AE, CB, DC, DISC, MC, V.
Open: Dinner only, Mon–Sat 5–9pm.

⭐ The Silverbow Inn has a menu and atmosphere reminiscent of a European country inn. The renovated building it occupies between Main and Seward Streets was known during Juneau's wild-and-woolly gold-rush days as the San Francisco Bakery; owners Richard and Mindy Lee refurbished it with antiques in 1984. Intimate dining today is in large parlors, surrounded by works of stained glass and Alaska watercolors, or on an outdoor porch.

The food is a delightful surprise. The menu changes with regularity. Candlelit dinners can start with smoked Alaskan salmon or Cajun oysters, followed by salad, vegetable, French bread, and potato, rice, or pasta; try the rosemary lamb chops, pecan chicken Acadiana, salmon Florentine, or bouillabaisse. There's an outrageous dessert selection, with the likes of sour cream–pecan cheesecake and homemade ice cream, and a brief but provocative international wine list. Vegetarian meals and light dinners are specialties. Smoking is not permitted.

SUMMIT RESTAURANT, 455 S. Franklin St., downtown. Tel. 586-2050.
Cuisine: STEAK/SEAFOOD. **Reservations:** Recommended.
$ **Prices:** Appetizers $7–$10; main courses $15–$32. AE, CB, DC, MC, V.
Open: Dinner only, daily 5–10pm.

The Summit—the chief reason to visit the Inn at the Waterfront, at the south end of the historic People's Wharf district—has long been considered one of Juneau's premier spots for steaks. It also offers a broad choice of chicken and seafood dinners, served in an intimate, masculine decor of maroon carpets and mauve walls.

All entrees include soup; salad; potatoes, rice, or pasta; and freshly baked bread. You can start with steamed clams or spicy buffalo wings, then move to an entree like sautéed abalone, sesame salmon, coquilles St-Jacques, chicken Teklanika (with scallops, green peppers, and mushrooms), or the ever-popular New York steak à la bleu. Dessert features include a chocolate miners pie and apple crisp à la mode; the restaurant also offers an extensive wine list.

MODERATE

CANTON HOUSE, Capital Plaza Building, 8588 Old Dairy Rd., Mendenhall Valley. Tel. 789-5075.
Cuisine: CHINESE. **Reservations:** Recommended evenings and weekends.
$ **Prices:** Main courses $8.25–$16; lunch specials $5.75. AE, CB, DC, DISC, MC, V.
Open: Mon–Thurs 11:30am–10pm, Fri 11:30am–11pm, Sat–Sun 10:30am–10pm.

This is probably Juneau's most authentic Chinese restaurant. Traditional, melodic Far Eastern music filters through trailing ivy draped over chandeliers. The simple blue-and-white color scheme and rattan-backed chairs are in stark contrast to the tendency of many Chinese restaurants to overdecorate in gaudy hues.

Here the food does the talking. Cantonese and Szechuan are the featured cuisines, with dishes ranging from almond chicken to sliced abalone in black-bean sauce. If there are quite a few of you, you can order a nine-course, family-style dinner for $14.50 per person, with crispy duck, Four Happiness, and Sam Sing in the Nest. Lunch specials include your choice of two items (such as egg foo yong and chicken chow mein) plus soup, rice, and tea. On weekends there's an all-you-can-eat brunch.

THE COOK HOUSE, 200 Admiral Way, downtown. Tel. 463-3658.
Cuisine: AMERICAN. **Reservations:** Recommended in summer.
$ **Prices:** Appetizers $5.45–$9.95; main courses $5.95–$17.95 at lunch, $8.25–$19.95 at dinner. AE, CB, DC, MC, V.
Open: Mid-May to mid-Sept, Sun–Thurs 11am–10pm, Fri–Sat 11am–11pm; mid-Sept to mid-May, daily 11am–9pm.

S The atmosphere of a turn-of-the-century mining camp is recalled at the Cook House. At the front entrance stand a steam engine and stamp mill, and inside the building, crafted to have a rustic, half-finished look, is a 20-part photomural of Juneau-area mining operations, courtesy of the State Historical Library. The open kitchen goes hand-in-hand with the scaffold and noose in one corner: THE COOKING HAS NEVER KILLED ANYONE, BUT THE MINERS HAVE HUNG MORE THAN ONE COOK reads a sign.

The lunch menu offers such choices as barbecued ribs and a halibut burger. Dinner selections (with soup and salad, bread, baked potato or french fries) include Alaskan spot prawns, Cajun-blackened prime rib, or a 16-ounce grub steak. Perhaps the most popular item is the three-pound Cook House burger, undoubtedly the largest you've ever seen, served in a 9½-inch, pizza-size bun with two pounds of fries on the side.

FERNANDO'S, 9200 Glacier Hwy., Mendenhall Valley. Tel. 789-3636.
   Cuisine: MEXICAN. **Reservations:** Not required.
$ Prices: Appetizers $4–$7; main courses $6–$14. AE, CB, DC, DISC, ER, MC, V.
   Open: May–Sept, daily 7am–10pm; Oct–Apr, daily 7am–9pm; brunch Sun 10am–2pm.

This is as close as you'll find to hacienda-style Mexican dining in southeast Alaska. A fountain spurts in the center in an atmosphere of painted tiles and decorative iron, and festive decor is all around. If you're a salad lover, try the ensalada suprema, which has shrimp, two types of cheese, eggs, tomato, avocado, and lettuce on a tortilla shell. Full dinners are just that—full. Consider the enchiladas Suizas. Fernando's also boasts a busy cantina.

GOLD CREEK SALMON BAKE, end of Basin Rd. Tel. 586-1424.
   Cuisine: AMERICAN. **Reservations:** Required of large groups. **Transportation:** Bus service from the Baranof Hotel.
$ Prices: Full meal $21 adults, $10.50 children. AE, MC, V.
   Open: Mid-May to mid-Sept, lunch Mon–Sat 11:30am–1:30pm; dinner daily 5:30–9pm.

☆ This excellent salmon bake just outside downtown is near the site of Harris's and Juneau's first gold discovery. You get all the alder-smoked salmon, salad, bread, and lemonade you can consume, and your first beer is free.

From here you can take a short hike to explore the remnants of the Alaska-Juneau Mining Company, now incorporated in the Last Chance Basin Historic District. (Pick up a walking-tour brochure at the Juneau–Douglas City Museum.)

GRANDMA'S FARMHOUSE RESTAURANT, 2358 Mendenhall Loop Rd., Mendenhall Valley. Tel. 789-5566.
   Cuisine: AMERICAN. **Reservations:** Recommended.
$ Prices: Main courses $5–$9.50 at lunch $11–$20 at dinner. AE, CB, DC, DISC, MC, V.
   Open: May–Sept, breakfast/lunch Mon–Fri 7am–3pm, Sat–Sun 8am–3pm (including Sun brunch); dinner Sun–Thurs 5–9pm, Fri–Sat 5–10pm. Oct–Apr, dinner only, Tues–Sun 5–8:30pm.

You'll really feel as if you're in Grandma's house, with calico patterns on cushions and armchairs and antique toys mounted on shelves. Dinners include salad bar, homemade soup, vegetable, potato, and bread; the 14-ounce prime rib is a favorite. Turkey and dressing, pastas and salad dishes are recent additions to the menu. Gourmet sandwiches and a huge Petersburg shrimp Louie are lunchtime favorites. The bakery sells fresh bread and pastries, while a gift shop specializes in quilts and country handcrafts. Grandma's is licensed for wine and beer only. The upstairs floors are occupied by an elite Victorian bed-and-breakfast.

LUNA'S, 210 Seward St., downtown. Tel. 586-6990.
   Cuisine: MEDITERRANEAN. **Reservations:** Recommended for dinner.
$ Prices: Main courses $3.50–$11 at lunch, $10–$19 at dinner. AE, MC, V.
   Open: Lunch Mon–Fri 11am–5pm; dinner Mon–Sat 5–9:30pm.

Juneau's best Italian food may be served at Luna's, where even grownups are provided crayons to scribble on their butcher-paper tablecloths over the lunch hour. Lunch might be minestrone with Luna's famous homemade bread, pasta, pizza, or something more international, like Greek salad. Dinners—chicken, steak, veal, and fresh seafood—include soup or salad, bread, vegetable, and pasta. Lighter eaters can get calzone or a pasta dish. Gelato and espresso top off the meal. Wine and beer are served.

THANE ORE HOUSE, 4400 Thane Rd. Tel. 586-3442.

Cuisine: AMERICAN. **Reservations:** Not required. **Transportation:** Evening bus service from the Baranof Hotel, or call for pickup.
$ Prices: All-you-can-eat dinner and show $19.95 (children under 12½ pay their age plus $4); dinner without the show $16; the show without dinner $6. AE, MC, V.
Open: Early May to early Oct, daily noon–9:30pm (one show nightly at 6:30pm).

⭐ Eat all the salmon, halibut, or barbecued ribs you can handle in a replica of a 19th-century miners' mess hall near the tailings of the old Alaska-Gastineau mine. Each evening, the Gold Nugget Revue, a family-oriented dinner show, treats you to song, dance, and the humorous historical adventures of Joe Juneau. You can also pan for gold or see an exhibit of historic photos and artifacts.

INEXPENSIVE

ARMADILLO TEX-MEX CAFE, 431 S. Franklin St., downtown. Tel. 586-1880.

Cuisine: MEXICAN. **Reservations:** Not required.
$ Prices: Main courses $5.75–$15.95. MC, V.
Open: Mon–Thurs 11am–9pm, Fri–Sat 11am–10pm, Sun 4–10pm.

⑤ Chips and salsa are free with all meals here, where you place counter orders beneath the casual glances of armadillo miniatures. Prices range from $5.75 for a bowl of Texas chili to $15.95 for a large order of barbecued ribs with potato salad, beans, and cornbread. Or you can build your own fajita—a gourmet steak taco—for $10.95 or try the barbecued chicken. Mexican import beers are only $1.50 between 4 and 6pm Sunday.

BULLWINKLE'S, 318 Willoughby Ave. E., downtown. Tel. 586-2400.

Cuisine: PIZZA. **Reservations:** Not required.
$ Prices: Pizzas $10–$18. MC, V.
Open: Mon–Thurs 11am–midnight, Fri–Sat 11am–1am, Sun noon–midnight.
This is probably Juneau's favorite venue for pizza. For a bargain, come on Friday night, when imported beers are $1.50, and try to ignore the blips and blurps from the video machines.

CITY CAFE, 439 S. Franklin St., downtown. Tel. 586-4180.

Cuisine: ASIAN/AMERICAN.
$ Prices: Breakfast $3.95–$9.95; lunch $4.25–$9.50; dinner $6–$13.95. No credit cards.
Open: Mon–Fri 6am–11pm, Sat–Sun 7am–11pm.
This nondescript café is an old Juneau standby. Chinese combination dinners, including Mongolian beef, and an extensive Filipino menu, with dishes like pork adobo, complement the usual American offerings. The City Café is licensed for wine and beer.

HERITAGE COFFEE CO. AND CAFE, 174 S. Franklin St., downtown. Tel. 586-1088.

Cuisine: DELI.
$ Prices: Average meal $2.85–$4.50. No credit cards.
Open: Mon–Wed 7am–11pm, Thurs 7am–7pm, Fri 7am–11pm, Sat 8am–11pm, Sun 9am–11pm.

Okay, so say you're from Seattle and you haven't had your caffè con latte fix in two weeks. This spot will reestablish your caffeine blood level and tempt you with savory croissants, deli-style sandwiches, and homemade soups to boot. And you'll see more sippers gathered to read their copies of the just-arrived *USA Today* or *Seattle Post-Intelligencer* than anywhere else in the city.

THE 2ND COURSE, 119 S. Seward St., downtown. Tel. 463-5533.
  Cuisine: CHINESE. **Reservations:** Recommended.
$ **Prices:** Lunch $7–$10. MC, V.
  Open: Lunch only, Tues–Fri 11:30am–2pm.
      Canton-born, Hong Kong–raised Heidi Grimes opened this tiny (six-table) café and gift shop on the second floor of a commercial block in 1990. Now, you must wait in line for a seat. Heidi serves a set menu each day—usually soup, stir-fry meat or fish, vegetables, rice, and tea—with Friday left for bite-size dim sum. Remarkably, she never serves the same menu twice. It's always low sodium and without monosodium glutamate; no alcohol is served. Cooking classes are offered from 11:30am to 1:30pm on Saturday for $40.

THE VIKING, 218 Front St., downtown. Tel. 586-2159.
  Cuisine: AMERICAN.
$ **Prices:** Appetizers $4.95–$7.95; main courses $9.95–$19.95; breakfast $3.50–$11.95; lunch $4.95–$11.95. AE, DISC, MC, V.
  Open: Mon–Fri 7:30am–midnight, Sat 9am–midnight. **Closed:** Sun.
Nautical decor pervades this long-established Juneau coffee shop, which dominates one of the key downtown street corners. Locals flock here for burgers, pork chops, chicken-fried steaks, grilled seafood, and other staples of American culture. There are also a few Chinese dishes on the menu, including stir-fries.

VINTAGE FARE CAFE, Glacier Hwy. at Egan Expwy., Mendenhall Valley. Tel. 789-1865.
  Cuisine: DELI.
$ **Prices:** Average meal $3–$5.50. No credit cards.
  Open: Mon–Fri 9am–8pm, Sat 9am–6pm, Sun 11am–5pm.
Shoppers and others visit the Vintage Fare for its soups, salads, sandwiches, desserts, and the Valley's only espresso bar. There are daily breakfast and luncheon specials.

EVENING ENTERTAINMENT

If you think of Juneau as a wild-and-woolly town in terms of nightlife, you're right. But you'd be just as right to call it a cultural oasis.

THE PERFORMING ARTS

The **Juneau Arts and Humanities Council,** 206 N. Franklin St. (tel. 586-ARTS), presents an annual winter-spring concert season that in the past has included jazz artists such as Dizzy Gillespie, dance troupes such as the Theatre Ballet of Canada, and European performers such as the Vienna Boys' Choir and the Warsaw Philharmonic Orchestra. The council can also inform you of the activities of other local performing arts groups, such as the **Juneau-Douglas Little Theater** and the **Juneau International Folkdancers.**

The *Juneau Empire*'s Thursday "Preview" section includes a calendar of arts, entertainment, gallery exhibits, and special events in the Juneau area for the following week.

MOVIES If you're in the mood for a movie, the **20th Century Theater,** 222 Front St. (tel. 586-4055), and the **Glacier Cinema,** 3303 Mendenhall Loop Rd. (tel. 789-9191), both have twin theaters showing first-run movies nightly, with weekend matinees.

LADY LOU REVUE, Merchants Wharf, 2 Marine Way at Egan Dr. Tel. 586-3686.

⭐ If you like live theater, or even if you don't, you'll enjoy the melodramatic *Lady Lou Revue*. Based on a pair of Robert Service ballads, "The Shooting of Dan McGrew" and "The Cremation of Sam McGee," this rollicking 75-minute show re-creates some of the romance and excitement of the 1898 Klondike Gold Rush.

Admission: $14 adults, $7 children.
Open: Mid-May to mid-Sept; the schedule isn't consistent, but there are shows at 8pm almost daily, and frequent 2pm matinees as well. **Closed:** Mid-Sept to mid-May.

PERSEVERENCE THEATER, 914 3rd St., Douglas. Tel. 364-2421.

The *Lady Lou Revue* is a production of this nationally respected professional company which has toured to New York, France, and Guam, as well as throughout Alaska. Between September and May the company stages five separate productions, each for four-week runs, at its 150-seat theater. Productions range from Shakespeare to Tennessee Williams to Theater of the Absurd.

Admission: Varies; inquire at Big City Books or Hearthside Books (see "Shopping" in "What to See and Do," above) for tickets and schedule information.
Open: Performances, Sept–May, Thurs–Sat at 8pm, Sun at 2pm.

THE BAR & MUSIC SCENE

RED DOG SALOON, 278 S. Franklin St. Tel. 463-3777.

⭐ Nearly every visitor sooner or later ducks his or her head into the Red Dog Saloon. The sawdust floor, bearskins, and collection of old firearms—including a gun that Wyatt Earp supposedly deposited for safekeeping in the 1880s and never returned to pick up—are straight out of the last century. The ceiling is bedecked with autographed life rings and other memorabilia of ships passing through port; management swears that the *Exxon Valdez* flag is the one the vessel was flying when it went aground in Prince William Sound in 1989. There's frequently live music, including small rock combos, blues, and Alaskan bush balladry, but mainly this is just a friendly main-street saloon—with a bustling souvenir shop adjoining (open summers only). Like most Alaskan bars, the Red Dog opens at 11am and doesn't close until 2am.

ALASKAN HOTEL & BAR, 167 S. Franklin St. Tel. 586-1000.

⭐ If the Red Dog is typical of the miners' turn-of-the-century watering holes, then the nearby Alaskan Hotel & Bar was where the privileged class drank. Many of them still swap pleasantries here today. Reminiscent of a bygone era, this lounge is truly elegant, with its upholstered furnishings, stained wood and brass decor, imitation stained glass, upstairs balcony, and long bar. The piano is 19th century, but the beautiful Wurlitzer and big-screen television are admittedly of more recent vintage. Live entertainment is featured on a new stage.

THE PENTHOUSE, on the top floor of the Senate Bldg., 175 S. Franklin St. Tel. 586-5656.

The Penthouse is a huge ballroom divided into two sections: a dance floor with an enormous video screen, and a four-sided bar surrounded by high stools. The Penthouse is frankly un-Alaskan—it's a place where you dress to impress. Disc jockeys hold forth Wednesday through Sunday from 8pm to 2am.
Admission: Free Wed–Thurs, $2 Fri–Sat.

Other Possibilities

Elsewhere downtown, you'll find jazz weekends at **The Fiddlehead** restaurant; a light rock combo playing dance music at **The Diggings** in the Prospector Hotel; a lounge singer in the Westmark-Juneau's **Woodcarver Room;** and a piano bar in the Baranof Hotel's **Bubble Room.**
There's also a proliferation of skid-row bars along South Franklin and Front

Streets—you'll quickly recognize them by the inebriated locals stumbling as they exit. If you *must* absorb some of this local flavor, the **Rendezvous,** 184 S. Franklin St., is a hangout for ships' crews, and the **Triangle Club,** 251 Front St., is the most infamous.

Out in the Mendenhall Valley, where half of Juneau's population makes its home, there are a few more lounges. **The Sandbar,** 2055 Jordan Ave. (tel. 789-3411), is Juneau's best blue-collar country-western venue, with Stetson-hatted musicians playing most nights and occasional strip shows during the after-work happy hour.

EASY EXCURSIONS

One voyage most visitors thoroughly enjoy is a trip south down the Stephens Passage to ✪ **Tracy Arm,** a long, fingerlike fjord 50 miles from Juneau. The inlet, contained within the Tracy Arm–Fords Terror Wilderness Area, is fed by spectacular glaciers and is a good place to spot seals, whales, and porpoises.

Full-day cruises offered by **Tracy Arm Glacier Cruises,** P.O. Box 20438, Juneau, AK 99802 (tel. 907/586-3311), depart from Juneau at 11am and return at 10pm; they run $130 and include two hot meals. Half-day trips, including one way by seaplane, are $180.

A similar trip offered by **Alaska's Glacier Bay Tours and Cruises,** 76 Egan Dr., Suite 130, Juneau, AK 99801 (tel. 907/463-5510), leaves Juneau at 8am and returns at 5:30pm; it costs $99 for adults ($59 for children 12 and under) including lunch. The half-day trip, including one way by seaplane, is $164 ($114 for children).

Alaska Rainforest Tours, 369 S. Franklin St., Suite 200, Juneau, AK 99801 (tel. 907/463-3466), also offers a 10-hour Tracy Arm cruise, with an early-morning departure and including lunch only, for $140.

If you plan to head north from Juneau to Skagway, consider Westours' **Lynn Canal Tour** aboard the *Fairweather.* The 4½-hour cruise, offered mid-May to mid-September, is available one way ($139) or round-trip ($199), with return to Juneau via air. Note that the ferry makes the same Juneau–Skagway trip, without the luxury frills, for $24 one way.

ADMIRALTY ISLAND   Admiralty Island National Monument, encompassing all but a small northern spur of the 1,709-square-mile island across Stephens Passage from Douglas Island, preserves the land that Tlingit Indians know as Xootsnoowu (*Hoots*-new-woo), Fortress of Bears. On densely forested Admiralty Island the huge Alaskan brown bear outnumbers its most dangerous foe—man. Some naturalists estimate, in fact, that there is one bear per square mile of land area.

The **Pack Creek Bear Preserve** on the island's northeastern shore is considered the best place to view the grizzlies of Xootsnoowu. Individuals and groups of up to 12 can obtain permits to visit the site—accessible only by small boat—from June 1 to September 10, between 9am and 9pm. A sandspit and observatory tower provide safe viewing of the huge creatures. A ranger is on site throughout the summer.

A great variety of other wildlife also populates this pristine wilderness. There are no regularly scheduled trips to the island; visits are normally prearranged and are by charter boat or plane. For information, contact Admiralty National Monument Headquarters, 8461 Old Dairy Rd., Juneau, AK 99801 (tel. 907/586-8790), or the U.S. Forest Service Information Center, Centennial Hall, 101 Egan Dr., Juneau, AK 99801 (tel. 907/586-8751).

The Forest Service, while discouraging overuse of the fragile ecosystem, has improved access to the island's natural wonders by creating the **Kootznoowoo Wilderness** and the **Admiralty Lakes Recreation Area,** some 110,000 acres accessible by canoe or kayak on lakes, rivers, and portages. Seven primitive Forest Service cabins, out of 16 on the island, are within the recreation area. They must be reserved in advance (at $20 a night) by visiting the Forest Service at Juneau's Centennial Building. Visitors are warned that the risks of bear attack, exposure to storms, and geographical disorientation are very real on Admiralty Island.

Within the recreation area is the **Thayer Lake Wilderness Lodge,** one of several well-known fishing lodges on the island. Located about 50 air miles due south of Juneau, it offers all meals and lodging plus fully guided lake and stream trout fishing for $130 per day (children 3–8 are charged half price), two-day minimum, transportation not included. Private cabins are also available at $90 (with a wood stove) or $105 (with a gas stove) per day. Service is seasonal: June 1 to September 10 only. Contact the lodge at P.O. Box 211614, Juneau, AK 99821 (tel. 907/789-5646), in summer; or P.O. Box 5416, Ketchikan, AK 99901 (tel. 907/225-3343), in winter.

Whalers' Cove Sport Fishing Lodge, in Killisnoo Harbor at Angoon, about 10 air miles south of Thayer Lake, accommodates up to 24 guests in 11 units, including five beachfront cabins. They're served by a fleet of charter boats. The spacious lodge also has a lounge and hot tub. All-inclusive package rates, including full board and daily guided fishing trips, are $2,695 per person for seven days and seven nights. For more information: P.O. Box 101, Angoon, AK 99820 (tel. 907/788-3123, or toll free 800/423-3123).

A third lodge, at Funter Bay on the northwest edge of Admiralty Island, is the **Admiralty Inn,** which serves a maximum of eight people interested in salmon and halibut fishing, crabbing, and photography. Rates start at $1,950 for five nights, with discounts for early booking. Contact the lodge at 1414 Mary Ellen Way, Juneau, AK 99801 (tel. 907/789-3263).

There's only one town on Admiralty Island, the Tlingit village of **Angoon** (pop. about 640). The ferry *LeConte* stops here twice a week; otherwise transportation is by floatplane or charter boat. Angoon is situated on the west coast of the island at the mouth of scenic but turbulent Kootznahoo Inlet, a maze of wooded islets, reefs, and channels that leads to Mitchell Bay and the cross-Admiralty canoe trail. Salmon fishing supplements subsistence hunting and gathering (shellfish, seaweed, and berries) to support the population in this most traditional of Tlingit communities in southeast Alaska. Angoon means "village on the beaver trail."

If you intend to stay in Angoon, a bed-and-breakfast establishment called the **Favorite Bay Inn,** P.O. Box 101, Angoon, AK 99820 (tel. 907/788-3123, or toll free 800/423-3123), will accommodate you for $55 single, $65 double. The owners operate a booking service for guides and transportation services. There is also a small motel: the **Kootznahoo Inlet Lodge,** P.O. Box 134, Angoon, AK 99820 (tel. 907/788-3501), with a dining room and 11 units, including six with kitchenette, priced at $59 single, $69 double. The local tax is 2%. You'll find a public **campground** near the ferry landing, three miles from town.

There is one café in town, **The Surf** (tel. 788-3535). Angoon is a dry community, which means you cannot purchase liquor locally.

If you appreciate Native crafts, Angoon is a good place to buy blankets, moccasins, and handmade beadwork. Many of these items are for sale at a shop in the Municipal Building. The nearby Community Services Building contains the headquarters of Admiralty Island National Monument (tel. 788-3166).

CHICHAGOF ISLAND The Chatham Strait separates Admiralty Island from Chichagof Island. (Together with Baranof Island, south of Chichagof, they comprise the "ABC islands.") **Tenakee Springs,** on the north side of Tenakee Inlet near the island's east coast, has a permanent population of about 140, most of them retirees who regularly take advantage of the therapeutic hot (106°–108°F) sulfur spring for which the town is named. A bathhouse on the waterfront was reconstructed after a devastating Thanksgiving 1984 storm. There's no mixed bathing—women use the spring from 9am to 2pm and 6 to 10pm, and men all other hours—which discourages honeymooners.

Tenakee is intentionally remote. Only a fire truck and an old oil truck are allowed on the one street, Tenakee Avenue, two miles long and 4–12 feet wide. But the *LeConte* ferry stops twice a week, and Wings of Alaska flies two round-trips daily from Juneau ($60).

If you want to stay over, you could do worse than the **Tenakee Inn and Tavern,** a lovely Victorian-style hotel between the ferry terminal and boat harbor, opened in 1985 by the same Adams family that operates the Alaskan Hotel & Bar in Juneau. Singles with shared bath are $40, and doubles run $45, plus 6% tax; rooms with private bath are $5–$10 more. All rooms have kitchenette facilities. Bunkhouse beds go for just $15. Write to P.O. Box 54, Tenakee Springs, AK 99841 (tel. 907/736-2241 or 736-9238).

You can also rent efficiency cabins on the beach (bring your own sleeping bag) for $25 a night from **Snyder Mercantile Co.,** P.O. Box 505, Tenakee Springs, AK 99841 (tel. 907/736-2205). There's a primitive **campground** at Indian River, two miles east of town, but you'll have to share it with bears. The **Blue Moon Café,** next to the dock, serves meals.

The sheltered village of **Hoonah**—literally, "place where the north wind doesn't blow"—is a Tlingit settlement in Port Frederick on the north shore of Chichagof Island, closer to Glacier Bay than to Juneau. About 860 people, most of them involved in fishing or logging, make their homes here. According to Tlingit tradition, Hoonah was founded centuries ago by tribespeople fleeing the advance of ice into Glacier Bay.

The *LeConte* stops three times a week. But the village's only public lodging—the 28-unit **Huna Totem Lodge,** Hoonah, AK 99829—was closed in 1992 seeking new management. **Mary's Inn** (tel. 945-3228) is a popular local café. The local tax is 4%.

Ask directions to the **Hoonah Indian Association Cultural Center** (tel. 945-3600), a small hillside museum containing Tlingit artifacts donated by local residents. It's open Monday through Friday from 9am to 5pm and by request. The **Glacier Winds** gift shop has excellent local craft items.

Tiny **Elfin Cove,** population 28 (at last count), is located near Chichagof Island's northwest extremity. The ferry doesn't call here, but for those who charter boats or planes or have their own transportation, there are several lodges with weekly fishing packages May to September. Contact the **Elfin Cove Sportfishing Lodge,** P.O. Box 44, Elfin Cove, AK 99825 (tel. 907/239-2212), in summer, or P.O. Box 4007, Renton, WA 98057 (tel. 206/228-7092), in winter, which hosts 10–12 guests at $2,850 per person for six nights; the **Tanaku Lodge,** General Delivery, Elfin Cove, AK 99825 (tel. 907/239-2205), a new cedar lodge with a hot tub, priced at $1,395 for five nights; or **Louie's Place,** P.O. Box 704, Juneau, AK 99802 (tel. 907/586-2032), a vacation home which accommodates four to six at $350 per week.

6. GLACIER BAY NATIONAL PARK

70 miles W of Juneau

GETTING THERE By Plane   The only access to Glacier Bay is by air or private boat. **Alaska Airlines** (tel. toll free 800/426-0333) offers daily late-afternoon jet connections from Juneau, mid-May to mid-September only. Flight time is 20 minutes. **Glacier Bay Airways** (tel. 907/697-2249, or 789-9009 in Juneau) and **Air Excursions** (tel. 907/697-2375) both have daily scheduled service between Juneau and Gustavus, with flightseeing tours and connections anywhere between Skagway, Elfin Cove, and Angoon. **L.A.B. Flying Service** (tel. 907/697-2203, or toll-free 800/426-0333) and **Skagway Air Service** (tel. 907/983-2219 in Skagway) offer daily service year-round.

A **shuttle bus** operates between the Gustavus airport and the Glacier Bay Lodge at Bartlett Cove (for $8); it will let you off at any intermediate point. **TLC Taxi** (tel. 697-2239) charges $18 for the first person, $3 for each additional person, between town and Bartlett Cove. Some of the accommodations in Gustavus also provide transportation to and from the cove.

By Ferry   No ferries run to this corner of the southeast.

ESSENTIALS Orientation   Airport and boat docks are in the hamlet of Gustavus (pop. about 150), 10 miles from Bartlett Cove via a graded gravel road. The residents of Gustavus live in wood houses scattered amid pasture and meadows sprinkled with wildflowers in early summer. The community has a post office, chapel, school, grocery store, and two cafés.

Information   The **Gustavus Visitors Association,** P.O. Box 167, Gustavus, AK 99826, will send a free brochure, with a map and a listing of local businesses, on request. For park information, contact **Glacier Bay National Park and Preserve,** Park Headquarters, Gustavus, AK 99826 (tel. 907/697-2230). Maps, nautical charts, and brochures are available at the visitor center opposite the Bartlett Cove dock.

Fast Facts   There is no bank, so visitors should plan on taking care of their financial needs before arrival. For emergency services, phone 911.

A trip through Glacier Bay is a trip through natural time, a brief but powerful glimpse of the irrepressible forces of creation. Glacier Bay was among the first of Alaska's federally protected lands, established in 1925 as Glacier Bay National Monument. In 1980, when Congress passed the Alaska National Interest Lands Conservation Act, it increased the protected area to 3.3 million acres (4,400 square miles) and changed its status to "national park and preserve." (The preserve, where hunting, trapping, and subsistence agriculture are allowed, comprises some 57,000 acres at the mouth of the Alsek River in the park's northwest corner.)

Only two centuries ago—the blinking of an eye in geologic terms—massive glaciers up to 4,000 feet thick occupied the modern bay's entire 800-foot-deep channel, all the way to its outlet on Icy Strait opposite Chichagof Island. In 1794 an exploration party sent by Capt. George Vancouver found an impassable wall of "compact solid mountains of ice" blocking what is now the entrance to the bay; yet by the time of naturalist John Muir's first visit in 1879, the ice had retreated over 45 miles. Since then glacial regression has unveiled a 65-mile-long, Y-shaped bay—and still the retreat continues.

As receding glaciers uncover land cloaked for centuries by ice, nature reclaims it. Glacier Bay visitors who travel up the bay by water, northward toward the existing great tidewater glaciers, have a unique opportunity to observe this reclamation process. The most popular trip, aboard the motor vessel *Spirit of Adventure,* begins in dense spruce forest at Bartlett Cove, where park headquarters is located. Voyagers traverse 200 years in time as they travel first past hardwood forest of alder and willow, then sedge and horsetail tundra, and finally to barren rock and glacial moraine. Here, where the Muir or Riggs or Grand Pacific Glacier spews enormous chunks of ice into the frigid water while hundreds of seals bark their approval, it's difficult not to feel awed, even humbled, by the might of nature.

The glaciers, of course, are the primary reason that people visit Glacier Bay. The national park and preserve contain 16 tidewater glaciers (those whose faces reach the sea) and myriad other, mostly nameless glaciers sliding down the flanks of 15,320-foot Mount Fairweather and other high peaks. Not all of them are retreating; those on the stormy Gulf of Alaska coast, west of the Fairweather Range, are slowly advancing.

Glaciers are frigid rivers formed when heavy snowfall compresses under its own weight to form ice, which then is caused by temperature, slope, and gravity to flow downhill. The face of a glacier where it reaches the water dwarfs even large cruise ships: It can be a few hundred yards to several miles wide, and is commonly 150–200 feet high. Many times each day large chunks of ice break off the face—the process is called "calving"—and float away as small icebergs.

The ice floes attract harbor seals by the hundreds and bald eagles by the dozens. Elsewhere in Glacier Bay, humpback whales breach with thunderous claps and colorful puffins flutter around their burrows on bird-filled islets. Some 40 varieties of mammals and more than 220 species of birds have been recorded in the park; naturalists recommend that serious animal- and birdwatchers come armed with binoculars.

Binoculars don't help much, though, in pouring rain and dense fog. Glacier Bay gets its share of both. What Harry Fielding Reid wrote during an 1892 expedition to Glacier Bay still applies today: "We have concluded that there are many infallible signs of rain in this region. If the sun shines, if the stars appear, if there are clouds, or if there are none; these are all sure indications. If the barometer falls, it will rain; if the barometer rises, it will rain; if the barometer remains steady, it will continue to rain."

Annual rainfall, depending on which part of the park you're in, varies from 55 to 125 inches, with an additional 12 feet of snowfall. Bartlett Cove experiences summertime highs in the 60s, winter lows in the 20s, but the upper reaches of the bay can be 20°F cooler in both seasons. You can expect some rain to fall, on average, 228 days a year. Your chances of clear skies are best in May and June; as summer progresses into autumn, the probability of bad weather grows.

WHAT TO SEE & DO

A **boat cruise** is the highlight of any visit to Glacier Bay. Accompanied by a National Park Service ranger/naturalist (and 100 or so other passengers), you'll cruise up the bay past island bird rookeries and floating icebergs to enormous tidewater glaciers. With luck, you'll see some whales along the way.

The ✪ *Spirit of Adventure* leaves the Bartlett Cove dock daily from May 24 to September 13 promptly at 7am daily and returns at about 3:30pm after voyaging up the west arm of Glacier Bay. Tickets are $144.50 for adults and $72 for children 2–11, lunch included. Beer and wine are cheaper (by 50¢) on the boat than at the lodge. The vessel is heated, but most passengers like to spend a fair amount of time with camera or binoculars on deck, so dress warmly.

Sometimes these trips can get more exciting than advertised. In June 1986 a tour boat actually collided with a humpback whale that suddenly surfaced about 15 feet from the boat. There were no injuries either to the whale or to any of the passengers.

Some private operators offer overnight sightseeing trips up Glacier Bay's 65-mile west arm to Tarr and Johns Hopkins Inlets. **Grand Pacific Charters,** P.O. Box 5, Gustavus, AK 99826 (tel. 907/697-2288), has two staterooms on its 42-foot yacht. Half- or full-day whale-watching trips to Glacier Bay are also available. Rates are $160 per person for a full day or $90 per person for a half day. **Fairweather Fishing and Guide Service,** P.O. Box 164, Gustavus, AK 99826 (tel. 907/697-2335 or 735-2253), specializes in whale-watching and wildlife photography.

Many of the Gustavus innkeepers—among them the Gustavus Inn, the Glacier Bay Country Inn, and the Puffin—offer packages that include lodging, cruise, meals, and transfers.

SPORTS & RECREATION

FISHING The Bartlett and Salmon Rivers and some small inland lakes can be good for Dolly Varden and cutthroat trout and river-run salmon in season. Halibut and salmon are the main game fish in Glacier Bay and Icy Strait. Remember that an Alaska fishing license is required even though the park is federally operated.

Grand Pacific Charters, P.O. Box 5, Gustavus, AK 99826 (tel. 907/697-2288); **Gustavus Marine Charters,** P.O. Box 81, Gustavus, AK 99826 (tel. 907/697-2233); and **Mike Mills Charter Service,** P.O. Box 151, Gustavus, AK 99826 (tel. 907/697-2236), operate private charters from Glacier Bay, providing all tackle and bait. Their seasons run May through September. Rates vary according to number of people and size of boat; figure $100 per person (minimum of two) for a half day, $180 for a full day, including preparing and freezing your catch.

HIKING & BACKPACKING There are only two formal trails in Glacier Bay National Park, both at Bartlett Cove. The **Beach and Nature Trail** winds through a spruce rain forest and returns to the lodge via the rocky bay shore. A naturalist leads a tour along this mile-long trail at 2pm daily. The **Bartlett River Trail** skirts a tidal lagoon, then cuts through the forest to the river estuary, 1½ miles from the lodge. Birds and small mammals are usually seen on this route.

Outside of Bartlett Cove, steep rocky slopes, dense underbrush, glacial streams, and tides that fluctuate as much as 25 feet daily make backpacking treacherous. Be sure to read the Forest Service publication "Hazards Ashore and Afloat." No open fires are permitted; you must carry your own portable stove and white-gas fuel bottle, as well as water. Be sure to include warm clothing, rain gear, and insect repellent in your pack. Park rangers sell topographical maps on backcountry areas. Bring a compass and know how to use it.

The *Spirit of Adventure* will drop you off or pick you up anywhere along the shore of Glacier Bay for a per-stop charge of $24 above the normal tour cost. Other private charter-boat and floatplane operators can also provide backcountry transportation.

Backpacking expeditions are sometimes arranged by **Alaska Travel Adventures,** 9085 Glacier Hwy., Juneau, AK 99801 (tel. 907/789-0052). The same group also leads occasional cross-country ski trips in winter.

HUNTING Capturing, injuring, or killing animals is strictly prohibited in the park. Firearms are allowed only in the backcountry, and then for emergency use only. Special regulations apply to the preserve along the Alsek River, where sport hunting for moose and bear is permitted in late summer and fall. Consult a ranger or write the park superintendent for details.

KAYAKING Among outdoor types, this is the most popular way to see the park. Kayaks are preferable to canoes because they ride lower and therefore can buck wind and waves more easily. Keep your distance from floating ice and tidewater glaciers, whose calving can create waves that will swamp a small craft and throw you into 34°F water. Park rangers at Bartlett Cove can provide nautical charts, tide tables, and local knowledge of hazardous areas.

Five saltwater wilderness areas have been designated within the park for the use of self-propelled boats only. These areas are unique in the national park system; rangers will direct you to them.

As with backpackers, kayakers can be dropped anywhere by the park boats for a $24 charge; there is no additional fee for carrying a kayak or other equipment.

You can rent two-person kayaks for $40 a day (discounts available for rentals of four days or longer) from **Glacier Bay Sea Kayaks,** P.O. Box 240F, Gustavus, AK 99826 (tel. 907/697-2257). **Spirit Walker Expeditions,** P.O. Box 122, Gustavus, AK 99826 (tel. 907/697-2266), offers guided trips through Icy Strait and along the coast of Chichagof Island from May through September. Day trips are $94 per person, including lunch; all-inclusive overnight trips of three to seven days average $200 per day per person.

Alaska Travel Adventures (see above) and **Chilkat Guides,** P.O. Box 170, Haines, AK 99827 (tel. 907/766-2409) operate thrilling 9- to 13-day river-raft trips down the Tatshenshini and Alsek Rivers from the Yukon Territory. Prices start around $1,300. If you've never been on a raft before, this is probably not the place to start!

WHERE TO STAY

There is no room tax in Gustavus or Glacier Bay.

EXPENSIVE

GLACIER BAY LODGE, P.O. Box 199, Gustavus, AK 99826. Tel. 907/ 697-2225. Reservation requests to 520 Pike St., Suite 1610, Seattle, WA 98101 (tel. 206/623-7110, or toll free 800/622-2042; fax 206/623-7809). 55 rms.
$ **Rates:** $115–$126 single; $138–$149 double; $26 dormitory bed. MC, V.
Closed: Sept 16–May 21.

Most package tourists and many independent travelers park their bags here, the only lodging available in the park. Located at Bartlett Cove, the lodge—constructed of natural wood—is set in a spruce and hemlock rain forest. Boardwalks lead to the rooms, interconnected cabins that are adequate for the location, as most visitors will want to spend their time out-of-doors. Each room has a table, chair, and beds for two to four.

Between the restaurant and the lounge is a plush seating area around a large fireplace. An information board stands by the door, announcing nature walks and other activities. Upstairs, next to a National Park Service wildlife exhibit, films and lectures are presented nightly. The boat dock is about a 300-yard walk south on a well-lit path. Visitors who consider it important to be at the center of the action will be very happy here.

Dining/Entertainment: The busy restaurant in the main lodge building has a diverse menu. A buffet-style breakfast is served from 6 to 7am for $8.50 (or $4.50 for a continental), and a regular breakfast menu is available from 7:30 to 9am. Lunches, served from 11:30am to 1:30pm, include sandwiches and salads priced $5–$12, while full steak or seafood dinners, served from 5:30 to 9:30pm, are in the $17–$22 range. Budget- and weight-watchers are disappointed to find, however, that lunch offerings are unavailable at dinner—and the next-closest restaurant is 10 miles away in Gustavus. The Icebreaker Lounge is open from 5:30pm to midnight.

Services: Rooms available for nonsmoking and for disabled guests.

Facilities: Gift shop, nightly films and lectures.

MODERATE

GLACIER BAY COUNTRY INN, P.O. Box 5, Gustavus, AK 99826. Tel. 907/697-2288. Fax 907/697-2289. In winter contact P.O. Box 2557, St. George, UT 87441 (tel. 801/673-8480; fax 801/673-8481). 9 rms (8 with bath).

$ Rates (including all meals): $139 single; $218 double. Additional adult $69 extra; additional child 3–11 $54 extra. AE, MC, V.

⭐ Al and Annie Unrein's rambling inn, which opened in 1986, is in the center of a 160-acre farmstead. Al himself built the home as a labor of love (he even milled his own wood!). It has log-beam ceilings, large porches, and dormer windows. A circular staircase leads from the library to a turret with a sitting room. There's a telescope in the lounge. Outside, the root cellar is covered by sweet hybrid strawberries. Eventually the Unreins plan to have their own airstrip.

All the rooms, decorated with a garden, nautical, or forestry theme, have thermopedic beds with flannel sheets. Gourmet meals are prepared by a graduate of the Culinary Institute of America; dinners (at $24) are also served to non–inn guests by reservation. The lodge offers free use of bicycles and has its own boat, a 42-foot Sunnfjord, to take guests on sightseeing and fishing trips.

GUSTAVUS INN AT GLACIER BAY, P.O. Box 31, Gustavus, AK 99826. Tel. 907/697-2254. Fax 907/697-2291. In winter, contact 7920 Outlook Dr., Prairie Village, KS 66208 (tel. 913/649-5220). 14 rms (8 with bath).

$ Rates (including full board): $120 per adult (double occupancy); $60 per child 4–12. AE, MC, V. **Closed:** Sept 16–May 14.

⭐ David and JoAnn Lesh's big gray farmhouse, an original Alaskan homestead, has been totally refurbished to offer full-board packages. There are comfortable guest rooms, a homey dining room, a six-seat wine bar, and a library. Outside, on the five-acre property, are a children's playground in a big grassy field, a large vegetable garden and greenhouse, and a huge wine and root cellar.

The inn's food is famous—so much so that Juneau residents frequently charter a plane to fly in just for dinner. Local catches of salmon, halibut, and crab are supplemented by home-grown vegetables and wild berry pies. Visitors pay $26 for a full-course dinner (included in the price for inn guests). The rates also include transfers to and from the airport and Bartlett Cove and use of bicycles and fishing poles.

W. T. FUGARWE LODGE, P.O. Box 27, Gustavus, AK 99826. Tel. 907/697-2244. Fax 907/697-2373. In winter, contact P.O. Box 459, Georgetown, CO 80444 (tel. 303/623-7108; fax 303/569-2632). 8 rms (none with bath).

Transportation: Free transfers from the airport.

$ Rates (including full board): $110 per person. MC, V. **Closed:** Sept 16–May. Ask him and owner J. L. ("Doc") Bailey will gladly relate to you the "Indian legend" for which he named his inn. Suffice it to explain that "W. T." stands for "where the." If the name strikes your funny bone, you'll be ready for the back-slapping humor shared by Bailey and other former airline pilots who frequently visit. Several world records have been set by guests fishing off the lodge's three salmon and halibut boats. Basic rates for charter fishing are $100 per half day (4½ hours). The lodge also offers flightseeing charters on a private Cessna for $140 an hour and rents bicycles.

The lodge itself resembles nothing so much as a hangar. The large but simply appointed rooms accommodate two to four guests in double beds or bunks. Private toilets are attached, but showers are down the hall. The hearty meals include homemade breads and soups, which are served family style in a cozy dining room.

INEXPENSIVE

GOOD RIVER BED & BREAKFAST, P.O. Box 37, Gustavus, AK 99826. Tel. 907/697-2241. 2 rms (both with bath).
$ **Rates** (including breakfast): May–Sept, $60 single; $75 double. Oct–Apr, $40 single; $50 double. MC, V.

This spacious log home provides comfortable beds, modern baths, home-cooked breakfasts, and free use of bicycles. Those who prefer more self-sufficiency can ask about "Beyond Good River," a nearby fully furnished log cabin with electricity for cooking, but no running water.

A PUFFIN'S BED AND BREAKFAST, P.O. Box 3F, Gustavus, AK 99826. Tel. 907/697-2260, or toll free 800/478-2258 in Alaska. Fax 907/697-2258. 5 cabins (all with bath).
$ **Rates** (including full breakfast): $40–$65 single; $60–$65 double. Additional adult $15 extra; additional child 2–12 $8 extra. MC, V.

⑤ Five modern cabins with wood heat or electricity surround a central lodge nestled amid spruce and hemlock trees. Sandy and Chuck Schroth offer free van service from the airport, provide complimentary bicycles, and make all touring and kayaking arrangements for guests. Glacier Bay Puffin Charters offers fishing trips and sightseeing.

SALMON RIVER RENTALS, P.O. Box 13, Gustavus, AK 99826. Tel. 907/697-2245. 10 cabins (none with bath).
$ **Rates:** $50 per cabin per night, $250 per week. MC, V. **Closed:** Sept 21–May 19.

Bring your own sleeping bag to spread on a bed or couch in one of the rustic housekeeping cabins. Each cabin holds one to four guests and has a wood-burning stove, electric hotplate, outdoor grill, all eating and cooking utensils and towels, as well as a sink and a table with four chairs. Restroom facilities and showers are in a central building.

WHALESONG LODGE, P.O. Box 5, Gustavus, AK 99826. Tel. 907/697-2288. Fax 907/697-2289. In winter, contact P.O. Box 2557, St. George, UT 87441 (tel. 801/673-8480; fax 801/673-8481).
$ **Rates** (including breakfast): Condominiums, $300 per day for one to three days, $250 per day for four to six days, $225 per day for a week or longer. Bed-and-breakfast, $70 per person. Hostel beds, $32 per person. AE, MC, V.

Scheduled to open in 1993 is this new lodge, owned by Glacier Bay Country Inn proprietors Al and Annie Unrein. It is composed of three distinct units: two three-bedroom condominium units, each with large living room and fully equipped kitchen; several bed-and-breakfast rooms with shared baths; and separate men's and women's bunkrooms, the least expensive accommodations in Gustavus short of pitching a tent.

CAMPGROUNDS

Backpackers and kayakers can set up tents and camp free of charge at the **Bartlett Cove Campground,** about half a mile south of the Glacier Bay Lodge. A bear-proof food cache, wood, and firepits are provided, but there's a 14-day limit on stays. You can shower and use the laundry facilities at the lodge, where you must go for check-in and orientation.

WHERE TO DINE

HITCHING POST, west side of Salmon River north of Main Rd. Tel. 697-2206.
Cuisine: AMERICAN. **Reservations:** Not required.
$ Prices: Dinner $10–$16. MC, V.
Open: Dinner only, Tues–Sun 5:30–10:30pm.
Charcoal-broiled steaks, including tenderloin filets, are the specialty of this rustic restaurant, a bit off the beaten path on the Salmon River. Lighter eaters can opt for a burger and leave room for homemade pie and ice cream.

OPEN GATE CAFE, ¼ Mile, Dock Rd. Tel. 697-2227.
Cuisine: AMERICAN.
$ Prices: Lunches $4–$7; dinners $9–$14. MC, V.
Open: Mon and Wed–Thurs 6:30am–4pm, Tues and Fri–Sat 6:30am–9pm.
Lunches at this local favorite include homemade breads and pastries, deli sandwiches, and burgers. Light dinners include stir-fried vegetables and pepper steaks. The café is located off the Main Road en route to the Gustavus dock.

AN EASY EXCURSION TO YAKUTAT

The small town of Yakutat (pop. about 450) is a gateway to the Dry Bay/Alsek River edge of Glacier Bay National Park and Preserve, 50 miles southeast, and to the Yakutat Bay/Malaspina Glacier precincts of Wrangell–St. Elias National Park and Preserve, fewer than 20 miles northwest.

A Tlingit fishing town, Yakutat has much to attract sport fishermen and nature lovers. You can rent a car and drive to the acclaimed trout grounds of the Situk River and Harlequin Lake, where there are U.S. Forest Service primitive **cabins** ($20 a night). More cabins are at Dry Bay, abutting Glacier Bay National Preserve. Contact the U.S. Forest Service (tel. 784-3359) for full information. **Gulf Air Taxi,** P.O. Box 37, Yakutat, AK 99689 (tel. 784-3240), can fly you there. Halibut and salmon, crab, and scallops are the most commonly taken ocean fish. **Yakutat Bay & River Charters** (tel. 784-3415) will arrange trips, and the Alaska Department of Fish and Game (tel. 784-3222) can offer additional information.

Yakutat is the home of the rare glacier or "blue" bear. Believed to have become isolated from other black bears during the Ice Ages, this creature adapted to its treeless situation by acquiring a protective pale-bluish color. Snow geese and trumpeter swans are frequently seen along this stretch of shoreline.

Across Yakutat Bay, the Malaspina Glacier covers 850 square miles, making it the largest in North America. It's within the **Wrangell–St. Elias National Park,** which maintains a Yakutat District office (tel. 784-3295).

Alaska Airlines (tel. 784-3366) flies through Yakutat twice daily—in the late morning from Juneau en route to Cordova and Anchorage, and in the late afternoon from those same destinations en route to Juneau. If the skies are clear, the view of the Malaspina Glacier is spectacular.

There are two year-round accommodations in Yakutat, both with restaurants and lounges. My choice is the **Glacier Bear Lodge,** P.O. Box 303, Yakutat, AK 99689 (tel. 907/784-3202), which has 30 rooms with private bath. Rates vary from $70 to $130, depending on whether you desire a full-meal package.

7. HAINES

90 miles N of Juneau, 15 miles S of Skagway,
775 road miles E of Anchorage

GETTING THERE By Plane Haines-based **L.A.B. Flying Service,** 480

Main St. (tel. 907/766-2222, or toll free 800/426-0333), is the Alaska Airlines commuter carrier. L.A.B.'s routes cover the Lynn Canal area from Juneau to Skagway to Glacier Bay. **Haines Airways,** P.O. Box 61, Haines, AK 99827 (tel. 907/766-2646), and **Wings of Alaska,** 574 Second Ave. (tel. 907/766-2030, or toll free 800/478-9464 in Alaska), have similar routes. **Skagway Air Service,** P.O. Box 357, Skagway, AK 99840 (tel. 907/983-2218), and **Glacier Bay Airways,** P.O. Box 1, Gustavus, AK 99826 (tel. 907/697-2249), also fly into Haines. The airport is 3½ miles west of downtown, on Chilkat Inlet. The various carriers will provide transportation to motels.

By Bus   **Alaskon Express** connects Haines with Anchorage, Fairbanks, Skagway, and Whitehorse, Yukon Territory, three times a week, May 26 to September 13. Buses leave Haines at 8:15am on Sunday, Tuesday, and Friday and make afternoon connections at Haines Junction. Buses arrive in Haines at 6:30pm on Monday, Thursday, and Saturday. The trip to Anchorage takes 35 hours (at a cost of $182, not including overnight lodging at Beaver Creek, Yukon Territory); to Skagway, 11 hours ($128); to Whitehorse, a little over 8 hours ($75). Purchase tickets in Haines at Wings of Alaska, 574 Second Ave. (tel. 907/766-2030). Alaskon Express is associated with Gray Line of Alaska (tel. toll free 800/544-2206).

By Car   The Haines Highway connects Haines with the Alaska Highway at Haines Junction, Yukon Territory, 150 miles or a four-hour drive northwest. The all-weather road (over three-quarters of it is paved) follows the old Dalton Trail to the Klondike. It's maintained year-round.

By Ferry   The **Alaska Marine Highway ferry terminal** (tel. 766-2111) is 4½ miles north of downtown Haines on Lutak Road, just before the cruise-ship dock. Each week seven northbound boats (to Skagway) and seven southbound boats call. The **Haines Street Car Co.** (tel. 766-2819) runs a shuttlebus service from town to the ferry terminal, meeting all arrivals and departures. The charge is $5 one way. **Haines Taxi** (tel. 766-3138) is the best alternative.

SPECIAL EVENTS   The year's big event in Haines is the **Southeast Alaska State Fair,** held the third week of August. What began as a Strawberry Festival in the early 1900s evolved in 1969 into the premier fair for all southeast Alaska and Canada's Yukon. It includes a five-day horse show, a logging carnival, miniature train rides, and outdoor entertainment of all types. Contact P.O. Box 385, Haines, AK 99827 (tel. 907/766-2478), for information. The fair also includes the week-long **Bald Eagle Music Festival,** where over 50 local musicians join headline artists. The 21-acre fairgrounds are on the south side of the Haines Highway near its junction with Main Street, about halfway between downtown and the airport.

The **Alcan 200** international snow-machine rally and **Dalton Trail Sled Dog Races** take place in late January. The **Fourth of July** is a big day, with raft races, logging events, parades, and a carnival atmosphere. Other special events include the **Master Anglers Fishing Tournament** (the last two weeks of August) and **Alaska Day** (October 18), with a parade, costume ball, and pioneer contests on the anniversary of Alaska's 1867 purchase from Russia.

The quiet town of Haines on the northern Lynn Canal is rich in scenery and Native traditions. Its approximately 2,000 people, though they live only 15 miles from bustling Skagway, have a relaxed pace of life, with an economy more attuned to fishing, logging, and the arts than to seasonal tourism.

The Chilkat Valley is the site of the world's largest American bald eagle preserve, where as many as 3,500 of the national symbol gather in the autumn months to feast on a late run of chum salmon. There is a tribal arts center at historic Fort William H. Seward where the Chilkat clan of Tlingit Indians carve totem poles and perform tribal dances. Local art galleries feature local craftsmanship. A network of rivers and trails cater to fishermen, hikers, and cross-country skiers.

Set against a backdrop of forested peaks and glaciers, Haines occupies a narrow portage in a peninsula at the head of the Lynn Canal, between the mouths of two rivers, the Chilkat and the Chilkoot. Visited many times in the 19th century by white traders and trappers, it was established as a mission town in 1881 after Presbyterian missionary S. Hall Young and naturalist John Muir conferred with local Tlingit chieftains to determine an appropriate site. Called Dehshuh ("end of the trail") by Tlingits, Chilkoot by traders, it was renamed Haines in honor of the Presbyterian home missions secretary.

Haines's economy grew on fishing and gold mining. Several salmon canneries were operating here by the 1890s. The Porcupine Mining District produced thousands of dollars of gold in the early 1900s, and the Dalton Trail—named after the notorious Jack Dalton, who charged an outrageous fee to guide people over the trail to the Klondike and posted armed guards to prevent nonpayers from using it—began in Haines. Lumber and tourism have replaced gold mining as key industries, but fishing (mainly gill-net salmon and halibut) remains important.

Fort Seward was built by the U.S. Army as a permanent military post a half mile south of Haines at Port Chilkoot in 1904. Renamed Chilkoot Barracks in 1922, it was the only army base in Alaska until the outbreak of World War II. After the war it was deactivated and sold to a group of veterans who dreamed of starting their own town. Port Chilkoot merged with Haines in 1970; two years later the post was designated a National Historic Site.

Haines is drier than most other southeast towns, with an average annual precipitation of about 60 inches. The average July high temperature is 66°F (with extremes in the 80s); the average January low is 17°F (with extremes below −10°F). Spring and fall drizzle and consistent winter snowfall are the norms.

ORIENTATION

INFORMATION   Haines's very helpful **Visitor Information Center** shares a small wood cabin with the chamber of commerce, just off Second Avenue on Willard Street (P.O. Box 518), Haines, AK 99827 (tel. 907/766-2202 or 766-2234, or toll free 800/458-3579 in the U.S., 800/478-2268 in Canada's Yukon Territory and British Columbia). It's open daily from 8am to 8pm. For outdoor information, try the **Alaska Division of Parks** in the Gateway Building on Main Street (tel. 755-2292). If you plan to cross into Canada from Haines, you may want to contact **U.S. Customs** (tel. 766-2374) or **Canadian Customs** (tel. 766-2541).

CITY LAYOUT   Most of Haines faces east. It looks out on Portage Cove and the Chilkoot Inlet, which is the eastern arm of the Lynn Canal. The Haines Highway separates Haines proper (downtown) from Port Chilkoot (the fort); each is on its own low hill, with downtown a half mile north of the fort. Many businesses, including motels and restaurants, are within a couple of blocks' walk of Second Avenue and Main Street. The principal exceptions are those around the parade grounds at Fort Seward. Front Street (Beach Road), Second Avenue, and Third Avenue (Mud Bay Road) connect the two parts of town.

GETTING AROUND

Car rentals are available from **Hertz** at the Thunderbird Motel (tel. 766-2131), from **Avis** at the Halsingland Hotel (tel. 766-2733), and from **Eagle's Nest** at the Eagle's Nest Motel (tel. 766-2352).

Sockeye Cycle & Tours, located in the alley off Main Street, between Second and Third Avenues (tel. 766-2869), rents and services bicycles and runs bike tours for all ages.

FAST FACTS

Emergencies   In an emergency, call 911. For medical assistance, the Chilkat Valley Medical Center is on First Street (tel. 766-2521), adjacent to the Visitor Information Center.

Newspaper   Haines's *Chilkat Valley News* is published weekly.

Post Office   The post office is on the Haines Highway near Second Avenue.

WHAT TO SEE & DO

ATTRACTIONS IN TOWN

FORT WILLIAM H. SEWARD, Fort Seward Dr. at Portage St.

Otherwise known as Port Chilkoot, Fort Seward was the army regimental headquarters for all Alaska from 1904 to 1942. Two full companies plus detachments of headquarters and quartermaster personnel were assigned here. After the fort's deactivation in 1946, a group of American veterans bought the fort with the idea of creating a small-business cooperative. That idea faltered, but many of the families involved have succeeded in Haines as artists and entrepreneurs.

Pick up a walking-tour map of the fort from the visitors center or museum. And don't expect a walled fortress with sentries posted. Signs are being placed to commemorate many of the individual buildings, and there are plans to renovate some of the structures for tourist visitation.

In particular, you should visit the former hospital building, No. 13, on the southern side of the fort. It now houses the **Alaska Indian Arts Skill Center** (tel. 766-2160), where Tlingit artists tutor students in traditional arts like mask and totem pole carving, silver jewelry making, and blanket weaving. Visitors are welcome daily except Sunday from 9am to noon and 1 to 5pm. There is a display and sale room with excellent prices on quality woodcrafts.

Immediately behind No. 13 is the **Chilkat Center for the Arts** (tel. 766-2160), a barnlike building that was formerly the army's recreation hall. Completely renovated in 1967, it now has a modern 350-seat theater and ample meeting rooms and facilities for conventions. In summer the colorful Chilkat Dancers share the auditorium with a melodrama, *Lust for Dust* (see "Evening Entertainment," below).

The parade ground, at the center of the fort, is now the site of a replica of a small Tlingit community, **Totem Village.** The Hotel Hälsingland's nightly salmon bake is served in the Indian Tribal House.

Admission: Free.

Open: Fort grounds, daily 24 hours.

SHELDON MUSEUM AND CULTURAL CENTER, Main St. at First Ave. Tel. 766-2236.

The town museum has a fine collection of Tlingit artifacts, exhibits of Presbyterian mission and pioneer history, free Russian tea, and a book and gift store. I like the reconstructed shop of the pioneer who reputedly wore several pairs of glasses at once with this reasoning: "If one pair helps me see a little, more will help me see a lot." If you can't visit Haines between November and January, be sure to see the film *Last Stronghold of the Eagles.* The museum is named for longtime resident Steve Sheldon (1885–1960), who willed much of his collection to the museum.

Admission: $2; children under 18 free when accompanied by an adult.

Open: Mid-May to mid-Sept, daily 1–5pm; mid-Sept to mid-May, hours vary (call ahead).

THE EAGLES

For centuries, as far back as the Natives' earliest memories, eagles by the thousands have gathered on the Chilkat River in the fall and winter months to feast on chum salmon. To help protect them, the state created the 48,000-acre ✪ **Alaska Chilkat Bald Eagle Preserve** in 1982. Visitors can park their vehicles in turnouts at the side of the Haines Highway, 18–22 miles north of town at the "council grounds," and scan the trees and riverbanks with binoculars and cameras.

A particularly good time to scout for eagles is in November, when the resident population of about 200 eagles soars to as many as 4,000—some coming from as far away as the state of Washington. Upwelling warm water keeps a three-mile stretch of the river free of ice, and it is here that the eagles gather to feed. See "Organized Tours," below.

NEARBY ATTRACTIONS

Mud Bay Road leads south nine miles from Fort Seward, halfway out the Chilkat Peninsula. The glaciers tumbling from rocky peaks across the Chilkat Inlet originate over the mountain crest in Glacier Bay National Park. Only one, **Davidson Glacier,** is a tidewater iceflow; you'll also see a spectacular hanging glacier known as the **Rainbow Glacier.**

Chilkat State Park, reached down a steep grade on a two-mile gravel side road, is southeast Alaska's largest state park. It offers picnicking, camping, beachcombing, and fishing, plus whale- and seal-watching in Chilkat Inlet. The Parks Division hosts coffee klatches, campfire talks, and slide shows at a centrally located log cabin.

Northeast of Haines, the **Lutak Road** runs past the ferry terminal and cruise-ship dock to Chilkoot Lake and **Chilkoot State Park,** 11 miles from downtown. The lake is a popular venue for boating, fishing, and picnicking, as well as camping.

ORGANIZED TOURS

Haines Street Car Co., P.O. Box 703, Haines, AK 99827 (tel. 907/766-2819), offers various three-hour tours of Haines, the Chilkat River valley, Chilkat Park, and Chilkoot Lake. All are priced at $16 (half price for kids 7–11; children under 7, free). A dinner and theater tour lets you take in the salmon bake and a show at the Chilkat Center, for $32, all-inclusive. Drivers meet all ferry arrivals and will transport you to your hotel ($5 one way) or give you a whirlwind tour of Haines and get you back to the dock before departure for $8.

Alaska Sightseeing, based locally at the Hotel Hälsingland (tel. 766-2435), also conducts three-hour local tours, including the fort and museum, for $18 ($9 for kids 5–11), May 15 to September 30. Departure times vary.

Chilkat Guides, P.O. Box 170, Haines, AK 99827 (tel. 907/766-2409), offers raft floats through the bald eagle preserve to see America's majestic national bird close up. Daily four-hour raft trips cost $45 for adults, $25 for children under 14. Chilkat Guides also offer four-wheel-drive excursions to Glory Hole Spring at the head of Chilkoot Lake. **Alaska Cross Country Guiding & Rafting,** P.O. Box 124, Haines, AK 99827, also offers eagle preserve tours. There are also guided photo tours offered by **Eclipse Alaska,** P.O. Box 698, Haines, AK 99827 (tel. 907/766-2670), and **Alaska Nature Tours,** P.O. Box 491, Haines, AK 99827 (tel. 907/766-2876); and jet boat tours by **River Adventures,** P.O. Box 556, Haines, AK 99827 (tel. 907/766-2050).

All local air-taxi operators offer flightseeing over Glacier Bay National park and surrounding areas. See "Getting Around," above, for a listing.

SPORTS & RECREATION

The Haines High School **swimming pool** is open to the public, with open swims scheduled Monday through Saturday from 1 to 3pm and 7:30 to 9pm. A $2 fee is charged. The high school also has free **tennis courts** and a **jogging** track. **Bicycles** can be rented from the Bike Shop (tel. 766-2249), in the basement of the Gateway Building. A **miniature golf** course has been set up on Second Avenue behind the visitor center.

FISHING The waters of the Chilkoot and Chilkat Inlets are rich in salmon and halibut. Troll for kings in the upper Lynn Canal in early summer—the Haines King Salmon Derby is held the last weekend of May and the first weekend of June. Pinks proliferate in the Chilkoot and Lutak Inlets in July and August. Chums and coho are excellent in the Chilkat Inlet and Chilkat River from September to early November. Trout fishermen go after Dolly Varden in Lutak Inlet and Chilkoot Lake June through November, or fly-fish for cutthroats in the Chilkoot and Chilkat Rivers.

You can get licenses and tackle at the **Alaska Sport Shop,** Fourth Avenue and Main Street (tel. 766-2441), or **Haines Tackle Company,** FAA and Battle Roads just south of Fort Seward (tel. 766-2255). Fishing charters carry four to six passengers and provide all bait and gear. Try **Lynn Canal Charter Service** (tel. 766-2254), at

$20 per person per hour, for a minimum of two passengers and three hours. There's also a wilderness fishing camp on Chilkat Lake, accessible only by floatplane or riverboat. Contact **Don's Camp,** P.O. Box 645, Haines, AK 99827 (tel. 907/766-2303).

For additional information on fishing in the Haines area, contact the Alaska Department of Fish and Game, Division of Sport Fish (tel. 766-2625), or the Division of Fish and Wildlife Protection (tel. 766-2533).

HIKING Pick up the green "Haines Is for Hikers" brochure at the visitor center. This short guide to local trail systems suggests numerous day trips of varying length and difficulty. The shortest and easiest trip is the 2.4-mile **Battery Point Trail,** beginning at the end of Beach Road on the south side of Haines. It offers beautiful views across the Lynn Canal. There are three trails to the summit of 1,760-foot **Mount Riley,** ranging from a steep 2.1-mile hike off Mud Bay Road to a more gentle 5½-mile hike from Portage Cove. The peak of 3,920-foot **Mount Ripkinsky** is a difficult all-day climb from the top of Young Road overlooking Lutak Inlet. On clear days there's a view all the way to Admiralty Island south of Juneau. The **Seduction Point Trail** follows the west side of the Chilkat Peninsula 6.8 miles south from the Chilkat State Park visitor center to spectacular viewpoints across the Davidson Glacier. You may encounter bear or moose on any of these trails.

The more adventurous might enjoy an outing with **Ice-Field Ascents,** P.O. Box 170, Haines, AK 99827 (tel. 766-2097 or 766-2409), which specializes in the "art of negotiating variable terrain." The agency offers unusual guided hiking and glacier-walking trips, such as Haines-to-Skagway (10–14 days for $550). Experience with an ice axe and crampons is essential, but novices who sign on for a longer trip can pay half price for a weekend crash course at the Davidson Glacier, normally $150. Outings are strenuous, but the client-to-guide ratio is kept at two to one.

RIVER RAFTING Besides the half-day trip down the Chilkat River, through the eagle preserve, there are numerous other rafting opportunities—many of them breathtaking in their scenery and their waterborne adventure. **Alaska Cross Country Guiding & Rafting,** P.O. Box 124, Haines, AK 99827, flies visitors into its Tsiruku River wilderness lodge, then rafts them out through the preserve on two-day trips. **Chilkat Guides,** P.O. Box 170, Haines, AK 99827 (tel. 907/766-2409), also has two-day Tsiruku trips, which include a walk on the LeBlondeau Glacier (price: $250). Chilkat Guides' 11-day epic voyage down the Tatshenshini and Alsek Rivers has been called one of the last great adventures on the planet: Starting at Dalton Post, Yukon Territory, it cuts a swath through the St. Elias Mountains, and at one point disappears into the eight-mile-wide Alsek Glacier. The trip ends at Dry Bay in Glacier Bay National Park/Preserve. Trips are seasonal, from June 1 to October 1. Prices start at around $1,300.

WINTER SPORTS With average snowfall of 8–10 feet and a six-month cold season lasting from mid-November to mid-May, Haines appeals to many winter-sports enthusiasts—especially after February, when daylight hours are longer.

There is **cross-country skiing and snowshoeing** with trails down the Chilkat River through the eagle preserve, and on the many other lakes and trails in the area. Telemarkers often head for Chilkat Pass, just across the Canadian border in British Columbia. **Telemark Line,** P.O. Box 491, Haines, AK 99827 (tel. 907/766-2876), a Nordic ski shuttle and outfitting service, has daily charters for trailhead pickups and dropoffs along the Haines Highway and into the Yukon Territory.

There's a 100-strong local **snow machine** club, the Chilkat Snowburners, who sponsor the Alcan 200 rally in late January, with over $20,000 in prize money. Those **ice fishing** often strike it big at Mosquito Lake, while **dog-sled teams** practice along the lower Chilkat River and Chilkoot Lake.

SHOPPING

Haines is an artists' town, so it's no accident that there is a proliferation of fine art galleries around the Chilkat Valley.

At the **Northern Arts Gallery,** on Second Avenue behind the post office, look for Pete Andriesen's pen-and-ink drawings (and silkscreen reproductions thereof), Jenny Lyn Smith's silver pieces and wood carvings in totemic designs, and Linda Matthews's pottery. You can see Sue Folletti's silver pieces and wood carvings at **Chilkat Valley Arts,** 307 Willard St. **The Sea Wolf,** on the Fort Seward parade grounds, and **The Whale Rider,** at Second Avenue and Willard Street, by the visitor center, are both operated by Tresham Gregg III, who has made his name as a multimedia artist by applying Tlingit themes to metal and wood sculptures.

Knute's Shop, No. 5 Officers' Row in Fort Seward, is the studio-gallery of custom woodworker Lowell Knutson. Two other fine shops—**Alaskan Indian Arts** and **Wild Iris**—are in the old hospital building on the south side of the Fort Seward Parade Ground at No. 13 Officers' Row.

You can handle your photographic needs at **Bell's Store** on Second Avenue.

WHERE TO STAY

Haines offers a variety of accommodations, nearly all of them in the moderate or inexpensive price ranges.

Tax   City tax of 5% should be added to all quoted rates.

MODERATE

CAPTAIN'S CHOICE MOTEL, Second Ave. and Dalton St. (P.O. Box 392), Haines, AK 99827. Tel. 907/766-3111, or toll free 800/247-7153, 800/478-2345 in Alaska. 40 rms (all with bath), 5 suites. TV TEL
$ Rates: Mid-May to mid-Sept, $85 single; $95 double; $125 suite. Mid-Sept to mid-May, $75 single; $85 double; $100 suite. AE, CB, DC, MC, V.

A natural-wood nautical theme carries from the lobby into the rooms, many of which overlook Portage Cove. Earth-toned carpeting, drapes, and bedspreads complement the wood decor. All rooms have courtesy coffee, a refrigerator, desk-dresser combinations, and electric baseboard heat. Several suites have kitchenettes; the bridal suite has a wet bar and in-room Jacuzzi. Pets are allowed in some rooms.

EAGLE'S NEST MOTEL, Mile 1, Haines Hwy. (P.O. Box 267), Haines, AK 99827. Tel. 907/766-2352. Fax 907/766-2891. 9 rms (all with bath). TV TEL
$ Rates: Mid-May to mid-Sept, $67 single; $76 double; $86 twin. Mid-Sept to mid-May, $57 single; $66 double; $76 twin. AE, CB, DC, MC, V.

You'll feel welcome at this motel as soon as you see the big stone fireplace in the lobby. Each quiet room has a white calico bedspread to go with rust-colored carpets, a queen-size bed, desk-dresser, couch or easy chair, thermostat-controlled hot-water heating, and courtesy coffee. There's a pay phone in the lobby. This is the closest motel to the airport and the eagle preserve. Eagles Nest car rental is located at the motel.

FORT SEWARD BED & BREAKFAST, No. 1 Officers' Row, Fort Seward (P.O. Box 5), Haines, AK 99827. Tel. 907/766-2856. 3 rms, 2 suites (2 with bath).
$ Rates (including tax and breakfast): May–Sept, $58 single without bath; $68 double without bath; $95 suite for two; $105 suite for four. Oct–Dec 15, $38 single without bath; $48 double without bath; $75 suite for two; $85 suite for four. MC, V.
Closed: Dec 16–Apr.

Haines's original B&B is the pride of owner Norm Smith, a 30-year resident of the town. Smith has worked hard to renovate this former chief surgeon's quarters, a grand Victorian (1904) structure in the classic Jeffersonian architectural style. Art students will appreciate its cross-gabled slate roof, decorated box cornices, and original leaded- and beveled-glass china cabinets. Selections from Smith's personal print and historic photo collection adorn the walls of the rooms and corridors, while an open veranda looks across the parade grounds to the Lynn Canal. Belgian tile fireplaces warm the three spacious bedrooms, which share a main-floor bathroom. One flight up the oak-bannistered staircase are two fully furnished suites with private bath. Breakfast is Alaska-size with sourdough pancakes and fresh-ground coffee.

INEXPENSIVE

FORT SEWARD CONDOS, Nos. 2 and 3 Officers' Row, Fort Seward (P.O. Box 75), Haines, AK 99827. Tel. 907/766-2425. 4 suites (all with bath).
$ Rates (including utilities and parking): $70 per unit per day, $420 per week. Minimum stay of three days required. MC, V.
Ted and Mimi Gregg's fully furnished one- and two-bedroom apartment units overlook the parade grounds on the west side of Fort Seward. Located in a historic residence, they all have cooking facilities, and some have fireplaces. Families in particular find the apartments handy.

HOTEL HÄLSINGLAND, Officers' Row, Fort Seward (P.O. Box 1589), Haines, AK 99827. Tel. 907/766-2000, or toll free 800/542-6363 in U.S., 800/478-2525 in Alaska, 800/478-2003 in Canada. Fax 907/766-2445. 60 rms (50 with bath).
$ Rates: May 15–Sept 15, $29.50 single without bath, $65 single with bath; $33.50 double without bath, $65–$70 double with bath; $70–$75 twin with bath. Mar–May 14 and Sept 16–Nov, $24.50 single without bath, $55 single with bath; $28.50 double without bath, $55–$60 double with bath; $60–$65 twin with bath. AE, CB, DC, DISC, MC, V. **Closed:** Dec–Feb.

The Hotel Hälsingland is not the newest, nor the best-maintained, nor the most centrally located accommodation in Haines. But it has more charm and ambience than any other. Directly facing the Fort Seward parade grounds, the hotel has taken over what were the commanding officer's quarters in the days before World War II. The big white houses were purchased in 1947 by Clarence and Hilma Mattson; Hilma came from the Swedish province of Hälsingland, and so the name. A huge hand-woven tapestry from Hälsingland still hangs above a landing on the stairs. Hilma's nephew, Arne Olsson, and his wife, Joyce, operate the hotel today.

No two of the Hälsingland's rooms are alike. Many contain such unusual touches as a settee and a hanging lamp over the bed. All rooms have thermostat-controlled hot-water heating and wall-to-wall carpeting. Wildlife photographs decorate the walls. Most of the rooms have TV and phone, and two pay phones are available for use in the lobby. The hotel's Commander's Room Restaurant is popular among Haines residents for its local seafood dinners and generous portions of all meals (see "Where to Dine," below). Meanwhile, the Port Chilkoot Potlatch salmon bake is offered in the parade grounds nightly from June through August.

MOUNTAIN VIEW MOTEL, Mud Bay Rd. at Second Ave. (P.O. Box 62), Haines, AK 99827. Tel. 907/766-2900, or toll free 800/478-2902 in Alaska and Canada. 8 rms (all with bath). TV TEL
$ Rates: Mid-May to mid-Sept, $54 single; $69 double. Mid-Sept to mid-May, $45 single; $58 double. AE, CB, DC, DISC, MC, V.
This small motel's biggest plus is that every unit is equipped with a small kitchenette. Located just above the Haines post office, it has a quiet, convenient location. Each room has a dining table, two double beds, a couch, and a dresser. The decor is uninspired, with brown carpeting, white trim, and Arizona Indian paintings on the walls.

THUNDERBIRD MOTEL, 242 Dalton St. (P.O. Box 589), Haines, AK 99827. Tel. 907/766-2131, or toll free 800/327-2556. 20 rms (all with bath). TV TEL
$ Rates: $56 single; $66 double, $76 double with kitchenette. AE, MC, V.
The Thunderbird Motel ushers you into the lobby on Astroturf carpeting, then announces your arrival to front-desk clerks with a loud buzzer. Bright floral bedspreads brighten the otherwise dreary wood-paneled rooms of this single-story motel. Six units have kitchenettes; all feature electric baseboard heating.

BUDGET

BEAR CREEK CAMP AND YOUTH HOSTEL, Mile 1, Small Tracts Rd. (P.O. Box 1158), Haines, AK 99827. Tel. 907/766-2259. Cabins (none with bath) and dormitory beds. **Transportation:** Free shuttle from ferry terminal.
$ Rates (including tax): $30 cabin; $10 dorm beds for Youth Hostel Association members, $12 for nonmembers. No credit cards.

Bear Creek has sourdough-type cabins—one step above a tent, with canvas stretched over a wood frame—for one to four people, as well as dormitory lodging. Communal kitchen facilities are available. The hostel is basic and operates year-round.

CAMPGROUNDS

There are numerous private RV or camper parks and several public campgrounds in the area immediately surrounding Haines.

The **Port Chilkoot Camper Park,** P.O. Box 473, Haines, AK 99827 (tel. 907/766-2755), on Mud Bay Road in Fort Seward between the Hotel Hälsingland and the Mountain View Motel, has 60 spaces for $9 a night with electricity, $6.50 without; tent sites are $3.50 a night. A laundry and coin-op showers are also available. The **Eagle Camper Park,** P.O. Box 28, Haines, AK 99827 (tel. 907/766-2335), closer to downtown on Union Street near Main, has 62 units with full hookups at $14, tent sites at $3.50, and showers. The **Haines Hitch-Up RV Park,** on the Haines Highway at the entrance to town (tel. 907/766-2882), has 92 spaces at $14 a night for full electric, sewer, and water hookups. It also has a gift shop, laundry, and showers. **Oceanside RV Park,** Front Street at the foot of Dalton Street (tel. 907/766-2444), also caters to recreational vehicles.

Backpackers without vehicles won't find a better place to set up their tents than the **Portage Cove Wayside,** three-quarters of a mile south of downtown Haines on Beach Road. On a small promontory extending into the Chilkoot Inlet, the campground provides picnic tables, water, and toilets. Farther away from town, there are 32 sites at **Chilkat State Park,** 7 miles south on Mud Bay Road, and 33 sites at **Chilkoot Lake Wayside,** 11 miles north of Haines but only 4 miles from the ferry terminal.

WHERE TO DINE

EXPENSIVE

COMMANDER'S ROOM, in the Hotel Hälsingland, Officers' Row, Fort Seward. Tel. 766-2000.
Cuisine: STEAK/SEAFOOD. **Reservations:** Recommended for dinner.
$ Prices: Appetizers $6–$10; main courses $17–$26; breakfast/lunch $5–$8. AE. CB, DC, DISC, MC, V.
Open: Breakfast daily 7–10am; lunch daily 11am–2pm; dinner daily 6–10pm.

The commanding officer of Fort Seward once made his home in this building, so it's only fitting that Haines's best restaurant be housed in the hotel. Tall windows look out on the spacious parade ground. Free transportation to and from the restaurant is provided for dinner guests not staying at the hotel.

Full dinners include both salad bar and potato bar; featured dishes include halibut Humboldt (in white wine and cheese sauce), sautéed prawns, and a variety of steaks. The "Stars and Stripes" special—steak and scallops—highlights the menu.

MODERATE

FORT SEWARD LODGE, Totem at Fort Seward. Tel. 766-2009.
Cuisine: STEAK/SEAFOOD. **Reservations:** Recommended.
$ Prices: Appetizers $4–$7; main courses $11–$17. MC, V.
Open: Dinner only, daily 5–10pm.

Located in the former post exchange building, the Fort Seward Lodge offers diners a beautiful evening view across the Lynn Canal, especially from its second-floor balcony. A hardwood floor and tasteful wood decor give it a spacious yet cozy feeling. The steak-and-seafood menu includes Chilkoot Inlet salmon, Lynn Canal crab, prime rib, and a 12-ounce sirloin steak.

LIGHTHOUSE RESTAURANT, Main St. at Front St. Tel. 766-2442.
   Cuisine: AMERICAN. **Reservations:** Not accepted.
$ **Prices:** Breakfast $4–$8.50; lunch $5.50–$13.50; dinner $15–$22. MC, V.
   Open: Daily 8am–10pm. **Closed:** Dec–Feb.
It's only appropriate that the Lighthouse should be decorated in nautical fashion. Fishing floats and greenery hang from the beams beside windows showcasing the harbor's busy activity. Dinner specials, such as barbecued spareribs and eastern oysters, include salad bar, potato, and bread. Lunches range from burger and fries to a big fish-and-chips platter with salad, and breakfasts feature three-egg omelets.

PORT CHILKOOT POTLATCH, Totem Village Tribal House, Fort Seward. Tel. 766-2000.
   Cuisine: SALMON BAKE. **Reservations:** Recommended.
$ **Prices:** $17.50 adults, $9 children. AE, CB, DC, DISC, MC, V.
   Open: June–Aug, daily 5–8pm.
⭐ Operated by the Hotel Hålsingland, this salmon bake is as good as any of its genre, and better than most. Offered up in a re-created Tlingit Indian longhouse—the Totem Village Tribal House on the Fort Seward parade ground—it's an all-you-can-eat extravaganza of alder-smoked salmon, corn, beans, and other side dishes. The highlight is a performance by Haines's highly acclaimed Chilkat Dancers. Not to be missed.

INEXPENSIVE

BAMBOO ROOM, Second Ave. between Main and Dalton Sts. Tel. 766-9101.
   Cuisine: AMERICAN. **Reservations:** Not required.
$ **Prices:** Breakfast/lunch $3.50–$8; dinner $5–$12. No credit cards.
   Open: Daily 6am–10pm.
An informal, down-home café, the Bamboo Room offers hotcakes and coffee for breakfast, quarter-pound burgers for lunch, and the likes of fried chicken for dinner. The house special is hot apple pie with brandy-cinnamon sauce.

CHILKAT RESTAURANT & BAKERY, Fifth Ave. north of Main St. Tel. 766-2920.
   Cuisine: AMERICAN/MEXICAN. **Reservations:** Recommended for dinner.
$ **Prices:** Breakfast $4–$6; lunch $4.50–$7.50; dinner $7–$11. MC, V.
   Open: Mid-May to mid-Sept, Mon–Sat 7am–8pm. Mid-Sept to mid-May, Mon–Thurs 7am–5pm, Fri 7am–8pm, Sat 8am–4pm.
Ⓢ This country kitchen greets families with open arms. From the embroidered welcome sign on the front door to the daintily curtained windows in the dining room, you'll feel as if you're at Aunt Millie's place. Dinners like roast beef and Hawaiian ham are reasonably priced. Luncheon sandwiches include a reuben grill or halibut steak; and there are big breakfast omelets. Homemade pastries are a favored dessert. Friday has been "Mexican Night" since 1981. The Chilkat has chosen not to apply for a liquor license.

PORCUPINE PETE'S, Second Ave. at Main St. Tel. 766-9199.
   Cuisine: PIZZA/DELI.
$ **Prices:** Sandwiches $3.50–$6; pizzas $10–$24. MC, V.
   Open: Mon–Sat 11am–11pm, Sun noon–9pm.
If you're in the mood for pizza, this is the place that may satisfy your appetite. In a natural-wood, ice-cream-parlor atmosphere with video games blaring away, the open kitchen prepares grinders and hoagies, and sourdough pizza for $2 a slice. Its pride

and joy is the "kicking horse combo," four meats and nine vegetables on a 15-inch crust.

EVENING ENTERTAINMENT

The ✪ **Chilkat Dancers** perform throughout the summer at the Chilkat Center for the Arts on Monday at 7:30 and 8:30pm, and on Wednesday, Thursday, and Saturday at 8:30pm. This troupe, composed of Native and non-Native adults and children performing tribal dances in traditional costume, has won international acclaim—they put on a great show. Adult admission is $6; kids 5–18, $4; children under 5, free. Call 766-2160 for more information.

On many nights that the dancers are not doing their thing at the Chilkat Center, the **Lynn Canal Community Players** are. From June to August, characters like the notorious Jack Dalton, miner Porcupine Pete, Sgt. Justin Time, and sweet Patience Steadfast take the stage on Friday and Sunday at 8:30pm in a melodrama known as *Lust for Dust*. Tickets are $6 for adults, $4 for children. The theater group also presents several short-run plays at the Chilkat Center in the winter months, and hosts the biennial State Drama Festival of the Alaska State Community Theater Association in April of odd-numbered years. You can get more information by calling 766-2540.

Night lights are much dimmer in Haines than in Skagway or Juneau. The large lounge at the **Lighthouse Restaurant,** Front Street at Main (tel. 766-2442), occasionally books live bands. A good-size dance floor, a jukebox, and pool tables will keep you hopping in any event. The **Pioneer Bar,** on Second Avenue between Main and Dalton Streets, and the **Fogcutter Bar,** on Main Street between First and Second Avenues, are popular local watering holes.

THE HAINES HIGHWAY

The Alaska Chilkat Bald Eagle Preserve is not the only point of interest on the Haines Highway as it heads north to the Canadian border. The mountain scenery is equally spectacular. The highway weaves its way up the Chilkat River valley as it leaves Haines.

In the middle of the eagle preserve, just past Milepost 21, there's a bumpy dead-end turnoff to the Tlingit village of **Klukwan** (pop. about 100). This was once the main village of the Chilkat clan, famous for their blankets woven from cedar-bark fibers and mountain-goat hair. Today there's little to see—some newer houses, a handful of ramshackle older ones, and a log tribal house with a faded eagle-and-raven design painted on it. There are no facilities, and the Natives don't enjoy being subjects of photographic curiosity. Things may change if a cultural center, now under consideration, is built here.

The final miles to the border ascend through the Klehini River canyon, surrounded by snow-covered peaks. At Milepost 27, pristine **Mosquito Lake** (don't let the name scare you) has a campground and other facilities. Historic **33 Mile Roadhouse** (tel. 767-5510) is the last gas station before the border; open daily, it serves light meals and is licensed for beer and wine. A couple of miles farther, look across the Klehini River to pick out the remnants of the once-flourishing **Porcupine Mine ghost town,** destroyed by a flood in 1906.

The international border is 40 miles from Haines. **Canadian Customs** is open 8am to midnight, Pacific time, year-round. If you are coming from the north, **U.S. Customs** is open the same hours.

8. SKAGWAY

15 miles N of Haines, 105 miles N of Juneau

GETTING THERE   By Plane   Skagway's 3,300-foot airstrip runs along the west side of Alaska Street, with the terminal on 12th Avenue. **L.A.B. Flying Service** (tel. 983-2471) has its office at the airport; associated with Alaska Airlines, this commuter service flies Pipers, a Navajo Chieftain, and two Britten-Norman Islanders to Juneau, Haines, Glacier Bay, and Hoonah. Skagway is also served by **Wings of Alaska** (tel. 983-2442), sharing offices with **Skagway Air Service** (tel. 983-2218), at Fourth Avenue and Broadway. You can't miss the latter's colorful logo (a high-kicking dance-hall girl) or slogan ("We can can can.").

By Train A novel way to get to Skagway is from Whitehorse, in Canada's Yukon Territory, aboard the **White Pass & Yukon Route** railway (tel. 907/983-2217, or toll free 800/343-7373 in the U.S., 800/478-7373 in Canada). There's service daily, May to late September; you must bus from Whitehorse to Fraser, B.C., then travel by train to Skagway. The trip takes 4½ hours. Connecting buses leave Whitehorse at 8:15am daily Yukon time (one hour earlier than Alaska time); trains depart Skagway at 7:45am and 1pm daily. Fare is $92 for adults, half price for kids.

By Bus Whitehorse, capital of the Yukon, is 110 miles north of Skagway on the Klondike Highway. This bustling town of 17,000 is traditionally regarded as the midway point of the Alaska Highway. There's daily bus service from Whitehorse to Skagway, as well as to Fairbanks, Anchorage, and points between on Gray Line's **Alaskon Express** (tel. 983-2241), mid-May to mid-September.

From Skagway, buses leave the Westmark Hotel for Whitehorse at 7:30am daily. Buses for Anchorage and Fairbanks depart at 7:30am on Tuesday, Wednesday, Friday, and Sunday. The fare is $59 to Whitehorse (4 hours), $184 to Fairbanks (32½ hours), and $227 to Anchorage (35½ hours). Journeys to Fairbanks and Anchorage require overnight stays at Beaver Creek, on the Yukon-Alaska border. Contact Gray Line of Alaska, 300 Elliott Ave. W., Dept. AE1, Seattle, WA 98119 (tel. 206/286-3203, or toll free 800/544-2206).

By Car It's 110 miles from Whitehorse south to Skagway over Klondike Highway 2. The route branches south off the Alaska Highway about 11 miles east of Whitehorse. For northbound travelers, a shortcut is the Tagish Road (Klondike Highway 8), an all-weather gravel road that departs the Alaska Highway at Jake's Corner and cuts off about 40 miles of travel via Whitehorse.

By Ferry The ferries of the Alaska Marine Highway System (tel. 983-2229) visit Skagway eight times a week in summer, remaining in port for anywhere from 45 minutes to 9¼ hours before heading back south. The ferry dock empties directly onto Broadway. Cruise ships anchor in Taiya Inlet and unload passengers on the Skagway waterfront.

SPECIAL EVENTS The year's big party is on the **Fourth of July.** There's a twice-around parade, which has been the tradition since 1898, when the notorious Jefferson Smith (see below) rode his tall white horse up Broadway as the grand marshal of the Independence Day parade; four days later he died in a gunfight.

Other summer events include the **Skagway Windfest,** with competition in ore-truck pulling and chain-saw throwing in mid-March (very early spring); the **Summer Solstice picnic,** June 21; the **Eastern Star Flower Show** and Skagway Garden Club competition, mid-August; and the **Klondike Trail of '98 Road Relay** from Skagway to Whitehorse, mid-September.

Skagway is the end of the trail . . . and the beginning of it. It's the final stop of Alaska's Inside Passage for ferry or cruise-ship passengers (see map of Skagway in Section 2, "Wrangell"). For the gold-seekers of 1898 who shed their sea legs here en route to the Klondike, and for modern-day adventurers who seek to retrace that adventure, it's the takeoff point for the famed Chilkoot Trail.

But don't get the idea that Skagway is merely a stopping-off point. It's a community that begs you to become immersed in its history and unique atmosphere.

Broadway, Skagway's main drag, looks almost as it did eight decades ago. More than 30 buildings along a five-block stretch were built between 1897 and 1903, and nearly all of them are still active places of business. In fact downtown Skagway is now a unit of the Klondike Gold Rush National Historical Park, a designation that aids with its preservation and adds to its interest.

Skagway's permanent population of 700 or so more than doubles during the May-to-September tourist season. Temporary hotel workers (most of them college students from the Pacific Northwest and California) and other part-time residents flock in to cater to the lucrative cruise-ship crowd, whose numbers often reach 3,000 or more a day. Visitors who arrive in Skagway between October and April will find only four hotels and one hostel open for business.

Skagway is located at the northern extreme of the Inside Passage, on a long finger of the Lynn Canal called the Taiya Inlet. The town was built where the Skagway River, tumbling from the 7,000-foot heights of the Canadian boundary ranges, flattens into a narrow plain nestling between high ridges.

Because of its extremely sheltered location, Skagway has a much drier climate than the rest of the southeast. The average annual precipitation is only 29 inches—less than half that of Haines, only 15 miles south. Temperatures average 57°F in July, 23°F in January. The north wind can be biting.

But it was more than pleasant climate that attracted Capt. William Moore in 1887 to build a homestead in the valley the Indians called Skagua, "Home of the North Wind." Moore was a riverboat skipper who had amassed a small fortune delivering miners and goods to British Columbia's Cassiar goldfields in the 1870s, and who now was convinced that the Klondike would yield the next great lode. With the vision of a seer he began laying out city streets, planning a wharf, and even musing about a railroad in preparation for the coming gold rush.

And come it did, in 1897 and 1898. Over 20,000 anxious fortune hunters boarded ships in Seattle and disembarked at this boom town at the mouth of the Skagway River, en route to Dawson City. The first boatload landed in July 1897 and overran Moore's settlement with a tent city. By October, Broadway was lined with frame buildings and three new wharves were under construction. By 1899 the tracks of the White Pass & Yukon Route railroad were snaking over the mountains.

Many of the new arrivals were less interested in panning streams or sluicing mud than in stripping the golden fleece from those who had already done so. Thousands remained in Skagway; Moore had not foreseen the proliferation of saloons and gambling halls (80 at one count), the thriving red-light district, the wolfpacks of thieves and con men. Skagway became known as "the roughest town on earth." Certainly it was among the most lawless.

Jefferson Randolph ("Soapy") Smith was the most nefarious of all the wolves. Surrounding himself with a cadre of compliant lieutenants, he launched scam after unpunished scam to relieve the miners of their hard-won gold dust. His reign finally ended in a shootout with town surveyor Frank Reid on the city dock on July 8, 1898, a duel that left both men dead. Their graves are found in Skagway's Gold Rush Cemetery; their story is recounted daily in summer in Gold Rush Productions' *Skaguay in the Days of '98* show at the Eagles Hall. The cast honors Smith on the anniversary of his death with a wake at his grave, beginning about 10pm (after the last show). Smith's grandson, a resident of California, provides champagne for the party each year!

It wasn't long thereafter that the strike-it-rich miners heard about a new gold find—this one in Nome, in 1899—and all but abandoned the Klondike. Only the existence of the railroad shuttling freight between Whitehorse and the Inside Passage kept Skagway alive at all. The population shrank to a few hundred people, except during World War II when a couple of thousand federal workers channeled goods and personnel through Skagway to build the Alaska Highway. Skagway's economy staggered in 1982 when the railroad was shut down; when it reopened as a summer tourist attraction in 1988, it gave the economy a shot in the arm.

ORIENTATION

INFORMATION Your single best source of information is the **Klondike Gold Rush National Historical Park Visitor Center,** in the old White Pass & Yukon

Route railroad depot, at Second Avenue and Broadway (tel. 907/983-2921). The park rangers will give you a sheaf of printed materials, answer your questions, and steer you to the daily schedule of films, lectures, and historical walks. The **Skagway Convention and Visitors Bureau,** P.O. Box 415, Skagway, AK 99840 (tel. 907/983-2854 or 983-2297), is located at City Hall, Seventh Avenue east of Broadway. (From May through September, the visitor center operates in the Arctic Brotherhood Hall, Broadway between Second and Third Avenues.) You might also try the **Skagway Chamber of Commerce,** P.O. Box 194, Skagway, AK 99840 (tel. 907/983-2297).

If you have any questions before heading into (or after arriving from) Canada, check with the **U.S. Customs and Immigration Service,** Second Avenue and Spring Street (tel. 983-2325 for Customs, 983-2725 for Immigration).

CITY LAYOUT Skagway's streets are laid out in a straight grid pattern. Paralleling Broadway on the east is Spring Street; on the west are, in order, State, Main, and Alaska Streets. These five thoroughfares are crisscrossed by numbered streets, from First Avenue to 23rd, which crosses the Skagway River and turns north as the Klondike Highway.

GETTING AROUND

For local taxi service, try **Frontier** (tel. 983-2512), **Pioneer Taxi and Tours** (tel. 983-2623), **Sourdough Shuttle and Tours** (tel. 983-2523), or **Southeast Tours** (tel. 983-2617).

You can rent cars in Skagway from **Avis** (tel. 983-2247), at the Klondike Hotel during the months of May through September, or from **Sourdough Shuttle and Tours** (tel. 983-2523)

FAST FACTS

Banks See "Post Office," below.

Emergencies For emergency services, call the Skagway Police Department (tel. 983-2301) or the fire department and ambulance (tel. 983-2300). For maritime search and rescue, contact the Coast Guard (tel. toll free 800/478-5555).

There's a medical clinic on 11th Avenue between Broadway and State Street (tel. 983-2255).

Newspaper The *Skagway News* is published biweekly from May to October, monthly the rest of the year.

Post Office The post office and the National Bank of Alaska (tel. 983-2264) share a building at Sixth Avenue and Broadway.

WHAT TO SEE & DO

SIGHTS & ATTRACTIONS IN TOWN

The ✪ **Klondike Gold Rush National Historical Park,** P.O. Box 517, Skagway, AK 99840 (tel. 983-2921), comprises many of the buildings of the Historic District of Skagway, as well as the nearby ruins of Dyea, the Chilkoot and White Pass Trails, and a museum in Seattle commemorating the fortune-hunters' seaborne departure for the Klondike.

Start your visit at the park headquarters and visitor center in the recently restored White Pass & Yukon Route depot building, Second Avenue and Broadway, open May through September, daily from 8am to 6pm. There's something happening every hour, from films and slide presentations to lectures and a permanent exhibit. Especially recommended are the movie *Days of Adventure, Dreams of Gold,* and the 45-minute guided walk (usually beginning at 11am and 3pm).

Among the circa-1898 city structures visited on the walking tour, the one that's worth more than a passing glance is the **Arctic Brotherhood Hall** on Broadway between Second and Third (site of the visitor center from May to September). With a facade assembled from more than 20,000 pieces of tideflat driftwood, the headquarters of this now-defunct fraternal order (the last person initiated was President Warren Harding in 1923) is easily the most-photographed building in Skagway. Today the hall has become a minitheater where *The White Pass Railroad Story* is recounted in photo, word, and song. It's presented daily in summer from 9am to 9pm. Admission is $2.50.

Another building worth visiting is **City Hall,** one block east of Broadway on Sixth Avenue. Built in 1899 as Bishop McCabe College, it's also the state's oldest granite structure. From 1901 to 1956 the building was a federal courthouse. Today the ground floor contains city offices.

City Hall's second floor is occupied by the **Trail of '98 Museum** (tel. 983-2420). The most interesting items in the collection are the odds and ends from early Skagway—stampeders' sleds and snowshoes, settlers' Victorian-era appliances, casinos' roulette wheels and game boards. You can also peruse a multitude of old scrapbooks with historical photos and documents, a taxidermy display of local wildlife, and a variety of Native artifacts. It's open May through September, daily from 9am to 5pm; other months, by appointment. Admission is $2 for adults, $1 for children.

The narrow-gauge **○ White Pass & Yukon Route** railway was built at the turn of the century to handle the shipment of goods between here and the Yukon. Today old Steam Engine No. 73 pulls the 1890s parlor cars 1½ miles through town, from the dock to the railroad yards off 23rd Avenue, where regular diesel engines take over for the 2,885-foot climb to the summit of White Pass. The 41-mile round-trip spans spider-web trestles over gorges like Dead Horse Gulch, past cataracts like Bridal Veil and Pitchfork Falls, to panoramic spectacles like Inspiration Point.

The train operates daily from May 1 to late September. Trains leave Skagway at 8:45am and 1:15pm for the 2¾-hour round-trip run to White Pass. The fare is $72 for adults, half price for children 12 and under. For full information, contact White Pass & Yukon Route, P.O. Box 435, Skagway, AK 99840 (tel. 907/983-2217, or toll free 800/343-7373 in the U.S., 800/478-7373 in Canada).

NEARBY ATTRACTIONS

Skagway was not the only township on the Taiya Inlet in 1898. Nearby **Dyea**—2½ miles by water, 9 miles by road—rivaled Skagway as the largest community in Alaska. It was the gateway to the Chilkoot Trail until the railroad from Skagway opened up an easier route to the Yukon in 1899.

The dirt road to Dyea branches west off the Klondike Highway about 2½ miles north of Skagway. It also leads to a National Park Service campground and to the **Chilkoot Trailhead,** about 6½ miles from the junction.

Prospectors had the option of two trails to reach the Klondike—the easier 40-mile White Pass Trail from Skagway or the shorter, steeper 33-mile Chilkoot Trail from Dyea. Naturally, most of them chose the latter. It was a costly mistake. The final half-mile climb over the snow-covered 3,739-foot pass took a severe toll on humans and horses, who were required to ascend 20–30 times to tote over the top their ton of food and gear (enough for a year's prospecting, as stipulated by the Canadian government).

Back on the Klondike Highway, there's one more point of interest before the rapid climb to White Pass begins. Take a turnoff to the east about half a mile past the Dyea Road and you'll discover **Tent City,** a recent attempt by the proprietor of the famed Red Onion Saloon to re-create the atmosphere of the first few gold-rush months in old Skaguay (as it was originally spelled). Among the canvas-covered "buildings" are a cookhouse, general store, saloon, Chinese laundry, miner's home, and harlot's crib. The store contains a private collection of antique furnishings and ladies' wardrobes from the Red Onion, which was in fact a brothel. Summer visitors are given a chance to pan for gold from a sluice box. They are treated to refreshments in the mess hall and serenaded with gold-rush ballads and stories. Tickets are $10; check at the Red Onion Saloon, Broadway and Second Avenue (tel. 982-2222), for show times.

The 15 miles on the **Klondike Highway** from downtown Skagway to the

Canadian border at White Pass (3,290 feet) afford one of the most beautiful drives in Alaska, with spectacular waterfalls, gaping chasms, and even a unique cantilever bridge for engineering students to appreciate. Canadian Customs is another eight miles past the summit. Returning south, U.S. Customs is just six miles out of Skagway. Both are now open 24 hours.

ORGANIZED TOURS

My personal favorite among the numerous Skagway tour operators is the ☺ **Skagway Street Car Co.,** P.O. Box 400, Skagway, AK 99840 (tel. 907/983-2908). Steve and Gayla Hites have set out to re-create the early 20th-century tours hosted by Martin Itjen, a Skagway prospector, hotelier, undertaker, roulette spinner, and Ford dealer. Conductors dressed in period costume now squire visitors around Skagway in a fleet of antique 1937 touring coaches. The tour takes in historic Skagway from the waterfront, where the prospectors arrived, to the Gold Rush Cemetery, where the unlucky ones were laid to rest. At the conclusion of the trip, Steve concertizes on guitar and harmonica in the Arctic Brotherhood Hall. The tour takes 2¼ hours and costs $38 ($19 for children under 12). It operates from 9am to 9pm daily, mid-May through September.

Similar historical tours by van or motorcoach are offered in the summer by **Gray Line** at the Klondike Hotel (tel. 983-2241), **Atlas Tours** at Fourth Avenue and Broadway (tel. 983-2402), and **Princess Tours** (tel. 983-2895). Typical tours last 2–2½ hours and cost $20 for adults, $10 for children 5–11.

Flightseeing tours over Chilkoot Pass (45 minutes) and to Glacier Bay (1½ hours) are offered by all local air charters, usually with a passenger minimum and on advance request. Check with **Skagway Air Service** (tel. 983-2218) or **L.A.B. Flying Service** (tel. 983-2471). The Glacier Bay tour costs $100 per person. Even more exciting than Pipers and Cessnas are helicopters: **Temsco Helicopters,** 1650 Maplesden Way, Juneau, AK 99801 (tel. 907/983-2909), depart from the ferry dock for glacier and gold-rush tours. Prices average $135.

SPORTS & RECREATION

There are **tennis courts** at Skagway Public School, on State Street between 11th and 13th Avenues, and **softball** diamonds at 12th Avenue and Main Street and at 16th Avenue and Alaska Street. Skagway's slow-pitch teams have games every Monday through Thursday night, May through August.

FISHING You can angle for silver and pink salmon from Skagway's beaches and wharves, but you'll need a boat to get deep enough for the big king salmon. Local lakes and streams contain rainbow trout, Dolly Vardens, and arctic char. **Skagway Sports Emporium,** on Fourth Avenue between Broadway and State Street (tel. 983-2480), and **Skagway Hardware,** at Fourth Avenue and Broadway (tel. 983-2233), sell fishing equipment and licenses.

HIKING & BACKPACKING The 33-mile **Chilkoot Trail** follows the path of the gold seekers of 1898 over the Chilkoot Pass to Lake Bennett, Canada, from which they could travel down the Yukon River to Dawson City. A unit of the Klondike Gold Rush National Historical Park, this difficult but well-maintained trail is used by about 1,500 modern-day adventurers a year. The trip takes three to five days. Gold-rush ruins and relics (all of them federally protected) are scattered along the route; bear and moose are frequently encountered.

The trailhead is in Dyea. From June to mid-September taxis will carry you and your gear the nine miles from Skagway for $12. At the Canadian end you must hike an additional eight miles from Lake Bennett to Log Cabin on the Klondike Highway and there catch either the bus to Whitehorse ($38) or Skagway ($16), or the White Pass and Yukon Route railway to Fraser, B.C. ($15), or Skagway ($72). The train leaves Lake Bennett at 8:30am and 1:15pm daily. For additional information and trail conditions, contact the National Park Service, P.O. Box 517, Skagway, AK 99840 (tel. 907/983-2921). Ask for their detailed brochure on the trail.

There are several fine day hikes closer to Skagway. The **Dewey Lake Trail System** starts in downtown Skagway across the railroad tracks from the Klondike Hotel. Nine miles of trails connect numerous lakes, waterfalls, and historic sites. The 5½-mile **Denver Glacier Trail** begins about three miles up the railroad right-of-way, ascending 2,000 feet up the east fork of the Skagway river to the glacier. Contact the Skagway Convention and Visitors Bureau (see "Orientation," above) for a map of area hiking trails.

SHOPPING

Attracted by the historic atmosphere and the potential for sales to tourists, many artisans have chosen to make Skagway their home. You can find good buys in gold and silver jewelry, scrimshaw, wood carving, ivory sculpture, paintings, and photography. The boardwalks of Broadway are lined with gift shops from Second to Sixth Avenue. My favorites are a couple of long-established businesses: **Kirme's Curio Shop,** at Fifth and Broadway (tel. 983-2341), and **Corrington's Alaska Ivory Co.,** on Broadway between Fifth and Sixth (tel. 983-2452). I'm also impressed by the fine ivory work at the **David Present Gallery,** at Third and Broadway (tel. 983-2873).

The best place in Skagway to get your photo and reading requirements handled is **Dedman's Photo Shop,** on Broadway between Third and Fourth (tel. 983-2353).

WHERE TO STAY

With well over 300 rooms available in a town of 800, you might expect to have no problem finding accommodations. That's not always true. Because so many disembarking cruise-ship passengers stay overnight in Skagway before making onward connections, midsummer reservations are essential.

Tax Add 8% room tax to all prices quoted.

EXPENSIVE

WESTMARK INN, Third Ave. and Spring St. (P.O. Box 515), Skagway, AK 99840. Tel. 907/983-6000, or toll free 800/544-0970 in the U.S., 800/999-2570 in Canada. Fax 907/258-0560 (reservations) or 907/983-2952 (front desk). For off-season information or reservations, contact 300 Elliott Ave. W., Seattle, WA 98119 (tel. 206/281-5194). 209 rms. TEL

$ Rates: By reservation, $118 single; $132 double. Space available, $75 single or double, $49 backpacker rate. AE, CB, DC, DISC, MC, V. **Closed:** Sept 26–May 19.

Two-thirds of the rooms in Skagway are at this hotel, owned and operated by Seattle-based Holland America Line/Westours primarily for its tour clientele. The interior decor of this rambling inn, which spills over two city blocks, is evocative of the gold-rush era of the Gay '90s. Red carpets and red-velvet wallpaper, brass fixtures, and historical photos are its earmarks.

The gold-rush theme is carried over into the 100- and 200-numbered rooms in the main hotel building north of Third. An oval brass mirror hangs above the desk in each room; white loge-style drapes hide the midsummer midnight sun from the two double beds. There are thermostat-controlled electric baseboard heating, a clock radio, and complimentary sundries in the bathroom. The 300- through 600-numbered rooms south of Third are more like motel units with outside entrances; they're smaller and less atmospheric than the lower-numbered units.

Dining/Entertainment: The Westmark has two restaurants. The spacious Chilkoot Dining Room adjoins the main lobby, serving outstanding dishes in the moderate to expensive range. The informal Sourdough Café is an Alaska-style Italian restaurant. (For full descriptions, see "Where to Dine," below.) The Bonanza Lounge, open from 4pm to midnight, is a climb up a circular staircase from the lobby; live musical revues are sometimes featured.

Services: Courtesy van to the airport, ferry, and Chilkoot Trail; car-rental and travel agency.

Facilities: Gift shop, guest laundry.

MODERATE

GOLDEN NORTH HOTEL, Third Ave. and Broadway (P.O. Box 431), Skagway, AK 99840. Tel. 907/983-2294 or 983-2451. Fax 907/983-2755. 33 rms (all with bath).

$ Rates: $60 single; $70 double; $75 twin. Additional person $5 extra. AE, CB, DC, MC, V.

The Golden North Hotel, one of four accommodations in Skagway that remain open year-round, is believed to be the oldest hotel in Alaska in continuous operation since it opened in 1898. It's a living museum of Victoriana—beginning with the lobby, whose reception desk, display sideboard, and even the settees facing the fireplace hail from another time.

A small plaque dedicates each room to a different gold rush–era family. Contained within are the original furnishings of that family: beds with oak or brass frames, hardwood dressers, portraits on the walls. Although all the rooms have red carpeting and gaily patterned wallpaper, no two are the same. All have private baths (showers but no tubs), and heating is done the old-fashioned way: with hot water. There are no TVs or phones, by the way. But there's a beauty salon, and a courtesy van is available.

The Golden North Restaurant is open from 6am to 9pm daily. It features a soup-and-salad bar at lunchtime, steak and seafood entrees ($12–$21) for dinner. A lounge is adjacent to the restaurant.

GOLD RUSH LODGE, Sixth Ave. and Alaska St. (P.O. Box 514), Skagway, AK 99840. Tel. 907/983-2831. Fax 907/983-2742. 12 rms (all with bath). TV

$ Rates: $65 single; $75 double; $80 triple. MC, V.

Rooms at this motel, one of the few to remain open year-round, are comfortable but hardly flamboyant: orange carpet, twin beds, electric baseboard heating. All rooms have outside entrances. Cable television features Showtime. There's no phone, though; you'll have to use the booth outside. Complimentary juice, coffee, and pastry are offered. A courtesy car provides service to the ferry terminal and downtown. Senior rates and no-smoking rooms are also available.

GRAMMA'S BED & BREAKFAST, Seventh Ave. and State St. (P.O. Box 315), Skagway, AK 99840. Tel. 907/983-2312. 4 rms (with shared bath). TV TEL

$ Rates (including continental breakfast): $50 single; $55 double; $65 triple. MC, V.

Rooms at Gramma's are aptly named: They'll remind you of a visit to your grandmother's house. There's plenty of Victorian lace together with antique furnishings in a cozy, home-style atmosphere.

SGT. PRESTON'S LODGE, Sixth Ave. and State St. (P.O. Box 538), Skagway, AK 99840. Tel. 907/983-2521. 22 rms (12 with bath). TV TEL

$ Rates (including continental breakfast): $55 single without bath, $65 single with bath; $65 double without bath, $75 double with bath. Additional person $5 extra. AE, CB, DC, DISC, MC, V.

Never mind that the TV character of the 1950s after whom the lodge is named, Sergeant Preston of the Yukon, was a member of the Royal Canadian Mounted Police: In pursuit of his man, Sergeant Preston and his lead sled dog, King, did make occasional trips into Skagway. The lodge's rooms, all on ground level and open year-round, are decorated in autumn colors and vary in spaciousness, bed size, and amenities. They are kept warm by central forced-air heating. Courtesy van service is included in the room rate.

SKAGWAY INN, Seventh Avenue and Broadway (P.O. Box 500), Skagway, AK 99840. Tel. 907/983-2289. 12 rms (all with shared bath).

$ Rates (including breakfast): $55 single; $66 double; $79 twin; $91 quad. AE, MC, V. **Closed:** Sept 16–Apr.

Built in 1897 as a rooming house for women, the Skagway Inn today has rooms named in remembrance of those hardy gals who survived rough-and-ready Skagway, including Alice, Essie, Flo, and Grace. Each of them was a little bit different—and so is each of the period-style rooms. Everyone shares the charming living room, however, with its couches and easy chairs, piano, and television. A hearty full breakfast is provided. Smoking is not permitted. There's courtesy car service to the airport, ferry dock, and Chilkoot Trail.

WIND VALLEY LODGE, 22nd Ave. and State St. (P.O. Box 354), Skagway, AK 99840. Tel. 907/983-2236. Fax 907/983-2236. 30 rms (all with bath). TV

$ Rates: $59 single; $69 double. Additional person $10 extra; children under 12 stay free in parents' room. AE, MC, V. **Closed:** Dec to mid-Mar.

Like many ex-railroadmen, owner Les Fairbanks, a former brakeman on the White Pass & Yukon Route, couldn't stand to be far from the tracks. So he built his motel across the street from the old railroad yard and even decorated his spacious rooms with rail photographs he took in the 1950s. The property caters as much to motorists and business travelers as to short-term tourists. Each room has a queen-size bed or twin beds, table and chairs, desk and dresser, and electric baseboard heating. Cribs are free. Six rooms are designated no-smoking, and one is available for disabled travelers. Public phones are in a vending room; there's a coin-operated guest laundry, as well as a spa. The lodge provides courtesy transportation to those who need it, but it's a pleasant one-mile walk into town.

INEXPENSIVE

IRENE'S INN, Sixth Ave. and Broadway (P.O. Box 538), Skagway, AK 99840. Tel. 907/983-2520. 10 rms (2 with bath).

$ Rates: $35 single without bath, $60 single with bath; $50 double without bath, $65 double with bath. Additional person $5 extra. AE, CB, DC, DISC, MC, V. **Closed:** Oct–May 14.

Despite a boost in rates to keep pace with extensive remodeling, Irene's continues to attract budget-conscious guests. Rooms are small and simple, with twin beds, a towel rack, and a nightstand with a lamp. Venetian blinds and lace curtains are on the windows, and a hot-water baseboard heater is against the wood-paneled walls. Guests check in at the ground-floor bakery (open from 7am to 11pm daily) and restaurant (open from 11am to 2pm and 5 to 10pm daily).

BUDGET

SKAGWAY HOME HOSTEL, Third Ave. and Main St., Skagway, AK 99840. Tel. 907/983-2131. 10 beds.

$ Rates: $10 for card-carrying members of the American Youth Hostel Association, $15 for nonmembers. No credit cards.

This 10-bed home is a member of the American Youth Hostel network. It provides year-round housing for all ages. Pets, drinking, and smoking are not permitted, and there's an 11pm curfew. There are shared baths, a kitchen, and common facilities.

CAMPGROUNDS

Back Track Camper Park, 12th and Broadway (tel. 983-3333), has 70 RV sites at $15 per night and 15 tent sites at $8 per night. Facilities include restrooms and showers, a guest laundry, and a TV room. **Hanousek Park,** 14th and Broadway (tel. 983-2768), has 10 tent sites and 40 RV spaces that go for $8 per night. **Pullen Creek Park,** on Congress Way near the small-boat harbor (tel. 983-2768), has 42 RV sites that cost $13.50 per night. **Hoover's,** at Fourth and Main (tel. 907/983-2454), has 10 RV sites at $10 per night. Showers are available. The **Liarsville** campground (tel. 983-2061), located north of the Skagway River Bridge on the Klondike Highway, has tent and RV sites for $6 per night.

There's also a small National Park Service campground for backpackers at **Dyea,** near the Chilkoot Trailhead, nine miles by dirt road from Skagway. This one costs $10, but it'll cost you around $12 to get there by local taxi.

WHERE TO DINE
EXPENSIVE

CHILKOOT DINING ROOM, in the Westmark Inn, Third Ave. and Spring St. Tel. 983-6000.

   Cuisine: AMERICAN. **Reservations:** Recommended.

$ **Prices:** Appetizers $5–$8; main courses $13–$24; breakfast $5.50–$9; lunch $8.50–$11. AE, CB, DC, DISC, MC, V.

   Open: May 20–Sept 25, breakfast daily 5:30–10am; lunch daily 11:30am–1pm; dinner daily 5–9pm. **Closed:** Sept 26–May 19.

A world-record 126-pound king salmon is mounted over the entrance to the Chilkoot Room from the Westmark's main lobby. It's a clue to try the salmon baked with brown sugar, a dish acclaimed by the press all the way to New York. If you're not a fish eater, the apple-almond chicken is a house specialty. At lunchtime, there's a generous all-you-can-eat seafood buffet. The Chilkoot Room's garden-trellis atmosphere is given gold-rush flavor by historical photos on the walls.

MODERATE

NORTHERN LIGHTS PIZZERIA, Broadway between Fourth and Fifth Aves. Tel. 983-2225.

   Cuisine: INTERNATIONAL. **Reservations:** Recommended for dinner.

$ **Prices:** Breakfast $3.75–$6.75; lunch $4.50–$9.95; dinner $4.50–$16.95. AE, V.

   Open: Mid-May to mid-Sept, daily 6am–10pm. **Closed:** Mid-Sept to mid-May.

This informal restaurant has a truly eclectic menu. The specialty is pizza, but you can also dine on a Greek salad and gyros or Mexican tacos and burritos. Burgers and sandwiches are served evenings as well as lunchtime—even full porterhouse steak dinners don't break the bank. The restaurant is also known for its hearty breakfasts.

SOURDOUGH CAFE, in the Westmark Inn, Third Ave. and Spring St. Tel. 983-6000.

   Cuisine: ITALIAN. **Reservations:** Recommended.

$ **Prices:** Lunch $4–$8; dinner $8–$14. AE, CB, DC, DISC, MC, V.

   Open: May 20–Sept 25, lunch daily 11:30am–3pm; dinner daily 5–8pm. **Closed:** Sept 26–May 19.

Checkered tablecloths, painted benches, and turn-of-the-century photos highlight the Sourdough Café, where the menu is Italian. Spaghetti dinners, including bread and salad, start around $8, while featured dishes like veal parmigiana are a little higher. Pizza is also a featured item. Wine is served by the glass. Cafeteria-style lunches include a by-the-pound salad bar.

INEXPENSIVE

DEE'S SALMON BAKE, First Ave. and Broadway. Tel. 983-2200.

   Cuisine: STEAK/SEAFOOD. **Reservations:** Not required.

$ **Prices:** Main courses $5–$13. MC, V.

   Open: Daily 11am–9pm.

There's both indoor and outdoor seating at Dee's, where the fare goes beyond salmon. The menu features a variety of steak and seafood dishes, such as halibut, steaks, and burgers.

PROSPECTOR'S SOURDOUGH RESTAURANT, Broadway between Fourth and Fifth Aves. Tel. 983-2865.

   Cuisine: AMERICAN. **Reservations:** Recommended for dinner.

$ **Prices:** Breakfast $3.50–$6.75; lunch $5.50–$8.75; dinner $5.50–$11.50. AE, MC, V.

Open: Daily 6am–9pm.

Oil paintings of mountain scenery hang on the walls of this spacious coffeehouse. It's the only place in town where you can get a fresh salmon dinner for $10.50, including soup or salad, potato, and vegetable. Steak sandwiches are a good bet at lunch, and Goldie's Grubstake, an Alaska-size breakfast with three hotcakes, two eggs, meat, and coffee, highlights the morning menu.

SWEET TOOTH SALOON, Broadway at Third Ave. Tel. 983-2405.
    Cuisine: AMERICAN. **Reservations:** Not accepted.
    $ Prices: Average meal $1.50–$3.50. No credit cards.
    Open: Daily 6am–6pm.
This place is tiny (only seven tables) but has great cinnamon rolls and the cheapest eggs in town.

EVENING ENTERTAINMENT

There aren't a lot of places to choose from, but those that do exist can really get wild when the ships are in port. Everyone—tourist, local, and seasonal worker—seems to gravitate to Madame Jan's ✪ **Red Onion Saloon and Gold Rush Brothel,** Broadway and Second Avenue (tel. 983-2222). It's no longer a house of ill repute, but you can buy a monogrammed garter and pretend you were there when it was. The Red Onion has live jazz frequently, honky-tonk piano and jukebox always, and dancing wherever you can find empty floor space. Great lunch sandwiches too.

Don't spend all your evening hours in the Red Onion, though. Take a break for ✪ *Skaguay in the Days of '98,* staged daily from mid-May to mid-September in the Eagles Hall, Broadway and Sixth Avenue. A musical production on a Gay '90s dance-hall set, the show recounts the flamboyant career and demise of Jefferson ("Soapy") Smith during Skagway's heyday. Gold Rush Productions, P.O. Box 1897, Skagway, AK 99840 (tel. 907/983-2545), has been presenting this show since 1926! The box office is open daily from 10am to 9pm; tickets are $12 for adults, $6 for kids. You may also book through cruise-ship excursion offices. Forty-five minutes of casino-style gambling (with phony money) precedes the 8:30pm evening curtain—the winner earns an opportunity to remove a garter from a dance-hall queen. A matinee schedule is geared to cruise ships.

Another worthwhile summer evening pursuit is a visit to the **Buckwheat Show,** presented by the so-called Bard of Skagway. Every night at 7:30pm, Buckwheat Donahue recites Robert Service ballads in the Arctic Brotherhood Hall, Broadway between Second and Third Avenues. Admission is $6.

If you're merely looking for a cold beer and a pinch of conversation, **Moe's Frontier Bar,** on Broadway between Fourth and Fifth (tel. 983-2238), does a thriving business with the local crowd.

SETTLING INTO ANCHORAGE

Half of all Alaskans live in Anchorage, the state's largest city and commercial center. Its approximately 250,000 residents make their homes within sight of Mount McKinley, on a large, flat triangle of land bounded on the east by the rounded peaks of the Chugach Mountains and on the northwest and southwest by the tidal fluctuations of the Cook Inlet.

The residents of Anchorage are mainly young (average age: 26) and affluent (average annual income: $28,000). They like sophisticated restaurants, shops, music, and theater. They like to live in suburbia, drive to a secure job in the morning and return home in the evening, and take their weekends to visit the wilderness.

That wilderness is never far away: Moose frequently stroll through backyards and beluga whales frolic in the inlet. Within an easy day's trip are rugged mountains, mighty glaciers, and wild rivers.

Once an Athabaskan Indian fishing camp, the site of Anchorage was first visited by the ubiquitous Capt. James Cook in 1778. Miners en route to rich inland goldfields used the deep-water anchorage at the mouth of Ship Creek before the turn of the 20th century. But it wasn't until 1914 that the town was established as a tent city for Alaska Railroad workers. The first permanent buildings were constructed the following year on the bluff overlooking the creek.

Anchorage remained primarily a rail headquarters, with its population stagnated at around 2,000, until World War II military spending gave impetus to the local economy. With the opening of Fort Richardson and Elmendorf Air Base, and the construction of the Alaska Highway, the city became directly linked to the outside world. By 1950 some 40,000 people called themselves permanent residents.

No one who lived in Alaska in 1964 will ever forget the Good Friday earthquake. No one who has moved here since can ignore it. At 5:36pm on March 27, the largest tremor ever felt on the North American continent devastated large sections of the city. Seismographs measured it between 8.4 and 8.6 on the Richter scale. Only nine people died in Anchorage itself, but property damage was estimated at over $300 million. With federal disaster aid, Anchorage quickly rebuilt. Today, Earthquake Park and museum displays graphically recall nature's wrath.

Anchorage owes its current stature to the building of the Trans Alaska Pipeline. The largest private construction project in history brought tens of thousands of new workers to Alaska in the 1970s. Many of them chose to remain and build their lives in the Anchorage area after the 779-mile pipeline was completed in 1977.

WHAT'S SPECIAL ABOUT ANCHORAGE

Natural Attractions

☐ White beluga whales in the Cook Inlet, visible from the windows of many downtown buildings.

☐ Tour boats crossing a lake to the foot of Portage Glacier, the most visited attraction in Alaska.

☐ Anchorage Coastal Wildlife Refuge at Potter Marsh, which lures more than 130 species of birds to a 2,300-acre wetland.

Culture

☐ The Anchorage Museum of History and Art, displaying the work of such noted Alaska painters as Sydney Laurence and Fred Machetanz.

☐ The Alaska Center for the Performing Arts, a $67-million complex that attracts major symphonies and theater companies.

☐ The Fur Rendezvous, a 10-day winter festival in February, combining music and dance with athletic contests, Native heritage, and a big parade.

Heritage

☐ Exhibits at Earthquake Park describing the devastation of the 1964 tremor, 8.4 on the Richter scale.

☐ Crow Creek Mine in Girdwood, where a late 19th-century goldmining community is preserved in its entirety.

Winter Recreation

☐ Mount Alyeska, the state's leading ski resort, which has been proposed as a site for Winter Olympics alpine events.

☐ Over 120 miles of groomed cross-country ski trails in Anchorage parks, converted in summer to bicycle paths.

Because of its unique geographical location—roughly equidistant between Tokyo and New York, only slightly farther to London—Anchorage has become an international crossroads city and a world trade center. Since the late 1970s, over 75% of all Alaskan exports have gone to Japan, the major consumer of Alaska's seafood, petroleum products, and timber. Korea and China are also important markets for Alaska.

Anchorage's climate, thanks to the warming Japanese Current, is surprisingly mild for a city at 61° North Latitude. Its winters have been compared to those of Innsbruck, Austria, with temperatures commonly in the teens and 20s; its 60°F and 70°F summers are like those of San Francisco. Summer days last over 19 hours in mid-June. Winter nights, kept bright by the aurora borealis, can seem almost interminable in the days before Christmas. Average annual precipitation is only about 15 inches, much of that falling in the form of winter snow (60 inches average).

1. ORIENTATION

ARRIVING

As Alaska's transportation hub, Anchorage is easily accessible by air and road, less readily by scheduled ship.

BY PLANE

Well over 100 flights a day originate or terminate at **Anchorage International Airport** (tel. 907/266-2525). The international terminal serves about a dozen airlines, many of them foreign flag carriers, which consider Anchorage an ideal stopover and refueling point between the Orient and Europe or the U.S. East Coast. The domestic terminal handles all flights arriving and departing within Alaska and between Anchorage and the Lower 48. Curb-side check-in is not provided and some travelers report waiting as much as an hour to check bags, so take this into account when making your departure plans. The Anchorage Convention and Visitors Bureau staffs information desks on the ground floors of both terminals (tel. 266-2437). There are also several restaurants or quick-serve cafés, lounges, and gift shops, as well as prominent displays of Alaskan wildlife and art in both terminals. The two terminals, about 500 yards apart, are connected by a free shuttle bus, operating at 15-minute intervals from 5:30am to 2:30am daily.

Domestic airlines serving Anchorage are: **Alaska Airlines,** 4750 W. International Airport Rd. (tel. 907/243-3300, or toll free 800/426-0333), and also in the Anchorage Hilton and Sheraton Hotels; **Continental Airlines,** at the airport (tel. 907/266-2830, or toll free 800/525-0280); **Delta Airlines,** 3830 W. International Airport Rd. (tel. toll free 800/221-1212), and also in the Hotel Captain Cook; **Northwest Airlines,** 4300 W. International Airport Rd. (tel. toll free 800/225-2525), and also in the Anchorage Hilton Hotel; **United Airlines,** at the airport (tel. 907/562-4020, or toll free 800/241-6522); and **MarkAir,** 4100 W. International Airport Rd. (tel. 907/243-6275, or toll free 800/426-6784, 800/478-0800 in Alaska).

GETTING TO & FROM THE INTERNATIONAL AIRPORT Anchorage International Airport is located about five miles southwest of downtown. If you've just arrived and are driving a rental car, the easiest way to reach the city center by road is to head east on International Airport Road to a cloverleaf intersection with Minnesota Drive, then turn left (north) and proceed until, after a big S-curve, you find yourself entering downtown on I Street. The drive takes 15–20 minutes.

There are two alternatives. **Taxis** cost around $12 to downtown. The city bus, known as the **People Mover** (tel. 343-6453 weekdays from 7am to 6pm), also serves the airport. Route 6 stops hourly on the lower level and plies the byways to downtown via Minnesota Drive. The adult fare is 75¢, students pay 25¢, and preschoolers and senior citizens ride free with a pass.

SMALLER AIRPORTS In a state with eight times the national average number of pilots and 15 times the average aircraft per capita, it isn't surprising to learn that Anchorage International is not the only airport in the city (there are 17). In fact, International—though it ranks as the nation's 30th busiest airport—is not even the busiest in the city. That honor goes to **Merrill Field** (tel. 276-4044), east of downtown between Fourth and 15th Avenues, which is said to have more takeoffs and landings than any other airport in the world: over 375,000 a year. If you're flying to an airstrip in the bush, chances are you'll do so from here.

If you're traveling to a fishing lodge, there's a good chance you'll visit **Lake Hood Air Harbor,** the world's busiest floatplane base with about 85,000 flight arrivals and departures annually. Most of those are in summer, of course, but don't be surprised to see ski-equipped planes taking off and landing on the winter ice. Lake Hood is immediately north of the international airport.

BY TRAIN

The **Alaska Railroad,** 411 W. First Ave., on Ship Creek (P.O. Box 107500), Anchorage, AK 99510 (tel. 907/265-2494 or 265-2623, or toll free 800/544-0552), operates daily express service in summer (May 20 to September 20) between Anchorage and Fairbanks via Denali National Park (departs 8:30am). From September to May, service is twice a week. The one-way fare is $115 for adults, $57.50 for children 5–12. Additional local service between Anchorage and Denali Park operates twice a week, May through September. Daily from June to August the Alaska Railroad operates an all-day excursion between Anchorage and Seward.

A rail shuttle runs during the summer months between Portage and Whittier several times daily to serve Prince William Sound ferry arrivals and departures. (The ferry doesn't operate to Whittier in winter.) There is no Anchorage–Portage train, but Eagle Custom Tours (tel. 907/277-6228) provides bus service for the 40-mile connection twice daily (departing Anchorage at 8:30am and 5:15pm, departing Portage at 10:15am and 7pm). Reservations are required for the bus. Pray that it isn't raining or snowing when you reach Portage, because there's no town or station, or even a covered seating area. What settlement existed was wiped off the map by the 1964 earthquake.

BY BUS

Anchorage is served by scheduled bus lines, charter lines, and tour-bus lines. During the summer only, it's possible to travel by bus from the Lower 48 all the way to Anchorage.

Canadian Greyhound Lines operates year-round, six times a week in summer, from Vancouver and Edmonton to Whitehorse, capital of the Yukon Territory. From there, connecting service to Anchorage is available mid-May to mid-September on Tuesday, Friday, and Sunday aboard Gray Line's **Alaskon Express**, 547 W. Fourth Ave., Anchorage (tel. toll free 800/544-2206). In addition to Whitehorse, the Alaska towns of Skagway and Haines, at the northern end of the Alaska Marine Highway ferry system, are served three times weekly. It's $151 one way from Whitehorse to Anchorage (not including overnight accommodation in Beaver Creek) and $200 from Skagway. **Alaska-Denali Transit,** P.O. Box 4557, Anchorage, AK 99510 (tel. 907/273-3331), provides connections to Anchorage from Fairbanks. **Caribou Express,** 501 L St., Anchorage (tel. 907/278-5776), offers year-round service from Fairbanks, Denali National Park, Tok Junction, and points between. **Denali Overland Transportation Co.,** P.O. Box 330, Talkeetna, AK 99676 (tel. 907/733-2384), provides transportation between Anchorage, Talkeetna, and Denali Park, March 15 to September 15 only.

BY CAR

Contrary to popular belief, Anchorage is not the end of the Alaska Highway. That's up north, in Delta Junction. But the Glenn Highway, which originates in Anchorage, wends its way 180 miles northeast to Glennallen, and the Tok Cutoff joins the Alaska Highway 138 miles farther on at Tok Junction. From there it's a mere 1,311 miles to Milepost 0 of the Alaska Highway at Dawson Creek, B.C., and another 712 miles to the nearest U.S. border crossings at Sumas, Wash., and Babb, Mont. Anchorage is 2,463 road miles from Seattle, 3,608 from Los Angeles, 3,690 from Chicago, 4,285 from Houston, 4,499 from New York, and 5,074 from Miami.

If you're heading north to Fairbanks, take the Glenn Highway as far as Palmer, 40 miles northeast; turn west onto the George Parks Highway, which will carry you the remaining 335 miles to Alaska's second city. The Seward Highway is the only route south to the Kenai Peninsula. It's 126 miles to Seward. Homer is 225 miles via the Sterling Highway, which branches off the Seward Highway near Kenai Lake.

BY SHIP

There's little regularly scheduled passenger-ship service to Anchorage. The fickle tides of the Cook Inlet ebb and neap over 38 feet in the springtime—second only to Nova Scotia's Bay of Fundy (43 feet) on the North American continent. An occasional cruise liner puts the city on its schedule, but the vast majority of ships dock at the deep-water port of Whittier and carry their passengers overland to Anchorage.

Although the Alaska Marine Highway system operates to Valdez, Whittier, and Seward, all of which have direct road or rail access to Anchorage, there is no interconnecting ferry to southeast Alaska and beyond.

If you really want to travel to Anchorage from the Lower 48 by ship, you may have to check with freighter companies or join a West Coast fishing crew.

TOURIST INFORMATION

The best source of information in Anchorage is the **Anchorage Convention and Visitors Bureau,** 1600 A St., Suite 200, Anchorage, AK 99501-5162 (tel. 907/257-2331; fax 907/278-5559). On arrival, don't fail to visit the bureau's **Log Cabin Information Center,** at Fourth Avenue and F Street (tel. 907/274-3531), for full information on all area attractions, right down to restaurant menus. It's open daily: from 7:30am to 7pm June through August, 8:30am to 6pm in May and September, and 9am to 4pm the rest of the year. There's also a **24-hour events line** (tel. 276-3200) with recorded information on current attractions, including cultural and sports events. The **Anchorage Chamber of Commerce** is at 437 E St., Suite 300, Anchorage, AK 99501-2365 (tel. 907/272-7588). For statewide tourist information, contact the **Alaska Division of Tourism,** 3601 C St., Suite 722, Anchorage, AK 99503 (tel. 907/563-2167).

The glass-paned **Egan Civic and Convention Center,** 555 W. Fifth Ave. (tel. 907/263-2800), has nearly 100,000 square feet of space for meetings and exhibits.

For information on outdoor pursuits, try the **U.S. Forest Service** (Chugach National Forest), 201 E. Ninth Ave., Suite 206, Anchorage, AK 99501 (tel. 907/261-2500); the **Alaska Division of Parks and Outdoor Recreation,** 3601 C St., Suite 1280 (P.O. Box 7001), Anchorage, AK 99510 (tel. 907/762-2617); and the **Alaska Public Lands Information Center,** 605 W. Fourth Ave., Anchorage, AK 99501 (tel. 907/271-2737).

AAA Alaska is affiliated with the American Automobile Association. Members can call 24 hours for emergency road service (tel. 907/337-6921) or during weekday office hours for travel assistance (tel. toll free 800/367-7020). For up-to-date information on winter road conditions, dial 337-9481.

For foreign visitors, the visitors bureau maintains a language bank of 26 languages, from Indonesian and Inupiat to Armenian and Serbo-Croatian. In addition, Anchorage has two foreign consulates general (Japan and Korea) and consuls or honorary consulates for Denmark, Finland, France, Germany, Norway, Sweden, and the United Kingdom.

CITY LAYOUT

When locals talk about the Anchorage Bowl, the subject isn't a New Year's Day football game or a 10-pin alley. That's the name given to a mountain- and sea-ringed swath of land on which the city is built. Sprawling for some 10 miles north-south, from Elmendorf Air Force Base to Rabbit Creek, and 10 miles east-west, from Chugach State Park to Point Campbell, Anchorage city encompasses about 75 square miles of land. The Municipality of Anchorage, stretching over 50 miles from the Portage Glacier to the head of Cook Inlet, covers 1,955 square miles.

Despite this vastness, it's easy to find your way around downtown Anchorage. All **numbered avenues** run east-west, and all **lettered streets** run north-south. The city is divided neatly in two by **A Street.** West of it, streets proceed alphabetically, B through U. Eastward, they're also alphabetical, but with names—Barrow, Cordova, Denali, Eagle, Fairbanks, Gambell, Hyder, Ingra, and so on through Orca. Fifth Avenue, going one-way west, and Sixth Avenue, running one-way east, are extensions of the **Glenn Highway,** which runs east and north to Eagle River and beyond.

Gambell Street, going one-way south, and Ingra Street, running one-way north, connect with the **Seward Highway,** the main thoroughfare to the Kenai Peninsula.
   Downtown is generally defined as that area west of Merrill Field between Ship and Chester Creeks. The **main business district** runs from Third to Sixth Avenues between A and L Streets. **Midtown,** a growing business and restaurant area, lies west of the Seward Highway and south of Chester Creek as far as International Airport Road. **Spenard,** the city's traditional (and often notorious) entertainment district, weaves along Spenard Road connecting midtown with the international airport. Large parks and suburban shopping malls speckle the outlying areas to the south and east.

2. GETTING AROUND

Bus, taxi, and rental cars are the preferred means of getting around Anchorage. The more energetic travel on foot or bicycle—or, in season, on cross-country skis.

BY BUS   The Anchorage public bus network—properly called the **People Mover Mass Transit System**—operates 22 routes to all corners of the city, providing easy access to most visitor attractions and activities. Regular service is available Monday through Friday from 5:30am to 11:05pm and on Saturday from 7:30am to 11:05pm. A few routes also have Sunday service from 9:30am to 6:30pm. Fares (exact change, please) are 75¢ for adults, 25¢ for students, free for preschoolers and senior citizens.
   The downtown **Transit Center** at Sixth Avenue and G Street has free information and maps of all routes. It's open from 6am to 10pm daily. Every route but one makes a stop here. Until you get familiar with the route system, you can call the People Mover's **"Ride Line"** (tel. 343-6453 from 7am to 6pm weekdays) and tell the operator where you are, where you'd like to go, and at what time of day. There's even a "Ride Line" for the hearing impaired (tel. 343-4775).

BY TAXI   They're expensive but often indispensable, especially if the weather's bad or you have to get somewhere in a hurry. Try **Alaska Cab** (tel. 563-5353), **Checker Cab** (tel. 276-1234), or **Yellow Cab** (tel. 272-2422). All have similar rates. It's about $12, for example, from downtown to the international airport, a distance of five miles. Some folks insist they get the fairest fares from **Eagle Cab** (tel. 694-5555).

BY CAR   All major car-rental firms, and many privately owned local companies, are represented at Anchorage International Airport and downtown offices. I have had good service and fair prices renting from both **Avis,** Fifth Avenue and B Street (tel. 243-4300, or toll free 800/331-1212), and at the airport (tel. 243-2377), and **National,** 509 W. Third Ave. (tel. 274-3695, or toll free 800/227-7368), and at the airport (tel. 243-3406). Other large rental agencies include **Budget,** 521 W. Third Ave. (tel. 276-2100, or toll free 800/527-0700), and at the airport (tel. 243-0150); **Dollar,** 940 W. International Airport Rd. (tel. 562-1412, or toll free 800/800-4000); and **Hertz,** at the airport (tel. 243-3308, or toll free 800/654-3131). Among cut-rate agencies, **Rent-a-Wreck,** 854 E. 36th Ave. (tel. 562-5499, or toll free 800/478-5499), and **Thrifty,** 3730 Spenard Rd. (tel. 276-2855, or toll free 800/FOR-CARS), offer free pickup and delivery service for clients. Check the Anchorage phone directory's *Yellow Pages* or the Anchorage Convention and Visitors Bureau for a complete list.
   As availability of rental vehicles decreases in summer, rates increase. It's wise to make advance reservations at that time. Expect to pay $40–$50 a day, limited mileage, for a compact model.
   For information on current **road conditions,** call 243-7675.

BY BICYCLE   Bicycling is very popular in Anchorage, and the city has catered to its young population by installing a 121-mile network of bicycle trails. For rentals of touring or mountain bikes, check with **Downtown Bicycle Rental,** Sixth Avenue and B Street (tel. 279-5293), or **Borealis Backcountry Cycling,** 300 W. 36th Ave. (tel. 562-4493).

FAST FACTS: ANCHORAGE

American Express   The local Amex office is located at 2522 Arctic Blvd. (tel. 276-2310).

Area Code   The telephone area code for Anchorage and the rest of Alaska is 907.

Babysitters   Call Rent-a-Mom, 7926 Old Seward Hwy., Suite C-8 (tel. 349-4463).

Barbers   See "Hairdressers/Barbers," below.

Business Hours   In summer, shops are generally open from 9am to 9pm Monday through Saturday and 10am to 6pm on Sunday. Winter hours are more limited. Banks, easily located in the downtown area and major suburban shopping areas, are generally open Monday through Friday from 10am to 6pm.

Car Rentals   See "Getting Around," above.

Cleaners   See "Laundry/Dry Cleaning," below.

Climate   See "When to Go," in Chapter 2.

Crime   See "Safety," below.

Currency Exchange   There is an exchange counter at the international terminal of Anchorage International Airport. Deak International has a downtown office in the Anchorage Hilton Hotel, 311 F St. (tel. 278-2822).

Dentist   An emergency dental line is available 24 hours (tel. 279-9144).

Doctor   Anchorage has several outpatient clinics, including Anchorage Medical & Surgical Clinic, downtown at 718 K St. (tel. 272-2571); and FirstCare, 3710 Woodland in Spenard (tel. 248-1122) or 1301 Huffman in South Anchorage (tel. 345-1199). For physician referral, call Providence Hospital (tel. 562-3737) Monday through Friday between 8am and noon or 1 and 3pm.

Drugstores   Most times, you can visit Longs Drugs, 200 E. Northern Lights Blvd. (tel. 279-8410) or 601 E. Dimond Blvd. (tel. 349-4508). After hours, call the hospitals (see below).

Emergencies   For emergency assistance from police, fire department, or ambulance, dial **911.**

Eyeglasses   In downtown Anchorage, there's a good optical shop at JC Penney, Fifth Avenue and E Street (tel. 279-5656). In midtown, visit The Mall at Sears, 700 E. Northern Lights Blvd. at Old Seward Highway.

Film   See "Photographic Needs," below.

Hairdressers/Barbers   There are salons throughout the greater Anchorage area including The Mall at Sears, 700 E. Northern Lights Blvd. at Old Seward Highway. Another reliable choice is the styling salon in JC Penney, Fifth Avenue and E Street (tel. 279-5656).

Hospitals   The major institutions are Providence Hospital, 3200 Providence Dr. (tel. 562-2211), and Humana Hospital, 2801 DeBarr Rd. (tel. 276-1131).

Hotlines   Crisis line (tel. 562-4048 or 563-3200), battered women (tel. 272-0100), pet emergency (tel. 274-5636), poison control (tel. 261-3193), rape and assault (tel. 276-7273).

Information   See "Tourist Information" in "Orientation," in this chapter.

Laundry/Dry Cleaning   For one-hour dry cleaning, try Alaska Cleaners, with 15 locations in greater Anchorage, including Fourth Avenue and I Street (tel. 274-7753), open daily from 7:30am to 6pm. A couple of good coin-op laundries are Cleaning World, 1120 Huffman Rd. at Old Seward Highway (tel. 345-2311), and Tudor Coin-Laundry and Dry Cleaning, 2494 E. Tudor Rd. (tel. 561-7406).

Libraries For reading materials, check out the Z. J. Loussac Public Library, 3600 Denali St. (tel. 261-2844); the University of Alaska Library, 3211 Providence Dr. (tel. 786-1871); or the National Bank of Alaska's Heritage Library and Museum, 301 W. Northern Lights Blvd. (tel. 265-2834).

Lost Property Call the police (see below).

Newspapers/Magazines The *Anchorage Daily News* is the city's only major daily newspaper, having purchased the *Anchorage Times*, its sole competition, in 1992. It is published mornings. *Alaska* magazine, a high-quality glossy, comes out monthly and is widely available on newsstands.

Photographic Needs Stewart's Photo Shop, at 531 W. Fourth Ave. (tel. 272-8581), has a large selection of photographic supplies and services, including photofinishing and rentals. Dan's Camera Repair, 735 W. Fourth Ave., is recommended if you have camera trouble.

Police In case of emergencies, call 911. For normal business, dial 786-8500 for the Anchorage police, 269-5511 for Alaska State Troopers.

Post Office The downtown station is located on the lower level of the Post Office Mall, next to the Holiday Inn on West Third Avenue between C and D Streets. The main post office is located near the airport and is open 24 hours.

Radio Nineteen radio stations call Anchorage home, six of them AM stations and the remaining 13 FM.

Safety Even though Anchorage is Alaska's largest city, it's extremely safe by standards elsewhere. Nonetheless, whenever you're traveling in an unfamiliar city or region, you should stay alert. Be aware of your immediate surroundings. Keep a close eye on your possessions. Be particularly careful with cameras, purses, and wallets, all favorite targets of thieves and pickpockets.

Taxes The city of Anchorage tacks an 8% room tax onto all individual hotel bills.

Taxis See "Getting Around," in this chapter.

Telegrams/Telex/Fax Major hotels provide these services for guests at a nominal fee.

Television Anchorage has one public TV station, KAKM (PBS), Channel 7; and five commercial stations: KTUU (NBC), Channel 2; KTBY (independent), Channel 4; KYES (independent), Channel 5; KTVA (CBS), Channel 11; and KIMO (ABC), Channel 13.

Transit Information See "Getting Around," in this chapter.

Useful Telephone Numbers Road conditions in winter (tel. 243-7675), weather forecast (tel. 936-2525), visitor information (tel. 274-3531), calendar of events (tel. 276-3200 for a recording), language bank (tel. 276-4118).

Weather Call 936-2525.

3. ACCOMMODATIONS

With more than 4,000 guest rooms available in Anchorage, one might expect no shortage of space for travelers. Not necessarily so! During the height of the summer tourist season, in July and August, rooms are at a premium. So it's essential to book ahead.

If you do get stuck without a room, the Anchorage Convention and Visitors Bureau sometimes operates a **lodging hotline** (tel. 276-7655) during the summer months and other peak periods. Contact the **Log Cabin Visitor Information Center** (tel. 907/274-3531) if the line is not connected.

FROMMER'S SMART TRAVELER: HOTELS

1. Always remember that at any time of year a hotel room is a perishable commodity: If it's not sold, the revenue is lost forever. Therefore, rates are linked to the hotel's occupancy rate. If it's 90% occupied, the price goes up; if it's 50% occupied, the price goes down. So always try negotiating by stating *your* price.
2. Travel before Memorial Day or after Labor Day, if possible. Off-season rates at Alaskan hotels are half to two-thirds of the summer rates.
3. Hotels typically offer corporate rates, industry rates, government rates, active military rates, educational rates, and senior citizens' rates. If you're a member of any special-interest group whatsoever, ask about discounts.
4. Consider staying at a bed-and-breakfast establishment, which often has lower rates than hotels and saves you money by including your first meal of the day.

In the pages that follow I have categorized hotels and motels according to location and price. **Downtown** is between Ship Creek and Chester Creek, from Ingra Street (Seward Highway) to the Cook Inlet's Knik Arm. **Midtown/Spenard** includes everything south of Chester Creek and west of Seward Highway as far as International Airport Road—as well as the airport itself. **South Anchorage** is everything else along the Seward Highway corridor, heading toward the Kenai Peninsula. **East Anchorage** comprises all lodgings along the Glenn Highway, heading toward the Matanuska Valley.

Price Ranges The price breakdown is based on the walk-in rate for a standard double room during the summer season (room tax not included). "Very Expensive" hotel rooms run $180 and up per day; "Expensive," $125–$175; "Moderate," $90–$125; "Inexpensive," $60–$90; "Budget," under $60. Rates are significantly lower during the off-season from Labor Day to Memorial Day.

Tax The Anchorage room tax is 8%.

DOWNTOWN

Most of the downtown hotels are concentrated between Third and Sixth Avenues and between Gambell and L Streets.

VERY EXPENSIVE

ANCHORAGE HILTON, 500 W. Third Ave. (P.O. Box 100520), Anchorage, AK 99510. Tel. 907/272-7411, or toll free 800/245-2527 (800/HILTONS). Fax 907/265-7140. 577 rms, 23 suites. TV TEL
$ Rates: June–Sept 15, $160–$220 single; $180–$260 double; $185–$900 suite. Sept 16–May, $99–$160 single or double; $185–$900 suite. AE, CB, DC, DISC, ER, JCB, MC, V.

The Bristol Bay Native Corporation owns the Hilton. It was built in 1972, a 22-story tower on the site of the old Anchorage Hotel, and Hilton assumed management in 1977. In 1986 the hotel completed a $30-million renovation and expansion program, which included a new 15-story tower and a shopping mall.

The new guest rooms in the Hilton's Westward Tower sport a proud burgundy-and-jade color scheme. The older rooms, in the Anchorage Tower, have a similar mauve-toned look. All rooms are spacious and well lit, with handsome stained-wood furniture, including six-drawer dressers. The very large closet has floor-to-ceiling mirrors. Heating is thermostat-controlled. The television, with built-in AM/FM radio, has cable pickup and in-house movies. Beside the bed is an alarm clock. In the bathroom you'll find an array of hair-care products, lotion, soaps, and a sewing kit.

Dining/Entertainment: Atop the Westward Tower is the Top of the World restaurant, noted for its Sunday champagne brunches and its 360° view. Enjoy, too, the art deco setting, with its pastel tones: lilac carpeting, blue-green chairs, brass railings, etched-glass dividers, and huge pots of silk flowers. Dinner entrees, $18–$28, include such innovative recipes as breast of duckling with juniperberry sauce and apples, and fresh Hawaiian mahimahi with macadamia-nut butter sauce. In seasons with long days and warmer weather, a rooftop terrace is open for drinks and hors d'oeuvres.

On the ground floor, the Berry Patch coffee shop, decorated in shades of pastel peach with modern-art prints, serves omelets, salads, sandwiches, pastas, and half a dozen dinner dishes. Lunch runs $7–$11; dinner, $10–$16. The days of the old Anchorage Hotel are recalled in the festive decor of the Sports Edition lounge, which features a deli buffet lunch and a compact-disc sound system.

Services: Room service, valet laundry, no-smoking rooms and rooms adapted for disabled guests.

Facilities: Health club, free to guests, with heated swimming pool, sauna, Jacuzzi, and Universal gym; shopping mall with gift shops, art galleries, boutiques, and newsstand; hair salon; Alaska and Northwest airlines desks; banquet and conference facilities.

HOTEL CAPTAIN COOK, Fifth Ave. and K St., Anchorage, AK 99501. Tel. 907/276-6000, or toll free 800/323-7500, 800/478-3100 in Alaska. Fax 907/278-5366. Telex 9025340. 562 rms, 77 suites. TV TEL

$ Rates: May 22–Sept 22, $170 single; $180 double; $180–$500 suite. Sept 23–May 21, $118 single; $115–$128 double; $180–$500 suite. AE, CB, DC, DISC, ER, JCB, MC, V.

This landmark hotel, whose three gold-colored towers are easily seen from anywhere in downtown Anchorage, is probably the finest accommodation in Alaska. Owned by Alaska Gov. Walter J. Hickel and managed by his son, Wally Jr., it's a member of the independent Preferred Hotels group that also includes such prestigious names as the Imperial Hotel in Tokyo, the Dorchester in London, and the Breakers in Palm Beach. The coordinating themes of the Captain Cook are its rich decor of teakwood and polished brass and its art, much of it original oil paintings of the famous 18th-century English navigator who explored this coast of Alaska and most of the South Seas.

The guest rooms are located in three towers connected by a spacious ground level of restaurants, shops, and guest services. The rooms are decorated in muted shades of maroons, browns, and beiges, with teakwood furnishings and rattan lamps. All rooms have queen-size beds, plush chairs or couches, desk/dressers, large closets, and individually controlled electric baseboard heating. Local phone calls cost 50¢. Cable television is provided. There's an alarm clock, plus shampoo, soaps, and a sewing kit in the bathroom. All rooms are supplied with robes and morning newspaper, and turn-down service is provided. Executive suites in the 17th-floor penthouse of Tower II include such special touches as a velour bathrobe, a shoeshine machine, and complimentary breakfast in a private lounge.

Dining/Entertainment: The elite Crow's Nest serves continental cuisine, fresh Alaskan seafood, and wild game in a rooftop room designed like the underdeck of a ship. For $38–$50 a person, not including wine, you can enjoy a "menu gastronomique prix fixe," a five- to seven-course gourmet dinner. Main courses are priced at $24 à la carte, from crevettes à la "dry martini" to poussin rôti aux truffes. It's open Tuesday through Sunday from 6 to 11pm (from 7pm to midnight in summer). The lounge opens at 4pm. A popular Sunday champagne brunch is served from 10am to 2pm.

Among the Cook's other restaurants, I like Fletcher's, an informal pub in the lobby level of Tower III. The hand-molded copper ceiling, Italian marble floor and bar, and mahogany walls contrast with the simple menu of gourmet pizzas (Fletcher's special

0.5 mi
0.8 km
N

Knik Arm

Area of Inset

Earthquake Park

Westchester Lagoon

West 1st Ave.
West 3rd Ave.
Delaney Park

East 1st
East 3rd

Barrow St.
Cordova St.
Gambell St.
Ingra St.
Karluk St.

11th Ave.
12th Ave.
15th Ave.
16th Ave.

C Street
A Street
Denali St.
Eagle St.

Chester Cre

Fireweed Lane

Northern Lights Blvd.

Benson Blvd.

C Street
A Street
Denali St.

36th Ave.

Aircraft Dr.

Lakeshore Dr.

Lake Hood

Wisconsin St.

McRae Rd. Spenard Rd.

Northwood St.

Arctic Blvd

Lake Spenard

Int'l Airport Rd.

Tudor Rd.

Old Seward Hwy.

Anchorage International Airport

Connors Lake Park

Minnesota Dr.

International Airport Rd.

C Street

Connors Lake

Dowling Rd.

Raspberry Rd.

5585

Alaska Samovar **30**
Anchor Arms **29**
Anchorage Eagle Nest **10**
Anchorage Hilton **22**
Anchorage Hotel **23**
Anchorage International
  Hostel **19**
Arctic Inn Motel **15**

Arctic Tern Inn **1**
Best Western
  Barratt **12**
Best Western Golden
  Lion Hotel **16**
Big Timber Motel **2**
Days Inn **27**
Hillside Motel **6**

Holiday Inn **24**
Hotel Captain Cook
Inlet Inn **20**
Kobuk Hotel-Motel **4**
Midtown Lodge **7**
Mush Inn **3**
Northern Lights Inn
Puffin Inn **11**

ANCHORAGE ACCOMMODATIONS

Ship Creek

Davis Park

Commercial Dr.

1 ①

3 ① **2**

✈ Merrill Field

Bragaw St.

Russian

Jack

DeBarr Rd.

Springs

Park

Boniface Pkwy.

Greenbelt

Lake Otis Pkwy.

Goose Lake Park

Northern Lights Blvd.

University Dr.

Providence Dr.

DOWNTOWN ANCHORAGE

Rail Depot ■

Ship Creek

Warehouse Ave.

Knik Arm

Christiansen Dr.

W. 1st Ave.

E. 1st Ave.

W. 2nd Ave.

E. 2nd Ave.

22 Post Office ✉

25 **26**

Resolution Park

W. 3rd Ave.

E. 3rd Ave.

23

Elderberry Park

W. 4th Ave.

24

E. 4th Ave.

18

I St.

H St.

W. 5th Ave.

B St.

A St.

E. 5th Ave.

27 **29**

M St.

L St.

K St.

17

21

20

G St.

W. 6th Ave.

Barrow St.

Cordova St.

28

E. 6th Ave.

W. 7th Ave.

19

F St.

E St.

D St.

C St.

B St.

City Cemetery

N St.

M St.

W. 8th Ave.

Denali St.

Eagle St.

Fairbanks St.

Gambell St.

30

W. 9th Ave.

E. 9th Ave.

Delaney Park

W. 10th Ave.

E. 10th Ave.

Post Office ✉

Quality Inn Towers **5**
Regal Alaskan **13**
Sheraton Anchorage **28**
Super 8 Motel **9**
The Uptown **26**
Voyager Hotel **17**
West Coast
  International **14**

Westmark Anchorage **21**
Westmark Inn
  Third Avenue **25**

has duck sausage and goat cheese, at $9), fresh pastas, salads, and sandwiches. The bar features 31 imported beers and a world-class selection of 28 cognacs. It's open Monday through Friday from 11am to midnight, from 5pm on Saturday.

Also in the lobby is the Pantry, open daily from 6am to 10pm. It's a pleasant coffee shop, but priced on the high side: A chicken-salad sandwich is $7.75; two eggs with bacon, $8.75. A children's menu is available.

The Quarter Deck, on the 10th floor of Tower I, is a private restaurant for club members and hotel guests only. Guest chefs prepare regional dishes and creative surprises like wild mushroom omelets and grilled Thai shrimp with coconut-cream chili sauce. Lunch items, served Monday through Friday from 11am to 2pm, run $7–$12; dinner entrees, offered Monday through Saturday between 6 and 10pm, run $18–$26 per person.

Just off the lobby is the Whale's Tail, with live entertainment—usually a small Top-40 combo for dancing—Tuesday through Saturday until 1am, in an upscale Polynesian atmosphere. Fondue and hors d'oeuvres are served beginning at 5pm.

Services: 24-hour full-menu room service, concierge service, valet laundry, multilingual staff, no-smoking rooms and rooms for the disabled.

Facilities: Captain Cook Athletic Club, with a five-lane swimming pool, three racquetball courts, Nautilus weight room, sauna, Jacuzzi, steam room, solarium, tanning parlor, and masseur; shopping mall with boutiques, art galleries, gift shops and newsstand; barbershop and beauty salon; airline travel desk; 13 meeting rooms, banquet seating for 1,000, and covered guest parking.

SHERATON ANCHORAGE HOTEL, 401 E. Sixth Ave., Anchorage, AK 99501. Tel. 907/276-8700, or toll free 800/325-3535, 800/478-8700 in Alaska. Fax 907/276-7561. Telex 25325. 341 rms, 33 suites. TV TEL

$ Rates: Mid-May to mid-Sept, $195 single; $205 double; $260–$500 suite. Mid-Sept to mid-May, $90–$145 single; $90–$165 double; $160–$400 suite. AE, CB, DC, DISC, ER, JCB, MC, V.

The Sheraton calls itself a "showcase for Alaska art." The spacious lobby, with its giant sun roof, certainly has a museum feel to it. The theme is drawn from the art of the state's five major Native groups: Athabaskans, Aleuts, Tlingits, Haidas, and Eskimos. Look around the lobby. The free-standing marble staircase has genuine jade tiles from Alaska's southwest. The huge columns are decorated in the fashion of Yupik Eskimo arrow cases. The etched-marble murals—one shows a caribou migration, another a man being carried to the moon by an eagle—are Native designs that depict the kinship between animal and hunter.

Dark winter days are made brighter by a pastel color scheme of peaches and lime greens in the rooms and corridors. Business travelers are pleased to find a writing desk, modem jack (for laptop computers), and two phones in every room (local calls are 50¢). Each room has an armoire and a queen-size bed or two double beds. AM/FM radio and an alarm clock are built into the remote-control cable television, and in-house films can be viewed for an additional charge. Bathroom amenities include a hairdryer, three soaps, shampoo, lotion, shoe polish, and a sewing kit.

Dining/Entertainment: A departure from the Native theme is Josephine's, the Sheraton's highly regarded continental restaurant in the 15th-floor penthouse. The decor here is Napoleonic: It's named after Bonaparte's empress because Josephine's emblem, the trumpeter swan, frequently migrates in Alaska. You'll find the symbol embossed in crystal. You'll also find six French Empire-style chandeliers, and magnificent carpets and fabrics patterned after those in Napoleon's last palace. Cuisine is French provincial and Northwest. A favorite is potpourri Napoléon—medallions of veal, Scottish red deer, and stuffed quail, served with fresh linguine. If you start with steak tartare or escargots bourguignons and have a bottle of wine with your meal, you'll pay about $80 for a dinner for two. It's open for dinner Tuesday through Sunday from 5 to 10pm, and 10am to 2:30pm for Sunday brunch.

More down to earth is the Bistro, whose sidewalk-café adjoins the lobby. Pastas and other dishes are $6–$12. It's open daily from 6am to 10pm. On the other side of the lobby is the high-tech Legends Lounge. Hot hors d'oeuvres are served nightly from 5 to 7pm, and a disk jockey spins Top-40 records or live music is presented Wednesday through Saturday nights.

Services: Room service (5am–midnight), valet laundry, no-smoking rooms and rooms for disabled guests, tour package service.

Facilities: Small health club with weight equipment, sauna, and Jacuzzi; gift and sundry shop; spacious banquet and conference facilities, including the Grand Ballroom, which seats up to 1,300.

EXPENSIVE

ANCHORAGE HOTEL, 330 E St., Anchorage, AK 99501. Tel. 907/272-4553, or toll free 800/544-0988. Fax 907/277-4483. 21 rms, 10 suites. TV TEL
$ Rates (including continental breakfast): June–Sept 14, $129 single; $139 double; $159–$179 suite. Sept 15–May, $79 single; $89 double; $109–$129 suite. AE, CB, DC, DISC, JCB, MC, V.

The oldest hotel in Anchorage was established when the city itself was a mere infant, and it's still going strong. Built in 1916 on the site of the present-day Anchorage Hilton, it was the hub of city social life for decades. When the original structure was torn down in 1972 to make way for the Hilton, the hotel annex (erected in 1936 in the Late Gothic Revival style) became the Anchorage Hotel. But it had become run-down when Alaska native Bob Neumann bought it in 1988 and put it through a thorough restoration.

Today the elegant lobby—once the studio of famed Alaska landscape artist Sydney Laurence—features a comfortable seating area and handsome paintings. A broad staircase, which sweeps up to two floors of guest rooms, is lined with sepiatone photographs of Anchorage's earliest years. Rooms are of ample size and offer a queen-size or two double beds, a desk, a dresser, and other furnishings—including a deep, old-style bathtub. Ten parlor suites feature wet bars, refrigerators, and coffee makers. There's cable TV in all rooms, and local phone calls are free.

Services: Room service (from Cyrano's Café), valet laundry, complimentary newspaper, no-smoking rooms.

DAYS INN, 321 E. Fifth Ave., Anchorage, AK 99501. Tel. 907/276-7226, or toll free 800/633-1414. Fax 907/278-6041. 111 rms, 7 suites. TV TEL
$ Rates: Mid-May to mid-Sept, $119 single; $129 double. Mid-Sept to mid-May, $52–$59 single; $62–$69 double. AE, CB, DC, DISC, JCB, MC, V.

The Days Inn is built in the shape of a square, three-story doughnut. That's not as strange as it sounds, because the central courtyard is used for parking. The rooms typically have maroon carpeting, gray drapes, orange or blue bedspreads, and bare white walls. The hotel is soundproofed, but its lighting could be improved. Each room has double beds, a long desk/dresser, table and chair, and electric baseboard heating. On the negative side, three floors are served by a single slow elevator—but while you wait, you can take advantage of the soft drinks and ice on each floor.

Dining/Entertainment: The 24-hour Daybreak Coffee Shop is reasonably priced, with eggs Benedict for $5.50, cheeseburgers at $5, and a full steak-and-prawns, $12.50. The Plaza Lounge is open until 2am.

Services: Valet laundry, courtesy van, no-smoking rooms.

HOLIDAY INN OF ANCHORAGE, 239 W. Fourth Ave., Anchorage, AK 99501. Tel. 907/279-8671, or toll free 800/465-4329 (800/HOLIDAY). Fax 907/258-4733. Telex 09026647. 252 rms. TV TEL
$ Rates: May 23–Sept 8, $110–$115 single; $125–$130 double. Sept 9–May 22, $60–$65 single; $65–$70 double. AE, CB, DC, MC, V.

Alaska's only Holiday Inn is a great place for families. Its heated indoor swimming pool is a favorite with kids, who can purchase swimsuits from the hotel if they didn't bring their own. Each room has a king-size or double bed with reading lamps, a clock radio, a long dresser, chairs, and table. The carpets are green, the walls beige, the bedspreads rose patterned. Prints decorate the walls. Satellite TV and in-room movies are available.

Dining/Entertainment: The Greenery restaurant on the second floor serves a homemade soup-and-salad bar to complement the standard coffeeshop fare of omelets, sandwiches, and several entrees ($11–$15). It's open daily from 5am to 2pm and 5 to 11pm in summer, 7am to 2pm and 5 to 10pm in winter. Lucy's Lounge adjoins the restaurant.

Services: Room service (mornings and evenings), valet laundry, courtesy van, no-smoking rooms and rooms for the disabled.

Facilities: Heated indoor swimming pool, sauna, coin-operated laundry.

VOYAGER HOTEL, 501 K St., Anchorage, AK 99501. Tel. 907/277-9501, or toll free 800/247-9070. Fax 907/274-0333. 38 rms. TV TEL

$ Rates: May, $89 single; $99 double. June–Sept 15, $109 single; $129 double. Nov–Apr, $74 single; $79 double. Discounts for seniors. AE, CB, DC, DISC, MC, V.

Owned by Stan Williams, who was born in Anchorage when the population was 2,100 and has never left, the Voyager has an international flavor. There's an antique barometer on the wall, an antique chest with coffee service, a lighted globe, and a big world map.

Each of the Voyager's clean, spacious rooms is a minisuite, complete with kitchen facilities. The rooms are tastefully appointed with mauve carpets, blue upholstery, and light floral bedspreads. Modern-art prints adorn the walls. Each room has a queen-size bed, lamps that turn on at the touch of a finger, a large desk, a four-drawer dresser, a divan, and wheeled chairs. There's also plenty of closet space, and electric baseboard heating and hairdryers are provided in all rooms. Local phone calls are free. The office will provide a "kitchen kit," with pots, dishes, and silverware, on request.

Dining/Entertainment: In the lower level of the Voyager is the privately owned Corsair restaurant, one of Anchorage's finest (see "Where to Dine," below). The Voyager Lounge, with a street entrance, adjoins the lobby.

Services: Valet laundry, no-smoking rooms.

Facilities: Snack and sundry machines on second floor.

WESTMARK ANCHORAGE, 720 W. Fifth Ave., Anchorage, AK 99501. Tel. 907/276-7676, or toll free 800/544-0970, 800/274-6631 in Alaska, 800/999-2570 in Canada. Fax 907/258-4958. Telex 25414. 167 rms, 33 suites. TV TEL

$ Rates: Mid-May to mid-Sept, $154 single; $164 double. Mid-Sept to mid-May, $114 single; $126 double. AE, CB, DC, DISC, ER, MC, V.

The Westmark's location, near the Egan Convention Center and the new Performing Arts Center, isn't lost on business travelers, who make up a hefty portion of the regular clientele. Small trees (in planters) and rock pillars surround couches located in the cozy lobby. The newly renovated rooms boast rich wood furnishings, king-size and double beds, armoires, blue serge chairs, and landscape paintings on the walls. Heating is by electric baseboard. There is cable television with Showtime and ESPN; there are also direct-dial phones (local calls are free). Vanities are provided with shampoo and sewing kits.

Dining/Entertainment: A garden-style coffee shop, the Manor House, has an entrance right off the lobby. A 14th-floor cocktail lounge, the Penthouse, also serves businessmen's lunches on weekdays (11:30am to 1:30pm; summer hours extended 8:30am to 10pm).

Services: Room service, valet laundry, courtesy van, no-smoking rooms and rooms for the disabled.

Facilities: Gift and sundry shop.

WESTMARK INN THIRD AVENUE, 115 E. Third Ave., Anchorage, AK 99501. Tel. 907/272-7561, or toll free 800/544-0970, 800/274-6331 in Alaska, 800/999-2570 in Canada. Fax 907/272-3879. Telex 25224. 91 rms. TV TEL

$ Rates: Mid-May to mid-Sept, $125 single; $135 double. Mid-Sept to mid-May, $89 single; $92 double. AE, CB, DC, DISC, ER, MC, V.

This former TraveLodge has good-sized rooms—those on the ground floor even have private entrances. They've been newly renovated with powder-blue carpeting and pastel drapes and bedspreads. Heating is electric baseboard. TVs have local reception and cable with Showtime. Local telephone calls are free. Shampoo and a sewing kit are provided in the bathroom.

Dining/Entertainment: The Coach House Restaurant and Lounge have a nice warm feeling, with lots of greenery and a big fireplace. It's open daily during the winter from 6am to 2pm and 5 to 8pm. Hours are extended to 9pm in summer for food, to 11pm for drinks.

Services: Courtesy van, no-smoking rooms.

MODERATE

QUALITY INN TOWERS SUITES, 1200 L St., Anchorage, AK 99501. Tel. 907/276-0110, or toll free 800/544-0786. Fax 907/258-4914. 182 rms (all with bath). TV TEL

$ Rates: Mid-May to mid-Sept, $115–$120 studio for one or two people; $130 one-bedroom suite; $145 two-bedroom suite. Mid-Sept to mid-May, $60–$70 studio for one or two; $70–$75 one-bedroom suite; $90–$100 two-bedroom suite. AE, CB, DC, ER, JCB, MC, V.

This 14-story former residential apartment building is one of Anchorage's best hotel bargains. For less than the price of a standard first-class hotel room elsewhere, you can get a full one-bedroom or two-bedroom suite, complete with kitchenette. All rooms are decorated in tones of brown and beige with floral upholstery and rustic wall paintings. They have double beds with reading lamps, dressers, armchairs, and electric baseboard heating. Minikitchens have electric stoves, refrigerators, toasters, and coffee percolators. Suites have extra closet and shelf space, and large living rooms with couches and dining tables. You can rent a VCR and videotapes in the lobby, and there's a 10% surcharge on long-distance calls. There are men's and women's saunas and exercise rooms and a beauty salon on the premises, and a coin-op guest laundry in the basement.

THE UPTOWN, 234 E. Second Ave., Anchorage, AK 99501. Tel. 907/279-4232, or toll free 800/478-4232 in Alaska. Fax 907/278-8995. 19 suites (all with bath). TV TEL

$ Rates: June–Sept 15, $80–$100 single or double. Sept 16–May, $50–$70 single or double, $330–$350 per week, $800–$1,200 per month. AE, CB, DC, MC, V.

A converted apartment building, the Uptown has simple but clean one-bedroom suites. Each unit has a living room and full kitchen; some also have sofa beds and fireplaces. Cable TV is provided. A second location, at 5308 Arctic Blvd. (tel. 907/561-7488, or toll free 800/478-7488 in Alaska), is just 10 minutes from Anchorage International Airport; that location has another 19 units, some of them two-bedroom suites. A laundry is open to all guests at both locations.

INEXPENSIVE

ALASKA SAMOVAR INN, 720 Gambell St., Anchorage, AK 99501. Tel. 907/277-1511, or toll free 800/478-1511 in Alaska. Fax 907/272-5192. Telex 09025340. 68 rms (all with bath), 4 suites. TV TEL

$ Rates: Late May to mid-Sept, $70–$79 single or double. Mid-Sept to late May, $45–$60 single or double; from $105 suite. AE, CB, DC, DISC, MC, V.

Picture this, if you can: a motel room with one wall covered by orange wool, a second by a green-and-beige tartan fabric, a third by a velvety batik-style print, and a fourth of simple plaster painted lime green. Add a double Jacuzzi and a few antiques, like a love seat and early 20th-century headboard, and—*presto!*—you have a deluxe room at the Samovar Inn. Standard rooms have queen-size beds, a small Jacuzzi bath, and a full double mirror beside the dressing table. O'Toole's restaurant is open for three meals daily.

ANCHOR ARMS MOTEL, 433 Eagle St., Anchorage, AK 99501. Tel. 907/272-9619. Fax 907/272-0614. 46 suites (all with bath). TV TEL
$ Rates: Mid-May to mid-Sept, $59 single; $69–$89 double. Mid-Sept to mid-May, $39 single; $49–$69 double. Weekly rates available. DISC, MC, V.
Formerly the crew lodgings for Lufthansa German Airlines, these one-bedroom suites, just around the corner from the Sheraton, are clean and spacious. All are furnished with double beds and dressers, couches, coffee tables, and dining tables, and all have cable TV and gas heating. The kitchen has a refrigerator and stove with oven; dishes and pots are provided. There is a coin-op guest laundry. If you don't mind yellow-brick walls, you can't beat the price.

INLET INN, 539 H St., Anchorage, AK 99501. Tel. 907/277-5541. Fax 907/277-3108. 93 rms (all with bath). TV TEL
$ Rates: Mid-May to mid-Sept, $50 single; $60 double; $65 twin. Mid-Sept to mid-May, $40 single; $45 double; $48 twin. AE, CB, DC, DISC, MC, V.
Built in 1952, the Inlet Inn is still well maintained. The narrow wood-paneled corridors lead to small, sparsely furnished rooms with double or twin beds and desk/dressers. Wildlife prints accent the dark-wood walls. The baseboard heating is centrally controlled.

BUDGET

ANCHORAGE INTERNATIONAL HOSTEL, 700 H St., Anchorage, AK 99501. Tel. 907/276-3635. 60 beds.
$ Rates: $12 for American Youth Hostel members, $15 for nonmembers. Annual AYH memberships, $25 adults, $10 youths under 17, $15 seniors 55 and over, $35 families. No credit cards.
The hostel has separate men's and women's dormitories, plus a few family rooms for parents with children. It also has a full kitchen, showers, and a laundry room. Bring your own sleeping bag or bedroll, or rent linens at the hostel; blankets are free. The hostel permits maximum stays of six consecutive nights, longer in winter if space is available. The building is closed—and must be vacated—from noon to 5pm daily. A midnight curfew is strictly enforced. Smoking, alcohol, illegal drugs, and pets are forbidden.

MIDTOWN/SPENARD

This area includes the midtown business district, the Spenard Road entertainment strip, and the international airport area. Geographically, it comprises the section of Anchorage west of the Seward Highway and south of downtown as far as International Airport Road.

VERY EXPENSIVE

REGAL ALASKAN HOTEL, 4800 Spenard Rd., Anchorage, AK 99517. Tel. 907/243-2300, or toll free 800/544-0553, 800/478-2100 in Alaska. Fax 907/243-8815. 245 rms, 3 suites. TV TEL **Transportation:** Courtesy car.
$ Rates: Mid-May to Sept, $185–$195 single; $200–$215 double; $275–$645 suite. Oct to mid-May, $130–$140 single; $140–$150 double; $250–$550 suite. AE, CB, DC, DISC, ER, JCB, MC, V.
⭐ The Regal Alaskan (formerly the Clarion) combines the best of two worlds. It's a city hotel, barely five minutes' drive from the international airport, yet it has many of the attributes of an opulent wilderness fishing lodge, including a private dock for chartered seaplanes on adjacent Lake Spenard. The Regal Alaskan's odd key shape was dictated by airport-area building codes (which kept the height to three stories) and by a desire to give the restaurant and bar lake frontage.
The low-ceilinged lobby is casually elegant. The first thing you'll notice as you

FROMMER'S COOL FOR KIDS: HOTELS

Hillside Motel (*see p. 186*) Located beside Chester Creek Park, the Hillside offers year-round access to a network of bicycling, jogging, and, in winter, cross-country skiing trails.

Holiday Inn of Anchorage (*see p. 179*) A heated indoor swimming pool will keep the youngsters occupied; if they didn't bring suits, they can purchase them from the hotel.

Puffin Inn (*see p. 185*) Everyone loves the little black-and-white birds that swoop around Alaskan ferries and cruise ships; everything here pursues the puffin theme, from the pictures in the guest rooms to the gift items sold at the front desk.

Regal Alaskan Hotel (*see p. 182*) From the restaurant or the private dock, kids can watch seaplanes take off and land on Lake Spenard and adjacent Lake Hood, the world's largest seaplane base.

enter is the wide, red-carpeted staircase with the mahogany banister leading to the third-floor ballrooms. Reception is to your left; the concierge, an expert in booking "Alaskan experience" wilderness trips, has a desk to your right, near the gift shop. In the far corner, surrounded by plush seating, is a big fireplace shared with the Fancy Moose Lounge.

The Regal Alaskan's rooms contain special touches that can't be found in other Anchorage hotels. Every room has track lighting with dimmer switches, a mini-refrigerator built into the dressing table, a hairdryer, a working desk, and Stonington Gallery art on the walls. In addition, the hotel virtually guarantees that noise from the nearby airports won't disturb your slumber: The double five-inch-thick walls are separated by a one-inch air gap. A pastel color scheme (with blue-green carpeting and pink-and-brown covers on the queen-size beds) enhances the units. Each room also has an easy chair, entertainment console, clock radio, and thermostat-controlled hot-air heating. Bathroom amenities include shampoo, conditioner, and hand cream. Two large suites have fireplaces.

Dining/Entertainment: The Flying Machine Restaurant emphasizes the aeronautic theme in its decor: Byron Birdsall watercolors and prints depicting the seaplane in Alaska, historical aviation photos, an antique aviator's jacket, aerial topographical maps. But the cuisine is more California than Alaska. Consider a healthy breakfast of granola and yogurt parfait ($4.25), a lunch of halibut and chips ($8.50), and a national-award-winning dinner of salmon filets in yellow-and-blue cornmeal with a shrimp hollandaise ($19). In warm weather, food and beverage service are available on an outdoor patio. It's open from 6am to midnight.

Next door is the Fancy Moose Lounge, with a video jukebox and three television screens.

Services: 24-hour room service, summer concierge, valet laundry, airport courtesy car, no-smoking rooms and rooms adapted for disabled guests.

Facilities: Private dock for chartered seaplanes on adjacent Lake Spenard, health club, bicycle rentals, conference and banquet facilities.

EXPENSIVE

BEST WESTERN BARRATT INN, 4616 Spenard Rd., Anchorage, AK 99517. Tel. 907/243-3131, or toll free 800/221-7550, 800/478-7550 in

Alaska. Fax 907/243-5620. Telex 4955510. 213 rms, 4 suites. TV TEL **Transportation:** Courtesy car.

$ Rates: Mid-May to mid-Sept, $110–$125 single; $120–$145 double. Mid-Sept to mid-May, $65–$80 single; $75–$95 double. AE, CB, DC, DISC, ER, JCB, MC, V.

The Best Western offers a real choice of accommodation styles. The four separate buildings—two on each side of busy Spenard Road, connected by a tunnel—house a variety of moderate and deluxe rooms. Buildings I and II have newly remodeled rooms. They contain queen-size beds, two armchairs, desk/dresser, satellite TV with built-in radio, electric baseboard heating, and hairdryer. Buildings III and IV have spacious rooms with such extras as king- and queen-size beds, sofa, easy chairs, dresser, clock radio, and TV stand with drop-leaf desk. Rooms in Building III have refrigerators and some kitchenettes. A hairdryer is provided in the bathroom, along with standard amenities.

Dining/Entertainment: The Susitna Restaurant, open daily from 6am to 10pm has good food at good prices; try the specialty four-egg omelet ($6.50) for breakfast or a Susitna burger ($5.50), with Swiss cheese, bacon, and avocado, for lunch. Most dinners are priced at $9.95–$14.95; a specialty is fresh seafood.

Services: Room service, 24-hour airport courtesy car, valet laundry, no-smoking rooms and rooms for disabled guests.

Facilities: Coin-operated laundry.

WEST COAST INTERNATIONAL INN, 3333 International Airport Rd., Anchorage, AK 99502. Tel. 907/243-2233, or toll free 800/544-0986, 800/478-2233 in Alaska. Fax 907/248-3796. 128 rms, 14 suites. TV TEL **Transportation:** Courtesy car.

$ Rates: June to mid-Sept, $116 single; $126–$136 double; $140–$215 suite. Mid-Sept to May, $99 single; $109–$119 double; $125–$175 suite. AE, CB, DC, DISC, MC, V.

This is the closest accommodation to the airport, and with six clocks in the lobby giving the current time in New York, Seattle, Honolulu, Tokyo, and London, as well as Anchorage, there's no excuse for missing your flight. A lodge theme carries through the lobby into the Trophy Room lounge.

The inn's newly renovated rooms are impressively appointed with light-wood furnishings and wildlife prints on the white walls. Each room has one king- or two queen-size beds, dresser, easy chair, and electric baseboard heating. The dressing table has a lighted makeup mirror. Cable TV features HBO. For a few dollars more than the regular rate, the inn's "suite deal" gives you a minirefrigerator stocked with beverages, complimentary coffee with your morning paper, and other special touches.

Dining/Entertainment: The International Dining Room, open daily from 6am to 2pm and 5 to 11pm, serves a wide range of dinner courses, priced $12–$22, including salad, dessert, and coffee.

Services: 24-hour room service, 24-hour airport courtesy car, valet laundry, no-smoking rooms and rooms for disabled guests, room/car packages with Budget Car Rental.

Facilities: Weight/exercise room, sauna, freezer facilities for sportsmen, meeting facilities.

MODERATE

ANCHORAGE EAGLE NEST HOTEL, 4110 Spenard Rd., Anchorage, AK 99503. Tel. 907/243-3433, or toll free 800/848-7852, 800/478-3433 in Alaska. Fax 907/248-9258. 28 rms (all with bath). TV TEL **Transportation:** Courtesy car.

$ Rates (for one or two guests): May–Oct, $99–$109 studio; $125 one-bedroom suite; $195 two-bedroom suite. Oct–May, $60 studio; $75–$95 one-bedroom suite; $135 two-bedroom suite. AE, CB, DC, MC, V.

S One of the nicer touches here is an enclosed summer wildflower garden with a pair of barbecue pits. In the lobby of this rustic-looking, two-story lodging are a gift shop that sells Native crafts and jewelry and a snack corner, complete with freezer and microwave.

The well-lit rooms, decorated in dark earth tones, include studios as well as one- and two-bedroom suites. All contain queen-size beds, round tables, and two comfortable chairs, and have courtesy coffee and electric baseboard heating. The TV features HBO. Wildlife or scenic photos hang on the walls. Each unit has a kitchen with stove and oven, refrigerator, dishwasher, toaster, and coffee maker. A coin-op guest laundry is available, and free airport transportation is provided. The hotel also leases two-bedroom apartments off-site for $140–$160 per night.

NORTHERN LIGHTS INN, 598 W. Northern Lights Blvd., Anchorage, AK 99503-3899. Tel. 907/561-5200, or toll free 800/447-9559. Fax 907/561-7817. 143 rms (all with bath). TV TEL **Transportation:** Courtesy car.
$ Rates: Mid-May to mid-Sept, $105 single; $120 double. Mid-Sept to mid-May, $65 single; $71 double. Children 12 and under stay free in parents' room. AE, CB, DC, DISC, MC, V.

This newly renovated, eight-story hotel, affiliated with Grand Tradition Hotels, doesn't depend on the aurora borealis for an Alaskan atmosphere. Early dog-sledding photos are reproduced on the walls of the spacious lobby, and foods like sourdough pancakes and reindeer stew highlight the menu at its Cama'i Restaurant. The rooms are nicely appointed, with a heavy use of wood paneling. All have queen-size or double beds, refrigerators, coffeemakers, direct-dial phones (local calls are free), and cable TV with built-in radio. No-smoking rooms are available.

The hotel restaurant, open daily from 6am to 2pm and 5 to 10pm, uses imaginative curves in the design of its booths and partitions. Daily luncheon specials, including prime rib, London broil, and baked salmon, are priced at $7. Dinner runs $9–$15. Hotel services include room service, valet laundry, and free guest memberships in the nearby GreatLand Gold Health Club.

INEXPENSIVE

ARCTIC INN MOTEL, 842 W. International Airport Rd., Anchorage, AK 99518. Tel. 907/561-1328. 23 rms (all with bath). TV TEL
$ Rates: Mid-May to mid-Sept, $69 single; $79–$84 double; $99.20 suite. Mid-Sept to mid-May, $54 single; $64–$67.50 double; $91.80 suite. 10% discount for seniors and active military. Weekly rates year-round, monthly rates in winter only. AE, MC, V.

Music from a popular country-and-western establishment next door, the Flight Deck Bar and Restaurant, often keeps Arctic Inn guests rocking into the wee hours. Each room has two double or two twin beds, a desk/dresser, cable TV, telephone (free local calls), and gas heating with individual thermostats. Rustic prints decorate the walls. There's a guest laundry; pets are permitted with approval from the management.

PUFFIN INN, 4400 Spenard Rd., Anchorage, AK 99517. Tel. 907/243-4044, or toll free 800/4-PUFFIN in Alaska. Fax 907/248-6853. 52 rms (all with bath). TV TEL **Transportation:** Courtesy car.
$ Rates (including continental breakfast): Mid-May to mid-Sept, $69 single; $74 double; $79 twin. Mid-Sept to mid-May, $47 single; $52 double; $57 twin. AE, CB, DC, DISC, MC, V.

If you enjoy watching the black-and-white birds that swoop and dive around Alaskan ferries and cruise ships, you'll love this inn. Everything here pursues the puffin theme, from the pictures in the guest rooms to the gift items sold at the front desk: stuffed toy birds, etched ulus (Eskimo knives), cards, jewelry, cups, potholders. The rooms are simple but nice, with a light beige-and-red decor. All have queen-size beds and desk/dressers. Older units have hot-water rather than electric baseboard heating, and shower instead of tub/shower combinations. Rates include muffins, coffee, and the morning paper delivered to your room.

SUPER 8 MOTEL, 3501 Minnesota Dr., Anchorage, AK 99503. Tel. 907/276-8884, or toll free 800/843-1991. Fax 907/279-8194. 84 rms (all with bath). TV TEL **Transportation:** Courtesy car.
$ Rates: Mid-May to mid-Sept, $78.90 single; $89.90 double; $99.90 suite. Mid-Sept to mid-May, $70.90 single; $80.90 double; $90.90 suite. AE, CB, DC, DISC, JCB, MC, V.

The Super 8 has a big double entranceway where you can stomp the snow off your boots on winter days. Throughout the year it offers 24-hour courtesy van service to and from the airport, baggage-storage facilities, and a coin-operated guest laundry. The rooms have queen-size beds, a built-in desk and luggage rack, and electric baseboard heating. Watercolors on the walls complement brown carpets and autumn-pattern bedspreads. Soft drinks and snacks are sold in the second-floor vending room. Some no-smoking rooms and rooms for disabled guests are available. Pets are permitted with a deposit.

BUDGET

HILLSIDE MOTEL, 2150 Gambell St., Anchorage, AK 99503. Tel. 907/258-6006, or toll free 800/478-6008 in Alaska. 26 rms (all with bath). TV TEL
$ Rates: Year-round, $46 single; $56 double; $66 family room with kitchenette. MC, V.

The Hillside has a lovely location: just southeast of downtown, adjacent to Chester Creek Park with its bicycling, jogging, and (in winter) cross-country skiing trails. The quiet, wood-paneled units have double beds, desk/dressers, in-room coffee, and electric baseboard heating. There's also a coin-op guest laundry, as well as a gift counter in the spacious lobby.

MIDTOWN LODGE, 604 W. 26th Ave., Anchorage, AK 99503. Tel. 907/258-7778. 60 rms (none with bath). TV TEL
$ Rates: Year-round, $35 single; $40 double or twin. Weekly rates available. MC, V.
Some folks have lived at the lodge since 1968! Budget travelers who don't require a private bath will be comfortable here. The carpeted rooms are uninspired in decor, but most contain a small refrigerator as well as a bed, nightstand, desk/dresser, chair, satellite TV, and telephone (local calls are free). Electric heating is centrally controlled. Towels and soap are provided to guests, who share a central men's or women's lavatory. There's also a coin-op laundry. You can watch in-house movies in the TV lounge. Drinks, snacks, and cigarettes are sold.

SOUTH ANCHORAGE

These lodgings are located near the Seward Highway as it heads south out of Anchorage en route to the Kenai Peninsula.

MODERATE

BEST WESTERN GOLDEN LION HOTEL, 1000 E. 36th Ave., Anchorage, AK 99508. Tel. 907/561-1522, or toll free 800/528-1234. Fax 907/561-1522, request fax. 83 rms (all with bath). TV TEL
$ Rates: Mid-May to mid-Sept, $100 single; $106 double. Mid-Sept to mid-May, $85 single; $91 double. AE, CB, DC, DISC, MC, V.
The only lion in the state of Alaska may be the big African cat poised, with fangs bared, just inside the lobby doors at the hotel. Don't worry—it's stuffed. But it's an

imposing sentinel as it guards the wide, red-carpeted stairway leading to the Lion's Pride Restaurant and Lion's Den lounge on the second floor.

The spacious and newly refurbished rooms are decorated in neutral tones. Each soundproofed room has two queen-size beds (or a queen-size bed and a sofa bed), a big dresser, table and chairs, and individual heating and air-conditioning.

Dining/Entertainment: Pictures of lions decorate the walls of both dining room and lounge. The restaurant, open daily from 6:30am to 1:30pm and 5:30 to 10pm, has a popular Sunday brunch ($10). Regular dinner entrees range from $8.50 for teriyaki chicken to market price for Australian lobster tail. Top-40 dance music is played in the lounge several nights a week.

Services: Room service, valet laundry, no-smoking rooms and rooms for disabled guests.

Facilities: Hair salon, meeting rooms.

BUDGET

ALASKA'S TUDOR MOTEL, 4424 Lake Otis Pkwy., Anchorage, AK 99507. Tel. 907/561-2234. 15 rms (all with bath). TV TEL

$ Rates: Mid-May to mid-Sept, $49 single; $54 double; $83.25 suite (for four). Mid-Sept to mid-May, $39 single; $44 double; $73.25 suite. Weekly rates. AE, CB, DC, DISC, MC, V.

It's nothing fancy, but this former apartment complex has reasonably priced one-bedroom housekeeping units with private entrances. The full kitchenettes come with cooking utensils. Furnishings include double beds and dressers, and there's covered electric baseboard heating. Pets are permitted, but keep in mind that maid service is offered only twice weekly (or upon departure). The office is open for check-ins from 8am to 10pm.

EAST ANCHORAGE

This area includes all accommodations east of the Seward Highway and north of Chester Creek; it's mainly the Glenn Highway corridor, heading east from Anchorage toward Eagle River.

INEXPENSIVE

ARCTIC TERN INN, 5000 Taku Dr., Anchorage, AK 99508. Tel. 907/337-1544. Fax 907/337-2288. 4 rms, 33 suites (all with bath). TV TEL

$ Rates (single or double): June–Oct 1, $65 studio; $70 one-bedroom suite; $85 two-bedroom suite. Oct 2–May, $45 studio; $52 one-bedroom suite; $64 two-bedroom suite. AE, CB, DC, MC, V.

This small motel suits a tight budget. You'll register in the pleasant, carpeted lobby with a small snack shop. The management will tell you how to find the coin-op guest laundry, then direct you down the well-lit, carpeted corridors to your room. The motel's four small studios and 33 spacious one- and two-bedroom suites have wood-paneled walls and orange or chocolate-brown carpeting. Utensils for the kitchenette are furnished for a small deposit. Each nice, clean suite has queen-size, double, or twin beds, together with a desk and dresser, in the bedroom; in the main room it has a hideaway couch, chair, coffee table, and kitchen table with chairs. You also get thermostat-controlled hot-water baseboard heating.

MUSH INN, 333 Concrete Ave., Anchorage, AK 99501. Tel. 907/277-4554, or toll free 800/478-4554 in Alaska. Fax 907/277-5721. 94 rms (all with bath). TV TEL

$ Rates (single or double): Year-round, $60–$80 standard room; $80–$120 specialty room. AE, CB, DC, DISC, MC, V.

Watercolors of historic Russian Orthodox churches, the only such collection in Alaska, cover one wall of the lobby. Guest rooms, located in four separate two-story buildings, vary considerably, from tiny rooms with little more than a bed and shower to large family-size accommodations with kitchenette. Standard units contain two double or queen-size beds, desk/dresser, cable TV with HBO and built-in radio, telephone (free local calls), and baseboard heating. Many have small kitchens with a stove, refrigerator, and table. "Specialty rooms" include the Korean Room, with Oriental antiques, a colorful butterfly collection, and a dragon lamp hanging over the Jacuzzi; and the Sweetheart Room, with a heart-shaped waterbed and Jacuzzi. Pets are permitted, and there's a coin-op guest laundry.

BUDGET

BIG TIMBER MOTEL, 2037 E. Fifth Ave., Anchorage, AK 99501. Tel. 907/272-2541. 23 rms (all with bath). TV TEL
$ Rates: Year-round, $55 single or double; $70 family room; $80–$120 specialty suite. AE, CB, DC, DISC, MC, V.
Most of the Big Timber's clean, spacious, well-maintained rooms have paneled walls and red carpets. They come furnished with king- or queen-size beds, desk/dressers, large closets, cable TV, baseboard heating, portable fans, and, in most cases, small Jacuzzi/steambath combinations. About half a dozen are family rooms with kitchenettes. Twelve "specialty" rooms have large Jacuzzis or waterbeds; they include the Cave Room, with imitation flagstone walls and a Neanderthal fur chair; and the intimate, all-green Islander Room.

KOBUK HOTEL-MOTEL, 1104 E. Fifth Ave., Anchorage, AK 99501. Tel. 907/274-1650. 56 rms (all with bath). TV TEL **Transportation:** Courtesy car.
$ Rates (single or double): Year-round, $47–$50 standard room; $52–$54 room with kitchenette; $55 Jacuzzi room; $69 specialty room. AE, CB, DC, DISC, MC, V.
Historical photos hang in the rooms and line the narrow corridor walls of this hotel. Its rooms, most of them in the newer annex, have double beds and reading lamps, desk/dressers, chairs, cable TV, telephones (local calls are free), and electric baseboard heating. Many rooms have a Jacuzzi/steambath, and five have kitchenettes.

BED-&-BREAKFAST

Weary of hotel rooms? Anchorage is proud of its bed-and-breakfast associations, which pair visitors with local families for $45–$90 a night, including breakfast. At last count, there were 171 B&Bs in Anchorage. Most give discounts to guests staying longer than one night. In all cases, whether through a private owner or an association, it's essential to book ahead.
The two principal associations offer similar services. **Alaska Private Lodgings,** P.O. Box 20047, Anchorage, AK 99520 (tel. 907/258-1717), has private rooms, suites, and apartments available downtown, in the suburbs, or out of town in Fairbanks, Healy, Homer, Palmer, Seldovia, Seward, Soldotna, Talkeetna, Valdez, Wasilla, and Willow. Car-rental discounts can be arranged. Singles are $45–$70; doubles, $55–$85. There is a $5 surcharge for stays of only one night.
Accommodations Alaska Style—Stay with a Friend, 3605 Arctic Blvd., Suite 173, Anchorage, AK 99503 (tel. 907/278-8800), has guest rooms for prices ranging from budget ($45 single, $50 double) to luxury ($90 double). There are also some one- and two-bedroom suites starting at $60, with TVs or recreation rooms, hot tubs, saunas, or Jacuzzis; and fully furnished apartments starting at $60. Statewide, some 70 B&B operators are listed with this agency, including those with homes in Denali Park, Fairbanks, Girdwood (Alyeska), Gustavus (Glacier Bay), Hatcher Pass, Homer, Juneau, McCarthy, Palmer, Seward, Sitka, Seldovia, Soldotna, Talkeetna, Valdez, and Wasilla.

There are far too many B&Bs in the Anchorage area to mention each individually, but here is one of my personal favorites:

Sixth & B Bed & Breakfast, 145 W. Sixth Ave., Anchorage, AK 99501 (tel. 907/279-5293), is a downtown oasis just one block west of the Anchorage Museum of History and Art. Seven spruce trees surround the 1930s home, once a Lutheran parsonage; a 25-foot flagpole declares it the world headquarters of the Far from Fenway Fan Club, an organization founded by B&B owner Peter Roberts for displaced Boston Red Sox baseball fans. Two double rooms with shared bath cost $50 single, $60 double, a night, and a third-floor penthouse with private bath runs $88, single or double. Bicycles come with the rooms (Downtown Bicycle Rental is also based at the B&B). Roberts's basement is occupied by Arctic Images T-shirts, featuring his own designs.

Among the dozens of other B&Bs in Anchorage are these, recommended by friends: **All the Comforts of Home,** 12531 Turk's Turn, Anchorage, AK 99516 (tel. 907/345-4279); **The Cassel,** 1040 W. 27th Ave., Anchorage, AK 99503 (tel. 907/277-7746); **The Green Bough,** 3832 Young St., Anchorage, AK 99508 (tel. 907/562-4636); **Heart of Anchorage,** 725 K St., Anchorage, AK 99501 (tel. 907/279-7066); and **Hillcrest Haven,** 1449 Hillcrest Dr., Anchorage, AK 99503 (tel. 907/276-1491). Each undoubtedly has its charms. I suggest writing ahead for information.

CAMPGROUNDS

Two areas are open to tent and RV campers, both in East Anchorage. **Russian Jack Springs Park,** off the Boniface Parkway, just south of the Glenn Highway, contains Lion's camper park, with 50 RV spaces, 10 tent sites, restrooms, hot showers, and pay phones. Facilities at Russian Jack Springs Park include picnic grounds, hiking trails, a nine-hole golf course, softball fields, and tennis courts.

Centennial Park has 89 campsites, with picnic tables and fire pits, suitable for either RV or tent camping. There are restrooms, hot showers, and pay phones. Access is from Muldoon Road and Boundary Avenue, just south of the Glenn Highway. Rates at both parks are $12 a night, with stays limited to seven nights.

For further information, contact the **Anchorage Parks and Recreation Department,** 2525 Gambell St., Room 404, Anchorage, AK 99503 (tel. 907/264-4474).

4. DINING

It wasn't too many years ago that a mention of Anchorage restaurants would have brought a chorus of guffaws. "What are they serving today?" someone might have asked. "Whale blubber? Reindeer stew?" Although *that* sort of diet has traditionally been the exclusive fare of Eskimo communities in the far north and west, it's true that Anchorage cuisine was pretty much of the steak-and-potatoes variety.

As the city has grown more cosmopolitan, however, so has its tastes. Anchorage is a long way from becoming the fine-food capital of North America, but it's no longer difficult to find sushi or coquilles St-Jacques, linguine, or a big chimichanga.

Anchorage is not *so* cosmopolitan, though, as to require that you wear a coat and tie everywhere you go. In fact, about the only places where you may be looked at cross-eyed if you arrive in clean, ironed jeans and a wool sweater are the premier establishments in the big international hotels—the **Crow's Nest** at the Cook, **Josephine's** at the Sheraton, or the **Top of the World** at the Hilton.

Price Ranges The restaurants listed below are categorized like the accommodations, by area and price. As a rule of thumb, figure $25 and up per person for a complete dinner at an "Expensive" restaurant, $13–$25 at a "Moderate" restaurant, and $5–$13 at an "Inexpensive" restaurant. I will frequently save on my personal

0 0.5 mi
N 0.8 km

Knik Arm

Area of Inset

West 1st Ave.
West 3rd Ave.
East 1st A
East 3rd A

Barrow St.
Cordova St.
Denali St.
Eagle St.
Gambell St.
Ingra St.
Karluk St.

Delaney Park

11th Ave.
12th Ave.
15th Ave.
16th Ave.

C Street
A Street

Westchester Lagoon

Chester Cre

Earthquake Park

Northern Lights Blvd.

Fireweed Lane

7

8 9

Benson Blvd.

6

10

Denali St.

Aircraft Dr.

Wisconsin St.

Lakeshore Dr.

McRae Rd. Spenard Rd.

5

11 12

36th Ave.

C Street
A Street

Arctic Blvd.

13

Lake Hood

Lake Spenard

4

14 15

16 17 18

Tudor Rd.

Old Seward Hwy.

Northwood St.

Int'l Airport Rd.

International Airport Rd.

19

Anchorage International Airport

Connors Lake Park

Connors Lake

Minnesota Dr.

C Street

Dowling Rd.

Raspberry Rd.

5586

Ah Sa Wan 16	Daruma 17	Harry's 10
Akaihana 27	Downtown Deli & Café 30	Hogg Bros. Café
Armen's Mazzi's 20	Elevation 21	Imperial Palace 2
Café Europa 12	Garcia's of Scottsdale 15	Jens' 11
Club Paris 31	Garden of Eatin' 5	Kumagoro 29
The Corsair 25	The Greek Corner 8	La Cabaña 33
Cyrano's 32	Gwennie's Old Alaska 4	La Mex 26

ANCHORAGE DINING

Davis Park

Commercial Dr.

①

◆**2**

①

3

Bragaw St.

✈ **Merrill Field**

Russian

Jack

DeBarr Rd.

Springs

Park

Boniface Pkwy.

Greenbelt

Lake Otis Pkwy.

20

Northern Lights Blvd.

Goose Lake Park

University Dr.

Providence Dr.

DOWNTOWN ANCHORAGE

Knik Arm

Rail Depot ■

Ship Creek

Warehouse Ave.

Christiansen Dr.

W. 1st Ave.

E. 1st Ave.

W. 2nd Ave.

E. 2nd Ave.

Post Office

Resolution Park

21 **22**

23

W. 3rd Ave.

E. 3rd Ave.

34

Elderberry Park

M St.

L St.

K St.

J St.

24

29 **30**

W. 4th Ave.

E. 4th Ave.

28

32

B St.

A St.

E. 5th Ave.

25 **27**

31

W. 5th Ave.

33

26

W. 6th Ave.

E. 6th Ave.

N St.

M St.

W. 7th Ave.

H St.

G St.

F St.

E St.

D St.

C St.

B St.

Barrow St.

Cordova St.

† † † † †
City Cemetery
† † † † †
† † † † †

W. 8th Ave.

Denali St.

Eagle St.

Fairbanks St.

Gambell St.

Post Office

Delaney Park

W. 9th Ave.

E. 9th Ave.

W. 10th Ave.

E. 10th Ave.

☒

Marx Bros. Café **23**
Natural Pantry **13**
Old Anchorage Salmon Bake **22**
One Guy from Italy **6**
Peggy's **1**
Red Robin Burger & Spirits
    Emporium **3**

Romano's **9**
Sacks Fifth Avenue Café **28**
Sea Galley **14**
Simon and Seafort's **24**
Sourdough Mining Co. **19**
Stuart Anderson's Cattle Co. **18**
Tundra Club **34**

FROMMER'S SMART TRAVELER: RESTAURANTS

1. Prices are significantly lower at lunchtime, especially at the best restaurants. Eat your main meal at midday, when you can hit the hot spots and save.
2. There are some fine delis and take-out cafés in the city. Grab a sandwich or picnic fixings, and enjoy a meal in one of Anchorage's lovely parks—or better yet, take it with you on a day's outing.
3. Limit your beers and wines. Alcohol isn't cheap, and adds greatly to the cost of any meal.

expenses by having my main meal at lunchtime at a better restaurant, when prices are much lower than at dinnertime.

DOWNTOWN

EXPENSIVE

CLUB PARIS, 417 W. Fifth Ave. Tel. 277-6332.
 Cuisine: CONTINENTAL. **Reservations:** Highly recommended.
$ Prices: Appetizers $7–$23; main courses $14–$40; lunch $6.50–$9.50. AE, CB, DC, DISC, MC, V.
 Open: Lunch Mon–Sat 11:30am–2:30pm; dinner Mon–Sat 5–11pm, Sun 5–10pm.

Don't let the less than sophisticated facade fool you: Club Paris is famous for its charcoal-broiled steaks. In the rear of a dimly lit cocktail lounge, in a plush booth or at a table, you can feast on a dinner of escargots, filet mignon, sautéed mushrooms, crème de menthe parfait, and a bottle of Châteauneuf du Pape for two.

THE CORSAIR, in the Voyager Hotel, 944 W. Fifth Ave. Tel. 278-4502.
 Cuisine: CONTINENTAL. **Reservations:** Recommended.
$ Prices: Appetizers $7–$10; main courses $18–$32. AE, CB, DC, DISC, MC, V.
 Open: Dinner only, Mon–Sat 5–11pm.

Some say that the best continental cuisine in Anchorage is served here, across from the Hotel Captain Cook. European chef Hans Kruger's establishment is elegantly designed like a ship's hold, with rigging above each intimately secluded table. The service is timed to allow you to savor your meal, not rush through it.

You might start with oysters Corsair (baked on the half shell with foie gras), followed by roast duckling Madagascar (with red wine and green-peppercorn sauce) or rack of lamb Armenonville, and topped off with strawberries Devonshire. Main courses also include a wide selection of seafood, steaks, and veal dishes. *Wine Spectator* magazine says that the Corsair has one of the top 100 wine lists in the United States. Kruger recommends the Trockenbeerenauslese, perhaps because he likes to hear patrons try to say the word.

THE MARX BROS. CAFE, 627 W. Third Ave. Tel. 278-2133.
 Cuisine: NEW AMERICAN. **Reservations:** Recommended.
$ Prices: Appetizers $7–$10; main courses $18–$25. AE, CB, DC, MC, V.
 Open: Dinner only, Mon–Sat 6–9:30pm.

Squeezed into a refurbished 1916 wood-frame house, this culinary tribute to the famed family of comedy is nothing to joke about. The menu changes regularly to offer a variety of gourmet specialties such as seafood mousse and venison. You can open with Dungeness crab ravioli with lemon-basil-beurre sauce or a homemade eggplant pâté, then enjoy grilled halibut with macadamia nuts and mango chutney, black-horned antelope with smoked caribou-ham sauce, or New York steak with black-bean sauce. In summer, the café's own garden produces a variety of lettuces, edible flowers, and over 50 herbs for unique salads. The dessert menu features homemade cheesecake, and the Captain's List of wines offers some 350 vintages.

MODERATE

AKAIHANA, 930 W. Fifth Ave. Tel. 276-2215.

Cuisine: JAPANESE. **Reservations:** Recommended.
$ Prices: Main courses $4.50–$8.50 at lunch, $9.25–$15.50 at dinner; sushi $4–$6. AE, JCB, MC, V.
Open: Lunch Mon–Sat 11am–2pm; dinner Mon–Sat 5–9pm.

Akaihana ("red flower") offers Japanese meals in an informal setting. Sit at the delightful sushi bar for two-bite servings of such ocean denizens as tuna, shrimp, octopus, and sea urchin; or enjoy a full-course dinner of miso soup, tempura, pork tonkatsu, and chicken teriyaki. A cook-your-own seafood yosenabe is also on the menu.

ELEVATION 92, 1007 W. Third Ave. Tel. 279-1578.

Cuisine: SEAFOOD. **Reservations:** Recommended.
$ Prices: Appetizers $3.95–$10.95; main courses $7.95–$11.95 at lunch, $14.95–$19.95 at dinner. AE, CB, DC, MC, V.
Open: Mon–Fri 11am–midnight, Sat 5pm–midnight, Sun 10am–2pm and 5pm–midnight.

Bob Sparks, proprietor of Elevation 92, once owned a Sun Valley restaurant called Elevation 6000. When he moved to Alaska in the mid-1970s and started this restaurant overlooking the inlet, he adapted the name to his new elevation. There's a garden feel to the dining room, with hanging ferns and tall potted plants beside stained-wood trellises with cut-glass panels.

Local salmon, halibut, and king crab headline the summer menu: Seafood selections change according to availability and season. You can start with crab-stuffed mushrooms, then follow with Cajun-style king salmon. If seafood isn't your menu choice, try the tournedos bordelaise. Praline cheesecake makes a tasty dessert. A popular wine and seafood bar serves as a lounge.

LA MEX, 900 W. Sixth Ave. Tel. 274-7678.

Cuisine: STEAK/MEXICAN. **Reservations:** Recommended.
$ Prices: Main courses $3.95–$15.95. AE, DISC, MC, V.
Open: Mon–Thurs 11am–10:30pm, Fri 11am–11pm, Sat noon–11pm.

This downtown restaurant, a two-story hacienda in pueblo style, is famous for its prime rib and barbecued rib specials, as well as its gourmet shrimp and chicken selections. It also serves standard taco-enchilada combination meals. You can even dine well at the bar with a "grande"—the house specialty giant margarita—and a plate of tostaditos (chips smothered in beans, cheese, lettuce, jalapeños, and house dressing).

La Mex has another outlet at 2550 Spenard Rd. (tel. 274-7511), open Monday through Thursday from 11am to 10:30pm, on Friday and Saturday from 11am to midnight, and on Sunday from 2 to 10pm.

OLD ANCHORAGE SALMON BAKE, Third Ave. and K St. Tel. 279-8790.

Cuisine: SEAFOOD. **Reservations:** Accepted for large parties only.
$ Prices: Full meals $14.95–$19.95. MC, V.
Open: Memorial Day weekend to Labor Day, daily 4–10pm. **Closed:** Rest of the year.

A gold-panning exhibition in a re-created "Tent City" lends an authentic atmosphere to Anchorage's leading outdoor dining attraction. Diners feast on fresh Alaskan salmon, halibut, snow crab, reindeer sausage, and New York steak, accompanied by an all-you-can-eat salad bar, barbecued beans, and sourdough bread. Afterward, they're invited to roast marshmallows over an open-pit fire. There's seating for 400, including 150 under cover in case of rain. A bush balladeer or strolling classical guitarist performs nightly, all summer long.

SACKS FIFTH AVENUE CAFE, 625 W. Fifth Ave. Tel. 276-3546.
  Cuisine: CREATIVE INTERNATIONAL. **Reservations:** Recommended.
$ **Prices:** Appetizers $6.75-$8.50; main courses $10.50-$16.50; lunch $6.50-$9. AE, MC, V.
  Open: May-Sept, Sun-Thurs 11am-10pm, Fri-Sat 11am-11pm. Oct-Apr, dinner only, Sun-Thurs 5-9pm, Fri-Sat 5-10pm.

⭐ Sacks serves homemade pastas and deli sandwiches in a bright, airy garden atmosphere, with Scandinavian-style furnishings and large potted plants. Light jazz is piped in, and there are changing art and photo exhibitions on the walls.
For lunch you might try an Alaskan reindeer-sausage sandwich with melted cheese and red onions, or a Japanese noodle salad (udon noodles and shiitake mushrooms in a spicy sauce). Popular dinner dishes include skewered scallops with a Chinese pesto-cream sauce, and broiled beef tenderloin with a port wine and Stilton cheese sauce.

SIMON AND SEAFORT'S SALOON AND GRILL, 420 L St. Tel. 274-3502.
  Cuisine: SEAFOOD. **Reservations:** Recommended.
$ **Prices:** Appetizers $3-$7; main courses $6.95-$11.95 at lunch, $14.50-$29.95 at dinner. AE, MC, V.
  Open: Memorial Day-Labor Day, lunch Mon-Sat 11:15am-2:30pm; dinner Mon-Thurs 5-10pm, Fri-Sat 5-10:30pm, Sun 5-9pm. Labor Day-Memorial Day, lunch Mon-Sat 11:15am-2:30pm; dinner Mon-Thurs 5:30-9:30pm, Fri-Sat 5-10pm, Sun 5-9pm.

Simon and Seafort's goes to great lengths to re-create the atmosphere of a circa 1900 grand saloon, with white marble and brass trim throughout. Ask for the fresh fish list. You might go for the baked Alaska halibut in dill sauce or something more exotic such as Hawaiian ono with hazelnut butter or toasted almonds. Simon and Seafort's also makes its own pasta daily, and offers a superb selection of desserts. At lunchtime, consider the sesame chicken salad or a bowl of homemade clam chowder. The bar, a popular after-work gathering place, features gourmet beer and 70 different brands of scotch.

INEXPENSIVE

CYRANO'S, 413 D St. Tel. 274-1173.
  Cuisine: DELI. **Reservations:** Not accepted.
$ **Prices:** Average meal $2.50-$9.95. MC, V.
  Open: May-Sept, Mon-Thurs 10am-6pm, Fri-Sat 10am-midnight, Sun noon-5pm. Oct-Apr, Mon-Thurs 10am-6pm, Fri 10am-9pm, Sat 10am-midnight, Sun noon-5pm.

This unusual café in the center of downtown Anchorage serves light meals—soups, salads, sandwiches, quiches, and pastas—with wine and cappuccinos beside the stacks of one of Alaska's thought-provoking bookstores. The name honors 17th-century French writer Savinien Cyrano de Bergerac, legendary for his love of word play and fine cuisine. Book reviews, poetry readings, and light musical performances are frequent evening events; an improvisational theater group often performs Saturday night. Foreign and art films are presented at Cyrano's adjoining cinema.

DOWNTOWN DELI & CAFE, 525 W. Fourth Ave. Tel. 276-7116.
  Cuisine: INTERNATIONAL. **Reservations:** Not accepted.
$ **Prices:** Breakfast $4.25-$7.95; lunch $5.25-$9.95; dinner $9.95-$12.95. AE, DISC, MC, V.

Open: May–Sept, daily 6am–11pm. Oct–Apr, Mon–Sat 7am–10pm, Sun 9am–4pm.

Former mayor Tony Knowles is a part-owner of the Downtown Deli & Café, Anchorage's closest approximation of a New York deli. The atmosphere is campuslike, with ivy hanging over smoked-glass room dividers and seating on wooden benches. The visitor can come for lox and bagels, pickled herring, matzohs, and other noshes. Breakfast is served anytime: Try the Bavarian omelet. The seafood melt, a heaping open-face sandwich, and fresh spinach salad are popular lunches. Dinner dishes, served from 4 to 10pm, range from chicken tarragon with artichoke hearts to seafood pasta primavera. Barbecued reindeer ribs are often on the menu.

KUMAGORO, 533 W. Fourth Ave. Tel. 272-9905.
   Cuisine: JAPANESE. **Reservations:** Not required.
$ Prices: Main courses $4.50–$7 at lunch, $10–$13 at dinner; sushi $4–$6. AE, CB, DC, DISC, JCB, MC, V.
   Open: Daily 11am–11pm.
When Japanese visitors are in town, many of them head for Kumagoro, a casual Japanese eatery with shoji screens and bamboo dividers. One favorite dish is champon ramen, a stew of vegetables and seafood (shrimp, squid, octopus), and a full meal in itself. The Kumagoro also has a good sushi bar.

LA CABAÑA, 312 E. Fourth Ave. Tel. 272-0135.
   Cuisine: MEXICAN. **Reservations:** Not required.
$ Prices: Lunch $5–$7; dinner $7–$10. AE, DC, MC, V.
   Open: Lunch Mon–Fri 11:30am–3pm; dinner Mon–Fri 3–11pm, Sat 5–11pm, Sun 5–10pm.
La Cabaña was Alaska's first Mexican restaurant when the Torres family opened it in 1953 at another location. It's still in the same family. The decor is unpretentiously south-of-the-border, with curtained alcoves, wrought-iron railings and chandeliers, and wall murals. Piped-in mariachi music completes the feeling. Complimentary chips come with all meals, from burritos to chimichangas. The bar serves excellent margaritas.

TUNDRA CLUB, 250 Gambell St. Tel. 278-4716.
   Cuisine: ALASKAN. **Reservations:** Not accepted.
$ Prices: Lunch courses $5; dinner courses $8. No credit cards.
   Open: Mon–Fri 7am–3pm.
When Native Alaskans come to Anchorage, they often gather at the Alaska Native Medical Center to visit with friends. The center's Tundra Club café has therefore become the city's most popular spot for authentic Native cuisine, including sourdough pancakes, berry dumplings, fish pie, reindeer sausage, Indian fry bread, and akutak (Eskimo ice cream). Lunch—usually meat, potatoes, and vegetables—is served on a paper plate. And don't expect a lot of atmosphere; the building has worn out at least two dozen coats of paint.

MIDTOWN/SPENARD

MODERATE

AH SA WAN, 560 W. Tudor Rd. Tel. 562-7788 or 563-0044.
   Cuisine: CHINESE. **Reservations:** Recommended.
$ Prices: Lunch $5.50–$7; dinner $10–$16. AE, CB, DC, MC, V.
   Open: Sun–Thurs 11:30am–10pm, Fri–Sat 11:30am–11pm.
Colorfully painted masks are the unifying theme in this elegant Mandarin and Cantonese restaurant. (You'll recognize it immediately—it looks like a temple gate from the outside.) For under $15 per person you can have a Mandarin feast of sizzling rice soup, eggroll, Mongolian beef, sweet-and-sour pork, shrimp with lobster sauce,

FROMMER'S COOL FOR KIDS: RESTAURANTS

Old Anchorage Salmon Bake (see p. 193) A gold-panning exhibition in a re-created "Tent City," live music by an Alaskan bush balladeer, and the opportunity to roast marshmallows over an open fire make this all-you-can-eat attraction a popular event for the whole family.

Gwennie's Old Alaska Restaurant (see p. 198) Every kind of Alaskana you might imagine is on the walls or ceilings of Gwennie's, from photos of Anchorage after the 1964 earthquake to Eskimo sleds made of whale baleen and a 45,000-year-old bison skull.

Sea Galley (see p. 197) An ample children's menu makes the smell of fresh fish that much sweeter. Nets and other nautical decor hang from the ceilings and walls.

Sourdough Mining Co. (see p. 199) A mining tunnel leads you into this replica of an authentic 19th-century gold mill, with its extensive collection of hunting and fishing trophies. Kids love the mesquite-grilled baby back ribs.

and fried rice. The kung pao chicken is also excellent. Adventuresome? Try moo goo gai pan, sautéed sea cucumber, or Ma-po's tofu.

DARUMA, 550 W. Tudor Rd. Tel. 561-6622 or 561-6633.
    Cuisine: JAPANESE. **Reservations:** Recommended.
$ Prices: Lunch $6.50–$13; dinner $9.50–$24.50. AE, CB, DC, MC, V.
    Open: Mon–Sat 11am–11pm, Sun 11am–10pm.
Traditional Japanese prints decorate the walls of this restaurant, which is simple in decor (natural-wood chairs, a large aquarium). Lunch dishes include donburi, yaki soba, and tsukimi udon. A good choice might be the special, which includes miso soup, salad, three kinds of nigiri sushi, shrimp tempura, sesame chicken, rice, and azuki (red bean) ice cream. For under $20 you can feast on beef or chicken sukiyaki, chicken teriyaki, shrimp tempura, miso soup, salad, rice, and tea. Wash it down with hot sake or plum wine.

GARDEN OF EATIN', 2502 McRae Rd. Tel. 248-FOOD (248-3663).
    Cuisine: STEAK/SEAFOOD. **Reservations:** Recommended.
$ Prices: Appetizers $3.50–$8.50; main courses $12.50–$29.50. AE, CB, DC, DISC, MC, V.
    Open: Dinner only, Tues–Sat 5:30–9:30pm.
Some may find it hard to take seriously a restaurant lodged in a World War II Quonset hut. Besides, the light-hearted management obviously sees dining as a time for amusement: The Garden's "calor'o'fare" menu for weight-watchers offers items like shredded egg skin, mosquito knuckles sautéed in vinegar, and boiled tablecloth stains. Fortunately, you're not locked into that regimen. In this garden setting you can enjoy an elegant dinner of plank steak or prime rib, fresh salmon, and halibut (in season) or crab imperial. All meals come with salad, homemade bread, two vegetables, and potatoes or rice.

JENS', 701 W. 36th St. Tel. 561-JENS (561-5367).
    Cuisine: DANISH/CONTINENTAL. **Reservations:** Recommended.
$ Prices: Lunch appetizers $3.50–$4, main courses $7–$10.50; four-course dinners $18–$28. MC, V.

Open: Lunch Mon–Fri 11:30am–2pm; dinner Tues–Sat 6–10pm.

✪ Owned and operated by the former head chef at the Hotel Captain Cook, Jens' bills itself not just as a restaurant but as a *bodega* and gallery: The art collection on the walls of the two dining rooms is impressive, and the wine collection would make any oenophile happy. The menu changes daily according to whim. Lunches typically include grilled seafood, pasta, and continental specialties like wienerschnitzel and osso buco. Dinners may start with a homemade pâté or gravad laks (marinated salmon), follow with a Caesar salad, and climax with a seafood entrée (such as oven-poached king salmon in crab-cognac sauce) or a meat dish (perchance roast loin of venison with a cranberry-orange-peppercorn sauce). Dessert is more simple: cheese, fruit salad, or ice cream.

ROMANO'S, 2415 C St. Tel. 278-1414.

Cuisine: ITALIAN. **Reservations:** Recommended.

$ Prices: Appetizers $5–$8; main courses $10–$16.50. AE, CB, DC, MC, V.

Open: Dinner only, Sun–Thurs 5–11pm, Fri–Sat 5–11:30pm.

Romano's is Anchorage's no. 1 choice for a romantic trattoria dinner with fine wine and candlelight. You can listen to Pavarotti belt out a Puccini aria as you dine in a Venetian atmosphere, complete with arches and a wall-size mural of gondoliers on the canals. Pastas range from spaghetti and ravioli to linguine. Dinners include chicken cacciatore and veal dishes like scaloppine piccata. There's also a selection of seafoods and steaks. Escape to the Vesuvio Room for after-dinner cocktails.

SEA GALLEY, 4101 Credit Union Dr. Tel. 563-3520.

Cuisine: SEAFOOD. **Reservations:** Recommended.

$ Prices: Appetizers $4.50–$8.50; main courses $9–$22; lunch $7–$12. AE, CB, DC, DISC, MC, V.

Open: Mon–Thurs 11am–10pm, Fri–Sat 11am–11pm, Sun 11am–10pm.

Here you're guaranteed fresh fish—and only fresh fish. The fish menu and daily blackboard specials list only the day's catches, either from Alaskan waters or flown in (often from Hawaii). Prices vary from $9 to $12 for a full fish meal, and up to $21 for a pound of king crab legs. The Sea Galley also has steaks and salads ($7 for an unaccompanied salad bar), plus a children's menu. An oyster bar attached to the lounge serves the misshapen shellfish for $6–$6.50 the half dozen. Nets and other nautical decor hang from the ceilings and walls over the rustic, light-wood construction.

STUART ANDERSON'S CATTLE COMPANY, 300 W. Tudor Rd. Tel. 562-2844.

Cuisine: STEAK/SEAFOOD. **Reservations:** Recommended.

$ Prices: Appetizers $3–$6; main courses $6–$12 at lunch, $10–$22 at dinner. AE, CB, DC, DISC, MC, V.

Open: Mon–Thurs 11am–10:30pm, Fri–Sat 11am–11pm, Sun 4–10:30pm.

Stuart Anderson's is like all others in this chain of western steakhouses—a low-lit, intimate restaurant with comfortable private booths and a noisy, bustling disco lounge. Soundproofing is guaranteed. Full steak and chicken dinners cost under $12 and include soup or salad, potato or rice, and bread. Prime rib and lobster are at the top end of the menu. Fresh catches of the day, such as rainbow trout and Hawaiian thresher shark, are based on market price. The lounge stays open into the wee hours, with DJ entertainment nightly.

INEXPENSIVE

CAFE EUROPA, 601 W. 36th Ave. Tel. 563-5704.

Cuisine: INTERNATIONAL. **Reservations:** Recommended.

$ Prices: Breakfast $4.95–$8.95; lunch/dinner $5.95–$10.95; Sun brunch $10.95. MC, V.

Open: Mon–Sat 7am–10pm, Sun 9am–4pm.

⭐ Garden-style decor marks this spacious café, with potted ferns and pandanus plants standing on the light-green carpet, fresh flowers on the white linen tablecloths, and ivy accenting the rotating exhibits of paintings from the Visual Arts Center on the walls. An all-day café menu is offered beginning at 11am; it

Ⓢ features a variety of salads, deli-style sandwiches, quiches, and pastas (including Cajun chicken fettuccine and tricolor Alfredo), served with soup or salad. Dinner specials (served after 5pm) vary daily, but usually include fresh seafood and a meat dish (such as teriyaki steak or London broil). Sunday champagne brunches are superb: You can have a gourmet egg or crêpe dish with fruit compote, fresh croissant, and juice for $10.95, and pay just another $3 for a split of champagne. The Europa also has a gourmet espresso bar and its own bakery.

GARCIA'S OF SCOTTSDALE, 4140 B St. Tel. 561-4476.
  Cuisine: MEXICAN. **Reservations:** Not required.
$ Prices: Lunch $5.25–$7.50; dinner $8.25–$11. AE, CB, DC, MC, V.
  Open: Mon–Thurs 11am–10pm, Fri–Sat 11am–midnight, Sun noon–10pm.
There's always a fiesta at Garcia's. Multicolored balloons dangle from the ceiling of this vibrant hacienda garden, giving it a permanent party feel. As befits a party, the portions are generous. At lunch, you might have a taco salad or the pollo fundido—a deep-fried flour tortilla filled with chicken, covered with melted cheese, and served with rice. Dinner combinations start at $8.75, but if you want a little of everything—enchilada, taco, tostada, rice, and beans—it will come on two plates: Garcia's calls it "el supremo sampler."

THE GREEK CORNER, 302 W. Fireweed Lane. Tel. 276-2820.
  Cuisine: GREEK. **Reservations:** Recommended.
$ Prices: Appetizers $3.95–$5.95; main courses $6.95–$8.95 at lunch, $8.95–$14.95 at dinner. MC, V.
  Open: Mon–Fri 11am–11pm, Sat 4–11pm, Sun 4–10pm.
Athenian music sets the pace at the Greek Corner. Spanakopita (spinach pie), dolmades (stuffed grape leaves), and lamb dishes, as well as baklava (a honey-and-walnut pastry), highlight the menu here, supplemented by a variety of pastas and pizzas. Beer and wine are served.

GWENNIE'S OLD ALASKA RESTAURANT, 4333 Spenard Rd. Tel. 243-2090.
  Cuisine: ALASKAN. **Reservations:** Not accepted.
$ Prices: Breakfast/lunch $3.75–$8.50; dinner $4.75–$12. MC, V.
  Open: Mon–Sat 6am–10pm, Sun 8am–10pm.
Ⓢ No restaurant in Anchorage can beat the pioneer atmosphere of this place. A spacious, two-story cabin of log and stone, Gwennie's is chock-full of every kind of Alaskana you can think of, from photos of Anchorage in 1915 and after the 1964 earthquake to Eskimo sleds made of whale baleen and a 45,000-year-old bison skull. Dug into the middle of the ground floor is a wishing well, 3 feet deep and 12 feet across, whose proceeds are periodically donated to charity. There's an old Wurlitzer in the lounge, and lots of hanging plants everywhere. Breakfast is served anytime; try the reindeer sausage omelet. A bowl of chili makes a great lunch, and barbecued ribs are popular at dinner. You don't need to ask for ice water: Every table gets a big pitcher.

HARRY'S, 101 W. Benson Blvd. Tel. 561-5317.
  Cuisine: AMERICAN. **Reservations:** Recommended.
$ Prices: Appetizers $3.95–$7.95; main courses $9.95–$14.95; lunch $5.50–$9.25. AE, CB, DC, MC, V.
  Open: Mon–Thurs 11am–10pm, Fri–Sat 11am–11pm, Sun 11am–9:30pm.
Harry's is dedicated to the memory of Harry R. Truman, the old man who refused to leave his Spirit Lake lodge when Washington's Mount St. Helens erupted in 1980. "His outlook on life and his rugged individualism would have been right at home here on the Last Frontier," explains a plaque. A life-size statue of Truman with binoculars, sitting on a barrel surrounded by wildlife, greets guests who can look past the video

games. The restaurant itself serves a wide selection of soups, salads, burgers, and baked potato dishes midday; in the evening, diners often opt for such house specials as garlic shrimp, honey-lime chicken, and blackened prime rib. The lounge's numerous specialty drinks include the Griz Killer ($3.25), "a drink that'll stop a rampaging bear dead in its tracks, lights out, forever."

HOGG BROS. CAFE, 2421 Spenard Rd. Tel. 276-9649.

Cuisine: ALASKAN. **Reservations:** Not accepted.
$ Prices: Average meal $4–$9. No credit cards.
Open: Daily 8am–4pm.

This Anchorage breakfast institution shares a saloon-style building with Chilkoot Charlie's nightclub. It's open only eight hours daily, but as the management proclaims, "Everything else is just eggs" compared with the generous and unusual breakfasts offered here—such as 20 different omelets, the Hogg McKinley and El Breakfast de Roberta. For lunch, try an asparagus burger. But the food actually takes second place to the people-watching. You'll have to drop in to see what I mean.

NATURAL PANTRY, 300 W. 36th Ave. Tel. 563-2727.

Cuisine: NATURAL FOODS. **Reservations:** Not required.
$ Prices: Average meal $3.50–$7.50. MC, V.
Open: Mon–Fri 11am–7:30pm, Sat 11am–6:30pm.

Daily vegetarian casserole specials, just $5 a plate, make this place one of Anchorage's best bargains. There are also a variety of soups, sandwiches, and quiches.

ONE GUY FROM ITALY, 3020 Minnesota Dr. Tel. 277-9231.

Cuisine: ITALIAN. **Reservations:** Recommended.
$ Prices: Appetizers $3–$6; main courses $7–$14. MC, V.
Open: Daily 11am–11pm.

The service isn't the speediest, but the food is good at this spacious neighborhood restaurant, with red-upholstered seating on two levels. There's an extensive menu of meat-free items, such as eggplant parmigiana, as well as dishes like veal parmigiana and seafood cannelloni. Spaghetti dinners include soup or salad and garlic bread. One Guy is licensed for wine and beer.

SOUTH ANCHORAGE

Most of these restaurants are within shouting distance of the Seward Highway as it heads out of town toward Girdwood and the Kenai Peninsula.

MODERATE

ARMEN'S MAZZI'S, 2052 E. Northern Lights Blvd. Tel. 279-9547.

Cuisine: ITALIAN. **Reservations:** Recommended.
$ Prices: Appetizers $6–$9; main courses $11–$18. AE, MC, V.
Open: Lunch Mon–Fri 11am–2pm; dinner Sun–Thurs 5–10pm, Fri–Sat 5–11pm.

Armen's Mazzi's bills itself as "the best little Italian restaurant this side of New York." Owner Armen Kevrekian claims to have been the first Italian restaurateur in Anchorage to serve deep-dish Sicilian pizza, calzone, and homemade pasta, and the first to offer a no-smoking room. Those points may be in doubt, but the richness of the decor is not. Enjoy the Persian carpets, fine carved wooden chairs, stained glass, wrought-iron work, and reproductions of Michelangelo's *David* and other classic sculptures. You have your choice of pastas à la carte or as full dinners, with soup or salad and garlic bread. Spaghetti, fettuccine, and manicotti are favorites. Veal dinners—parmigiana, francese, marsala, Tuscany, and contadine—start at $14. There's a highly palatable wine list, and an espresso bar.

SOURDOUGH MINING CO., 5200 Juneau St. Tel. 563-2272.

Cuisine: ALASKAN. **Reservations:** Recommended.
$ **Prices:** Appetizers $4–$8; main courses $12–$21; lunch $6–$11. AE, CB, DC, DISC, MC, V.
Open: Daily 11am–11pm.

Did you ever want to dine at a gold mine? The Sourdough Mining Co. is a replica of the abandoned mill house at Independence Mine on Hatcher Pass. Enter through a mining tunnel to a collection of 1890s antiques and hunting and fishing trophies. Mesquite-grilled baby back ribs, by the full or half rack, are the house specialty. Other choices include king crab, Alaskan-style catfish rolled in cornmeal and spices, and New Orleans pepper steak. Arctic lime pie tops the dessert list. The Creekside Saloon overlooks Campbell Creek, where you can watch spawning salmon in season. Folk and ballad singers frequently perform on weekend nights.

WARSAW RESTAURANT, 7550 Old Seward Hwy. Tel. 344-8193.
Cuisine: EASTERN EUROPEAN. **Reservations:** Recommended.
$ **Prices:** Lunch $5–$8; dinner $9–$17. MC, V.
Open: Lunch Mon–Sat 11am–3pm; dinner Mon–Sat 5–10pm, Sun 4–10pm.

Alaska's only glimpse across the former Iron Curtain is afforded by this restaurant. Polish sausage, stuffed cabbage, pirozhkis, and wienerschnitzel dinners are some of the offerings.

INEXPENSIVE

MEXICO IN ALASKA, 7305 Old Seward Hwy. Tel. 349-1528.
Cuisine: MEXICAN. **Reservations:** Not required.
$ **Prices:** Lunch $5–$8; dinner $9–$12. MC, V.
Open: Mon–Thurs 11am–9pm, Fri 11am–10pm, Sat noon–10pm, Sun 4–9pm.

Anchorage residents insist, with good reason, that this is the most authentic Mexican restaurant in the city—maybe in Alaska. Its chefs come straight from the state of Michoacán. Sure, you can get your tacos and enchiladas here, but why not step out and have pollo en mole (chicken in a spicy chocolate sauce) or lengua en salsa de aceituna (beef tongue in olive sauce)? Sunday-night dinner buffets draw big crowds.

ANCHORAGE EAST

These are just a few of the restaurants along the Glenn Highway heading east from downtown.

INEXPENSIVE

IMPERIAL PALACE, 400 Sitka St. Tel. 274-9167.
Cuisine: CHINESE. **Reservations:** Not required.
$ **Prices:** Lunch $4.25–$6.50; dinners $10–$14. AE, DISC, MC, V. -
Open: Mon–Sat 11am–10:30pm, Sun noon–10:30pm.

The Imperial Palace is arguably the best Chinese restaurant on the east side of Anchorage. Lunch specials, consisting predominantly of San Francisco–style chop suey, chow mein, and egg foo yung, run $4.25–$5.50. Spicy Mandarin and Szechuan specialties make tasty dinners for $9–$13.50 per person.

PEGGY'S, 1675 E. Fifth Ave. Tel. 258-7599.
Cuisine: AMERICAN. **Reservations:** Not accepted.
$ **Prices:** Breakfast $2.25–$6.75; lunch $3.50–$8.50; dinner $7–$12. MC, V.
Open: Daily 6am–10pm.

Ⓢ Peggy's calls itself Alaska's oldest family restaurant. Anchorage residents know it best for its fruit and cream pies. But Peggy's offers generous portions of all meals. There's a working man's breakfast—three eggs, ham, potatoes and gravy, two pancakes, and toast. The sirloin luncheon steak (with salad and fries) is a full nine ounces. And for dinner there are the jumbo prawns.

RED ROBIN BURGER & SPIRITS EMPORIUM, 3401 Penland Pkwy. Tel. 276-7788.

Cuisine: AMERICAN. **Reservations:** Not required.
$ Prices: All-day menu $5–$12. AE, CB, DC, MC, V.
Open: Mon–Thurs 11am–midnight, Fri–Sat 11am–2am, Sun 10am–11:30pm
(brunch until 2pm).

Hamburger lovers will find Anchorage's best here. The only Alaskan installment of a Seattle-based chain that has recently expanded into Japan, the Red Robin couples a party atmosphere with an imaginative variety of gourmet burgers.

SPECIALTY DINING

Most of the following recommendations are covered in greater detail above in this dining section or in "Anchorage Accommodations," earlier in this chapter.

Local Alaskan Flavor   Check out Gwennie's Old Alaskan Restaurant, the Hogg Bros. Café, or the Garden of Eatin'.

Hotel Dining / Dining with a View   You'll find the best hotel dining at the Crow's Nest, in the Hotel Captain Cook; Josephine's, in the Sheraton Anchorage; and the Top of the World, in the Anchorage Hilton. All have outstanding (and expensive) continental cuisine; all are in the penthouses of their respective hotels, and thus also offer Anchorage's finest view dining.

For Breakfasts   The Hogg Bros. Café is famous for its breakfasts. I'd also recommend Peggy's, the Café Europa, and the Downtown Deli & Café.

Afternoon Tea   While tea time isn't exactly institutionalized in this rough-edged culture, you can grab a cup (without the scones) at the major hotels or visit the espresso bars at Café Europa or Cyrano's.

Late-Night Dining   Although it's easy to drink well into the morning, it's hard to find a place to eat: Most restaurants close by 11pm, even on weekends. Your best bets for late-night dining are the Red Robin Burger & Spirits Emporium, open until midnight weeknights, until 2am on weekends; and Hollywood All-Night Pizza (see "Fast Food," below), open from 4pm to 4am daily.

FAST FOOD   Like any good-sized American city, Anchorage has its share of national fast-food franchises. Unless you're a devotee of McDonald's and Burger King, consider some of the locally owned outlets: **Wings 'n' Things,** 529 I St. (tel. 277-6257), for buckets of chicken or submarine sandwiches; **Hollywood All-Night Pizza,** 343 W. Benson Blvd. (tel. 562-3666), for Italian pies and Chinese food into the wee hours; and **Larsons Homemade Ice Cream and Yogurt Garden,** 425 E. Fifth Ave. (tel. 338-6054), for quarter-pound scoops of gourmet ice cream made with a 16% fresh-cream base.

CHAPTER 6

WHAT TO SEE & DO IN ANCHORAGE

Many Anchorage visitors are under the impression that while the city has lots of guest facilities, it doesn't have a whole lot for one to see and do.

Granted, the more spectacular sights and activities—the Portage Glacier, for example—are at least a two-hour drive from downtown Anchorage. But there's more than enough in the central city to fill up two or three days' time.

1. ATTRACTIONS

SUGGESTED ITINERARIES

IF YOU HAVE ONE DAY   Give yourself a walking tour of downtown Anchorage, stopping for lunch en route and concluding with a visit to the Anchorage Museum of History and Art. Then take an afternoon drive around the Anchorage Bowl, perhaps pausing to watch the plethora of seaplanes take off and land at Lake Hood.

IF YOU HAVE TWO DAYS   On your first day, follow the suggestions above. On Day 2, follow the Seward Highway south past the Anchorage Coastal Wildlife Refuge at Potter Marsh, then west along the north shore of Turnagain Arm, with its remarkable bore tides, to Girdwood—site of Mount Alyeska and Crow Creek Mine. After lunch, continue to Portage Glacier, where you can travel by boat to the foot of this river of ice.

IF YOU HAVE THREE DAYS OR MORE   For Days 1 and 2, follow the suggestions above. On Day 3 and beyond, get involved in an activity: bicycling, hiking, or (in winter) cross-country skiing. Or go shopping for Native crafts in the city's fine shops and department stores.

MUSEUMS

ANCHORAGE MUSEUM OF HISTORY AND ART, 121 W. Seventh Ave. Tel. 343-4326.

✪ This is Alaska's premier permanent exhibit of art, from prehistoric to contemporary. Since opening in 1968, the museum has twice been expanded, and now has 93,000 square feet of floor space plus underground parking for 100 cars.

Galleries on the west side of the ground-floor exhibit holdings of the permanent collection, with such noted Alaskan artists as Sydney Laurence, Fred Machetanz, and Eustace Ziegler well represented. The east-side galleries have temporary special exhibits (sometimes from the Smithsonian Institution) as well as an excellent children's gallery and activity rooms. Also on the ground floor are a museum shop and café, and an auditorium for the presentation of public programs, often

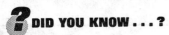

DID YOU KNOW . . . ?

- Turnagain Arm boasts the second-greatest tide variation in North America—as much as 38 feet.
- Lake Hood is the world's busiest floatplane base.
- The Good Friday earthquake that struck Anchorage and surrounding areas in 1964 was the strongest ever recorded in North America.
- The Iditarod, the world's longest and richest sled-dog race, begins in Anchorage every March.

including lectures, film series, and jazz performances.

A large second-floor gallery contains a comprehensive display of Alaskan history, from Native cultures through Russian occupation up to the present day. The museum offices and a research library, containing many valuable books and more than 150,000 historical photos of Alaska, are also upstairs.

The museum is supported by the Municipality of Anchorage, but donations are accepted to develop educational programs and temporary exhibits.

Admission: Free, but donations accepted.

Open: June–Aug, daily 10am–6pm; Sept–May, Tues–Sat 10am–6pm, Sun 1–5pm.

ALASKA AVIATION HERITAGE MUSEUM, 4721 Aircraft Dr. Tel. 248-5325.

A fascinating display of aircraft that played a part in Alaska's history, such as pioneer bush planes, is presented here. Aircraft include a 1928 Stearman 2B and a Stinson A Trimotor, thought to be the only one in existence. There are exhibits about aviator Wiley Post's flight with humorist Will Rogers (they died in a crash near Barrow in 1935) and on the Aleutian campaign of World War II. The museum lends itself to self-guided exploration, but guided tours are available on request, as are video presentations.

Admission: $5 adults, $3.75 seniors and military, $2 children 12 and under.

Open: June–Sept, daily 9am–6pm; Oct–Apr, daily 11am–4pm. **Closed:** Holidays.

ELMENDORF AIR FORCE BASE WILDLIFE MUSEUM, Building 4-803. Tel. 552-2282.

There are excellent mounted displays of Alaskan wildlife here. The collection includes polar, grizzly, and black bears; other mammals, such as coyotes, foxes, buffalo, moose, and musk ox; and a variety of birds. Interpretive materials consist of descriptions accompanying the animals on display, brochures, and maps. Hunters have been known to avail themselves of the map resources. There are hands-on exhibits for children where they can feel animal fur or handle bones. Group tours on request. There's a more limited taxidermy display at Fort Richardson, east of Anchorage off the Glenn Highway.

Admission: Free.

Open: Mon–Fri 9am–4pm, Sat 10am–3pm.

HERITAGE LIBRARY AND MUSEUM, 301 W. Northern Lights Blvd. Tel. 265-2834.

In midtown, the National Bank of Alaska's library and museum has an outstanding private collection of rare books, paintings, photographs, and Native artifacts of Alaskan cultures. The reference library covers Alaskan subjects and is open to the public. Leave about an hour in your itinerary to view this small but interesting collection. Parking is free for visitors.

Admission: Free.

Open: Mon–Fri noon–5pm.

REEVE AVIATION PICTURE MUSEUM, 343 W. Sixth Ave. Tel. 272-9426.

Housed in the Reeve Aleutian Airways offices, this collection includes over 1,100 photographs. They show the wide variety of aircraft flown by Reeve Airways over the years and commemorate the accomplishments of bush aviation pioneers. The exhibit also includes photographs of the historic flights, military aircraft, and the Lockheed

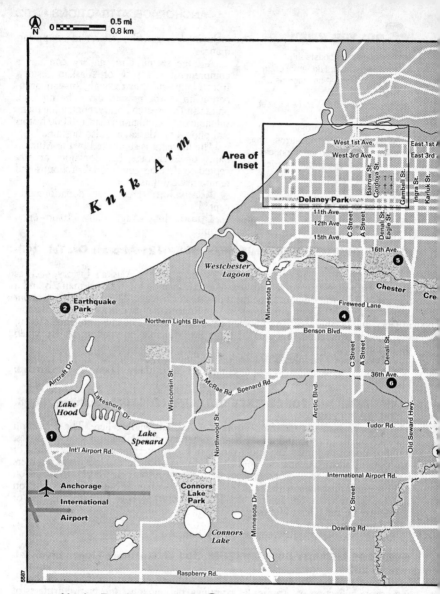

N
0 ‖‖‖‖‖ 0.5 mi
0.8 km

Knik Arm

Area of Inset

West 1st Ave.
West 3rd Ave.
East 1st
East 3rd

Barrow St.
Cordova St.
Gambell St.
Ingra St.
Karluk St.

Delaney Park

11th Ave.
12th Ave.
15th Ave.
16th Ave.

C Street
A Street
Denali St.
Eagle St.

Westchester Lagoon

Earthquake Park

Chester
Cre

Fireweed Lane
Benson Blvd.

Northern Lights Blvd.

C Street
A Street
Denali St.

Minnesota Dr.

36th Ave.

Aircraft Dr.

McRae Rd.
Spenard Rd.

Wisconsin St.

Arctic Blvd.

Old Seward Hwy.

Lake Hood

Lakeshore Dr.

Lake Spenard

Northwood St.

Tudor Rd.

Anchorage International Airport

Connors Lake Park

Minnesota Dr.

International Airport Rd.

C Street

Connors Lake

Dowling Rd.

Raspberry Rd.

5587

Alaska Pacific University ⑨
Alaska Public Lands Information
   Center ⑭
Anchorage Avation Heritage
   Museum ①
Anchorage Museum of History
   and Art ⑰

Centennial Park ⑪
Earthquake Park ②
George M. Sullivan
   Sports Arena ⑤
Goose Lake ⑧
Heritage Library and
   Museum ④

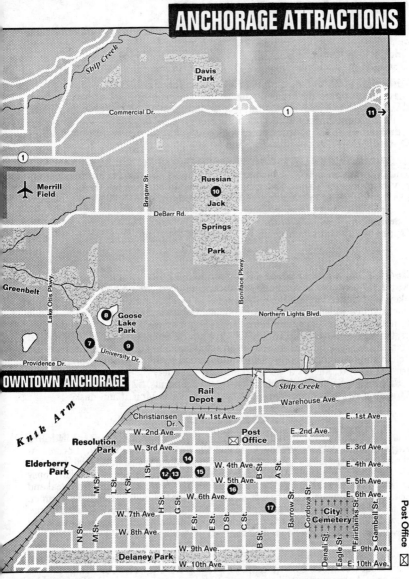

ANCHORAGE ATTRACTIONS

Ship Creek

Davis
Park

Commercial Dr.

1

11 →

1

Merrill
Field

Bragaw St.

Russian
10
Jack

DeBarr Rd.

Springs

Park

Boniface Pkwy.

Greenbelt

Lake Otis Pkwy.

Northern Lights Blvd.

8 Goose
Lake
Park

7

9

University Dr.

Providence Dr.

OWNTOWN ANCHORAGE

Knik Arm

Rail
Depot ■

Ship Creek

Warehouse Ave.

Christiansen
Dr.

W. 1st Ave.

E. 1st Ave.

Resolution
Park

W. 2nd Ave.

Post
Office

E. 2nd Ave.

Elderberry
Park

W. 3rd Ave.

E. 3rd Ave.

14

W. 4th Ave.

E. 4th Ave.

M St.

L St.

K St.

I St.

H St.

G St.

12 13

15

B St.

A St.

E. 5th Ave.

W. 5th Ave.

16

E. 6th Ave.

W. 6th Ave.

F St.

E St.

D St.

C St.

17

Barrow St.

Cordova St.

City
Cemetery

W. 7th Ave.

N St.

M St.

W. 8th Ave.

B St.

Denali St.

Eagle St.

E. Fairbanks St.

Gambell St.

E. 9th Ave.

W. 9th Ave.

Delaney Park

W. 10th Ave.

E. 10th Ave.

Post Office

Post Office ⊠

Imaginarium 12

Log Cabin Information
Center 15

Z. J. Loussac Public Library 6

Reeve Aviation Picture
Museum 16

Russian Jack Springs Park 10

University of Alaska—
Anchorage 7

Visual Arts Center 13

Westchester Lagoon
Waterfowl Sanctuary 3

Vega flown by Wiley Post and Will Rogers (see the Alaska Aviation Heritage Museum, above).
Admission: Free.
Open: Mon–Fri 10am–5pm.

VISUAL ARTS CENTER, 713 W. Fifth Ave. Tel. 274-9641.
Alaskan artists are the focus of this center, which hosts local and national art exhibits, workshops, and studios for visiting and member artists. Call for current schedules for new shows and receptions, open to the public.
Admission: $2 for galleries; receptions cost extra.
Open: Mon–Fri noon–8pm, Sat–Sun noon–6pm.

Z. J. LOUSSAC PUBLIC LIBRARY, 3600 Denali St. Tel. 261-2846.
This $17-million edifice, which opened its doors in 1986, is an architectural fantasy of cylindrical shapes and geometric forms. In addition to Alaska books, it houses the Anchorage municipal council chambers and a public auditorium. Numerous fine paintings and bronze sculptures are located inside.
Admission: Free.
Open: Mon–Thurs 9am–9pm, Fri 9am–6pm, Sat 10am–6pm, Sun noon–6pm.

PARKS

ALASKA ZOO, 4731 O'Malley Rd. Tel. 346-3242.
At this 25-acre zoo in southeastern Anchorage, there are no lions and tigers, no monkeys and giraffes. In fact the only concession to a traditional wild-animal park is the inclusion of Indian and African elephants. Otherwise, every animal and bird is indigenous to Alaska. Come and learn the difference between black, blue, and brown bears, between reindeer and caribou. Observe moose and musk oxen in their natural habitat, and see seals and otters frolic in an aquarium. The zoo is also a sanctuary for the rehabilitation of injured or orphaned animals and birds that are being prepared for return to the wild. There's a gift shop near the entrance.
Admission: $5 adults, $4 senior citizens, $3 students, $2 children 3–12.
Open: May–Sept, daily 9am–6pm; Oct–Apr, Wed–Mon 10am–dusk.

CITY PARKS

Wildlife lovers can see multitudes of birds at the **Anchorage Coastal Wildlife Refuge** and the **Westchester Lagoon Waterfowl Sanctuary.** Located at Potter Marsh in the city's southernmost extreme, along the Seward Highway as it heads along the Turnagain Arm, the Anchorage Coastal Refuge is especially busy when waterfowl migrate in late April and early May. Over 130 species, from teal and geese to whistling swans, visit the refuge, and many birds remain through the summer. Look for small mammals like muskrat, mink, and beaver as you walk the interpretive boardwalk. Westchester Lagoon, a broadening of Chester Creek at the southwest end of downtown, has a half-mile marked nature trail starting on 19th Avenue off Spenard Road.

If you continue south on Spenard Road to Northern Lights Boulevard, then turn west and follow it about three miles, you'll come to **Earthquake Park,** arguably the best place in Anchorage to still get a picture of the damage done by the Good Friday quake of '64. From a pavilion of photographs and geological diagrams you can get a good idea of the disaster. On a clear day you can see all the way to Mount McKinley.

Other parks in Anchorage include the **Bicentennial Native Heritage Park,** 5,000 acres south of Tudor Road, including 18 miles of trails for summer hiking and winter dog mushing; **Centennial Park,** 78 acres at Glenn Highway and Muldoon Road, with camping, sledding, and skiing; **Kincaid Park,** site of the 1983 World Cup cross-country championship, west of the international airport at Point Campbell; and **Russian Jack Springs Park,** with a wide range of sports and recreation facilities (including a municipal greenhouse) on either side of DeBarr Road off Boniface Parkway.

You shouldn't be surprised to find wildlife—of the large variety—in these parks. In fact you might even expect it, especially in winter, when big game descend from the surrounding mountains. Moose warnings regularly punctuate midwinter traffic reports on Anchorage radio stations, and bear tales occur and recur in residential districts. City jail inmates once complained when a bear wandered outside their fence because it made them feel as if they were in a zoo.

If you're planning to look for wildlife in Denali National Park or on other federal lands, you might benefit from a visit to the **Alaska Public Lands Information Center,** Fourth Avenue West and F Street (tel. 271-2737). You can talk to a ranger, pick up brochures and maps, look at some displays, and see free films.

UNIVERSITIES

Anchorage is the home of two four-year universities, the **University of Alaska– Anchorage** and **Alaska Pacific University.** They're located on "College Row," beside Providence Hospital along Providence Drive and University Drive, east of midtown.

Privately owned Alaska Pacific (tel. 561-1266), formerly Alaska Methodist University, was the site of the 1971 convention of the Alaska Federation of Natives, which approved the Alaska Native Settlement Act passed by Congress. The U.S. Geological Survey has an office on campus that sells topographical maps.

UAA (tel. 786-1800), one of several campuses of the state institution (the main campus is in Fairbanks), has a performing arts center and sports complex that may be of interest to visitors.

The university campuses lie next to Goose Lake, with bicycle and cross-country ski trails, swimming and ice skating, picnic areas, and a playground. Dog-sled tours are offered in winter.

COOL FOR KIDS

In addition to the Imaginarium (below), there's a children's gallery at the **Anchorage Museum of History and Art,** an interesting exhibition of bush planes at the **Alaska Aviation Heritage Museum,** hands-on exhibits at the **Elmendorf Air Force Base Wildlife Museum,** and real-life Alaskan animals at the **Alaska Zoo** (all described above).

IMAGINARIUM, 725 W. Fifth Ave. Tel. 276-3179.

This is a hands-on science discovery center geared toward children but enjoyable for adults as well. Hands-on displays focus on natural history, such as polar bears and marine life, and illustrating principles of physics in a fun and educational way. The center houses a planetarium, and videos are shown in the Galaxy Room.

Admission: $4 adults, $2 children under 12.

Open: June–Sept, Mon–Sat 7am–8pm, Sun noon–5pm; Oct–May, Tues–Sat noon–6pm, Sun noon–4pm.

WALKING TOUR —— DOWNTOWN ANCHORAGE

Start: Log Cabin Visitor Information Center.
Finish: Anchorage Museum of History and Art.
Time: Three to five hours, depending on whether you return to the Log Cabin from Egan Convention Center or continue your walk through Delaney Park to the museum.
Best Times: Any warm day between May and September, especially Wednesday through Sunday.
Worst Times: Monday and Tuesday when attractions may be closed, especially before Memorial Day and after Labor Day.

A good way to get oriented in Anchorage is to take a downtown walking tour. The one assembled by the Anchorage Convention and Visitors Bureau, included in the city's annual visitor's guide, is considerably longer and more detailed than the one suggested here.

Begin at the:

1. **Log Cabin Visitor Information Center,** at the southeast corner of Fourth Avenue and F Street, a sod-roofed structure operated by the Anchorage Convention and Visitors Bureau. A milepost in front stresses Anchorage's location as the "Air Crossroads of the World." You may be surprised to find the mileages from East Asia, Western Europe, and the eastern and southern United States almost identical. Also outside are a 5,114-pound jade boulder from the Kobuk River area of northwestern Alaska and a "peace pole" erected in 1985 by a Japanese group.

Many of the buildings along this stretch of Fourth Avenue date from the early days of the city's history. If you turn west down Fourth from the Log Cabin and look across the street, you'll see the:

2. **Old Federal Building and U.S. Courthouse,** between F and G Streets. With the passage by the U.S. Congress of the Alaska Statehood Bill in 1958, the entire facade of this building was covered by a gigantic 49-star American flag. The structure, which dates from the late 1930s, is on the National Register of Historic Places. So is the:

3. **Fourth Avenue Theater,** across the street. Built in 1947 by a redoubtable Alaskan millionaire named Cap Lathrop, it was the venue of many stage productions until completion of the new Performing Arts Center in 1988, when it reverted to small playhouse and cinema. The interior is handsomely designed, with handcrafted woodwork, bronze and silver murals, and ceiling lights outlining the North Star and Big Dipper of Alaska's flag.

Reverse course, traveling east on Fourth Avenue. Next door to the Log Cabin is the:

4. **Old City Hall.** On the grounds is a white sculpted memorial to former Secretary of State William H. Seward, who engineered the purchase of Alaska from Russia in 1867. The first floor of the former municipal building, now occupied by the Alaska Pacific Bank, has a rotating exhibit of historical photos of Anchorage.

Turn north (left) on E Street. Between Second and Third Avenues you'll see a small:

5. **Bureau of Land Management monument,** with a bronze memorial plaque commemorating the original 1915 townsite survey. Four etchings depict the first land auction, the original tent city, an aerial view of Anchorage, and a 1985 street map. This is a good viewpoint from which to see the train station at the foot of the hill, Ship Creek just behind it, and Elmendorf Air Force Base in the near distance.

Wind your way down the hill to the:

6. **Alaska Railroad Depot** on First Avenue. In front is Engine No. 1, a small locomotive first used in the construction of the Panama Canal in the early 1900s. There are also some Native totem poles outside and historical photos inside the station. Anchorage was built as a railroad town, the headquarters of a line connecting the port of Seward with the gold-rush city of Fairbanks.

Just behind the station is:

7. **Ship Creek,** the historic site of Tanaina Indian summer fishing camps and the small Native village of Zludiat. Upstream, to the east are an interpretive salmon-viewing platform and a waterfowl-nesting area in a pond beside a power plant. One of the nine people who lived by Ship Creek in 1914, when federal railroad surveyors arrived, was the ranger for the 5.8-million-acre Chugach National Forest, established in 1907 by President Theodore Roosevelt.

Unless you're feeling especially energetic, you may not want to cross Ship Creek to climb Government Hill, an isolated residential district where federal

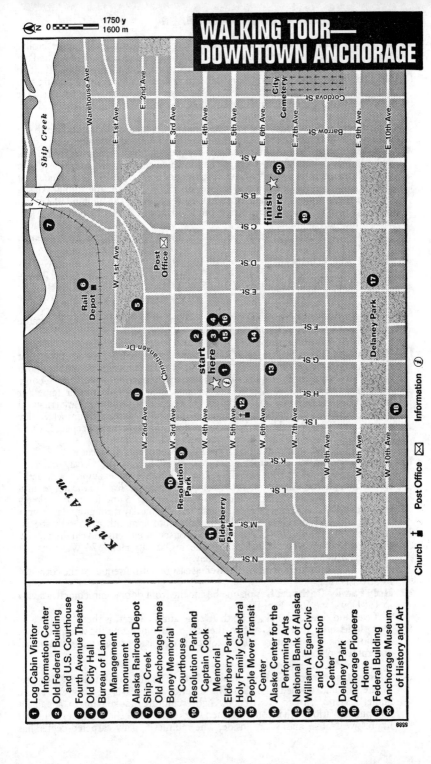

WALKING TOUR—
DOWNTOWN ANCHORAGE

1750 y
1600 m

1 Log Cabin Visitor Information Center
2 Old Federal Building and U.S. Courthouse
3 Fourth Avenue Theater
4 Old City Hall
5 Bureau of Land Management monument
6 Alaska Railroad Depot
7 Ship Creek
8 Old Anchorage homes
9 Boney Memorial Courthouse
10 Resolution Park and Captain Cook Memorial
11 Elderberry Park
12 Holy Family Cathedral
13 People Mover Transit Center
14 Alaska Center for the Performing Arts
15 National Bank of Alaska
16 William A Egan Civic and Convention Center
17 Delaney Park
18 Anchorage Pioneers Home
19 Federal Building
20 Anchorage Museum of History and Art

Church **†**   Post Office ⊠   Information ⓘ

employees were housed in the city's early days. Californians, take note: Hollywood and Vine run parallel here, not at right angles as in Los Angeles. The Port of Anchorage (tel. 272-1531) is at the north end of Government Hill. Built in 1951, the port handles more than 400 tanker and container ships bearing two million tons of cargo a year. A new visitor observation deck is a great place for spotting small, white beluga whales in the Cook Inlet during the spring and fall. Tours of the port can be arranged.

From the station, follow First Avenue west to Christensen Drive, and climb the hill back to Second Avenue. Along this stretch of Second are a series of:

8. Old Anchorage homes. Noteworthy are the Andrew Christensen House (no. 542), former home of the General Land Office director who auctioned the original townsite; the Leopold David House (no. 605), built by Anchorage's first elected mayor; the William Edes House (no. 610), built for the former Alaska Engineering Commission chairman; and Cottage 23 (no. 618), built in 1917 for an AEC storekeeper and occupied from the 1930s to the 1950s by noted Alaskan artist Mildred Hammill.

Follow Christensen Drive to H Street, then turn west (right) on Third Avenue. Two blocks down, you'll find the:

9. Boney Memorial Courthouse, with its main entrance on K Street. There are numerous fine examples of Native arts on display inside, including a totem pole, a steel wall panel engraved to show an Eskimo dance ceremony, and a teak wall panel carved to represent 19th-century scrimshaw on walrus ivory. There are more carvings on the doors.

Across K Street, in front of the office building at no. 310, is a fiberglass statue titled *The Last Blue Whale* by Anchorage sculptor Josef Princiotta.

At the westward end of Third Avenue, where it joins L Street, is:

10. Resolution Park. The Captain Cook Memorial, featuring a statue of the great English navigator looking seaward, was built in 1978 to commemorate the 200th anniversary of Cook's exploration of the inlet bearing his name. George Vancouver and William Bligh, later to gain their own degree of fame (or notoriety), were with him on the voyage. On a clear day Resolution Park is a good place from which to see the mountains on Anchorage's flanks: Mount McKinley and Mount Foraker to the north, volcanic Mount Spurr and the Sleeping Lady to the west.

Downhill and west one block from Fifth Avenue and L Street is:

11. Elderberry Park. The chief point of interest here is the Oscar Anderson House, at 420 M St. (tel. 274-2336), a well-preserved example of a 1915 wood-frame home. Anderson, a coal company executive, lived in the house until 1969. His widow donated the house to the city in 1976 and it was completely restored in 1982. It's open May to September, Wednesday through Friday from 1 to 4pm and on Saturday and Sunday from noon to 4pm; other times, by special arrangement. Admission is $2 for adults, $1 for senior citizens and children 6–12. For a guided tour, you can meet the guide at Old City Hall (524 W. 4th St.) at 1pm on Monday, Wednesday, and Friday.

Head back toward downtown, traveling east on Fifth Avenue. At the corner of H Street is the:

12. Holy Family Cathedral. A plaque beside the front door commemorates a visit in 1981 by Pope John Paul II.

Over and down a block, at Sixth Avenue and G Street, is the:

13. People Mover Transit Center, the hub of Anchorage public transportation. It adjoins the Hill Building, 632 W. Sixth Ave., the site of all major municipal government offices.

Across the street is the:

14. Alaska Center for the Performing Arts. The $67-million facility, 10 years in the making, opened in 1988. The exterior features New York artist Eric Staller's *Visual Music,* a $100,000 light sculpture hooked up to a pair of computers. Various other commissioned works of over $120,000 value, including impressive Native masks, are inside. The multilevel, gaily carpeted center has three main theaters: the 2,100-seat Evangeline Atwood Concert Hall, the 800-seat Discovery Theatre for dramatic performances, and the 350-seat Sydney Laurence Theatre. The lobby is open Monday through Saturday from 11:30am to 6pm and prior to all events.

Adjacent to the Performing Arts Center is Town Square, a three-quarter-block landscaped park with picnic tables between Fifth and Sixth Avenues and E and F Streets. At Fifth Avenue and F Street, note the:

15. National Bank of Alaska building. Across the mezzanine balcony stretches a 160-foot-long mural depicting 200 years of Alaskan history, from Russian colonization to the construction of the Trans Alaska Pipeline. During the summer months, free concerts are held on Friday at noon in the plaza in front of the building.

Across F Street is the:

16. William A. Egan Civic and Convention Center, stretching a full block to E Street. Named after Alaska's first governor, it's a common site of national and regional conventions and trade expositions. In the lobby are examples of modern Native artworks.

If you've walked enough, the Log Cabin lies immediately to the north of the Egan Center. Otherwise, turn south on E Street and proceed four blocks to:

17. Delaney Park, better known to Anchorage citizens as, simply, "The Park Strip." A block wide and a mile long, it extends east to A Street and west all the way to P Street, between Ninth and Tenth Avenues. Once the site of the city's first airfield, it now contains ballfields, skating rinks, tennis courts, picnic tables, the Delaney Community Center, a centennial rose garden (on N Street), and several monuments and memorials—the most impressive is a veterans' memorial flanked by an American flag atop a huge spruce tree. A 50-ton bonfire was held here to mark statehood in 1959, and Pope John Paul II celebrated outdoor mass here in 1981.

Across the street from the park at Tenth Avenue and I Street is the:

18. Anchorage Pioneers Home, built for senior Alaskans who have lived in the state for at least three decades, and also the home of Star the Reindeer, probably the most photographed individual of the species. The current "Star" is the fourth one. No. 2 was kidnapped (to much public indignation) and was never heard from again (he presumably became sausage). No. 3 choked on the plastic wrappers of "goodies" he was thrown by well-wishers.

Wander Delaney Park to its eastern end, then turn north on A Street. Two blocks north are the:

19. Federal Building, U.S. Courthouse, and the Federal Building Annex, on either side of Eighth Avenue between A and C Streets.

Another block north on A Street is the main entrance to the:

20. Anchorage Museum of History and Art, at Seventh and A. Conclude your walk here, spending an hour or two in the collections (see "Museums," above). Afterward, if you want, you can walk three blocks due east to the Anchorage Cemetery, between Cordova and Eagle Streets along Seventh. Several famous Alaskans are buried here. Artist Sydney Laurence's tombstone is marked by a painter's palette. Upright whalebones identify the graves of notable Eskimos, while crosses with extra diagonals denote Russian Orthodox plots.

ORGANIZED TOURS

Numerous agencies operate half-day tours of Anchorage. Each company covers similar ground—everyone seems to hit Earthquake Park and the Lake Hood seaplane base—but itineraries vary depending on whim or weather conditions.

I believe locally owned and operated tours cover the city better than larger brokers, which emerge from the woodwork only during the summer months. You won't find the little guys operating out of the big hotels, but you will find their makeshift booths outside the Log Cabin Visitor Information Center.

Eagle Custom Tours, 329 F St. (tel. 277-6228; fax 272-7766), offers a variety of tours year-round, from summer cruises to winter dogsledding and northern lights viewing. The three-hour city tour costs $30 and has morning and afternoon departures. A six-hour tour of Portage Glacier and Alyeska is $60 for adults, and a six-hour tour of the Matanuska Valley costs $65. In summer, full-day northern and southern tours are offered as well as the Kenai Fjords one-day cruise/tour package. Eagle Custom Tours can also book for Denali Park, fishing trips, bear-viewing camps, and flightseeing.

A 2½-hour walking tour offered by **Back Trails Tours,** 2316 Galewood St. (tel. 276-5528), leaves from the Log Cabin Monday through Friday in summer, at 8:30am and 1pm. The $14 price includes a snack and drink. This tour puts its emphasis on views and natural attractions, such as salmon and wildflowers. Hikes and cross-country ski excursions in the greater Anchorage area are specialties of this little company.

Among the larger companies, **Alaska Sightseeing Tours,** 543 W. Fourth Ave. (tel. 276-1305), or at the Sheraton and Westmark Hotels, operates a three-hour city tour May 15 to September 30, with daily departures at 3pm. The fare is $22 for adults, $11 for children 5–11. This tour includes the Museum of History and Art, the universities, military bases, railroad, and port. There's also a full-day tour, leaving at 8am daily, which, at $48 for adults, $24 for children, combines the city tour with a trip to Alyeska and the Portage Glacier (see "Easy Excursions from Anchorage," below).

Gray Line of Alaska, the largest tour company in Alaska, is located at 745 W. Fourth Ave. (tel. 277-5581) and has sales desks at the Hilton, Hotel Captain Cook, and the Westmark. One of the most popular tours is the daily 7-hour tour/cruise to Portage Glacier. The cost is $49.50 for adults, $24.75 for children 11 and under. The 3½-hour city tour includes the Museum of History and Art, Lake Hood, and the Aviation Heritage Museum. Tours depart twice daily at 8am and 3pm May 15 to September 15. Tickets are $26.50 for adults, $13.25 for children.

Princess Tours, 329 F St. (tel. 276-7711), and at the Hotel Captain Cook, offers a 2½-hour Anchorage tour May 1 to September 30, departing at 9am. This tour, priced at $20 for adults, $10 for children under 12, stops at the wildlife museum.

FLIGHTSEEING   A large number of local flightseeing services offer trips over the Anchorage Bowl. **Airlift Alaska** (tel. 276-3809), departing from Merrill Field, charges $85 per person for a 75-minute look at the Anchorage Bowl and Knik Glacier. Other carriers include **Anchorage Air Center** (tel. 278-9752), at Merrill Field, and **Regal Air** (tel. 243-8535), at Lake Hood.

Helicopters have some advantages over fixed-wing aircraft. They have a much larger window area, and can hover in one spot for an extended period of time. **HeliTour Alaska,** P.O. Box 190283, Anchorage, AK 99519 (tel. 243-1466), offers three tours, including a 2½-hour picnic-lunch trip to the Knik and Colony Glaciers ($250 per person), a one-hour excursion into the Chugach Range and surrounding area ($150 per person), and an approximately 5½-hour excursion to the Mount McKinley Park area (call for rates). Charter rates are also available. Round-trip transportation from Anchorage hotels is offered with tour packages by HeliTour and other flightseeing firms.

2. SPECIAL & FREE EVENTS

The **۞ Fur Rendezvous,** Anchorage's annual 10-day winter carnival, is Alaska's biggest party. Its reputation stems from days long past, when fur trappers and gold miners, escaping winter's grip, came to the "big town" to replenish their supplies and get rowdy for a few days. They'd race their sled-dog teams, auction off their caribou skins and otter pelts, and grab a saloon girl for a fling. Revived in 1936, it has been held annually ever since.

"Rondy," as it's known locally, begins on the second Friday of February. Some 140 different events are scheduled, from snow-sculpture contests to snowshoe softball, sled-dog races to dog weight-pulling, Telemark ski races to hot-air ballooning, snowmobile races to auto rallies, beer-drinking contests to the Eskimo blanket toss. The first weekend highlight is the Miners and Trappers Ball, a gigantic masquerade party that limits tickets to 4,000 lucky Alaskans (or visitors). On the final weekend, the big Rondy Parade is held through downtown.

Don't worry about snow. On the rare occasions when it's been in short supply, the city fathers have stockpiled enough of the white stuff to stage events. The Anchorage Fur Rendezvous office, at 327 Eagle St. (tel. 907/277-8615), is the clearinghouse for information on that annual event.

As befits a city of a quarter of a million people, Anchorage has a full slate of happenings throughout the year. After Rondy, the most important is the start of the **Iditarod Trail Sled Dog Race** (about 1,100 treacherous miles to Nome), the first Saturday in March (call 907/376-5155 for information). Other popular occasions are the three-day **Renaissance Festival** at Tudor Center in mid-June; the **Mayor's Midnight Sun Marathon** on June 21, the longest day of the year; **Spirit Days**, with Native story telling and a potlatch, the last weekend of June; the **Freedom Days Festival** over the July 4 weekend; **Quiana Alaska**, a festival of Native singing, dancing, and storytelling in mid-October; and the **Christmas Tree Lighting Ceremony** in early December. There are many more events throughout the year; check with the Log Cabin Visitor Information Center for a full events calendar.

3. SPORTS & RECREATION

A great variety of summer and winter, indoor and outdoor sports are available for participants and spectators in the Anchorage area.

SPECTATOR SPORTS

BASEBALL Two semipro teams—the **Anchorage Glacier Pilots** (tel. 274-3627) and the **Cook Inlet Bucs** (tel. 272-2827)—play in the eight-team Alaska League that attracts some of the nation's top college players from June through August. Many current and former big-league stars (including Tom Seaver and Dave Winfield) played in this local league. Home games are at Mulcahy Ball Park, East 16th Avenue and Cordova Street. Check local papers for schedules.

BASKETBALL The **Great Alaska Shoot-Out** is one of the nation's leading preseason major college tournaments. Since this eight-team confrontation began in 1978, North Carolina, Louisville, Indiana, and many other nationally ranked teams have performed at the George M. Sullivan Sports Arena in late November. The tourney is hosted by the NCAA Division II University of Alaska–Anchorage Seawolves. In February the UAA women's team sponsors its own tournament, the **Northern Lights Invitational.** Some of the finest university teams in the country participate, and some of the great players, such as former UCLA Olympian Cheryl Miller.

DOG SLEDDING Mushing is the official state sport, and throughout the winter months you'll see teams training and racing. Even in summer you'll often see dry-land training runs, the sleds having converted their runners to wheels. The two biggest races in Anchorage (with purses valued in thousands of dollars) are the **World Sled Dog Championships** during the Fur Rendezvous in February and the grueling 1,100-mile ☼ **Iditarod Trail Sled Dog Race,** an Anchorage-to-Nome marathon, in early March. Every Sunday from January to March, the Tudor Sled Dog Track of the **Alaska Sled Dog Racing Association,** off East Tudor Road near Bragaw Street (tel. 248-5796), hosts races at 10am and 1pm.

ICE HOCKEY The University of Alaska–Anchorage is a leading hockey power in national collegiate competition, regularly scheduling matches against large schools from the Midwest and Northeast. Home contests (admission is $4 for adults, $2 for seniors and children) are played in the **UAA Sports Center,** 2801 Providence Dr. (tel. 786-1233). Local high schools and community groups also have teams. The annual **Nissan/Jeep Hockey Classic,** an international college tournament, is held at Sullivan Arena in mid-December.

SOCCER   Municipal Parks and Recreation (tel. 264-4365) operates the **Anchorage Metro Soccer leagues.** You can write ahead for information to P.O. Box 196650, Anchorage, AK 99519.

RECREATION

BALLOONING   Have a yen to go around the world in 80 days or around the Anchorage Bowl in 80 minutes? Contact **Hot Air Affair,** 3605 Arctic Blvd., Suite 1575 (tel. 349-7333), or any of nine other operators listed in the *Yellow Pages.* Prices are typically $150 per person for a one-hour flight in a 10-passenger balloon. Launch sites vary according to weather conditions.

BICYCLING   There are 121 miles of bike trails in the city of Anchorage. Inquire at the Log Cabin Visitor Information Center about the "Earth Cycle" summer program for free use of bikes. Or rent all-terrain bikes or 10-speed touring bicycles from **Goose Lake Services,** East Northern Lights Boulevard at the University of Alaska (tel. 276-2960); or **Downtown Bicycle Rental,** Sixth Avenue and B Street (tel. 279-5293). **Engle Expeditions,** P.O. Box 90375, Anchorage, AK 99509 (tel. 907/563-0706), organizes bicycle tours.

BOATING   Cook Inlet waters are treacherous because of tides, mud flats, and silty waters. Local knowledge is essential. Turnagain Arm is off-limits for all boats, period. The best motorboating is in Big Lake and other Susitna Valley lakes north of Anchorage. You can rent boats and trailers from **Big Boy Toys,** 5610A Old Seward Hwy. (tel. 563-0660).

BOWLING   Downtown, the public can strike down the tenpins at **Elks Anchorage Lodge No. 1351,** 717 W. Third Ave. (tel. 276-1351). The closest major bowling alley to the city center is **Center Bowl,** 3717 Minnesota Dr., at Spenard Road (tel. 562-2695), with 30 lanes, a restaurant, and lounge.

DIVING   Tours are available through **Underwater Safaris—Alaska,** 6161 A St. (tel. 562-3483). For equipment, supplies, and personalized instruction, try **Dive Alaska,** 3002 Spenard Rd. (tel. 276-6479).

DOG SLEDDING   **Chugach Express** (tel. 783-2266), which takes visitors on three-hour dog-sled tours near Girdwood (see "Easy Excursions from Anchorage," below), also offers various mushing options at Kincaid Park, starting with a 30-minute excursion costing $25 for adults, $15 for children. You're guaranteed some time behind the sled. Short loops of the Delaney Park strip near downtown are also possible, especially during Rondy.

FISHING   Within the Municipality of Anchorage there are 19 creeks, four rivers, and numerous lakes. For fishing charters, consult the Log Cabin Visitors Information Center. Most charters operate out of towns on Prince William Sound or the Kenai Peninsula. A good place to buy or rent equipment is **Angler's Habitat,** 700 E. Benson Blvd. (tel. 276-7847). **Sport Fishing Alaska,** 1401 Shore Dr. (tel. 344-8674), plans personalized fishing trips year-round.

For information on regulations, contact the **Alaska Department of Fish and Game,** 333 Raspberry Rd. (tel. 344-0541). The department also has a recorded message of current fishing conditions (tel. 349-4687). Nonresident licenses cost $10 for 3 days, $20 for 14 days, and $36 for one year.

GOLF Four Anchorage courses are open to the public: **Eagle Glen Golf Course,** Elmendorf AFB (tel. 552-2773), has 18 holes, open June to October. **Moose Run Golf Course,** Fort Richardson (tel. 428-0056), is Alaska's oldest; it also has 18 holes and is open May to October. Rentals are available at both; civilian greens fees are $12 weekdays, $15 on weekends. **Russian Jack Springs Park,** on Boniface Parkway south of DeBarr Road (tel. 333-8338), has a nine-hole, par-30 course open mid-May to mid-September, daily from 7am to 10pm. Adult greens fees are $6 weekdays, $8 on weekends. **O'Malley's on the Green,** 3651 O'Malley Rd. (tel. 522-3322), the newest course, has 18 holes and a restaurant.

HEALTH CLUBS Among the numerous fitness centers in Anchorage are the **Alaska Athletic Club,** with two locations, at 745 W. Fourth Ave. (tel. 274-4232) and 630 E. Tudor Rd. (tel. 562-2460); the **Alaska Club,** 5201 E. Tudor Rd. (tel. 337-9550); **Gold's Gym,** 5011 Arctic Blvd. (tel. 561-2214); and **GreatLand Golden Health Club,** 360 W. Benson Blvd. (tel. 561-5535).

HIKING Hiking is a year-round activity in Anchorage. The Log Cabin Visitors Information Center has trail maps and information on scheduled hikes.
  Of special interest within the city are the **Westchester Lagoon** nature trail, off 19th Avenue between Arctic Boulevard and Spenard Road, with facilities for the disabled, and a fitness trail in **Muldoon Park,** starting at the corner of Muldoon Road and East Northern Lights Boulevard. A good day hike for families is the 3½-mile (round-trip) climb of 4,050-foot **Rendezvous Peak.** The trail begins at about 2,500 feet elevation in the parking lot of Arctic Valley Ski Area, 15 miles east of downtown. Allow three to five hours for the climb.
  For a longer trip, consider the 27-mile Iditarod Trail segment between Crow Creek Road in Girdwood and the Eagle River Visitor Center of **Chugach State Park.** You can get full information from park headquarters in the Frontier Building, 3601 C St. (tel. 561-2020, or 694-6391 for a recorded message on current trail conditions). Park officials offer a planning service for overnight backpackers. Make sure you know how to deal with bears, should you encounter any. You can get additional help from the **Chugach National Forest** office at 201 E. Ninth Ave., Suite 206 (tel. 271-2500).

HORSEBACK RIDING The **Wallace Brothers Mountain Ranch,** Wallace Mountain Road (P.O. Box 670632), Chugiak, AK 99567 (tel. 907/688-2161), is the nearest location, about a half-hour drive north of downtown. The ranch is open daily from 8am to 9pm, year-round.

HUNTING Within the Municipality of Anchorage there are seasons (some by permit only) for sheep, goat, moose, black bear, waterfowl, and small game such as rabbit and ptarmigan. Nonresident hunting licenses cost $60, plus tag fees for species hunting. Call the **Alaska Department of Fish and Game,** 333 Raspberry Rd. (tel. 344-0541), for full information.

ICE SKATING Eight outdoor skating rinks are maintained by Anchorage Parks and Recreation. Some have skate rentals. Closest to downtown is the **Delaney Park Community Center,** Tenth Avenue and E Street (tel. 264-4291), with warm-up facilities. The **Ben Boeke Ice Arena,** 334 E. 16th Ave. (tel. 274-5715), has two year-round rinks, skate rentals, and instruction. Times are also set aside for public use at **Dempsey Anderson Ice Arena,** 1741 W. Northern Lights Blvd. (tel. 277-7571), and the **UAA Sports Center,** 2801 Providence Dr. (tel. 786-1233). Serious skaters can get instruction and training with the **Anchorage Figure Skating Club,** P.O. Box 4-2222, Anchorage, AK 99502 (tel. 345-6325).

KAYAKING **Adventures and Delights,** 441 K St. (tel. 276-8282), runs kayak trips in Prince William Sound and the Kenai Fjords area.

RIVER RAFTING   Half-day raft trips are offered by **Eagle River Raft Trips,** P.O. Box 142294, Anchorage, AK 99514 (tel. 337-7238). The trip down the Eagle River, only about a 15-minute drive from downtown Anchorage, costs $75 (free transportation to and from the river included). This trip provides opportunities for wildlife viewing and fishing. Extended trips are available on request.

SAILING   Small boats can test on Westchester Lagoon and Jewel Lake, although serious sailors usually head for Prince William Sound. Check with **Pilot Rock Sailing Charters,** 2220 Paxson Dr. (tel. 338-2401). **Sailing Inc.,** 8125 Jewel Lake Rd. (tel. 243-7649), offers instruction.

SKIING   Remember those 121 miles of bicycle trails? They're all groomed as cross-country ski trails during the winter. **Kincaid Park** (tel. 264-4365), once proposed as the Nordic site for the 1994 Winter Olympics, has another 19 miles of trails, including 5 miles lit for night (or short winter day) skiing, and warm-up facilities. **Russian Jack Springs Park** (tel. 337-4444) has 6½ miles of Nordic trails (3 miles lit), a beginners' rope tow, and a chalet with ski rentals.

Most summer hiking trails are also appropriate for Nordic skiers. The **Nordic Ski Association of Anchorage,** P.O. Box 103504, Anchorage, AK 99510 (tel. 277-0827), can get you together with other cross-country skiers for day and weekend outings. There's also a recorded Nordic ski report number: 277-5114.

The best-known (and rightly so) downhill ski resort in the Anchorage area is Alyeska, at Girdwood (see "Easy Excursions from Anchorage," below). But there are a couple of other smaller areas in the Chugach Mountains nearer to the city center.

To reach **Alpenglow at Arctic Valley** (tel. 522-3645), head 5 miles northeast on the Glenn Highway, then take the Arctic Valley turnoff as it winds another 10 miles uphill. The resort has two chair lifts, a T-bar, and three rope tows, plus a ski school and a day lodge with a cafeteria. Shuttle buses run from downtown Anchorage. Open weekends and holidays December through April. Call 349-SNOW for up-to-date information on conditions.

The **Hilltop Ski Area** (tel. 346-2165) is 10 miles south of downtown on Abbott Road in Hillside Park, 4 miles east of the Seward Highway near the Service High School. Hillside operates daily from 9am to 10pm, November to mid-April, as snow permits. Facilities include a chair lift and three lighted runs, plus some cross-country trails. Rates are $11 for a full day (9am to 5pm), $9 for night skiing (5 to 10pm). Instruction is offered daily. Hillside is on the People Mover bus route. Call 346-1446 for ski conditions.

You can buy or rent ski equipment in Anchorage at **Gary King Sporting Goods,** 202 E. Northern Lights Blvd. (tel. 279-7454), or **Sunshine Sports,** 1231 W. Northern Lights Blvd. (tel. 272-6444). **Recreational Equipment, Inc.** (REI), 2710 Spenard Rd. (tel. 272-4565), and **Barney's Sports Chalet,** 906 W. Northern Lights Blvd. (tel. 561-5242), are strong in Nordic, Telemark, and ski mountaineering gear. **The Rental Room,** 5905 Lake Otis Pkwy. (tel. 562-2866), deals strictly in rentals.

Call the **Avalanche Forecast Center** (tel. 271-4500) for a recorded message of backcountry avalanche danger before setting out on a cross-country tour.

SLEDDING   There's a special sledding hill with warm-up facilities maintained by Anchorage Parks and Recreation in **Centennial Park** (tel. 264-4365). It's limited to plastic sleds, cardboards, or inner tubes. With an 80° vertical drop and 600-foot outrun, it's a challenge.

SNOW MACHINING   The World Championship Cross-Country Snow Machine Race, a two-day, 200-mile challenge from Talkeetna to Anchorage, is an integral part of the Fur Rendezvous. Most winter weekends, snowmobilers frequent Bicentennial Park or Connors Lake. Chugach State Park trails are more popular. Contact the **Alaska Motor Mushers Club,** 3931 Edinburgh Dr. (tel. 243-0888), for full information.

SWIMMING   Five indoor pools—four at local high schools, plus the **UAA**

Sports Center—have public schedules. Admission is $3.50 for adults (over 18), $2 for children and students, 75¢ for senior citizens. Call 264-4474 for locations and hours.

YMCA members can visit the **Anchorage YMCA,** 5353 Lake Otis Pkwy. (tel. 563-3211), and get discounts.

Supervised public swimming is offered outdoors in summer at three city lakes, administered by Anchorage Parks and Recreation (tel. 264-4365). All have lifeguards (noon to 8pm), picnic areas, and playgrounds. **Goose Lake** (Northern Lights Boulevard and Providence Drive) also has tennis courts and a bathhouse. The others are **Jewel Lake** (Jewel Lake Road and Dimond Boulevard) and **Spenard Beach** (Spenard Road and Lakeshore Drive).

TENNIS No fewer than 49 public courts are maintained by Anchorage Parks and Recreation, including five courts in the **Delaney Park** strip at Ninth Avenue and C Street. For further information, call 264-4365. Private clubs include the **Anchorage Racquet Club,** 700 S. Bragaw St. (tel. 278-3621), and **Four Seasons Sports Center,** 1133 N St. (tel. 279-4189).

4. SAVVY SHOPPING

As the state's largest market, it stands to reason that Anchorage has the greatest variety of Alaskan merchandise of any community in the state.

SHOPPING A TO Z
ARTS & CRAFTS

Most visitors are first attracted by the handcrafted work of Eskimos, Aleuts, Athabaskans, Tlingits, and other indigenous peoples. Here are some crafts to keep an eye out for:

Walrus-tusk ivory, used in scrimshaw (etching) work, jewelry, and figurines. Only Alaskan Natives are permitted to harvest or possess unworked ivory; it can be sold only after it has been crafted. Walrus-tusk ivory has a distinctive cross-hatch pattern; this is one way experts tell it apart from illegally imported elephant tusks.

Gold, jade, and hematite jewelry. Gold is synonymous with Alaska, but few people realize that green jade is quarried near Kotzebue, and hematite (a shiny black semiprecious stone) is native to iron ore deposits.

Soapstone sculptures, varying in color from dark green to brown and gray. This easily carved stone must be waxed or oiled to preserve its appearance.

Wood carvings. Southeast Alaska Indians carve colorful masks, totem poles, and boxes from yellow cedar. Athabaskans, from the Interior, employ birch in manufacturing a variety of household utensils. Eskimos and Aleuts, who rarely see trees in their home regions, nevertheless craft driftwood into masks and other items.

Baskets, woven with all manner of material from marsh grasses and willow roots to birch bark, and sometimes whale baleen or sealskin.

ALASKA HERITAGE ARTS, 400 D St. Tel. 278-4787.

Natives own and operate this downtown store, where you can watch and talk to carvers as they create works of ivory, soapstone, bone, horn, and wood. It's open Monday through Saturday from 10am to 7pm and on Sunday from noon to 5pm.

ALASKA NATIVE ARTS & CRAFTS, 333 W. Fourth Ave., in Post Office Mall. Tel. 274-2932.

This is a good place to start your search for something authentically native Alaskan. The broad selection of items sold here is purchased directly from the Native artists themselves. Even if you choose not to buy something here, you'll have a good idea of competitive pricing when you browse elsewhere. Open Monday through Friday from 10am to 6pm and on Saturday from 10am to 5pm.

BOOKS

Among the most interesting bookstores in Anchorage is **The Book Cache,** with 11 locations, including downtown at 436 W. Fifth Ave. (tel. 277-2723). Also check out **Cyrano's,** a bookshop and café at 413 D St. (tel. 274-2599). **Adventures and Delights,** 441 K St. (tel. 276-8282), has a travel-book store and coffeehouse, in addition to its adventure travel service. The nationwide chain stores of **B. Dalton** and **Waldenbooks** are well represented in Anchorage.

CAMERAS

Established in 1942, **Stewart's Photo Shop,** 531 W. Fourth Ave. (tel. 272-8581), is the oldest photo shop in Anchorage. It has a large selection of photographic supplies and services, including photo finishing and camera repairs and rentals. I've also visited **Dan's Camera Repair,** 735 W. Fourth Ave. (tel. 277-7214), for work on my equipment, and I've been pleased with the results.

FINE ARTS

There is no shortage of artisans or art galleries in the Anchorage area. Perhaps best known is the **Stonington Gallery,** in Old City Hall behind the ACVB log cabin, at 415 F St. (tel. 272-1489). If you're shopping for paintings or small sculptures, you should also visit **Stephan Fine Arts,** in the Hotel Captain Cook (tel. 278-9555); and **Artique Ltd.,** with a downtown gallery at 314 G St. (tel. 277-1663), features the work of watercolor specialist Byron Birdsall, oils by premier Alaska artist Fred Machetanz, and the work of 60 other artists. Unique gifts, jewelry, and prints are also available.

Less well known, but equally interesting, galleries are **Lefors Academy of Fine Arts,** 2823 E. Tudor Rd. (tel. 562-1066), which features classes and the quaint LaPalette Café; **Amniote Egg,** 1123 F St. (tel. 272-9072), with an interesting array of "alternative" artwork; and the **Alaska Art Print Company,** 1236 W. 10th Ave. (tel. 278-4975), with a collection of silkscreened and limited-edition prints. The **Arctic Rose Gallery,** 720 D St. (tel. 258-7673), is worth a look.

Many excellent **photographers** are represented in these and small private galleries. Two whose work I especially like are Johnny Johnson, a superb wildlife photographer, and Myron Rosenberg, who does some intriguing cultural studies. Rosenberg has a public gallery at 400 W. Fourth Ave. (tel. 274-1369).

FURS & QIVIUT

Anchorage's winter festival wouldn't be called the Fur Rendezvous if there weren't **furs.** Trappers throng to the big city in February with hundreds of pelts from animals large (bear) and small (beaver), and all sizes in between. The big fur auctions, well advertised, are worth attending if you're in the market for furs.

Qiviut is the soft, warm underwool of the musk-ox, known to Eskimos as oomingmak, "bearded one." Each spring the musk-oxen are combed and the qiviut comes off in big fleecy puffs that are spun into yarn. This silky yarn is knitted by Eskimo women into hats, vests, and scarves, bearing signature patterns from remote villages in the Yukon–Kuskokwim Delta region.

ANCHORAGE FUR FACTORY, 105 W. Fourth Ave. Tel. 277-8414.

From June through September you can get free guided tours here to see how pelts are treated in preparation for garment making. The factory outlet sells parkas, fashion coats, Eskimo mukluks (boots), and other fur garments. Open daily from 9am to 7pm.

DAVID GREEN & SONS, 130 W. Fourth Ave. and 423 W. Fifth Ave. Tel. 277-9595.

The finest-quality furs (and the most expensive) are sold at these two boutiques. Established in 1922, this furrier also boasts the largest selection of furs. They have parkas, coats, jackets, and skins and will custom-design a garment or service furs in-house.

OOMINGMAK, 604 H St. Tel. 272-9225.
This little shop is the principal outlet for the Alaskan Musk Ox Producers' Co-operative. It markets qiviut garments hand-knit from the yarn of domesticated musk-oxen. It's not cheap—scarves and caps are in the $65–$105 range, but the light, silky wool is very soft to the touch and is said to be eight times warmer than sheep's wool by weight.

GIFTS

One of the first items you'll see in any souvenir shop is a fan-shaped knife with a wooden handle in the "wrong place." This is an *ulu*. Traditionally made of bone and used by Eskimos for skinning and fileting seals and whales, the tourist ulu of today has a stainless-steel blade and a walnut handle. Many sold at Anchorage gift shops for $14–$20 are made at the **Ulu Factory,** 298 Warehouse Ave. (tel. 276-3119).

You'll be confronted by gift shops on nearly every block in downtown Anchorage. There's really no "best" one, but I like the selection at **JC Penney,** 406 W. Fifth Ave. (tel. 279-5656); the **Caribou Trading Company,** 326 E St., near the Hilton (tel. 276-3960); **The Rusty Harpoon,** 411 W. Fourth Ave., in the Sunshine Plaza (tel. 278-9011); and **Arctic Artisans,** in the University Center Mall on Old Seward Highway (3901 Old Seward, no. 8; tel. 562-2801).

SEAFOOD & GAME

Seafood gift packs, with salmon, crab, halibut, and other treats, make great items to carry home or to ship to friends overseas. The **Alaskan Food & Gift Cache,** 419 D St. (tel. 279-3912), and **Tenth and M Seafoods,** 1020 M St. (tel. 272-3474), can handle all arrangements.

If you have more of a taste for wild game, contact **Indian Valley Meats,** P.O. Box 8809, Indian, AK 99540 (tel. 907/653-7511), off the Seward Highway south of Anchorage. The folks there will cut, grind, wrap, label, freeze, box, or can moose, mountain goat, dall sheep, caribou, and deer meat.

5. EVENING ENTERTAINMENT

Recent years have seen the rapid growth of a variety of cultural attractions. Anchorage has its own symphony, its own ballet, modern-dance, and opera companies; and its own theatrical troupes.

When the ✪ **Alaska Center for the Performing Arts (ACPA),** 621 W. Sixth Ave. (tel. 263-2900), opened in 1988, its facilities immediately became the focus of Anchorage cultural life. The $67-million structure, 10 years in the making, contains the 2,100-seat Evangeline Atwood Concert Hall, the 800-seat Discovery Theatre, and the 350-seat Sydney Laurence Theatre, as well as other facilities. Tickets for all events are sold in the lobby from 11:30am to 6pm Monday through Saturday and immediately prior to events. Ticket prices vary, but typically range from $10 to $25. For schedule and ticket information, call 343-ARTS.

Performances take place all over the city, in the suburbs as well as downtown. To keep up on the action, pick up the Friday morning *Anchorage Daily News* and turn to its 24-page "Weekend" tabloid section. The *News* has complete daily events calendars. The Anchorage Convention and Visitors Bureau has a daily recorded listing of doings around town (tel. 276-3200), while the **Anchorage Arts Council** announces visual and performing arts events (tel. 263-ARTS).

Tickets to many events can be purchased from **Tickets, Inc.,** catercorner from the Log Cabin in the lobby of the Alaska Pacific Bank Building, 524 W. Fourth Ave. (tel. 279-9695).

THE PERFORMING ARTS
CLASSICAL MUSIC, OPERA, DANCE

Even before Anchorage had a paved street it had an orchestra. The first music teacher arrived here by ship in 1928 and immediately began organizing a choir and producing an operetta.

The **Anchorage Concert Association** (tel. 272-1471) and **Anchorage Symphony** (tel. 274-8668) were both founded in the late 1940s, and they've been going strong ever since. The Concert Association brings "name" performers to Anchorage for two series of shows—Discover Dance and the Celebrity Series— during an October-to-April season. The symphony plays an October-to-May season, performing everything from the European masters to traditional Eskimo chants. A Winter Classics series, in October and February, brings many top-name musicians who also perform at the Sitka Summer Music Festival. A mid-June Basically Bach Festival highlights the music of Johann Sebastian and such other composers as Mozart and Haydn, and in early May a Viennese Waltz Night is hosted by the Anchorage Symphony League.

The **Anchorage Opera** (tel. 279-2557) has a short March and April season of lavish productions, with guest artists boosting local talent in classic tales, plus a wintertime dinner opera. **Ballet Alaska** (tel. 279-2871), the **Alaska Contemporary Dance Company** (tel. 276-2088), and the **Alaska Dance Theater** (tel. 562-5707) get lots of support. The ballet's big event is Tchaikovsky's popular *Nutcracker Suite* during Thanksgiving weekend.

Many of these concert and dance groups use the fine auditorium at **West High School,** 1700 Hillcrest Dr. (tel. 274-2502).

THEATERS

The **Anchorage Light Opera Theater** (tel. 561-7515) is among those performing at the ACPA. Look also for the **Anchorage Community Theater** (tel. 344-4713), which presents four major shows annually; the **Theater Guild** (tel. 276-2008), with a September-to-May season; and **Way-Off Broadway Productions** (tel. 563-3075). Some of these groups may use the University of Alaska–Anchorage Performing Arts Center. Contact the Log Cabin Visitor Information Center for specifics. *The Great Alaskan Opry,* a summer revue at the Hotel Captain Cook, attracts many visitors.

THE CLUB & MUSIC SCENE
NIGHTCLUBS

Nightlife in Anchorage hotels tends toward quiet cocktails. If you're looking for more excitement than that, you'll have to leave downtown. Spenard Road is the area where nightlights burn the brightest and longest.

CHILKOOT CHARLIE'S, 2435 Spenard Rd. Tel. 272-1010.

Anchorage's most stereotypically "Alaskan" bar—with sawdust floors, padded tree-stump stools, and gold rush–era decor—is marked by a giant windmill near the corner of Fireweed Lane. It was once a rowdy saloon where no self-respecting person would take a date, but strict management measures have toned down the old image. The result is that "Koot's" may now be the most popular club in Anchorage.

The club is actually six separate rooms strung together. Between them are three bars, including an upstairs wine lounge; a snack bar; an enclosed courtyard with horseshoe and barbecue pits; a big slate fireplace; a games room for pool and darts;

and two stages for live music. One of them vibrates to the beat of high-decibel rock music for dancing, starting at 9:30pm, 365 days a year. The other features mainly country, folk, and ballad singers starting at 6pm weekdays. The bar is open till 2:30am Sunday through Thursday, to 3am on Friday and Saturday.

Drink prices are reasonable; the bar's slogan, in fact, is: "We cheat the other guy and pass the savings on to you!" If you're there on your birthday, you can get a free pitcher of beer or a mixed drink.

Chilkoot Charlie, by the way, was a legendary sourdough (immortalized by balladeer Ruben Gaines) who performed feats that could be ascribed only to an Alaskan. He once, for instance, staved off starvation on an ice floe by eating the tail of a polar bear and giving the bear the bone to chew on. That's why the modern polar bear has only a stump for a tail.

Admission: Free most weekdays; varies on weekends.

FLY BY NIGHT CLUB, 3300 Spenard Rd. Tel. 279-7726.

Perhaps because I appreciate a little eccentricity and subtle, tongue-in-cheek humor along with good music, this is my favorite nightspot in Anchorage. The whimsical owner, a jazz musician known only as Mr. White Keys, serves his guests Spam hors d'oeuvres—half price with champagne by the glass, free with Dom Perignon (the club's phone number can be read 279-SPAM). But he slaps a 50¢-per-bottle tax on Budweiser beer because, as he explains: "In spite of our attempt to offer a tremendous selection of little-known but excellent American and Canadian beers, you nitwits continue to drink nothing but Budweiser."

The musical selection here is as enigmatic as Mr. White Keys. Slapstick revues like *The Whale Fat Follies* are normal fare at 8pm Tuesday through Saturday. Dance music starts at 10:30pm, featuring the owner's own Spamtones on Tuesday and Wednesday, while some of the state's best rock bands play Thursday through Saturday. The Fly by Night is closed Sunday and Monday. Special occasions—and there are more than you might imagine—are times for celebration. Fats Domino's birthday, for example, calls for a '50s party.

Admission: Revue tickets, $9.50 and $11.50; otherwise no cover except for major guest acts

COMEDY

THE PIERCE STREET ANNEX, 701 E. Tudor Rd. Tel. 563-JOKE.

Anchorage's leading comedy club, located just west of the Old Seward Highway, attracts popular young comedians like Vince Champ, Glenn Farrington, and Bill Tucker, who perform stand-up routines nightly except Sunday. The Annex has a restaurant (meals: $5.25–$8.50), a bar and games room in front, and the cabaret-style theater at the rear.

FOLK & COUNTRY

Although Alaskan bush ballads are a unique form of folk music, opportunities to hear them are catch-as-catch-can. Chilkoot Charlie's occasionally features balladeers, as do other small taverns around town. If you're into bluegrass, try to catch the Bluegrass Festival in late July at the Alaska State Fairgrounds in Palmer, sponsored by radio station KSKA.

ADVENTURES AND DELIGHTS, 552 K St. Tel. 276-8282.

This small adventure-travel bookstore and coffee shop often features balladeers evenings and weekends.

CREEKSIDE SALOON, Sourdough Mining Co., 5200 Juneau St. Tel. 563-2272.

Alaskan folk balladeers like Doc Schultz perform at this southside restaurant Tuesday through Saturday nights. It's off International Airport Road.

MIDNIGHT EXPRESS, 2612 Spenard Rd. Tel. 279-1861.

Located across the street from Chilkoot Charlie's, the Express attracts solid country-western and rock bands; it also has two big-screen TVs for afternoon sports events. The dance floor is advertised as Alaska's largest.

THE PINES, E. Tudor Rd. and Lake Otis Pkwy. Tel. 563-0001.
Anchorage's most popular country-and-western saloon draws folks from throughout the area to two-step around the dance floor to live bands nightly.

ROCK

When headliners come to town with rock concerts, they draw capacity crowds to the 8,000-seat **George M. Sullivan Sports Arena.** Call the arena's recorded event-information line (tel. 279-2596), read the city's newspaper, or consult Tickets, Inc., to find out who, if anyone, will be in Anchorage during your visit. Apart from that, there are a couple of clubs where you can hear modern music.

GRAND CENTRAL STATION, 549 W. International Airport Rd. Tel. 562-4934.
A generation has passed since Little Eva set the nation on fire with "The Locomotion," but trains remain big in the Anchorage rock scene. Colorful locomotives light up the walls of the glittery disco-style showroom at this spacious cabaret, where contemporary rock groups and occasional touring stars play to crowds of up to about 300. Dancing begins at 9:30pm Tuesday through Saturday. If you come early, Pedro's Mexican restaurant, adjoining the station, has south-of-the-border dinners starting at $7.

HOT RODS, 4848 Old Seward Hwy. Tel. 562-5701 or 562-4251.
This classic recollection of a bygone era is actually two establishments in one. The top floor is a popular disco with decor that recalls the cars, chrome, glass, and mirrors of the 1950s and '60s. The basement comprises the Anchorage Billiard Palace, a spacious and upscale games room featuring 16 antique pool tables. Both are open daily from 11am to 2:30am; lunches and dinners run $5–$7.

JAZZ

Anchorage doesn't have a lot to offer jazz enthusiasts on a regular basis. Some clubs, like the Fly by Night, have jazz nights, and the Anchorage Museum has occasional Sunday performances.

KEYBOARD LOUNGE, 939 W. Fourth Ave. Tel. 276-8131.
Situated beside the Hotel Captain Cook, the Keyboard Lounge draws an older crowd, which listens to jazz bands Tuesday through Sunday nights.

THE OFFICE, 545 E. Northern Lights Blvd. Tel. 276-9150.
This is a small, second-story cocktail lounge with a circular bar, small dance floor, and frequent solo jazz artists.

BURLESQUE

Anchorage's best-known evening attraction may be the **Great Alaskan Bush Co.,** 631 E. International Airport Rd. (tel. 561-2609). Designed like a high-class, Old West saloon, the showroom boasts wagon-wheel chandeliers and a full balcony. The scantily clad dancers who perform at this strip club aren't shy about dancing on a patron's table or trading a conversation for a drink—especially if the patron has just come in from the Bristol Bay fishing grounds or North Slope oil fields with a wad of bills to spend. Strict licensing laws, however, prevent the meeting from going beyond conversation (in the club, at least). Visitors without bucks can sip on a beer and enjoy the show from a distance. There is a one-drink minimum; drinks cost $3.75 each.

THE BAR SCENE

Outside of the hotels, downtown Anchorage has two especially popular bars. The **F Street Station,** 325 F St. (tel. 272-5196), is a fashionable establishment with round wooden tables, brass trim, and a grill that serves up seafood and pasta to supplement the oyster bar. **Darwin's Theory,** 426 G St. (tel. 277-5322), is a lively local tavern that can at once be more crowded and less civilized than the F Street; popular among Alaska media folks, it tends to be more evolutionary than revolutionary.

Two other downtown bars cater to gay men and women: **Blue Moon,** 530 E. Fifth Ave. (tel. 277-0441), and **The Raven,** 618 Gambell St. (tel. 276-9672).

MOVIES

Perhaps because its winter nights are so long, Anchorage has a sizable population of regular moviegoers. As long as the Fourth Avenue Theatre is hosting the Alaska Rep, no first-run, major-studio films are shown downtown; elsewhere, however, movie theaters are prolific. At last count, there were 34 in Anchorage. The largest is the eight-screen **Fireweed Cinemas,** Fireweed Lane at Gambell Street (tel. 277-3825). Slightly farther from downtown is the six-screen **University Cinemas,** 3901 Old Seward Hwy. (tel. 562-1250).

For art and foreign films, check the current schedule at **Cyrano's Cinema,** associated with the coffeehouse-bookstore of the same name at 413 D St. (tel. 274-2599). You can see recent movies for $1 at the **Capri Cinema,** 3425 E. Tudor Rd. (tel. 562-2478); and at 7pm on Tuesday only, foreign films and revivals are shown at the **Anchorage Museum,** 121 W. Seventh Ave. (tel. 264-4326).

The **Campus Center Cafeteria** at the University of Alaska–Anchorage (tel. 786-1204) has a Saturday-night film program; and two universities—UAA (tel. 786-1731) and Alaska Pacific (tel. 564-1266)—have Sunday-night discount shows.

There is one downtown theater—the domed ✪ **Alaska Experience Center,** 705 W. Sixth Ave., at G Street (tel. 272-9076), and its breathtaking 40-minute presentation of *Alaska the Greatland* in three-dimensional Omnivision is definitely worth the price of admission. Filmed from helicopters, rafts, and trains, the movie makes you feel a part of all you see. It's shown hourly, every day of the year, from 9am to 10pm in summer, 11am to 8pm in winter. Adjoining the theater is an Alaska Earthquake Exhibit, which uses newsreels to re-create the Good Friday 1964 quake in a room that rumbles and shakes. Adult tickets are $6 for the movie and $5 for the quake exhibit, or $10 for both. Children and seniors pay about 30% less.

6. EASY EXCURSIONS FROM ANCHORAGE

Many of Anchorage's residents think of urban life as a necessary evil. The city, to them, is not a place where they want to be "cooped up" any longer than necessary. With spectacular scenery and many wilderness attractions within easy driving distance, why stay in the Big Smoke?

Within the Municipality of Anchorage there are two directions to travel: southeast on the Seward Highway, along the Cook Inlet's Turnagain Arm; and northeast on the Glenn Highway, through Eagle River toward the Matanuska Valley.

We'll head south first.

TURNAGAIN ARM

Heading out of downtown Anchorage, you'll cross Rabbit Creek Road, then descend to this long bay near the Anchorage Coastal Wildlife Refuge at Potter Marsh. You'll trace the shoreline of Turnagain Arm all the way to Portage, a distance of about 37 miles. Turnagain Arm, it is said, got its name in 1778 when Capt. James Cook took the *Resolution* up the inlet just far enough to realize it wasn't the fabled Northwest Passage, then told his crew to "turn again." Don't be foolish, however, and get out of your vehicle to scavenge on the mudflats. For one thing, some of it is quicksand. For another, when the tide comes in you might not have time enough to run to safety. Turnagain Arm has the second-greatest tide range in North America—nearly 39 feet in the spring, regularly 25–30 feet—and watching the bore tide rushing in can be a memorable experience, from a safe spot.

Twelve miles from downtown Anchorage you enter **Chugach State Park.** McHugh Creek State Wayside, three miles farther, is a nice place to stop for lunch beside a pretty waterfall. You'll pass several trailheads, the tiny community of Indian, the Bird Creek State Campground with 19 sites, and (27 miles from downtown Anchorage) the renowned **Bird House Bar,** a collapsing log shanty half-buried in sod. You'll know it by the large blue bird's head protruding from its outer wall. The interior is, in a word, bizarre. Everything slants in a different direction—floors, walls, bar, you name it. Some say you've had too much to drink when things begin to look normal! The walls are covered with business cards, photos, and expired driver's licenses, and the bartender may insist that you cannot leave until you leave something behind from your own person. Ask about calling the ptarmigan.

GIRDWOOD

Ten miles farther, at the Girdwood Station shopping center, turn left on the Girdwood–Alyeska Access Road. This three-mile paved road leads to the community of Girdwood and Mount Alyeska, Alaska's no. 1 ski resort. Girdwood's full-time population is only around 300, but that figure mushrooms into the thousands on winter weekends and holiday periods with the influx of Anchorage snow lovers to privately owned condominiums.

WHAT TO SEE & DO

The open meadows of Glacier Valley are the best place in the Anchorage area to try your hand at mushing, if you're here in the winter. Contact **Chugach Express,** P.O. Box 261, Girdwood, AK 99587 (tel. 783-2266), and ask about its dogsledding trips, which range in duration from 30 minutes to three days.

There are two big annual events in the valley, aside from the Alyeska-sponsored spring carnival (in April) and occasional World Cup ski races. The **Girdwood Forest Fair,** a two-day craft, food, and entertainment fair, is held in early July. The **Alaska Festival of Music,** a Labor Day weekend bash, has folk, rock, jazz, country, classical, and big-band music ringing throughout the valley, from outdoor amphitheaters to indoor stages.

ALYESKA RESORT, P.O. Box 249, Girdwood, AK 99587. Tel. 907/783-2222.

When Anchorage bid for the 1994 Winter Olympic Games, the Alyeska Resort on Mount Alyeska was proposed as the site for all alpine ski events. It's a challenging mountain with excellent facilities: five chair lifts (including a high-speed quad) handling over 5,000 skiers an hour, a 3,125-foot vertical drop, two rope tows for novices, a 60-acre snow-making capability, National Ski Patrol, equipment rental-repair shop, professional ski school, and Reliable racing program. A tramway was planned for the 1993–94 season. The timberline on this 3,939-foot mountain is just 1,500 feet, so there's plenty of open snow for experts. If there seem to be a surprising number of Japanese skiers, that may be because Alyeska is owned by the Seibu Group, a Japanese hospitality-industry conglomerate.

The 1¼-mile-long Chair 1 transports you to the glass-enclosed Skyride Restaurant. From the sun deck at 2,350 feet elevation, you get an eagle's-eye view of Girdwood's Glacier Valley and, if you're lucky, of the bore tide steaming in on Turnagain Arm. The restaurant is open daily during lift hours, serving homemade soups, deli sandwiches, wine, and beer.

Snow conditions vary from year to year (tel. 783-2121 for daily reports), so be sure to phone the resort to check the open hours. Spring skiing, on a reduced schedule, may last until June. Tickets are $30 for adults on the weekend and $26 midweek, $24 for students, and $15 for children (to 13) and seniors (over 59); $14 for all ages for night skiing. Full ski-boot-pole rental packages cost $18 all day for adults, $10 for those 12 and under. If the children are too young to ski, plant them for the day at the nearby Little Bear's Playhouse child-care center (tel. 783-2116).

Open: Mid-Nov to mid-Dec, Wed–Sun 10:30am–5:30pm; mid-Dec to mid-Mar, daily 10:30am–5:30pm, Wed–Sat 4:30–9:30pm.

CROW CREEK MINE, P.O. Box 113, Girdwood, AK 99587. Tel. 278-8060 (messages).

⭐ One of the first gold strikes in Alaska was made here in Glacier Valley in 1888; it didn't become anything enormously big, but argonauts are still pursuing the dream, and you can too. The mine's 19th-century buildings—a blacksmith's shop, bunkhouse, mess hall, barn, icehouse, and meat cache—have all been preserved, and are in fact still lived in. You'll see here a fine example of a turn-of-the-century placer mine as well as the first non-Native settlement in the Anchorage area; as such, the mine has been included in the National Register of Historic Places. Crow Creek Road, on which the mine is located (3½ miles off the Girdwood–Alyeska road), was part of the original Seward-to-Nome Iditarod Trail through Crow Pass.

Current owner Cynthia Toohey estimates that more gold remains on the site than was recovered during the life of the mine (1898–1940), when it was producing an average of 700 ounces a month. If you want to try your hand at panning or sluicing, the Tooheys will be glad to provide you with a pan, shovel, cup, and guaranteed bag of gold for $4 a day. "Look in the side of the hill for gold, not in the creek," cautions Cynthia, who should know: The 2½-ounce gold nugget she wears on a chain around her neck was found in the side of a Crow Creek hill. Other finds, many crafted into jewelry, are sold in the gift shop. Primitive overnight camping adjacent to the mine costs $2 per unit.

If you're visiting in the winter, you'll find that although the mine is closed, the Toohey family still lives here—without electricity, without well water, and without a telephone. They communicate with the outside world by citizens band radio, keep warm around a wood stove and kerosene lantern, and go shopping in a snowmobile or on cross-country skis.

Admission (for sightseeing only): $2.
Open: May 15–Sept 15, daily 9am–6pm.

WHERE TO STAY

Alyeska's Japanese owners began construction of a new, 311-room hotel, the **Alyeska Prince Hotel,** which was scheduled for completion in December 1993. The hotel will have four restaurants, a lounge, a health club with an indoor swimming pool, and meeting and convention facilities. The 80-acre site is three-quarters of a mile from the slopes, but will be connected by a special access lift.

Several condominium-rental agencies are active in Girdwood, providing temporary tenants for the expensive condos owned mainly by Anchorage professional people. Leading agents include **Golden Eagle Property Rentals,** P.O. Box 1196, Girdwood, AK 99587 (tel. 907/783-2000; fax 907/783-2425), and **Vista Alyeska Accommodations,** P.O. Box 1029, Girdwood, AK 99587 (tel. 907/783-2010; fax 907/783-2011). The homes they offer are scattered along the lower slopes of the mountain on narrow streets bearing the names of famous ski resorts: Cortina, Davos, Garmisch, Kitzbuhel, Megeve. Every home is different but fully furnished, often with a full kitchen, television and VCR (rent videos at the Girdwood mercantile), stereo system, telephone, laundry facilities, hot tub or sauna, even waterbeds. Rates vary, but start around $65 a day and $250 a week for studios, $100 and $395 for two-bedroom suites, $200 a night and up for luxury chalets.

And there's a year-round youth hostel at Girdwood, the tiny **Alyeska International Youth Hostel,** P.O. Box 10-4099, Anchorage, AK 99510 (tel. 907/277-7388). Located on Alpina Way half a mile from the ski lifts, it has four beds and an outdoor sauna.

Tax The hotel room tax is 8%.

ALYESKA NUGGET INN, Alyeska Resort, P.O. Box 249, Girdwood, AK 99587. Tel. 907/783-2222. Fax 907/783-2814. 29 rms (all with bath). TV TEL

$ Rates: Dec–Apr, $79 single; $89 double. Mid-May to mid-Sept, $89 single; $99 double. **Closed:** Spring and fall (dates vary). AE, CB, DC, DISC, JCB, MC, V.

This foot-of-the-mountain lodge offers spacious hotel rooms and several condominium units. Hotel rooms are furnished with queen-size beds, desk/dressers, and special closets for skis and ski boots. The rooms have a television, and you can phone Anchorage without charge.

The Nugget Inn restaurant on the second floor is open daily from 8am to 10pm. You can have blueberry hotcakes for breakfast or a steak dinner of anywhere from eight ounces to four pounds. Burgers and pizzas are good too. Summer fare features soups, salads, and sandwiches, with meals in the $8.50 price range. Winter dinner entrees range from $15 to $22. Enjoy a hot rum toddy at the adjoining Sitzmark Lounge and dance to live bands on weekends in winter.

ALYESKA VIEW B&B, P.O. Box 234, Girdwood, AK 99587. Tel. 907/ 783-2747. 3 rms (none with bath).

$ Rates (including full breakfast): Nov 15–Apr 15, $50 single; $65 double. May 15–Sept, $45 single; $60 double. MC, V.

The home of Austrian natives Heinrich and Emmy Gruber is off Vail Drive, reached via Timberline Drive off the Alyeska Access Road. The B&B has three deluxe guest rooms, one of them with a Jacuzzi, TV loft, ski-waxing area, and lots of gemütlichkeit. Emmy also runs a hair salon out of the home.

WHERE TO DINE

BAKE SHOP, in the Alyeska Nugget Inn. Tel. 783-2831.

Cuisine: DELI. **Reservations:** Not accepted.
$ Prices: Average meal $3.50–$6.50. MC, V.
Open: Sun–Fri 7am–7pm, Sat 7am–9pm.

This small deli-bakery, with an entrance on the lodge's exterior shop row, has superb soups, sandwiches, and pastries, as well as pizza. Many folks come just for the sourdough pancakes before a day on the slopes.

CHAIR 5, Linblad Ave. Tel. 783-2500.

Cuisine: AMERICAN. **Reservations:** Recommended at dinner.
$ Prices: Breakfast/lunch $4–$8; main courses $8–$15. AE, MC, V.
Open: Daily 9am–midnight.

The scene here is Alaskan rustic, with a big wood stove heating up the building—located behind the Girdwood post office and near the fire station, off Mile 2.4 of Alyeska Access Road. Rock 'n' roll and country-western music add a little life, while the menu lists 54 beers from all over the world. There's an extensive steak and seafood menu, as well as a variety of pizzas and pastas. Every night features a different all-you-can-eat special; on Monday, for instance, it's Mexican food.

DOUBLE MUSKY INN, Crow Creek Rd. Tel. 783-2822.

Cuisine: CAJUN. **Reservations:** Not accepted.
$ Prices: Appetizers $6–$10; main courses $20–$26. MC, V.
Open: Dinner only, Tues–Thurs 5–11pm, Fri–Sun 4–11pm.

Many faithful patrons insist that this Cajun restaurant, decorated with mirrors and harlequin masks, has the best cuisine in Alaska. Cajun cooking, as owner Bob Persons explains, is "400-year-old French country food adapted to the locally available game, seafood, vegetables, and spices." All the food is spicy, but it's cooked to order, hot or mild, depending on the diner's preference. The specialties of the house are 16-ounce pepper steak in a burgundy sauce and blackened redfish (salmon) à la (chef Paul) Prudhomme.

By 6pm on a Friday or Saturday the Double Musky bar is already packed with people willing to wait two hours or longer for a table. To me, however, the restaurant fell short of its lofty reputation. The food was superb; but if I'm paying $80 or more for a dinner for two—as one can easily do here with appetizer, dessert, and wine—I do not expect less than gracious service, as I received here.

EDELWEISS GASTHAUS, Mile 3, Alyeska Access Rd. Tel. 783-2526.
   Cuisine: GERMAN. **Reservations:** Recommended at dinner.
$ Prices: Lunch/dinner $6–$14. AE, MC, V.
   Open: Memorial Day–Labor Day, daily 10am–9pm; Labor Day–Memorial Day, daily 11am–9pm.

Back up at Alyeska is this Tyrolean A-frame a few steps below the lodge. Pretend you're at Garmisch or Innsbruck and enjoy home-cooked German food, like grilled Bratwurst mit Sauerkraut or Wiener Schnitzel mit Kartoffelsalat. The menu is written on skis behind the bar, which serves beer and wine. Espresso coffees and Teutonic desserts are also served, and a variety of German-Austrian gifts, from steins to lederhosen, are sold.

PORTAGE GLACIER

This natural wonder isn't as awe-inspiring as the glaciers of Glacier Bay or Prince William Sound, but it has an attribute shared by only one of Alaska's other great glaciers: easy accessibility by road from a metropolitan center. (The other is Juneau's Mendenhall Glacier.) Portage Glacier is, in fact, the most visited attraction in the state of Alaska. The access road is off the Seward Highway 48 miles from downtown Anchorage, 11 miles from the Girdwood junction.

Portage Glacier and four others—Byron, Middle, Explorer, and Placer—overhang or drop into the Portage Valley, a historically important pass connecting Prince William Sound with Turnagain Arm. When the Pleistocene Age ended 10,000 years ago, they were all part of a single massive glacier that covered the entire valley. What you see now are but remnants. Portage is the most spectacular because it terminates in a photogenic three-mile-long lake, speckled with small icebergs throughout the year.

All visitor activity at Portage Glacier focuses on the $8-million **۞ Begich, Boggs Visitor Center** (tel. 783-2326), opened in 1986 in memory of U.S. Congressmen Nick Begich of Alaska and Hale Boggs of Louisiana, who died in a plane crash in this area in 1972. The picture windows of the center's 400-seat theater look directly upon the lake and glacier, underscoring every point made by Chugach National Forest rangers as they explain the geology of the region. They also show a 20-minute movie (charge: $1). Excellent exhibits and displays introduce the flora and fauna of the area, including the obscure iceworm, a tiny invertebrate that lives between glacial ice crystals and feeds on pollen and algae.

A short nature trail interprets natural and geologic history on the terminal moraine where the visitor center is built. Another three-quarter-mile-long trail leads to Byron Glacier. Three campgrounds with 55 campsites and six picnic sites are located in the valley.

Within snowball-throwing distance of the lake is **Portage Glacier Lodge,** where you can enjoy soup, sandwiches, and pie while sitting around a warm fireplace. The lodge also has a gift shop.

Another 1¼ miles up the shore of Portage Lake, the **M.V. Ptarmigan** departs seven times daily from May to September, on a more or less hourly basis, to take visitors on a cruise through the iceberg-studded lake. The boat is the only way to reach the foot of Portage Glacier, unless you come equipped with winter mountaineering gear. The *Ptarmigan,* an 80-foot vessel capable of carrying up to 200 passengers, is owned and operated by Holland America Line/Westours. Tickets on-site are $19.50 for adults, $10 for children under 12.

Gray Line of Alaska (tel. 277-5581) offers twice-a-day bus tours from Anchorage, including the Portage Lake cruise. The tours leave at 7:15am and 3:30pm and are priced at $49.50 (children pay $25). **Alaska Sightseeing / Cruise Alaska** (tel. 276-1305) and **Princess Tours** (tel. 276-7711) run similar tours.

My favorite Portage Glacier tour is the one operated by a unique service called **Bed**

and Meals on Wheels, P.O. Box 190411, Anchorage, AK 99519 (tel. 248-3747). John Regan, Jr., puts four adults (and perhaps a child or two) in a 25-foot motorhome for a full-day spin around Turnagain Arm. The trip starts in Anchorage at 9am, takes about nine hours, and costs just $32 per person, including lunch.

HOPE

A minor gold-rush town in the late 19th century, a virtual ghost town by the second decade of the 20th, Hope (pop. about 100) is 88 road miles from Anchorage but only about 15 air miles. Built on the south side of Turnagain Arm opposite Indian, it is today an isolated weekend getaway destination at the mouth of Resurrection Creek.

Modern gold-rush bravado may have been responsible for the creation of **Paystreke.** A replica 1800s mining camp five miles upstream from Hope on rutted Resurrection Creek Road, it began construction in 1984. A year later, it gained national attention when gold-miner Tom Williams placed a newspaper ad for "mail-order brides" for his all-male crew and drew nearly 4,000 responses. Williams wound up as a media hero, even appearing on "The Phil Donahue Show." He lived with one of the responding women for several months until she tired of an Alaska winter without running water or electricity. But although the relationship fizzled, he couldn't have asked for better national publicity for his enterprise.

Unfortunately, the infusion of publicity was temporary, and when interest dried up, so did money for the enterprise. Nevertheless, Williams, a burly man now in his 40s, clings to the hope that the 17 buildings so far erected will someday become more than a mere shell of a town. At present, the only lodging available is in tent cabins that sleep four for $20 a night (bring your own sleeping bag), and the only commercial establishment is a tiny shop with a few gift items and photographic memories of Paystreke's brief moment in the national spotlight.

Williams has at least one built-in market. His camp is at the trailhead of the 38-mile **Resurrection Pass Trail** across the northern Kenai Peninsula, a pathway used by some 8,000 backpackers a year. There are seven public-use cabins along the trail, where hikers can stay for $20 a night. Permits can be obtained from the Chugach National Forest supervisor's office, 201 E. Ninth Ave., Anchorage (tel. 271-2599).

Hope township itself has few buildings remaining. Most of the old streets, since abandoned, were absorbed by the 1964 earthquake. Joyce and Don Ohr's **Seaview Café,** on Main Street (tel. 782-3364), built in 1896, is the center of what activity remains in town. The Ohrs are also experts on local history, and will sell you a walking guide map to the townsite.

If you plan on staying overnight in Hope, I recommend the **Bear Creek Lodge,** P.O. Box 90, Hope, AK 99605 (tel. 907/782-3141), at Milepost 15.9 of the Hope Highway. The lodge has seven log cabins nestled around a pond frequently visited by geese. The cabins are charming, each with a double bed and hideaway couch, wood stove, radio, table and chair, and frilly drapes on the windows. A central bathhouse is clean and well maintained. Rooms go for $55 a night.

The tiny restaurant seats but 12 at three tables, but it serves good home-style cooking, and you can't beat the price—steak dinner and champagne for two, including after-dinner coffee and dessert, just $29.50! The restaurant is open daily except Tuesday from 8am to 8pm.

For campers, the U.S. Forest Service **Porcupine Creek Campground,** with 24 tent sites, toilets, and firepits, is at the end of the Hope Highway, two miles past Bear Creek. The overnight fee is $5.

EAGLE RIVER

This community of about 9,000, 12 miles northeast of downtown Anchorage on the Glenn Highway, has become a well-to-do bedroom community for Alaska's metropolis. For the visitor, it's the primary gateway to 495,000-acre **Chugach State Park.**

The park's **Eagle River Visitor Center** (tel. 694-2108) is a beautiful 12½-mile drive east of town, up the Eagle River Valley. Eagles, bear, moose, and other animals populate the densely forested valley floor, and dall sheep can often be seen on the sheer mountainsides.

From the veranda of the visitor center, you can study those sheep through telescopes and gaze out on the glaciated Chugach Mountains. Excellent wildlife displays include a "hands-on" exhibit for children. The center also has a three-quarter-mile interpretive nature trail, accessible to the disabled, a beaver pond, and a salmon-spawning area. There are other short trails from the center and a series of ranger-led hikes and naturalist programs. Eagle River Visitor Center is open in summer Thursday through Monday from 11am to 7pm, and in winter Friday through Sunday from 11am to 5pm.

The visitor center is the northern trailhead for the popular 27-mile **Old Iditarod Trail** segment connecting Eagle River and Girdwood over Crow Pass. Get full information on trail conditions from Chugach State Park headquarters, 2601 Commercial Dr., Anchorage, AK 99501 (tel. 907/694-6391), and file a trip plan with park rangers (tel. 907/279-3413).

Eagle River itself is a Class II white-water trip for canoers, kayakers, and rafters. Canoe trailheads are at miles 7.5 and 9 of the Eagle River Road. Half-day paddle excursions from Anchorage are offered May to September and cost $75 (minimum age is 13). Contact **Alaska Whitewater,** P.O. Box 142294, Anchorage, AK 99514 (tel. 907/337-RAFT), or **Eagle River Raft Trips,** P.O. Box 142294, Anchorage, AK 99514 (tel. 337-7238).

Eagle River, of course, isn't the only point of access to this huge state park. About 10 miles north of town, look for signs on the Glenn Highway pointing to **Thunderbird Falls.** This twin cataract, hidden in a canyon near a picnic area, is an easy one-mile hike from road's end. Turquoise **Eklutna Lake,** a 10-mile drive east from Glenn Highway Milepost 26, is the largest lake in Chugach Park. Seven miles long and one mile wide, it gets its color from glacial silt. It's popular for fishing, camping, swimming, and hiking.

Near the lake turnoff, just west of the highway, is a tiny Indian settlement, the **Eklutna Village Historical Park.** Its St. Nicholas Russian Orthodox Church, which dates from the 1860s, is almost certainly the oldest-surviving building in the Municipality of Anchorage. A hand-hewn log prayer chapel stands nearby, surrounded by dozens of "spirit houses"—family graves brightly painted in traditional colors. The village is open to tourism daily, mid-May to mid-September. Most Tanaina Indians—Athabaskans who have lived along the Knik Arm of Cook Inlet since the mid-17th century—were converted to Russian Orthodox more than 150 years ago by missionaries.

If you've been too long in the park to return to Anchorage, don't despair: Eagle River has ample visitor services. For a bed, check out the comfortable **Eagle River Motel,** Lynn Drive, Eagle River, AK 99577 (tel. 907/694-5000). **Garcia's Cantina,** in Valley River Center (tel. 694-8600), has excellent Mexican food and a convivial atmosphere.

Further information on the area is available from the **Chugiak–Eagle River Chamber of Commerce,** P.O. Box 353, Eagle River, AK 99577 (tel. 907/694-4702).

CHAPTER 7

SOUTH-CENTRAL ALASKA

1. **THE KENAI PENINSULA**
- **WHAT'S SPECIAL ABOUT SOUTH-CENTRAL ALASKA**
2. **PRINCE WILLIAM SOUND**
3. **THE COPPER RIVER BASIN**
4. **THE MATANUSKA-SUSITNA VALLEYS**

All south-central Alaska is within a day's trip of Anchorage. Yet it's a wildly diverse region. It incorporates the halibut fleets of Homer, the seal and bird rookeries of Kenai Fjords National Park, the awesome splendor of the great Columbia Glacier thundering into deep-blue Prince William Sound, oil tankers steaming fully loaded out of the port of Valdez, white-water rivers plummeting from the high peaks of Wrangell–St. Elias National Park, and gentle agricultural colonies in the Matanuska Valley.

1. THE KENAI PENINSULA

Were it not for the narrow isthmus between Portage and Whittier, the Kenai Peninsula would be an island. That geographical anomaly is responsible for its unique character. Connected by road to Anchorage and interior Alaska, it hasn't suffered 20th-century influence; yet its semi-isolation has allowed it to evolve in its own way, and in its own time. Happy to be a vacation playground for Anchorage sportsmen and women, it has nevertheless fallen comfortably into a slower, more casual lifestyle.

That's not to say that every corner of the Kenai Peninsula is alike. Far from it. Some 150 miles long and 60–110 miles wide, larger than Vermont, this protrusion is almost a microcosm of the entire state of Alaska in its variety. From the low-lying lake and river country of the Kenai National Wildlife Refuge to the rugged shoreline of the Kenai Fjords, from the enormous ice fields cloaking the Kenai Mountains to the halibut banks and clam beds of Kachemak Bay, there's something for everyone here.

The towns of the Kenai Peninsula are as different as the topography. **Seward** (pop. about 3,200) is a growing industrial center, a deep-water port and fishing community surrounded by snow-covered mountains. **Kenai** (pop. 6,700) has emerged from a fascinating Russian history to become an important oil town. **Soldotna** (pop. 3,800), founded only in the 1940s, has become the seat of peninsula government and a sportsman's heaven on the Kenai River. **Homer** (pop. 4,100) is an artists' and fishermen's community in a spectacularly beautiful setting on Kachemak Bay.

Package tours of the Kenai Peninsula are offered from Anchorage. **Gray Line of Alaska,** 547 W. Fourth Ave., Anchorage, AK 99501 (tel. 907/277-5581, or toll free 800/544-2206), offers full-day Kenai River fishing trips, leaving Anchorage daily from June 1 through September 15. Fares range from $175 to $249. **Princess Tours,** 519 W. Fourth Ave., Anchorage, AK 99501 (tel. 907/276-7111), offers packages that include flightseeing, fishing, and accommodations at the Kenai Princess Lodge.

Trails North, P.O. Box 923, Seward, AK 99664 (tel. 907/224-3587), provides customized tour packages of the Kenai Peninsula for groups and individuals.

WHAT'S SPECIAL ABOUT SOUTH-CENTRAL ALASKA

Natural Attractions

☐ Kenai Fjords National Park, home to tens of thousands of sea birds and marine mammals.

☐ Wrangell–St. Elias National Park, comprising a spectacular mountain range capped by a pair of 16,000-foot peaks.

☐ Columbia Glacier, one of the world's largest tidewater glaciers, 440 square miles in breadth.

History

☐ Palmer, founded as a Depression-era farm colony, which preserves its old buildings in Colony Village.

☐ Reminders of gold and copper wealth at the Independence Mine in Hatcher Pass and the Kennicott Mine in McCarthy.

☐ Russian heritage, flourishing from Kenai town's fort and church to villages of "Old Believers" near Homer.

☐ Valdez, the southern terminus of the cross-state Alaska Pipeline and the focus of Alaska's mid-1970s oil boom.

Sports and Recreation

☐ The Kenai River, known as the richest king-salmon stream in Alaska, which once yielded a 97-pound salmon.

☐ The Chitina and Copper Rivers, adjacent to Wrangell–St. Elias National Park, offering some of North America's finest rafting.

☐ Homer, the home base for a halibut fleet that takes sport fishermen onto Kachemak Bay.

Wildlife

☐ Moose and dall sheep, oft-seen denizens of the Kenai National Wildlife Refuge.

☐ Humpback whales and other marine mammals, which attract droves of whale-watchers to Prince William Sound.

☐ The Center for Alaskan Coastal Studies on Kachemak Bay, which preserves a unique marine ecosystem, best seen in tidepools reached by boat from Homer.

Events

☐ The Alaska State Fair which is held in Palmer the week before Labor Day and offers first-hand inspection of enormous Matanuska Valley vegetables.

☐ The Cordova Iceworm Festival in February, which fetes a rarely seen glacial creature with parades and exhibits.

☐ The Iditarod Trail Sled Dog Race, held every March, with its headquarters in Knik, home of the Dog Mushers Hall of Fame.

For detailed information, contact the **Kenai Peninsula Tourism Marketing Council,** 110 Willow, Suite 106, Kenai, AK 99611 (tel. 907/283-3850), or the **Kenai Chamber of Commerce,** P.O. Box 497, Kenai, AK 99611.

GETTING THERE By Plane Each of the main communities on the peninsula has a small airport and is served by regional airlines. A surprising number of Kenai residents, in fact, commute to Anchorage daily in private planes. Options include **South Central Air,** with reservations offices in Anchorage (tel. 243-8791) and Kenai (tel. 283-7343), and ticket offices in Soldotna (tel. 262-9820) and Homer (tel. 235-6171). Serving only the Kenai Peninsula, its 12-seat, twin-engine aircraft give passengers a great fly-over view. Another choice is **ERA,** the Alaska Airlines commuter line; you can call toll free (tel. 800/843-1947 outside Alaska) or contact reservations offices in Anchorage (tel. 248-4422), Kenai (tel. 283-3168), or Homer (tel.

235-5205). ERA flies larger jets several times daily between Anchorage, Kenai, and Homer, as well as Valdez. **Harbor Air,** based in Seward, flies two nonstop round-trips a day to Anchorage during the week and one trip a day weekends; call the airline in Anchorage (tel. 243-1167) or Seward (tel. 224-3133).

By Train From Memorial Day weekend through Labor Day only, Thursday through Sunday, the **Alaska Railroad** runs an all-day excursion from Anchorage to Seward and back. The train leaves Anchorage at 7am and reaches Seward at 11am; it departs Seward at 6pm and gets back to Anchorage four hours later. The fare is $70 round-trip or $40 one way. For information, contact the railroad at P.O. Box 7-2111, Anchorage, AK 99510 (tel. 907/265-2494 or 265-2623, or toll free 800/544-0552), or P.O. Box 330, Seward, AK 99664 (tel. 907/224-5550).

By Car The two main highways on the Kenai Peninsula are fully paved and well maintained. The **Seward Highway,** which covers the 127 miles from Anchorage to Seward, climbs through the Kenai Mountains after leaving Turnagain Arm and then drops through scenic lake and river country to Resurrection Bay on the Gulf of Alaska. The **Sterling Highway,** which branches west off the Seward Highway 38 miles north of Seward, runs across the middle of the peninsula to Soldotna, then down the coast of the Cook Inlet to Homer, 225 miles from Anchorage.

By Ferry Seward, Homer, and tiny Seldovia are also served by the southwest sector of the **Alaska Marine Highway System.** The M.V. *Tustumena* runs between these ports, Kodiak Island, and Prince William Sound twice weekly throughout the year, except for a one-week-long trip to Dutch Harbor in the Aleutians each month between May and September, and a 10-week maintenance period in Seattle beginning January 1. The passenger fare between Seward and Homer is $94. For specific schedule and fare information, contact the Alaska Marine Highway, P.O. Box R, Juneau, AK 99811 (tel. toll free 800/642-0066), or call the ferry office in Anchorage (tel. 272-4482), Seward (tel. 224-5485), or Homer (tel. 235-8449).

SEWARD

High, snowy peaks surround Seward, nestled at the head of lovely Resurrection Bay. Founded in 1902 as the starting point for the federally financed Alaska Railroad, Seward, 127 miles south of Anchorage, was named after William Seward, the secretary of state who arranged the purchase of Alaska from Russia in 1867. Even before that the year-round ice-free harbor was the southern terminus of the Iditarod Trail, the overland route to the Nome goldfields. Seward attracted adventurers of all kinds—miners, trappers, loggers, and fishermen—who thronged to the town for business dealings, supplies, and entertainment.

Despite several devastating setbacks, including the 1964 earthquake and tidal wave (which destroyed over 90% of the town's economy), Seward has shown great resiliency. It has fisheries and shipping industries, a Pacific Rim coal port, a lumber mill, marine research center, vocational training center, and the new state penitentiary.

The climate is mild—average summer highs in the 60s, average winter lows in the 20s. Precipitation is moderate, about 60 inches annually, including seven to eight feet of snow.

ORIENTATION & ESSENTIAL INFORMATION

Seward is the only community on the Kenai Peninsula with a traditional "downtown." The Seward Highway enters town three miles from Milepost 0 when it crosses the Resurrection River near the airport. As you continue into town, you'll see Mount Marathon towering above you on your right, and on your left, the Suneel Alaska coal terminal, Alaska Railroad depot, and small-boat harbor. When you pass a lagoon and cross Van Buren Street, the highway becomes Third Avenue and you're in downtown Seward.

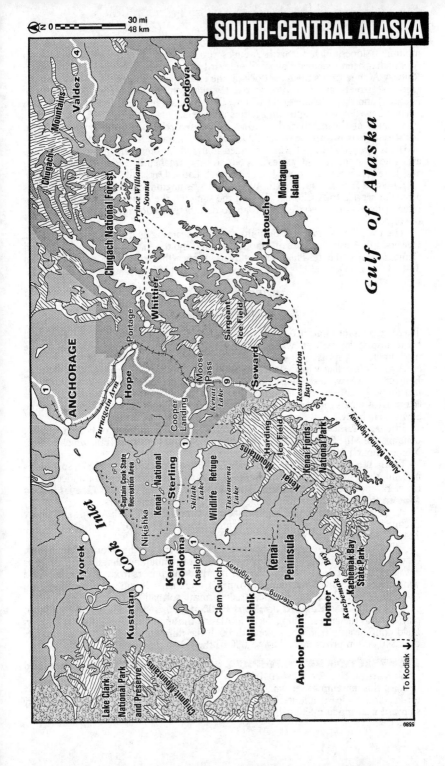

SOUTH-CENTRAL ALASKA

Downtown streets are laid out in a traditional grid pattern. Starting on the mountain slopes, First to Sixth Avenues run north-south; the beachside Seventh Avenue has been renamed Ballaine Boulevard after a turn-of-the-century city father. Railway Avenue fronts the ferry dock (at the end of Fourth Avenue). From there, the east-west streets are first presidential (Washington, Adams, Jefferson, Madison, Monroe) and then alphabetical (A, B, C, D). The main business district is on Fourth Avenue between Washington and Jefferson Streets.

Located at the north end of town, the **Seward Chamber of Commerce Visitor Information Center,** P.O. Box 749, Seward, AK 99664 (tel. 907/224-8051), is open year-round with extended hours in the summer. Information is also available from the early-day Alaska Railroad car permanently resting at Third Avenue and Jefferson Street. It's open June 1 through Labor Day, daily from 10am to 4pm.

Seward Bus Lines, Fourth Avenue and Washington Street (tel. 224-3608), runs a regular service to Anchorage. During the summer, the **Alaska Trolley Car Co.** offers daily $1-a-ride service from 10am to dark between downtown, the harbor, and the airport.

The town has as many institutions of higher learning as it has banks (two). The University of Alaska Institute of Marine Research and the Alaska Vocational Technical Center are located here. There's a weekly newspaper (the *Seward Phoenix Log*) and a 33-bed Seward General Hospital, at First Avenue and Jefferson Street (tel. 224-5205).

WHAT TO SEE & DO

Sights and Attractions

There aren't a lot of attractions in Seward itself. The Visitor Information Center will try to inspire you with its walking tour. I find the attractions cited below to be the most interesting spots.

Alaska's first flag was designed in Seward. A 13-year-old orphan named Benny Benson was a Seward schoolboy when his "eight stars of gold on a field of blue" was unanimously chosen the territorial flag in a 1926 contest. A **Benny Benson Memorial** stands today in a small park opposite the boat harbor at Milepost 1 of the Seward Highway.

Iditarod Trailhead Park, near the ferry terminal at the foot of Fourth Avenue, contains the Mile 0 monument of the Iditarod National Historic Trail, which ends in Nome, about 1,100 miles northwest.

Trails North, P.O. Box 923, Seward, AK 99664 (tel. 907/224-3587), specializes in land tours for cruise-ship passengers, but will arrange tours for independent travelers upon request. **Seward Bus Lines** (tel. 224-3608) and **Gray Line of Alaska** (tel. 277-5581 in Anchorage) also offer local charter tours.

At the end of the day, you might visit **Dreamland Bowl,** Fifth Avenue at Railway Avenue (tel. 224-3544), a town social center. **Liberty Theater,** 305 Adams St. (tel. 224-5418), has first-run movies.

July 4 is the big occasion in Seward. All eyes focus on the **Mount Marathon Race,** an annual trudge up and down the 3,022-foot mountain that began in 1909 as a wager between two sourdoughs. Today hundreds of runners from all over the world compete in three divisions—junior, women's, and men's. If you're not a runner, you can enjoy a Fourth of July parade, street carnival, softball tournament, and more.

During July, the **Seward Jackpot Halibut Tournament** is held. Seward also plays host to the largest fishing derby in Alaska, the annual **Silver Salmon Derby.** Held continuously from the second through the third weekend of August, it offers over $40,000 in prizes, including $5,000 to the grand champion.

RESURRECTION BAY HISTORICAL SOCIETY MUSEUM, Third Ave. and Jefferson St. Tel. 224-3902.

Visit this museum to see what destruction nature wrought on Seward in the 1964 quake, and to learn about Russian Gov. Alexander Baranov's late 18th-century shipyard near modern Seward.

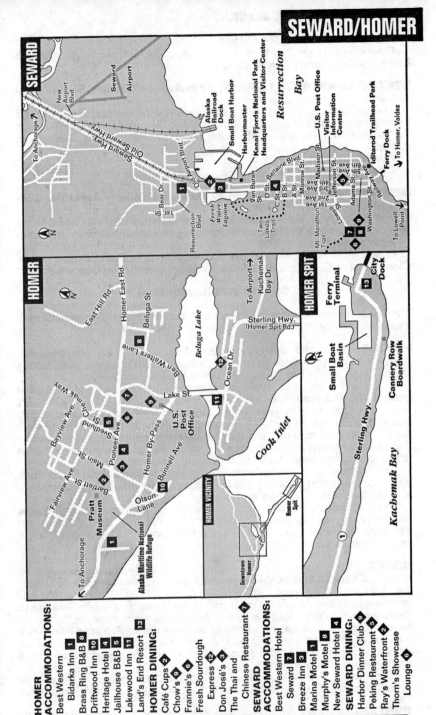

SEWARD/HOMER

SEWARD

Seward Airport

New Airport Blvd.

To Anchorage

Old Seward Hwy.

Old Airport Blvd.

Bear Dr.

1st St.

Resurrection Blvd.

Fresh Water Lagoon

Two Lakes Trail

1

2

3

Alaska Railroad Dock

Small Boat Harbor

Harbormaster

Kenai Fjords National Park Headquarters and Visitor Center

Resurrection Bay

U.S. Post Office

Visitor Information Center

Iditarod Trailhead Park

Ferry Dock

→ To Homer, Valdez

Van Buren St.

D St.

C St.

B St.

A St.

Ballaine Blvd.

Monroe St.

Madison St.

Jefferson St.

Adams St.

Washington St.

Railway Ave.

5th Ave.

4th Ave.

3rd Ave.

2nd Ave.

1st Ave.

Lowell

Mt. Marathon Trail

4

5

6

7

8

9

To Lowell Point

N

HOMER

East Hill Rd.

Homer East Rd.

Beluga St.

Ben Walters Lane

Beluga Lake

Ocean Dr.

Lake St.

Sterling Hwy. (Homer Spit Rd.)

To Airport → Kachemak Bay Dr.

Bayview Ave.

Fairview Ave.

St. Charmak Way

Svedlund St.

Main St.

Pioneer Ave.

Bartlett St.

Pratt Museum

Homer By-Pass

Bunnell Ave.

Olson Lane

U.S. Post Office

Alaska Maritime National Wildlife Refuge

To Anchorage

8

7

9

6

5

4

3

10

11

12

1

N

Cook Inlet

HOMER VICINITY

Downtown Homer

Homer Spit

HOMER SPIT

Ferry Terminal

City Dock

Small Boat Basin

Sterling Hwy.

Cannery Row Boardwalk

Kachemak Bay

13

1

N

5590

Admission: $1 adults, 50¢ children.
Open: June–Labor Day, Mon–Fri 11am–6pm, Sat–Sun noon–5pm. **Closed:** Labor Day–May, except by appointment.

SEWARD COMMUNITY LIBRARY, Fifth Ave. and Adams St. Tel. 224-3646.

The earthquake is also of abiding interest here. A slide program called "Seward Is Burning!" is presented at 2pm daily, June to Labor Day, and free films are shown at 7:30pm on Friday. The original Alaska flag, signed by designer Benny Benson, is on display.
Admission: Free.
Open: Mon–Fri 1–8pm, Sat 1–6pm.

INSTITUTE OF MARINE SCIENCE, Third and Railway Aves. Tel. 224-5261.

This University of Alaska facility has marine displays, slide shows, and a film at 3pm daily. You can learn about aquaculture projects and oceanographic research.
Admission: Free.
Open: Memorial Day–Labor Day, Mon–Fri 1–5pm, Sat 8am–noon and 1–5pm. **Closed:** Labor Day–Memorial Day, except by appointment; holidays year-round.

Sports and Recreation

The Visitor Information Center will give you directions to Seward's swimming pool, ice skating rink, gymnasium, tennis courts, and softball fields.

FISHING Resurrection Bay is a saltwater fishery, one of Alaska's most popular. Boats are nearly gunwale to gunwale in August during the annual Silver Salmon Derby. Locals say the best fishing is off Lowell Point or Fourth of July Creek.

The consensus choice as Seward's most complete fishing supply and information center is **The Fish House,** P.O. Box 1345, Seward, AK 99664 (tel. 907/224-3674), open daily from 6am to 9pm. Dale Clemens and his staff can make charter arrangements for you on any of 14 different boats. Some 20 charter operators work out of Seward, and most maintain dockside booths where you can make your own decision about which one to fish with. Typical full-day rates for salmon or halibut fishing are $90 per person, including all bait and equipment.

The most popular nearby freshwater holes are at **Grayling Lake,** 13 miles north, where you can fly-fish for grayling May to October, and **Grouse Lake,** 8 miles north, with excellent winter ice-fishing for Dolly Varden.

Some 30 miles north of Seward, on the Seward Highway, the **Trail Lakes Hatchery,** operated by the Alaska Department of Fish and Game, will show you where many of Resurrection Bay's salmon get their start. The visitor center here is open daily from 8am to 4:30pm in summer.

HIKING A wide variety of trails—short and long, level and steep—are open for hiking in **Chugach National Forest.** Check with forest headquarters, 334 Fourth Ave. (P.O. Box 275), Seward, AK 99664 (tel. 907/224-3374), for complete trail information. Among the more popular trails in the Seward area are the **Two Lakes Trail,** a one-mile loop along the base of Mount Marathon, beginning behind the VoTech at Second Avenue and B Street; and the gently sloping **Johnson Pass Trail,** a 23-mile segment of the Old Iditarod Trail connecting Upper Trail Lake (Mile 33 on the Seward Highway) with Granite Creek (Mile 64). Wildlife, especially black bear, is common.

The Forest Service also maintains 17 walk-in **cabins** for public use at $20 in the Seward district of Chugach National Forest. You can book up to 180 days in advance.

HUNTING Black and brown bear, moose, mountain goat, and dall sheep roam the Chugach National Forest around Seward. Small game, such as snowshoe hare, ptarmigan, and grouse, are also hunted. Waterfowl hunting can be some of the best in Alaska. For details, contact the **Alaska Department of Fish and Game** at 333 Raspberry Rd., Anchorage, AK 99502 (tel. 907/344-0541, or 224-3017 in Seward).

KAYAKING & CANOEING The sheltered inlets of Resurrection Bay and the Kenai Fjords are ideal for small man-powered craft. **Alaska Treks 'n' Voyages,** P.O. Box 210402, Anchorage, AK 99521 (tel. 907/224-3960 in summer, 907/276-8282 in winter), and **Adventures and Delights,** 441 K St., Anchorage, AK 99501 (tel. 907/276-8282), are the foremost purveyors in the area of three- to eight-day sea-kayak voyages in the Kenai Fjords.

WINTER SPORTS Cross-country skiing, snowshoeing, and snow machining are popular on trails frequented by hikers in the summer. **Turnagain Pass,** at Mile 68 on the Seward Highway, reserves the west side of the road for snow machiners and the east side for skiers. Another good bet is **Summit Lake,** at Mile 46. Owners Marty and June Arnoldy, who fled the madness of running an Oregon singles bar, can fix you a meal or put a rustic roof over your head at the log **Summit Lake Lodge,** Mile 45.8 on the Seward Highway, Moose Pass, AK 99631 (there are no phone lines in this remote locale).

WHERE TO STAY

In addition to the listings below, the Visitor Information Center has a listing of local residents offering **bed-and-breakfast** facilities.

Camping is also possible at several locations around Seward, including the Resurrection Bay beachfront, downtown along Ballaine Boulevard. Rates are $6 a night per campsite. Contact City of Seward, P.O. Box 167, Seward, AK 99664 (tel. 907/224-3331). Miller's Landing at Lowell Point, down an unpaved road south of town, offers primitive camping at $7.50 per night. Contact P.O. Box 81, Seward, AK 99664 (tel. 907/224-5739). There are three Chugach National Forest campgrounds 17–25 miles north of town on the Seward Highway.

Recreational vehicles can stay overnight at **Bear Creek Mobile Home Park,** Bear Lake Road, Mile 6.6 on the Seward Highway (P.O. Box 386, Seward, AK 99664; tel. 907/224-5725); or at **Kenai Fjords RV Park** at the small boat harbor (P.O. Box 2779, Seward, AK 99664).

Expensive

BEST WESTERN HOTEL SEWARD, 221 Fifth Ave. (P.O. Box 670-FG), Seward, AK 99664. Tel. 907/224-2378, or toll free 800/478-4050 in Alaska. Fax 907/224-3112. 38 rms. TV TEL
$ Rates: Mid-May to mid-Sept, $139–$159 single; $149–$169 double. Mid-Sept to mid-May, $79–$89 single; $89–$99 double. Inquire about off-season discounts. AE, DC, DISC, MC, V.
Under the same ownership as the adjacent New Seward Hotel, this hostelry, in the heart of downtown, offers a quiet, luxurious lodging option. The rooms feature colorful contemporary decor with turn-of-the-century elements, like the Tiffany lamps in view rooms. Bay windows offer outstanding views of Resurrection Bay. The property underwent a $1-million expansion in 1991.

All rooms have king- or queen-size beds, refrigerators, and coffee makers. Remote-control cable TV with free in-room movies and a VCR are provided. Complementary shuttle-van service is provided.

Moderate

BREEZE INN, 1306 Seward Hwy. (P.O. Box 2147), Seward, AK 99664. Tel. 907/224-5238. Fax 907/224-7024. 50 rms (all with bath). TV TEL

$ Rates: Mid-May to Sept, $78–$88 single; $88–$98 double. Oct to mid-May, $68–$78 single; $78–$88 double. AE, DC, DISC, MC, V.

Refurbished under new management, this three-story motel has clean and spacious rooms with decor in shades of brown and gray. Everyone gets cable TV; deluxe rooms also have a free movie channel. A coffee shop serves breakfast, plus lunch and dinner buffets daily, and an adjoining lounge features Top-40 bands weekend nights.

MARINA MOTEL, 1603 Seward Hwy. (P.O. Box 1134), Seward, AK 99664. Tel. 907/224-5518. 18 rms (all with bath). TV TEL

$ Rates: Mid-May to Sept, $75 single; $85 double. Oct to mid-May, $45 single; $55 double. DC, DISC, MC, V.

Flower boxes greet guests at the entrance. The wood-paneled rooms are decorated in earth tones and furnished with double beds. One room is a kitchenette. There's courtesy coffee and juice in the rooms. A small library in the office lends magazines and paperbacks, and there are adjacent picnic grounds for summertime feasts. Courtesy car service is available.

MURPHY'S MOTEL, 911 Fourth Ave. (P.O. Box 736), Seward, AK 99664. Tel. 907/224-8090. 10 rms (all with bath). TV TEL

$ Rates: Mid-May to mid-Sept, $74 single; $84 double. Mid-Sept to mid-May, $48–$52 single; $58–$62 double. AE, DC, MC, V.

Antique lovers appreciate Murphy's: Although the rooms are rather standard, the reception area is a private museum of beautiful antique furniture. The cozy guest rooms—done in shades of brown—all have double beds, free local phone calls, and courtesy coffee. Courtesy car service is available.

NEW SEWARD HOTEL, 217 Fifth Ave. (P.O. Box 670-FG), Seward, AK 99664. Tel. 907/224-8001, or toll free 800/478-4050 in Alaska. Fax 907/224-3112. 32 rms (10 with bath), 4 suites. TV TEL

$ Rates: Mid-May to mid-Sept, $62 single without bath, $82 single with bath; $72 double without bath, $92 double with bath; $175 suite. Mid-Sept to mid-May, $35 single without bath, $45 single with bath; $45 double without bath, $55 double with bath; $175 suite. AE, DC, DISC, MC, V.

This downtown hotel offers central location and European-style ambience. Owner-manager Brad Snowden advertises that "we pamper you," and that's no empty boast. The rooms are red carpeted and wood paneled, with paintings on the walls, drapes on the windows, nice wood furnishings, and hot-water radiator heating. They aren't particularly large, and there's no elevator to the second floor, but the "little things" truly make a difference—such as remote-control cable TVs with 24-hour in-house movies, and amenity packs (with razor, comb, shampoo, sewing kit) in every room. The lobby has courtesy coffee and a well-stocked gift shop. In the basement is a games room with a pool table and darts. Shuttle-van service is provided between the hotel and the harbor, ferry dock, and train station. The New Seward serves as a booking point for Kenai Fjords tours.

The cozy hotel saloon, decorated in turn-of-the-century San Francisco style, is easily spotted by the antique gargoyle street lamps on the sidewalk outside. It's downtown Seward's most popular after-work gathering place. A seafood bar offers light meals, and solo guitarists frequently perform.

Inexpensive

ALASKA NELLIE'S INN, Mile 23.3 Alaska Railroad (P.O. Box 88), Moose Pass, AK 99631. Tel. 907/288-3124. 8 rms (none with bath). **Directions:** Drive about 30 minutes north of Seward on the Seward Highway to Kenai Lake; when you reach Lawing townsite, take the first turnoff south of Rouge's Gallery Gift Shop.

$ Rates (including continental breakfast): $50–$60 single or double. No credit cards.

Nestled in the mountains on the bend of Kenai Lake, Alaska Nellie's is a rustic B&B that offers beautiful views and a historic flavor. Two of the log cabins on the site were built by the original Nellie, a fiercely independent pioneer woman who was awarded the first federal contract to feed Alaska Railroad construction crews in the early 1900s. She later operated a roadhouse that accommodated the likes of humorist Will Rogers, actor Tom Mix, and two U.S. presidents, Herbert Hoover and Warren Harding. The eight rooms are spread among three structures: the main house, an annex, and a single cabin by the lake. Rooms have twin, double, queen- or king-size beds. A telephone and TV-viewing room are located in the main house.

WHERE TO DINE

HARBOR DINNER CLUB, 220 Fifth Ave. Tel. 224-3012.

Cuisine: STEAK/SEAFOOD. **Reservations:** Recommended.
$ Prices: Appetizers $5.50–$13; main courses $6–$45; breakfast $4–$9; lunch $4.50–$10.50. AE, DC, DISC, MC, V.
Open: Memorial Day–Labor Day, breakfast daily 6–10am; lunch daily 11am–2:30pm; dinner daily 4:30–11pm. Labor Day–Memorial Day, breakfast daily 6–10am; lunch daily 11am–2:30pm; dinner daily 4:30–10pm.

The Harbor Dinner Club has a long-established reputation as one of Seward's best restaurants. It has a light nautical theme: Model ships, fishermen's floats, and driftwood decorate the walls. The cuisine is likewise maritime; try the seafood special, a cornucopia of deep-fried, sautéed, or poached prawns, scallops, and halibut for $16.50, including vegetable, potato, and soup or salad. For beef eaters, the largest steak on the menu weighs in at a whopping 32 ounces. Pork, veal, and chicken dishes are also served. The lunch menu features 57 different sandwiches.

LE BARN APPETIT RESTAURANT AND BAKERY, Mile 3.7, Seward Hwy.

Tel. 224-8706 or 224-3426.
Cuisine: CONTINENTAL. **Reservations:** Recommended.
$ Prices: Main courses $3.50–$5 at lunch, $14.50–$19 at dinner. MC, V
Open: Daily 11am–9pm.
Le Barn is a B&B, but it also provides a bit of European elegance for midday and evening diners. In addition to continental coffees, tea, and pastries, entrees such as omelets, crêpes, and quiches are offered. Homemade soups and salads are popular at lunch; dinner entrees include ham and flank steak. Frequently, there is live music. A part of the establishment functions as a health-food store.

PEKING RESTAURANT, 338 Fourth Ave. Tel. 224-5444.

Cuisine: CHINESE. **Reservations:** Recommended.
$ Prices: Appetizers $3.95–$9.95; main courses $5.50–$9.75 at lunch, $9.50–$14.50 at dinner. MC, V.
Open: Sun–Thurs 11:30am–10:30pm, Fri–Sat 11:30am–11pm.
The Peking gets an "A" for atmosphere: hanging lanterns, bronze Oriental casts, and a prevailing phoenix-and-dragon theme. The meals are Americanized Cantonese, Szechuan, and Mandarin. Local seafood, such as fresh halibut, is often a featured entree.

RAY'S WATERFRONT, 1316 Fourth Ave. Tel. 224-5606.

Cuisine: STEAK/SEAFOOD. **Reservations:** Recommended.
$ Prices: Appetizers $4–$6; main courses $6–$12 at lunch, $13–$20 at dinner. AE, MC, V.
Open: Daily 11am–2am (regular menu, 11am–10pm; bar menu, 10pm–2am).
The atmosphere here is enough to inspire any would-be fisher to toss a line into the briny. Ray's is built on pilings in the small-boat harbor, so diners can watch vessels carry their catch right to the docks. On the cedar walls are 55 mounted fish from local waters, including a 300-pound halibut and a beluga whale. Lunches feature burgers,

seafood pastas, and halibut and chips. Dinners include broiled salmon and halibut, prime rib, and steaks.

THORN'S SHOWCASE LOUNGE, 208 Fourth Ave. Tel. 224-3700.
    Cuisine: STEAK/SEAFOOD. **Reservations:** Recommended.
$ Prices: Appetizers $3.95–$7.95; main courses $9.95–$14.95. No credit cards.
    Open: Dinner only, daily 5:30–11pm.

This place is big among local steak lovers. Although the menu is not extensive, the featured items are very good. In a bar atmosphere of dim red lighting, you can get a 13-ounce New York steak with potato and salad for under $15. The steak sandwich and halibut dinner are local favorites.

KENAI FJORDS NATIONAL PARK

Encompassing steep-sided ocean fjords and a vast wilderness of ice, the 580,000-acre Kenai Fjords National Park, established in 1980, is home to thousands of sea birds and marine mammals. Stretching for about 50 miles along the southeastern shore of the Kenai Peninsula, just south and west of Seward, it's one of Alaska's most dramatic protected landscapes.

Visitors can reach the seacoast by chartered boat from Seward, the icefield by foot, and either by small plane. But your first stop should be at the Kenai Fjords National Park **headquarters and visitor center,** located in Seward at the small-boat harbor (P.O. Box 1727), Seward, AK 99664 (tel. 907/224-3175). From Memorial Day to Labor Day, it's open daily from 8am to 7pm; the rest of the year it's open weekdays from 8am to 5pm. The visitor center has a photo exhibit, slide programs, and a variety of publications and maps.

The park's most accessible corner is about 12 miles from downtown Seward. Head north to Mile 3.7 on the Seward Highway, then turn west onto a gravel road which leads nine miles up the Resurrection River to the **Exit Glacier Ranger Station.** Open daily in summer, it has exhibits, weekend campfire programs, and naturalist-led hikes.

Exit Glacier is but a remnant of a much larger glacier that once extended all the way to Resurrection Bay. As it retreats, it reveals the process of plant succession from lichen to hemlock and spruce. A half-mile walk from the visitor center gives you a chance to reach out and touch the highly compacted ice. But *be cautious:* A California woman was killed here by calving glacial ice in 1987. There is access for the disabled to within a quarter mile of the glacier.

A steep three-mile trail follows the flank of the glacier to the top of the **Harding Icefield,** 35 miles long and 20 miles wide. This alpine desert, 4,000 feet above sea level, wasn't even discovered until the early 1900s, when surveyors realized several coastal glaciers were part of the same system. Only a few isolated mountain peaks, called *nunataks* by Eskimos, interrupt its rolling surface.

Harbor Air, based at Seward Airport (tel. 224-3133), offers dramatic one-hour flightseeing tours of the icefield for $85 per person (minimum of three people). Landings can be arranged for one-day or long-term winter expeditions.

Some 35–65 feet of snow falls annually on the icefield. Its increasing pressure slowly forces fingers of ice—glaciers—in all directions. Eight of them are tidewater glaciers that tumble into the Kenai Fjords, producing myriad icebergs. Harbor seals, pups as well as adults, love the icebergs. They share the waters of the fjords with sea lions, sea otters, porpoises, and several species of whales. Thousands of puffins, kittiwakes, murres, and gulls nest on the steep cliffs and rocky islands of the fjords.

The best way to see the maritime portion of the park is by charter boat from Seward. **Kenai Fjords Tours, Inc.,** P.O. Box 1889, Seward, AK 99664 (tel. 907/224-8068), operates eight-hour national park trips for $80 per person (children pay half price), mid-May to early September. Half-day wildlife cruises in Resurrection Bay are $50. Other tour operators that provide service to Kenai Fjords National Park include **Major Marine Tours,** P.O. Box 338, Seward, AK 99664 (tel. 907/224-8030); **Mariah Charters,** 3812 Katmai Circle, Seward, AK 99664 (tel. 907/224-8623, or 243-1238 in Anchorage); and **Kenai Coastal Tours, Inc.,** 524 W. Fourth

Ave., Suite 101, Anchorage, AK 99501 (tel. 907/277-2131 or 224-7114). **Alaska Treks 'n' Voyages** in Anchorage (tel. 276-8282) offers daily kayak trips ($95 per person) and five-day Kenai Fjords and Prince William Sound expeditions ($795 per person).

SOLDOTNA

The youngest town on the Kenai Peninsula, Soldotna, 148 miles southwest of Anchorage and 78 miles north of Homer, was just a fork in the road as recently as 1947. When the area was opened to homesteading in that year, Soldotna boomed. It has since become the major commercial and recreation center of the central peninsula. For a stretch of several miles down the Sterling and Kenai Spur Highways, you'll see nothing but shopping malls, motels, and small restaurants.

But there's plenty of wilderness just off the "strip." Soldotna is headquarters for the nearly two-million-acre Kenai National Wildlife Refuge, covering most of the western half of the peninsula, and is the main stepping-off point for fishing expeditions on the Kenai River, Alaska's best king salmon stream.

Located a few miles upstream from the mouth of the Kenai River, Soldotna gets slightly warmer in summer (68°F average high) than neighboring Kenai town, but still has chilly winters (19°F average daytime high) and minimal precipitation (18 inches annually, most of it as snow).

ORIENTATION & ESSENTIAL INFORMATION

The easiest place to orient yourself is the Y junction, at the east end of the downtown, where the Kenai Spur Highway branches northwest toward Kenai town while the Sterling Highway continues in a northeast-to-southwest direction. The residential district lies west of here, along with most of the Kenai Peninsula Borough government buildings (on Binkley Street). Kalifornsky Beach Road intersects the Sterling Highway south of the Kenai River bridge and leads west to Kenai Peninsula Community College and Kenai town. Funny River Road winds east two miles to the airport.

The **Greater Soldotna Chamber of Commerce,** P.O. Box 236, Soldotna, AK 99669 (tel. 907/262-1337 or 262-9814), maintains a **Tourist Information Center** from May 15 through Labor Day, open from 9am to 7pm, in a new building on the Sterling Highway just south of the Kenai River bridge. From Labor Day to mid-May, it's open from 9am to 5pm.

Central Peninsula General Hospital, off Mary Dale Drive (tel. 262-4404), is staffed 24 hours a day for emergencies. To get around town you can rent a car from **Nye Peninsula Ford,** 43925 Sterling Hwy. (tel. 262-5491), or **Hutchings Chevrolet,** 44055 Sterling Hwy. (tel. 262-5891).

WHAT TO SEE & DO

Sights and Attractions

Soldotna isn't a town you can "do." It's the center of a region you must "see." Start your exploration at the headquarters and visitor center of the **Kenai National Wildlife Refuge,** P.O. Box 2139, Soldotna, AK 99669 (tel. 907/262-7021), on Ski Hill Road one mile south of the Kenai River bridge. Signs on the Sterling Highway will point you in the right direction. Open Monday through Friday from 8:30am to 4:30pm and on Saturday and Sunday from 10am to 5pm throughout the year, it has lifelike wildlife dioramas, a bookshop, and free brochures. Nature films are shown hourly from noon to 5pm on weekends.

Formerly the Kenai National Moose Range, this is the most accessible of all Alaskan wildlife refuges. It stretches 110 miles north-south from Turnagain Arm to the 6,600-foot heights of the Kenai Mountains, and another 40 miles west-east from Soldotna to the Chugach National Forest. Over two-thirds of this expanse is designated wilderness. It includes 15 campgrounds (most of them improved), 15 hiking trails, two canoe trails—and of course, a great deal of wildlife.

In particular, many people come here to see the moose, the largest antlered deer on earth. Alaskans are a bit jaded when it comes to moose sightings, but it's very exciting to watch a 1,400-pound bull moose grazing by the side of a road. Calves are born in the late spring; you'll often see them with their mothers in swampy areas during the summer. But don't approach them too closely; the bull in particular can be dangerous when feeling protective.

You're likely to spot dall sheep on mountainsides in the rugged Kenai River canyon terrain along the Sterling Highway on the east boundary of the refuge. Black bears often visit campsites, and brown bears congregate at salmon-spawning streams. Mountain goats are found mainly in the glaciated Kenai Mountains; caribou and wolves are relatively scarce. You may see many small mammals, including beaver, lynx, and wolverine; the trumpeter swan and a variety of other waterfowl; and 146 species of resident and migratory birds. The visitor center has checklists for amateur ornithologists.

Apart from the Sterling Highway, there are two pleasant drives for car-bound travelers. The **Swanson River Road** (turn off the highway at Mile 83) leads 30 miles through an area of low lakes and marshland rife with wildlife. Even more scenic is the **Skilak Lake Loop Road,** a 19½-mile side road that follows a ridge overlooking deep valleys, lakes, and rivers.

Soldotna's two biggest annual events are focused on the Rodeo Grounds off Kalifornsky Beach Road. **Soldotna Progress Days,** held since 1961 on the last weekend of July, include a horse show and rodeo, parade, air show, auto races, the Crimebusters 10K Run, dances, and arts and crafts exhibits. The **Peninsula Winter Games** take place at the rodeo grounds the third weekend in January. It includes broom hockey, ice sculpting, sled rides, snow golf, and the Alaska State Championship Dog Weight Pulling Contest. The **Soldotna Silver Salmon Derby** runs during the third week in August.

Sports and Recreation

Soldotna has its requisite bowling alley, tennis courts, softball fields, and high school swimming pool, open to the public during scheduled hours. Further information can be obtained from the Greater Soldotna Chamber of Commerce (tel. 262-9814 or 262-1337).

The **Central Peninsula Sports Center,** 538 Kalifornsky Beach Rd. (tel. 262-3150), has an Olympic-size ice-hockey rink, weight room, racquetball courts, and an indoor jogging track. It's open Monday through Friday from 7:30am to 9pm and on Saturday from 9am to 6pm.

CANOEING Two canoe routes in the northern lowlands of the Kenai National Wildlife Refuge have been designated as National Recreational Trails: the **Swanson River Route,** 80 miles long, connects 40 small lakes with 46 miles of stream; and the **Swan Lake Route,** 60 miles long, connects 30 small lakes with 33 miles of stream. The longest portage on either route is less than a mile. Either circuit can be traveled leisurely in a week or less, and portions thereof make good weekend trips. You're guaranteed relative isolation: No more than 15 people are permitted within the canoe-system lakes at any one time. Contact refuge headquarters in Soldotna (tel. 907/262-7021) for route maps and complete canoeing regulations. Rent canoes at the **Sports Den,** 44176 Sterling Hwy. (tel. 262-7491), or from **Stephan's Services** (tel. 262-2113). For kayak rentals, you have to go to Homer; try **Discovery Adventures** (tel. 235-6942).

FISHING The Kenai River boasts 11 different sport fish, but everybody comes for the king salmon, which range from 20 to 70 pounds, with some reaching 85 pounds or more. The world-record king, a 97-pounder, was taken out of the river in May 1985 by a Soldotna fisherman. Kings usually peak in mid-June and late July. Red salmon run in June and July, pinks in August, silvers from July to October. The river also yields trophy-size rainbow trout and Dolly Varden, as well as smaller grayling and other species. Big Eddy's Jetty and Poacher's Cove, both on the river near Soldotna, are among the most popular fishing holes. For a daily updated fishing report March 1 to October 15 you can call **Alaska Fishing News** (tel. 900/288-FISH) for $2.50 per minute, or contact the company directly (tel. 907/262-2897) for travel planning assistance.

Many fishing services operate out of the Soldotna area, and I hesitate to recommend one over any other. Full-time Kenai River residents are usually more reliable than "weekend guides" from Anchorage. Rates vary from $80 to $140 per person for a day's excursion. Many guide services have packages with area motels. Write to the chamber of commerce and ask for a current list of guides or inquire at the **Sports Den,** 44176 Sterling Hwy. (tel. 262-7491), where you can get not only up-to-the-minute fishing information but also rent equipment, including boats and canoes.

Some say that **Big Sky Charter and Fish Camp,** near Sterling on the bank of the Kenai River, is a sterling operation. Rates for a fully furnished private cabin with kitchen are $100 a day, $600 per week. Charter drift or powerboat fishing costs $125 per person for a half day (gear included). Shore fishing is good here too. Contact 13120 Saunders Rd., Anchorage, AK 99516 (tel. 907/345-5760 in winter or 907/262-9496 in summer). Other guide services include **Great Alaska Fish Camp & Safaris** (tel. toll free 800/544-2261) with day trips and fishing/lodging packages of up to 10 days; **Irish Lord Charters** (tel. 907/262-9512); and **Rod 'N Reel Sport Fishing Guides and Charters** (tel. 907/262-6064).

For a customized fishing/lodging package with fly-out trips available, contact **Silver Salmon Creek Lodge** (tel. 907/262-4839) or **Alaska's Bear Trap Lodge** (tel. 907/262-7409).

Because the Kenai River is the most heavily used freshwater fishery in Alaska, the Alaska Department of Natural Resources has established the Kenai River Special Management Area to protect the spawning grounds and wildlife habitat of this 80-mile stream. The **Alaska Department of Fish and Game,** P.O. Box 3150, Soldotna, AK 99669 (tel. 907/262-9368), is keeping a close watch on human impact: Fishing is subject to suspension on 12-hour notice.

Nonresident sportfishing licenses cost $15 for 3 days, $30 for 14 days, $50 for a year.

You must also have a fishing license to dig for clams. Razor clams are in season along the shore of Cook Inlet from April to October. Clam Gulch, on the Sterling Highway 40 miles south of Soldotna, is the most popular location, although anywhere from Kasilof to Anchor Point is regarded as prime clamming ground during low tide. The bag limit is 60 clams, regardless of size.

For fish and game processing or storage, try **Echo's Gourmet Meats** (tel. 283-9456).

GOLF   The Kenai Peninsula's first golf course, the nine-hole **Birch Ridge Golf Course** (tel. 262-5270), is east of downtown on the Sterling Highway.

HIKING   More than 200 miles of trails and routes wind through the Kenai National Wildlife Refuge. Hikers should have staunch rubber boots for the marshy lowland muskeg, and should be in reasonably good shape for more strenuous hill climbs; get a map at the Kenai refuge visitor center. Nearest to Soldotna is the **Funny River Trail,** which climbs nearly 21 miles (with an elevation gain of 2,000 feet) into the Kenai Mountain foothills. The trailhead is near the municipal airport.

A plus for hikers is the proliferation of wild berries free for the picking. Look for blueberries, cranberries, lingonberries, raspberries, strawberries, rose hips, and currants, and ask someone to describe cloud, crow, salmon, service, and nagoon (!) berries.

HUNTING   Hunting is permitted throughout the Kenai National Wildlife Refuge in accordance with state game regulations. Big-game animals plus snowshoe hare, ptarmigan, spruce grouse, and waterfowl are the most sought-after species. A nonresident annual hunting and sportfishing license costs $135. Contact the Alaska Department of Fish and Game, P.O. Box 2-5525, Juneau, AK 99802 (tel. 907/465-2376), for additional information.

RIVER RAFTING Alaska Rivers Co., P.O. Box 827, Cooper Landing, AK 99572 (tel. 907/595-1226), offers a Kenai River canyon trip ($80 per person, half price for children under 12) plus a less rigorous three-hour scenic float ($39 per person) and a variety of custom white-water trips. Canoe and kayak instruction is available.

Alaska Wildland Adventures, P.O. Box 26, Cooper Landing, AK 99572 (tel. 907/595-1279, or toll free 800/478-4100 in Alaska), has three-hour Kenai River floats for $39 ($24 for children), seven-hour trips for $95 ($45 for children), and half-day ($95 per person) and full-day fishing trips ($160 per person). It also has picnic lunches for $7.50 at its headquarters, Mile 50.1 on the Sterling Highway.

Rafting season is mid-May to mid-September, depending on the water level in the river.

WINTER SPORTS Cross-country skiing, snowshoeing, ice fishing, and skating on frozen lakes are all popular cold-weather pursuits on the Kenai Peninsula. Add dog sledding to that list: Soldotna hosts the state championship sled-dog races the last weekend of February (after the Anchorage Fur Rendezvous). The start and finish lines are at the airport. Soldotna has outdoor ice-skating rinks and a new Olympic-size hockey rink in the sports center on Kalifornsky Beach Road.

WHERE TO STAY

The City of Soldotna (tel. 262-9107) runs two **campgrounds,** both in wooded settings on the Kenai River. **Swift Water Park,** off East Redoubt Avenue, east of the Sterling Highway, on the north side of town, has 45 campsites. **Centennial Park,** at the south end of Soldotna off Kalifornsky Beach Road, has 170 units, 32 of them for tents. The charge is $7 a day. No reservations are required.

There are several B&Bs in the city; inquire with the Soldotna Chamber of Commerce (tel. 262-1337) for a current listing.

BEST WESTERN KING SALMON MOTEL, 35545 Kenai Spur Hwy. (P.O. Box 430), Soldotna, AK 99669. Tel. 907/262-5857 or 262-6106. 49 rms (all with bath). TV TEL

$ Rates: May–Sept, $99 single; $109 double. Oct–Apr, $89 single; $99 double. AE, MC, V.

About half the units here have kitchenettes, and the office provides dishes and pans on request. The others have refrigerators, and all have coffee makers. Each spacious, nicely appointed room has plush brown carpeting, queen-size beds, and hot-water baseboard heat. There's always a pot of coffee on in the pleasant lobby, and the folks in the office will pack and freeze the fish you catch. The motel is conveniently located with a grocery, bakery, restaurant, and liquor store next door.

BUNK HOUSE INN, 44715 Sterling Hwy., Soldotna, AK 99669. Tel. 907/262-4584. 34 rms (all with bath). TV TEL

$ Rates (including tax): $75 single; $95 double. MC, V.

Spacious rooms are decorated in earth tones; two units have kitchenettes with gas stoves. Satellite TV and telephones are provided (local calls are free). The Bunk House Restaurant, open from 4am to 10pm in summer, 7am to 10pm the rest of the year, specializes in prime rib and steaks, and there are daily specials. Prices start at $5 for burgers; full dinners run $10–$17.95. The unfinished-wood decor carries to the friendly Brand X Lounge.

KENAI RIVER LODGE, 393 Riverside Dr., Soldotna, AK 99669. Tel. 907/262-4292. Fax 907/262-7337. 30 rms (all with bath). TV TEL

$ Rates (including continental breakfast): May–Sept, $89 single; $93 double; from $195 luxury suite. Oct–Apr, $60 single; $70 double. MC, V.

Nestled on the riverbank, the Kenai River Lodge was built as a permanent home in the early 1970s by retired bush pilot Bob Green and his wife, June. Now a hunting and fishing guide, Bob provides a fishing charter service just a few steps from your room—at $125 per person per trip for king salmon fishing and $90 for the feisty silver salmon.

The motel units have modern decor with wildlife photos on the walls, queen-size beds, full baths, controlled heat, cable TV, and telephone (local calls are 50¢). Each room has a view of the river and easy access to private river frontage. A full-service shopping mall is within walking distance. Breakfast is served in the newly remodeled lobby, where you can always find a pot of coffee. The Upper Deck Lounge overlooks the Kenai River and serves cocktails and food. There's also a deck for summer barbecues.

SOLDOTNA INN, 35041 Kenai Spur Hwy. (P.O. Box 565), Soldotna, AK 99669. Tel. 907/262-9169. 24 rms (all with bath), 4 suites. TV TEL
$ Rates: $75 single; $85 double; $100–$150 suite. AE, DC, DISC, MC, V.

Of all the motels in the central Kenai Peninsula, I was most impressed by this one. The management is very friendly and the rooms are spacious and thoughtfully maintained; there's a TV and refrigerator in every room, and there's no charge for local phone calls. There's also a guest laundry, and special amenities—shampoo, conditioner, and lotion—in the bathrooms. A red-brown color scheme decorates most rooms, which have king- and queen-size beds, nature pictures on the walls, and hot-water heating. Four lovely suites contain full kitchens. Some rooms have waterbeds, and two rooms have been set aside for nonsmokers. In the lobby, mounted moose and dall sheep heads overlook a small gift and sundry shop. The hotel includes Mykel's restaurant (see "Where to Dine," below) and banquet facilities.

WHERE TO DINE

FOUR SEASONS RESTAURANT, 43960 Sterling Hwy. Tel. 262-5006.
   Cuisine: CREATIVE AMERICAN. **Reservations:** Recommended.
$ Prices: Appetizers $4.95–$8.95; main courses $10.95–$21.95; lunch $3.50–$5.60; Sun buffet $7.95 adults, $3.95 children 12 and under. MC, V.
   Open: May–Sept, breakfast buffet Sun 9:30am–1pm; lunch Mon–Sat 11am–3pm; dinner daily 5:30–10pm. Oct–Apr, lunch Tues–Sat 11am–3pm; dinner Tues–Sat 5:30–10pm. **Closed:** Four weeks beginning Christmas.

The finest restaurant in Soldotna, the Four Seasons is concealed in a grove of trees. Classical music, hanging ferns, and solid-wood decor have you feeling as if you're in the Vienna Woods, or at least taking a walk in the Black Forest. All the food is made from scratch. The chefs specialize in new variations on old favorites, like honey-spiced chicken breast, made with honey, Dijon mustard, and fresh limes and herbs; Cook Inlet halibut, baked in parchment with a tangy sauce of sake, soy, and ginger; and a 12-ounce New York steak with mushrooms. All dinners include homemade soup and hors d'oeuvres, vegetable, and potato. There's also a full wine list.

MYKEL'S, 35041 Kenai Spur Hwy. Tel. 262-4305.
   Cuisine: STEAK/SEAFOOD. **Reservations:** Not required.
$ Prices: Breakfast $2.95–$10.95; lunch $4.50–$10.25; dinner $14.95–$19.95. AE, DC, MC, V.
   Open: Mon–Sat 6am–11pm, Sun 7am–10pm.
This is a low-lit, fully licensed restaurant with red decor and private booths. Breakfast items range from biscuits and gravy to steak and eggs. The soup-and-salad bar is very popular for lunch. For dinner, you can have halibut grilled, blackened, or with mornay sauce, or even couple it with prime rib on a seafood combination plate.

PIZZA PETE'S, 35320 Kenai Spur Hwy. Tel. 262-5306.
   Cuisine: ITALIAN/AMERICAN. **Reservations:** Not required.
$ Prices: Lunch $4.25–$5.95; dinner $5.95–$15.95. DISC, MC, V.
   Open: Daily 11am–midnight.

This restaurant has one of the most varied menus in Soldotna. You can get 29 varieties of pizza and 15 different kinds of sandwiches, plus a salad bar. Mexican lunch specials include chicken enchiladas with rice and beans. Dinner dishes include a variety of Italian dishes, such as lasagne, spaghetti, and ravioli, as well as seafood, steaks, and shish kebabs.

SIZZLER FAMILY STEAK HOUSE, 44900 Sterling Hwy. Tel. 262-1005.
   Cuisine: STEAK/SEAFOOD. **Reservations:** Not required.
$ Prices: Salad bar $6–$7; main courses $9–$13. AE, MC, V.
   Open: Sun–Thurs 11am–10pm, Fri–Sat 11am–11pm.
This is like the Sizzler Steakhouses in the Lower 48, with some added Alaskan touches. The building is constructed of large round logs. The interior is accented by rough pine and Alaskana photos and wildlife mountings. Place your order at the counter, pick it up when your number is called, and enjoy steaks, seafood, and combination plates featuring local specials like halibut and king crab. At lunch, the salad/soup/tostada/fresh fruit/pasta bar is $6 by itself, $2.30 with a meal. At dinner it's $7 by itself, $3 with a meal.

EVENING ENTERTAINMENT

Nightwatch, on Sterling Highway at Funny River Road (tel. 262-7020), occupies a new building overlooking the Kenai River on the southeastern side of the bridge. This popular lounge and bar features local entertainment on weekends. About half a mile north on the Sterling Highway is the **Maverick Club** (tel. 262-7979), a tavern with live rock 'n' roll several nights a week.

   The **Orca Twin Theaters,** in the Red Diamond Center on Kalifornsky Beach Road (tel. 262-7003), regularly show first-run movies. Tickets are $6 for adults, $3 for children and seniors.

AN EXCURSION FROM SOLDOTNA

Sterling, a small town 13 miles east of Soldotna, is the location of the **Izaak Walton State Recreation Site** at the confluence of the Kenai and Moose Rivers. Archeological excavations in this area have revealed that Eskimos had fishing settlements here more than 2,000 years ago. Interpretive displays will help you find the ancient house sites.

   Cooper Landing (pop. about 350) stretches along the banks of the upper Kenai River for nearly 10 miles, 39–49 miles east of Soldotna. Aside from its fishing and rafting lures, it's a nesting place for bald eagles and the site of the **Charley Hubbard Gold Mining Museum,** Mile 51 on the Sterling Highway. The museum, with artifacts and photographs, is open daily, Memorial Day through August. The Resurrection Pass and Russian River trailheads are nearby.

Where To Stay and Dine

GWIN'S LODGE, Mile 52, Sterling Hwy., Cooper Landing, AK 99572.
   Tel. 907/595-1266. 5 cabins (all with bath).
$ Rates: $65 per cabin. DISC, MC, V.
A handful of modern cabins, each fully carpeted and with two double beds, surround a log-cabin café that's a four-decade institution near the confluence of the Russian and Kenai Rivers. If you're merely passing through at lunchtime, stop for a cheeseburger ($6.50 with a Pepsi and fries). The café, which is open from 7am to 11pm daily, has a bar and a liquor store, as well as fishing-tackle sales.

KENAI PRINCESS LODGE, Bean Creek Rd. (P.O. Box 676), Cooper Landing, AK 99572. Tel. 907/595-1425. (For reservations year-round, write to 329 F St., Suite 207, Anchorage, AK 99501, or call toll free 800/426-0500.) Fax 907/277-8255. 50 rms (all with bath), 4 minisuites. TV TEL
$ Rates: May–Oct, $160 single or double; $200 minisuite. Nov–Apr, $99 single or double; $150 minisuite. Additional person $10 extra. AE, MC, V.
In 1990, Princess Tours opened this luxury 50-unit wilderness inn on a 35-acre plot

on the Kenai River, adjacent to the Kenai National Wildlife Refuge. The old Resurrection Lodge was resurrected to become the main lodge, with a dining room and bar, gift shop, and huge stone fireplace. Log buildings, spread along 1,900 feet of the Kenai River, contain regular rooms and minisuites, all with wood stoves, vaulted ceilings with skylights, screened veranda decks, and private entrances. Suites have Jacuzzis. Two rooms are equipped for disabled patrons.

Guests may participate in a variety of activities, including fishing, hiking, horseback riding, river rafting, and a salmon bake. Adjacent is a 37-site RV park with full water, sewage, and electric hookups, plus grocery, laundry, showers, and toilets.

VINTON'S ALPINE INN MOTEL, Mile 48.2, Sterling Hwy. (P.O. Box 801), Cooper Landing, AK 99572. Tel. 907/595-1212. 12 rms (all with bath). TV TEL

$ Rates: May–Sept, $68 single; $75 double; $85 triple. Oct–Apr, $45 single; $55 double. AE, DISC, MC, V.

Each modern unit is self-contained with a private bath and a full kitchenette. A gold-nugget jewelry shop is attached.

KENAI

The peninsula's largest town, Kenai, 11 miles northwest of Soldotna and 159 miles southwest of Anchorage, can lay legitimate claim to being both its oldest and its most progressive. In 1791, Russian fur traders built a fort, Nikolaevsky Redoubt, near a Tanaina Indian village on a low bluff overlooking the Cook Inlet and the mouth of the Kenai River. In 1869, two years after the American purchase of Alaska, the U.S. Army erected Fort Kenay. A replica of the fort and early Russian Orthodox church stand today in Old Town. Commercial fishing became prominent in the late 19th century and remains of major importance today.

The boom that built modern Kenai began in 1957, when oil was discovered in the Cook Inlet. The companies exploiting the field—Amoco, Atlantic Richfield, Marathon, Mobil, Phillips, Shell, Standard, Union, and Tesoro Alaska—could be a *Who's Who* of the oil industry. Several of them have built refineries at Nikiski, 12 miles north of Kenai town, in an industrial area where two liquefied natural gas plants and an ammonia-urea chemical factory are also in operation. Fifteen offshore platforms are now producing 200,000 barrels of crude oil and 800 million cubic feet of natural gas per day.

Kenai's climate is cool and dry, with average summer temperatures in the low 60s and winter in the mid teens. Extremes can be up to 80°F and down to −40°F. Only about 20 inches of precipitation falls a year, much of it as snow (an annual average of 69 inches).

ORIENTATION & ESSENTIAL INFORMATION

Located on the western shore of the Kenai Peninsula at the mouth of the Kenai River, Kenai township comprises a fistful of residential pockets mainly along the Kenai Spur Highway. The **Kenai Bicentennial Visitors and Cultural Center,** operated by the Greater Kenai Chamber of Commerce, is at 11471 Kenai Spur Hwy. (P.O. Box 1991), Kenai, AK 99611 (tel. 907/283-1991). It's open year-round, Monday through Friday from 9am to 5pm.

There is hourly air-taxi service to and from Anchorage, 30 minutes away by air, as well as to Homer and Kodiak. **Kenai Airport,** the peninsula's largest, is a 15-minute walk north of downtown at 305 N. Willow St. **Triple A Taxi** (tel. 283-6000) or **The Cab Co.** (tel. 283-7101) can transport you from there to your destination, or you can get transportation from **Payless Car Rental** (tel. 283-7865) or one of the three car-rental agencies that have outlets at the airport—**National** (tel. 283-9566), **Avis** (tel. 283-7900), or **Hertz** (tel. 283-7979).

The *Peninsula Clarion,* a tabloid newspaper, is published daily. There is a shopping mall, **Kenai Mall** on the Kenai Spur; there are also several banks and three medical clinics, including the **Kenai Medical Center,** at 11355 Kenai Spur Hwy.

(tel. 283-4611). The nearest hospital is in Soldotna. Kenai also has a **Women's Resource Center** (tel. 283-9479).

WHAT TO SEE & DO

Sights and Attractions

Most of Kenai's visitor attractions are in **Old Town.** Pick up a walking-tour map from the visitors center and begin there. Among the stops you will make are:

Fort Kenay, Mission Street at Overland Avenue (tel. 283-7294), a 1967 reconstruction of the circa 1869 U.S. Army stockade, houses the one-room **Kenai Historical Museum** of local and natural history. It's open daily June 1 to September 14, 10am-5pm Monday through Saturday.

The **Holy Assumption of the Virgin Mary Church,** opposite the fort on Mission Street, is a National Historic Landmark. This sky-blue, onion-domed but spartan Russian Orthodox church is still actively used as a place of worship. The adjacent **St. Nicholas Chapel** is a shrine; its first resident priest, Igumen Nikholai, and other church leaders are buried under the floor. If you want a tour, contact Fr. Paul Merculies at the parish house (the oldest building in Kenai), next door to the fort (tel. 283-4122).

The **Kenai Fine Arts Center** and Olde Towne Gallery, 816 Cook St., near Main (tel. 283-7040), is a combination art school, studio, and shop. You'll see here the work of some outstanding central Kenai artists, especially in pottery and fiber crafts. It's open Monday through Saturday from 10am to 4pm.

Twenty-five miles north of Kenai, as far as the fully paved North Kenai Spur Road will take you, the 4,000-acre **Captain Cook State Recreation Area** nestles by the mouth of the Swanson River. Many local folks come out here to picnic, to look for wildlife, or to walk the beach in search of agates. Canoeing in the river, swimming in Stormy Lake, fishing, and (in winter) cross-country skiing are also popular. Camping facilities are provided for RVs, tent campers, and boaters. State park rangers are based in Soldotna (tel. 262-5581).

Sports and Recreation

Kenai's **Peninsula Oilers,** who play in the Alaska Baseball League, are *the* game in town in the summertime. They play a 54-game, June-to-August schedule against teams from the Anchorage and Fairbanks areas, including 27 home games at their park on Tinker Lane. Among their alumni are major-league pitchers Dave Stieb and Frank Viola.

The **swimming pools** at Kenai Central High School and Nikiski's North Peninsula Recreation Area are open to the public during scheduled hours. The **Kenai Recreation Center** has weight and exercise rooms, as well as racquetball, volleyball, and basketball courts. It's open from 6am to 10pm Monday through Saturday and 1 to 10pm on Sunday. Softball is a popular summer activity. For information, call **Kenai Parks and Recreation** (tel. 283-3855).

FISHING   More than a dozen outfitters call Kenai home. A five-hour morning or afternoon outing to the banks of the Kenai River, including transportation to and from a Kenai motel, typically costs $125 per person, all inclusive. Check with **Atland's Guides** (tel. 283-7466), or **Gary King Sporting Goods,** 405 Overland St. (tel. 283-2665 or 283-4648). **Ron's Alaska Lodge** (tel. 283-4333) provides hunting and fishing guide services and lodging packages. For a floatplane flight into a remote lake or stream, call **Alaska West Air, Inc.** (tel. 907/776-5147 or 776-8600).

GOLF   The new 18-hole **Kenai Golf Course,** 1420 Lawton Dr. (tel. 283-7500), has a pro shop and driving range.

WINTER SPORTS   There's a lighted outdoor rink for **ice skating** in Kenai, and an Olympic-size indoor arena (with an extended season) at the North Peninsula Recreation Area in Nikiski. For **cross-country skiing,** there's hundreds of square miles of flat, treeless terrain for skiers to lay their tracks across.

WHERE TO STAY

Besides the accommodations listed below, you can try the **Kenai Municipal Campground,** located on Forest Drive overlooking the Cook Inlet. It has 40 units on a wooded site which also features a children's playground. Stays are limited to three days. Contact the chamber of commerce (tel. 907/283-1991) for information.

Recreational vehicles can hook up at **Overland RV Park,** 410 Overland St. (tel. 283-4227). Shopping, restaurants, and visitor information are within walking distance.

For bed-and-breakfast–style accommodations, try **Irene's Lodge** (see below); **The Chalet** (tel. 907/283-4528), located midway between Soldotna and Kenai; or **Coyle's Landing** (tel. 907/283-5378 or 283-3223), on the Kenai River.

COUNTRY APARTMENTS, Poppy Ridge Rd., off College Rd. (write 10819 Kenai Spur Hwy., Suite 349), Kenai, AK 99611. Tel. 907/262-7881. 8 units (all with bath). TV TEL
$ Rates: $75 single; $85 double; $120 triple. Additional person $20 extra. No credit cards; personal checks accepted.
Families who like an unhurried place to stay and enjoy doing their own cooking would find it hard to beat this arrangement. The four lovely one-bedroom log cabins and four condominium units near the Kenai River are completely furnished with towels, linens, and kitchen utensils.

DANIELS LAKE LODGE, Drift Circle at Daniels Lake (P.O. Box 1444), Kenai, AK 99611. Tel. 907/776-5578. 4 rms (2 with bath).
$ Rates: $60–$75 single or double; $130 two-bedroom suite. No credit cards.
It's a bit of a drive—about 20 miles from downtown Kenai—but well worth it if you value waking up to the sight of the sun rising over a pristine woodland lake. Karen Walters has turned over her entire downstairs to guests. Three rooms, the Swan, Wood Duck, and Wildflower, open onto a large living room with a big wood stove. The Wood Duck and Wildflower combine to make a two-bedroom suite with private bath. The Pheasant room is located upstairs. The walls are decorated with photos of the same wildlife you're likely to see on the lakeshore, including moose and bears. For lonely evenings, there's a TV, radio, and tape player, and local phone calls are free. The shared bathroom has a large sunken shower and a sauna. Laundry facilities are off the kitchen. You cook your own meals, but Karen will keep you supplied with duck eggs, goat milk, and other country fixings.

IRENE'S LODGE, 702 Lawton Dr., Kenai, AK 99611. Tel. 907/283-4501. 5 rms (2 with bath).
$ Rates (including breakfast): $62.50 per person. MC, V.
River guide Herman Fandel and his educator wife, Irene, have turned their spacious, antique-furnished home into a year-round bed-and-breakfast inn. Two rooms have private entrances; there is a central telephone and some rooms have a TV. The Fandels prepare a full Alaska-size breakfast for guests and provide a complimentary cocktail or non-alcoholic drink in the evening. Guests can take advantage of a free fish fry on Tuesday and Friday nights. The Fandels also enjoy assisting guests with tour arrangements.

KATMAI HOTEL, 10800 Kenai Spur Hwy. (P.O. Box 2840), Kenai, AK 99611. Tel. 907/283-6101. Fax 907/283-6217. 30 rms (all with bath). TV TEL
$ Rates: $79 one bed; $89 two beds; $109 three beds. AE, MC, V.
This hotel was once the *belle dame* of Kenai. A 1986 renovation with Scandinavian-

style furniture helped revive its image a bit, but additional noise-proofing is still needed. On the plus side, there's room service and complimentary airport transportation. The Katmai Restaurant (open 24 hours daily) is famous for breakfast, with specials for $4.50, lunch specials for $6.45, and dinner entrees for $8.95 and up. The Katmai Lounge, a popular country-and-western bar with dancing, may be the best reason to visit.

KENAI KINGS INN, Kenai Spur Hwy. at Airport Way (P.O. Box 1080), Kenai, AK 99611. Tel. 907/283-6060. Fax 907/283-3874. 51 rms (all with bath). TV TEL

$ Rates: June–Sept 16, $94 single; $104 double. Sept 17–May, $74 single; $84 double. AE, DC, DISC, MC, V.

Formerly King Oscar's Motel, this property offers modern, spacious rooms with queen-size beds and color TVs. Amenities include a guest laundry, disabled accessibility, conference and meeting facilities, airport transportation, and fish cleaning and freezer space. A restaurant is open for three meals daily (with room service available), and a lounge features live entertainment.

UPTOWN MOTEL, 47 Spur View Dr. (P.O. Box 1886), Kenai, AK 99611. Tel. 907/283-3660, or toll free 800/777-3650. 52 rms (all with bath), 1 suite. TV TEL

$ Rates: May–Sept, $99.50 single; $109.50 double; $129.50 suite. Oct–April $69.50 single; $89.50 double; $109.50 suite. AE, DC, MC, V.

Two barrackslike buildings contain a full deck of rooms, each decorated in a red color scheme. All have satellite TV, in-room movies, and electric heat. Ten rooms are set aside for nonsmokers, and the one suite contains a private Jacuzzi. The lobby features a taxidermist's delight of game heads and trophy fish. Louie's Restaurant and Back Door Lounge adjoin the motel.

WHERE TO DINE

JUNIOR'S, Nikishka Mall, 51805 N. Kenai Spur Hwy., Nikiski. Tel. 776-5489.
Cuisine: AMERICAN. **Reservations:** Not required.
$ Prices: Main courses $6–$9. No credit cards.
Open: Daily 8am–10pm.

An informal restaurant that welcomes families with children, Junior's serves a varied menu with all-American food as well as pizza and tacos.

LOUIE'S RESTAURANT, 47 Spur View Dr. Tel. 283-3660.
Cuisine: STEAK/SEAFOOD. **Reservations:** Not required.
$ Prices: Breakfast/lunch $3.25–$7.50; dinner $11–$16. AE, DC, MC, V.
Open: May–Aug, daily 5am–11pm, Sept–Apr, daily 6am–10pm.

A motel lobby with an extensive collection of trophy animals and fish leads into Louie's, arguably the Kenai area's finest steak-and-seafood spot. Big steaks and local salmon and halibut highlight the menu. The Back Door Lounge adjoins.

PARADISOS, 33222 Kenai Spur Hwy. Tel. 283-7008.
Cuisine: ITALIAN. **Reservations:** Not required.
$ Prices: Lunch $6–$9; dinner $9.95–$13.95. DC, MC, V.
Open: Daily 11am–10:30pm.

Paradisos focuses on Italian cuisine, but you can also get steaks and seafood, like fresh halibut. Pizza and pasta dishes are the featured entrées, and are best accompanied by the salad bar.

EVENING ENTERTAINMENT

The **Rainbow Bar,** on Main Street at Overland Avenue (tel. 283-9929), is cramped, crowded, smoky, and has live country music seven nights a week. **Larry's,** 12656 N. Kenai Spur Hwy. (tel. 283-9935), a couple of miles north of downtown, has live rock 'n' roll Monday through Saturday nights. The **Katmai Lounge,** in the Katmai

Hotel, 10800 Kenai Spur Hwy., serves up live C&W and rock oldies in a big, well-lit room, with lots of seating and a friendly crowd.

First-run movies and occasional revivals are shown downtown on the three screens at the **Kambe Theater,** 215 Willow St. (tel. 283-4554). Admission is $5.50 for adults and $3 for seniors and children under 12.

EN ROUTE TO HOMER

About 750 people live in the old Russian fishing village of **Ninilchik,** halfway between Soldotna and Homer. The new town on the Sterling Highway doesn't look like much more than a wide spot in the road, but seek out the winding road that turns downhill toward the shore of Cook Inlet, just past the Ninilchik River bridge. A handful of ramshackle log houses are still occupied by about two dozen descendants of 19th-century Russian colonists. Most today are commercial set-net beach fishermen who worship at the turn-of-the-century Russian Orthodox church overlooking the community from the top of a bluff. Visitors to the village and church are encouraged to park their cars in designated areas, travel on foot, and avoid cutting through private property.

It seems like an out-of-the-way location, but Ninilchik is the site of the annual **Kenai Peninsula State Fair** on the third weekend of August. There's a parade, horse and livestock shows, garden produce and flower exhibits, arts and crafts displays, and carnival entertainment—everything you'd expect of a small state fair.

HOMER

Few, if any, sights in Alaska surpass the arresting view of Kachemak Bay that one gets upon rounding the last big turn before Homer on the southbound Sterling Highway. The heavily glaciated peaks of the Kenai Range rise dramatically above the deep-blue waters of the bay, while the Homer Spit—said to be the second longest in the world—paints a curlicue pattern from the forested foreshore. Off to the west you may see volcanic Mount Augustine island steaming away.

A 40-minute flight from Anchorage (226 miles southwest of Anchorage and 78 miles south of Soldotna), Homer has in recent years gained a reputation as the "Acapulco of Alaska"—for all the right reasons. It has great natural beauty, a warm mild climate (by Alaskan standards), numerous fine artisans, a fleet of deep-sea fishing boats, and a booming tourist industry.

Established in 1895 and named after an early gold prospector, Homer (see map in the section on Seward earlier in this chapter) owed most of its turn-of-the-century settlement to the Cook Inlet Coal Fields Company, which built a town and dock on the 4½-mile-long spit and a railroad to the mines, 7 miles away. Coal production dwindled, but fishermen and homesteaders arrived in the 1920s. Today fishing and seafood-processing are the most important industries. The construction of a $355 million hydroelectric project at Bradley Lake, just east of Kachemak Bay, began in 1986 and is expected to bring more people and money to the town. The population of 4,100 swells with summer tourists and fishery workers.

Moderated by the warm Japan Current, summer temperatures in Homer hover in the balmy 60s and low 70s, while midwinter temperatures are commonly 10°–20°F. The Kenai Range protects Kachemak Bay from the storms of the Gulf of Alaska; average annual precipitation in Homer is only 23 inches.

ORIENTATION & ESSENTIAL INFORMATION

For purposes of getting acquainted, one can divide Homer into four sections: Homer Bluffs, downtown, Ocean Drive, and the Spit. Entering Homer from the west, the Sterling Highway forks, with the upper (left-hand) road becoming **Pioneer Avenue,** the main drag of downtown, and the lower road, the **Homer Bypass,** heading toward the Spit. Above downtown rise the bluffs, peppered with residences. **Lake Street** intersects both Pioneer Avenue and the Bypass at their eastern ends and crosses a lagoon known as Beluga Lake to reach **Ocean Drive.** This east-west strip of motels, restaurants, and businesses ends at **Homer Spit Road,** which turns straight out to sea for nearly five miles.

Homer Airport (tel. 235-8588), served by two commercial carriers and several smaller air-taxi services, is on Kachemak Drive, which runs east from Homer Spit Road just below its intersection with Ocean Drive. Beluga Lake is used by floatplanes in summer, skiplanes in winter. The **Alaska Marine Highway System** (tel. 235-8449) connects Homer with Kodiak and Seldovia, as well as Seward and Valdez; the M.V. *Tustumena* ties up at the City Dock on the Spit.

Nick's Taxi (tel. 235-6921) or **Lynx Taxi** (tel. 235-5969) can meet you at the ferry or airport and shuttle you to your hotel. Car-rental agencies include **National** (tel. 235-5115) and **Peninsula Ford Rentals** (tel. 235-5229).

The **Visitor Information Center,** located on Homer Spit Road, is open Memorial Day to Labor Day only (tel. 235-5300). For year-round information, contact the **Homer Chamber of Commerce,** P.O. Box 541, Homer, AK 99603 (tel. 907/235-7740).

Homer has a weekly newspaper, the **Homer News;** a 38-bed hospital, the **South Peninsula Hospital,** on Bayview Avenue (tel. 235-8101); three banks; 22 churches; and numerous community organizations.

WHAT TO SEE & DO
Sights and Attractions

⭐ **THE HOMER SPIT** The very existence of a commercial community on the Spit represents an uneasy truce between humans and nature. Turned into a tidal island by the '64 earthquake, rebuilt but again washed out by a storm in 1979, the Spit has been resurrected by steel bulkheads and concrete blocks. As a visitor, you'll travel about 3½ miles out on the Spit before you see much of anything but sand, rocks, and water. Then, suddenly, you're right in the middle of the action.

Businesses are built around the newly enlarged **Small Boat Basin.** Located on the Spit's east (leeward) side, this is the home of the 120 boats operated by 60 charter-boat firms, as well as a great many private fishing and pleasure craft. In total, the Small Boat Basin has 734 slips.

As you drive out the Spit, three boardwalk "villages" on your right are sure to catch your eye. All three are populated by fishing-charter operators, gift shops, and small cafés. First is **Thompson's Boardwalk,** then **Seabreeze Boardwalk,** followed by **Cannery Row Boardwalk,** which has a collection of gray Cape Cod–style shanties.

The ramshackle lighthouse across Spit Road from the Boardwalk is the ✪ **Salty Dawg** (tel. 235-9990). Built in 1897, it has somehow survived all Spit catastrophes as a school, a post office, a grocery store, a railroad station, a coal-mining office, and an oil company headquarters. Today it's a saloon, famous statewide as a sometimes-rowdy hangout for fishermen and "tent city" denizens.

On the grounds of Land's End Resort is a rustic sign that reads: THE EAGLE'S SPOT: KEEP OUT. From late January to May at ✪ **The Eagle's Spot** you may see more American bald eagles in this one spot than you have collectively seen in your entire life up until then. I counted more than 100 on the beach in a five-minute sitting. But if you picture a bald eagle as a perpetually majestic raptor, your romanticism may be shattered by the scavenger practices of these birds of prey.

DOWNTOWN HOMER So much of Homer's summertime activity centers on the Spit that it's easy to overlook the downtown area. Start a half-mile walk at the west end of Pioneer Avenue where it branches off the Sterling Highway.

On your left, just before the intersection of Bartlett Street, you'll see the hexagonal headquarters of the **Alaska Maritime National Wildlife Refuge,** 202 W. Pioneer Ave. (tel. 235-6546); and just around the corner, the **Pratt Museum,** 3779 Bartlett St. (tel. 235-8635). Farther east on Pioneer Avenue is the **Homer Public Library,** the Tourist Information Center, and a co-op art gallery, the **Arctic Wolf Gallery/Snow Geese Originals,** at 510 Pioneer Ave. (no phone).

Across the street is **○ Ptarmigan Arts,** 471 E. Pioneer Ave. (tel. 235-5345). Of the numerous galleries in Homer, this is probably the single best place to survey the work of the town's artists. Ptarmigan Arts is a co-op, and each of the 45-50 member artisans contributes time and energy to run the shop and studios. They work in many media, including painting, sculpture, pottery, basketry, weaving, leatherwork, wood carving, stained glass, metalsmithing, jewelry, scrimshaw, and photography. It's open from 10am to 7pm daily.

Don't miss a visit to **○ Alaska Wild Berry Products,** 528 E. Pioneer Ave. (tel. 235-8858). Homer's most famous shop and "factory" gathers the numerous tasty berries from the meadows and hillsides of the Kenai Peninsula, then juices, pulps, and blends them into natural jams, jellies, and sauces. No preservatives are used in the process, which visitors can watch from beginning to end through showcase windows. Sample the jams, homemade fudge, and candies in a tasting room. Wild Berry Products has an excellent gift shop of various souvenir items as well as their own gift packs, and a mini-museum of local pioneer and prehistoric artifacts. Open daily from 9am to 7pm.

ALASKA MARITIME NATIONAL WILDLIFE REFUGE HEADQUARTERS AND VISITOR CENTER, 202 W. Pioneer Ave. Tel. 235-6546 or 235-6961.

The Alaska Maritime refuge comprises more than 2,500 islands, islets, rocks, reefs, and headlands of the Alaskan coast, from the southeast rain forest to Arctic Ocean tundra. Most of the Aleutian Islands and the smaller islands of the Gulf of Alaska and Bering Sea are part of the 3.5-million-acre refuge. Some 15-30 million birds of 55 species nest in the refuge, as well as thousands of sea lions, seals, walruses, and sea otters. Closest to Homer are designated shore areas and islands of Kachemak Bay and the Cook Inlet.

The visitor center here stimulates interest through displays, interpretive exhibits, maps, and literature on the birds and sea mammals of the refuge. A new $5-million visitor center is under construction.

Admission: Free.
Open: Daily 9am-5pm.

PRATT MUSEUM, 3779 Bartlett St. Tel. 235-8635.

One of Alaska's finest museums, the Pratt has two floors of exhibits of nature, ecology, and anthropology. There are dioramas of large land animals, mounted bird displays, two saltwater aquariums which show the deep-sea life of Kachemak Bay, a depiction of the tragic effect of oil spills on marine life, artifacts of modern industry, exhibits of prehistoric tools, and a botanical garden of Alaskan wildflowers.

A museum shop sells gifts and publications. The museum, which is operated by the Homer Society of Natural History, also has a reference library and media collection, functions as a Marine Mammal Information Center, and hosts adult education workshops.

Admission: $3 adults, $2 seniors, free for children under 18.
Open: Memorial Day weekend-Labor Day, daily 10am-5pm; the rest of the year, Tues-Sun noon-5pm. **Closed:** Jan and public holidays.

Special Events

Homer has three main festival periods. The town awakens from the frozen doldrums when the three-day **Winter Carnival** is staged beginning the first Friday of February. It opens with the Miss Homer pageant at the high school, picks up steam with a Saturday parade down Pioneer Avenue, and climaxes on Sunday with stock-car races—on frozen Beluga Lake. It includes such diversions as cherry-pit spitting and outhouse racing, iceboat and cross-country ski races, and arts-and-crafts exhibits. There are contests for seafood chowder cooking, home-brewing, and dog weight-pulling.

The **Spring Arts Festival,** held over several weeks in late April and early May, is an annual "coming out" for area artisans to show what they've produced in the winter. Painters and photographers, craftspeople and musicians, dancers and dramatists are all featured.

Memorial Day is the official opening of the tourist season, and the starting date of the **Homer Jackpot Halibut Derby,** which runs until Labor Day weekend. The **Taste of Homer,** an opportunity to snack on a variety of foods, is held over Labor Day; **Kachemak Appreciation Days,** which honor the commercial fishing community and area pioneers, are scheduled Columbus Day weekend in October; and an arts-and-crafts–oriented **Christmas Bazaar** occurs the second weekend of December.

Organized Tours

Gert Seekin's **Homer Tours,** P.O. Box 1264, Homer, AK 99603 (tel. 907/235-8996), takes visitors high above Homer on Skyline Drive for superb views of the city, the Spit, and the bay. Tours also stop at the Pratt Museum, the Norman Lowell Art Studio and other galleries, and Wild Berry Products; visit with an Eskimo doll-maker; and finish up with a tour of the Spit fish-processing area. Custom trips can also be arranged. Standard rates are $25 per person (entrance fees included) for a four-hour tour (family discounts available).

Homer Vacations and Conventions, P.O. Box 1050, Homer, AK 99603 (tel. 907/235-2575), specializes in tailoring reasonably priced packages of 2–10 days for independent travelers. Various fishing, wildlife, sightseeing, and statewide touring packages include everything from Homer's own Halibut Derby to glacier flights and trips through Denali and Kenai Fjords National Parks. Host "Johnny B" is the piano player for humorist Tom Bodett's National Public Radio show, "The End of the Road," and the Bodett brand of homespun hospitality is evident in B's agency.

The fastest way to the wilderness, including the maritime wilderness, is by air. Whether you're sightseeing or on a fishing or hunting expedition, there are numerous charter-flight operators in Homer. **Kachemak Air Service,** P.O. Box 1769, Homer, AK 99603 (tel. 907/235-8924), offers scenic flights in DeHavilland Beavers and Otters at a rate of $75 per seat. Other flight operators include **SouthCentral Air,** 2100 Kachemak Dr., Homer, AK 99603 (tel. 907/235-6172, or toll free 800/478-6172 in Alaska), and **Beluga Lake Float Plane Service,** P.O. Box 2072, Homer, AK 99603 (tel. 907/235-8256).

Sports and Recreation

Kachemak Bowl, Pioneer Avenue at Lake Street (tel. 235-8666), has eight lanes. Bicyclists can rent wheels from **Quiet Sports,** 144 W. Pioneer Ave. (tel. 235-8620), across from the library. A one-mile public **orienteering** course starts behind Homer High School at the wooden bridge. There's a **roller skating** rink at Lakeside Mall. The **Kachemak Bay Gun Club** (tel. 235-7442 or 235-6894) has a pistol range and trapshooting. The public can use the **swimming pool** and **tennis courts** at the high school (tel. 235-7416 or 235-6090). Weightlifters will find Nautilus equipment at **Hot Tub Emporium,** on Pioneer Avenue in the basement of the Acropolis Building.

For information on these and other sports activities, contact the **Homer Recreation Department** (tel. 235-6210).

FISHING Many Anchorage residents and other Alaskans come to Homer specifically for the fishing. There's no shortage of craft here to take them out into Kachemak Bay and the Cook Inlet looking for halibut and other species: At last count, 60 charter-boat firms had 98 vessels available.

One good way to choose your boat and skipper is to wander around the Small Boat Basin on the Homer Spit as charters are coming in with their catches, and see who has been most successful in snaring the "big ones." I had good luck with **North Country Halibut Charters,** P.O. Box 889, Homer, AK 99603 (tel. 907/235-7620). They have an office on the Cannery Row Boardwalk. **Central Charters Booking Agency,** 4241 Homer Spit Rd., Homer, AK 99603 (tel. 907/235-7847), will be happy to line you up quickly with any available boat. Typical rates are $147 per person for a 12-hour excursion (starting at 7am) or until you've caught your limit.

Summer anglers can enter the **Homer Jackpot Halibut Derby,** running from Memorial Day to Labor Day. The largest fish caught in the summer of 1991 won a jackpot $18,434; it usually takes a 350-pounder to capture the prize. Monthly prizes for first ($1,000), second ($750), and third ($500) place are offered, and there are over 35 tagged fish from local sponsors worth $500–$1,000.

You can get licenses and buy tackle, or camping gear from sporting goods shops. Try **Sportsman Marine Supply** (tel. 235-8918) or **Kachemak Gear Shed II** (tel. 235-5562), both on the Spit.

If you do catch that big one, **Katch Canning,** on the Spit (tel. 235-6241), will vacuum-pack, smoke, freeze, and ship it to your home.

DIVING Given Kachemak Bay's rich underseas life, this is a natural. **C & C Aquatics** (tel. 235-2415) gives diving lessons and recommendations, and will help you with equipment rental.

HIKING Most of it is across the bay in Kachemak Bay State Park. Nearer to Homer, the **Diamond Creek Trail,** opposite Diamond Ridge Road west of town, winds down a creek valley to a lonely stretch of beach. Figure 45 minutes each way.

HORSEBACK RIDING **Trails End,** P.O. Box 1771, Homer, AK 99603 (tel. 907/235-6393), or **Seaside Farms,** 58335 East End Rd., Homer, AK 99603 (tel. 907/235-7850), will take you for country or seaside lopes.

HUNTING Contact the **Alaska Department of Fish and Game** on Ocean Drive (tel. 235-8191) for regulations and other information.

✪ **KAYAKING** **Ageya Kayak Tours,** 1266 Ocean Dr., Suite D, Homer, AK 99603 (tel. 907/235-6624), offers guided voyages into Kachemak Bay State Park as well as kayaking seminars and wilderness studies courses. Kachemak Bay day trips run $75 per person. From Kusitna Bay near Seldovia, Ageya also takes remote five- and seven-day paddles into Kenai Fjords National Park and around Shuyak Island, off Kodiak Island. Prices—which include equipment, food, and a guide/instructor—begin at $685 per person for five days or $960 for seven, plus an additional air-charter fee of $375 for Shuyak Island and $275 for Kenai Fjords. The company's Homer office is open mid-May to Labor Day only; during the off-season, contact P.O. Box 141506, Anchorage, AK 99603 (tel. 907/248-7140).

Experienced kayakers may contact **Central Charters Booking Agency,** 4241 Homer Spit Rd., Homer AK 99603 (tel. 907/235-8302) for rentals. They do not offer instruction or guide service.

WINTER SPORTS If you're not into ice-racing stock cars, you can at least put on a pair of skates and go **ice skating** around Beluga Lake. For **skiing,** downhill skiers will find a rope tow on Ohlson Mountain; cross-country skiers enjoy the terrain out East End Road. Inquire at Quiet Sports, 144 Pioneer Ave. (tel. 235-8620), about possible equipment rentals. Those into **snowmobiling** usually head farther afield, into the Caribou Hills or 20 miles out East End Road.

WHERE TO STAY

There are numerous motels and other accommodations in Homer and its immediate vicinity. You can pay as much as $140 for an oceanfront suite or as little as $40 for a comfortable room if you're willing to share a bath. Camping, of course, is much cheaper yet. Summer rates apply from Memorial Day to Labor Day.

Tax All rates are subject to a 5.5% city tax.

Moderate

BEST WESTERN BIDARKA INN, 575 Sterling Hwy. (P.O. Box 1408), Homer, AK 99603. Tel. 907/235-8148, or toll free 800/528-1234. 75 rms (all with bath). TV TEL

$ Rates: May–Sept, $78 single; $88 double, $98 double with kitchenette. Oct–Apr, $66 single; $75 double, $84 double with kitchenette. AE, DISC, MC, V.

If staying on the Spit isn't essential, this Best Western might satisfy you if you prefer a standard motel to other options. The spacious rooms, with orange carpets and cream trim, are furnished with queen-size beds and electric heat. There is a guest laundry, and shuttle service is available. A fitness center includes exercise equipment and hot tubs. Service can be abrupt, however.

A marine display hangs on the walls of the small lobby, through which you enter the Bidarka Inn's Periwinkle Gardens restaurant (open from 5am to 10pm daily) and lounge. A *bidarka,* by the way, is a sealskin Aleut kayak.

DRIFTWOOD INN, 135 W. Bunnell Ave., Homer, AK 99603. Tel. 907/ 235-8019, or toll free 800/478-8019 in Alaska. Fax 907/235-9940. 20 rms (11 with bath). TV TEL

$ Rates: May–Sept, $60–$85 single; $65–$90 double. Oct–Apr, $45–$65 single; $50–$70 double. AE, DISC, MC, V.

S Entering this inn is like walking into someone's living room. Merlin Corde's guest mansion in old Homer has a stone fireplace surrounded by couches and chairs, a well-lit library alcove, and hanging plants. To your left is the reception desk and a community kitchen, with tables, a refrigerator, microwave, and complimentary coffee and tea for all. There's also a TV in the living room, as well as a community phone in the kitchen area, laundry facilities, and a courtesy car. On a deck facing Bishop's Beach are a picnic table and barbecue. The inn has a playground for kids, five dog kennels (available by advance arrangement), conference facilities for up to 30 people, and fish-cleaning, shellfish-cooking, and freezing facilities.

The rooms vary considerably in size and furnishings, but two main themes prevail. The upstairs "Grandma's Place" rooms have calico curtains, patchwork quilts on double beds, wood and brass fittings, and other touches reminiscent of the 1920s and '30s; most have private baths. The small downstairs "Ship's Quarters" units are like cabins on the Alaska ferry, with nautical decor and outside entrances; they share baths. All rooms have a desk and dresser, hot-water baseboard heat, color TV, and AM/FM radio.

LAND'S END RESORT, 4786 Homer Spit Rd., Homer, AK 99603. Tel. 907/235-2500. Fax 907/235-6695. 65 rms (all with bath), 12 suites. TV TEL

$ Rates: Mid-Mar to mid-Sept, $55–$140 single or double. Mid-Sept to Nov, $40–$100 single or double. **Closed:** Dec to mid-Mar. AE, MC, V.

Land's End is the last stop on the Spit: Beyond here, in all directions but the one from which you came, it's all water. Sea otters, seals, and bald eagles frolic in the water and ashore, within easy sight of the hotel. Wood carvings of a fisherman and mermaid stand on the roof over the entrance, luring you in. Rooms have twin beds, dressers, satellite TV, individually controlled heat, and new lighting. All but 12 rooms have private decks facing the ocean. The 12 suites have queen-size beds and sofa beds to sleep additional guests. Twenty newly built rooms offer bay windows, sitting areas and private decks and can accommodate up to four people.

There's a beautiful view of Kachemak Bay from the picture windows of the Chart Room restaurant, open from 6am to 10pm daily. Seafood dinners are in the $15–$20 range, and include mesquite-broiled salmon and halibut, and fresh Dungeness crab. The wine list has 50 domestic and foreign selections. The adjoining Wheelhouse Lounge has live entertainment Thursday through Sunday. It can get loud and boisterous during musical shows and football games: The big-screen TV is a popular attraction.

Inexpensive

BAY VIEW INN, 2851 Sterling Hwy. (P.O. Box 804), Homer, AK 99603. Tel. 907/235-8485. 13 rms (all with bath), 1 suite, 1 cottage. TV

$ Rates: May–Sept, $69 single; $74 double; $104 suite or cottage. Oct–Apr, $52 single; $56 double. AE, MC, V.

Remember that staggering view as the Sterling Highway turns toward Homer? From your room here, you can wake up to that scene every morning. The units are decorated in Cape Cod gray with white trim and furnished with double beds, desks, private facilities with showers, and hot-water heating. A phone is available in the office. Five rooms have kitchenettes; there's also a honeymoon suite with a fireplace as well as a separate guest cottage with a loft.

Summer visitors can use the barbecue pit and picnic tables on the lawn; for winter visitors, a five-kilometer (three-mile) cross-country ski track begins across the highway.

LAKEWOOD INN, 984 Ocean Dr., Homer, AK 99603. Tel. 907/235-6146, or toll free 800/478-LAKE in Alaska. Fax 907/235-6774. 23 rms (all with bath), 5 suites. TV TEL

$ Rates: June–Aug, $65 single; $70 double; $120 suite. Sept–May, $50–$55 single; $55–$65 double; $70–$85 suite. AE, DC, DISC, MC, V.

Built on a bluff overlooking Beluga Lake with its waterfowl population and winter ice racing, the Lakewood's rooms include five suites with kitchenettes. The cozy standard rooms, decorated in pastel tones against bare white walls, have electric heat.

From the windows of the 24-hour Lakewood Inn restaurant, you can watch the ducks as you enjoy breakfast or a Sunday brunch for $6.75. Lunch entrees are $5 and up and dinner entrees, served from 5 to 10pm, are in the $9 range. The Mallard Lounge has specialty drinks; upstairs, the Raven's Nest sometimes has live music on weekends.

Budget

HERITAGE HOTEL, 147 E. Pioneer Ave., Homer, AK 99603. Tel. 907/ 235-7787. 45 rms (33 with bath). TV TEL

$ Rates: May–Sept, $45 single without bath, $50–$60 single with bath; $50 double without bath, $55–$65 double with bath; $90 suite. Oct–Apr, $40 single without bath, $45–$50 single with bath; $45 double without bath, $50–$55 double with bath; $70 suite. AE, CB, DC, DISC, MC, V.

The log-construction Heritage is the one hotel on Homer's downtown strip. Its homey front lobby, with couches, chairs, and lots of green plants, gives you a comfortable feeling right away. Rooms are decorated in earth tones and have a queen-size bed or two doubles, radio, electric heat, and courtesy coffee or tea. Rooms have satellite TV with in-house movies.

Bed-and-Breakfasts

BRASS RING BED & BREAKFAST, 987 Hillfair Court, Homer, AK 99603. Tel. 907/235-5450. 6 rms (1 with bath).

$ Rates (including breakfast): May–Sept, $55 single without bath; $65 double without bath, $75 double with bath. Oct–Apr, $45 single; $55 double. MC, V.

Just a couple of blocks from downtown, Guy and Renée Doyle's house has 2½ baths, a wood stove and electric heat, hot tub, laundry facilities, and freezer space for fish. The beautiful home was custom-built of white spruce in late 1984 specifically as a B&B. Each guest room is furnished with antiques and decorated with Norwegian country stenciling. Breakfasts are made to order in the big kitchen, and guests are encouraged to make themselves at home in the living room and den (with TV/VCR and library). No smoking, please.

JAILHOUSE BED AND BREAKFAST, 190 E. Pioneer Ave., Homer, AK 99603. Tel. 907/235-2575. 3 rms (none with bath).

$ Rates (including breakfast): $100–$140 for three to four people in two or three rooms. No credit cards.

Though it was built as Homer's first jail in 1940, the Jailhouse never housed a single prisoner: It failed to pass state codes, so was turned into a private home. Today it's a unique "no-host" B&B. The owners, who live off-premises, provide keys to the house and full breakfast fixings, leaving guests in complete privacy. There are three bedrooms, one bathroom, and a sofa bed in the living room. It's ideal for families or couples traveling together.

MAGIC CANYON BED AND BREAKFAST, 40015 Waterman Rd., Homer,

AK 99603. Tel. 907/235-6077. (In winter, write P.O. Box 20354, Oak Creek, AZ 86341.) 3 rms (1 with bath).
$ Rates (including breakfast): Summer, $50–$85. Winter, $50–$60. No credit cards.
Guests are invited to share in guided nature walks and lectures on Alaskan history and anthropology at this 75-acre homestead, which overlooks Kachemak Bay, glaciers, and the Kenai Mountains five miles east of Homer. There is a sun deck with a hot tub and a library of Alaskana. Also here are Carrie Reed's fiber-art studio and a riding stable. Kids can check out the llamas and other livestock or take a pony ride. Guests stay in the aptly named Glacierview, Northern Lights, or Garden Rooms. A full farm breakfast is prepared each morning.

SEEKINS' HOMER BED & BREAKFAST, East Hill Race Rd. (P.O. Box 1264), Homer, AK 99603. Tel. 907/235-8996. 4 rms (all with bath).
Directions: Turn left off Pioneer Avenue three-quarters of a mile east of Lake Street, then drive uphill two miles to Cottonwood Lane and Race Road.
$ Rates (including continental breakfast): $40–$45 single; $50–$60 double. MC, V.
Moose occasionally wander through the yard of this place, high on Homer Bluffs overlooking the city and bay. There's a variety of accommodations here—a one-bedroom cabin, a three-bedroom guesthouse atop a garage, a single room, and a family room in the main house—all of which have a warm decor. All but one of the units also has its own kitchen. You're invited to share breakfast with hosts Floyd and Gert Seekins, who probably know Homer as well as or better than anyone else: They also operate Homer Tours (see "Organized Tours" in "What to See and Do," above) and arrange fishing charters. Call 235-8998 for referral to other B&Bs if Seekins' is full.

Campgrounds

First-time summer visitors are always stunned by the sea of tents and RVs set up just above the high-water mark on the Spit. The **Homer Spit Campground**, P.O. Box 1196, Homer, AK 99603 (tel. 907/235-8206), is open May to September and accepts reservations. For $10, campers get restrooms, tap water, hot showers, and a dump station. Electrical hookups for recreational vehicles are an additional $5. For information on camping elsewhere on the Spit, contact the Harbormaster's Office, 4350 Spit Rd., Homer, AK 99603 (tel. 907/235-3160).
The City of Homer (tel. 907/235-6090) operates the **City Campground** on Mullican Drive, near the hospital on the slopes overlooking town, offering barbecue pits, picnic tables, and restrooms. The fee is $4. The city also permits camping on the Spit at $7 for RVs and $4 for tents. Water, restrooms, and a dump station are available. Reservations are not accepted.
Also available for camping are the **Oceanview RV Park**, P.O. Box 891, Homer, AK 99603 (tel. 907/235-3951), and **Land's End RV Park** (tel. 907/235-2500) at the end of the Spit.

WHERE TO DINE

Aside from hotel eateries, there are ample restaurants at all price levels. The more elegant among them offer a similar range of steak and seafood dishes. There are also several Asian-food restaurants. On the Spit you'll find numerous seasonal fast-food hamburger and fish-and-chips shops; consensus favorites are **Addie's Big Patties** and **Boardwalk Fish and Chips.** There's even a **McDonald's** on Lake Street.

Moderate

CAFE CUPS, 162 W. Pioneer Ave. Tel. 235-8330.
   Cuisine: CREATIVE AMERICAN. **Reservations:** Recommended for dinner.

$ Prices: Appetizers $7.50–$8.95; main courses $9.50–$16.50; breakfast $2.95–$7.50; lunch $3.50–$7.50. MC, V.

Open: Memorial Day–Labor Day, breakfast/lunch daily 7am–3pm; dinner daily 5–9pm. Labor Day–Memorial Day, breakfast/lunch Tues–Sat 7am–3pm; dinner Tues–Sat 5–9pm.

A self-labeled "coffee, art, and dinner house," Café Cups is a center for Homer's prolific artists' and writers' community. A private art collection, featuring the works of Picasso and Dalí along with leading local talents, adorns the walls; the café is the frequent venue for improvisational theater performances and readings by the likes of local humorist Tom Bodett, nationally known poet Tess Gallagher, and former Iditarod champion Libby Riddles.

The cuisine is characterized by creative combinations of gourmet ingredients and fresh local seafood. For breakfast you can have eggs Benedict or Florentine or take advantage of the 7 to 9am "early bird" special: two eggs, home-fries, and toast for only $2.95. Lunch dishes include sourdough grinders, soup, and salad. On the dinner menu are a half dozen pasta dishes, including linguine carbonara, clams Créole, and scallops sherry; sautéed halibut; chicken Mediterranean; and a tenderloin pepper steak.

FRANNIE'S, 177 E. Pioneer Ave. Tel. 235-3956.

Cuisine: AMERICAN. **Reservations:** Recommended for dinner.

$ Prices: Breakfast $1.95–$8.95; lunch $5.25–$12.95, dinner $8.95–$16.95. MC, V.

Open: Mid-May to Sept, daily 5:30am–10pm. Oct to mid-May, daily 7am–5pm.

Housed in a log cabin, Frannie's offers good, hearty meals at fair prices in the casual atmosphere of a diner. The extensive breakfast menu includes pancakes, waffles, omelets, and specialties like reindeer sausage and eggs and the "kitchen sink scramble." Lunches feature hot sandwiches and a good selection of salads. Dinner at Frannie's is an event even for the gourmet, including halibut Alyeska (topped with sour cream, bay shrimp, and cheddar cheese), oysters Françoise (pan-grilled, served on a bed of fresh spinach and topped with lobster sauce), and a variety of steak and chicken dishes. You won't want to miss the ice-cream bar at the rear of the restaurant.

FRESH SOURDOUGH EXPRESS BAKERY AND RESTAURANT, 1316 Ocean Dr. Tel. 235-7571.

Cuisine: AMERICAN. **Reservations:** Not required.

$ Prices: Breakfast $4–$8.50; lunch $5–$11.95; dinner $8.95–$19.95. AE, CB, DC, DISC, MC, V.

Open: Daily 6am–10pm.

Homer's favorite lunch stop began in 1982 as a green bakery van on the Spit; now the owners grind their own flour daily for 19 varieties of sourdough breads and five yeast breads. Breakfasts are typically stuffed savory croissants, pastries, muffins, and sourdough waffles. Deli-style sandwiches reign at lunchtime; there are also homemade soups and an espresso bar. In the evening you can dine light on burgers or mini-pizzas, or feast on barbecued chicken, salmon, or halibut combinations. There's even an all-you-can-eat option for $19.95.

Inexpensive

CHOW'S, 435 E. Pioneer Ave. Tel. 235-6226.

Cuisine: HAWAIIAN/AMERICAN. **Reservations:** Not required.

$ Prices: Appetizers $2.75; main courses $3.75–$12.75. No credit cards.

Open: Mon–Fri 11am–8:30pm.

Enter through the rear of this small café to a virtual greenhouse of potted plants and cacti. There are a few booths and tables, plus counter space. They offer plates like sweet-and-sour pork, broccoli beef, and teriyaki chicken. Full stir-fry shrimp-and-vegetable dinners with rice cost less than $10. Diners with allergies will be pleased that the chefs refuse to use monosodium glutamate. If you crave American food, they also have hamburgers on the menu. Chows has take-out service too.

DON JOSE'S, 127 W. Pioneer Ave. Tel. 235-7963.
  Cuisine: MEXICAN/ITALIAN. **Reservations:** Recommended on weekends.
$ Prices: Appetizers $5.25–$7.75; main courses $8.75–$11.50. DISC, MC, V.
  Open: Mon–Fri 11am–8:30pm, Fri–Sat 11am–midnight.
A wrought-iron fence and hanging ivy divide the split-level restaurant in two.
Oil-on-black-velvet paintings hang on the walls, and mariachi music is piped in. You
can have a full burrito or enchilada dinner for less than $10 and wash it down with a
raspberry margarita, or dine on lasagne for $8.75. Lunch specials are served until
2pm.

**THE THAI AND CHINESE RESTAURANT, 601 E. Pioneer Ave. Tel.
235-7250.**
  Cuisine: THAI/CHINESE. **Reservations:** Recommended for dinner.
$ Prices: Appetizers $1.25–$8.25; main courses $5–$10.75. DISC.
  Open: Daily 11am–10pm.
Separate Thai and Chinese menus come together at lunch, when this popular
restaurant is packed for its $6.30 all-you-can-eat buffet, served from 11am to 3pm. At
other times, the cuisines rarely mix. Thai dishes include tom yum gai, a lemongrass
soup with chicken; beef, chicken, shrimp, or crab curry with coconut milk and fresh
basil; and various sautés rich in ginger or peanut sauce. Traditional Chinese dishes
include sweet-and-sour pork, Szechwan chicken, chow mein, fried rice, and wonton
soup. The dinner special ($8.95), served family style, includes soup, eggroll, fried rice,
and choice of entrees.

EVENING ENTERTAINMENT

Homer's hot spot is **Alice's Champagne Palace,** a big, barnlike building on
Pioneer Avenue (tel. 235-7650), just west of the Heritage Hotel. Alaska's best rock
bands play here, unless they're preempted by national or international recording
artists. Dance to the live music Wednesday through Sunday from 10pm to 3am.
There's also a pool table, pinball machines, and video games. Margie's Kitchen serves
burgers, tamales, and other fast food Sunday through Wednesday from 11:30am to
midnight, until 2am Thursday through Saturday.
  Two other downtown spots also do a brisk business. **Hobo Jim's Alaskan Bar,**
on Pioneer Avenue across from Alice's (tel. 235-9932), has been remodeled since
Hobo Jim, a noted bush-ballad and sea-shanty singer, bought what previously was
Jack's Other Place. Open from 10am to 5am daily, it offers live entertainment on
Sunday night. There's also the **Bayside Lounge,** 445 E. Pioneer Ave. (tel. 235-9921).
  The Waterfront, a ramshackle old restaurant at 120 Bunnell Ave. (tel. 235-8747),
in old Homer near the Driftwood Inn, has live rock 'n' roll Wednesday through
Saturday nights, a karaoke machine, and a snack bar/grill. It's open from 1pm to 5am
daily. Some 4½ miles east of Homer on East End Road, **Rawley's Roadhouse** (tel.
235-8644) has a big dance floor with local rock or country-and-western bands.
  Out on the Spit, the **Wheelhouse Lounge** at Land's End Resort (tel. 235-2500)
is open from 10am to midnight and always does good business. But for real Spit
atmosphere you must visit the ramshackle **Salty Dawg** (no phone). It's nearly a
century old, and looks it, with a sawdust floor, initials carved into all the counters and
tables, and flags, lifebuoys, and T-shirts hanging from the ceilings and walls. This
saloon is famous throughout Alaska as a fishermen's den. When it's stormy out, some
of them come at 11am when the Salty Dawg opens and stay till closing around 5am.
  The bar scene aside, Homer has a very active performing arts schedule throughout
the year. Dance troupes, theatrical companies, musicians, and others frequently visit
the town. Contact the **Homer Council on the Arts,** P.O. Box 1764, Homer, AK
99603 (tel. 235-4288), for this year's schedule.
  Pier One Theatre (tel. 235-7333), Homer's community theater group, presents a
series of summer plays in an old warehouse on the Spit. It also has a regular season
running October to May, featuring contemporary and classical drama and comedy. A
new group called **Fresh Produce** specializes in improvisational theater, and there
are several small local dance companies.

The **Homer Family Theater,** at Main Street and Pioneer Avenue (tel. 235-6728), presents first-run films.

AN EASY EXCURSION TO HALIBUT COVE

✪ Halibut Cove, with its spruce-cloaked islet and peninsula surrounding a deep green lagoon, is one of the most charming small communities in the state of Alaska. It's kept that way in part because it cannot be reached by road—only by boat or floatplane.

The **Kachemak Bay Ferry** (tel. 235-7847 in Homer, 296-2223 in Halibut Cove) is the 34-passenger *Danny J*, a fishing-boat-cum-shuttle service. It leaves the Spit daily at noon for Halibut Cove via Gull Island (more on which later). After a 1½-hour layover it departs the cove at 4pm for the return run to Homer. The round-trip fare for this tour is $35 cash, $36 with credit card. The ferry leaves again for the cove at 5pm, returning at 10pm; on this trip it carries only cove residents or visitors with dinner reservations at the Saltry. The fare is $17.50, $18.50 with a credit card. Reservations are required.

Between 1911 and 1928 this isolated location was the site of a thriving herring fishery, with 36 salteries (fish-curing plants) supporting a population of nearly 1,000. After waste pollution in the cove drove the fishermen out of business, bootleggers concealed their stills here during Prohibition times.

In its late 20th-century incarnation, the community of Halibut Cove owes its existence to Clem Tillion, who bought Ismailof Island as a young man in 1943 and established it as a family estate. Tillion, who retired as speaker of the Alaska House of Representatives but remains a member of the North Pacific Fisheries Commission, is the father figure for a tightly knit artists' community of about 65 year-round residents, swelling to about 125 in summer.

About a mile of boardwalks connects the boat dock with the large green Tillion home—you'll recognize it by the birdhouses for nesting swallows (they eat the mosquitoes) under the eaves. Clem's wife, Diana Tillion, an artist renowned for her octopus-ink paintings, operates the **Cove Gallery.** Within this geodesic dome structure you can see the paintings and sculptures of many of Halibut Cove's artisan residents.

Where to Stay

If you feel you'd like to stay awhile, there are several accommodation options in the cove.

HALIBUT COVE CABINS, P.O. Box 1990, Homer, AK 99603. Tel. 907/296-2214 in Halibut Cove or 235-8110 in Homer. 2 cabins (with private outhouses).
$ Rates: $75 double per night, $350 per week. No credit cards.
Artist Sydney Bishop's two cozy cabins are situated at the eastern end of Ismailof Island. Bring your own food and bedding; cushions, kitchen appliances, a wood stove, well water, and a shower at the main house are provided.

ISMAILOF ISLAND LODGE, P.O. Box 6430, Halibut Cove, AK 99603. Tel. 907/296-2217. 5 rms (none with bath), 1 cabin (with private outhouse).
$ Rates: $250 per person all-inclusive, $125 per person with bed-and-breakfast; $175 cabin for four people, $40 per additional person. No credit cards.
There are a range of accommodations, from all-inclusive (room, all meals, and guide service) and B&B style to rental of the self-contained cabin. The rustic cabin has dishes, propane heat, cold running water, and its own outhouse. Unless you have a boat, arrange to be picked up at the Saltry restaurant. The proprietors also provide water-taxi service to Kachemak Bay State Park for $12 per person.

QUIET PLACE LODGE, P.O. Box 6474, Halibut Cove, AK 99603. Tel. 907/296-2212. 5 cabins (none with bath).
$ Rates (including breakfast): $125 double; $175 quad. No credit cards unless booked through Central Charters in Homer (tel. 235-7847).
The cozy cabins here huddle around the main lodge, in which are located joint bath

facilities, a library, and a dining area, where hearty, country-style breakfasts are served. There's a sauna too. Rowboats are available for energetic fishermen.

Where to Dine

There's only one restaurant in Halibut Cove, but it's a good one.

THE SALTRY, Halibut Cove. Tel. 296-2223, 235-7847 for ferry and reservations.

Cuisine: SEAFOOD. **Reservations:** Required for dinner.
$ Prices: Appetizers $8-$10; main courses $14-$17. MC, V.
Open: Daily 1-9pm.

The fare here, at the cove's first and only restaurant, is exotic seafood like sushi, mussels, salmon caviar, ceviche, pickled salmon, salmon pâté, and sable-fish chowder. Occasionally there are pasta dishes or pescado Veracruz with black beans and corn salsa. Queasy stomachs can get a cheese platter. The ample wine list includes sake, and Black Hook Premium Ale is on tap.

AN EASY EXCURSION TO KACHEMAK BAY

This long inlet's entire south shore—not just Halibut Cove—is a world unto itself.

Most of the land here, from the bayshore over the crest of the Kenai Mountains to the Gulf of Alaska, is part and parcel of **Kachemak Bay State Park** or the adjoining **Kachemak Bay State Wilderness Park.** Together they comprise some 350,000 acres of primitive mountain and fjord terrain. There are only three short hiking trails in the preserves, two of them from near Halibut Cove (to the Grewingk Glacier and to Leisure Lake). Hunting, fishing, and trapping are allowed in the parks, but horses and motorized vehicles are not. The *Danny J* offers drop-off service to adventurous hikers and campers. The Alaska Division of Parks and Outdoor Recreation (tel. 235-7024) has detailed information.

Of chief interest to Homer visitors are several coastal enclaves. The first of note is a community of birds. **Gull Island,** about three miles off the Spit, is a major bird rookery and a part of Alaska Maritime National Wildlife Refuge. An estimated 8,000 puffins, guillemots, kittiwakes, murres, cormorants, and gulls nest on this barren, rocky outcropping, and numerous other species frequently visit.

Nearby, in Peterson Bay, is the **Center for Alaskan Coastal Studies** (tel. 235-6667). Kachemak Bay has a unique marine ecosystem, which the society was established to protect. An astonishing variety of invertebrate species, mollusks, and crustaceans make their homes in the tidepools of Peterson and China Poot Bays, two small inlets on opposite sides of a peninsula just west of Halibut Cove. The entire bay is rich in fish, marine mammals, and sea, shore, and woodland birds. Visitors to the marine research center are treated to explorations of tidepools, subarctic rain forest, and prehistoric archeological sites. Call the center for tour information and reservations.

A few miles west are two long, fingerlike fjords, Sadie Cove and Tutka Bay, each with a lodge of its own. Near the Tutka Bay Lodge is one of the Alaska Department of Fish and Game's most remote facilities, the **Tutka Lagoon Hatchery** (tel. 235-8191 in Homer). Built in 1976, it has a capacity of 30 million salmon eggs, mainly pink and chum. Visitors are welcome.

Seventy miles west of Kachemak Bay, on the western side of the Cook Inlet, is **Mount Augustine,** a volcanic island that may rumble or emit smoke plumes during your visit to Homer. Mount Augustine was very active in the late 1980s, sending ash clouds over Homer and Seldovia, grounding planes, and sending citizens running for dust masks and air filters. During a volcanic eruption a tsunami (tidal wave) is always a danger. If you hear sirens, head for high ground!

Rainbow Tours, on Homer's Cannery Row Boardwalk (tel. 235-7272), offers daily tours on the 99-passenger *Rainbow Connection* to Gull Island and Peterson Bay, departing from the Spit at 9am and 4:30pm. An all-day Natural History Tour to the Center for Alaskan Coastal Studies departs at 9am daily for $49 ($29 for children). A cruise to Seldovia leaves daily at 11am and returns at 4pm; the price is $36 ($26 for children). Other tour operators offering Kachemak Bay tours include **Kachemak Bay Adventures,** P.O. Box 1196, Homer, AK 99603 (tel. 235-8206), and **Alaska Maritime Tours,** P.O. Box 3098, Homer, AK 99603 (tel. 907/235-2490, or toll free 800/478-2490).

Where to Stay

KACHEMAK BAY WILDERNESS LODGE, P.O. Box 956, Homer, AK 99603. Tel. 907/235-8910. Fax 907/235-8911. 1 rm, 4 cabins (with bath). **$ Rates** (including round-trip transfer from Homer): $1,950 per person, all-inclusive, for minimum stay of five days/four nights. No credit cards. **Closed:** Mid-Dec to Apr.

⭐ Acclaimed by the newsletter *The Hideaway Report* as "America's best wilderness lodge," this lodge on China Poot Bay offers days of leisure spent in a beautiful natural environment. Host Mike McBride is a member of the prestigious Explorers Club and is a registered guide and naturalist, a licensed skipper, and a former bush pilot. His wife, Diane, a biologist and emergency medical technician, is the lodge's gourmet chef. Together with a staff of eight, they have created an experience that begs to be embraced—for those who can afford it.

Everything is provided, from hip boots and guide service to French wine. The lodge has its own electric generator, a sod-roofed Finnish sauna, and a Jacuzzi. A maximum of 10 guests at a time stay in the single lodge room and four private two-bedroom cabins with wood stoves and electric lights. Family-style meals, served in the huge main lodge, are prepared from fresh-caught seafood, fruits and berries from the hills, vegetables from a backyard garden, and homemade bread from a wood oven.

SADIE COVE WILDERNESS LODGE, P.O. Box 2265, Homer, AK 99603. Tel. 907/235-7766. 3 cabins (1 with bath). **$ Rates** (including round-trip transfer from Homer): $500 per person. Minimum stay three nights. No credit cards.

Seventeen-year resident and lodge owner Keith Iverson has a colorful past, as described in his autobiography, *Alaska Viking.* His accomplishments include construction of this lodge by hand. Two of the three cabins have one bedroom and share a bath; one two-bedroom cabin has a private bath. Rates include gourmet meals in the spacious dining room, and guide service for wildlife photography or salmon and halibut fishing.

TUTKA BAY LODGE, P.O. Box 960, Homer, AK 99603. Tel. 907/235-3905. 3 cabins (2 with bath). **$ Rates** (including use of mountain bikes, guide service, meals, and round-trip transfer from Homer): $200 per person without bath, $225 with bath, $275 luxury with bath. No credit cards.

John and Nelda Osgood's lodge has deluxe accommodations for up to 15 guests in three separate cabins. Tutka Bay Lodge's seafood dishes are renowned: some of Nelda's recipes have found their way into the pages of *Gourmet* magazine.

AN EASY EXCURSION TO SELDOVIA

Spread across a low promontory, surrounded by water and mountains, Seldovia's secluded charm makes it a popular destination for many visitors.

This fishing village of about 700 people was settled by the Russians in the late 18th century as a year-round harbor and coal port. Salmon and crab processing are the main industries. Seldovia was once famed for a half-mile boardwalk which served as its main street; this was destroyed when the land mass dropped about four feet into the bay during the 1964 earthquake. Only a small portion of the boardwalk was preserved when the town was rebuilt. Some of the town's past does remain intact, however: **St. Nicholas Russian Orthodox Church,** long the social hub of Seldovia, was built in 1891 on a hill overlooking the harbor. Restored in 1981, it's still in use today.

Visitors come to Seldovia not to visit indoor attractions, but to enjoy fishing, hiking, birdwatching, and cross-country skiing. For information, write to the **Seldovia Chamber of Commerce**, P.O. Drawer F, Seldovia, AK 99663, or call the Boardwalk Hotel (tel. 907/234-7816).

Seldovia is served by the **Alaska Marine Highway System** (tel. 234-7868). The ferry M.V. *Tustumena* usually operates between Homer and Seldovia twice weekly in summer. In winter, the ferry usually sails once a week. Service is erratic, so you need to call about specific dates and times. There's no service while the *Tustumena* is in maintenance from January to mid-March. One-way fares are $16 for adults, $8 for children 6–11, and considerably more if you bring your vehicle. Have information on the length and width of your vehicle available when you call for reservations.

Daily year-round passenger ferry service is offered by **Rainbow Tours** (tel. 235-7272 in Homer), leaving Homer at 11am, returning from Seldovia at 4pm. Adult fares are $36 round-trip, $24 one way; children are charged $26 and $14, respectively.

For customized tours, with or without guide service, contact **Jakolof Ferry Service**, P.O. Box 235, Seldovia, AK 99663 (tel. 907/234-7686). The company specializes in active adventures, like mountain biking, sea kayaking, hiking, climbing and camping.

Where to Stay

BOARDWALK HOTEL, P.O. Box 72, Seldovia, AK 99663. Tel. 907/234-7816. 13 rms (all with bath). TEL
$ Rates (including breakfast): $58 single; $84–$98 double. No credit cards.
Annie McKenzie's bed-and-breakfast hotel has modern rooms on the waterfront and friendly service. Rooms have great views and there is a large deck facing the harbor. The comfortable interior furnishings include an exhibit of local art. Relax in the library or borrow one of the bicycles available to guests. The hotel offers courtesy transportation from the airport or harbor.

SELDOVIA LODGE, P.O. Box 136, Seldovia, AK 99663. Tel. 907/234-7654. 10 rms (all with bath). TV
$ Rates: $36 single; $42 double; $48 triple. MC, V.
Each room has a private bath and can accommodate three people comfortably. The restaurant, which specializes in steak and seafood, is open for three meals daily and has a salad bar and Saturday barbecue. There is also a bar, open until 2am daily.

STAMPER'S BAYVIEW LODGE, P.O. Drawer A, Seldovia, AK 99663. Tel. 907/234-7631. Fax 907/234-7461. 3 apts (all with bath). TV
$ Rates: $50–$60 single; $60–$70 double. Additional person $10 extra. MC, V.
True to its name, Stamper's offers beautiful views across Kachemak Bay. Each fully furnished, self-contained unit has a kitchen, bath, and television; two of the units have microwave ovens. You can cook your fresh fish on the deck on a barbecue grill overlooking the bay. For an additional $5 per day, you can get continental breakfast delivered to your room; $10 gets you a gourmet breakfast.

Where to Dine

CENTURION RESTAURANT, Seldovia. Tel. 234-7676.
Cuisine: SEAFOOD. **Reservations:** Not required.
$ Prices: Appetizers $3–$8; main courses $6–$16. No credit cards.
Open: May–Sept, daily 11:30am–8pm. Oct–Apr, hours vary.
This harborfront diner features local art on the walls and seafood on the plates. Halibut fish and chips, served in generous portions, is a local favorite. Full dinners with salad and bread include king salmon, New York steak, and local butter clams. For dessert, try the cheesecake. Beer and wine are served.

KACHEMAK KAFE, 233 Main St. Tel. 234-7494.
Cuisine: AMERICAN. **Reservations:** Not required.

$ Prices: Breakfast $3–$7.50; lunch $1.50–$8. No credit cards.
Open: Daily 7am–4pm.
Home-style cooking at reasonable prices is the mark of this café. Even Homerites rave about its breakfasts, especially its enormous cinnamon rolls and apple pancakes. If you're really hungry, try the earthquake scramble or a breakfast burrito with homemade salsa. For lunch, the fresh halibut comes highly recommended.

AN EASY EXCURSION TO ANCHOR POINT

This small community on the Sterling Highway, 16 miles northwest of Homer, has one chief claim to fame: It represents the westernmost point on the North American continent that can be reached by a continuous road system. (The easternmost is Cape Breton, Nova Scotia.) A marker designates the spot.

The town's population of 226 swells in the summer with the arrival of hordes of fishermen seeking the steelhead and silver salmon that run in the Anchor River.

Four miles east of Anchor Point is the **Norman Lowell Studio and Gallery,** Mile 161 on the Sterling Highway (tel. 235-7344), billed as Alaska's largest private art gallery. Lowell, an artist who has made his home here since 1959, also shares his original homestead and garden with visitors. Open Monday through Saturday from 9am to 9pm and on Sunday from 1 to 5pm.

Inland from Anchor Point, up the North Fork road, is a unique community of Russian-Americans known in Homer as the Old Believers. In their settlement of **Nikolaevsk,** they pursue the original lifestyles of their 17th-century ancestors, who refused to conform to mandated changes in their traditional Orthodox faith. While the people don't appreciate curious visitors in their isolated village, they can frequently be seen in their colorful costumes in Anchor Point and Homer.

Where to Stay

ANCHOR RIVER INN, Mile 157, Sterling Hwy. (P.O. Box 154), Anchor Point, AK 99556. Tel. 907/235-8531. Fax 907/235-2296. 20 rms (all with bath). TV TEL
$ Rates: $38–$55 single; $42–$60 double. AE, DC, DISC, MC, V.
Modern, comfortable rooms with queen-size beds and electric heat are popular among vacationers. The spacious newer units are more expensive, but the cozy older rooms are a budget bargain. A restaurant is open for three meals a day, and a lounge, grocery store, and liquor store are on the premises. Near both the Anchor River and the beach, this place offers plenty of fishing opportunities.

2. PRINCE WILLIAM SOUND

The sparkling blue waters of forest-shrouded, isle-studded Prince William Sound are a playground both for Anchorage boaters and myriad marine mammals. The fjords and inlets of this magnificent expanse see a regular traffic of pleasure boats and cruise ships, ferries and oil tankers, trollers and kayaks. They also see a wealth of humpback and other whales, seals and sea lions, porpoises and sea otters.

Many Alaska visitors venture into Prince William Sound specifically to view the Columbia Glacier. Truly, it's worth the trip. This massive tidewater glacier, 5 miles wide at its terminus and 40 miles long, covers as much ground as does the city of Los Angeles. To moor among harbor seals a short distance from the roar of the glacier's calving ice, or to hover over it in a helicopter, is an experience not easily forgotten.

But the sound is more than one glacier, of course. In all, well over a dozen glaciers tumble into its waters. Almost completely encompassed in Chugach National Forest,

Prince William Sound has 15 public-use cabins and numerous other recreational opportunities on its shores. Each of its three main settlements has a character all its own—tiny Whittier (pop. about 330), the jumping-off point for Anchorage visitors; Valdez (pop. 3,700), Alaska pipeline oil port and center of a thriving tourist trade; and Cordova (pop. 2,500), a laid-back fishing town near the mouth of the Copper River.

Shielded from Gulf of Alaska storms by two large islands at its southern entrance, Montague and Hinchinbrook, Prince William Sound enjoys a mild if wet climate. Summer temperatures are usually in the 50s and 60s Fahrenheit, while the midwinter average is in the 20s. But precipitation in different corners of the sound ranges from 60 to 180 inches annually. Good rain gear is essential.

In March 1989 the oil tanker *Exxon Valdez* ran aground in Prince William Sound, affecting many species of marine animals and birds and fouling pristine shorelines. The town of Valdez became one of the staging centers for a massive cleanup effort. By mid-1992, little evidence of the spill was visible to the tourist's eye. A cleanup technique known as "bioremediation" was continuing: Oiled beaches were being regularly sprayed with a special fertilizer to encourage the growth of oil-eating organisms. The dynamic forces of nature, over time, provide the most effective cleansing of all.

For general information on Prince William Sound, contact the offices of **Chugach National Forest,** 201 E. Fourth Ave., Anchorage, AK 99501 (tel. 907/271-2500); the Valdez Convention and Visitors Bureau; or the chamber of commerce in Cordova.

GETTING THERE   By Plane   Valdez and Cordova both are served by regularly scheduled flights. Cordova is a daily stop (each way) for **Alaska Airlines** on its Anchorage–Juneau run. Call the airline's toll-free number (tel. 800/426-0333) or the offices in Cordova (tel. 907/424-7151), Anchorage (tel. 907/243-3300), or Juneau (tel. 907/789-0600). Valdez is served four times daily to and from Anchorage by **ERA,** an Alaska Airlines commuter line; call toll free (tel. 800/426-0333), or in Valdez (tel. 907/835-2636) or Anchorage (tel. 907/243-3300). Air-taxi lines are based in all three towns on the Sound. (In Whittier there are float planes only.) Cordova is also served by **Markair** (tel. 907/424-5982).

By Train   The only practical way to reach Whittier from Anchorage is by train via Portage. The half-hour Whittier Shuttle runs six times daily in summer, less often in winter. The fare is $15 one way for foot passengers and $70 for vehicle and driver; passengers are bused from the **Alaska Railroad** station in Anchorage (tel. 265-2685) to meet the shuttle at Portage.

By Car   Currently, the only town on Prince William Sound with road access is Valdez. The Richardson Highway connects Valdez with Glennallen, 121 miles north via snowy Thompson Pass; from there it's a straight drive to either Anchorage (another 181 miles west) or Fairbanks (250 miles north). Various tour buses ply the six-hour route regularly in summer. Plans have been laid to extend the Copper River Highway from Chitina to Cordova.

By Ferry   Unquestionably the best way to see Prince William Sound is by sea. The ferries of the **Alaska Marine Highway System** do it most often and for the least cost. The M.V. *Bartlett* is a permanent fixture in the sound, shuttling back and forth between Cordova and Valdez (a six-hour voyage) several times a week. From mid-May through mid-September the route is extended to include Whittier and the Columbia Glacier five times weekly; as an added bonus, a U.S. Forest Service naturalist accompanies these trips as a narrator. When the *Bartlett* goes into port for nine weeks' annual maintenance in mid-March, travelers must depend on the weekly visits of the M.V. *Tustumena,* which connects Valdez and Cordova with Seward, Homer, Kodiak, and occasionally, other points west. Typical deck-class fares are: Whittier–Valdez, $56 (plus $13 for the train); Valdez–Cordova, $28; Cordova–Seward, $56. Taking a vehicle costs more. For further information, contact the Alaska Marine Highway System, P.O. Box R, Juneau, AK 99811 (tel. toll free 800/642-0066, 800/551-7185 in Alaska), or call the terminal in Valdez (tel. 907/835-4436) or Cordova (tel. 907/424-7333).

Package Tours   Most major Alaskan tour companies offer Prince William Sound cruises via the Columbia Glacier. I like the service and narration provided by **Columbia Glacier Cruises,** run by Gray Line of Alaska, 745 W. Fourth Ave., Suite 200, Anchorage, AK 99501 (tel. 907/277-5581), aboard the M.V. *Glacier Queen II.* The *Queen* is a luxury yacht with two seating decks, a full bar, and a galley. The tour can be taken as a one- or two-day trip, either eastbound or westbound, with road or air connections between Anchorage and Valdez. The one-day fly/cruise price is $250; the standard two-day trip, including overnight shared accommodation in Valdez, is $329 single, $275 twin. Tours operate from the Memorial Day holiday to mid-September.

   Alaska Sightseeing Tours, 543 W. Fourth Ave., Anchorage, AK 99501 (tel. 907/276-1305), offers one- and two-day cruises in the sound aboard the sleek M.V. *Glacier Seas.* The tour operators promise gourmet meals and more scenery aboard this luxury yacht than others can provide. The one-day fly/cruise price is $335; the two-day drive/cruise price, including hotel in Valdez, is $435 single, $345 twin. If you travel between mid-May and June 15 or after September 1 (until September 15), you'll pay $335 for the one-day trip, and just $289 (twin) for the two-day trip. Children 5–11 pay $175 for the two-day trip, but there are no discounts on the one-day trip.

WHITTIER

Tour brochures say Whittier is "unique . . . even in Alaska." How right they are! Well over half of the town's population lives in a single building, the 14-story Begich Towers, which also contains the city hall, post office, library, grocery store, café, museum, and art gallery. Most of the other inhabitants live in a private condominium.

   If the community is reminiscent of a military camp—well, that's what it was. Whittier was a prime debarkation point for cargo and troops of the Alaska Command after the Portage–Prince William Sound railroad spur was completed in 1943. About 1,200 people lived here until 1960, when the command was deactivated. The Buckner Building, now a hollow concrete skeleton awaiting renovation, was then the primary residence: A city under one roof, it held 1,000 apartments, a hospital, school, library, bank, restaurants, shops, radio station, theater, bowling alley, gymnasium, swimming pool, jail, and morgue.

   Although ferries and summer cruise ships tie up in Whittier, the community—located 75 miles southeast of Anchorage—really cannot be considered more than a jumping-off place. Most activities in Whittier are of the outdoor variety, mainly hiking and boating. But these are often put on hold by days on end of wind gusting to 90 m.p.h. (chiefly in winter) and an average annual precipitation of 173 inches, including 22 feet of snow.

   If you're inclined to tarry in Whittier, you can get information at the **information kiosk** at the Harbor Triangle or the **City Office** in Begich Towers (tel. 907/472-2327).

WHAT TO SEE & DO

The **Whittier Historical & Fine Arts Museum,** on the first floor of the Towers, is open on Monday, Wednesday, and Friday through Sunday from 1 to 6pm.

   Most visitors to Whittier restrict their wanderings to the shoreward area between the railroad tracks, ferry dock, and small-boat harbor. Numerous fishing and cruise boats and sailing charters operate out of the harbor, frequently run by weekend sailors commuting from Anchorage. The **Harbor Office** (tel. 907/472-2330) can give you a full list and make recommendations depending on your needs and desires.

   Alaskan Wilderness Sailing Safaris, P.O. Box 1313, Valdez, AK 99686 (tel. 907/835-5175), offers a variety of sailing options, from skippered charters to bareboat flotillas. Experienced skippers and naturalist guide service is provided. Skippered trips range from $340 per person for 3 days to $1,420 per person for 10 days. Bareboat flotillas, where you have the privacy of your own vessel but sail in a group, range from $550 per person for 3 days to $2,700 per person for 10 days. Voyages are planned from mid-May into September. Write or call for details. **Sound Water Adventures,**

P.O. Box 652, Whittier, AK 99693 (tel. 907/472-2455), provides casual, personalized service on its 12-person, disabled-accessible vessel. Tours of four hours to overnight are led by experienced naturalists and navigators.

Whittier is a point of departure for sea kayaking. Folks aged 12–70 have enjoyed paddling through the quiet coves and bays of the sound from May until September. **Prince William Sound Kayak Center** (tel. 907/472-2452) rents single kayaks for $35 per day and doubles for $55 per day. For escorted trips, contact their Anchorage office at 2205 E. Tudor Rd., Anchorage, AK 99501 (tel. 907/562-2866). Guided trips are not regularly scheduled, but escorts are provided on a limited basis.

The world's largest **kittiwake rookery** is just across Passage Canal from Whittier, beside a glacier-fed cascade. For many boaters, including ferries and cruise liners, the rookery is the first or last stop before arriving in, or after departing from, Whittier.

WHERE TO STAY

The two visitor accommodations are *not* in Begich Towers.

SPORTSMAN'S INN, 88 Front St. (P.O. Box 698), Whittier, AK 99693. Tel. 907/472-2352. 20 rms (all with bath). TV TEL
$ Rates: $56 single or double. AE, MC, V.
Located on a low bluff overlooking the sea-train terminal, the Sportsman's has a guest laundry and sauna in addition to its 20 guest rooms. It has a pleasant restaurant that's open 24 hours a day and a bar open until midnight.

ANCHOR INN, Whittier St. (P.O. Box 746), Whittier, AK 99693. Tel. 907/472-2354. 18 rms (all with bath). TV TEL
$ Rates: $50 single. Additional person $5 extra; room with kitchenette $5 extra. AE, MC, V.
Rooms at the Anchor Inn, situated between Begich Towers and the railroad shop, belie the somewhat weathered outward appearance of the building. Some rooms have kitchenettes and waterbeds. There is an upper-floor lounge with good views of the water and a full-service restaurant open 24 hours in the summer. A grocery store and laundrette are on the premises.

WHERE TO DINE

The **Sportsman's Inn** and the **Anchor Inn** are the places to go for restaurant food in Whittier. For deli-style food and liquor sales, try **Irma's Outpost,** at the Harbor Triangle (tel. 907/472-2461). Irma's will provide orders to go and charter lunches on request.

EN ROUTE TO VALDEZ

The ✪ **Columbia Glacier** is so large—440 square miles in area—that to see the entire ice flow you'd have to be a good distance above it in a plane or helicopter. Cruise boats can approach the glacial terminus to within about half a mile; even from there, the thunder of ice chunks falling from its 200-foot cliff face is almost deafening. Ferries are restricted from approaching within 3½ miles.

At the face of the glacier, Columbia Bay is teeming with life. Great numbers of sea mammals and birds are drawn by an abundance of plankton, microscopic animal and plant life swarming amid the glacial debris. Harbor seals are the most photographed: Adults and young pups are seen by the hundreds swimming in the near-freezing water or reclining on ice floes. There are also a great many bald eagles, kittiwakes, and gulls, and an occasional sea otter.

The glacier starts just beneath the summit of 12,023-foot Mount Witherspoon in the Chugach Mountains. The weight of 100 feet of annual snowfall squeezes it out of its icefield much like toothpaste from a tube, and gravity does the rest. The ice is so densely compacted that it absorbs every color but blue, which is reflected back when the glacier is fractured.

But after nearly two centuries of remarkable stability, the glacier began to retreat in the 1970s. As it recedes deeper back into its fjord, an increased number of icebergs break off into the sound—about 10 million tons of ice daily, geologists estimate. At its current rate of retreat, the Columbia Glacier may be only 25 miles long (instead of the present 40) by the third decade of the 21st century.

VALDEZ

They call it the "Switzerland of Alaska," though in many regards Valdez (say "Val-*deez*") is more reminiscent of Norway. Surrounded by steep mountains dropping into fjordlike Port Valdez Bay, it is at once a gateway to the marine world of Prince William Sound and the alpine wonderland of Thompson Pass and the Chugach Mountains. Since the mid-1970s it has also been a busy oil port, the southern terminus of the Trans Alaska Pipeline.

A Hispanic name was pinned on Valdez in 1790 when Spanish-Mexican caravels discovered the inlet, but no real effort was made to settle the fjord until the Klondike gold rush of 1897 and 1898 sent thousands of stampeders scampering through Thompson Pass toward the Yukon. After a road was pushed through to Fairbanks at the turn of the century, Alaskans quickly established the value of Valdez's deep-water, ice-free port. The town grew and flourished.

Then came the Good Friday earthquake of 1964. Valdez was literally wiped off the map by the tremor and a series of tidal waves. Few buildings were left standing as the surviving population fled to higher ground. There was little question in their mind but to rebuild the town, though the old site at the tip of the bay was no longer appropriate. A new town site was chosen four miles up the north shore. With the construction of the pipeline terminal across the bay and the growth of tourism in Prince William Sound, the economy again boomed. Recently the town has added a $51-million terminal and a $7-million civic center.

Valdez's climate is quite mild, with midsummer temperatures in the 50s and 60s, midwinter temps in the 20s. Rainfall is fairly heavy in the spring and summer (though not as heavy as in Whittier), while snow falls from October to April.

ORIENTATION & ESSENTIAL INFORMATION

As the Richardson Highway enters Valdez from the east, it becomes **Egan Drive,** the town's main street, at the intersection of Meals Avenue. (William Egan, Alaska's first state governor, was born and raised in Valdez.) At the other end of downtown, two long blocks away, **Hazelet Avenue** runs north-south toward Mineral Creek. The ferry terminal is near the south (bay) end of Hazelet. The boat harbor faces North Harbor Drive, which runs parallel to Egan Drive two blocks south via Meals. **Valdez Airport** is about four miles east of town, near the old town site. The Alyeska Pipeline Terminal is south across Port Valdez Bay, about 4 miles by boat but 13 by road.

The **Valdez Convention and Visitors Bureau,** P.O. Box 1603, Valdez, AK 99686 (tel. 907/835-2984), has its main offices at 200 Chenega Ave., across from City Hall. The bureau also operates a **visitor information center** (tel. 835-INFO) during the summer months. There is a 24-hour recorded **"hotline" for parks and recreation information** (tel. 835-2555). You can get city information from the **Valdez Chamber of Commerce,** P.O. Box 512, Valdez, AK 99686 (tel. 907/835-2330).

Valdez has a hospital, **Valdez Community Hospital** (tel. 835-2249), and a weekly newspaper, the *Valdez Vanguard.*

There's one taxi service in town, **Valdez Yellow Cab** (tel. 835-2500), and three car-rental outfits: **AAA Auto Rentals** (tel. 835-5282 or 835-2774), **Avis** (tel. 835-4774), and **Valdez U-Drive Car Rental** (tel. 835-4402), at the airport. In addition to **ERA** (tel. 835-2636), Valdez Airport is served by **Valdez Aero Service** (tel. 835-2453). Many people arrive in town by ferry on the Alaska Marine Highway System (tel. 835-4436) or by bus aboard **Alaskon Express** (tel. toll free 800/248-7598) or **Caribou Express** (tel. 907/235-2350).

WHAT TO SEE & DO
Sights and Attractions

Aside from fishing derbies, there are two important annual festivities. **Gold Rush Days,** held for five days through the second weekend of August, includes a parade, dance, casino night, and community fish fry. **Winter Carnival,** lasting five days in March, takes advantage of the heavy snowfall while celebrating the beginning of spring. Other special occasions include the **Ice Climbing Festival,** in February over President's Day weekend; the **World Extreme Skiing Championships** in April; and the **Whitewater Weekend** in early June. In May 1992, the first annual **Royal Flush Regatta**—a floating poker game and water carnival—was held.

The Valdez walking tour brochure produced by the Convention and Visitors Bureau pinpoints some of the 50 or so buildings that were moved from the old town site after the 1964 earthquake. But there's little to be seen on the **Old Town Site.** A plaque, dedicated to those who lost their lives during the '64 quake is located at the end of the road.

The **Valdez Civic Center,** overlooking the ferry dock on Clifton Avenue near Hazelet (tel. 835-4440), is a state-of-the-art convention and performing arts center. Nearby is a **U.S. Coast Guard Station,** 105 Clifton Dr. A **Native head** sculpted from wood, standing in front of Prince William Sound Community College on Pioneer Avenue, is one of a planned series in all 50 states of sculptures on a Native theme by Peter Toth.

One mile east of the Alyeska Pipeline Terminal (see below) is the **Solomon Gulch Salmon Hatchery,** on Dayville Road. The Valdez Fisheries Development Association (tel. 835-2594) gives guided tours by appointment. Visiting hours are 8am to 5pm daily.

If you're interested in a tour by car, several drives can be recommended to visitors who appreciate alpine scenery. The narrow **Mineral Creek Canyon** road winds 5½ miles north to sites of gold- and copper-mining endeavors. Seven miles from Valdez, up the airport road, is the rapidly receding **Valdez Glacier.** The first miners' trail to the Copper River Basin and interior went over this glacier. Thirteen miles east of Valdez along the Richardson Highway is the beginning of sheer **Keystone Canyon** with its two beautiful waterfalls, Bridal Veil Falls and Horsetail Falls. **Thompson Pass,** 24 miles from (and 2,771 feet above) Valdez, has wildflower meadows in spring and summer, downhill skiing in winter, and always a fine scenic overlook.

VALDEZ MUSEUM, 217 Egan Dr., at Chenega Ave. Tel. 835-2764.

Located in downtown Valdez, this is one of the best small museums in Alaska. Even if you think you have little interest in local history, go. Valdez senior citizens have volunteered to make three of the exhibits come alive—a wood carver in a sportsman's display, a seamstress in a sewing room, and a bartender (serving apple juice) across a bar rescued from the Pinzon Hotel in Old Valdez. Other exhibits include early 20th-century fire trucks and firefighting equipment in almost mint condition, mining tools in an old cabin, a scale model of the pipeline terminal across the bay, and earthquake information and photos.

Admission: $2 adults, free for children.

Open: Mid-May to mid-Sept, daily 10am–6pm; mid-Sept to mid-May, Tues–Sat 10am–6pm.

ALYESKA PIPELINE TERMINAL, c/o Alyeska Pipeline Service, Valdez Airport. Tel. 835-2686 or 235-6983.

Next to the Columbia Glacier, Valdez's most popular attraction is the Alyeska Pipeline Terminal. The drive to the terminal is an interesting one, and there are interpretive signs outside the facility describing operations, but only authorized bus tours may enter the terminal. (Bus service from the airport is free.) There's a visitor information office at the outer gate where interpretive displays and brochures are available for the non-engineers among us, and where almost any question regarding the pipeline and oil shipment can be answered.

When crude oil arrives at the terminal after completing its 800-mile journey from

Prudhoe Bay, it is temporarily stored here in 18 tanks (each with a capacity of 510,000 barrels) until it's loaded onto tankers. That's a total storage capacity of 378 million gallons of oil. Tankers of 50,000–265,000 deadweight tons dock at four berths; oil is gravity-fed to them through hydraulically controlled metal arms with loading rates up to 110,000 barrels an hour. The arms simultaneously pump out ship-ballast water.

You may be impressed to see the precautions taken to minimize the effects of natural disasters or those caused by human error. There are oil-spill cleanup equipment, vapor recovery systems, facilities for the treatment of sewage, water and ballast water, firefighting equipment, and more. (After the 1989 *Exxon Valdez* oil spill, however, many question whether these precautions are sufficient.)

Even more fascinating is the Operations Control Center, from which the entire 800-mile pipeline system is monitored and directed by remote control. Computer consoles with data displays and pushbutton controls enable pipeline controllers to initiate actions at every working level, including emergency procedures where necessary. The system depends on a microwave communications network with satellite backup.

Only 300 men and women are currently employed at the marine terminal, down from the 3,500 who occupied the Alyeska barracks during mid-1970s construction. But the others haven't been forgotten. All the 70,000 people who worked on the pipeline are commemorated in the **Pipeline Monument,** a 13-foot bronze casting just outside the terminal gate. Sculptor Malcolm Alexander's acclaimed work, commissioned in 1977 and completed in 1980, depicts a surveyor, engineer, welder, teamster, and workman.

Admission: Free.

Open: Memorial Day–Labor Day, daily 8am–8pm; off-season, Mon–Fri 8am–8pm. **Directions:** Drive seven miles east on the Richardson Highway and turn west (down the south shore of Port Valdez Bay) on Dayville Road for six miles.

Organized Tours

Gray Line of Alaska, with travel desks in the Westmark Valdez and Westmark Inn (see "Where to Stay," below), has two tours. A two-hour tour of the Alyeska Pipeline marine terminal—offered daily at 7pm, mid-May to mid-September—costs $19 for adults, $8.50 for children under 12. A full-day Columbia Glacier cruise, priced at $79 full fare, includes the 13-hour round-trip passage to Whittier via the Columbia Glacier with two stops, with the separate pipeline terminal tour thrown in.

Valdez Sightseeing Tours (tel. 835-4776 or 835-2500) is the only agency giving land tours of the entire Valdez area. Day tours take in the old town, Keystone Canyon, and Worthington Glacier, while evening tours visit the Solomon Gulch Hatchery.

The most adventuresome local charter-boat operator is Stan Stephens, captain of the custom-built 80-foot *Glacier Spirit.* **Stan Stephens Charters,** P.O. Box 1297, Valdez, AK 99686 (tel. 835-4731), offers a wide variety of waterborne opportunities, from daily Columbia Glacier cruises (leaving the Westmark Dock at 1pm, Memorial Day to Labor Day) for $87.50 ($59.50 for children), to chartered dinner parties and wildlife cruises up to 10 days long. Hunting and fishing expeditions are available throughout the year, except February through April when Stephens operates cross-country ski charters to remote parts of Prince William Sound.

Local air taxis like **Ketchum Air Service** (tel. 835-3789) and **Alpine Aviation Adventures** (tel. 835-4304) will fly you over the Columbia and other glaciers for rates beginning at $149 per person. An even more spectacular way to see the Columbia Glacier is aboard a helicopter. A 50-minute tour with ✪ **ERA Helicopters** (tel. 835-2595), costs $145 per person (two-person minimum). My flight over the glacier was one of the most awe-inspiring experiences I have had in Alaska, one that I highly recommend.

Sports and Recreation

For general information, call the 24-hour activity hotline sponsored by the **Valdez Parks and Recreation Department** (tel. 835-2555). The recorded information will include schedules for open **swimming** at Valdez High School on Robe River Drive; **racquetball** at Hermon Hutchins Grade School on West Klutina Drive; and many other activities, including the local **rifle range.** The Black Gold Park Strip on the west side of Valdez off Cottonwood Drive has **tennis, basketball,** and **volleyball courts** and some **horseshoe pits. Softball** fields are east of town at Mile 1.5 on Richardson Highway. A **bicycle path** parallels the highway for several miles.

FISHING   The waters of Valdez Arm are rich in sea life. Five species of salmon, halibut, red snapper, rock bass, ling cod, and gray cod are sought by fishermen in the salt water, while Dolly Varden and rainbow trout are pursued in Robe Lake and the Robe and Lowe Rivers. Shrimp and crab are also popular catches, and there are excellent clamming beaches. A **halibut derby** is held in late May or early June, a **pink salmon derby** is held over the Fourth of July weekend, and a **silver salmon derby** attracts fishermen from all over Alaska during the month of August.

More than a dozen private operators charter boats from the small-boat harbor for day trips and longer excursions; there's very little difference between them. You can either visit the boats in the harbor and book a trip right at the docks, or consult an outdoor store like **Hook, Line and Sinker** (tel. 835-4410) or **Beaver Sports** (tel. 835-4727). They can advise you on private boat rental and also sell licenses.

HIKING   The possibilities are almost endless. Two favorite areas are **Mineral Creek Canyon,** where a trail at the end of the rutted 5½-mile road leads an additional mile to an abandoned gold stamp mill, and 1½-miles farther to the foot of the Mineral Creek Glacier; and the **Worthington Glacier,** accessible by a short road and trail off Keystone Canyon.

RAFTING & KAYAKING   The favorite excursion offered by Mike Buck's **Keystone Raft & Kayak Adventures,** P.O. Box 1486, Valdez, AK 99686 (tel. 835-2606), is a short but spectacular run down the Lowe River, through the precipitous Class III Keystone Canyon. Rafters cover 6 miles of river past Bridal Veil and Horsetail Falls in one hour, starting 17 miles east of Valdez. There are several trips a day between June 10 and September 8, at a rate of $30 for adults, $20 for children. They also offer a five-day Chitina River trip. All transporation is provided, plus rubber boats, rain suits, and lifejackets. Expect to get wet anyway. **Anadyr Sea Kayaking Adventures,** P.O. Box 1821, Valdez, AK 99686 (tel. 835-2814), offers day trips to Shoop Glacier, Columbia Glacier and Galena Bay, as well as extended trips.

WINTER SPORTS   One thing there's never any shortage of in Valdez is snow. An average of 25–30 feet falls on the city annually (though not all at once). Thompson Pass once received 81 feet of snow in a winter, and 5 feet in a single 24-hour period. So the popularity of winter sports in Valdez comes as no surprise.

Cross-country **skiing** is probably no. 1 on the list. There are trails and meadows everywhere; the Mineral Creek Canyon road is kept groomed in winter. East of town, on Salmonberry Hill at Mile 5.5 on Richardson Highway, is a short poma lift and warming hut for beginning skiers. Advanced skiers go to Thompson Pass: There are no lifts, but a 2,000-foot car shuttle works just as well, and the powder is always good. Thompson Pass is also popular for **snowmobiling** and **dog sledding,** while **ice climbing** is the domain of an adventuresome few in Keystone Canyon.

WHERE TO STAY

The hospitality industry in Valdez is highly seasonal. Hotels jack their prices up $30–$50 a room during the summer season—and they get it, no problem.

You could also try a bed-and-breakfast—the B&B business has burgeoned so rapidly in Valdez that the visitors bureau now lists 51 establishments. **One Call Does It All** (tel. 835-4988) has a free reservation service for B&B accommodations.

There are also three Valdez camper parks near the small-boat harbor. **Sea Otter RV Park,** on the South Harbor Drive spit (P.O. Box 947), Valdez, AK 99686 (tel. 907/835-2787), has restrooms, showers, a laundry, and dump station. Full hookups are $17 a day; electric only, $14. **Bearpaw Camper Park,** North Harbor Drive (P.O. Box 93), Valdez, AK 99686 (tel. 907/835-4558), has similar facilities and rates, but without the sea life that visits the end of the spit. **Eagle Claw RV Park,** at the corner of Richardson Highway and Pioneer Drive (P.O. Box 610), Valdez, AK 99686 (tel. 907/835-2373), has full and partial hookups, tent camping, showers, bicycle rentals, and a booking service.

The city operates the 101-site **Valdez Glacier Campground,** six miles from town at the end of the airport road. You'll find tap water, firepits, picnic tables, and outhouses.

Tax   All room charges are subject to a 6% local bed tax.

TOTEM INN, Mile 0.2, Richardson Hwy. (P.O. Box 648), Valdez, AK 99686. Tel. 907/835-4443. 27 rms (all with bath). TV TEL

$ Rates: May–Sept, $95 single or double. Oct–Apr, $45 single; $50 double. AE, MC, V.

This may be one of Valdez's better bargains, especially in the off-season. With big-game heads mounted on the walls surrounding the restaurant–cum–reception area and a big fireplace to one side, it looks for all the world like a hunting lodge. Aquariums and totem poles add interesting touches to the dimly lit main room. The guest rooms, somewhat worn, are decorated in blues and whites; each has a queen-size bed, comfortable older furnishings, electric heat, and a small refrigerator. A guest laundry is free of charge; bring your own soap. Dinners are served in a fully licensed restaurant, with most entrees in the $17 range. A local seafood platter is the specialty of the house.

VALDEZ MOTEL, 136 Egan Dr. (P.O. Box 65), Valdez, AK 99686. Tel. 907/835-4444. 15 rms (all with bath). TV TEL

$ Rates: May–Sept, $90 single; $95 double. Oct–Apr, $60 single or double. AE, DISC, MC, V.

The Valdez Motel is Valdez's oldest-existing accommodation (it had been the Port of Valdez Hotel in the old town prior to the quake) and it's one of the least expensive during the tourist season. The wood-paneled rooms contain two twins or a king-size bed, essential furnishings, courtesy coffee, and steam heating. Three rooms have small kitchenettes.

VILLAGE INN, 201 Meals Ave. (P.O. Box 365), Valdez, AK 99686. Tel. 907/835-4445. Fax 907/835-2437. 100 rms (all with bath), 16 cottages. TV TEL

$ Rates: May–Sept, $109 single; $119 double. Oct–Apr, $78 single; $88 double. Year-round, $85 cottage; $135 two-bedroom condo. AE, DC, DISC, MC, V.

The Village Inn is a step down from the Westmark Inn in standard but not in facilities. There are standard units with two double beds and the usual furnishings in a decor of earth tones and natural wood. Each room has electric heat. Also rented are 16 six-person rustic cottages (all without phones, some without TVs) and two-bedroom condominium units just outside town. Within the building are the Body Works Spa and Fitness Center, offering hotel guests a reduced rate; two electronic Par-T-Golf courses; a sauna; and a courtesy car. Alaska Sightseeing Tours books its clients at this hotel.

Next door to the Village Inn, under the same management, the Sugarloaf Restaurant and Saloon (tel. 835-4600) has all-you-can-eat breakfasts for $7.95. It's usually open for lunch, but call ahead to make sure. There's a dinner buffet for $12.95 or an à la carte menu.

WESTMARK INN, 208 Egan Dr. (P.O. Box 1915), Valdez, AK 99686. Tel. 907/835-4485, or toll free 800/544-2206. Fax 907/835-2308. 40 rms (all with bath). TV TEL

$ Rates: Late May to mid-Sept, $124 single; $134 double. AE, DC, DISC, MC, V.
Closed: Mid-Sept to late May.

This is a seasonal property with a clientele that is 80% tour groups, most of them booked with Westours. It also serves as overflow accommodations for the Westmark

Valdez. It has several things in its favor, not least a spacious, comfortable lobby—the only one in Valdez. The rooms are nicely appointed in orange tones with white trim and prints of watercolors on the walls. Each room has two double beds and other standard furnishings, plus electric heating. Amenities include shampoo, hand lotion, and a vanity kit.

The restaurant, open for three meals daily, specializes in fresh seafood, with dinners in the $15–$20 range. There's also a bar and a deli.

WESTMARK VALDEZ, 100 Fidalgo Dr. (P.O. Box 468), Valdez, AK 99686. Tel. 907/835-4391, or toll free 800/544-0970, 800/478-1111 in Alaska. Fax 907/835-2308. 98 rms (all with bath). TV TEL
$ Rates: May–Sept, $118 single; $125 double. Oct–Apr, $78 single; $88 double. AE, DC, DISC, MC, V.

The town's largest hotel is guaranteed to be full most of the summer. Each room has two double beds, a four-drawer dresser, dressing table, and thermostat-controlled hot-water heating. The rooms, with brown carpets, red-purple bedspreads (it works), and cream-colored fabric walls, are well lit.

The Captain's Table restaurant, overlooking the harbor, offers a breakfast buffet ($7.95) and à la carte breakfasts after 9:30am; and full dinners, most in the $16–$21 range. It's open daily from 6am to 11pm in summer, 6:30am to 9pm in winter. The adjoining Wheelhouse Lounge, open daily from 11am to 1am, has a nautical theme underscored by a collection of oil supertankers' lifebuoys.

WHERE TO DINE

When Valdezans go out for dinner, it's likely they'll dine at one of the hotels—commonly the Westmark Valdez or the Totem Inn. Other establishments are listed below.

ALASKA HALIBUT HOUSE, Meals Ave. and Fairbanks Dr. Tel. 835-2788.
Cuisine: SEAFOOD. **Reservations:** Not required.
$ Prices: Breakfast $1.85–$5.75; lunch/dinner $2.95–$7.75. No credit cards.
Open: Breakfast daily 6–10:30am; lunch/dinner daily 11am–11pm.
Near the center of town, this informal dine-in or take-out restaurant is known for its seafood-and-chips baskets with halibut or prawns. It's also the place to come for a burger and shake, or even a low-price salad bar. Breakfast items include cinnamon rolls and breakfast sandwiches, with eggs and choice of meat. Senior discounts are available.

FU KUNG, 203 Kobuk St. Tel. 835-5255.
Cuisine: CHINESE. **Reservations:** Recommended.
$ Prices: Appetizers $1.50–$9.95; main courses $8.50–$14.95; lunch $6.25–$6.75. MC.
Open: Mon–Sat 11:30am–11pm, Sun 5–11pm.
Mandarin and Szechuan dishes are the specialty here, along with a few Korean dishes. A choice of luncheon specials is served with soup, rice, salad, and choice of appetizers. Dinner entrees include beef, poultry, and seafood dishes, such as Mandarin beef with black-bean sauce and king crab with ginger-scallion sauce. Take-out service is available.

PIPELINE CLUB, 112 Egan Dr. Tel. 835-4891.
Cuisine: STEAK/SEAFOOD. **Reservations:** Recommended.
$ Prices: Appetizers $4.25–$11.25; main courses $9–$24; breakfast/lunch $6.50–$10.75. AE, DC, DISC, MC, V.
Open: Lunch daily 6am–2:30pm; dinner daily 5–11pm (to midnight on summer weekends).
The Pipeline Club is first and foremost a steakhouse, with red upholstery and brick

walls, and atmospheric dim lighting. Steak and eggs costs $10.75 for breakfast; a steak sandwich is $10.25 for lunch. For dinner, the management recommends the Pipeline pupus, sliced steak with sautéed bell peppers, onions, tomatoes, and soy sauce; the Pipeliner, a 14-ounce New York steak; or the prime rib, served on Friday, Saturday, and Sunday only. There are also cheaper meals like halibut and chips and spaghetti. The lounge, which keeps kicking till 5am, is a great place to meet local Valdezans and hear some impromptu musical talent.

PIZZA PALACE, 201 N. Harbor Dr. Tel. 835-2365 or 835-4686.
   Cuisine: INTERNATIONAL. **Reservations:** Required for parties of seven or more.
$ Prices: Appetizers $1.75–$5.95; main courses $8.95–$14.95. MC, V.
   Open: Daily 11am–11pm.
The Pizza Palace is a lot of fun simply for the decor: old newspapers on the walls, photos of the earthquake, a fine doll collection, and more. The food is good too. The menu at this family restaurant offers a lot of variety: Italian food, Mexican food, Greek food, steaks, seafood, sandwiches. A large pizza is generally around $16, depending on the toppings, and a large pizza with the works costs $24.95. Take-out service is available.

CORDOVA

The charming community of Cordova is nestled between dense evergreen forests and the rocky peaks of the Chugach Mountains at the eastern end of Prince William Sound. Surrounded by water—Orca Inlet is to the west, freshwater Eyak Lake to the east—it comes as no surprise that most of its 2,504 residents depend on fishing for their livelihood. About 20 miles east of town is the Copper River Delta, one of the richest salmon-spawning grounds in the world. Cordova is also a regional headquarters for the Chugach National Forest and a major wildlife-viewing destination.

Cordova's raison d'être was copper—the mineral and the river. The discovery in 1889 of a major copper vein on the Chitina River, a tributary of the Copper, created a need for an ice-free port and railroad center. A small Orca Inlet cannery site filled the bill. Construction of the Copper River & Northwestern Railway began in 1906 with the arrival of a steamship-load of materials at the new town site. It was completed in 1911, running 196 miles up the Copper River to the Chitina and on to the great Kennicott mine.

Once Cordova was established as a railroad town, fishing gradually grew in importance. When the Kennicott mine shut down in 1938, fishing kept Cordova from becoming a ghost town. Miles of track were sold for scrap iron, and the Copper River Highway was laid on the old rail bed. Intended to link Cordova by road with the rest of the state, it was started from both ends, but before the ends could join, the 1964 earthquake destroyed the Million Dollar Bridge across the Copper River (downtown survived the quake). Work on the road had finally been scheduled for completion in 1993.

The climate is typical of Prince William Sound—mild and wet. Summer temperatures average in the 50s and low 60s, winter temperatures in the 20s. Average annual precipitation is 167 inches, much of it snow and most of it falling in the winter and spring, especially in March and April.

ORIENTATION & ESSENTIAL INFORMATION

It's hard to get lost in Cordova. **First Street,** the main drag through the two blocks of downtown, continues north about a mile to the state ferry dock, and south (then east) to become the Copper River Highway. It looks west, across the boat harbor to Orca Inlet and Spike Island. One block below it, running up against the harbor, is **Railroad Avenue.** Second Street is a block east and uphill. **Council Avenue** connects the three. Eyak Lake is half a mile east and a few hundred feet higher than downtown.

The **Cordova Chamber of Commerce,** P.O. Box 99, Cordova, AK 99574 (tel.

907/424-7260), has an office in the National Bank of Alaska Building on 1st Street that provides visitor information. When that office is closed, ask for assistance at the **Cordova Museum,** 1st Street near Adams Avenue (tel. 424-7443).

Cordova has a weekly newspaper, the **Cordova Times,** and a beautiful 22-bed hospital, the **Cordova Community Hospital,** on Railroad Row near 2nd Street (tel. 424-8000; dial **911** in an emergency).

Cordova Airport is 13 miles east on the Copper River Highway. It's served from Anchorage and Juneau by **Alaska Airlines** (tel. 424-7151) and **MarkAir** (tel. 907/424-5982, or toll free 800/426-6784, 800/478-0800 in Alaska). Three air-charter services are based at the gravel city airstrip on Eyak Lake—**Fishing and Flying** (tel. 424-3324), **Chitina Air Service** (tel. 424-3524), and **Cordova Air** (tel. 424-3289). Their prices run between $250 and $350 an hour for a four- or six-seater.

For ferry arrival and departure times, call the **Alaska Marine Highway System** (tel. 907/424-7333, or toll free 800/642-0066).

Harbor Cab (tel. 424-7575) and **A Cab** (tel. 424-7131) will get you around town. **Copper River Express** (tel. 424-5463) meets Alaska Marine Highway ferries and Alaska Airlines flights as a matter of course, and others by special arrangement. Car rentals are available from the town's major motel, the **Reluctant Fisherman** (tel. 424-3272), and **Imperial Car Rental** (tel. 424-3201).

WHAT TO SEE & DO
Sights and Attractions

The year's big event is the ✪ **Cordova Iceworm Festival,** held Thursday through Sunday of the first full weekend of February. Festivities include a boat parade and the blessing of the fleet, art exhibits, carnivals, square dances, and a grand parade highlighted by the annual appearance of the many-legged Cordova Iceworm. In fact, the rarely seen iceworm (*Mesenchytraeus solifugus*) is only slightly larger than microscopic in size. It feeds on pollen carried to the surface of glacial ice, but its legend is far greater than its reality. Turn-of-the-century sourdoughs frightened greenhorns with overblown tales about the worms, and poet Robert Service immortalized the creatures with a ballad about the iceworm cocktail. Cordova's unique railroad and mining history is celebrated on **Copper Day,** the second Saturday in April.

Start your visit to Cordova by following the **walking tour** compiled by the Cordova Historical Society. Brochures are available from the chamber of commerce or city offices.

The tour starts at the Centennial Building, 1st Street and Adams Avenue, built in 1967 to house the city museum and library. Before you begin, spend some time in the **Cordova Museum** (tel. 424-7443). The eclectic collection has brought together many bits and pieces of memorabilia relating to local history, including some wonderful early 20th-century photographs. You'll also find a Native canoe, an enormous lighthouse lens, a beaver-paw tobacco pouch, a copper still, and a giant harmonica. You can learn all you'd ever care to know about the tiny iceworm and the festival created in its name in 1961. The museum is open Tuesday through Sunday from 1 to 5pm with extended hours on Saturday for the showing of a film, *The Cordova Story,* at 7:30pm.

Climb Adams Avenue to 2nd Street and the historic **Red Dragon Mission** and **St. George's Episcopal Church.** Founded in 1908 and 1919, respectively, to bring religion to the miners and railroad workers, they are still in active use today. Both are listed on the National Register of Historic Sites.

Just north on 2nd Street, in the Federal Building, is the Cordova district office of the **U.S. Forest Service,** P.O. Box 280, Cordova, AK 99574 (tel. 424-7661). Nearly 2.7 million acres of Chugach National Forest are administered from here. Wildlife habitat, waterfowl-nesting areas, and recreation lands are managed and protected. The rangers are happy to share their knowledge of recreational opportunities and wildlife viewing Monday through Friday from 7:30am to 5pm.

Directly west two blocks is the **small-boat harbor,** home of Prince William

Sound's largest commercial fishing fleet. It's fun to browse down the docks and chat with fishermen. Near the Harbormaster's Office (tel. 424-3351) on the South Containment Field is the **Cordova Fishermen's Memorial,** a bronze statue by sculptor Joan Bugbee Jackson dedicated in 1985 to all Cordova fishermen who have lost their lives at sea. Called *The Southeasterly,* it depicts a raincoated pilot at the helm of his boat, shaking his fist at the weather with a look of frightened rage.

Facing the harbor on Breakwater Avenue is the **Bahay Kubo Gallery** (tel. 424-5842), Cordova's best art gallery and gift shop. The work of many local artists, sculptors, photographers, and writers is displayed and sold here.

On the north side of the harbor are several **canneries,** which will arrange tours on request. South of the harbor near Odiak Slough is the **Eyak Packing Company** (tel. 424-5300), a family-operated smokery which also offers tours.

Photographer Rose Arvidson and her husband, Bob, have taken their beachfront property on Whitshed Road and created a little park, **Odiak Gardens,** on a promontory jutting into Orca Inlet. You'll see it from several vantage points: a small lighthouse, ship's mast, and pavilion surrounded by flowers. Visitors are welcome.

Behind the city, at the end of Ski Hill Road off upper Council Avenue, is the **Eyak Ski Hill,** on the slopes of Mount Eyak. The views of Prince William Sound and downtown Cordova are outstanding here.

Eyak Lake, the beautiful glacier-fed lake on the east side of Cordova, is a real treat. Waterfalls cascade down the sides of surrounding mountains into its basin and trumpeter swans feed year-round near the lake outlet. Brown bear can often be seen in early summer pursuing spawning salmon at the lake's north end, where it's fed by Power Creek. The Eyak River, which flows from the Y-shaped lake's east end to the Gulf of Alaska, is a popular scenic route for kayakers, canoeists, and hikers.

At the west end of Eyak Lake, nearest the city, is **Nirvana Park,** a meditative retreat built in the 1930s by eccentric Henry Feldman. The **Pioneer Cemetery** is across Lake Avenue. The **Eyak Village Building,** at Chase Avenue and LeFevre Road, which serves as headquarters for the Eyak Native Corporation, displays artifacts Monday through Friday from 9am to 5pm, and the coffee pot is always on.

Sports and Recreation

The **Bob Korn Memorial Swimming Pool,** a five-lane, Olympic-size pool on Railroad Avenue (tel. 424-7200), has lockers and shower facilities, classes, and open swim times. The **Bidarki Recreation Center,** in the old city hall at 2nd Street and Council Avenue (tel. 424-7282 or 424-3277), has a weight room and gymnasium with public hours, equipment rentals, and aerobics classes. Usual hours are 2 to 10pm Monday through Saturday. The **Cordova Trap & Gun Club** has a shooting range on Sheridan Glacier Road. **Whiskey Ridge Cycle Shop** (tel. 424-3354) rents bicycles.

FISHING The possibilities are almost endless. Commercial fishermen gill-net for red and king salmon in the Copper River Delta, and purse-seine for pink and chum salmon in the sound. Silver salmon fishing is excellent right from the ferry dock. Halibut, herring, crabs, shrimp, and clams are other easily found seafoods.

Eyak Lake is closed to salmon fishing, but like many other freshwater lakes and rivers, is open year-round to Dolly Varden and cutthroat trout fishing—including in winter for ice fishing.

Fishing-guide services based in Cordova include the **M.V. Auklet** (tel. 424-7602), **Cordova Charters** (tel. 424-5895), and **Lucky Strike Charters** (tel. 424-3234).

HIKING Surrounded as Cordova is by national forest lands, there's no shortage of trails. Many folks enjoy walking the mile from road's end onto the **Sheridan Glacier.** The 3.7-mile **Lake Elsner Loop Trail** starts from Cabin Lake, at the Eyak Corporation campground near the airport. The **Crater Lake Trail** up the steep slopes of Mount Eyak is one of the most accessible and worthwhile for day trekkers. About 2½ miles long, it begins at Skater's Cabin, just past the city airport on Power Creek Road.

When hiking on the Copper River Flats or other boggy areas, the terrain may demand the use of rubber boots as well as sturdier hiking shoes. No matter where you're hiking, be on the lookout for bears and know what to do if you encounter one.

HUNTING   Moose, bear, deer, mountain goat, ducks, and geese are the most commonly sought species. Get full information on license fees and hunting seasons from the **Alaska Department of Fish and Game,** P.O. Box 669, Cordova, AK 99574 (tel. 907/424-3215).

WINTER SPORTS   **Mount Eyak Ski Area,** at the top of Ski Hill Road off upper Council Avenue (tel. 424-7766), has a 3,600-foot chair lift that's a true relic: It formerly operated at Sun Valley, Idaho, where it was erected in the 1930s as one of the first ski lifts in the western United States. Today the city-owned lift runs up Tripod Hill on Mount Eyak. The small but challenging ski area also has a beginners' rope tow and ski school. There's ice skating on Lake Eyak, and cross-country skiing is great on the lake or in the Copper River Flats.

WHERE TO STAY

In addition to the establishments listed below, the City of Cordova has a campground, the **Odiak Camper Park,** on Whitshed Road (P.O. Box 1210), Cordova, AK 99574 (tel. 907/424-7311). A tent-camping and RV facility, it has 25 slots with restrooms, hot showers, and a dump station.

The **U.S. Forest Service** has cabins in the Prince William Sound and the Copper River Delta areas. Contact them at P.O. Box 280, Cordova, AK 99574 (tel. 424-7661).

Bed-and-breakfast accommodations in Cordova include the **Oystercatcher,** P.O. Box 1735, Cordova, AK 99574 (tel. 424-5154), and the **Queen's Chair,** P.O. Box 1475, Cordova, AK 99574 (tel. 424-3000).

Tax   The city room tax is 4%.

ALASKA HOTEL, 1st St. and Browning Ave. (P.O. Box 484), Cordova, AK 99574. Tel. 907/424-3288. Fax 907/424-5276. 11 rms (3 with bath).
$ Rates: $35 single without bath; $45 single with bath; $40 double without bath, $50 double with bath. MC, V.
The Alaska Hotel hearkens back to an earlier day Built in 1908, it is today a workingman's hotel with budget-priced rooms. None of them has a phone or TV, but all have twin or double beds and adequate furnishings, plus fluorescent lighting and radiator heating. The hotel is worth a visit if only to see the honky-tonk bar downstairs, featuring a backbar carried by boat from a hotel in the defunct coal-boom town of Katalla.

CORDOVA HOUSE, 1st St. (P.O. Box 700), Cordova, AK 99574. Tel. 907/424-3388. 12 rms (all with bath).
$ Rates: $50 single; $60 double. MC, V.
Recently redecorated and refurbished, the Cordova House—built in 1908—has two floors of rooms above a bar. The steam-heated rooms are small, but they all have private baths with showers. Some of the rooms have TVs, but there are no private phones.

PRINCE WILLIAM MOTEL, 2nd St. (P.O. Box 848), Cordova, AK 99574. Tel. 907/424-3201, or 424-7406 after 8pm. 14 rms (all with bath). TV TEL
$ Rates: $65 single or double. AE, MC, V.
This motel doesn't look like much from the outside, and the reception area isn't much bigger than a closet. But its wood-paneled rooms are nicely decorated in tones of orange, yellow, and off-white. Each room has good-sized beds, a love seat, dressing tables, TV, telephone, and thermostat-controlled steam heating. Six rooms have kitchenettes with pots and utensils at no additional charge. There's also a guest laundry. Adjacent to the Prince William are the Club Restaurant and bar and a grocery store.

THE RELUCTANT FISHERMAN, 401 Railroad Ave. (P.O. Box 150),

Cordova, AK 99574. Tel. 907/424-3272. Fax 907/424-7465. 50 rms (all with bath). TV TEL
$ Rates: $85 single; $95 double. Additional person $10 extra. CB, DC, MC, V.

This is Cordova's only first-class lodging, with a full-service restaurant and coffee shop, lounge, guest laundry, gift shop, and travel agency. The wood-paneled rooms, decorated in earth tones with floral bedspreads, are amply furnished and quiet—except when the fleet is in, but then tranquility has no meaning in Cordova. They've all got dressing tables and electric heat.

Cordova's rich history is reflected in the solid-copper ceilings of the dining room and lounge. The dining room is also a showcase of Alaskan native art, and its big picture windows gazing upon the small-boat harbor let diners ruminate on which boat their dinner came from. Meal prices are reasonable: $14 for a salmon dinner, including soup, salad, and potato; $6.50 for a lunch of halibut and chips. Note the copper bar top in the lounge; like many other hotel fixtures, including the "cage" at reception, it came from a late, lamented Cordova bank building.

WHERE TO DINE

AMBROSIA RESTAURANT, 1st St. Tel. 424-7175.
   Cuisine: ITALIAN. **Reservations:** Not required.
$ Prices: Appetizers $3–$5; main courses $9.75–$14.50. MC, V.
   Open: Daily 11am–11pm.

A fine little Italian restaurant, Ambrosia overlooks the harbor from the west side of 1st Street. Housed in a former blacksmith's shop built in 1908, it has a cozy wood-paneled decor of red-checkered tablecloths and hanging ivy. Full spaghetti, lasagne, and other pasta dinners are served, along with gourmet veal parmesan and chicken cacciatore. Pizzas range in price from $9.75 (11-inch, with one topping) to $29.75 (17-inch, with the works). The restaurant is licensed for beer and wine.

CLUB RESTAURANT, 1st St. at Council Ave. Tel. 424-3405.
   Cuisine: STEAK/SEAFOOD. **Reservations:** Not required.
$ Prices: Appetizers $3.95–$7.95; main courses $12–$20; breakfast $4–$8.95; lunch $5–$10.50. No credit cards.
   Open: Mon–Sat 6am–9pm, Sun 7am–9pm.
This isn't a 24-hour eatery, but it seems as if it's never closed. Starting with breakfast, it remains open until the last-callers depart from the bar well after the witching hour. Pleasant nautical decor is the restaurant's trademark, with cork and rope lining the walls. Huge omelets are the breakfast specialty, but lighter fare is also available. Lunch is mostly soup and sandwiches; dinner features steaks and seafood specialties. Hearty nachos with ground beef or chicken are an appetizer favorite. Wednesday through Saturday from 10pm, the lounge is hopping with live bands and dancing.

KILLER WHALE CAFE, 507 1st St. Tel. 424-7733.
   Cuisine: DELI. **Reservations:** Not required.
$ Prices: Breakfast $5–$8; lunch $3.50–$8. No credit cards.
   Open: Daily 8am–4pm (3pm in winter).

A breakfast and lunch spot on a deck above a book and record store, the Killer Whale features pastries and eggs, deli-style sandwiches, homemade soups, and specialty salads. There are daily specials too, and decadent desserts like homemade cheesecake and brownies. Also served are gourmet teas and espresso coffee drinks.

OK RESTAURANT, 606 1st St. Tel. 424-3433.
   Cuisine: CHINESE/JAPANESE/KOREAN. **Reservations:** Not required.
$ Prices: Appetizers $2.95–$6.95; main courses $10–$16.95. MC, V.
   Open: Daily 11am–2am.
Kuk Kim's restaurant serves standard chop suey and chow mein lunches and a variety of Asian dinners: Mandarin, Szechuan, Japanese, and Korean. There's a good appetizer menu with selections like wonton, eggrolls, and tempura vegetables or meat.

POWDER HOUSE, Copper River Hwy. Tel. 424-3529.
   Cuisine: DELI. **Reservations:** Not required.
$ Prices: Average meal $3.50–$7. MC, V.
   Open: Daily 10am–midnight.

Once a railway gunpowder warehouse, the Powder House is a rustic building with a deck looking out on Eyak Lake. (You can buy a T-shirt that says "I got blasted at the Powder House.") The soup-and-sandwich deli provides light lunches and suppers. It's more of a bar than a full-service restaurant, so the Powder House doesn't usually serve dinner. Occasionally it has moderately priced salmon barbecues and the like; call for days and times. Entertainment in the bar runs the gamut from the jukebox to live folk and country.

EASY EXCURSIONS FROM CORDOVA

Until the road is completed to Chitina, you can head out the Copper River Highway only as far as the Million Dollar Bridge, 48 miles from Cordova—but that's far enough to spend time in some of the finest birdwatching country in North America. Several million birds pass through here on their annual migrations, and more than 240 species of shorebirds, waterfowl, and other birds have been spotted on the **Copper River Flats,** including the largest-known concentration of trumpeter swans on the continent. You should also look for beavers, mink, otters, and brown and black bears in the vast tidal marsh that is the **Copper River Delta.** Moose wander down the highway as a matter of course, except during the short September moose-hunting season. There's superb berry picking here in the summer and fall, but it's best to ask first at the Cordova Sea Grant office for a guide to berries. There are some poisonous wild fruits in the area.

A mile and a half past the airport an access road leads four miles to a picnic ground with a view of the **Sheridan Glacier.** It's a one-mile hike through bear country to the glacier's terminal moraine. At 41 miles on the Copper River Highway you'll have a beautiful view of the **Sherman and Goodwin Glaciers** flowing down 6,263-foot Mount Murchison.

The **Million Dollar Bridge** is at Mile 49, wedged between the spectacular **Childs and Miles Glaciers.** The 1964 quake toppled the bridge's north span into the Copper River and damaged the other spans. Makeshift repairs have been made, but until the new highway is completed, travel beyond this point is strictly at your own risk; anyway, the road peters out in another mile.

With its marine setting, cruising by boat is a natural option for seeing Cordova. Humpback, killer, and minke whales are at home in Prince William Sound, and harbor seals, Steller sea lions, and porpoises frequent Orca Inlet. Sea otters can sometimes be seen from the docks or in the small-boat harbor, floating on their backs while feeding on crabs and clams.

Cordova is the home of some of the world's foremost fish hatcheries. The nonprofit **Prince William Sound Aquaculture Corporation** (tel. 424-7511), founded in 1974, operates the world's largest pink salmon hatchery at Port San Juan on **Evans Island,** near the southwestern entrance to the sound between Cordova and Seward. A new hatchery on **Esther Island,** east of Whittier, will be three times larger and will eventually raise all species of salmon. The state of Alaska also operates two hatcheries in the Prince William Sound islands. All these hatcheries love to give tours.

A few miles across Orca Inlet from Cordova is **Hawkins Island** with its Native village site of **Palugvik,** a national historic landmark. Palugvik marks the southeasternmost point of Eskimo settlement and a place of cross-cultural adaptation: When Tlingit and Eyak (Athabaskan) Indians migrated into the area, the Chugach Eskimos borrowed their tools and foods, and began to assume private ownership of objects, including slaves. This noncommunal social behavior had been unknown to most Eskimos.

Some 62 miles southeast of Cordova is isolated **Kayak Island.** Captain Vitus Bering's landing here in 1741 is believed to have been the first European landfall on the west coast of North America. Today this remote 22- by 1½-mile island, administered as a part of Chugach National Forest, offers only beach and forest wilderness. The totally automated Cape St. Elias Lighthouse at the southwestern end of the island has been a beacon to sailors since it was built by the Coast Guard in 1916.

A majority of the 14 U.S. Forest Service public-use **cabins** in the Cordova Ranger District are located on Prince William Sound islands. Priced at $20 a night, these cabins go fast, so advance reservations and prepayment are essential. From late August to October in particular they are heavily booked by hunters stalking the Sitka black-tailed deer. Contact the **U.S. Forest Service,** P.O. Box 280, Cordova, AK 99574 (tel. 907/424-7661), for reservations and assistance in trip planning.

A number of charter-boat operators can be found in the small-boat harbor. You can contact **Alaska Pacific Expeditions** (tel. 424-7742), **Alaska Expedition Co.** (tel. 424-4317), and **Winter King Charters** (tel. 424-7170), or check with the chamber of commerce (tel. 424-7260) for information on additional charter services.

3. THE COPPER RIVER BASIN

The dominant features of the Copper River Basin are not its towns but its geography. And that's what makes this region special.

Here are the Wrangell Mountains, their ice-covered masses starkly visible from nearly every point in the basin. Here are the Copper and Chitina Rivers, their white-water canyons challenging intrepid outdoorsmen. Weathered homesteaders share their domain with the ghosts of copper miners and a variety of wildlife. Fishermen rush to test their skills and patience against trout and salmon in the many small lakes and streams, while mountaineers relish the challenge thrown their way by the massifs of Wrangell–St. Elias National Park and Preserve. And right through the middle of it all runs the Trans Alaska Pipeline, a reminder of man's mettle in modern Alaska.

This land was the traditional home of the Ahtna Indians, a seminomadic clan of the Athabaskan tribe that hunted and fished and repelled Russian incursions. But the Indians couldn't keep back the horde of half-crazed gold seekers who traversed the basin en route to the Klondike in 1898.

Some of the newcomers, upon finding sizable veins of copper, stayed. Kennicott and McCarthy, on the southern slopes of the Wrangell Range, established huge copper-mining operations, and the river junction town of Chitina, a gateway on the railroad to Cordova, boomed as an outfitting center. By 1938, however, the expense of working the deposits had grown greater than the potential profits. Today Kennicott is merely a picturesque reminder of the boom-and-bust cycles, so much a part of Alaskan history.

Only about 3,100 people live in the entire Copper River Basin. That's about one for every seven square miles of land area. About 600 of them are Ahtna Indians, many of whose elders still speak the ancestral language. Ahtna, Incorporated, the Native corporation, has been especially active in construction, mining, and tourism in the region.

The corporation makes its headquarters in the region's hub and largest town, Glennallen (pop. about 1,000), at the junction of the Glenn and Richardson Highways. No other community in the basin has more than 300 permanent residents. That perhaps is not surprising in a virtual wilderness where temperatures are often −50°F on long winter nights. Midsummer temperatures, on the other hand, frequently top 70°F (the mercury once hit 90°F). Annual precipitation is only about 10 inches, including 50 inches of snow accumulation.

GETTING THERE The **Richardson Highway,** running south-north from Valdez to Fairbanks, and the **Glenn Highway,** running northeast-southwest from Tok to Anchorage, are the principal arteries of the Copper River Basin. They overlap for about 14 miles from Glennallen north to Gakona Junction. Seventeen miles south of Copper Center on the Richardson Highway, the **Edgerton Highway** follows the Copper and Chitina Rivers east 33 miles to Chitina, whereupon a summer-only dirt road continues 60 more miles along the old railroad bed to what remains of McCarthy. When the Copper River Highway from Cordova is completed, it will join the Edgerton Highway at Chitina.

Private car is the most practical way to visit, though bus and small plane are also options. **Alaska Sightseeing Tours** (tel. 907/277-7282) provides bus service between Anchorage and Valdez through Glennallen; the fare to Valdez is $80 for adults and $40 for children. Local transportation options are limited, but **Backcountry Connections** (tel. 907/822-5292, or toll free 800/478-5292 in Alaska) does operate out of Glennallen.

Three air taxis serve the area. **Gulkana Air Service,** P.O. Box 31, Glennallen, AK 99588 (tel. 907/822-5532 or 822-3221), three miles north of Glennallen on the Richardson Highway, provides charter flights for fishing, hunting, and sightseeing at rates of about $240 an hour. Flights between Anchorage and Glennallen are about $250 per person, one way (two-seat minimum). **McCarthy Air,** P.O. Box MXY, McCarthy, AK 99588 (no phone), has flightseeing trips to Wrangell–St. Elias National Park and Preserve for about $50 depending on the length of the flight and number of passengers (rates for other flights generally run about $200 an hour). Flights from McCarthy to Anchorage are $200. You can catch the **Ellis Air Taxi** (tel. 822-3368) mail run on Wednesday and Friday from Glennallen to Anchorage for $150 per person or from Glennallen to McCarthy for $40.

INFORMATION For information about the Copper River Basin, contact the **Greater Copper Valley Chamber of Commerce,** P.O. Box 469, Glennallen, AK 99588 (tel. 907/822-5555).

SPORTS & RECREATION Salmon and trout fishing are popular year-round in hundreds of lakes and streams throughout the region. Hunters seek bear, moose, mountain goats, and especially dall sheep, with August and September the popular big-game-hunting seasons. About one-third of the national parkland is designated a "preserve" where hunting is permitted.

Backpacking, mountaineering, and cross-country skiing are also very popular on marked trails or self-created ones. The sport surging in popularity here is river rafting, mainly on the Copper and/or Chitina Rivers.

A five-day excursion down the Chitina River is offered by **Keystone Raft and Kayak Adventures,** P.O. Box 1486, Valdez, AK 99686 (tel. 907/835-2606). Most of the first day is spent traveling by road from Chitina to McCarthy; the second day is free for exploring. Then follow three days on the river, through undisturbed wilderness surrounded by spectacular mountains and ever-present wildlife. The price of $600 includes meals, lodging, equipment, and transportation from Anchorage or Valdez.

At the park's northern extreme, Carey Davis's **Nabesna Whitewater Rafting,** Star Route A, Box 1455, Slana, AK 99586 (c/o tel. 907/822-3426), works out of the Devils Mountain Lodge at the end of the 42-mile Nabesna Road. Davis offers several fly-in/raft-out trips, but the most intriguing is an excursion from the headwaters of the Copper River on Mount Sanford. Trips are run from June through early August. Room and full board at the **Devils Mountain Lodge** (same address and phone number as Nabesna Whitewater Rafting) is $70 a day. Lodging and meals are also available at the **Silvertip Inn,** Mile 25.5, Nabesna Road (Star Route A, Box 1260), Slana, AK 99586 (tel. 907/337-2065), for $25–$40 a night.

GLENNALLEN

The town proper is spread along the Glenn Highway about two miles west of the Richardson Highway junction. Most services in the Copper River Basin are focused here, including a state trooper station and offices for the Bureau of Land Management and the Alaska Department of Fish and Game. There's also a seven-bed, two-doctor Cross Road Medical Center (tel. 822-3202, or 911 in emergencies). There is a local newspaper called the *North Country Journal* (tel. 907/822-5233) and a summer visitors guide, the *North Country Companion.*

WHERE TO STAY & DINE

Midway between Glennallen and Gakona at Mile 118 on the Richardson Highway, the **Dry Creek State Recreation Site** has 58 campsites on 372 acres with well water and toilets. The Copper Basin district ranger for Alaska State Parks, P.O. Box 286, Glennallen, AK 99588 (tel. 907/822-5536), can inform you about other campsites and picnic grounds in the area.

CARIBOU HOTEL, Mile 187, Glenn Hwy. (P.O. Box 329), Glennallen, AK 99588. Tel. 907/822-3302. Fax 907/822-3010. 45 rms (all with bath), 3 suites. TV TEL

$ Rates: May–Sept, $79 single; $89 double, $109 double with spa; $150 two-bedroom suite. Oct–Apr, $69 single; $79 double, $99 double with spa; $140 suite. AE, CB, DC, DISC, JCB, MC, V.

Once a makeshift motor inn built of pipeline construction trailers, the Caribou underwent extensive remodeling in 1991. The result is a modern hotel. Each guest room has custom furnishings and is appointed with Alaska art; off the lobby are a gift shop and a full-service restaurant. Rooms for the disabled and conference facilities are available.

The restaurant is open for three meals daily, with breakfasts and lunches (including reindeer sausage specialties) in the $4–$8 range. Dinner selections, priced $9–$14, include steaks, seafood, chicken, and salads.

GAKONA JUNCTION VILLAGE, Richardson Hwy. at the Tok Cutoff (P.O. Box 222), Gakona, AK 99586. Tel. 907/822-3664, or toll free 800/962-1933, 800/478-3665 in Alaska. Fax 907/822-3696. 23 rms (all with bath). TV TEL

$ Rates: May 15–Sept 15, $75 single; $85 double. Sept 16–May 14, $55 single or double. Children under 12 stay free in parents' room. AE, CB, DC, MC, V.

Located 12 miles north of Glennallen, this motel has pleasant units and a reasonably priced restaurant. You'll feel right at home when you enter the lobby: It's like a living room, with couches and a coffee table flanked by a grandfather clock, heated by a big fireplace. The rooms, appointed in beige and white, are spacious and amply furnished, with two double or three single beds, dressing tables, and centrally controlled hot-water heating. There's a guest laundry down the hall, a gift shop and a Texaco gas station on the premises. The management will set you up with Alaska Fish Guides for a salmon-fishing excursion ($85 for five hours, $135 for eight hours including lunch) or the nightly Gulkana River Ranch dinner/trail ride/raft trip ($85 for adults, $55 for children).

Bunny's Café, open from 6am to 9pm daily, doubles as an art gallery. Have homemade pastries for breakfast, hot sandwiches for lunch, and Alaska seafood, beef, or chicken for dinner ($8–$16). Pasta dishes and lighter fare, like stir-fries, are new additions to the menu.

GAKONA LODGE, Mile 2, Tok Cutoff (P.O. Box 285), Gakona, AK 99586. Tel. 907/822-3482. 9 rms (none with bath).

$ Rates: Year-round, $25 single; $45 double. AE, MC, V.

The rooms here are unquestionably basic. They'll do in a pinch. But most folks stop by the Gakona Lodge—located two miles northeast of the Richardson Highway on the road to Tok—for food, not a bed. This historic way station serves perhaps the best charcoal-grilled steaks between Anchorage and Whitehorse. The log Carriage House restaurant has hunting trophies mounted all over its walls, but it also has a touch of coarse elegance: dim lighting and red tablecloths. You'll get a 16-ounce New York cut here for $17 or a 20-ounce T-bone for $19. Dinner specials like Yankee pot roast go for as little as $12. The lunch menu features hamburgers ($5.50) and other sandwiches. There's a full bar (the Trapper's Den) and a nice wine list. The restaurant is open from 11am to 10pm Monday through Saturday and from 11am to 8pm on Sunday; despite (or because of) its isolation, reservations are essential in the evening.

LAKE LOUISE

Some 27 miles west of Glennallen, the road to Lake Louise, a popular summer-winter resort area, branches north off the Glenn Highway. The gravel byway leads 17 miles to a state recreation area with campsites and a boat launch. The lake is held to be especially good for lake trout, turbot, and grayling fishing. Ice fishing, snow machining, and cross-country skiing are popular in winter.

Bear Mountain Outfitters, P.O. Box 688-5091, Chugiak, AK 99567 (tel. 907/688-5091), specializes in fly-in fishing expeditions in the Susitna–Copper River Basin and Wrangell–St. Elias National Park. They operate out of Lake Louise's Evergreen Lodge B&B, with a mailing address at HC01 Box 1709, Glennallen, AK 99588 (tel. 907/822-3250).

WHERE TO STAY

Several lodges accommodate long-term guests as well as overnight visitors. Two possibilities are listed below:

LAKE LOUISE LODGE, Mile 16.1, Lake Louise Rd. (HC01 Box 1716, Glennallen, AK 99588). Tel. 907/822-3311. 5 cabins (none with bath).
$ Rates: $35 single; $45 double. No credit cards.
Five rustic cabins and an Alaskan log lodge overlook the lake. There's no running water in the cabins, but the lodge has a shower facility for guests, as well as a dining room and lounge. Guests can take advantage of the private swimming beach or motorboat rentals.

WOLVERINE LODGE, Mile 16.2, Lake Louise Rd. (HC01 Box 1704, Glennallen, AK 99588). Tel. 907/822-3988. 8 rms, 1 cabin (none with bath).
$ Rates: $45 single; $50 double; $65 cabin. Additional person $5 extra. No credit cards.
Family owned and operated, the Wolverine offers easy access to the lake. Boats can be docked, rented or even repaired; gasoline is sold too, as well as fishing and hunting licenses. There is a full-service restaurant and lounge, open from 8am to 11pm daily.

COPPER CENTER

Established as a trading post in 1896, Copper Center turned into a mining camp by the 1898 gold rush and grew to become a principal supply center for the entire region. The **George I. Ashby Memorial Museum,** operated by the Copper Valley Historical Society, has preserved many fascinating pioneer and Native artifacts, including telegraph, mining, and trapping articles. It's open summers only, Monday through Saturday from 1 to 5pm, and also on Friday from 7 to 9pm.

WHERE TO STAY & DINE

COPPER CENTER LODGE, Mile 101.1 Richardson Hwy. on Loop Rd., Copper Center, AK 99573. Tel. 907/822-3245. 14 rms (6 with bath).
$ Rates: $50 single; $55 double. AE, MC, V.
A three-story log structure with no-frills rooms, the lodge was built in 1932. It replaced the historic Blix Roadhouse, constructed in 1898 but later destroyed by fire. You have your choice of private or adjoining baths. The lodge has a dining room and lounge; the Ashby Museum is housed in a bunkhouse annex. This spot offers easy access to fishing on both the Klutina and Copper Rivers.

CHITINA

About 64 miles southeast of Glennallen at the end of the Edgerton Cutoff, Chitina (pop. 42) has a couple of dozen homes, a National Park Service ranger station, minimal tourist facilities, and one public phone. Established in 1908, and once considered a likely candidate to become Alaska's capital, Chitina's star faded rapidly after the demise of copper mining in the Wrangell Range. The old town is still fun to walk through and reminisce. If you want to rent a room in Chitina, there are only two available, at **Chitina Fuel and Grocery Store** (tel. 907/823-2211), for $50 a night.

MCCARTHY–KENNICOTT

The narrow, winding McCarthy Road extends 61 unpaved miles up the abandoned Copper River & Northwest Railroad bed. It takes about three hours to make the trip in normal summer conditions; when it rains, the muddy conditions make a four-wheel-drive vehicle desirable, but not essential. From the parking area at the end of the road, two hand-pulled trams cross the Kennicott River to McCarthy. Travelers should ask ahead at the Chitina ranger station for current road conditions.

Only about a dozen people still live in McCarthy, one of the more remote Alaskan communities connected to the rest of the world by road. From 1910 to 1938 this was "town" to the men who worked at the ✪ **Kennicott Copper Mine,** six miles north. The colorful buildings of the abandoned mine are still basically intact. Kennicott is a National Historic Landmark with ongoing preservation efforts. It's being considered for acquisition by the National Park Service.

Historic artifacts and photographs are on display at the **McCarthy-Kennicott Museum.** There's also a country store in McCarthy.

McCarthy Trailrides offers rides up the Erie Mine wagon trail to the old mine and excursions to Root Glacier and Stairway Ice Falls for prices starting at $30 per person. Full-day trips, including lunch, run $130, and custom overnight rides are $150. **St. Elias Alpine Guides,** P.O. Box 111241, Anchorage, AK 99511 (tel. 907/277-6867), with headquarters in the Mother Lode Powerhouse, schedules Kennicott ghost town tours and hiking trips at rates from $25 per person.

WHERE TO STAY & DINE

Accommodation is available mid-May through September.

KENNICOTT GLACIER LODGE, Kennicott (P.O. Box 103940, Anchorage, AK 99510). Tel. 907/258-2350, or toll free 800/582-5128, 800/478-2350 in Alaska. Fax 907/248-7975. 12 rms (none with bath).
$ Rates: $109 single; $129 double. Vacation package, $150 single; $210 double. AE, MC, V. **Closed:** Oct to mid-May.

    Located at the old mine itself, this lodge offers the area's most deluxe trappings. Most visitors opt for the vacation package, which includes accommodations, three meals a day, transportation from the tram, and a guided tour of the ghost town. The lodge arranges hikes, history and photography tours, and flightseeing trips upon request. Independent travelers dine by reservation only; breakfast and lunch are in the $9 range and dinners are about $20.

MCCARTHY LODGE, McCarthy, AK 99588. Tel. 907/333-5402. Fax 907/694-6788. 14 rms (none with bath).
$ Rates: $85 single; $95 double. Additional person $20 extra; children are charged half price (under 3, free). May and Sept rates are discounted 50%. MC, V. **Closed:** Oct–Apr.

    Built in 1916 at the height of the Copper Rush, this quaint lodge is located right in McCarthy. Rooms have double or twin beds; three have a double and a daybed—ideal for families or groups of three. The tariff includes round-trip transfers to the mine; the lodge also arranges rafting, hiking, and sightseeing excursions. Special events include an annual Tall Tales contest in July.

Across the street from the lodge and under the same ownership is the local saloon (built in the early 1900s) and a restaurant where you can get breakfast ($6–$10) and lunch or dinner ($8–$22).

MCCARTHY WILDERNESS BED & BREAKFAST, Wrangell–St. Elias National Park and Preserve (P.O. Box 111241, Anchorage, AK 99511). Tel. 907/277-6867. 3 rms, 1 cabin (none with bath).

$ Rates: $60 single or double; $150 cabin. Two-day/night package $145 per person. No credit cards (50% cash deposit required). **Closed:** Oct to mid-May. In the heart of the Wrangell–St. Elias National Park and Preserve, you'll find three rustic rooms and a former territorial commissioner's cabin, which sleeps 10. Hosts Bob and Babbie Jacobs arrange Kennicott mine tours, white-water-rafting trips, and glacier hiking trips. A two-night minimum stay is required; most visitors prefer the two-day/two-night package, which includes bed and breakfast, a guided one-day tour of the area, and glacier hiking.

WRANGELL–ST. ELIAS NATIONAL PARK & PRESERVE

Chitina and McCarthy are encompassed in this 12.4-million-acre parkland, which stretches from the Gulf of Alaska at Yakutat Bay some 200 miles north to the headwaters of the Copper River and from the Canadian border about 150 miles west to Glennallen.

The Wrangell Mountains are the park's centerpiece. Of 20 peaks in the United States over 14,000 feet, 17 of them are in Alaska and 3 of them are here—Mount Blackburn (16,390 feet), Mount Sanford (16,237 feet), and Mount Wrangell (14,163 feet). In terms of sheer mass, Mount Wrangell is the largest—bigger by four times even than Washington state's Mount Rainier, no mole hill itself. Mount Wrangell is also a semi-active volcano. Though it hasn't formally erupted since 1912, when it sent a stream of lava to its base and threw ash beyond Glennallen, it has shown signs of reawakening since the mid-1970s. On cold, clear mornings it's easy to see wisps of steam rising from Mount Wrangell's vents.

The main park headquarters is at Mile 105 on the Old Richardson Highway, 10 miles south of Glennallen and 4 miles north of Copper Center. A **visitor center,** P.O. Box 29, Glennallen, AK 99588 (tel. 907/822-5234), is open daily during the summer months, making maps and other information available to the public. There are National Park Service district ranger stations at Chitina (tel. 907/823-2205) and Nabesna (tel. 907/822-5238).

Together with Kluane National Park in Canada's Yukon, Wrangell–St. Elias has been designated a World Heritage Site by the United Nations.

4. THE MATANUSKA-SUSITNA VALLEYS

The twin valleys of the Matanuska and Susitna Rivers, known to most Alaskans simply as "Mat-Su," comprise a rich agricultural region at the head of the Cook Inlet. The dual hubs of the district, Palmer and Wasilla, are about 11 miles apart, each 40 miles north of Anchorage: Palmer is on the Glenn Highway heading east to Glennallen and Tok; Wasilla is on the George Parks Highway heading north toward Denali National Park and Fairbanks.

It's easy to dismiss the Mat-Su Valley as a slightly distant suburb of Anchorage. A significant percentage of the population in fact commutes to the "big city." But tarry a while: The valley boasts such singular attractions as the headquarters of the Iditarod Trail Sled-Dog Race, the historic Independence Mine at spectacular Hatcher Pass, the state fairgrounds, and the Museum of Alaska Transportation and Industry. You'll also find excellent fishing, hiking, rafting, and other leisure pursuits.

Two factors played key roles in Mat-Su's historical development: the building of the Alaska Railroad and the establishment of the Matanuska agricultural colony. The Anchorage–Fairbanks rail line was completed in 1915, and within two years Wasilla had been established as the trade and commercial center for a growing community of Hatcher Pass gold miners and Mat-Su homesteaders. In 1935 the Matanuska Colony was created as a place to give a new start to Midwest American farmers ruined by the Great Depression. This federally sponsored agricultural experiment helped develop the 15,000 cultivated acres of farmland around Palmer; more than half of Alaska's farms today are in the Matanuska Valley. The growing season is short, but long hours of daylight produce record vegetables—like 80-pound cabbages!

The climate in the Mat-Su Valley is very much like that of Anchorage, with slightly greater extremes of summer heat (record high: 89°F) and winter cold (record low: −40°F). Temperatures typically range between 4°F and 21°F in midwinter, with 8–10 inches of monthly snowfall, and between 44°F and 68°F in midsummer, with two inches monthly rainfall.

For more information on Mat-Su facilities and activities, write the **Matanuska-Susitna Convention & Visitors Bureau,** HC01 Box 6616 J21, Palmer, AK 99645 (tel. 907/746-5000, or 907/745-8001 for the events line; fax 907/746-2688); or visit the **Visitor Information Center** (tel. 907/756-5002) June through September on Welcome Way, Mile 35.5 on the Parks Highway, just half a mile west of the Glenn Highway junction.

GETTING THERE   As noted, the two major highways serving the Mat-Su Valley are the **George Parks and Glenn Highways,** both emanating from Anchorage. Because many of the valley's best attractions are off the main roads, you're best served by driving a private vehicle. Charter bus service is provided, however, by **Alaskan Star Charters** (tel. 907/345-2432 in Anchorage). Tours of the valley are offered by a few operators. **Alaska Heritage Tours,** P.O. Box 210691, Anchorage, AK 99521 (tel. 907/696-8687), offers custom tours of the valley; among its specialties is tours for the disabled. Tour service to and from Anchorage is also provided by **Alaska Experience Tours** (tel. 907/373-1770).

The **Alaska Railroad** passes through Wasilla twice daily in summer and less frequently in winter. From Anchorage, it takes about 1½ hours to reach Wasilla (one-way adult fare: $15). From Wasilla, it takes 4¾ hours to Denali Park (fare: $85), and 8¼ hours to Fairbanks (fare: $115). Call for information and reservations (tel. 907/265-2685 in Anchorage, or toll free 800/544-0552).

As befits Alaska, there are **small airports** in both Palmer and Wasilla, as well as in several smaller communities in the valley. These serve private pilots and charter services. Regularly scheduled flights go through Anchorage.

PALMER

Palmer's 3,200 people owe the existence of their community to the Matanuska Colony. These 202 families were resettled here in 1935 under President Franklin D. Roosevelt's New Deal program to establish the only farm colony in American history. They drew lots for 40-acre tracts, then lived in tent camps while they cleared the land, planted it, and built their log homes and barns. The surviving structures are testimony to the colony's perseverance and success, as is the fact that the main street through downtown Palmer is called Colony Way, and the biggest local annual event (in June) is called Colony Days.

The **Greater Palmer Chamber of Commerce,** P.O. Box 45, Palmer, AK 99645 (tel. 907/745-2880), maintains its offices in the **Visitor Information Center and Museum** at 723 S. Valley Way (tel. 745-2880), just across the railroad tracks from the intersection of South Colony Way and East Fireweed Avenue. This rustic log cabin, open daily from 9am to 5pm, displays many memories of the colony era in its downstairs collection. It also has a gift shop.

Valley Hospital, 515 E. Dahlia Ave. (tel. 745-4813), serves residents for many miles around.

WHAT TO SEE & DO

Sights and Attractions

Start your exploration at the **Alaska State Fairgrounds,** which has a main entrance at Mile 40.2 on the Glenn Highway. Something is always going on here, even when the fair is not. **Colony Days** is celebrated annually over the third weekend of June. Events include a parade, open-air market, various games, and exhibits. The ✪ **Alaska State Fair** draws folks from all over the state during the 11 days ending Labor Day. The fair includes standard agricultural exhibits (a great place to see oversize Matanuska Valley vegetables), lots of animals, 4-H and home displays, a carnival and parade, horse shows, and a rodeo.

A free fairgrounds attraction is **Colony Village** (tel. 745-4827), comprising five of the early Matanuska Colony buildings. A church, barn, and two private homes house historical displays, open from 10am to 4pm daily except Sunday, June through August. The **Valley Performing Arts** group (tel. 745-2484) makes its home in the Lutheran church building, now a theater.

The last of the original three Colony churches still in regular use—the so-called **Church of a Thousand Logs,** a United Protestant church (Presbyterian)—is two blocks east of the visitor center on Elmwood Avenue. Built in 1936–37, it has handmade pews and a pulpit overlaid with birch bark.

MUSK OX FARM, Mile 50.1, Glenn Hwy. Tel. 745-4151.

✪ More than 100 shaggy musk-oxen live at an old colony farm, where their downy underwool (*qiviut*) is harvested to be knit into clothing by Natives of several western Alaska villages. There are numerous educational displays in the barn, and guided tours conducted half-hourly.

Admission: $5 adults, $3 seniors and students, free for children under 6; $12 family.

Open: June–Sept 15, daily 10am–6pm; winter, by appointment.

MUSEUM OF ALASKA TRANSPORTATION AND INDUSTRY, Mile 46.7, Parks Hwy. Tel. 745-4493.

This largely open-air museum appeals to kids, with its variety of trains, boats, planes (civilian and military), trucks, farm machinery, and parts thereof. Some of the vehicles are of the "climb aboard" variety. Inside three rail cars is a very interesting Alaska Railroad historical exhibit.

Admission: $3 adults, $7 family.

Open: Mon–Sat 8am–4pm.

PALMER TSUNAMI OBSERVATORY, Mile 0.5, Palmer–Wasilla Hwy. Tel. 745-4212.

Scientists at this headquarters of the Alaska Regional Tsunami Warning System, a division of the National Weather Service, record seismic and tidal information.

Admission: Free.

Open: Public tours, Fri 1–3pm; groups at other times by special arrangement.

REINDEER FARM, Bodenburg Butte Loop Rd., Mile 11.5, Old Glenn Hwy. Tel. 745-4000.

✪ This commercial operation welcomes visitors, especially families with children. Over 300 reindeer, descendants of a herd brought from Russia in the 1890s, can be hand-fed and photographed. The view of Pioneer Peak from the farm is also worth seeing. Large parties are asked to phone ahead.

Admission: $3 adults, $1 children.

Open: Daily 10am–6pm. **Directions:** Take the Old Glenn Highway (Arctic Avenue) east and south from downtown Palmer and turn west after 7 miles on Bodenburg Butte Loop Road opposite the Butte Quick Shop; the farm is 0.8 mile farther.

UNIVERSITY OF ALASKA AGRICULTURAL EXPERIMENT STATION, Trunk Rd. off Parks Hwy. Tel. 745-3278.

✪ The station was established in 1915. A center for dairy-farm testing, it also has developed numerous crop adaptations for subarctic growing conditions.

Admission: Free.

Open: June–Sept, Mon–Fri 8am–4pm.

Sports and Recreation

There's an indoor **swimming** pool at Palmer High School, West Arctic Avenue (tel. 745-5091), and an artificial lake on the Knik River for summer dips. Public **tennis** courts are four blocks east of the visitor center at South Gulkana Street and East Elmwood Avenue.

BASEBALL The semi-pro **Mat-Su Miners,** members of the Alaska Baseball League, play in June and July at Hermon Brothers Field on the state fairgrounds. Home games start at 7:30pm Monday through Saturday, with Sunday doubleheaders at 1pm.

FISHING Trout angling is popular in the Palmer area, mainly in the valley's numerous small lakes. Try the Kepler-Bradley Lakes, a half dozen of which are interconnected by foot trails starting at Mile 37.3 on the Glenn Highway. The **Alaska Department of Fish and Game** has an office in Palmer at the corner of South Alaska Street and West Cedar Avenue (tel. 745-4247).

GOLF Palmer has an 18-hole municipal course and driving range at 1000 Lepak Ave. (tel. 745-GOLF). There's a snack bar and a pro shop where you can rent equipment. Greens fees are $20 weekends, $18 weekdays.

HIKING Dozens of trails, ranging in difficulty from easy to strenuous, are in the Palmer area. **Chuck Kaucic** at the Mat-Su Borough office (tel. 745-9636) has detailed information on conditions and terrain. Cross-country skiers use the same trails in winter. One short steep trail that offers a fine view over the Mat-Su Valley and the Knik Glacier goes half a mile up Bodenburg Butte south of Palmer. Access is from Mile 11.5 on the Old Glenn Highway.

HORSEBACK RIDING No fewer than 10 different horse shows are held at the state fairgrounds between May and September. The **Rafter T Ranch,** Mile 50 on the Glenn Highway (tel. 745-2894), 2.2 miles north of Palmer, rents horses (weekdays $15 per hour, $10 each additional hour; $25 per hour on weekends). The ranch offers trail rides Friday through Sunday, and buggy and hay rides. Call ahead to make reservations.

RIVER RAFTING An hour's drive northeast of Palmer, **NOVA Riverrunners,** P.O. Box 1129, Chickaloon, AK 99674 (tel. 745-5753), offers a family-oriented white-water-rafting day trip on the scenic lower Matanuska River ($40 for adults, $20 for children under 12; minimum age of 5). They also have a thrilling adventure on the rugged Lions Head River (the upper Matanuska), complete with Class IV rapids ($60; minimum age of 12). Remote 2- to 12-day expeditions are also available on request. The rafting season is May through September.

WHERE TO STAY

In addition to the listings below, the 75-space municipal **Matanuska River Park** is in a wooded section of town on East Arctic Avenue (Mile 17.5 on the Old Glenn Highway). Intended for RVs, it has picnic tables, trails, toilets, showers, and sewage disposal. Contact the visitor center for information and rates. Several state park campgrounds are nearby, including the **Moose Creek Wayside,** five miles north on the Glenn Highway. Write to Department of Natural Resources, Division of Parks and Outdoor Recreation, HC 32, Box 6706, Wasilla, AK 99687. On the Parks Highway you'll find **Matanuska Lake Park and Campground** (tel. 746-3517). The **Kepler Lakes Campground** (tel. 745-8932) is located at Mile 37.5 on the Glenn Highway.

FAIRVIEW MOTEL, Mile 40.5, Glenn Hwy. (P.O. Box 745), Palmer, AK 99645. Tel. 907/745-1505. 20 rms (all with bath). TV TEL
$ Rates: May–Sept, $46 single; $56–$61 double. Oct–Apr, $41–$51 single; $46–$56 double. AE, MC, V.

All rooms have queen-size beds and other standard furnishings, and thermostat-controlled hot-water heating. Three rooms have kitchenettes; all have access to the guest laundry. The motel has a new full-service restaurant and lounge (closed in winter).

PIONEER MOTEL, 124 W. Arctic Ave., Palmer, AK 99645. Tel. 907/745-3425. 27 rms (all with bath). TV

$ Rates: May–Sept, $40 single; $55 double; $65 kitchenette room per day, $225 per week. Oct–Apr, $35 single; $50 double; $60 kitchenette room per day, $100–$150 per week. AE, MC, V.

These rooms are basic but comfortable, especially the eight rooms with kitchenette—which go fast to weekly renters. There's no telephone in the rooms but they do have cable TV. Across the street from the motel are a restaurant, doughnut shop, and convenience store; a liquor store is on the premises.

TANNENHOF LLAMA INN, Mile 2.5, Palmer–Wasilla Hwy. (P.O. Box 3434), Palmer, AK 99645. Tel. 907/745-2309, or 745-1361 days. 2 rms (neither with bath).

$ Rates: $55 single; $65 double. No credit cards.

This Tudor-style house on a small llama ranch 2½ miles west of Palmer has one room with a queen-size bed and another with two twin beds. Guests have access to television and laundry facilities. Llama pack trips can be arranged by reservation ($250 per day includes meals and guide). The German hosts don't accept children under 16, smokers, or pets.

TEDDY BEAR CORNER COUNTRY INN, Mile 1.6, Hatcher Pass Rd. (P.O. Box 1151), Palmer, AK 99645. Tel. 907/745-4156 or 745-6248. 4 rms (none with bath).

$ Rates (including breakfast): $45 single; $55 double. Additional person $10 extra. No credit cards; $20 nonrefundable deposit required.

With a panoramic backdrop of the mountains surrounding Hatcher Pass, this B&B is a favorite of many readers. The clean, newly refinished bedrooms offer special amenities (shaving cream, lotion, shampoo and conditioner). There's a cozy guest lounge with TV, and from 6 to 8am you can feast on an old-fashioned breakfast, including dishes like French toast and reindeer sausage. Continental breakfast is served on request. Pets may be accommodated by advance arrangement.

VALLEY HOTEL, 606 S. Alaska St., Palmer, AK 99645. Tel. 907/745-3330, or toll free 800/478-7666 in Alaska. 34 rms (all with bath). TV TEL

$ Rates: $50–$55 single or double. AE, MC, V.

This hotel was established in 1948, when farming began to grow in the valley and coal and gold mines prospered. Since then, the lower level has been converted to offices and shops. A 24-hour coffee shop continues to be the hot spot for the town's news of the day. The comfortable rooms include private baths, cable TV, and telephone. The hotel also boasts the Caboose Lounge and a liquor store.

WHERE TO DINE

Open seven days a week, the **Food Cache** at the Pioneer Square shopping mall, on the Glenn Highway at the Palmer–Wasilla Highway, provides a variety of take-out or eat-in fast-food restaurants. Restaurant options include the following establishments.

CHARDONNAY'S, Mile 0.3, Palmer–Wasilla Hwy. Tel. 746-6060.
   Cuisine: CONTINENTAL. **Reservations:** Recommended.

$ Prices: Appetizers $5–$10; main courses $18–$24; lunch $7–$10. AE, DISC, MC, V.

   Open: Lunch Wed–Fri 11:30am–2pm; dinner Tues–Sun 5:30–10pm.

Probably the Mat-Su Valley's finest restaurant, Chardonnay's features an intimate formal dining room with chandeliers and an informal café with potted plants brightening a light-wood decor. Fresh pastas and salads, like a Spanish salad with honey-mustard dressing, are popular for lunch. Appetizers feature seafood and include oysters on the half shell, clams, and duck or salmon pâté. A wide range of dinner dishes, from fresh fish to an excellent pepper steak, are served. Try the homemade ice cream or bread pudding for dessert. As might be expected with a name like Chardonnay's, wines are heavily promoted, by the glass or bottle.

COLONY KITCHEN, 1890 Glenn Hwy. Tel. 746-4600.
   Cuisine: AMERICAN. **Reservations:** Not required.
$ Prices: Appetizers $3.95–$8.50; main courses $8–$14.95; breakfast $4–$7; lunch $2.75–$7. MC, V.
   Open: Daily 6am–midnight.
Colony Kitchen serves home-style cooking in a clean and friendly atmosphere. Breakfast is served anytime; this is the only place in Palmer you can get eggs Benedict, but less elaborate fare like pancakes and waffles, biscuits, and gravy are even more popular. Baskets of shrimp or chicken strips and homemade chili are featured lunch items. For dinner, you may want to try the fried chicken, the prawns, or a New York steak, and save room for the homemade pie for dessert. There are daily lunch and dinner specials and a salad bar. Special menu items for seniors and children are available.

FRONTIER CAFE, 133 W. Evergreen Ave. Tel. 745-3392.
   Cuisine: AMERICAN. **Reservations:** Recommended for large parties.
$ Prices: Main courses $8–$12; breakfast $2–$7; lunch $4–$8. MC, V.
   Open: Daily 6am–9pm.
This popular restaurant features hearty home-style cooking. The $2 breakfast special is a good value. For lunch, consider homemade soup followed by a slice of pie. Every evening there's a steak-and-seafood special. The café is licensed for beer and wine and can accommodate large groups in a banquet room.

LA FIESTA, 816 S. Colony Way. Tel. 746-3335.
   Cuisine: MEXICAN. **Reservations:** Recommended.
$ Prices: Appetizers $2–$5; main courses $6–$9. No credit cards.
   Open: Daily 11am–9pm.
La Fiesta features traditional Mexican meals such as chile rellenos, enchiladas, and tostadas in a festive decor. Locals flock here for the nachos.

PIZZARIA DELPHI, W. Arctic Ave. at Alaska St. Tel. 745-2929.
   Cuisine: INTERNATIONAL. **Reservations:** Recommended.
$ Prices: Appetizers $5–$8; main courses $5–$15. MC, V.
   Open: Daily 11am–11pm.
You can eat well here for under $10 per person. As you'd expect, Pizzaria Delphi has pasta dishes and pizza, but it also has Mexican dishes. You can order à la carte items and combination plates. If ethnic food is not your preference, you can get steaks and seafood.

EASY EXCURSIONS FROM PALMER

The **Knik Glacier** is one of the closest glaciers to a major population center in Alaska, yet it's one of the least visited. It cannot be reached by road but is easily accessible by air or by boat up the Knik River. Between 1915 and 1966 this glacier was a natural wonder, damming its own meltwater in the winter to create a 25-square-mile lake, then overflowing the ice dam in late June in a two-week, 150-million-gallons-a-minute flood. By 1967 the glacier had receded to a point where the ice dam was no longer created, but it's still an impressive sight.
   Country Lakes Flying Service, 2651 E. Palmer–Wasilla Hwy. (tel. 907/376-5868), offers a floatplane tour of Knik Glacier and iceberg-laden Lake George, high in the Chugach Mountains. The plane lands on Lake George if conditions permit; you can often see wildlife like bear and moose. The tour costs $99 per person for one hour.
   An awesome sight about an hour's drive east of Palmer, at Mile 102 on the Glenn Highway, is the **Matanuska Glacier.** Some 27 miles long, 4 miles wide, and 1,000

feet thick, it is stable and accessible enough to allow visitors to walk on it. A side road gives access to a state park and campground at Mile 101 on the Glenn Highway, from which a trail leads a short distance to the foot of the glacier. Watch out for crevasses!

Stop for a snack at the **Long Rifle Lodge,** Mile 102.2 Glenn Hwy. (Star Route C, Box 8445), Palmer, AK 99645 (tel. 907/745-5151), with a deck overlooking the glacier; or stay at the **Sheep Mountain Lodge,** Mile 113.5, Glenn Hwy. (HCO 3-8490), Palmer, AK 99645 (tel. 907/745-5121), a well-kept secret since the 1940s. Dall sheep often clamber across the rocky peak behind the lodge. Six cabins, some with private baths, are priced at $70 double. A sauna and Jacuzzi are available. The restaurant specializes in sourdough pancakes, homemade soups and chili, and rich desserts. Twelve miles of groomed cross-country ski trails surround the lodge. From May to October, Sheep Mountain's dorm cabins are an official American Youth Hostel, also open to nonmembers.

At Mile 61.5 on the Glenn Highway (no phone), you'll find the **Alpine Heritage and Cultural Center.** Open from June to September, this historical park is located close to the navy coal-washing plant that operated in the early 1900s. It features museum displays on the development of the regional coal industry, Alaska's native heritage, and the construction of the Glenn Highway. You can see the original post office and residences.

A good source of information on the Matanuska River country northeast of Palmer is the **Greater Sutton Chamber of Commerce,** P.O. Box 24, Sutton, AK 99674 (tel. 907/744-4527).

WASILLA

Built between and around the shores of two beautiful long lakes—Wasilla Lake and Lake Lucille—it's no wonder that Wasilla is growing fast. Many of its 3,900 people commute to work in Anchorage. A few are descendants of the miners and homesteaders who gave the town its start in 1917.

Information can be obtained from the **Greater Wasilla Chamber of Commerce,** P.O. Box 871826, Wasilla, AK 99687 (tel. 907/376-1299; fax 907/376-1299), in Cottonwood Creek Mall where the Palmer–Wasilla Highway joins the Parks Highway. It's open weekdays from 9am to noon and 1 to 5pm.

To get around Wasilla and vicinity, you can rent a car from **Denali Car Rental,** 435 E. Knik St. (tel. 373-1230), or **Nye Frontier Ford,** Mile 40 on the Parks Highway (tel. 376-5656).

The train station is right in the middle of town, where Main Street crosses the Parks Highway, though it's not in active use: You'll have to stand up outside as you wait for the Alaska Railroad and hope it's not late (as it often is). Wasilla also has a small airport used by private planes and air-taxi services.

From their Wasilla offices, the semiweekly *Frontiersman* newspaper and weekly *Valley Sun* keep the Mat-Su area informed. **Valley Hospital** in Palmer (tel. 745-4813) serves Wasilla as well, though medical assistance can be obtained at the **West Valley Medical Campus** at 950 E. Bogart Rd. (tel. 376-5028).

Given Wasilla's location between the lakes, it's no surprise that the town's biggest celebration of the year makes use of them. **Wasilla Water Days,** over the Fourth of July weekend, includes a family picnic, parades (land and water), waterski competition, raft races, and even an underwater tricycle race. **Iditarod Days,** held the first weekend of March to coincide with the start of the Iditarod Trail sled-dog race, include a costume ball, a Monte Carlo night, and a golf tournament on frozen Wasilla Lake.

WHAT TO SEE & DO

Sights and Attractions

The Iditarod sled-dog race, called by some "The Last Great Race" on Earth, has its headquarters at the ✪ **Iditarod Trail Sled Dog Race Gift Shop and Visitors Center,** Mile 2.2 on Knik Road (tel. 907/376-5155; fax 907/373-6998). Slide or video shows of past races are shown on request. You can buy videotapes, photos, posters, and other gifts and souvenirs. Visitors get a free card autographed by the mushers. Open year-round, Monday through Friday from 8am to 5pm, and June through mid-September, also on Saturday from 8am to 4pm and on Sunday from 8am to noon.

There are those who claim that the musher who wins the arduous Iditarod race should be considered the world's most durable athlete. An Alaskan woman, Susan Butcher, has won the race four times since 1986. (Past winners have come from Alaskan villages with names like Red Devil, Coldfoot, Clam Gulch, and Trapper Creek.) Beginning on or about March 1, normally consuming two to three weeks of time, teams of 12–18 dogs and their solo musher follow the Iditarod National Historic Trail over two mountain ranges, down the great Yukon River, and around a corner of the frozen Bering Sea. They retrace the route used during the Nome gold rush to move mail, supplies, and (later) diphtheria serum from the ice-free port of Seward. Millions of dollars in gold were transported by dog teams returning from Nome along the same route. For information on the modern race, write to the Iditarod Trail Committee, Pouch X, Wasilla, AK 99687.

The "Father of the Iditarod," as he's called, is Joe Redington, Sr. Born in 1917, he competed in 18 races before 1993; in 1988, at the age of 71, he finished fifth. Redington moved to Knik in 1948, opened much of the trail to mushing, promoted the race to Nome, and launched it in 1973 with a $25,000 purse. Now it's $250,000 and rising. You might have seen Redington mush down Pennsylvania Avenue in President Ronald Reagan's 1981 inaugural parade. Redington's ✪ **Knik Kennels,** Mile 12 on Knik Road (tel. 376-5562), is said to be the largest sled-dog kennel in the world. Visitors are welcome, but call for an appointment.

An important stop along the trail, then as today, was **Knik,** the first white settlement in what is now the Mat-Su Borough. The trade and supply center for the Willow Creek and Iditarod gold-mining districts between 1898 and 1919, it is remembered today only by historians and by two surviving structures. One of them is the Bjorn Cabin, restored by members of the Knik–Wasilla–Willow Creek Historical Society. The other is the former pool hall, now the Knik Museum, listed below.

DOROTHY G. PAGE MUSEUM AND HISTORICAL PARK, 323 Main St. Tel. 376-2005.

Less than two blocks north of the George Parks Highway at Swanson Avenue, you can see many reminders of early Wasilla. A log house built in 1931 as a community social center, it was restored in 1967 by the Wasilla–Knik–Willow Creek Historical Society to preserve artifacts pertaining to local history. Displays include a wildlife diorama, a "Flying Dentist's" office, Eskimo artifacts, and a gold mining exhibit. After dropping into the museum, you can head out the back door to the historical park, a restoration of early Wasilla at Swanson Avenue. Two different styles of log cabins, Wasilla's first school, a smokehouse, a blacksmith shop, and a public bath have been preserved here.

Admission: $3 adults, $2.50 seniors, free for youngsters under 18.

Open: Daily 10am–6pm.

KNIK MUSEUM AND SLED DOG MUSHERS HALL OF FAME, Mile 14, Knik Rd. Tel. 376-7755.

✪ Many artifacts of the old town are preserved here. But most visitors come to see its dog-sled memorabilia and portraits of famous mushers, past and present— such as five-time Iditarod winner Rick Swenson. The curator is Vi Redington, wife of renowned racer Joe Redington, Sr.

Admission: $1.50 adults, 75¢ children.

Open: June–Labor Day, Wed–Sun noon-6pm; winter, by appointment (call the Wasilla Museum, above).

Sports and Recreation

There's year-round indoor activity at Wasilla High School's **Mat-Su Pool** on Bogard Road (tel. 376-4222), open daily from 6am to 9:30pm. Call for schedules and fees. At

Wasilla Lake, there's a roped-off municipal swimming area and picnic spot next to the Parks Highway.

The Wasilla city **tennis** courts are downtown on Swanson Avenue, at Town Site Park. Settlers Bay Village Inn, Mile 8 on Knik Road, has courts.

There's also **bowling** at Valley Lanes, on the Palmer–Wasilla Highway just east of town (tel. 376-9737), and **skating** at the Let the Good Times Roller Rink, just off the Parks Highway on Broadview Avenue (tel. 376-8858).

BOATING   The Little Susitna River, north and west of downtown Wasilla, is a favorite place for **canoeing. Chimo Guns,** next to Carr's Shopping Center on Yenlo Street (tel. 376-5261), open daily, rents canoes for $20 for one day, $15 per day for two or more days ($50 deposit required). The **Mat-Su Resort** (tel. 376-3228) has paddleboat and rowboat rental for use on Wasilla Lake.

FISHING   Wasilla Lake has good trout fishing. Lake Lucille and Finger Lake, east of Wasilla on Bogard Road, are stocked with silver (coho) salmon. **Chimo Guns** and **Carr's Shopping Center** sell fishing gear and licenses.

GOLF   The **Settlers Bay Country Club,** south of Wasilla on Knik–Goose Bay Road (tel. 376-5466), has a nine-hole public golf course, driving range, and pro shop.

HORSEBACK RIDING   The **Mountain Creek Guest Ranch** (tel. 373-7433) offers custom trail horse rides. **Scenes of Yesteryear,** Mile 1.7 on Pittman Road (tel. 376-2379), and **Wilosa Ranch,** Mile 5 on Wasilla-Fishhook Road (tel. 376-5617), offer horse-drawn carriage rides and rentals.

WINTER SPORTS   Cross-country skiing and skating, ice sailing, and ice fishing are popular on the lakes surrounding Wasilla. More serious skaters appreciate the **Mat-Su Ice Arena** at Wasilla Junior High School, Crusey Street at Bogard Road (tel. 376-9260).

The world's longest cross-country ski race, the 210-mile March **Iditaski,** begins on the Knik Arm just south of Wasilla, follows the Iditarod Trail to Skwentna, and returns to the Cook Inlet down rivers of the Susitna basin. Participants, who must tow a 35-pound sled full of survival gear *without* the assistance of dogs, usually require two to three days to complete the ordeal.

WHERE TO STAY

Bed-and-breakfast enthusiasts should contact the Matanuska-Susitna Convention & Visitors Bureau (tel. 907/746-8000) for a full listing of B&Bs in the valley. For campers, the **Finger Lake Wayside** on Bogard Road has 41 sites with water, toilets, and picnic tables. The **Greenridge Camper Park,** 1130 Vicky Way, Mile 29.4 on the Parks Highway (tel. 907/376-5899), has sites for $14 a night, and **Rainbow Acres RV Park,** Mile 49 on the Parks Highway (tel. 907/376-8897), has full hookups for $12 a night. Other accommodations are listed below.

EL TORO II MOTOR LODGE, Mile 40, Parks Hwy. (P.O. Box 874907), Wasilla, AK 99687. Tel. 907/376-4908. 10 rms (all with bath). TV TEL
$ Rates: May–Sept, $55 single; $60 double. Oct–Apr, $50 single; $55 double. AE, MC, V.

Check in at the El Toro II restaurant, then check out the tidy rooms. All are appointed in blue, with two queen-size beds, cable TV, and electric baseboard heat. Dogs may be permitted with approval from the management and payment of a $25 deposit.

The restaurant (open from 11am to 10pm Sunday through Thursday and 11am to 11pm on Friday and Saturday) features Mexican decor and cuisine, plus steak and seafood. South-of-the-border specialties include enchiladas rancheras and chiles rellenos for about $8. There's also peel-and-eat shrimp and a filet mignon special ($17 for petit and $20 for large). Lunches are priced from $5. The lounge, with its round bar and country-western band playing Wednesday through Sunday nights, is known as the favorite watering hole of the Wasilla City Council.

KASHIM INN, 181 W. Parks Hwy., Wasilla, AK 99687. Tel. 907/376-5800. 10 rms (all with bath). TV

$ Rates: Mid-May to mid-Sept, $51.50 single or double. Mid-Sept to mid-May, $41.50 single or double. AE, MC, V.

The small rooms here feel like grandma's house, with lacy calico bedspreads and drapes and mountain pictures on the green-striped walls. But it's hard to ignore the noise from the nearby highway and railroad tracks. The standard furnishings include a dressing table, a television, and hot-water thermostat heating.

The coffee shop, open 24 hours daily, offers burgers from $5.25, omelets from $5, and a New York steak dinner for $10.50. The lounge has a big dance floor and live entertainment Thursday through Saturday.

MAT-SU RESORT, 1850 Bogard Rd., Wasilla, AK 99687. Tel. 907/376-3228, or toll free 800/478-3229 in Alaska. Fax 907/376-7781. 37 units (all with bath).

$ Rates: May–Sept, $72 economy; $82 deluxe single or double; $82–$98 suite or cabin. Oct–Apr, $58 economy; $68 deluxe; $83 suite or cabin. AE, DISC, MC, V.

This quiet resort, built of split logs in 1939, was expanded and renovated in 1980. Here you can step out on the back porch of your deluxe room and gaze across Wasilla Lake. Each of the 15 deluxe units, including a dozen suites and three private cabins, has a kitchenette, queen-size bed, sofa and coffee table, cable TV, phone (free local calls), and more-than-adequate lighting. They're decorated in brown and rust tones, with slatted red blinds and rich wood furnishings. The older economy rooms do not have TV or telephone.

The main resort lodge houses a lakeside restaurant and lounge, with decor that includes a full-size grizzly bear and record-class moose and caribou racks. A wide variety of dinners such as petite filet mignon, scampi, and deep-fried frogs' legs are served, most in the $20–$25 range. It's open for lunch weekdays from 11am to 2:30pm, on Saturday to 3pm; for dinner, Sunday through Thursday from 5 to 10pm, on Friday and Saturday to 11pm. Sunday brunch is served from 10:30am to 2:30pm. In summer, the lounge has live music and dancing on weekend evenings. A banquet room is available, and in summer, there are lunch and dinner cruises.

Rowboats and paddleboats are available for rent in the summer, and there are covered picnic facilities for 600 people. During the winter, the lake is ideal for skating and cross-country skiing.

WASILLA LAKE B&B, 961 North Shore Dr., Wasilla, AK 99687. Tel. 907/376-5985. 2 rms (neither with bath), 2 apts (both with bath). **Directions:** In Wasilla, turn north on Crusey Street at Mile 41.8 on the Parks Hwy., east on Bogard Road for one mile, south on North Shore Drive, and left at the Y.

$ Rates: $45 single without bath; $55 double without bath, $65–$95 apt with bath and kitchenette. Additional person $15 extra. No credit cards.

One of your hosts is an Alaskan artist specializing in hand-painted porcelain. Guests are welcome to visit her studio. Accommodations include two antique-furnished upstairs rooms with shared bath in the main house, or two self-contained units in the two-story lakeshore cabin. One of the cabin units is a two-bedroom luxury apartment with a view of the lake and the Chugach Mountains. Guests can stroll by the vegetable and flower gardens or enjoy the solarium. Pontoon-boat cruises on Wasilla Lake are offered by appointment.

THE WINDBREAK, 2201 E. Parks Hwy., Wasilla, AK 99687. Tel. 907/376-4484, or 376-4209. (For reservations: 1890 Glenn Hwy. S., Palmer, AK 99645.) 10 rms (all with bath).

$ Rates: Mid-May to mid-Sept, $45 single or double. Mid-Sept to mid-May, $35 single or double. MC, V.

The small rooms here are basic but sufficient, appointed with blue carpeting and bedspreads, and wildlife pictures on the walls. TVs are available on request, and there's a courtesy phone at the foot of the stairs. Pick up your key at the bar. The noise of pool, darts, and big-screen TV penetrates to the second-floor rooms, but the price is right. This is a good place to get fishing information; the management can help you line up guided and unguided fishing trips.

The Windbreak Café, open daily from 6am to midnight in summer, to 10pm in winter, has simple wood decor and mounted trout on the walls. Breakfast is served all day (try the four-egg "Windbreak special", $7); a quarter-pound burger with "the works" costs less than $5; and for dinner you can feast on sirloin steak or all the shrimp you can eat for around $10. There's also a complete children's menu.

YUKON DON'S, Mile 1.5, Fairview Loop Rd. (HC31 Box 5086), Wasilla, AK 99687. Tel. 907/376-7472. 5 rms (none with bath), 1 suite (with bath).
Directions: Drive 4 miles east from Wasilla to Mile 38 on the Parks Hwy., then 1.5 miles south on Fairview Loop Road.
$ Rates (including breakfast): $60–$80 double. No credit cards.

Don Tanner is a Yukon River outfitter; his wife, Kristan, a former Miss *and* Mrs. Alaska, and their family help run this delightful bed-and-breakfast inn. The guest rooms and the suite have fishing, hunting, dog-sledding, or logging decor, and the 900-square-foot recreation room has a barrel stove, pool table, and bar. There's even a sauna and exercise room. The Tanners can help set up guided tours, retreats, seminars, or weddings upon request.

WHERE TO DINE

COUNTRY KITCHEN, Wasilla Shopping Center, Mile 43, Parks Hwy. Tel. 376-6357.
Cuisine: INTERNATIONAL. **Reservations:** Not required.
$ Prices: Breakfast $3.95–$6.95; lunch $3.95–$8.95; dinner $6.95–$13.95. MC, V.
Open: Sun–Thurs 6am–11pm, Fri–Sat 6am–midnight.

This friendly, family-style restaurant serves Mexican, French, and Italian meals, as well as homemade baked goods and soups. Breakfast is served all day; the all-you-can-eat taco bar and teriyaki chicken strips are good dinner bargains, while a T-bone steak caters to hearty appetites. Children are welcomed.

MONICO'S ALASKAN RESTAURANT, Land Company Building, Carr's Mall, Parks Hwy. Tel. 376-6939.
Cuisine: MEXICAN/STEAK/SEAFOOD. **Reservations:** Accepted for large parties only.
$ Prices: Appetizers $1.75–$6.50; main courses $7.25–$15.95; lunch $3.95–$9.95. AE, MC, V.
Open: Memorial Day–Labor Day, daily 7am–10pm; the rest of the year, daily 8am–10pm.

This simple but pleasant café offers a wide range of combination meals and à la carte selections, from tacos to chimichangas. For lunch, you can also choose from a large selection of sandwiches and burgers. Featured offerings are the house seafood platter, a 16-ounce New York steak smothered in mushrooms, and home-style fried chicken. Mexican dinners include fajitas and flautas. There's an all-you-can-eat salad bar for $5.95; you can purchase one instead with your meal for $3. The children's menu has Mexican food as well as burgers, spaghetti, and fish and chips.

SETTLERS BAY VILLAGE INN, Mile 8, Knik Rd. Tel. 376-5298.
Cuisine: STEAK/SEAFOOD. **Reservations:** Recommended.
$ Prices: Appetizers $5.50–$8.95; main courses $12.95–$38.95. AE, MC, V.
Open: Dinner Tues–Thurs 5–10pm, Fri–Sat 5–11pm; brunch Sun 10:30am–3:30pm.

An upscale spot for fine dining and cocktails, the inn looks across the Knik Arm of the Cook Inlet toward the Chugach Mountains. The appetizer menu includes shrimp cocktail, escargots, and tempura vegetables. Veal marsala and veal Oscar are recommended dishes, along with the filet mignon. This is also a favorite spot for its Sunday champagne brunch buffet. Settlers Bay Village Inn features a nine-hole golf course, and caters special events for up to 300 people.

YAMAKAWA JAPANESE RESTAURANT, 290 N. Yenlo St., Meta Rose Sq. Tel. 373-6117.
Cuisine: JAPANESE/KOREAN. **Reservations:** Recommended for large groups.
$ Prices: Appetizers $3.75–$6.50; main courses $10.75–$18.95; lunch $3.50–$11.50. AE, MC, V.
Open: Mon–Sat 10am–9pm.

Yamakawa has daily luncheon specials and full dinners with beer, wine, and sake available. The chicken and New York steak teriyaki are good, and there's an excellent variety of sushi items, as well as Japanese staples like gyoza (homemade dumplings) and udon (hot noodles in broth). Korean dishes like hwe dep bab (sashimi salad) and kal bi barbecued ribs are also served. If you want to go all out, try the special Yamakawa dinner: shrimp tempura, kal bi ribs, sushi, and sashimi.

HATCHER PASS

High above the timberline, yet only a short drive from Palmer or Wasilla, is spectacular Hatcher Pass. Dotted with decaying mine buildings, the narrow, winding, unpaved road follows the Little Susitna River to the summit (3,886 feet), yielding glorious alpine views of the Mat-Su Valley, Cook Inlet, and Chugach Mountains, and providing access to popular hiking, horseback riding, cross-country skiing, and snow-machining terrain.

This southern end of the Talkeetna Mountains was actively mined for gold from the early 20th century until World War II. Today the ✪ **Independence Mine State Historic Park** recalls that era. This mining complex, which once produced 48,194 ounces of gold ($1,686,790 in value) in a single year, is slowly being restored for public viewing. The visitor center in the former mine manager's quarters features interpretive displays on the mine, which opened in 1908 but never recovered from World War II closures, and was finally shut down in 1951. A "touch tunnel" at the entrance to the visitors center simulates a gold mine, complete with miners' voices. The park includes an assay building (which is being turned into a hard-rock mining museum), bunkhouses, mess halls, a tipple, and other structures.

The visitors center and other facilities are open from 11am to 7pm Thursday through Monday in summer. On weekends from July 4 to Labor Day (Friday through Monday), guided tours (at $3 for adults, $2 for seniors and children) follow the trails among a dozen abandoned buildings. At any time of year, trails wind throughout and beyond the park for self-guided tours.

The Alaska Division of Parks is also trying to work out an agreement for tours of the adjacent Gold Cord Mine, which reopened in 1979 to process the old Independence claims. For more information, contact the Parks Division's Mat-Su office at Finger Lake on Bogard Road (tel. 745-3975).

WHERE TO STAY

HATCHER PASS LODGE, Independence Mine State Historic Park, Mile 17, Willow-Fishhook Rd. (P.O. Box 763), Palmer, AK 99645. Tel. 907/745-5897. 4 rms (none with bath), 5 cabins (all with bath). **Directions:** Drive 17 miles north-northwest of Palmer on the Willow-Fishhook Road or 20 miles north-northeast of Wasilla on the Wasilla-Fishhook Road.
$ Rates: $58 single or double; $84 cabin for one or two. AE, MC, V.

Ⓢ Close by the Independence Mine at 3,000 feet elevation, this large, red A-frame nestles in spectacular terrain that has been compared to the Swiss Alps. Accommodations include five private cabins and four small attic rooms with double or bunk beds. A propane-heated sauna sits outside beside a "dipping hole" in the Little Susitna headwaters.

In summer the lodge serves three meals a day in its intimate restaurant. Specials are in the $5–$15 range and include bratwurst on a bun, Swiss-style fondue for two with Gruyère and Emmentaler cheeses, kirsch and wine, and beef Stroganoff. There's also an espresso bar and cocktail service.

Some 20 kilometers (12 miles) of set-track cross-country ski trails surround the lodge in winter. A ski school teaches cross-country and Telemark skiing, and a ski patrol is on duty every weekend.

MOTHERLODE LODGE, Mile 14, Willow-Fishhook Rd. (P.O. Box 240685), Palmer, AK 99645. Tel. 907/746-1464, or 907/274-7010 in Anchorage. 10 rms (all with bath).
$ Rates: $65 single or double. AE, MC, V.
Near the foot of Hatcher Pass Road, the Motherlode Lodge re-creates memories of mining days. Built in the 1940s as the little Susitna Road House, it has a bit of everything—lodging, dining, a large lounge with a karaoke machine and billiard tables, and a tent-camping area. The no-frills guest rooms are carpeted and include private baths. The dining room, open Friday through Sunday for breakfast, lunch, and dinner, seats 150 and looks like an upscale miners' bunkhouse with dog sleds on the walls and brass lamps hanging from the ceilings.

BIG LAKE

One of south-central Alaska's major recreational playgrounds, Big Lake is the largest of many dozens of small, low-lying, glacier-dug lakes that dot the lower Mat-Su Valley. Anchorage residents and others build vacation homes along the shore of this lovely island-studded body of water.

Big Lake Road joins the George Parks Highway at Mile 52. Turn southwest here and drive about six miles to a land of marinas, resorts, campgrounds, and picnic areas. Fishing (for salmon, trout, grayling, and burbot), swimming, sailing, boating, and waterskiing are the preferred sports here in summer; in winter, snow-lovers turn to ice fishing, skating, cross-country skiing, and snow-machining on the frozen lake. The year's big events reflect seasonal sports interest—the Big Lake Sailing Regatta is held the third weekend of July and the Big Lake 500 Snowmachine Race takes place in March.

WHERE TO STAY

There are several places to rest your head around the lakeshore. With a couple of the lodges having fallen on hard times and awaiting new ownership, my preference is listed below.

BIG LAKE MOTEL, Mile 5, Big Lake Rd. (P.O. Box 520728), Big Lake, AK 99652. Tel. 907/892-7976. 20 rms (all with bath). TV **Directions:** Drive 10 miles west of Wasilla on the Parks Highway; then go south on Big Lake Road for 5 miles.
$ Rates: $50 single; $55 double; $60 twin. MC, V.
Built in 1986, this accommodation is adjacent to the Big Lake Airport and a mile from the lake by road. Each room has a navy-blue color scheme, queen-size beds, custom-built oak furnishings, sliding windows with screens and blinds, a clock radio, a TV, indoor and outdoor entrances, and thermostat-controlled hot-water heat. There's a pay phone in the lobby.

WHERE TO DINE

The most popular restaurants on Big Lake itself are inaccessible most of the year except by water or ice. But that doesn't slow business down.

CALL OF THE WILD, southwest corner of Big Lake. Tel. 892-6274.
Cuisine: AMERICAN. **Reservations:** Not required. **Transportation:** See below.
$ Prices: Appetizers $4; main courses $6.50–$20. No credit cards.

Open: Memorial Day–Labor Day, daily noon–midnight; the rest of the year, Thurs–Mon noon–midnight.

On a promontory near the west end of the five-mile-long lake is this restaurant, locally famous for its half-pound hamburgers with all the fixings and 24-ounce rib-eye steaks. It features live music for dancing on Friday and Saturday nights.

To get here, take the 24-hour water taxi from the marina, or drive across the ice in winter. There's also a road into the site, but you may need a four-wheel-drive vehicle to use it.

THE ISLANDER RESTAURANT, Long Island, Big Lake. Tel. 892-7144.

Cuisine: STEAK/SEAFOOD. **Reservations:** Required. **Transportation:** See below.

$ Prices: Appetizers $3.75–$8.75; main courses $10.75–$28.75; lunch $5.75–$7.75. AE, MC, V.

Open: Mon 4–9pm, Wed–Thurs 1–9pm, Fri 1–10pm, Sat noon–10pm, Sun 10am–9pm.

Located on an island in the middle of Big Lake, the Islander—built in 1984—is a modern restaurant with fine cuisine. Steaks and lobster tails are the big sellers, but the menu features everything down to southern fried chicken and a half-pound hamburger with all the fixin's.

Get here by private boat or the restaurant's own floatboat, which picks up diners with reservations at Big Lake's Burkeshore Marina.

The Islander also operates the *Big Wheel Jessica A.*, a 58-foot paddlewheeler that carries 20–60 people on Big Lake sightseeing tours beginning at noon and 4pm Wednesday through Sunday in summer. The tour costs $27.50 with lunch, $34.50 with a steak or halibut dinner.

WILLOW

A Talkeetna Mountain gold-mining camp from 1897 to 1940, Willow was revived from virtual ghost-town status by the completion of the George Parks Highway in 1972. Its star flared in 1976 when Alaska voters selected a nearby 100-square-mile site as the location of their new capital city. Six years later when voters refused to release funds to move the capital from Juneau, however, Willow (pop. about 500) resigned itself to being just another outpost on the highway, 27 miles northwest of Wasilla.

Between Willow and tiny Houston (17 miles from Wasilla), the **Nancy Lake State Recreation Area** preserves a beautiful forested flatland speckled with 130 lakes, most of them interconnected by streams (to the delight of canoeists and fishermen). During the summer, rangers lead a variety of naturalist programs, including campfire talks and a children's discovery hike. Although swampy ground limits hiking, 40 miles of trails are maintained within the recreation area, including the mile-long Tulik Trail, a self-guided nature walk. The Lynx Lake Loop canoe trail makes a leisurely weekend excursion with few portages.

The **Alaska Division of Parks** maintains an office at the Nancy Lake Wayside, Mile 66.5 on the Parks Highway (tel. 495-6273). The Nancy Lake Parkway turns off the Parks Highway at Mile 67.3 and runs south and west 6½ miles to the **South Rolly Lake campground**, with 100 units open to campers. Nancy Lake Wayside has another 30 sites, and there are 11 more campsites along the canoe trail system.

WHERE TO STAY

NANCY LAKE MARINA AND RESORT, Mile 64.5, Parks Hwy. (P.O. Box 114), Willow, AK 99688. Tel. 907/495-6284. 6 cabins (none with bath).

Directions: 22 miles west of Wasilla.

$ Rates: $35 cabin for two. Additional person $5 extra. No credit cards.

Here you'll find rustic cabins in a lakefront birch forest. If you don't mind bringing your own bedding (sleeping bags) and using a separate bathhouse, you'll get a carpeted, wood-paneled cabin with beds, kitchen facilities, a dining table, and wood or electric heat. There are also 50 campsites without hookups. The lodge/general store rents everything from boats, motors, and fishing tackle to aircraft fuel and snow machines.

WILLOW TRADING POST LODGE, Mile 69.5, Parks Hwy. (P.O. Box 69), Willow, AK 99688. Tel. 907/495-6457. 5 rms (all with bath), 5 cabins (none with bath). TV

$ Rates: $40–$125 per unit. No credit cards.

This is Willow's community center. The nicely appointed rooms and small cabins beside a tiny lake vary in size and furnishings, but all are spacious and homey, with wall-to-wall carpeting and oil heat. Toilets are in a separate bathhouse; showers cost $3. You can use the pay phone in the bar, which prides itself on its beer selection and its live piano music on Saturday nights. Other facilities include a small café with limited menu (open from 8am to midnight), liquor store, gift nook, and laundry.

WHERE TO DINE

A short snack menu is offered at the Willow Trading Post, but for meals, you're best off heading back toward Wasilla.

DENALI NATIONAL PARK

Measured from its base to its summit, with its enormous girth taken into account, Mount McKinley is greater than any other mountain on earth.

The Athabaskan Indians called the mountain Denali, the "High One." The white man named it Mount McKinley in 1896, after Republican presidential candidate Sen. William McKinley. First scaled in 1913, it became the centerpiece of Mount McKinley National Park in 1917. The park area was tripled in size (to six million acres) in 1980 and its name (but not the mountain's) was changed to Denali National Park and Preserve.

At 20,320 feet, Mount McKinley is North America's highest point. The towering centerpiece of the approximately 600-mile-long Alaska Range, it dominates a wilderness of tumbling glaciers and braided, silt-filled rivers, of subarctic taiga and tundra vegetation, and of an exceedingly rich wildlife.

Indeed, it's the animals that attract most of Denali's annual visitors, now exceeding 500,000 during the brief summer season. Brown (grizzly) bears, moose, caribou, dall sheep, wolves, and numerous smaller mammals thrive in the park, along with a varied birdlife.

For all its 9,300 square miles, there are only about 100 miles of road in the park. Of that, only 18 miles is unrestricted. Because of the negative effect that the throngs of summer visitors were having on the wildlife population, park authorities several years ago began limiting private vehicle traffic, and operating a shuttlebus service and wildlife tours. The ploy worked; the bears, sheep, and caribou are now more commonly seen along the road than they were in the late 1970s.

Park headquarters is located about 3½ miles west of the George Parks Highway junction, where Riley Creek meets the Nenana River, 249 road miles north of Anchorage and 126 miles south of Fairbanks. Two miles nearer the highway are the Denali Park Hotel (the only private concession in the national park wilderness area) and the Denali railway station and post office. All other hotels and restaurants servicing park visitors are located outside the park boundary, along the Nenana River. Some are located half a mile north of the park road junction; another handful are scattered between 6 and 13 miles south. There are several campgrounds in the park and three wilderness lodges (of varying degrees of rusticity) at Kantishna, an almost-forgotten mining community at the western end of the park road, 88 miles from the next closest accommodation or food service.

There is no hospital within the park—the nearest clinic and rescue service are located in Healy, about 12 miles north—but the park does have a 24-hour number (tel. 683-9100) to report emergencies, accidents, or injuries.

Interdenominational Christian services are held at 6pm on Saturday and Sunday in the Riley Creek Campfire Circle, at 9am on Sunday at the Denali Park Hotel auditorium, and at 11am on Sunday at the McKinley Chalets activity center just outside the park.

As far as weather goes, only one rule applies: Be prepared for anything. Summer tendencies can be predicted—days will have temperatures in the low to mid-60s, while night temperatures will fall to 40°F and perhaps into the 30s; the precipitation (a 2.8-inch annual average in July, the wettest month) will likely come as rain. But those are only tendencies; the mercury climbed to 90°F one day in June 1969, and in a sudden August 1984 storm 10 inches of snow fell (and drifted to five feet). Weather can change very rapidly in high mountain regions.

For full information on the park, contact the **Superintendent, Denali National Park and Preserve,** P.O. Box 9, Denali Park, AK 99755 (tel. 907/683-2294), or the **Alaska Natural History Association,** P.O. Box 230, Denali Park, AK 99755. Denali National Park also has a year-round **information line** (tel. 907/683-2686). **Alaska Public Lands Information Centers** are located in Anchorage at 605 W. Fourth Ave. (tel. 271-2737) and in Fairbanks at 250 Cushman St. (tel. 451-7352).

GETTING THERE & GETTING AROUND

Private car is the choice of many; it's a 5- to 6-hour drive from Anchorage, 2½–3 hours from Fairbanks. Denali Park is served by tour buses and by **Alaska's Goldline Express,** P.O. Box 61654, Fairbanks, AK 99706 (tel. 907/474-0535). The company charges only $39 one way from Anchorage to Denali, $59 from Anchorage to Fairbanks via Denali, and $25 one way from Fairbanks to Denali. Departure times vary, so check with them for schedule information. There's also seasonal van service aboard the **Denali Express,** 405 L St., Anchorage (tel. 907/274-8539, or toll free 800/327-7651).

Two alternative means of arriving at the park can be spectacularly beautiful, if the weather cooperates. The **Alaska Railroad,** 411 W. First Ave. (P.O. Box 107500), Anchorage, AK 99510 (tel. 907/265-2494, or toll free 800/544-0552), operates daily service between Anchorage, Denali, and Fairbanks (via Wasilla, Talkeetna, and Nenana) from the last week of May until mid-September. The train leaves Anchorage at 8:30am and arrives in Denali Park at 3:45pm; the one-way fare is $85 for adults, $42.50 for children. Or you can buy an Anchorage–Fairbanks ticket (or vice versa) for $115 (children are charged $57.50), with no extra charge for a stopover at Denali Park. The train leaves Denali at 4pm and arrives in Fairbanks at 8:30pm.

Express-train passengers also have the option of riding in Gray Line's deluxe "McKinley Explorer" or Princess Tours' "Midnight Sun Express," private domed cars with more elegant service than is offered in the standard passenger cars. **Gray Line of Alaska** (tel. toll free 800/544-2206) charges $118 for Anchorage–Denali and $62 for Denali–Fairbanks; children pay half price. **Princess Tours** (tel. toll free 800/835-8907) asks $274 for adults, $137 for children, for one-way Anchorage–Fairbanks fare, including an overnight stay at the Harper Lodge and a three-hour natural-history tour.

A train does stop at Denali Park twice a month (both northbound and southbound) in winter, but you'd have to pack a tent and warm gear and plan on doing some snow camping were you to stay: All facilities close for the season in September and don't reopen until May.

The other transportation option is by air. **ERA Aviation,** the Alaska Airlines commuter line (tel. 907/248-4422, or toll free 800/426-0333), has daily Anchorage–Denali Park service in summer. But even if you come to the park by another means, you should try to set aside some time for a clear-weather flightseeing excursion around Mount McKinley. It's the only way to get a grasp of the mountain's true magnitude. Contact **Denali Air,** P.O. Box 82, Denali Park, AK 99755 (tel. 907/683-2261), or most Anchorage and Fairbanks air-taxi services for current schedules and rates.

The following companies are among those offering two-day one-night tour packages between Anchorage or Fairbanks and the park: **Alaska Sightseeing Tours,** 808 Fourth Ave., Battery Building, Seattle, WA 98121 (tel. 206/441-8687, or toll free 800/621-5557); **Atlas Tours,** 609 W. Hastings St., Dept. 104, 5th Floor, Vancouver, BC V6B 4W4 (tel. 604/669-1332); **Gray Line of Alaska (Westours),** 300 Elliott Ave. W., Seattle, WA 98119 (tel. 206/281-3535, or toll free 800/544-2206); **Midnight Sun Tours,** P.O. Box 103355, Anchorage, AK 99510 (tel. 907/276-8687, or toll free 800/544-2235); and **Princess Tours,** 2815 Second Ave., Suite 400, Seattle, WA 98121 (tel. 206/728-4202, or toll free 800/647-7750).

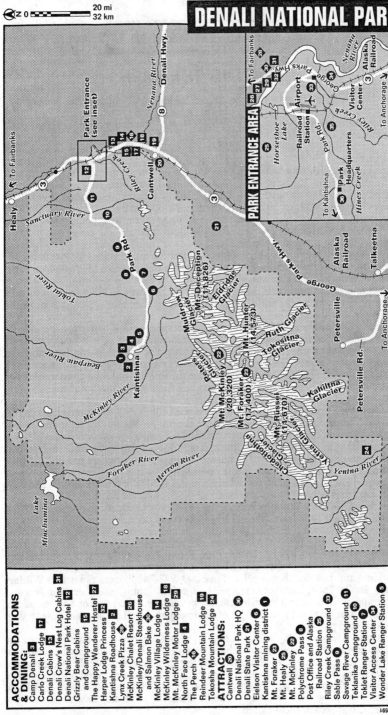

DENALI NATIONAL PARK

0 20 mi
0 32 km

PARK ENTRANCE AREA

ACCOMMODATIONS & DINING:

Camp Denali **3**
Carlo Creek Lodge **17**
Denali Cabins **13**
Denali Crow's Nest Log Cabins **31**
Denali National Park Hotel **12**
Grizzly Bear Cabins and Campground **15**
The Happy Wanderer Hostel **27**
Harper Lodge Princess **32**
Kantishna Roadhouse **2**
Lynx Creek Pizza **28**
McKinley Chalet Resort **30**
McKinley/Denali Steakhouse and Salmon Bake **29**
McKinley Village Lodge **14**
McKinley Wilderness Lodge **18**
Mt. McKinley Motor Lodge **29**
North Face Lodge **4**
The Perch **16**
Reindeer Mountain Lodge **19**
Tokosha Mountain Lodge **24**

ATTRACTIONS:

Cantwell **20**
Denali National Park HQ **36**
Denali State Park **21**
Eielson Visitor Center **6**
Kantishna mining district **1**
Mt. Foraker **23**
Mt. Healy **25**
Mt. McKinley **22**
Polychrome Pass **8**
Post Office and Alaska Railroad Station **35**
Riley Creek Campground **33**
Sable Pass **9**
Savage River Campground **11**
Teklanika Campground **10**
Toklat Ranger Station **7**
Visitor Access Center **34**
Wonder Lake Ranger Station **5**

1655

1. WHAT TO SEE & DO

TOURING THE PARK

The first thing every visitor wants to see is, appropriately, **Mount McKinley.** Ironically, the mountain cannot be seen from the central Denali National Park hotel area. **Mount Healy,** a mere baby at 5,716 feet, is the dominant peak in the park headquarters area.

If you arrived from the south on a clear day, you had a splendid view of McKinley and its huge neighbor, 17,400-foot **Mount Foraker,** as you drove up the George Parks Highway. For your first view of the mountain from within the park, though, you must drive about 10 miles down the park road, en route to the Savage River campground and check station (at 12 miles). You'll start to get good views of the Alaska Range from about 39 miles on. With few cloudless days in the park, especially in summer, you should plan on rising with the sun to maximize your chance of getting a good view. Early mornings are often cloudcap-free, and the rising sun paints a pinkish glow on the peaks' eastern faces.

Admission to the park is $3 for adults, and free for children and students under 17, seniors (62 and older), and disabled individuals. An annual pass is $15; a Golden Eagle Pass, providing annual access to all federal areas, is $25.

Because of the restriction on park traffic, the best way to see wildlife is to take either the park-operated shuttle bus or the private wildlife tour operated through the leading hotels.

Free ✪ **shuttlebus rides**—with no guides to provide a narrative—begin from the Visitor Access Center daily, late May to mid-September, at half-hourly intervals 6am to 4pm (except hourly from 1:30 to 3:30pm). The last round-trip bus returns to the center at 11:15pm. Disabled-accessible buses run on a regular basis. Because of the great number of people who sign up for the shuttle, you'll be given a ticket for boarding the next available bus. During July and August, that may mean the following day.

From mid-June, depending on snow and road conditions, the shuttle bus runs 85 miles (11 hours round-trip) to the Wonder Lake Ranger Station. Earlier in the season, it goes 53 miles (7 hours round-trip) to the Toklat Ranger Station or 66 miles (8 hours round-trip) to the Eielson Visitor Center. It makes scheduled stops, wildlife stops, and extra stops on a "flag" system: The bus will drop you off anywhere you like and pick you up again at no cost. There's just one catch: The bus must have an empty seat because there's no "standing room only" on this road. Bring warm clothes and your own food and drink, as there are no concessions along the road.

The ✪ **Tundra Wildlife Tour,** a six- to seven-hour excursion operated by ARA Outdoor World Ltd., leaves the McKinley Village Lodge, McKinley Chalet Resort, and Denali National Park Hotel twice daily in summer, at 6am and 3pm. Reservations are required. This tour features a driver and naturalist who acts as narrator for the journey. A trail lunch and hot beverage are included in the $41 cost ($20 for children 12 and under). Tours operate mid-May to mid-September.

The Kantishna Roadhouse (tel. toll free 800/942-7420) operates a deluxe **Wilderness Trails Tour,** leaving the Harper Lodge daily (until September 1) at 7am and returning at 7pm after a 95-mile round-trip odyssey. The price of $89 includes a narrated wildlife tour by van, stops for photography, lunch at the roadhouse, and an hour of gold panning.

Before Memorial Day weekend and after mid-September, road restrictions are lifted and you can drive your own vehicle. Should you choose to do this, be aware that the park road is narrow, winding, and mostly gravel. (The first 14 miles were repaved in 1989.) It's kept in tolerable condition, but the 35-m.p.h. speed limit often seems like speedway velocity, and you'll more often find yourself traveling 20–25 m.p.h. All wild animals are dangerous, so if you see some along the road, stay in your car. Do *not* attempt to approach them closely.

SIGHTS ALONG THE PARK ROAD

Some of the main sights you'll see along the road include:

Riley Creek Campground, Mile 0.2. This campground has 102 sites for RVs and tents. There's a 45-minute program each night at 8pm. A variety of information is presented, from glaciers to grizzlies to moose.

Visitor Access Center, Mile 0.7. This is the place to go for general park information, campground registration, and backcountry camping permits. The Alaska Natural History Association sells a variety of books and maps about the park and its wildlife in the information center. *The Denali Road Guide* is an especially worthwhile purchase. Be sure also to pick up a free copy of the *Denali Alpenglow* newspaper. Shuttle buses start from here.

Denali National Park Headquarters, Mile 3.4. About 15 families make this their year-round home; this is as far as the road is kept open in midwinter. As might be expected at an Alaskan winter outpost, there's a sled-dog kennel behind the headquarters, down a short trail from the parking lot. Half-hour **sled-dog demonstrations** are given daily at 10am, 2pm, and 3pm, with free transportation provided from the Denali Park Hotel.

Savage River Campground, Mile 12.8. From 1922 until 1938, when the park road was completed to Wonder Lake, this was as far as most tourists went. Horse-drawn stagecoaches carried visitors to the Savage River camp, where they slept overnight on cots in canvas tents. Today the paved road ends two miles farther, at the bridge over the Savage River. There are four campsites here.

Teklanika Campground, Mile 29.1. The park's second-largest campground with 50 sites, it is two miles from the broad, braided Teklanika River. (The Athabaskan Indian name means "Much gravel, little water.") Look for caribou here.

Sable Pass, Mile 39.1. This is prime grizzly bear country, being especially rich in berries, flowers, and other vegetation. The immediate vicinity is closed to any deviation from the park road.

Polychrome Pass, Mile 45.9. You'd almost feel as if you were in Arizona's Painted Desert here, were not the alpine scenery and wildlife so grand. Glacial chaos and wind and water erosion have created a spectacular and colorful landscape, especially on the east side of the pass. At the foot of the climb, on the east fork of the Toklat River, you'll see a cabin used today by scientific researchers, occupied in the 1930s by biologist Adolph Murie during his renowned study of wolves.

Highway Pass, Mile 58.3. At 3,980 feet in elevation, this is the highest point on the park road. (Park headquarters is at 2,055 feet.)

Eielson Visitor Center, Mile 66.0. Named for pioneer bush pilot Carl Ben Eielson, this facility is only 33 miles from the summit of Mount McKinley. Telescopes are set up to search for animals in the valley below and on the slopes of surrounding peaks. There's an information desk, exhibits on mountaineering and wildlife, restrooms, a water fountain, and a book sales counter. You can accompany a naturalist on a 30- to 60-minute tundra walk at 1:30pm daily. The visitor center itself is open from early June to mid-September, daily from 9am to 8:15pm.

Wonder Lake, Mile 84.6. This young glacial lake, about 4 miles long, is a home for lake trout, burbot, arctic char, and ling cod. Because of the fish, numerous diving and migratory birds often visit here, and caribou and moose are frequently seen. The Wonder Lake Ranger Station is 2 miles north, and the Wonder Lake Campground, with 30 tent sites, is 1½ miles south on a side road. This is the closest point to Mount McKinley—just 27 miles—on the park road, and mountaineering parties making north-side assaults usually start here.

Kantishna mining district. With its handful of lodges, this district begins at Mile 87.9, at the Denali National Park Wilderness boundary. The road ends about two miles farther on.

FLIGHTSEEING TOURS

Several times a day, from sunrise to sunset, pilots for **Denali Air,** P.O. Box 82, Denali Park, AK 99755 (tel. 907/683-2261), lift their wings for "totally awesome" trips around the park. Several tour packages are offered. One of the most popular, as it should be, is the 70-minute "Round Denali" trip, weather permitting. The tour costs $135 per person, based on a three-person minimum. Flights leave every hour starting at 8am.

ERA Helicopters (tel. 907/683-2574) offers 50-minute tours of Denali leaving hourly beginning at 9am. They cost $155 per person, with a three-person minimum and five-person maximum.

Many air taxis fly trips around Mount McKinley from the Anchorage and Fairbanks area. There are others in Talkeetna (see "Excursions South of the Park," below).

SPORTS & RECREATION

If you have any active blood in your veins at all, don't miss the opportunity to do some adventuresome exploring in this phenomenally beautiful park.

HIKING & BACKPACKING You can get your bearings with a one-hour "Morning Walk" beginning at 8am daily in summer from the porch of the Denali Park Hotel. Free hikes of a half day or longer, accompanied by a park naturalist, begin daily from the Park Hotel or the Eielson Visitor Center; times and locations are posted at all information centers.

Several day hikes, ranging from a half mile to nine miles, leisurely to strenuous, are recommended by park officials. Horseshoe Lake, just over a mile from the Park Hotel, and Mount Healy, overlooking the park headquarters area, are especially popular destinations.

Backpackers (those who intend to camp at least one night in the wilderness area) must obtain permits from a naturalist at the Visitor Access Center. The permit is free; it's simply a means of limiting and distributing park use within the backcountry units, each with a quota to protect the environment and enhance the visitors' experience. You must stay within the boundaries of the unit designated by your permit.

It's wise to attend an evening backpacking program at the Morino Campground, a half-mile walk from the railway station. There you'll learn how to hike the Denali backcountry, where there are no trails, few trees, plenty of subarctic tundra, and many glacial rivers to cross. You should boil all water because of the threat of giardiasis, a nasty parasite-transmitted disease. Campfires are prohibited, though you may use a small stove. No camping is allowed within half a mile of the park road, and your camp must be out of sight of the road.

In all hiking and backpacking, make sure before you start that you know how to handle yourself in the event of a bear encounter, should one occur, or other emergencies. There's good safety information on bears and backcountry safety in the park newspaper, the *Denali Alpenglow*.

MOUNTAINEERING Serious climbers from all over the world tackle Mount McKinley each year, mainly in the spring. There may be 40 or more expeditions on the mountain at once. Several thousand have stood on North America's pinnacle since it was first scaled in 1913. Nearly 50 have died trying, however, and more than 150 have been involved in serious accidents. In good years, the climbers' success ratio is about 50%. The whimsical weather, which can bring severe blizzards and gale-force winds at any time of year, is the biggest factor in success or failure.

Talkeetna, on the south side of the mountain, is the most popular start-off point. Most climbing teams prefer to begin their ascent from the 8,000-foot level of the mountain, after being dropped at the Kahiltna Glacier base camp by a ski plane. The **Talkeetna Ranger Station**, P.O. Box 588, Talkeetna, AK 99676 (tel. 907/733-2231), is set up as Denali National Park's main contact point for climbers on the mountain. Anyone contemplating a climb in the national park should write for general or specific information (free) and registration forms.

Six guide services are authorized by the National Park Service to lead trips to Mount McKinley and other Alaska Range peaks. Two are Alaska-based: **Alaska**

Denali Guiding, P.O. Box 326, Talkeetna, AK 99676; and **Mountain Trip,** P.O. Box 41161, Anchorage, AK 99509. The others are the American Alpine Institute of Bellingham, Wash.; Rainier Mountaineering of Tacoma, Wash.; the National Outdoor Leadership School of Lander, Wyo.; and Fantasy Ridge of Telluride, Colo.

RIVER RAFTING This is one of the most popular sports in the national park area. Several firms are ready to help you test your mettle against the Nenana. All operate from approximately mid-May to mid-September, depending on water conditions. Rain gear and lifejackets are provided, but you should dress warmly, with two pairs of wool socks if possible. Food is not provided, so bring your own if you're the munchie sort.

Owl Rafting (tel. 683-2684) will take you for a two-hour trip from the McKinley Chalet Resort to the town of Healy, through 10 miles of the Nenana River canyon. Departures are at 9am, 2pm, and 7pm daily. The cost is $45 per person; children must be at least 12.

Crow's Nest Rafting (tel. 683-2723 or 683-2321) offers two options, one for the adventurous and one for the slightly more faint-of-heart. The "Canyon Run" is a two-hour trip through the white water of the steep Nenana Canyon, while the "Scenic Float" starts farther upriver and gives more relaxation and wildlife-watching opportunities. Both cost $36 for adults, $26 for children under 12 ("McKinley Float" only). Departures are at 9am, 1pm, and 7pm for both trips.

Like Owl and Crow's Nest, **McKinley Raft Tours** (tel. 683-2392) begins from near the McKinley Chalet Resort. Tour A ($33) takes in 2½ hours of upriver scenery; Tour C ($33) is the standard 2-hour white-water run to Healy; Tour B ($48) combines the two, for a 22-mile voyage. Tours A and B start at noon daily; Tour C starts at 9am, noon, and 6:30pm.

Denali Raft Adventures (tel. 683-2234) leaves from the McKinley Village Lodge, Mile 231 on the George Parks Highway. The four-hour "Healy Express" run, covering 22 miles through the canyon for $54 per person, is a favorite (children must be at least 12). Departure is at 1:30pm daily. There's also a more gentle two-hour "McKinley Run," leaving at 9am, 1:30pm, and 7:30pm, and a two-hour, 10-mile "Canyon Run," leaving at 8:30am, 4pm, and 7:30pm. The latter two, suitable for families, cost $34 for adults, $24 for children under 12.

WINTER SPORTS Skiing and dog sledding are the main options. Cross-country skiers have the entire park road beyond headquarters at their disposal. Ski mountaineers enjoy flying into the Ruth Glacier from Talkeetna. Dog-sled enthusiasts, on the other hand, can take advantage of some organized trips.

Chugach Express Sled Dog Tours, P.O. Box 261, Girdwood, AK 99587 (tel. 907/783-2266), offers an all-inclusive three-day/two-night "family adventure" to the Ruth Glacier, with meals and overnight lodging at the Tokosha Mountain Lodge on the south side of the park. The charge of $675 per person includes round-trip transportation from Anchorage. Participants can drive the dog team, ride in the sled, or ski beside it. Other companies in the area that offer dog-sledding tours include **Denali Wilderness Safaris** (tel. 907/768-2550) in Cantwell and **Thunder Lodge** (tel. 907/683-2811) in Healy.

Denali Wilderness Freighters, P.O. Box 670, Denali Park, AK 99755 (tel. 907/683-2722), provide support for cross-country skiers, snowshoers, and mountaineers, but do not provide guided tours. Write for full information and requirements.

2. WHERE TO STAY & DINE

WHERE TO STAY

As noted, hotels serving park visitors are spread across more than a dozen miles of the George Parks Highway and a couple more miles of the park road. Because their number is limited, they are treated here as if they were all in the same community—

which, in a way, they are. Remember, hotels at Denali open no earlier than mid-May and shut their doors by late September. Few have TVs or room phones.

Tax There is no room tax.

EXPENSIVE

DENALI NATIONAL PARK HOTEL, Denali Park, AK 99755. Tel. 907/ 683-2215. (Year-round reservations: 825 W. Eighth Ave., Suite 240, Anchorage, AK 99501; tel. 907/279-2653; fax 907/258-3668.) 100 rms (all with bath).

$ Rates: $109 single; $119 double. Additional person $10 extra. Two nights for the price of one before June 6. MC, V.
Closed: Sept 20–May 21.

This hotel may be all things to all people. To those who don't stay here (as well as those who do), it's a focus of national park activities, a place to dine or drink, to hear a naturalist's lecture or to join a nature walk. To those who do rest their heads here, it's a quiet, luxury accommodation, owned and managed by ARA Outdoor World Ltd., the same group that operates the McKinley Chalet Resort and McKinley Village Lodge.

Surrounded by a rail depot theme, you feel as if you're walking to a ticket window when you step into the lobby to register. Giant blow-up photos of Mount McKinley decorate the lobby walls and usefully point out the major climbing routes to the summit. Behind you in the khaki-painted wood building, surrounding a pot-bellied wood stove, are the hard-backed benches typical of station seating. Old-time ceiling fans whir on the low rafters, and there are luggage lockers on the platform outside. Where you might expect to find arrival and departure timetables, however, are posted lists of the day's events. And when you sidle up to the sideboard where clerks await your arrival 24 hours a day, you'll be greeted with a room key rather than a train ticket.

The standard guest rooms are wood-paneled and decorated in earth tones with red-orange carpeting and upholstery. Each spacious room is furnished with a pair of double beds, a desk/dresser, working chair, and easy chair. There's hot-water heat, and outside the bathroom there's a sink with a large mirror.

Dining/Entertainment: At the far end of the lobby are the Denali Dining Room and Whistle Stop snack shop. The dining room—open daily from 7am to 10pm and 5 to 6:30am, with a light breakfast for those leaving on a wildlife tour—has a garden atmosphere, with high-backed chairs and wood dividers on green carpeting, surrounded by hanging plants and green-patterned wallpaper. Breakfasts, including blueberry pancakes and bagels with smoked salmon, are priced $5–$8; lunches and dinners, ranging from quiche and pasta to salmon and sirloin steaks, run $5–$13. The Whistle Stop, open from 10am to midnight daily, features burgers, chili, tuna sandwiches, and the like for about $5. Just beyond the rear of the main lobby is the Gold Spike Saloon (open from noon to midnight daily), crowded into a pair of railcars.

Services: Booking for wildlife bus tours, rafting, and flightseeing; no-smoking rooms and rooms designed for the disabled.

Facilities: Gift shop (open from 9am to 9:30pm daily) specializing in Native crafts; 300-seat auditorium where films (at 12:30 and 7pm daily) and a naturalist's presentation or slide show (most nights at 9pm) are shown.

HARPER LODGE PRINCESS, Mile 238.5, George Parks Hwy. (P.O. Box 110), Denali Park, AK 99755. Tel. 907/683-2282, or toll free 907/683-2545. (Year-round reservations: 329 F St., Anchorage, AK 99501; tel. 907/258-5993, or toll free 800/541-5174; fax 907/277-8255.) 192 rms and 6 suites (all with bath) TV TEL (? RANDELL COLE)

$ Rates: $136 single or double; $235 suite. Additional person $10 extra. AE, MC, V. **Closed:** Mid-Sept to late May.

★ An Athabaskan prospector named Walter Harper was the first to climb Mount McKinley (in 1913); the rustic theme and furnishings of this $6.3-million hotel are a tribute to his era. Exterior walls and interior front walls are done up in log siding, giving the appearance of entering the lobby and individual guest rooms through log passageways. The three wings are attached to a central lobby, with a gift shop and tour desk.

Rooms all have contemporary furnishings, including twin or double beds, dressers, and tables. Six VIP suites have Jacuzzis; two rooms are equipped for disabled travelers.

Dining/Entertainment: The Summit Restaurant is open from 5am to 10pm daily. Walter's Burger Bar offers light meals. The Base Camp Bar has a panoramic view of the Nenana River and Horseshoe Lake.

Services: Shuttle service to the train station and to various activities at park headquarters and the Denali Park Hotel.

Facilities: Three outdoor spas, gift shop, tour desk.

MCKINLEY CHALET RESORT, Mile 238.9, George Parks Hwy. (P.O. Box 87), Denali Park, AK 99755. Tel. 907/683-2215. Fax 907/683-2366. (Year-round reservations: 825 W. Eighth Ave., Suite 240, Anchorage, AK 99501; tel. 907/276-7234; fax 907/258-3668.) 218 rms and 36 suites (all with bath).

$ Rates: $130 single; $140 double; $210-$360 suite. Additional person (up to five) $10 extra. Two nights for the price of one before June 6. MC, V. **Closed:** Sept 27-May 14.

Elegant rooms in 18 one- and two-story cedar-log chalets are connected by covered boardwalks and gravel paths, high on a bluff overlooking the raging Nenana River. As you enter the hotel from its spacious parking area, you'll get the red-carpet treatment—literally. Reception is straight ahead. The restaurant and bar are to your right, the gift shop and theater to your left.

Some rooms have queen-size beds, but most have twins (they're more appropriate for package-tour groups, which constitute the largest part of the resort's clientele). Enter to a red-carpeted sitting room with a desk and hideaway sofa bed; the bedroom, with its orange-checked drapes and bedspreads, adjoins. All rooms have fabric walls and are electrically heated.

Dining/Entertainment: Wildlife photos, Native antiques, and fine woodwork set the Chalet Dining Room apart from other restaurants in the Denali area. One particular room, the Jewel Box, entered by sliding glass doors and featuring a pyramidal glass ceiling, affords a bird's-eye view of river rafting some 500 feet straight down. The restaurant offers full dinner entrees, such as poached salmon, veal piccata, and steamed king crab legs, for around $20, and for non-meat eaters the vegetable boutiquetière for $13. This is also the place to get an authentic baked Alaska dessert—individually baked as a "mini-McKinley." Lunches are priced at $5-$10; breakfasts, $5-$8. It's open daily from 5 to 6:30am for early breakfast, 7 to 10:30am for full breakfast, 11am to 2:30pm for lunch, and 5 to 9:30pm for dinner.

For more casual meals, the Denali Deli (open daily from 10:30am to midnight) has omelets, pastas, sandwiches, and light seafood and steak dinners. It also has outside seating around an array of flower boxes. The Chalet Lounge (open from noon to 2am daily) offers live solo entertainment five nights a week.

Located at the resort in a turn-of-the-century wilderness cabin near the Nenana River, Fannie Quigley's Alaska Cabin Nite Dinner Theatre is the Denali area's most popular nighttime attraction. An all-you-can-eat, family-style dinner of salmon, ribs, blueberry pie, and trimmings is followed by a 45-minute show of singing, dancing, and tall tales spun by a colorful troupe of prospectors, trappers, and other "sourdoughs." There are seatings at 5:30 and 8:30pm nightly, Memorial Day weekend through Labor Day weekend. Adults pay $22; children 11 and under, $14. Reservations are recommended.

Services: Shuttle service to the railroad station and Denali Park Hotel; booking for dinner theater, bus tours, and rafting.

Facilities: Chalet Club spa, with glassed-in swimming pools, Jacuzzi, sauna, masseur, Universal gym, sun table, and aerobics classes; meeting hall and convention center; theater featuring nightly movies and other programs; tasteful jewelry and gift shop.

MCKINLEY VILLAGE LODGE, Mile 231, George Parks Hwy., Denali Park, AK 99755. Tel. 907/683-2215. Fax 907/683-2398. (Year-round reservations: 825 W. Eighth Ave., Suite 240, Anchorage, AK 99501; tel. 907/276-7234; fax 907/258-3668.) 50 rms.

$ Rates: $103 single; $113 double. Additional person $10 extra. Two nights for the price of one before June 6. DISC, MC, V. **Closed:** Sept 13–May 28.

The late Gary Krabb, one of the pioneers of tourism in the Mount McKinley area (he lived here from 1959 until his death in 1987), built this lodge beside the Nenana River. (He also constructed the North Face Lodge: See "Wilderness Lodges," below.) Today it's owned by ARA Outdoor World Ltd., which also operates the Denali National Park Hotel and the McKinley Chalet Resort. The large hotel lobby presents access to a lovely candlelit lounge that is carpeted and upholstered in red, with a big fireplace and a small jukebox. On the wall of the Kantishna meeting room is a true relic: a dog sled pulled by 16 dogs to the 17,000-foot elevation of Mount McKinley.

The spacious rooms are brightly decorated with orange-gold carpeting and gold-colored bedspreads and drapes. All have two double beds, large hexagonal tables with chairs, desk/dressers, and thermostat-controlled hot-water heating. The walls are partially wood-paneled.

Dining/Entertainment: The contemporary restaurant specializes in steaks, chicken, and seafood in the $8–$16 range.

Services: Tour booking.

Facilities: Tavern with pool tables and fireplace; 200-seat meeting and banquet room showing national-park films nightly at 8pm; gift shop; coin-operated guest laundry; recreation center with covered and outdoor picnic tables; small sandy riverside beach.

MODERATE

DENALI CABINS, Mile 229, George Parks Hwy. (P.O. Box 229), Denali Park, AK 99755. Tel. 907/683-2643 mid-May to mid-Sept, or 907/258-0134 mid-Sept to mid-May. Fax 907/683-2595. 49 cabins (44 with bath).

$ Rates: $85 double with bath; $84 quad without bath, $104 quad with bath; $140 sextet with bath. 10% discount on Denali Raft Adventures trips. MC, V. **Closed:** Mid-Sept to mid-May.

Gary and Denae Kroll have a burgeoning village of varnished wood cabins of various configurations on nicely landscaped riverside grounds. The cabins sleep two, four, or six, and most have private baths; five units share a central facility. (The shower house is central to everyone; there are also two small hot tubs and a third, giant-size tub on the riverbank.) Two-thirds of the carpeted, propane-heated units are set up for four guests, with two double beds and private baths.

The village has its own generator, well, and sewage system. A grocery sells items for cooking on barbecue grills. There's a gift shop in the office. Courtesy pickup is provided to guests who arrive at the park via train or bus, and transportation is provided to the park Visitor Access Center.

DENALI CROW'S NEST LOG CABINS, Mile 238.5, George Parks Hwy. (P.O. Box 70), Denali Park, AK 99755. Tel. 907/683-2723. Fax 907/683-2323. 39 cabins (all with bath). **Directions:** 1.2 miles north of the Park Road junction; turn off the Parks Highway at McKinley/Denali Salmon Bake and drive 200 yards uphill.

$ Rates: $105 cabin for one to four, $132 cabin for six. 10% discounts on Crow's Nest raft trips. MC, V. **Closed:** Mid-Sept to mid-May.

These cabins are the pick of the litter in this category. Owners Carol and Mike Crofoot and their children, Tiko and Koro, began with a river-rafting operation, then added rough-hewn spruce cabins on three levels at the foot of the Sugarloaf Mountain reserve for dall sheep, across the Parks Highway from the McKinley Chalets. Each of the cabins is angled to provide a 180° vista of the mountains and river. They contain two double beds with calico bedspreads, picnic tables, propane heating, and historical photographs on the walls, personally selected by Carol from National Park Service archives. All windows are screened to keep pesky insects out. There are also two open-air hot tubs. Planter boxes with colorful flowers brighten decks on each cabin level, with benches to look across the river valley at Horseshoe Lake.

The Crow's Nest's Overlook Bar & Grill (tel. 683-2641) gives diners the choice of sitting either inside or on a large sunny deck looking across the Nenana River at the park. Open from 11am to 10pm, it serves a full lunch and dinner menu featuring moderately priced steaks, seafoods, chicken, and burgers. The bar—done up in the unlikely marriage of Fiji and Alaska motifs—serves cocktails, wine, and 45 varieties of beer. Box lunches will be packed on request. Courtesy transport is available throughout the Denali area.

MT. MCKINLEY MOTOR LODGE, Mile 238.6, George Parks Hwy. (P.O. Box 77), Denali Park, AK 99755. Tel. 907/683-1240, or 683-2567 Oct–Apr. 23 rms (all with bath). TV
$ Rates: $94 single or double. Additional person $5 extra; children under 6, free. MC, V. **Closed:** Mid-Sept to mid-May.
Keri and Rick Zarcone, longtime owners of the adjacent Lynx Creek Pizza restaurant and pub, established this new motel in 1990. Fully appointed rooms feature good views, color TV, and front-door parking. Guests can take advantage of the River View Trail to explore the Nenana River or have a cookout in the barbecue pavilion. The Zarcones will help you book tours and will develop an itinerary upon request.

BUDGET

CARLO CREEK LODGE, Mile 224, George Parks Hwy. (P.O. Box 103), Denali Park, AK 99755. Tel. 907/683-2576 or 683-2573. 6 cabins (all with bath).
$ Rates: $60–$85 cabin; $5 RV or tent site. MC, V. **Closed:** Mid-Sept to mid-May.
Carlo Creek Lodge consists of six rustic log cabins on a wooded 20-acre plot. All the cabins have standard furnishings, with toilets, showers, and propane heat; five have a double and a twin bed, and one has a double, a twin, and a king-size bed. Two of the cabins have kitchenettes. There are also 25 RV and tent sites with a dump station, and a large covered barbecue pit. The lodge includes a pay phone, a general store, and a gift shop. It's within walking distance of the Perch Restaurant, which serves steaks, seafood, and fresh-baked goods and has a full bar.

GRIZZLY BEAR CABINS AND CAMPGROUND, Mile 231.1, George Parks Hwy. (P.O. Box 7), Denali Park, AK 99755. Tel. 907/683-2696. (For reservations mid-Sept to mid-May: 5845 Old Valdez Trail, Salcha, AK 99714; tel. 907/488-3932.) 13 cabins (none with bath), 5 tent cabins.
$ Rates: $49–$99 cabin for two to six; $21–$23 cot in tent cabin; $14 RV, camper, or tent site (including tent). MC, V.
Here, 13 cabins, including two renovated prospectors' cabins, sleep two to six. Each of the cabins has wood heat; all but the smallest have running water and propane cooking stoves. Beds are doubles, singles, and hideaway sofas, in various combinations. These units—whose individual histories are described on plaques on the front walls—have a real pioneer feel, shrouded as they are in spruce and aspen forest overlooking the Nenana River. There are also a handful of unheated but rainproof tent cabins, with cots on wood floors. A central washhouse contains toilets, hot showers, and laundry facilities. RV, camper, and tent sites are available by the riverside.

THE HAPPY WANDERER HOSTEL, Mile 238.6, George Parks Hwy. (P.O. Box 108, Cantwell, AK 99729). Tel. 907/683-2690. 8 bunks.
$ Rates: $15 per person. No credit cards.
Shoestring travelers may be glad to find this hostel at a destination with normally high prices. A rustic two-room cabin across the road from Lynx Creek Pizza, it has eight bunks, with a curtain separating men from women. There's a community kitchen, but no indoor plumbing or running water.

MCKINLEY WILDERNESS LODGE, Mile 224, George Parks Hwy (P.O.

Box 89), Denali Park, AK 99755. Tel. 907/683-2277. 11 cabins (none with bath).
$ Rates (including continental breakfast): $65–$82 cabin single or double. MC, V.
Closed: Sept 8–June 1.

Here you'll find simple duplex cabins of unfinished wood beside gurgling Carlo Creek. Each unit contains single beds with light bedding, a dresser, a table and two chairs, venetian blinds on the windows, and propane heating. Six units sleep two and five sleep four. Showers and toilets are in the rear of the big, red A-frame that marks the facility from the highway.

CAMPGROUNDS

INSIDE THE PARK Within Denali National Park itself are seven campgrounds containing 232 sites and a backpacker campground that accommodates 60. No advance reservations are taken, so everything is on a first-come, first-served basis—and in the peak of the season is frequently gobbled up by 11am. You must register in person between 8am and 7pm at the Visitor Access Center. The maximum stay permitted is 14 nights.

The largest campground is at Riley Creek, with 102 sites. Facilities include flush toilets, piped water, and a sewage dump station. The cost per night is $12, as is the case in all but two of the park's campgrounds. Two of the campgrounds in the park's interior—Igloo and Wonder Lake—are off-limits to private vehicles and are reached by shuttle bus only. In the four-site Savage Group, sites cost $15 per night; the Morino Backpacker Campground costs only $2 per night.

OUTSIDE THE PARK The **Lynx Creek Campground,** at Mile 238.6 on the George Parks Highway (tel. 907/683-2548), has 46 campsites with a central bath and shower, piped water, laundry, and dump station. Rates are $20 with electricity, $15 without, $1.50 per additional person over four. It's open from May 16 to September 20. The **Grizzly Bear Campground** and **Carlo Creek Lodge** (see the listings above) charge $14 and $5 a night, respectively, for tent and vehicle campers.

WILDERNESS LODGES

If you're enthralled by the idea of waking up on a crisp, cloudless summer morning and gazing across a meadow of wildflowers at North America's largest mountain, you won't want to stay in the main Denali National Park resort area. You'll want to make the 90-mile trek west to Kantishna. Three lodges, each with its own distinct style, operate in or near this historic mining district within the national park but outside the wilderness boundaries. Two more, the Denali West Lodge on Lake Minchumina and the Denali Wilderness Lodge on the Wood River, are farther removed from the park but equally appealing.

CAMP DENALI, Denali National Preserve, near Kantishna (P.O. Box 67), Denali Park, AK 99755. Tel. 907/683-2290. Fax 907/683-2290 (request). (Off-season: P.O. Box 216, Cornish, NH 03746; tel. 603/675-2248; fax 603/675-9120.) 17 cabins (none with bath). **Transportation:** Shuttle from the Denali railway station to the camp three times every two weeks from early June to early September.
$ Rates (all-inclusive): $210 single; $420 double. Minimum stay three nights. No credit cards.

Camp Denali is the cream of the crop of Denali wilderness lodges. Composed of sleeping cabins, a dining cabin, a log lodge, and outbuildings spread across 60 acres of hills not far from Wonder Lake, it offers an all-inclusive vacation experience in the great outdoors. Hosts Wallace and Jerryne Cole place a great emphasis on environmental education: Full-time naturalist guides are among their 22-member staff, and frequent workshops are offered on such subjects as botany, ornithology, glaciology, photography, and local history. Activities include wildlife observation, hiking, canoeing, fishing, gold panning, and mountain biking. Lowell Thomas, Jr., son of the famous adventurer, offers flightseeing excursions from an airstrip four miles west.

Each cabin, of spruce construction with a pine interior, has a wood stove and propane hotplate; twin, double, or queen-size beds with handmade quilts; and a table with a mirror and washbasin. Each has its own outhouse, though there are also flush toilets in a central shower house. Smaller cabins sleep two; family cabins can accommodate up to five on bunks. Audiovisual programs are shown each evening in the lodge, which also houses a library, science resource center, photo darkroom, piano, and sports-equipment cache. The spacious dining room—decorated with an old-fashioned wood-burning cook stove, mountaineering photos, and nature prints—provides a family atmosphere. A self-sufficient operation, the lodge has its own vegetable garden and greenhouse, carpenters' shops, and hydroelectric system.

DENALI WEST LODGE, Lake Minchumina, AK 99757. Tel. 907/733-2630 or 907/276-8687. 3 cabins (none with bath). **Transportation:** Twice-weekly flights from Anchorage to Lake Minchumina airfield ($325); a boat shuttles guests across the lake to the lodge.

$ Rates (all-inclusive): Summer, $300 per person. Winter, $275 per person. No credit cards.

Just outside the park's northwestern boundary, on the shores of Lake Minchumina, is this remote bush getaway. The price includes lodging in private log cabins with wood stoves, use of a sauna, all meals in the main lodge, guided wildlife tours, and canoeing trips. For an additional $150–$300 per person, the lodge will provide fly-out trips for fishing, hiking, canoeing, or flightseeing (two-person minimum). Hearty gourmet meals are served (steak Diane is a dinner favorite).

DENALI WILDERNESS LODGE, Wood River (P.O. Box 50), Denali Park, AK 99755. Tel. 907/683-1287 in summer, or toll free 800/541-9779 year-round. Fax 907/683-1286 in summer, 907/342-6833 year-round. 23 cabins (all with bath). **Transportation:** By charter flight (included).

$ Rates (including meals and transportation): $260 per person for the first night, $160 for additional nights. AE, MC, V. **Closed:** Aug 26–June 9.

The flight to this turn-of-the-century mining camp doubles as a 20-minute flightseeing excursion, providing views of wilderness, glaciers, and wildlife. The lodge lies in a beautiful riverside setting and consists of 25 hand-hewn buildings. In addition to the main lodge, you'll find a trapper's cabin, guest cabins, a wildlife museum, greenhouses, and a sauna. You can relive gold-rush days by participating in such activities as nightly fireside entertainment, overnight horse trips, and gold panning. Hearty home-cooked meals are served.

KANTISHNA ROADHOUSE, Denali National Preserve, Kantishna (P.O. Box 130), Denali Park, AK 99755. Tel. 907/733-2535 or 907/683-2710, or toll free 800/942-7420. 28 cabins (all with bath).

$ Rates: $375 single; $475 double. **Closed:** Sept 16–June 6.

This roadhouse was established in 1905 as a way station for miners (more than 3,000 once prospected here) and other travelers. Today rustic cabins for two to four guests or heated tent cabins beside a stream recall the mining days of yore. Unlike the cabins of yesteryear, however, all now have private baths. A hot tub and sauna are centrally located, and family-style meals with homemade pastries are served in the dining hall. A cocktail lounge called the Topless Cabbage is open at night. Rates include lodging, meals, and transportation from and to the Denali railway station.

NORTH FACE LODGE, Denali National Preserve, near Kantishna (P.O. Box 67), Denali Park, AK 99755. Tel. 907/683-2290 in summer. Fax 907/683-2290 (request). (Off-season: P.O. Box 216, Cornish, NH 03746; tel. 603/675-2248; fax 603/675-9120.) 15 rms, 1 suite (all with bath). **Transportation:** See below.

$ Rates (all-inclusive): $235 single; $470 double. Minimum two-night stay required. No credit cards. **Closed:** Mid-Sept to mid-May.

The North Face Lodge was built in 1974 on a hilltop facing Mount McKinley. Wallace and Jerryne Cole, who also own Camp Denali, bought it in 1988. As you sit in plush leather chairs and couches in the lounge, you can gaze out full-size picture windows at the great mountain, or search for bears, caribou, or other animals through a telescope.

The lodge has carpeted, wood-paneled units, all with twin beds and gas heat, plus a family suite for a capacity of 35 guests. The big dining room, with long tables for communal eating, offers a menu ranging from New York charcoal-broiled steaks to grilled salmon. If you're in the mood for Arctic grayling for breakfast some day, show your Alaska fishing license and the lodge will outfit you with fishing gear and send you off to Moose Creek, behind the lodge. Gold pans are also available to would-be prospectors. There's shuttle service from the Denali railway station to the lodge three times in two weeks from early June to early September.

WHERE TO DINE

Beside the restaurants in the hotels, there are a few other eating places that are definitely worth visiting.

LYNX CREEK PIZZA, Mile 238. 6, George Parks Hwy. Tel. 683-2547.
   Cuisine: ITALIAN. **Reservations:** Not required.
   $ Prices: Pizzas $8.95–$20.95; sandwiches and calzones $6–$8. DISC, MC, V.
   Open: Mid-May to mid-Sept, daily 11am–11pm.
Lynx Creek offers deep-dish pizza with up to five toppings, as well as calzones, deli sandwiches, and a selection of beers and wines. The atmosphere is cozy, with a big fireplace and indoor-outdoor seating. The café is in the rear of a log cabin that also serves as a gas station, liquor store, and campground office.

MCKINLEY/DENALI STEAKHOUSE AND SALMON BAKE, Mile 238.5, George Parks Hwy. Tel. 683-2258 or 683-2733.
   Cuisine: STEAK/SEAFOOD. **Reservations:** Not required.
   $ Prices: Main courses $10–$18. AE, DISC, MC, V.
   Open: Mid-May to mid-Sept, daily 6am–10pm.
This is a freely constructed, wood-frame structure with crushed rock for a floor and transparent plastic for windows. A sourdough breakfast is served until 11am, after which you can choose from salmon, halibut, beef ribs, and steak, plus homemade soup and baked beans, a salad bar, and beverages (beer, wine, and soft drinks). A free shuttle service is provided from all local hotels.

THE PERCH, Mile 224, George Parks Hwy. Tel. 683-2523.
   Cuisine: STEAK/SEAFOOD. **Reservations:** Recommended.
   $ Prices: Main courses $11–$29. MC, V.
   Open: Memorial Day weekend to mid-Sept, dinner only, daily 5–10 pm.
Sitting high on a hill overlooking Carlo Creek, this new restaurant offers steaks and seafood, a full bar, and fresh-baked goods to diners on the south side of the park entrance. A few sleeping cabins, one with a kitchenette, are also available.

3. EXCURSIONS SOUTH OF THE PARK

Going south from Denali National Park, you'll travel 27 miles to get from the Park Road junction to **Cantwell,** a tiny community two miles west of the George Parks Highway, surrounded by magnificent snow-capped mountains. The main street of town, a 100-yard-long paved oasis in the middle of a gravel strip, has little more than a café, general store, and bar. There are a couple of restaurants and service stations at the junction of the **Denali Highway** (open summers only). Once the only route to the park from Anchorage, it threads its way 133 miles east to Paxson, where it intersects the Richardson Highway between Fairbanks and Valdez.

Six miles south of Cantwell, the George Parks Highway crosses the divide between the Gulf of Alaska and Yukon River drainages at Broad Pass. Though it sketches a line between peaks exceeding 12,000 feet elevation to its east and west, **Broad Pass** itself is only 2,300 feet above sea level.

Another 35 miles south, the highway enters the 421,000-acre **Denali State Park,** through which it runs for 47 miles. Camping, fishing, and hiking are popular in this state-administered reserve. At Mile 135, three miles from the south highway entrance to the park, a turnout with a display board is perhaps the best place to view and identify the peaks of the Alaska Range during fine weather.

WHERE TO STAY
SOUTH OF THE PARK

State parks division officials are developing plans for a multi-million-dollar tourist center and hotel in the southeastern corner of the park, near the Susitna River and the railroad community of Curry. Developers also have elaborate plans for a 150-room resort hotel in the state park, off the George Parks Highway. Until such time as either or both become reality, accommodations between the village of Talkeetna and the park road junction are limited. Those currently in existence are all in the budget category.

CHULITNA RIVER LODGE, Mile 156.2, George Parks Hwy. (Star Rte., Box 8396), Trapper Creek, AK 99683. Tel. 907/733-2521. 3 cabins (1 with bath).
$ Rates: $50 cabin for one or two without bath, $70 cabin for one or two with bath. Additional person $25 extra. MC, V.
The Chulitna River Lodge is more notable for its quaint log-cabin gift shop and café, as well as its overnight rafting expeditions, than for its rustic guest cabins. The café is open from 9am to 9pm and serves sandwiches, soup, and coffee. If you're interested in white-water rafting, the owners run a day-long trip for $100 per person. They sell gas here too.

REINDEER MOUNTAIN LODGE, Mile 209.5, George Parks Hwy. (P.O. Box 7), Cantwell, AK 99729. Tel. 907/768-2420 or 768-2942. Fax 907/768-2942. 16 rms (all with bath).
$ Rates: $65–$75 single or double. AE, DISC, MC, V.
The Reindeer Mountain Lodge has comfortable motel rooms with standard furnishings. There is no longer a café on the property, but there is a gift shop. The proprietors are a great source of information about Denali National Park and the surrounding area.

TOKOSHA MOUNTAIN LODGE, Denali National Preserve (P.O. Box 13188), Trapper Creek, AK 99683. Tel. 907/733-2821. 3 cabins (none with bath).
$ Rates: $100 per person; two-day package $400 in summer (fishing); three-day package $600, $675 in winter (dog sledding). No credit cards.
The only Denali National Park wilderness lodge on the south side of Mount McKinley, the Tokosha Mountain Lodge is located near the foot of the Ruth Glacier between the Tokositna River and Pirate Lake. It is accessible in summer by air or boat and in winter by dog sled or skis. There is a system of short trails around the lodge, including one to Pirate Lake, where summer guests can fish or canoe. Guests are housed in cabins with propane heat and lights, with access to outhouses. Hearty, all-you-can-eat, family-style meals are served in the lodge. Summer package rates

include round-trip jet boat from Mile 133 of the George Parks Highway; the winter package includes round-trip airfare from Anchorage.

TRAPPER CREEK TRADING POST, Mile 115.5, George Parks Hwy., Trapper Creek, AK 99683. Tel. 907/733-2315. 2 cabins (both with bath). **$ Rates:** $50 cabin for one or two. AE, DISC, MC, V.

This outpost boasts a café and grocery, a liquor store, a coin-op laundry, a gift shop, and two guest cabins. One cabin accommodates two people with a trundle bed, half-bath, and kitchenette. The other has a double and two twin beds and a full bath. The café (open from 8am to 9pm daily) offers fish, chicken, and Mexican dinners at less than $8. The trading post sells gas and propane, and operates a campground with six full hookups for $10 per night and tent camping for $5 per night.

TALKEETNA

At the end of a paved, 15-mile dead-end road branching off the George Parks Highway at Mile 98.7, is this quaint village of some 400 that is proud to remain just what it is: the hub of an old mining district, the jumping-off point for most Mount McKinley climbing expeditions, and a popular center for wilderness recreation.

Located near the confluence of the Talkeetna and Chulitna Rivers with the broad Susitna, some 80 miles upriver from the Cook Inlet, the community began as an Alaska Railroad construction camp in 1920 and as a freight and supply point for gold miners in the Talkeetna Mountains and other areas. Today it is what author Joe McGinniss described in *Going to Extremes* as "a quintessential Alaskan settlement: it had more pool tables (three) and more airfields (two) than it had gasoline stations (one)." Venture off the main street and you'll find yourself on dirt roads looking at log cabins built by some of the early miners and still occupied.

One of Talkeetna's attributes is that it's on the main Anchorage–Denali Park–Fairbanks railroad line. The *Denali Express* stops here daily in the summer season, at 11am northbound and 4pm southbound; during the winter the train stops only on its twice-monthly milk runs.

At festival time, Talkeetna is especially busy with outside visitors. The big occasions are **Miners Day** in May and the **Moose Dropping Festival** (yes, really) in July.

For information, you can contact the **Talkeetna Chamber of Commerce,** P.O. Box 334, Talkeetna, AK 99676 (tel. 907/733-2330). The new **Talkeetna Visitor Center,** located at the junction of the George Parks Highway and the Talkeetna Spur Road (tel. 907/733-2223), is open in summer.

WHAT TO SEE & DO

In Town

If any two men can be said to have been accorded the status of "immortals" in Talkeetna, they are mountaineer Ray Genet (1931–79) and bush pilot Don Sheldon (1921–75). Genet, sometimes called "The Pirate," was a Swiss-American who climbed Mount McKinley 25 times, including the first winter ascent (in 1967) and the first dog-team ascent (in 1979). He froze to death during an attempted climb of Mount Everest in the Himalayas. Sheldon, who knew McKinley as only a skilled pilot could, and who saved countless climbers from certain death on its flanks, died of cancer.

The **B&K Trading Post,** Main Street (tel. 733-2411), catercorner from the Fairview Inn, has a small museum devoted to local mountaineering, piloting, and outdoor life.

TALKEETNA HISTORICAL SOCIETY MUSEUM, Main St. Tel. 733-2487.

The museum, housed next to the downtown airstrip in a 1936 schoolhouse, contains many pioneer artifacts, local artworks, and a library of old papers and books. Most of all, it contains a series of displays on the history of climbing and flying around

Mount McKinley, featuring special sections on Genet and Sheldon. It boasts a 12-foot by 12-foot scale replica of the mountain and surrounding peaks, with 15 gigantic photographs by Bradford Washburn.

Admissions: Donations accepted.

Open: May–Sept, daily 10am–6pm.

TALKEETNA RANGER STATION, Main St. Tel. 733-2231.

To keep up with the history of Mount McKinley climbing, drop by the ranger station in the same downtown hub area. Denali National Park staffs this outpost—set up to register and monitor mountaineering expeditions in the park—with rangers who are also experienced McKinley climbers. New parties are shown a slide show, given a briefing, and asked to fill out an application to determine how prepared they are and to assist them on questions of equipment and skill. CB radios are monitored 24 hours a day here, at the Kahiltna Glacier airstrip at McKinley's 7,000-foot-level, and at a National Park Service camp at the 14,000-foot level, two days' climb from the top of the mountain. Between 800 and 1,000 climbers, from countries as far away as Brazil, Finland, and Vietnam, tackle the peak each year. Despite precautions, in a typical April-to-July climbing season, there will be 4–10 airlift evacuations and several deaths on McKinley.

Admission: Free.

Open: Mid-Apr to mid-Sept, 8am–5pm daily; mid-Sept to mid-Apr, intermittently.

Exploring the Environs

There are four ☉ **air-taxi services** in Talkeetna: **Doug Geeting Aviation,** P.O. Box 42, Talkeetna, AK 99676 (tel. 907/733-2366); **Hudson Air Service,** Main Street, Talkeetna, AK 99676 (tel. 907/733-2321); **K2 Aviation,** P.O. Box 290, Talkeetna, AK 99676 (tel. 907/733-2291); and **Talkeetna Air Taxi,** P.O. Box 73, Talkeetna, AK 99676 (tel. 907/733-2218). If you figure $200 an hour for the plane and divide it by the number of people in your party, you'll have a pretty good idea of your cost.

Geeting, a mountaineers' favorite, offers tourists an 80-minute, round-trip flight and landing on the Kahiltna Glacier, at the McKinley base camp. K2's Jim Okonek, a retired military pilot, includes a champagne lunch with his two-hour Circle McKinley tour; he also offers glacier landings and an "Overnight Adventure Triangle." David Lee of Talkeetna Air Taxi makes direct trips to Kantishna, on the north side of McKinley. All services do well with fly-in hunting and fishing packages.

If you're into **mountaineering** and looking for an expedition, you won't go wrong by talking to **Alaska-Denali Guiding,** P.O. Box 326, Talkeetna, AK 99676 (tel. 907/733-2649). The outfitter leads expeditions to the summit of McKinley and other Alaska Range peaks, as well as Denali National Park treks and cross-country ski expeditions. The prices are rather high, especially for the mountaineering trips, but so are the risks.

For **winter skiing,** a Nordic ski trail, with a 10-mile outer loop and 5-mile inner loop, begins in a park between the Fairview Inn and the Talkeetna Railway Station.

Several **boat operators** offer sightseeing tours of the Talkeetna Canyon and an adjacent gorge called Devil's Canyon, plus fishing and rafting opportunities on several rivers and jetboat excursions to the Tokosha Mountain Lodge. Check with **Talkeetna Riverboat Service,** P.O. Box 74, Talkeetna, AK 99676 (tel. 907/733-2281), in the Village Arts and Crafts Shop on Main Street; **Mahay's Riverboat Service,** P.O. Box 705, Talkeetna, AK 99676 (tel. 907/733-2223), on Boat Landing Road; or **Tri-River Charters,** P.O. Box 312, Talkeetna, AK 99676 (tel. 907/733-2400).

River waters around Talkeetna boast all species of salmon plus grayling, Dolly Varden, and rainbow trout. **Fishing-boat charters** may cost $135 per person for an eight-hour day, including guide service, lunch, and equipment, depending in part on the number of people sharing the boat. Shore fishing can also be excellent, especially at **Christianson Lake,** a short drive southeast of Talkeetna.

Denali Floats, P.O. Box 330, Talkeetna, AK 99676 (tel. 907/733-2384), offers a wide variety of one- to six-day rafting expeditions throughout the region. More experienced white-water rafters can contact **Nova Riverunners,** P.O. Box 1129, Chickaloon, AK 99645 (tel. 907/745-5753), about their Talkeetna River trips.

WHERE TO STAY

You have your choice of several accommodations in Talkeetna, ranging from moderate in price to downright pioneer.

Two Talkeetna-area bed-and-breakfasts are managed by **River Beauty B&B,** P.O. Box 525, Talkeetna, AK 99676 (tel. 907/733-2741). Rates are $50 single, $70 double. **Alaska Log Cabin B&B,** P.O. Box 19, Talkeetna, AK 99676 (tel. 907/733-2668), is a good value at $45 per night.

Talkeetna also maintains two **campgrounds,** both with shelters, outhouses, picnic tables, and boat launches. Talkeetna River Park is at the west end of the main street through town. Christianson Lake Camper Park is a few miles south and east, via Comsat Road.

FAIRVIEW INN, Main St. (P.O. Box 379), Talkeetna, AK 99676. Tel. 907/733-2423. 6 rms (none with bath).
$ Rates: $30 single; $40 double. MC, V.

S Located right on the main drag, Talkeetna's best-known building is famous for its bar, not for its six upstairs rooms. But the rooms (with shared toilets and bathing facilities) do have "character." Antique decor, including double beds with quilted comforters, would make them pleasant overnight stops were it not for the roars and laughter of successful mountaineering teams celebrating downstairs in the spring months. Their glee can be almost as deafening as the silence of expeditions turned away short of McKinley's summit. But at least the price is right, the people are friendly, and you can say you've stayed in a building listed on the National Register of Historic Sites. The white, wood-frame structure, built in 1923, was famed for years as *the* place for miners and trappers to congregate. There's no restaurant at the Fairview Inn, but wild-game potluck dinners are commonly sponsored during the winter.

While you're at the Fairview, inquire about the Talkeetna Bachelors Society. Nearly 50 strong at this writing, it's dedicated to "the preservation in perpetuity" of bachelorhood. Male members who succumb to nuptial bliss also surrender $100 to the society. Since its inception in 1980, less than $1,000 has been added in this manner to the society's party fund. More profitable is the annual Wilderness Women Contest and Bachelor Auction, at the Fairview the first weekend of December, at which a drink and dance with each of the society members is auctioned off to the highest-bidding woman. Eligible women are expected to demonstrate their prowess in such Alaskan bush skills as target shooting, water toting, and firewood hauling.

LATITUDE 62° LODGE/MOTEL, Mile 14, Talkeetna Spur Rd. (P.O. Box 478), Talkeetna, AK 99676. Tel. 907/733-2262. 12 rms (all with bath).
$ Rates: Apr–Sept, $55 single; $60 double. Oct–Mar, $45 single; $50 double. AE, MC, V.

The newest and nicest motel in Talkeetna is set back off the road in a spruce and birch forest. It has the feel of a modern hunting lodge, with animal heads and hides mounted on the walls, snowshoe chandeliers, and a honky-tonk piano beneath a mural of Mount McKinley. Small but comfortable rooms contain double or twin beds and hot-water heating. TV addicts can watch in the impressive bar, adjacent to the restaurant (open from 7am to 10pm daily), which serves such dinner dishes as 14-ounce charcoal-broiled steak and sautéed jumbo prawns for about $16 each. Winter is a big time here: Cross-country skiing, skating, ice fishing, and dog sledding are just out the door, and the lodge rents snow machines. The management arranges riverboat tours and flightseeing trips in summer.

SWISS-ALASKA INN, Boat Landing Rd. (P.O. Box 565), Talkeetna, AK 99676. Tel. 907/733-2424. 12 rms (all with bath).

$ Rates: $60 single; $70 double. Children under 12 stay free in parents' room. AE, MC, V.

As you might have guessed, the inn is run by Swiss immigrants (Renamary and Werner Rauchenstein). Their casual approach to business is indicated by a sign on the front door: OPEN MOST OF THE TIME. CLOSED PART OF THE TIME. Regardless, it's a favorite place for European mountaineering teams to stay. Located on an often-muddy backstreet, the inn has pleasant rooms decorated in blues, with twin or double beds and electric heat.

The spacious restaurant-bar, partially papered with old news clippings about climbing teams, is open daily for three meals—with such dinner dishes as chicken béarnaise and wienerschnitzel for around $12.

WHERE TO DINE

Outside of the hotels, there are limited choices for meals.

MCKINLEY DELI, Main St. Tel. 733-1234.

Cuisine: DELI. **Reservations:** Not required.

$ Prices: Sandwiches $6–$8; main courses $6–$10. No credit cards.

Open: Daily 6am–10pm.

The deli has full breakfasts, featuring a variety of omelets, reindeer sausage, and yummy baked goods. Later in the day, there are sandwiches, pizzas (priced $12.50–$18.50 for the "Kitchen Sink"), Italian dishes such as spaghetti and lasagne, and ribs, a local favorite.

TALKEETNA ROADHOUSE, Main St. Tel. 733-2341.

Cuisine: AMERICAN. **Reservations:** Recommended for large groups.

$ Prices: Sandwiches $5–$8; main courses $8–$16. MC, V.

Open: Breakfast/lunch daily 7am–3pm; dinner daily 5:30–8:30pm.

This homey café has three-egg omelets for breakfast starting at $4. Lunches include soup and sandwiches. During the busy tourist season, the dinner menu features steaks, seafood, and pasta dishes. In the winter, family-style dinners are served to parties of six or more at 7pm (reservations must be made by 3pm). Eat all you want for just $10 ($5 for children).

4. EXCURSIONS NORTH OF THE PARK

The George Parks Highway north of Denali Park Road junction follows the Nenana River 67 miles downstream to Nenana, then up the Tanana River valley another 58 miles to Fairbanks. As you leave the mountains and cross a broad basin, you'll know that you're in the Interior.

HEALY

It's 11 winding miles down the Nenana Canyon to the village of Healy (pop. 334). Alaska's largest commercial coal operation, the **Usibelli Mine**, is just across the river from here. It markets 1.7 million tons of the black mineral each year, mainly to South Korea; you'll see it put on trains for freighting to Seward and ultimate shipment to Pusan.

Healy Junction is at Mile 248.8. The town is spread for several miles east along the road to Usibelli; it has a medical clinic (Healy Clinic; tel. 683-2211), volunteer fire department, state trooper station, grocery, community center, schools, churches, and post office.

Almost exactly halfway between Healy and Nenana is the **Tatlanika Trading Co.,** Mile 276 on the George Parks Highway (tel. 582-2341). A unique gift shop with a museum atmosphere, it offers such items as moose-antler jewelry, trapper hats, and a variety of furs and original paintings. About 7½ miles farther north is a turnoff to

Clear Air Force Site, an integral part of the ballistic missile early-warning system. Sorry, you can't visit without advance permission.

WHERE TO STAY & DINE
NORTH OF THE PARK

In addition to the accommodations listed below, there is the nearby **McKinley KOA Kampground,** at Mile 248.5, George Parks Hwy. (P.O. Box 34), Healy, AK 99743 (tel. 907/683-2379). Open mid-May to mid-September, it's the only facility in the neighborhood of Denali National Park with full and electric hookups for RVs and campers. Full hookups cost $26 a night (based on two people). There are 77 sites in all, with fireplaces, picnic tables, and showers; reservations are accepted. Tent-camping sites go for $15.75 per night. The campground also has a grocery, laundry, and gift shop.

Tax   The room tax in Healy is 4%.

DENALI HOSTEL, Otto Lake Rd. (P.O. Box 801, Denali Park, AK 99755). Tel. 907/683-1295. 28 bunks. **Transportation:** Courtesy transportation to and from Denali National Park.
$ Rates (including continental breakfast): $22 per person. No credit cards.
The hostel provides bunk-style accommodations and continental breakfast. It has a community shower facility and a laundry.

HEALY HISTORIC HOTEL, Mile 248.8, George Parks Hwy. (P.O. Box 380), Healy, AK 99743. Tel. 907/683-2242. Fax 907/683-2248. 29 rms (all with bath).
$ Rates: June 15–Sept 15, $70 single; $80 double. Sept 16–June 14, $48 single; $56 double. MC, V.
This building was built in 1948 and moved to the site in 1986. It includes a gift shop and home-style restaurant (open daily from 6am to 10pm). Breakfast is in the $5–$7 range and dinners, featuring choices like halibut and shrimp, run $10–$20.

TOTEM INN, Mile 248.7, George Parks Hwy. (P.O. Box 105), Healy, AK 99743. Tel. 907/683-2420. 40 rms (23 with bath). TV
$ Rates: May–Sept, $40 single without bath, $70 single with bath; $50 double without bath, $80 double with bath. Oct–Apr, $30 single without bath, $60 single with bath; $40 double without bath, $70 double with bath. MC, V.
The 23 new rooms at this inn include full baths and satellite TV. Old Atco trailer units, a common sight in the Interior, contain 17 economy rooms (with communal baths) that house mainly transient workers year-round. The motel has a lounge (open from 4pm to midnight), a laundry, and a TV room with free use of videotapes. The café, a friendly log-cabin coffeehouse, is open 24 hours a day with hearty meals like a breakfast of steak and eggs for $8 and a full fried-chicken dinner for $8.95.

NENANA

The symbol of this river port of 640 people is a five-legged "tripod." Now, everyone knows that a tripod has only three legs—everyone, that is, but the residents of Nenana. This quintapod, as it were, set into the winter ice of the slow-moving Tanana River, is connected to a clock that stops at the exact moment of breakup. When that occurs, some lucky Alaskan wins $150,000 or more in the annual **Nenana Ice Classic.** Guess-the-time tickets, at $2 each, are sold throughout Alaska in February and March. (It's a fairly safe bet that breakup will occur some afternoon between April 28 and May 12.)

The Ice Classic aside, Nenana is a pleasant town to visit. The **Nenana Visitor Center** (tel. 832-9953), in a sod-roofed log cabin where A Street forks off the George Parks Highway, can get you started exploring. It's open Memorial Day to Labor Day, daily from 8am to 6pm. Several small gift shops are located near the visitor center.

Nenana is situated at the confluence of the Nenana and Tanana Rivers, 58 miles southwest of Fairbanks. It's the home of the **River Port Authority,** through which 80% of the villages along the Yukon River, from Fort Yukon to St. Michaels, are supplied with food and freight when the river is free of ice. A tug and barge fleet do the honors.

Also big in Nenana is dog mushing; you can drive past a large dog yard on C Street south of 3rd Street, and elsewhere around town you'll see dogs tethered beside small houses. The **Nenana Dog Mushers** headquarters is in a modern log building on 1st Street between A and Market Streets.

Local Athabaskan Natives, members of the Doyon Ltd. corporation, are active in cultural activities. Inquire at the visitor center about potlatches or dance performances scheduled around the time of your visit.

CHAPTER 9

FAIRBANKS & THE INTERIOR

O f all Alaska's cities, large and small, Fairbanks feels most like what an Alaskan city should feel like.

Spread for more than eight miles along the banks of the meandering Chena River, a tributary of the Tanana, this modern frontier settlement still carries reminders of the mineral wealth on which it was built. Gold dredges and mining camps speckle its outlying areas. Tom Sawyer paddlewheelers still ply the shallow, muddy rivers, sled-dog teams scamper through the long winter nights, and follies-style revues are a nightly occurrence in saloons and at the re-created Alaskaland pioneer village.

The Trans Alaska Pipeline, which crosses the rolling terrain a stone's throw northeast of the city, brought a new era of progress to Fairbanks in the mid-1970s. Today, at the University of Alaska's main campus, scientists study the aurora borealis and permafrost, the life cycles of arctic wildlife, and the effect on agriculture of 21-hour summer days. The university also has a superb museum. North of the city is a satellite-tracking station. And throughout Fairbanks are modern hotels and restaurants, the equal of those in other cities in Alaska and the American West.

Nowhere else in North America, and in few other places on earth, do as many people live in a community this far north. Only Tromsø, Norway, and three or four Russian cities scattered across the Arctic at this latitude are larger. The Arctic Circle is only about 200 miles north of Fairbanks, visitors are surprised to learn that Fairbanks experiences not only the lowest temperatures in the state of Alaska but also the highest!

Clear summer days, often reaching into the 90s (though the mean is around 60°F), never really get dark; the Fairbanks Goldpanners baseball team plays a game at midnight on June 20 without lights! On the other hand, average winter temperatures drop below −10°F from December through February, and there can be fewer than four hours of dim daylight. Springs are dry and cool; autumns, crisp with occasional light snow. No time of year is really wet, though August is the rainiest month (with frequent afternoon cloudbursts) and April is the driest. The only really unpleasant time to visit Fairbanks is when the temperature drops to −40°F, as it sometimes does in midwinter, and a stinging ice smog forms around pollutants caught in the air.

A SHORT HISTORY Fairbanks owes its existence to a low river and a lucky

WHAT'S SPECIAL ABOUT FAIRBANKS

Heritage

☐ A gold-rush flavor, which persists in such attractions as a historic gold dredge and reconstructed turn-of-the-century gold camps.

☐ Alaskaland, which preserves many relics of Fairbanks's bygone era, including a re-created gold-rush town, a pioneer riverboat, and a native village.

☐ The paddlewheeler *Discovery*, still plying the waters of the Chena and Tanana Rivers.

Natural Attractions

☐ Some of the world's largest vegetables, nurtured by summer days of 20 hours and longer, which are seen at local farms and greenhouses, including the Georgeson Botanical Garden of the University of Alaska–Fairbanks (UAF).

☐ The brilliant aurora borealis, or "northern lights," visible only between September and April (the UAF's Geophysical Institute has year-round exhibits).

☐ Musk-oxen, caribou, and reindeer, bred and studied at the UAF's Large Animal Research Station.

Culture

☐ The UAF Museum, which focuses on natural and cultural history.

☐ Athabaskan and Eskimo crafts, made and sold throughout the Fairbanks area.

☐ The World Eskimo-Indian Olympics, held annually in July, which includes such unique events as the ear pull and knuckle hop.

Technology

☐ The Trans Alaska Pipeline, which passes within a few miles of Fairbanks (it can be seen best from a site just eight miles north of the city).

Other Sights

☐ The nearby town of North Pole, built around Santa Claus House, where it's Christmas every day of the year.

☐ Chena Hot Springs, a lovely wilderness resort less than 90 minutes' drive from Fairbanks.

☐ Year-round dog-mushing demonstrations and a comprehensive exhibit of sled-dog racing at the Dog Mushing Museum or Tivi Kennels.

---

strike . . . and to two men, named E.T. and Felix—and I'm not talking movies or comic books.

E. T. Barnette, an ex-convict seeking to establish a trading post up the Tanana River in 1901, was marooned with his goods on the banks of the Chena River when the steamer on which he was traveling hit the shallows and was forced to turn back. While Barnette was contemplating how to move his supplies to a more marketable location, an Italian prospector named Felix Pedro happened upon gold near Fox, about 12 miles north. The date of the discovery, July 22, 1902, is still celebrated every year in Fairbanks with a full week of Golden Days festivities.

The rush was on, and Barnette's new trading post became the focus. E.T. became mayor, of course. As a favor to Judge James Wickersham, the first peacemaker to set up court in the Interior, he named the settlement after Indiana Sen. Charles Fairbanks, a Wickersham benefactor who later became vice-president under Theodore Roosevelt. Barnette had trouble staying on the right side of the law, however. He soon became the "most hated man" in Fairbanks for his role in a bank failure that cost many depositors their savings.

Fairbanks's history since then has been a series of peaks and valleys. Its population stood at around 11,000 in 1910, but dropped drastically during World War I, and slowly crept back up to around 4,000 with the construction of the Alaska Railroad and the establishment in 1922 of Alaska Agricultural College, now the University of Alaska. World War II saw the construction of the Alaska Highway and brought thousands of military personnel to Eielson Air Base and Ladd Field, now Fort Wainwright. A disastrous flood put much of the city under eight feet of water in August 1967, but the damage—though significant—was quickly forgotten when oil was discovered on the North Slope in 1968. The pipeline construction boom that followed in the mid-1970s brought new wealth and ballooned Fairbanks's population up over 70,000.

Today the 7,400-square-mile Fairbanks North Star Borough claims about 78,000 residents, of whom 20% are military personnel and dependents. Fairbanks itself has a population of around 31,000.

1. ORIENTATION

ARRIVING

Name your preferred means of arriving in Fairbanks. Any form of transportation but ship will get you there, and even then—if you're willing to seek out a Yukon Basin tugboat—you may get lucky.

BY PLANE Fairbanks International Airport is served by several leading carriers. On arrival, as you descend by escalator from an upper level where you'll find a restaurant, lounges, and gift shops, you'll see before you a black-and-white panoramic photo of the Fairbanks landscape. The main lobby contains a four-panel original oil painting of walruses on float ice and a single-engine antique bush plane suspended above the corridor linking the baggage-claim area with the car-rental counters. A detailed exhibit shares the history of aviation in the Interior. The Fairbanks Convention and Visitor Bureau maintains an information center at the airport.

Here are the Fairbanks phone numbers for leading airlines serving domestic traffic: **Alaska Airlines** (tel. 907/452-1661, or toll free 800/426-0333); **United Airlines** (tel. toll free 800/241-6522); **Delta Airlines** (tel. 907/474-0238, or toll free 800/221-1212); and **MarkAir** (tel. 907/474-9166, or toll free 800/426-6784). All have offices at the airport. Alaska Airlines offers many nonstop flights daily from Anchorage and direct daily flights via Anchorage from San Francisco, Seattle, Dallas, and Houston.

It's a six-mile, 15-minute drive east on Airport Way from the airport to downtown. Many hotels offer courtesy pickup service. If yours does not, you'll have to travel by taxi. **Taxis** are typically $8–$10 for the journey to downtown.

BY BUS Fairbanks is served by charter lines and tour-bus lines. Most of these operate in the summer only. They include three American lines: **Alaska Sightseeing Tours,** 553 First Ave., Fairbanks, AK 99701 (tel. 907/452-4518); **Princess Tours,** 3045 Davis Rd., Fairbanks, AK 99709 (tel. 907/479-9640); and **Gray Line of Alaska,** 1521 S. Cushman St., Suite 123, Fairbanks, AK 99701 (tel. 907/456-7742). **Atlas Tours,** P.O. Box 4340, Whitehorse, Yukon Territory Y1A 3T5 (tel. 403/668-3161), serves Fairbanks from Canada.

BY TRAIN The **Alaska Railroad,** P.O. Box 107500, Anchorage, AK 99510-7500 (tel. 907/265-2494 or 265-2685, or toll free 800/544-0552), operates daily express service in summer (May 24 to September 13) between Fairbanks and Anchorage via Nenana, Denali National Park, Talkeetna, and Wasilla. The train leaves Fairbanks at 8:30am, arriving in Anchorage at 8:30pm; the northbound train leaves Anchorage at 8:30am, reaching Fairbanks at 8:30pm. From September to May there is weekly service. The one-way fare is $115 for adults, $57.50 for children 5–12.

The Fairbanks passenger depot is across the Chena River bridge from downtown, at 280 N. Cushman St. (tel. 907/456-4155).

BY CAR As North America's northernmost major town, Fairbanks is a goal for many northbound drivers. The city is 206 miles west of Tok, at the junction of the

Alaska and Glenn Highways; 364 miles north of Valdez via the Richardson Highway; and 358 miles north of Anchorage via the George Parks Highway.

For a current report on road conditions, dial 452-1911 or 456-ROAD.

TOURIST INFORMATION

The **Fairbanks Convention and Visitor Bureau** maintains its headquarters and information center in a log cabin overlooking the Chena River, on First Avenue just east of Cushman Street. Visit the bureau at 550 First Ave. (tel. 907/456-5774, or toll free 800/327-5774) for full information on all area attractions, right down to restaurant menus and language services. It's open daily from 8am to 6:30pm in summer, 8:30am to 5pm in winter. Free guided walking tours are offered daily at 10am and 3pm, Memorial Day through September. You can also listen to a 24-hour recorded message of attractions and events (tel. 456-INFO).

The **Fairbanks Chamber of Commerce** office is at 250 Cushman St. (tel. 907/452-1105). For information on outdoor pursuits, try the **Alaska Public Lands Information Center,** 250 Cushman St., Suite 1A (tel. 907/451-7352), or the **U.S. Geological Survey,** 101 12th Ave. (tel. 907/456-0244).

CITY LAYOUT

The **Chena River** runs from east to west through Fairbanks, paralleling the course of the Tanana River until it turns south to meet the larger stream just past the Fairbanks Airport, five miles west of downtown. It's not difficult to keep your sense of direction if you remember where the river is.

Downtown Fairbanks is on the south side of the river. Numbered avenues curve around a bend in the Chena. The avenues are crossed by several north-south streets that fan out like spokes on a bicycle wheel. **Cushman Street,** running one-way north, is the main drag. **Barnette Street,** to its west, is the major southbound thoroughfare. To Cushman's east, Noble Street (northbound) and Lacey Street (southbound) are two other main byways.

Airport Way demarcates the southern limit of downtown, below 12th Avenue; it's a four-lane highway heading west to the airport and the George Parks Highway, which proceeds south to Denali National Park and Anchorage. At its eastern end, Airport Way divides the Richardson Highway, which heads south and east toward Delta Junction and the Alaska Highway, from the Steese Expressway, the major northbound artery. North of the Chena River, **College Road** wends its way west to the University of Alaska. Illinois Street provides the interface between the Cushman Street bridge and College Road.

2. GETTING AROUND

The preferred means of getting around the city are bus, taxi, and rental car. Fairbanks is flat enough, however, that bicycling and cross-country skiing are popular in the appropriate seasons.

BY BUS Fairbanks's city bus system is the **Metropolitan Area Commuter Service** (MACS). Its two color-coded routes link the downtown Transit Center at Fifth Avenue and Cushman Street (tel. 452-6623) with the university, Alaskaland, Fort Wainwright, and residential neighborhoods in all directions. Regular service is available Monday through Friday from 6:45am to 10:40pm and on Saturday from 7:15am to 9:40pm. Buses don't operate on Sunday.

Fares are $1.50 for adults; 75¢ for students through grade 12, seniors, and the disabled; free for children 5 and under. A day pass costs $3. For more information, write to MACS, 3175 Peger Rd., Fairbanks, AK 99701, or call the **public transit hotline** (tel. 907/452-3279).

BY CAR All the large automobile-rental agencies, and many smaller, locally owned firms, are represented at Fairbanks International Airport or at downtown offices. I've been pleased with **National,** at the airport (tel. 907/474-0151, or toll free 800/227-7368). Here's a short list of others: **All Star Rent-a-Car,** 4870 Old Airport Rd. (tel. 907/479-4229, or toll free 800/426-5243); **Avis,** at the airport (tel. 907/474-0900, or toll free 800/331-1212); **Budget,** at the airport (tel. 907/474-0855, or toll free 800/527-0700); **Hertz,** Airport Road and Cushman Street (tel. 907/452-4444, or toll free 800/654-3131) and at the airport (tel. 456-4004); **Holiday/Payless,** at the airport (tel. 907/452-0177, or toll free 800/729-5377); and **Rent-a-Wreck,** 2105 S. Cushman St. (tel. 907/452-1606, or toll free 800/421-7253 outside Alaska). Local firms include **Arctic Rent A Car,** at the airport (tel. 479-8044) and 1408 Turner St. (tel. 451-0111); and **Ford Leasing and Renting,** 1625 Old Steese Hwy. (tel. 452-1991).

BY TAXI If you have to get somewhere fast, you can't beat the convenience of a taxi. Fairbanks has a slew of them. Four majors, all with 24-hour dispatch, are **Fairbanks Taxi** (tel. 456-3535 or 452-3535), **United Cab Co.** (tel. 451-4444 or 451-0000), **King Cab** (tel. 479-5464 or 456-5464), and **Yellow Cab** (tel. 452-2121).

FAST FAIRBANKS

American Express The local office is easy to find on the corner of Cushman Street and Gaffney Road (tel. 456-7888).

Area Code The telephone area code, as with all of Alaska, is 907.

Barbers See "Hairdressers/Barbers," below.

Car Rentals See "Getting Around," in this chapter.

Cleaners See "Laundry/Dry Cleaning," below.

Climate See "When to Go" in Chapter 2.

Currency Exchange Banks, generally open Monday through Friday from 10am to 6pm, are easily located in the downtown and university areas. Mt. McKinley Mutual Savings Bank, 531 Third Ave. and 530 Fourth Ave. (tel. 452-1751), handles the greatest variety of foreign currencies. The National Bank of Alaska (tel. 474-4110), with six locations in Fairbanks, also exchanges currency.

Dentist Dr. Vaughan J. Hoefler practices general dentistry at 3535 College Rd., Suite 202 (tel. 479-4759).

Doctor The Fairbanks Clinic (tel. 452-1761) has physicians specializing in family practice, internal medicine, gynecology, orthopedics, and obstetrics. Located at 1867 Airport Way, near Super 8 Motel, the clinic is open Monday through Friday from 8am to 5pm and on Saturday from 8am to 4pm.

Emergencies For emergency assistance from police, fire department, or ambulance, dial **911.**

Eyeglasses Vista Optical (tel. 474-4900) is located in the University Center Mall at University Avenue South and Airport Way.

Film See "Photographic Needs," below.

Hairdressers/Barbers The New Design Hairstyling and Tanning Center, 3535 College Rd. at University Avenue (tel. 479-HAIR), specializes in haircuts and perms for men, women, and children.

Holidays

New Year's Day January 1
Martin Luther King Day Third Monday in January
Presidents Day Third Monday in February
Memorial Day Last Monday in May
Independence Day July 4
Labor Day First Monday in September
Columbus Day Second Monday in October

Veterans (Armistice) Day November 11
Thanksgiving Day Last Thursday in November
Christmas Day December 25

Hospitals Fairbanks Memorial Hospital, 1650 Cowles St. (tel. 452-8181), is located a short distance south of downtown.

Hotlines Crisis line (tel. 452-4403), Poison Control (tel. 474-0137).

Information See "Tourist Information" in "Orientation," in this chapter.

Laundry/Dry Cleaning B&L Laundromat, 418 3rd St. (tel. 452-1355), has self-service facilities or drop-off service. For dry cleaning, Norge Dry Cleaners is open from 8am to 8pm seven days a week at 1255 Airport Way (tel. 456-5211).

Libraries The Noel Wein Library, Airport Way and Cowles Street (tel. 459-1020), has a good Alaskan section. The University of Alaska–Fairbanks Rasmuson Library (tel. 474-7481) is the place to go for information on Alaskan history. North Pole has a library at 601 Snowman Lane (tel. 488-6101).

Newspapers The daily *Fairbanks Daily News-Miner* is a Gannett-affiliated newspaper. The *Pioneer All-Alaska Weekly* is also published in Fairbanks.

Photographic Needs For camera repairs, try Alaskan Photographic Repair Service, 551½ Second Ave., Room 221 (tel. 452-8819). For film and film processing, try Fairbanks Fast Photo and Video (tel. 456-8896, or toll free 800/478-8896), at the Shoppers Forum (Airport Way and Cowles Street), which has one-hour service. The Gavora Mall shop (Steese Highway and 3rd Street) has three-hour Ektachrome slide processing as well.

Police For emergency assistance, call 911.

Post Office The downtown station is at 315 Barnette St. (tel. 452-3203). There's a small branch in the Gavora Mall, 3rd Street near the Old Steese Highway. For customer service information, call 474-0938.

Radio Fairbanks has four AM and eight FM radio stations, including KFAR, 660 AM (news); KCBF, 820 AM (classic rock); KIAK, 970 AM and 102.5 FM (country and sports); KJNP, 1170 AM and 100.3 FM (Christian); KWLF, 98.1 FM (Top 40); KAYY, 101.1 FM (adult contemporary); and KSUA, 103.9 FM (album-oriented rock).

Religious Services In addition to the dozens of churches and religious organizations, there's also a Dial-a-Devotion phone line (tel. 452-2222).

Taxes Tax on hotel rooms in Fairbanks is 8%.

Taxis See "Getting Around," in this chapter.

Telegrams/Telexes Call Alascom (tel. toll free 800/478-9500).

Television Fairbanks has four television stations: KATN, Channel 2 (ABC/NBC) (tel. 452-2125); KJNP, Channel 4 (independent Christian broadcasting) (tel. 488-2556); KTVF, Channel 11 (CBS/NBC) (tel. 452-5121); and KUAC, Channel 9 (PBS) (tel. 474-7491).

Transit Information Call the public transit hotline (tel. 452-3279).

Useful Telephone Numbers The time and temperature number is 844. For a recorded local weather report, call 452-3553. For telephone information, the number is 411.

3. ACCOMMODATIONS

There are about 2,000 guest rooms available in Fairbanks and its immediate vicinity. Yet accommodation is at a premium in midsummer—and the innkeepers know it. Hotels typically raise their room rates 20%–95% for the May-to-September tourist season. When you tack onto this the city tax on rooms, you're staring at what could be a very big bill to visit Fairbanks during the summer months.

The following price breakdown for a double room is based on summer rates, though I've also listed the off-season rates with individual hotel descriptions. "Very

Expensive" hotels means $130 and up a day, "Expensive" is $100–$130, "Moderate" is $70–$100, and "Budget" is under $70. Quite often the winter rates are more indicative of the relative quality of the accommodation.

Tax   The city tax on hotel rooms is 8%.

DOWNTOWN

The downtown area is bounded by the Chena River on the north and Airport Way on the south, between the Steese Highway and Lathrop Street.

VERY EXPENSIVE

REGENCY FAIRBANKS, 95 10th Ave., Fairbanks, AK 99701. Tel. 907/452-3200, or toll free 800/348-1340, 800/478-1320 in Alaska. Fax 907/452-6505. 64 rms, 65 suites. TV TEL
$ Rates: May 15–Sept 15, $140 single; $150 double. Sept 16–May 14, $90 single; $100 double. AE, DC, MC, V.

⭐ Located within easy walking distance of the central downtown area, the Regency is a first-class hotel in every respect, with a feeling of opulence. Crystal chandeliers hang from the ceiling of the warm, two-level lobby. Plush lavender-and-burgundy carpeting lines the corridors.

Half the guest rooms contain kitchenettes with refrigerators, four-burner stoves, and microwave ovens. Dishes and other utensils are available on request from the bell stand at no charge. Forty of the units have Jacuzzis. Each room has two queen-size beds, nouveau antique wood furnishings, satellite television, telephones (free local calls), and thermostat-controlled hot-water heating. Burgundy and peach dominate the color scheme.

Dining/Entertainment: The pastel shades prevail in the decor of the restaurant and piano bar. A breakfast buffet (summer only) is priced at $8, while lunches are in the $7.50–$12 range. Dinner entrees, including veal Oscar, seafood fettuccine, and prime rib, cost $14–$20.

Services: 24-hour bell service, valet laundry, courtesy van, no-smoking rooms and rooms designed for disabled guests.

Facilities: Coin-op guest laundry; Princess Tours desk in lobby.

WESTMARK FAIRBANKS, 820 Noble St., Fairbanks, AK 99701. Tel. 907/456-7722, or toll free 800/544-0970. Fax 907/451-7478. 240 rms and 12 suites. TV TEL
$ Rates: May 15–Sept 15, $152 single; $162 double; $172 executive suite. Sept 16–May 14, $98 single; $102 double; $112 executive suite. AE, MC, V.

⭐ Fairbanks's finest full-service hotel is owned and operated by Westours (80% of the summer clientele is composed of tour groups). A rambling, four-story inn, it sprawls across two city blocks on the south side of downtown. As you drive in, you'll pass through a gateway dividing the lobby from the restaurant/lounge wing. The entry is informal and the staff friendly. The lobby features potted trees and vinyl-upholstered sofas on a tile floor.

Rooms are impressively decorated in pastel shades of mauve, gray, blue, and peach, with matching carpets, blackout drapes, and bedspreads. Silk-screened landscapes hang on the walls. Free local phone calls, 24-channel cable television, and thermostat-controlled hot-water heating are standard, as are a variety of complimentary toiletries. Executive suites have queen-size beds, large desks, elaborate sitting rooms, remote-control TVs, and clock radios—and in winter, complimentary continental breakfasts.

Dining/Entertainment: The Bear 'n Seal (tel. 456-7722 for reservations) is recognized by many as Fairbanks's no. 1 restaurant. Richly appointed and dimly lit, it specializes in continental cuisine. Plan on an outlay of $40–$50 per person, not including drinks or wine. Seafood appetizers, such as coquilles St-Jacques and lobster bisque, tempt the palate; entrees are mainly steaks and seafood, including steak Diane

FROMMER'S COOL FOR KIDS:
HOTELS

Captain Bartlett Inn (see p. 332) The authentic hunting-lodge flavor here—with big-game heads and skins and various gold rush–era Alaskana mounted on the log-cabin walls—fascinates all ages.

Sophie Station Hotel (see p. 330) Every room is a suite, which means that meals can be cooked at home—not bought in a restaurant night after night. Guests are welcome to use the tennis courts next door.

Wedgewood Manor (see p. 334) Another all-suite hotel, this one has an indoor swimming pool and other athletic facilities; and it's adjacent to the Creamers Field wildlife refuge, with many trails for summer hiking and winter cross-country skiing.

flambé and prawns Bombay. Flambé desserts are specialties. The hotel also has a midpriced coffee shop and a cocktail lounge, the Kobuk Room, with solo entertainment nightly except Sunday.

Services: Room service, valet laundry, courtesy car, no-smoking rooms and rooms for disabled guests; the *Wall Street Journal, USA Today,* and Anchorage and Fairbanks dailies are complimentary to guests.

Facilities: Westours/Gray Line desk, gift shop, hair salon, banquet seating for up to 500.

EXPENSIVE

BRIDGEWATER HOTEL, 723 First Ave., Fairbanks, AK 99701. Tel. 907/452-6661. Fax 907/452-6126. 90 rms. TV TEL
$ Rates: Mid-May to mid-Sept, $100 single; $110 double; $145 suite. Mid-Sept to mid-May, $55 single; $65 double; $100 suite. AE, MC, V.
The former Great Land Hotel has recently undergone a major renovation from the lobby up. Guest rooms, which overlook the Chena River, are not the largest in town, but they are clean and well kept. Rooms contain a queen-size, double, or twin bed, blackout drapes, easy chairs, desks, dressers, 12-channel satellite TV, and a telephone (local calls are free).
Dining/Entertainment: Cocktail lounge.
Services: Courtesy car.

POLARIS HOTEL, 427 First Ave., Fairbanks, AK 99701. Tel. 907/452-5571, or 907/452-5574 collect for reservations. Fax 907/456-2696. 111 rms, 24 suites. TV TEL
$ Rates: June–Labor Day, $94.50 single; $102.50 double; $110.70 suite. Sept 8–May, $69 single; $74 double; $82 suite. AE, CB, DC, DISC, MC, V.
At 10 stories, the Polaris is the tallest building in the Interior. Built in the early 1950s, it's one of the older hotels in the city, but through continued renovation it has kept its standards high.
The spacious guest rooms are tastefully appointed in earth tones, with wood paneling on some of the walls, reproductions of classic French paintings on the others. Most contain two double beds, a dresser, desks, chair and mirror, satellite TV, and phone (free local calls), plus lots of closet space. There's hot-water heating (but what's that Holiday Inn bathmat doing beside the toilet?). Suites have kitchenettes. Pets may be permitted with management approval.
Dining/Entertainment: The Black Angus, a coffee shop, is open daily from

6am to 10pm and features a salad bar, lunch sandwiches for $6–$8, filling beef and seafood dinners in the $16–$22 range, and king crab sold by the ounce. An adjoining lounge (open from 11am to 2am) has a jukebox and large-screen TV.

In the penthouse, the Tiki Cove restaurant (tel. 452-1484), open Monday through Saturday from 5pm to midnight and on Sunday from 2pm to midnight, offers Chinese and Polynesian cuisine. Most menu items are around $10; a deluxe combination dinner for two or more runs $20 per person. The decor alone is worth a trip up the elevator. As you disembark, you're greeted by hanging lanterns depicting a Chinese immortal and a Grecian maiden. Potted plastic bamboo stands on red or light-green carpeting. At the tables are wicker chairs with cushions featuring bamboo and bird-of-paradise patterns. The restrooms are marked with the Hawaiian words for man (*kane*) and woman (*wahine*).

Services: Valet laundry, courtesy shuttle from the airport or train station.
Facilities: Gift shop, liquor store, conference rooms.

BUDGET

ALASKAN MOTOR INN, 419 Fourth Ave., Fairbanks, AK 99701. Tel. 907/452-4800. 17 rms, 15 suites (all with bath). TV TEL
$ Rates: Mid-May to mid-Sept, $50 single; $60 double. Mid-Sept to mid-May, $40 single; $50 double. Suite with kitchenette $10 extra. AE, MC, V.
Each room has double or queen-size beds and other standard furnishings, including four-channel TV with HBO, free local phone, and hot-water heat. Native-theme prints are mounted on the wood-paneled walls. Suites have kitchenettes with four-burner stoves, but you must bring your own utensils. Courtesy coffee is provided. Pets are permitted.

FAIRBANKS HOTEL, 517 Third Ave., Fairbanks, AK 99701. Tel. 907/456-6440 or 456-7378. 36 rms (5 with bath).
$ Rates: $44 single; $59 double. No credit cards.
The Fairbanks Hotel is a survivor from the 1930s. Each room, small but clean, contains double or twin beds, a dresser, a desk, and chairs. Some have small private baths; most, however, share a central facility. A pay phone and television are in the lobby. Heating is by hot-water radiator.

WEST SIDE

This section of Fairbanks takes in a lot—from busy Airport Way to the university district and beyond.

VERY EXPENSIVE

SOPHIE STATION HOTEL, 1717 University Ave. S., Fairbanks, AK 99709. Tel. 907/479-3650. Fax 907/479-7951. 147 suites. TV TEL
$ Rates: Mid-May to mid-Sept, $150 suite for one, $160 suite for two. Mid-Sept to mid-May, $95 suite for one, $105 suite for two. AE, CB, DC, DISC, MC, V.
The centerpiece of an impressive condominium development on the east side of the airport, the Sophie Station presents itself as an elaborate railway depot. Walk in through double doors, with station-style seating in the entryway, to an elegant bilevel lobby featuring potted palms on green carpet and mirrored walls reflecting custom-made wood furnishings. Some 80% of the guests in this hotel are corporate businessmen and government workers.

The Y-shaped hotel's sophisticated rooms are all suites. They are richly appointed with wall-to-wall beige carpeting and burgundy upholstery and trim. Each living room has a couch and easy chair, coffee table, cable television, and desk. There's additional seating at the dining bar. The kitchen comes complete with cookware and utensils, from stove and refrigerator right down to toaster and coffee maker. The bedrooms are furnished with one or two queen-size beds, custom-made dressers, blackout drapes, and clock radios; there's a phone beside the bed as well as in the living room (local calls free). The wardrobe closet, with sliding mirror doors, is very

FAIRBANKS ACCOMMODATIONS & DINING

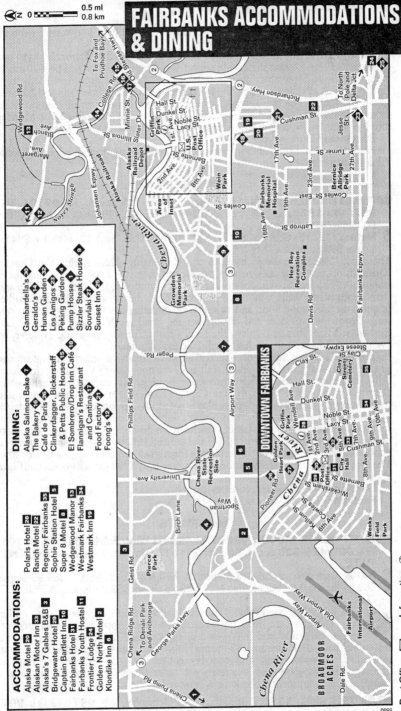

0.5 mi
0.8 km

ACCOMMODATIONS:

Alaska Motel 20
Alaskan Motor Inn 33
Alaska's 7 Gables B&B 3
Bridgewater Hotel 29
Captain Bartlett Inn 10
Fairbanks Hotel 31
Fairbanks Youth Hostel 11
Frontier Lodge 24
Golden North Motel 2
Klondike Inn 6

Polaris Hotel 28
Ranch Motel 22
Regency Fairbanks 33
Sophie Station Hotel 5
Super 8 Motel 8
Wedgewood Manor 13
Westmark Fairbanks 34
Westmark Inn 19

DINING:

Alaska Salmon Bake 7
The Bakery 16
Café de Paris 14
Clinkerdagger, Bickerstaff & Petts Public House 5
El Sombrero/Drop Inn Café 18
Flannigan's Restaurant and Cantina 17
Food Factory 21
Foong's 42

Gambardella's 30
Geraldo's 4
Hunan Garden 32
Los Amigos 23
Peking Garden 1
Pump House 40
Sizzler Steak House 9
Souvlaki 27
Sunset Inn 25

DOWNTOWN FAIRBANKS

Post Office ⊠   Information ⓘ

5592

large, and the dressing table is a nice addition. All units have hot-water baseboard heating.

Dining/Entertainment: Zach's restaurant is acclaimed by Fairbanksans as one of the city's finest. Elegant steak and seafood dinners are priced in the $12–$20 range. It's open May to September, daily from 6am to 10pm; October to April, daily from 7am to 9pm. A gift shop and deli, the Cornerstore (open daily from 6am to 12:30am), adjoin the lobby. The plush, relaxing Express Room lounge, on the second floor, serves as a meeting room during the day and is open for cocktail service Monday through Saturday from 4pm to midnight and on Sunday from 5 to 10pm.

Services: Courtesy van.

Facilities: Coin-op laundry; tennis courts and jogging track at adjacent Sophie Plaza Apartments.

EXPENSIVE

CAPTAIN BARTLETT INN, 1411 Airport Way, Fairbanks, AK 99701. Tel. 907/452-1888, or toll free 800/544-7528, 800/478-7900 in Alaska. Fax 907/452-7674. 191 rms, 6 suites. TV TEL

$ Rates: May 15–Sept 15, $110 single; $120 double. Sept 16–May 14, $64.50 single; $69.50 double. AE, MC, V.

The most "Alaskan-feeling" hotel in this thoroughly Alaskan city, the Captain Bartlett is of spruce-log construction, with totem poles and a food cache outside the front door. The log-cabin interior is like that of a hunting lodge, with a bearskin and rams' heads on the walls, a mounted wolf and dog sled in the rafters. Electric candles brighten the hardwood floor, and an antique grandfather clock tick-tocks against one wall. Down the corridors and throughout the hotel are historical photos of Old Fairbanks. (Capt. Robert Bartlett, the hotel's namesake, was an arctic explorer, an associate of Robert Peary on his North Pole expeditions.)

The hotel's rooms, simply decorated in green and mauve tones, contain queen-size or twin beds, desks, and dressers, as well as 27-channel cable TV, a phone (free local calls), and thermostat-controlled hot-water heating. Six units have kitchenettes. Despite its "expensive" category, the Captain Bartlett is not air-conditioned, and rooms can get hot and stuffy. Service also is not always up to the expected standards.

Dining/Entertainment: The Captain's Table restaurant, open daily from 6am to 10pm, offers a breakfast buffet, luncheon sandwiches ($5–$8), and such tasty dinner entrees as chicken Bartlett ($14) and sautéed scallops ($18). A small stage and dance floor are at the rear of the restaurant for after-dinner dancing to a jazz combo. The Dog Sled Saloon, entered through swinging circa 1900 gates, is open until 1am daily.

Services: Valet laundry, courtesy car.

Facilities: Captain's Treasure Chest gift shop.

MODERATE

GOLDEN NORTH MOTEL, 4888 Old Airport Way, Fairbanks, AK 99701. Tel. 907/479-6201, or toll free 800/447-1910 in Alaska. 62 rms (all with bath). TV TEL

$ Rates (including continental breakfast): Mid-May to mid-Sept, $69.95 single; $89.95 double. Mid-Sept to mid-May, $39.95 single; $59.95 double. AE, CB, DC, DISC, MC, V.

This motel is a good value if its slightly inconvenient location doesn't bother you. The units are small but exceedingly clean. Appointed with chocolate-brown carpeting and yellow-and-orange-checked bedspreads, they contain queen-size beds, desk/dressers, 12-channel cable TVs, free local phones, thermostat-controlled hot-water heat, and courtesy coffee. But the management provides courtesy van transportation wherever you want to go, even to dinner; and a complimentary continental breakfast is provided in the cozy lobby every morning.

KLONDIKE INN, 1316 Bedrock St., Fairbanks, AK 99701. Tel. 907/479-6241. Fax 907/479-4227. 46 suites. TV TEL

$ Rates: May 15–Oct, $59 suite for one, $70 suite for two. Nov–May 14, $54 suite for one, $65 suite for two. AE, DISC, MC, V.

For a single-story city motel, the Klondike Inn covers a lot of ground. These renovated apartment units spread like a ranch on both sides of Bedrock Street and across adjacent Rewak Drive. The friendliness and wide-open spaces are consistent throughout the motel.

There are one-, two-, and three-bedroom units, all with kitchenettes. Wood paneling, beige upholstery, and lush chocolate-brown carpeting set a tone of warmth. Bedrooms all are furnished with queen-size beds; a couch, chair, six-channel satellite TV and radio, and phone (free local calls) are in the living room. The kitchen area includes a four-burner stove, large refrigerator, microwave oven, and plenty of cabinet space—but you must provide your own utensils. Hot-water heating is thermostat controlled. Pets are accepted with a deposit, and there's a coin-op laundry on the premises. Courtesy car service is provided from the airport or train station.

The Klondike Lounge and Dining Hall (tel. 479-2224) has a good-time, rustic appeal. Prime rib is the specialty: You can get a prime-rib sandwich for lunch, with soup or salad, for around $8; or a 16-ounce dinner cut for less than $20, served au jus with sautéed mushrooms, and including baked beans, potato, hot bread, and soup or salad. The restaurant is open Monday through Saturday from 6am to midnight and on Sunday from 10am to 11pm. The lounge is open daily from 8am to 5am.

SUPER 8 MOTEL, 1909 Airport Way, Fairbanks, AK 99701. Tel. 907/ 451-8888, or toll free 800/800-8000. 73 rms, 2 suites (all with bath). TV TEL
$ Rates: May–Sept, $82.90 single; $88.90 double. Oct–Apr, $59.90 single; $66.90 double. AE, CB, DC, DISC, MC, V.

This is everything you expect a Super 8 to be—clean, well kept, reasonably priced . . . and a bit sterile. Each guest room has wall-to-wall brown or rust carpeting, matching patterned bedspreads, and watercolor prints on the walls. Rooms contain queen-size beds, desk, luggage rack (but no dresser), 12-channel cable TV, direct-dial phones (free local calls), and hot-water heating. One room is accessible to the disabled. There's a coin-op laundry and courtesy van service from the airport or train station.

There's no restaurant, but a Denny's (open 24 hours) is next door, and this stretch of Airport Way is fast-food city: Within one long block are McDonald's, Wendy's, Pizza Hut, Shakey's Pizza, Sizzler Steak House, and a 7-Eleven grocery.

SOUTH SIDE

Cushman Street heads south from downtown, eventually branching east as the Old Richardson Highway. Several restaurants are out this way.

VERY EXPENSIVE

WESTMARK INN, 1521 S. Cushman St., Fairbanks, AK 99701. Tel. 907/456-6602, or toll free 800/544-0970. Fax 907/451-7478. 173 rms. TV TEL
$ Rates: $135 single; $145 double. AE, MC, V. **Closed:** Mid-Sept to mid-May.

A charming pioneer atmosphere pervades the seasonal sibling property of the Westmark Fairbanks. The clean and spacious guest rooms are air-conditioned for the hot days of summer. The carpeting and bedspreads in the newer wing are in shades of burgundy and gray, with silk-screened landscapes on the walls and wicker furniture; the older wing is done up in rust tones with autumn-print bedspreads. Most rooms have two double beds, blackout drapes, vanities, free local phone calls, TVs with local reception, and thermostat-controlled hot-water heating.

Dining/Entertainment: A shake roof and railing mark the entrance to Felix's coffee shop, where old mining photos and rustic wood decor seem to add flavor to the barbecued rib specialties ($12 range) and potato bar. The adjoining Husky Lounge features a backyard patio.

Services: Valet laundry, courtesy car.

Facilities: Gift shop, Westours/Gray Line desk, guest laundry.

MODERATE

RANCH MOTEL, 2223 S. Cushman St., Fairbanks, AK 99701. Tel. 907/452-4783. 31 rms. TV TEL
$ Rates: Mid-May to mid-Sept, $70 single; $80 double. Mid-Sept to mid-May, $50 single; $60 double. MC, V.
Nicely appointed rooms with cobalt-blue carpets and floral wallpaper distinguish this motel. Each room has double or queen-size beds, two plush chairs, a smoked-glass coffee table, a handsome wood desk/dresser, and a closet with sliding mirror doors. The motel also has 10-channel cable TV, a phone (free local calls), gas heat for the winter and an electric fan for the summer.

BUDGET

ALASKA MOTEL, 1546 Cushman St. (P.O. Box 73766), Fairbanks, AK 99701. Tel. 907/456-6393. 9 rms, 28 suites (all with bath). TV
$ Rates: Mid-May to mid-Sept, $59 single; $69 double; seventh night free. Mid-Sept to mid-May, $49 single; $59 double; $160 weekly. DISC, MC, V.
Each room has two double beds, a desk and dresser, 12-channel cable television, free local phone, thermostat-controlled hot-water heating, light-brown carpeting, and wood-paneled walls. Kitchens, found in all the suites, have two-burner stoves, refrigerators, and tables with three chairs. A coin-op laundry and a barbershop are on the premises.

FRONTIER LODGE, 440 Old Richardson Hwy., Fairbanks, AK 99701. Tel. 907/456-4733. 20 rms (all with bath). TV
$ Rates: Mid-May to mid-Sept. $50 single; $55 double; $60 twin. Mid-Sept to mid-May, $40 single; $45 double; $50 twin. Weekly rates available. No credit cards.
A two-story log cabin faces the highway and a newer building, containing the office, sits at the rear. The rooms, all with kitchenettes, have double beds, dressers, couches, dining tables with chairs, large closets with shelf space, TVs (local reception), and hot-water baseboard heating. There are two pay phones in the lobby, and a coin-op guest laundry on the premises.

NORTH SIDE

This area takes in everything north of the Chena River and east of the university district.

VERY EXPENSIVE

WEDGEWOOD MANOR, 212 Wedgewood Dr., Fairbanks, AK 99701. Tel. 907/452-1442. Fax 907/451-8184. 150 suites. TV TEL
$ Rates: Mid-May to mid-Sept, $140 suite for one, $150 suite for two; additional person $10 extra. Mid-Sept to mid-May, $55 suite for one, $60 suite for two; additional person $5 extra. AE, DISC, MC, V.
A segment of an apartment complex has been set aside as a hotel, where guests get all the advantages of full-time residents and then some. It's bordered on the north and west by the Creamers Field state refuge, with trails for hiking or cross-country skiing year-round. During the off-season in particular, this is one of Fairbanks's best bargains. Reception is in Building R, near the center of the complex. As you enter, the desk is to your left, the lobby area two steps down to your right, with a central fireplace and wood-carved art set into the walls. A garden area is bathed in continuous light, and coffee is always available.

All rooms are one- or two-bedroom suites. Of the 150 units set aside for the hotel, a good third of them are in Building P, open year-round; the remainder, in Buildings M and N, are open summers only. Rooms are extremely spacious, clean, and well kept. The walls are wood paneled throughout. In the living room are two couches, two tables, and cable television (video, and VCR rentals are available). A balcony overlooks the complex's spacious lawn. The bedroom has two double beds and a double dresser, a clock radio, and an enormous wardrobe closet. Local calls are free. The full kitchen has all utensils and appliances, including toaster and coffeepot, and settings for four.

Dining/Entertainment: There's a restaurant in Building R where continental breakfasts are served from 6 to 11:30am for $5.95. It's also open (with full bar service) for a moderately priced lunch and dinner.

Services: Courtesy car, no-smoking rooms and rooms for disabled guests.

Facilities: Token-operated laundry, individual guest mailboxes, ramps for the disabled, indoor swimming pool, racquetball courts, four saunas, family-size Jacuzzi; equipment can be checked out at the front desk at no charge.

BUDGET

FAIRBANKS YOUTH HOSTEL, College Rd. and Aurora Dr. (P.O. Box 1738), Fairbanks, AK 99701. Tel. 907/479-4114 days.
$ Rates: $12 for American Youth Hostels members, $15 for nonmembers. No credit cards.

Located in a Quonset hut behind the Farmer's Market on the north side of the city, this hostel—open mid-May through mid-September—offers dorm space (provide your own sleeping gear), common bathrooms, showers, and laundry, but no kitchen. Registration is between 6 and 8pm. The hostel is easily reached via the Red Line of the city bus system.

BED-&-BREAKFAST

The main reservations and referral service in the city is **Fairbanks Bed & Breakfast,** P.O. Box 74573, Fairbanks, AK 99707 (tel. 907/452-4967). An effort is made to place travelers with families of similar interests. Most lodging is priced $55–$68 double, including a continental breakfast. About 50 B&Bs are located in Fairbanks, including the one recommended below. Contact the **Fairbanks Convention and Visitor Bureau,** 550 First Ave. (tel. 907/456-5774, or toll free 800/327-5774), for a complete listing.

ALASKA'S 7 GABLES BED & BREAKFAST, 4312 Birch Lane (P.O. Box 80488), Fairbanks, AK 99708. Tel. 907/479-0751. Fax 907/479-4742. 9 rms (5 with bath). TV TEL
$ Rates (including breakfast): $40–$70 single or double; $50–$95 suite. DISC, MC, V.

This spacious, Tudor-style home was originally designed as a fraternity house. The foyer is striking with seven-foot stained-glass icons above a seven-foot waterfall. The living room has cathedral ceilings and a balcony, and there is a two-story greenhouse. The wedding chapel with a fireplace adds a romantic touch. Gourmet breakfasts feature selections like salmon quiche, peachy pecan crêpes, and stuffed deviled eggs. Amenities include a laundry, Alaskan videotape library, and Jacuzzis. You can borrow bicycles or take a canoe down the nearby Chena River.

CAMPGROUNDS

There are several campgrounds within the city:

The **Chena River State Campground,** University Avenue on the south side of the river (tel. 907/451-2695), has 64 sites with restrooms, water, a dump station, tables, fireplaces, and a boat ramp. There's a $10 camping fee and a five-day limit.

The **Tanana Valley Campground,** at the fairgrounds where Aurora Drive meets College Road (tel. 907/456-7956), has 31 sites with restrooms, showers, water, a dump station, a laundry, tables, fireplaces, and wood for sale. There's space for recreational vehicles, but no hookups. The overnight charge is $10.

River's Edge RV Park and Campground, 4140 Boat St., off Airport Way (tel. 907/474-0286), is the area's newest RV facility, with over 100 sites. Full hookups with water, sewer, and electricity are $22, sites with water and electricity are $19, and sites with no hookups are $14 a night. Showers are free. You'll find a variety of facilities on site, such as a laundry, gift shop, and visitor information center.

The **Norlite Campground,** 1660 Peger Rd., just south of Airport Way (tel. 907/474-0206), has 25 tent sites and 250 trailer sites. Facilities include restrooms, showers, water, a dump station, a laundry, a grocery and liquor store, and full electric and sewer hookups for RVs. The fee is $13 for tents, $18 for electrical hookup, and $20 for full hookups (with sewer).

Goldhill RV Park, Mile 355, George Parks Hwy. (P.O. Box 60769), Fairbanks, AK 99706 (tel. 907/474-8088), charges $16 for units with electric hookups and $12 for sites without electricity. It's located about three miles west of Fairbanks.

Pioneer Trailer Park, 2201 S. Cushman St. (tel. 907/452-8788), has 40 units at $15 per day for full hookups and showers.

Self-contained RVs are also permitted overnight parking (with a five-night limit) at **Alaskaland,** on Airport Way, at $7 per night. Water and a dump station are provided.

There are numerous other state campgrounds within an hour's drive of downtown Fairbanks on the Elliot, Steese, and Richardson Highways and Chena Hot Springs Road. For information and a complete listing, contact the **Alaska Division of Parks,** 4420 Airport Way (on Sportsman's Way), Fairbanks, AK 99707 (tel. 907/451-2695).

4. DINING

As the gateway to the frontier, Fairbanks doesn't have the variety of restaurants you'll find in Anchorage. But neither is the city an ungourmandized outpost.

DOWNTOWN

Downtown has some of Fairbanks's highest-class restaurants—the **Bear 'n Seal** at the Westmark Fairbanks and the **Black Angus** and **Tiki Cove** at the Polaris Hotel. Its other restaurants, however, are very reasonably priced.

MODERATE

GAMBARDELLA'S, 706 Second Ave. Tel. 456-3417.
   Cuisine: ITALIAN. **Reservations:** Accepted only for parties of three or more.
$ Prices: Appetizers $2.50–$6; main courses $5.95–$14.95; deli $3.95–$8. MC. V.
   Open: Restaurant, dinner only, Mon–Thurs 5–9pm, Fri–Sat 5–9:30pm, Sun 4:30–9pm. Deli, Mon–Sat 11:30am–5pm.

Ⓢ   Alice Gambardella, once owner and chef of the San Remo restaurant in New Haven, Conn., sought to open a quiet hole-in-the-wall in Fairbanks. But her culinary touch gave her away, and lines now extend from this art deco Italian spot into the streets at midday.

This is really two different restaurants. In the afternoon it's a frenetic Italian deli with counter service and a blackboard menu of pasta, gourmet pizzas, and submarine sandwiches. In the evening it's a more serene sit-down restaurant, with veal, chicken, pasta, and other dinners. The house special is seafood Fra Diablo—calamari, shrimp, scallops, crab, and halibut in a tomato sauce with linguine. The lasagne is also excellent. Meals include homemade bread and house minestrone or salad. Alice's cheesecake is a great way to finish.

HUNAN GARDEN, 513 Fourth Ave. Tel. 474-8847.
   Cuisine: CHINESE. **Reservations:** Not required.

FROMMER'S COOL FOR KIDS: RESTAURANTS

Alaska Salmon Bake *(see p. 338)* While the young'uns are awaiting their dinner from the outdoor barbecue pit, they can explore the Mining Valley at the Alaskaland theme park, with its old mining tunnel, sluice boxes, and gold-dredge buckets.

The Food Factory *(see p. 339)* A strong step up from most fast-food places, this restaurant (there are three in the area) offers filling sandwiches and pizzas. Kids are welcome, even though the menu alerts parents that "Ropes and gags are available on request."

The Pump House *(see p. 338)* This national historic site preserves dozens of fascinating antiques, many of them up to 150 years old. From the Cook's Tent, children can wave at passengers on the paddlewheelers cruising down the Chena River.

Sizzler Steak House *(see p. 339)* No novelties here: Just good all-American food with a family accent. Order at the counter, then help yourself to the fruit, soup, salad, pasta, taco, and dessert bar.

$ Prices: Appetizers $1.25–$9.75; main courses $6.95–$12.95; lunch buffet $6.95. No credit cards.
Open: Mon–Sat 11:30am–10pm, Sun 4–9pm.

Before you climb the stairs to the second-story, pause a moment to drop a penny in the wishing well for Kuan Yin, the Chinese goddess of mercy. Then step up to this pleasant downtown eatery. It's not so much the decor (the red hanging lanterns, Japanese fan pattern on the wallpaper) that tells you this restaurant is authentic as the incense sticks and oranges on the altar devoted to Tien Kung, a major Chinese folk deity.

Five regional cuisines—Hunan, Szechuan, Mandarin, Shanghai, and Cantonese—are prepared here. As a lover of spicy food, I recommend the harvest beef or the Yushan chai tai (a pork dish), each $10. An all-you-can-eat buffet attracts lunchtime crowds Monday through Friday.

PEKING GARDEN, 1101 Noble St. Tel. 456-1172.
Cuisine: CHINESE. **Reservations:** Recommended for large groups.
$ Prices: Appetizers $3.95–$12.95; main courses $8–$20; lunch buffet $7. AE, MC, V.
Open: Mon–Sat 11:30am–11pm, Sun 3–10pm.

The interior of this restaurant is elaborate: After being greeted by a huge painted wood carving of a pair of sea dragons, you'll walk through a moon gate and beneath hanging lanterns into a gaudy Chinese art museum.

For under $40, a couple can dine on such Mandarin specialties as wonton or sizzling-rice soup, eggrolls, barbecued pork, Mongolian beef, garlic chicken, and steamed rice. Or you can order à la carte and try white-cucumber and bean-curd soup, "ants on a tree" (shredded pork with green onions and vegetables), or sautéed "happy family" (sautéed abalone, shrimp, scallops, and vegetables). There's an all-you-can-eat lunch buffet here too.

THE WEST SIDE

Some of the better moderately priced hotel restaurants, such as the **Captain's Table** in the Captain Bartlett Inn and the **Klondike Dining Hall** at the Klondike Inn, are located in this area. So, too, is Fairbanks's most famous restaurant, the Pump House.

EXPENSIVE

THE PUMP HOUSE, Mile 1.3, Chena Pump Rd. Tel. 479-8452.
   Cuisine: STEAK/SEAFOOD. **Reservations:** Recommended.
$ **Prices:** Appetizers $5–$11; main courses $11–$21; Sun brunch $13. AE, DC, MC, V.
   Open: Lunch daily 11:30am–2pm; oyster bar daily 2–5pm; dinner daily 5–11pm (5–10pm in winter); brunch Sun 10am–2pm.

⭐ Back in 1933 the Chena Pump House was built on the Chena River as part of an ingenious hydraulic system that sent river water 400 feet uphill through a three-mile ditch to a gold-dredging operation at Cripple Creek. In 1978 it was reconstructed as a fine restaurant, preserving many of the relics of that era. So successful was its effort at becoming a "period piece" that the restaurant has been designated a National Historic Site. One pool table, for example, was built in 1898 and used during the Klondike Gold Rush. Other antiques are as much as 150 years old.

The corrugated-iron exterior makes it look like a minor warehouse, but within its doors Sea Galley's Pump House exudes class. There's the Senator's Saloon, with a mahogany bar built in Kansas City; the Dining Room, whose hardwood floor and simple decor is reminiscent of a bygone era; and the Cook's Tent, a deck facing on the river, where you can wave at the paddlewheeler as it glides past.

For dinner, you can select prime rib, halibut, baked salmon, or chicken à la Oscar from the menu. Lunch features an all-you-can-eat buffet for $9.80. The Senator's Saloon—which boasts the Farthest North Oyster Bar in the World (mussels and clams too)—stays open till the wee hours. Call or ask your hotel about the restaurant's free transport service.

PIKES LANDING, 4438 Airport Way. Tel. 479-6500.
   Cuisine: CONTINENTAL. **Reservations:** Recommended.
$ **Prices:** Appetizers $5–$7.50; main courses $18–$26; Sun brunch $14.95. AE, CB, DC, DISC, MC, V.
   Open: Lunch daily 11:30am–2:30pm (lounge opens at 10am); dinner daily 5–10pm; brunch Sun 10am–3pm.

Pike's Landing takes advantage of its riverfront setting with an 11,000-square-foot deck, where lunch and dinner are served from May through August. Year-round, you can view the Chena River from inside this refined log structure, choosing from the lighter "broiler menu" (served from 2:30 to 11pm) in the lounge or the full menu in the fine dining room. The cuisine is elegant, but the atmosphere is relaxed and casual.

Recommended dinner entrees include the crab-stuffed filet mignon, rack of lamb, and the fresh halibut. Dinners come with all the fixings, including a Caesar or house salad, vegetable and bread. Pike's Landing also offers an all-you-can-eat Sunday brunch.

MODERATE

ALASKA SALMON BAKE, Alaskaland, Airport Way at Peger Rd. Tel. 452-7274.
   Cuisine: ALASKAN. **Reservations:** Recommended for large groups.
$ **Prices:** Lunch $9.95; dinner $16.95. Children pay 50¢ per year of age. No credit cards.
   Open: Lunch June 10–Aug 15, daily noon–2pm; dinner May 15–Sept 15, daily 5–9pm. **Closed:** Mid-Sept to mid-May.

⭐ Half the fun of this place is its location in the Mining Valley exhibit at Alaskaland. When you're not gathered around the outdoor barbecue pit (or in the covered seating), you can wander through an old mining tunnel and see sluice boxes, gold-dredge buckets, and other memorabilia of Fairbanks's roots, or you can visit the gift shop. Dinner—salmon, halibut, ribs, or a 16-ounce Porterhouse steak—includes salad bar, sourdough rolls, blueberry cake, and a non-alcoholic beverage. Beer and wine are extra.

The Palace Saloon opens at noon daily. You may want to take in the Palace Show, an old-fashioned music and dance performance. It costs $9.50 per person and performances are scheduled at 7:30pm and 9pm. Reservations are recommended (tel. 456-5960). Free transportation is provided several times nightly from larger hotels starting at 4:30pm.

SIZZLER STEAK HOUSE, 1694 Airport Way. Tel. 456-3581.
  Cuisine: STEAK. **Reservations:** Not required.
$ Prices: Main courses $7–$18. AE, MC, V.
  Open: Sun–Thurs 11am–9:30pm, Fri–Sat 11am–10pm.
This Sizzler is another one in the well-known chain of low-cost family steakhouses. Like the others, it's friendly and serves its purpose well. You can dine well on a small steak, or splurge for a steak-and-lobster combination plate. The restaurant also features fresh local fish. Sizzler is known for its all-you-can-eat fresh-fruit, soup, salad, pasta, taco, and dessert bar.

THE SOUTH SIDE
BUDGET

EL SOMBRERO / DROP INN CAFE, 1420 S. Cushman St. Tel. 456-5269.
  Cuisine: MEXICAN/AMERICAN. **Reservations:** Recommended for large groups.
$ Prices: Appetizers $5.50–$10.50; main courses $6.95–$18.25. AE, MC, V.
  Open: El Sombrero, Sun–Thurs 11am–10pm, Fri–Sat 11am–11pm. Drop Inn, daily 6am–5pm.
If you're in the mood for Mexican food but your companion is not, you might compromise at El Sombrero and the Drop Inn Café. Twin restaurants occupy this white-trimmed red building. The Drop Inn is strictly a breakfast-lunch spot (where you can get two poached eggs on toast for $4), while El Sombrero is open for lunch and dinner. If you're very hungry, try the Chihuahua combination, one each of a tostada, taco, taquito, enchilada, and chile relleno, plus rice, beans, chips, and salsa, for $14.50. The beef fajitas, made with prime rib, baby back pork ribs, and the steak bits appetizer are some of the most popular selections. Steaks like Porterhouses and New York cuts are on the menu, along with a vegetarian special. Live country-western music plays seven nights a week in the adjacent Greyhound Lounge.

THE FOOD FACTORY, 17th Ave. and Cushman St. Tel. 452-6348.
  Cuisine: DELI. **Reservations:** Not required.
$ Prices: Appetizers $3–$6; main courses $4–$10. AE, CB, MC, V.
  Open: Mon–Thurs 10:30am–11pm, Fri–Sat 10:30am–midnight, Sun noon–9pm.
You can dine in ("Parents: Ropes and gags available upon request," reads the menu note) or call for delivery ("Food just like Mom used to send out for!"). Cheese steaks are a specialty, but there are also hoagies, hamburgers, deli sandwiches, salads, and pizzas. The menu lists more than 100 domestic and imported beers and wine.
    There are Food Factory branches at 36 College Rd., at the Bentley Mall (tel. 452-3313), and in North Pole (tel. 488-3538).

LOS AMIGOS, 636 28th Ave. Tel. 452-3684.
  Cuisine: MEXICAN. **Reservations:** Not required.
$ Prices: Appetizers $5.25–$6.25; main courses $7–$14.95. CB, DC, MC, V.
  Open: Mon–Sat 11am–midnight.
Los Amigos was once a popular steakhouse called the Boardwalk. The boardwalk is still there, leading from the parking area to the front door, but the name and cuisine have changed. Tacos, tamales, enchiladas, and the like are available as combination meals. A weekday all-you-can-eat lunch buffet costs $6.50. In the basement, the Lower L.A. bar has pool tables and a big-screen TV.

SUNSET INN, 345 Old Richardson Hwy. Tel. 452-4696.
  Cuisine: AMERICAN. **Reservations:** Not required.
$ Prices: Appetizers $3–$5; main courses $7.95–$10.95; breakfast/lunch $4–$8. CB, DC, MC, V.

Open: Sun–Thurs 6am–10pm, Fri–Sat 24 hours, Sun brunch 10am–2pm.
The Sunset Inn offers reasonable prices in a rustic coffeehouse decor. Examples: a quarter-pound burger with fries for lunch is $4.95; a 10-ounce king salmon steak for dinner, with salad, potato, vegetables, and bread, is $10. The nightly specials always offer a substantial amount of food for less than $11. The Sunset Inn has good omelets, none priced over $6.50.

THE NORTH SIDE

This area takes in everything north of the Chena River and east of the university district, except for those restaurants several miles from downtown listed under "Fox and Chatanika."

MODERATE

CLINKERDAGGER, BICKERSTAFF & PETTS PUBLIC HOUSE, Bentley Mall, 24 College Rd. Tel. 452-2756.

Cuisine: STEAK/SEAFOOD. **Reservations:** Recommended.
$ Prices: Appetizers $5.95–$10.95; main courses $12.95–$18.95; lunch $5.95–$9.95. AE, MC, V.
Open: Lunch Mon–Fri 11:30am–2pm; dinner Sun–Thurs 5:30–9pm, Fri–Sat 5:30–9:30pm.

Better known simply as Clinkerdagger's, this is the crown jewel of the Bentley Mall. From the outside it looks like a Chaucerian manor. Within, it's a 17th-century English tavern, with high wood beams, brick fireplaces, and stone walls lined with prints and coats-of-arms, pewter mugs, and stained-glass windows. Even the waitresses get into the act, dressed in white as alehouse wenches.

The cuisine is hearty. Dinner favorites include teriyaki steak, fresh Alaskan and Hawaiian fish, and chicken Marlano with artichoke hearts. Don't miss the cheesecake for dessert. For lunch, you can count on fresh quiche and pasta dishes and homemade steak potage with vegetables and chopped beef. Maui-style kal bi ribs are popular. The full bar specializes in draft beer and Irish coffee, and features live blues or light rock music Thursday through Saturday night.

FLANNIGAN'S RESTAURANT AND CANTINA, Northgate Sq., Old Steese Hwy. Tel. 451-6100.

Cuisine: MEXICAN/AMERICAN. **Reservations:** Recommended.
$ Prices: Appetizers $2–$5; main courses $6–$18; lunch $5–$9. AE, CB, MC, V.
Open: Mon–Sat 11:30am–10pm, Sun 4–10pm.

Flannigan's is the Mexican equivalent of Clinkerdagger's, but perhaps just a bit overdone. The feeling of dining amid hanging plants in the courtyard of an adobe hacienda is nice . . . but neon sombreros? In the cantina (lounge), the neon extends to cactuses and beer mugs on stucco walls, and there are stained-glass scenes of Mexican desert life over the bar.

The menu is split between Sonoran specialties (pozole soup, avocado con pollo, tostada del rey) and gourmet American foods (steamed clams, scallops mornay, prime rib au jus). Lunch is strictly Mexican. A guitarist plays Tuesday through Saturday night in the cantina—which, of course, stays open late.

GERALDO'S, 701 College Rd. Tel. 452-2299.

Cuisine: ITALIAN. **Reservations:** Recommended (especially on spaghetti night).
$ Prices: Appetizers $5–$7; main courses $9.95–$23.95. AE, DC, MC, V.
Open: Mon–Thurs 11am–9pm, Fri–Sat 11am–11pm.

The most unforgettable feature of the decor here is the huge collection of beer cans and bottles around the rafters. But this Italian restaurant is no beer hall.

Dining in Geraldo's comfortable wooden booths, you can order such dinner entrees as steak, shrimp, veal Geraldo, chicken, and clams Geraldo. Geraldo sautés his specials with broccoli, cauliflower, green onions, red peppers, and mushrooms, and serves them in a lemon-garlic sauce. He also has daily specials, such as spaghetti and meat sauce, that include the salad bar.

BUDGET

THE BAKERY, 69 College Rd. Tel. 456-8600.
    Cuisine: AMERICAN/DELI. **Reservations:** Not required. **Directions:** Opposite Bentley Mall, just west of Old Steese Highway.
  $ **Prices:** Breakfast/lunch $3.50–$7.50; dinner $7–$13.95. No credit cards.
    Open: Breakfast/lunch Mon–Fri 7am–3pm, Sat 7am–4pm, Sun 8am–3pm; dinner Mon–Fri 3–9pm.

Baked goods, especially cinnamon rolls, are a favorite of patrons—as the restaurant's name implies. The café is also proud of its egg dishes, served at lunch (with soup or salad and a sandwich) as well as breakfast. In the evening, choose from a variety of dishes, including chicken, fish, and barbecued ribs, all served with potato or rice, mushrooms, soup or salad, bread, dessert, and coffee.

CAFE DE PARIS, 801 Pioneer Rd. Tel. 456-1669.
    Cuisine: FRENCH/DELI. **Reservations:** Recommended.
  $ **Prices:** Main courses $6–$10. AE, MC, V.
    Open: Mon–Sat 10am–3pm.
The Café de Paris occupies several rooms of a house. An old organ stands against one wall, and local artwork hangs on others; relaxing classical music is piped through the restaurant. A large deck allows diners to enjoy the sunshine. The blackboard menu changes daily but always features croissant sandwiches, crêpes, quiches, homemade soups, and salads.

FOONG'S, 1753 College Rd. Tel. 452-4399.
    Cuisine: VIETNAMESE/AMERICAN. **Reservations:** Recommended.
  $ **Prices:** Appetizers $1.50–$3; main courses $6–$9. MC, V.
    Open: Mon–Sat 11am–10pm (dinner 6–10pm), Sun 2–8pm.
This is a tiny but worthy palate-pleaser for anyone with a taste for Asian cooking. A faint odor of incense wafts from a Buddhist altar through hanging lanterns, and numerous family heirlooms, such as an ebony cabinet inlaid with intricate mother-of-pearl designs, decorate the room. There are only eight tables, but that allows Mai Foong to pamper her patrons. The menu shows Westernized Vietnamese dinners such as barbecued duck, pork, and fried chicken, including soup and rice, but if you have a special request, she'll try to oblige. An Oriental grocery and gift shop adjoins.

SOUVLAKI, 112 N. Turner St. Tel. 452-5393.
    Cuisine: GREEK/MEXICAN/AMERICAN. **Reservations:** Not required.
  $ **Prices:** Main courses $3.95–$5.95. MC, V.
    Open: Mon–Sat 10am–9pm.
Souvlaki is an informal restaurant, offering its sandwich and salad menu throughout the day. You can have Greek sandwiches (gyros) and salads; American fare, such as a ham-and-cheese sandwich; and light Mexican food, such as tacos and taco salad.

FOX & CHATANIKA

Some of the best restaurants in Fairbanks aren't in Fairbanks at all. That is, they aren't in the city itself—they're in the Fairbanks North Star Borough, several miles north or west, either in unincorporated areas or in the smaller communities of Fox, Chatanika, and Ester.

UNINCORPORATED FAIRBANKS
Moderate

IVORY JACK'S, Mile 1.5, Goldstream Rd. Tel. 455-6665.
    Cuisine: ALASKAN/STEAK/SEAFOOD. **Reservations:** Recommended. **Di-**

rections: Take the Steese Highway north 9½ miles and turn west on Goldstream Road; or take University Avenue north to Farmers Loop Road and turn east on Goldstream Road.

$ Prices: Appetizers $6–$12; main courses $14–$20. AE, CB, DC, DISC, MC, V.

Open: Dinner only, Sun–Mon and Wed–Thurs 5–10pm, Fri–Sat 5–11pm (cocktails till 1am).

Feel like something really different but typically Alaskan? Try the Nome reindeer Baden Baden. It's breaded in almonds and served with game sauce, mushrooms, and a stuffed pear. For a complete Alaskan meal, you might start with a king crab cocktail and finish off with strawberries Romanoff. Steak, prime rib, and stuffed prawns are other popular menu items. There's also an all-you-can-eat salad bar.

VALLATA, Mile 2.5, Goldstream Rd. Tel. 455-6600 or 455-6664.

Cuisine: ITALIAN. **Reservations:** Recommended. **Directions:** Take University Avenue north to Farmers Loop Road and then to Goldstream Road, the restaurant is at the intersection of Ballaine Road.

$ Prices: Appetizers $5–$7.50; main courses $7.50–$36.50. AE, DC, MC, V.

Open: Dinner only, daily 5:30–11pm.

A transplanted New Yorker named Sam Galindes serves arguably the best Italian cuisine in the Fairbanks area. The octagonal building has windows on all sides, offering views of Mount McKinley and other peaks from between hanging plants and chianti bottles. Specialties include clams oreganata, saltimbocca alla romana on a bed of spinach, and veal cutlet parmigiana with eggplant. New York–style pizzas and a variety of steaks and seafood are on the menu; there's also a nice Italian wine list.

FOX

This old gold-mining community, which grew up at the turn of the century around Felix Pedro's landmark discovery, is still the place to which many Fairbanksans head to dine on good steak.

Expensive

TURTLE CLUB, Mile 10, Steese Hwy. Tel. 457-3883.

Cuisine: BEEF/SEAFOOD. **Reservations:** Recommended.

$ Prices: Appetizers $7.95; main courses $11.95–$43.95. AE, MC, V.

Open: Dinner only, Mon–Sat 6–10pm, Sun 5–9pm.

The Turtle Club limits its menu to three main items: prime rib, seafood, and barbecued ribs. You can have them alone or in combination. It prepares them well enough to keep folks flocking back to the rustic atmosphere—and to stop into "Theotherbar" for a before-dinner drink.

Moderate

FOX ROADHOUSE, Mile 11, Steese Hwy. Tel. 457-7461.

Cuisine: STEAK/SEAFOOD. **Reservations:** Recommended.

$ Prices: Appetizers $4.50–$8.95; main courses $9.25–$32.95; lunch $4.95–$8.95. AE, DC, MC, V.

Open: Lunch Mon–Sat 11am–3pm; dinner Mon–Thurs 5–10pm, Fri–Sun 5pm–midnight; brunch Sun 10am–2pm.

The Fox Roadhouse has been sharing its homey atmosphere with travelers since 1908. Red-draped tables with high-backed wooden chairs nestle around a big stone fireplace. Steak, prime rib, and seafood dinners include a baked potato and salad bar. You might start with mushrooms amaretto, then try the steak montande, baked halibut, or simple liver and onions.

Budget

BUNKHOUSE BAR AND RESTAURANT, Gold Dredge no. 8, Mile 9, Old Steese Hwy. Tel. 457-6058.

Cuisine: AMERICAN. **Reservations:** Recommended.

$ Prices: Lunch $10; brunch $12.50. MC, V.

Open: Lunch Mon–Sat noon–1:30pm; brunch Sun 10am–2pm.
The rustic restaurant at this tourist attraction is open for lunch on a limited basis (it's best to call ahead and make sure they're serving) and for Sunday brunch. The buffet lunch features salads, lasagne, pot pie, and a beverage. The brunch buffet includes popular breakfast items like French toast, breads, and sausage. Attached is the Coffee Roaster, apparently without competition as North America's northernmost commercial coffee-roasting operation. A bar with turn-of-the-century brass decor is opposite the restaurant entrance.

CHATANIKA

It's about a 45-minute drive from downtown Fairbanks to this old mining community.

Moderate

CHATANIKA LODGE, Mile 28.5, Steese Hwy. Tel. 389-2164.
   Cuisine: AMERICAN. **Reservations:** Not required.
   $ Prices: Appetizers $5–$7; main courses $8.50–$12.50; lunch $4–$8. MC, V.
   Open: Daily 9am–10pm.
This place is like a pioneer roadhouse. Skins, traps and snowshoes, miners' cookware, carved walrus tusks, and various other knickknacks are mounted on the walls. The initials of visitors from all over the world are carved into the long bar. Yet this is only a reincarnation of the original lodge, built from a horse barn, hay barn, and tool shed after its turn-of-the-century predecessor burned to the ground in 1975. Cheese-steak sandwiches with onions and hot peppers are popular for lunch. The kitchen regularly serves up New York steak and grilled-chicken dinners, and halibut and catfish as the Friday and Saturday specials. Country-fried chicken is served for Sunday dinners only. At all evening meals, a trip through the salad bar is included.

NORTH POLE

This town of some 1,000 people about 14 miles east of Fairbanks on the Richardson Highway is more than just the home of Santa Claus. Anyway, the old guy in the white beard has to eat sometime, doesn't he? Unfortunately, Club 11 (a favorite steak-and-seafood place for Fairbanksans) was destroyed in a recent fire. In addition to the Food Factory (see the description in South Side budget restaurants), you'll find the establishment described below.

MODERATE

THE ELF'S DEN, Mile 14, Richardson Hwy. Tel. 488-3268.
   Cuisine: STEAK/SEAFOOD. **Reservations:** Recommended.
   $ Prices: Appetizers $5–$10; main courses $12–$22; lunch $5–$11. MC, V.
   Open: Mon–Sat 11am–10pm, Sun 10am–10pm.
Chef Tommy Tsakalos is a culinary wizard with such dishes as veal Cordon Bleu and stuffed capon. There's a huge (10-page) menu here, so everyone is sure to find something to his or her liking. The veal dishes and the prime rib are local favorites; there is also a wide variety of Alaskan seafood (with crab and lobster at market price). For lunch, try the souvlaki in pita bread.

CHENA HOT SPRINGS ROAD

Fairbanks's favorite escape is the hot-springs resort located more than an hour's drive east of the city. There's a fine restaurant and a coffee shop at the resort, and another about a third of the way there. The road branches east off the Steese Highway five miles north of the city.

MODERATE

CHENA HOT SPRINGS RESORT, Mile 56, Chena Hot Springs Rd. Tel. 452-7867.

Cuisine: AMERICAN. **Reservations:** Recommended.
$ Prices: Appetizers $4–$8; main courses $9–$20; breakfast $5–$9; lunch $7–$15. AE, MC, V.
Open: Daily 8am–8pm (breakfast only in the coffee shop, lunch and dinner in the fine-dining room).

The menu here is 20 pages long, but take heart—only four pages are devoted to food. The rest is a wine list and historical treatise. Dinner specials include "What a Crock," a hearty meat stew served with bread and salad. Drinks include the "Bathhouse Ax." As the menu explains: "A permanent fixture of the log bathhouse that graced the springs in early days was a heavy ax used to hammer open the rough-hewn door when it froze shut. But when even this failed, a cold miner warmed himself with 8-year-old Serbian plum brandy and orange juice . . . and waited for the ice to melt."

TWO RIVERS LODGE, Mile 16, Chena Hot Springs Rd. Tel. 488-6815.
Cuisine: STEAK/SEAFOOD. **Reservations:** Accepted only for parties of eight or more.
$ Prices: Appetizers $6–$8; main courses $16–$20. AE, DISC, MC, V.
Open: Dinner only, Wed–Sat 5–10pm, Sun 3–10pm.

This lodge is famous locally for its seafood, steaks, and cocktails, served in a relaxed and rustic log setting. You might start with sautéed soft-shell crab and follow it with flame-broiled rib-eye steak Delmonico or seafood Newburg Marsico in phyllo dough. The desserts are excellent.

SPECIALTY DINING

Most of the following recommendations are covered in greater detail above in this dining section or in "Accommodations," earlier in this chapter.

Local Alaskan Flavor It would be hard to top the Alaska Salmon Bake for gold-rush flavor, the Pump House for its fascinating decor, or Ivory Jack's for its menu.

Hotel Dining / Dining with a View There's outstanding hotel dining at the Bear 'n Seal in the Westmark Fairbanks and at Zach's in the Sophie Station Hotel. If it's dining with a view you're after, take the elevator to the Tiki Cove in the 10th-floor penthouse of the Polaris Hotel, the tallest building in Alaska's Interior. Or sit on a deck overlooking the Chena River at Pike's Landing.

For Breakfast At breakfast time, the Drop Inn Café and the Sunset Inn offer hearty meals to start the day, while the Bakery serves up fine baked goods and egg dishes. The restaurant in the Captain Bartlett Inn has one of the city's best breakfast buffets.

Late-Night Dining Late at night, your best bet is the Sunset Inn, which doesn't bother to close at all on Friday and Saturday nights; other nights it closes at 10pm. Open until midnight every night but Sunday are Los Amigos and Hot Licks (see below).

Fast Food There are a plethora of fast-food options. You'll know most of these names: Baskin-Robbins, Burger King, Dairy Queen, Denny's, Kentucky Fried Chicken, McDonald's, Royal Fork, Taco Bell, Wendy's, and Woolworth's. The Old Steese Highway and Airport Way are good places to find fast-food restaurants. And Fairbanks seems to have an unusually large number of pizza parlors per capita. National or regional chains represented here include Domino's, Godfather's, Pizza Hut, and Shakey's.

LIGHT FARE & DESSERTS For light fare and dessert, two establishments stand out. **Frère Jacques,** 4001 Geist Rd., in West Valley Plaza (tel. 479-0875), is a real French pâtisserie and bistro, open Monday through Saturday from 8am to 5pm. Also on the West Side, **Hot Licks,** 3549 College Rd. (tel. 479-7813), is more than just the neighborhood soda fountain. It's best known for its homemade ice cream and espresso bar, and is open Monday through Saturday from 11am to midnight and on Sunday from noon to 10pm.

5. ATTRACTIONS

You could easily spend a week in Fairbanks and not see everything the city has to offer. Indeed, tourist attractions are the gold nuggets of the "new" Fairbanks.

The **Fairbanks Convention and Visitor Bureau** has compiled excellent city walking and driving tours that take in most of the outstanding sights in the area. Brochures are available at their offices and at many other locations. Some sights, of course, will entice you to linger or to return for longer periods of time. But a walking tour is a good way to get oriented (see my "Walking Tour: Downtown Fairbanks," below).

SUGGESTED ITINERARIES

IF YOU HAVE ONE DAY If you're here during the peak summer season, start your day with a cruise down the Chena and Tanana Rivers aboard the pioneer sternwheeler *Discovery III*. Return to the city for lunch, then spend the last half of the afternoon and the early evening in Alaskaland, which re-creates Fairbanks's gold-rush era. Have dinner at the Alaska Salmon Bake, and don't miss the evening revue at the Palace Saloon.

IF YOU HAVE TWO DAYS Spend your first day as suggested above. On your second day in Fairbanks, focus your attentions on the fascinating facilities of the University of Alaska. Start with a 10am campus walking tour and be sure to take in the university's outstanding museum, agricultural research farm, and large-animal research station. The university is renowned worldwide for its studies of arctic phenomena; many of the laboratories are open to the public.

IF YOU HAVE THREE DAYS OR MORE After spending two days seeing the sights of Fairbanks itself (see the suggestions above), on the third day get out of the city. To see the natural-resource heritage of the Alaskan Interior, take a drive north out the Steese Highway. Along the way, you'll get a fine look at the Trans Alaska Pipeline; Gold Dredge no. 8, a national historic district; and two restored gold camps, Little El Dorado and Chatanika (the Old F. E. Company camp). Chena Hot Springs resort, about an 80-minute drive from Fairbanks, is another fine day-trip destination.

THE TOP ATTRACTIONS

ALASKALAND, Airport Way at Peger Rd. Tel. 459-1087.

This 44-acre theme park, built for the Alaska '67 Centennial Exposition and owned by the City of Fairbanks, may be a disappointment to visitors who expect something akin to Disneyland. That's not what Alaskaland is trying to be. Temper expectations and you'll enjoy several hours here. Transportation to the park is provided by a free tram that does a circuit of downtown hotels every day.

The retired riverboat **S.S. Nenana** was known as "The Queen of the Yukon" during its 1933–54 heyday. The boat, designated a National Historic Landmark, has been restored in drydock and now contains the visitor information center. From the boat, start your counterclockwise tour of the park. You may want to linger longest in **Goldrush Town,** composed of 29 early Fairbanks cabins and buildings donated by pioneers' descendants and moved here and renovated. More than half the homes are now occupied by gift shops and art galleries of one sort or another. (That's why there's no admission charge to the park.) Clerks and proprietors are dressed in period costumes. You'll also find a New York deli, a Greek souvlaki café, an ice-cream parlor, and a photo shop. The **Palace Saloon** has G-rated can-can revues every evening. The **Pioneer Hall** houses a small museum of Fairbanks history with narrated presentations several times daily.

Just past Goldrush Town is the depot for the narrow-gauge **Crooked Creek & Whiskey Island Railroad,** which takes passengers for a one-mile ride around the park grounds ($2 for adults, $1 for children). It's a good way to orient yourself. You'll see the **Pioneer Air Museum,** four structures in a re-created Native village called **Alaska Kkaayah,** a public boat launch and fishing pier on the Chena River, the Farthest North Square and Round Dance Center, a children's playground, and numerous picnic shelters. You can return to any or all of them when your ride is complete. In the park's southwestern corner is the **Mining Valley,** complete with a hard-rock mine tunnel and a waterfall with sluices for gold panning. The **Alaska Salmon Bake** also makes its home here (see "Dining," above).

On Barlett Plaza, facing the park's main entrance, is the **Fairbanks Civic Center.** The building contains a 384-seat theater (in use year-round), meeting rooms and exhibit halls, an important art gallery, and the offices of the Fairbanks Arts Association.

Admission: Free.

Open: Memorial Day weekend to Labor Day, daily 11am–9pm. **Closed:** Day after Labor Day to the Thurs before Memorial Day.

RIVERBOAT DISCOVERY, Mile 4.5, Airport Way at Dale Rd. Tel. 479-6673.

⭐ A cruise down the Chena and Tanana Rivers aboard the sternwheeler *Discovery III* is always a visitor favorite. Capt. Jim Binkley was apprenticed from childhood to be a river pilot, and no one has worked the waters of the Tanana longer than Binkley: He started in 1940. Binkley's knowledge of Alaska's Interior makes this narrated tour something quite out of the ordinary. You'll make stops at an Athabaskan Indian trapping camp and at a sled-dog training outpost, where you'll be given a demonstration of the dogs' prowess. You'll learn how fish wheels operate to assist commercial fishermen; how gold is trapped between layers of quartz, to be washed out by miners; and why ugly but efficient surplus truck tires are used to reduce erosion on riverbanks. The tour covers 20 miles of river in four hours.

Admission: $29.50 adults, $20 children 3–12. Advance reservations suggested.

Open: Mid-June to Labor Day, departures daily at 8:45am and 2pm; mid-May to mid-June and Labor Day to mid-Sept, departures daily at 2pm only. **Closed:** Mid-Sept to mid-May.

UNIVERSITY OF ALASKA MUSEUM, 907 Yukon Dr. Tel. 474-7505.

⭐ The university's most outstanding visitor attraction, the museum's exhibits focus on the five major geographical regions of Alaska and emphasize Native cultures, natural history, and mineral resources. A display incorporating Alaska's largest gold collection explains the formation of gold and various types of mining, and there is an exhibit on the Trans Alaska pipeline. Here also you can see "Blue Babe," the world's only fully restored Pleistocene bison. The museum also has an excellent shop specializing in publications on Alaska subjects.

Admission: $4 adults, $3.50 senior citizens and military, free for children under 12; $10 family.

Open: June–Aug, daily 9am–7pm; May and Sept, daily 9am–5pm; Oct–Apr, noon–5pm. **Closed:** New Year's, Thanksgiving, and Christmas Days.

UNIVERSITY OF ALASKA—FAIRBANKS, University Relations Office, 210 Signers Hall. Tel. 474-7581 or 474-6397.

There's so much to see and do at the university that visiting could easily take up two days of your time. Your best way to get acquainted with this 2,250-acre campus, located four miles west of downtown, is to join a free walking tour. Weather permitting, the 1½- to 2-hour tour begins at 10am Monday through Friday, June through August (except July 3–4). It begins at the UAF Museum and takes in several arctic research institutes, the Rasmuson Library (with its renowned collection of polar literature), the Constitution and Signers Halls (sites of the 1956 state constitutional convention), the Davis Concert Hall (home of the Fairbanks Symphony Orchestra and other performing arts groups), and the Patty Athletic Center (with its ice hockey arena and other facilities).

The UAF got its start in 1915 when Fairbanks was selected by Judge James Wickersham and approved by the U.S. Congress as the location of the land-grant Alaska Agricultural College and School of Mines. The college opened its doors in 1922 with one building, six students, and six professors. Today it has 120 buildings, 8,300 students, and 400 faculty. Renamed the University of Alaska in 1935, its system now includes two other university campuses (in Anchorage and Juneau) and 11 community colleges across the state.

The main Lower Campus area, reached by turning west on Taku Drive off Farmers Loop Road, is connected by a free shuttle bus to the West Ridge area, where the museum and most of the research institutes are located. Schedules are available at the Wood Center, the student union building.

Nearby the UAF Museum, in the Elvey Building on Koyukuk Drive, is the **Geophysical Institute** (tel. 474-7558), established in 1946 to study the aurora borealis and its effect on communications. Since then it has grown to become a center of expertise in arctic and subarctic geophysics, including permafrost, glaciation, ice dynamics, earthquakes, and volcanoes. Tours (at 2pm every Thursday from mid-June through August; other times, by appointment) include slide shows on the aurora and on quakes, a talk in the Globe Room, and visits to the remote-sensing and seismology laboratories.

The **Mineral Industry Research Laboratory** is on Lower Campus in the O'Neill Building (tel. 474-7135). Associated with the School of Mineral Engineering, it's devoted to finding, developing, and utilizing Alaska's mineral wealth. Prospectors and mine operators seek advice here throughout the year. Films on mining and permafrost are shown at 2pm every Wednesday from mid-June through August as a part of the campus walking tour.

Visitors marvel at the size of the vegetables grown at the **Georgeson Botanical Garden** of the Agricultural and Forestry Experiment Station on Tanana Drive, at the far west end of campus (tel. 474-6921). The station's purpose is twofold: to find out what crops (and animals) will grow and thrive in a subarctic climate, with short summers but long hours; and to discover how they can be made most economically feasible and competitive with outside markets. Free tours are offered at 2pm on Friday, mid-June through August, but you can drop by anytime between 8am and 8pm in summer (August is best) and look at the oversize veggies (note the cabbage, carrots, and broccoli) and flowers in the Demonstration Garden. There are displays of comparative farming techniques in the visitors center. A 40-minute round-trip walking trail leads through the experimental arboretum. Remember that this is a working farm with cows, swine, and other animals, so watch where you put your feet!

At the **Large Animal Research Station,** on Yankovich Road, on the north side of the campus a mile west of Ballaine Road (tel. 474-7207), herds of musk-oxen, caribou, reindeer, and moose are studied. It was established in 1962 as a division of the Institute of Arctic Biology, and its scientists study animal nutrition, physiology, breeding, and ecology. This may be your only chance to see suckling musk-oxen calves. Animals can often be seen from the road at nearby feeding stations, but you'll need binoculars if they're in the rear pastures. Tours ($4 for adults, $3 for seniors, $2 for students, and free for children under five) are offered at 1:30 and 3pm on Tuesday and Saturday, June through September.

Wood Center, the student union building on Yukon Drive opposite Chandalar Avenue North (tel. 474-7211), is the center of student activities. It includes a cafeteria and snack bar, Sir Walter's pub (open Monday through Friday for light lunches and dinners, at $4–$6), a bowling alley and games areas, and the headquarters for Wood Center Outdoor Programs to many wilderness areas around the state.

MORE ATTRACTIONS

STEESE HIGHWAY   The most-traveled highway north from Fairbanks, the Steese runs 162 miles to the village of Circle on the Yukon River. Only the first 44 miles are paved, but that includes the communities of Fox and Chatanika, where attractions of immediate interest to Fairbanks visitors are located. (There are two, roughly parallel roads as far as Fox: the Old Steese Highway and the newer Steese Expressway.) Take a drive up this road to see several old or re-created mining camps, a pair of scientific research stations, and the **Trans Alaska Pipeline.**

The best place to see the pipeline near Fairbanks is from a turnout at Mile 7 on the Steese Expressway. A small display and information board will tell you that the pipeline is 48 inches in diameter and pumps 1.9 million barrels of oil each day from Prudhoe Bay to Valdez. The pipeline parallels the highway for a short distance. If you're well equipped and feeling adventurous, you can turn left at Fox and follow the Elliott and Dalton Highways up the treacherous North Slope Haul Road 487 miles to Prudhoe Bay. (See Chapter 10, "The Arctic.")

Gold Dredge no. 8, at Mile 9 on the Old Steese Highway, south of Goldstream Road (tel. 457-6058), is a National Historic District. It preserves a fascinating floating factory, 250 feet long and five decks high, that dug gravel from the front edge of a pond, separated the gold out, then spewed the washed tailings behind. Built in 1928, it shut down in 1959 when the company that owned it refused to give union workers a 5¢-an-hour wage increase. Today the dredge is open May through September, Monday through Saturday from 9am to 9pm and on Sunday from 9am to 6pm; winter visits are by appointment. An admission fee of $8 (two for $15; children 8 and under, free) includes a tour and gold panning. The bunkhouse has been turned into the Bunkhouse Bar and Restaurant and Coffee Roaster (see "Dining," above).

One mile off the Steese Highway—turn left at Fox on the Elliott Highway and proceed to the sign—is the **Little El Dorado Gold Camp** (tel. 479-7613, or 456-4598 in Fairbanks). A narrow-gauge railroad, the *El Dorado Express,* carries visitors from the parking lot to a miners' tent city, where you have an opportunity to try your hand at drift and shaft mining and at using a gold hound, suction dredge, and sluice box. Gold panners can keep the nuggets they're guaranteed to find. A two-hour tour is priced at $20 for adults, $15 for children 5–12.

Free tours are offered year-round at the **Satellite Tracking Station** (tel. 451-1200), operated by the National Aeronautics and Space Administration and the National Oceanic and Atmospheric Administration. To reach it, turn off the Steese Highway at Mile 13.5 and climb about six miles into a wilderness area near Gilmore Creek.

Pedro's Monument, Mile 16.6 on the Steese Highway, commemorates the discovery of gold near here in 1902 by Italian immigrant Felix Pedro. His find started a gold rush that led to the removal of more than seven million troy ounces of gold from the Tanana Valley. Pedro died in Fairbanks in 1910; his remains were returned to Italy, where he was buried in Trignano.

In 1925 the Fairbanks Exploration Co. opened a gold camp near Chatanika, at Mile 27½ on the Steese Highway. As many as 400 men lived and worked in the 48-acre camp's 15 buildings until it closed in 1955. Today it has new life as the **Chatanika (Old F.E. Company) Gold Camp** (tel. 389-2414). You'll be welcomed to the camp year-round to see the vintage mining equipment, old foundry, and gold-panning equipment. The camp, registered as a national historic district, also has a restaurant, a newly refurbished hotel ($45 single, $55 double, $75 cabin), a mercantile store, and a gift shop. Call ahead to arrange the Aurora City Tour from Fairbanks (including brunch) for $55 per person or a shorter three-hour tour (without brunch) for $30 per person.

 CHENA HOT SPRINGS   Some 62 miles east of Fairbanks, at the end of a lovely wilderness road, is this mineral hot-springs resort. Ever since its discovery in 1907 it has been an important out-of-town getaway for Fairbanks residents.

Over the years a village of lodges and small cabins has grown up around Monument and Cold Spring Creeks, so that today this year-round resort offers a variety of indoor and outdoor activities in all seasons.

Mineral baths and hot pools are the main attractions. There are also whirlpool baths and a big indoor pool. Says the management: "Different soaks for different folks." Displays of pioneer mining and farming equipment stand beside the vegetable garden and sun deck. You can play volleyball, badminton, miniature golf, croquet, and horseshoes or opt to go fishing or hiking on 22 miles of trails. In winter, cross-country skiers have their run of the summer hiking trails; nordic rentals are available in the ski lodge. Ice skating, sledding, and snowmobiling are also popular.

The main lodge contains the dining room and bar (see "Dining," above) and a coffee shop, open for breakfast only. Prices for overnight lodging (swim passes included), single or double, are $50 for rooms (with single and double bed) and $80 for cabins (equipped with wood stove and electricity but no water, and bring your own linens). Children accompanied by adults are allowed free. For reservations and further information, contact Chena Hot Springs Resort, 331 Seventh Ave., Fairbanks, AK 99701 (tel. 907/452-7867).

En route to Chena Hot Springs, you might want to stop at Mile 22 on Chena Hot Springs Road and check out the **Pleasant Valley Animal Park** (tel. 488-3967), where you can take a horse-drawn buggy ride to see a variety of native animals in their natural habitat. There are pony rides and a petting zoo for the little ones.

NORTH POLE This Richardson Highway community of 1,000 happy souls, 14 miles east of Fairbanks, is indeed the home of Santa Claus. In fact, Con Miller's **Santa Claus House,** built even before the town was incorporated in 1953, is far and away North Pole's biggest attraction.

Miller, then the struggling young proprietor of a Fairbanks trading post, first donned a red Santa Claus outfit on business trips in 1949 to bring the Christmas spirit to hundreds of children in the Interior Alaskan bush. He moved to the current site of North Pole in 1952 and erected his new trading post. Miller served as the mayor of North Pole for 17 years and his two sons became state legislators (one also became lieutenant-governor), but they all stayed involved in the family business. Today it's a huge and unique gift shop, with a wide variety of Alaska souvenirs and a constant stock of tasteful toys and Christmas ornaments.

Every Christmas, Santa Claus sends a special letter to children all over the world from North Pole, along with a deed to one square inch of Santa Claus Subdivision. You can hear all about it here, or you can contact Santa Claus House, Santa Land, North Pole, AK 99705 (tel. 907/488-2200).

There's free overnight parking for self-contained RVs in the Santa Land lot.

Also in North Pole is **Jesus Town,** a missionary community of a dozen beautiful hand-hewn spruce-log cabins, all with sod roofs. Radio station KJNP ("King Jesus North Pole") broadcasts on a 50,000-watt AM station and a 25,000-watt FM frequency in the English, Inupiat, Athabaskan, and Russian (for Siberia) languages. TV station KJNP is local Channel 4. Visitors are welcome daily between 8am and 10pm (tel. 488-2216). To reach Jesus Town, turn north off the Richardson Highway at Mission Road, where the **North Pole Chamber of Commerce and Visitors Center** (tel. 488-2242) is located.

TANANA VALLEY FAIRGROUNDS In August, the finest horse show and rodeo in the Interior are held during the Tanana Valley Fair at this College Road site, two miles west of the Steese Highway. A **Farmers Market** is open during the summer months only. On the east side of the fairgrounds is **Creamer's Field National Wildlife Refuge,** where more than 100 species of resident and migratory birds might be seen during the various seasons.

MILITARY BASES Tours of the facilities near Fairbanks can be scheduled by appointment.

To visit **Fort Wainwright Army Post,** whose main gate is off Gaffney Road on the east side of the city, contact the Public Affairs Office, Building 3409, Fort Wainwright, AK 99703 (tel. 907/353-7117).

For information about **Fort Greely Army Post,** call Fort Wainwright (tel. 907/353-6211).

To see **Eielson Air Force Base,** 23 miles east of Fairbanks on the Richardson Highway, contact the Public Affairs Department, Eielson Air Force Base, AK 99702 (tel. 907/377-2116).

COOL FOR KIDS

There's a lot for children to enjoy in and around Fairbanks. The many attractions of **Alaskaland** include the Crooked Creek & Whiskey Island Railroad, Mining Valley, a Native village, and Goldrush Town. The riverboat trip on the sternwheeler **Discovery** is another sure favorite.

Young animal lovers will want to see the baby musk-oxen and caribou at the **University of Alaska–Fairbanks Large Animal Research Station,** the bird life at **Creamer's Field National Wildlife Refuge,** the petting zoo at the **Pleasant Valley Animal Park,** and perhaps even "Blue Babe," the world's only fully restored Pleistocene bison, at the **University of Alaska Museum.**

Other attractions: giant vegetables at the university's **Georgeson Botanical Garden;** gold panning at the **Little El Dorado Gold Camp;** the **Santa Claus House** in North Pole, where every day is Christmas; and **Chena Hot Springs,** a delightful small resort with year-round recreation.

WALKING TOUR — DOWNTOWN FAIRBANKS

Start: Visitor Information Center.
Finish: Visitor Information Center.
Time: About two hours, including a half hour browsing in the Alaska Public Lands Information Center.
Best Times: Any day during the warmer summer months.
Worst Times: Midwinter, when the ice smog sets in.

Start at the:

1. **Visitor Information Center,** at First Avenue and Cushman Street on the banks of the Chena River, operated by the Fairbanks Convention and Visitor Bureau. Built of white spruce, birch, and fir, it has a sod roof. Pioneers appreciated the insulation offered by sod during winter, and often used it as a garden in summer.

   Directly across the Cushman Street Bridge is the:
2. **Immaculate Conception Church,** built in 1904 on the south side of the Chena River at First Avenue and Dunkel Street. It was moved to this site seven years later, pulled across log rollers by horses when the Chena froze over. It still has an active congregation and is listed on the National Register of Historic Sites.

   Recross the bridge and walk west on First Avenue. At the corner of Wickersham Street is the:
3. **Masonic Temple,** from whose false facade President Warren Harding addressed Fairbanks in 1923 after driving the golden spike of the Alaska Railroad.

   A couple of blocks farther, past Kellum Street, visit:
4. **St. Matthew's Episcopal Church,** which features a stained-glass nativity scene depicting Mary and Joseph as Eskimos.

   Retrace your steps a block to Cowles Street and turn south. At the corner of Second Avenue, note the:
5. **Midnight Sun Mural,** one of 20 murals and two parks created in 1979 as part

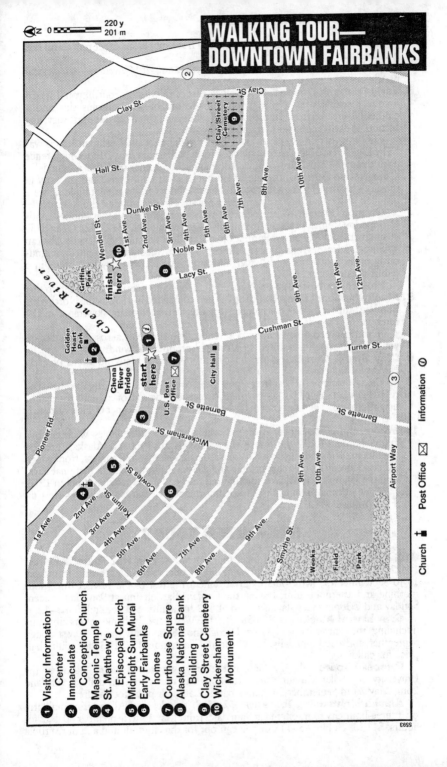

WALKING TOUR—DOWNTOWN FAIRBANKS

220 y
201 m

Chena River

Golden Heart Park

Chena River Bridge

Griffin Park

Clay St.

Hall St.

Dunkel St.

Noble St.

Lacy St.

Cushman St.

Turner St.

Wendell St.

Wickersham St.

Barnette St.

Pioneer Rd.

Kellum St.

Cowles St.

Smythe St.

Weeks Field Park

Airport Way

Clay Street Cemetery

City Hall

U.S. Post Office

start here

finish here

1st Ave.
2nd Ave.
3rd Ave.
4th Ave.
5th Ave.
6th Ave.
7th Ave.
8th Ave.
9th Ave.

1st Ave.
2nd Ave.
3rd Ave.
4th Ave.
5th Ave.
6th Ave.
7th Ave.
8th Ave.
9th Ave.
10th Ave.
11th Ave.
12th Ave.

9th Ave.
10th Ave.

① Visitor Information Center
② Immaculate Conception Church
③ Masonic Temple
④ St. Matthew's Episcopal Church
⑤ Midnight Sun Mural
⑥ Early Fairbanks homes
⑦ Courthouse Square
⑧ Alaska National Bank Building
⑨ Clay Street Cemetery
⑩ Wickersham Monument

Church †   Post Office ⊠   Information ⓘ

5583

of a Downtown Beautification Project. You'll see numerous other murals on this walking tour.

Farther down Cowles, between Fourth and Fifth Avenues, are several prestigious:

6. Early Fairbanks homes. In the block east of Cowles on Fourth, you'll spot a unique dwelling with a picket fence made out of army surplus skis and a clothesline created from moose antlers. Just beyond you'll cross the last surviving section of early Fairbanks's ubiquitous boardwalks.

Continue east on Fourth Avenue. Between Barnette and Cushman Streets was "The Line," a red-light district blocked from public view by a 10-foot-high fence until the mid-1950s. Turn left at Cushman; at the corner of Third Avenue is:

7. Courthouse Square, the site of Fairbanks's first courthouse and jail early in the city's history. The copper roof and marble floors of the present building were installed in 1934. There are numerous private offices and retail shops inside.

Of most interest to the short-term visitor is the Alaska Public Lands Information Center, in the basement off Third Avenue (tel. 451-7352). Open daily in summer from 8:30am to 9pm, it offers excellent dioramic displays of Alaskan wildlife, landscapes, and Native culture; 30 short videotapes presented continuously on mini-screens; and longer films and slide shows every two hours in a public theater.

Proceed one block east on Third Avenue to the corner of Lacey Street, to the:

8. Alaska National Bank Building. When completed in 1952 as the Northward Building, this eight-story structure was the first steel-girder skyscraper in the Interior.

If you proceed down Lacey to Seventh, then turn east across Noble Street, you'll pass through a restored 1930s neighborhood and wind up in the:

9. Clay Street Cemetery, the final resting place for many hundreds of early Fairbanks pioneers.

Cross through the cemetery and head west again on Fifth Avenue. The residences between Hall and Dunkel Streets are typical of an early Fairbanks neighborhood. Then turn north on Noble Street. At the corner of First Avenue is the:

10. Wickersham Monument, on the original site of Judge James Wickersham's frame house. (Today the house is in Alaskaland.) Probably Alaska's greatest statesman, Wickersham moved from a federal judgeship to Congress, from which he introduced the bills that created the Alaska Railroad, Denali National Park, and the University of Alaska, and offered the first Alaska statehood bill in 1916.

Your starting point at the Visitor Information Center is two blocks west on First Avenue.

ORGANIZED TOURS

BUS TOURS There are good local tour operators. **Red Hat Tours,** P.O. Box 10622, Fairbanks, AK 99710 (tel. 907/457-3000), offers a regular schedule from May 15 to September 15, with tours by arrangement the rest of the year. A three-hour morning and afternoon tour, leaving the Captain Bartlett Inn at 9am daily except Sunday and 2:30pm every day, is priced at $22 for adults, $11 for children 3–12.

Gray Line of Alaska (tel. 456-5816) at the Westmark Fairbanks) offers city tours (including the university and Gold Dredge no. 8) at 9am daily, May through September, and at 2:30pm daily, June 1 through September 15 ($21.50 for adults, half price for children).

Princess Tours (tel. 479-9660) is the only operator including a stop at the University of Alaska Museum; the three-hour city tour is offered daily at 9am and 2pm, May 20 to September 25 (adults pay $22.50; half price for children).

Alaska Sightseeing Tours (tel. 452-8518) includes the UAF experimental farm on a three-hour city tour, offered at 9am daily from May 15 to September 30 ($22 for adults, $11 for children 5–11), or you can opt for the city tour and a 2pm riverboat cruise for a full day's worth of activities ($57.50 per person). Check with any of these operators for additional tour options.

FLIGHTSEEING TOURS   No fewer than 10 different services offer flights from Fairbanks over the Interior, from Gates of the Arctic National Park to Denali National Park. Mainly based on University Avenue South near the airport, they include **Frontier Flying Service** (tel. 474-0014), **Larry's Flying Service** (tel. 474-9169), and **Wright Air Service** (tel. 474-0502). The Fairbanks Convention and Visitor Bureau can provide a complete list.

   If you prefer a helicopter trip, contact **Heli-Lift Inc.** (tel. 452-1197).

6. SPECIAL & FREE EVENTS

The year's biggest celebration is **Golden Days,** annually scheduled the second through third full weekends of July (it begins July 10, 1993, and July 9, 1994). Commemorating Felix Pedro's 1902 gold discovery, it started in 1952 with a 50th-anniversary fest; everyone had such fun, it has continued each year since. The whole town dresses up in turn-of-the-century attire; events include a parade, air show, concerts, beard and moustache contests, and even a Felix Pedro look-alike competition. You can get more information from the Golden Days Manager, Greater Fairbanks Chamber of Commerce, P.O. Box 74446, Fairbanks, AK 99707 (tel. 907/452-1105).

   Other annual events include the week-long **Fairbanks Winter Carnival** in March, including sled-dog races, ice sculptures, a parka parade, Native potlatch, and dances; the **Festival of Native Arts** at the University of Alaska, also in March; the **Nuchalawoyya Festival,** offering Athabaskan songs and dances, games, potlaches, and a footrace, and **Nenana River Daze** in June; the **Tanana Valley/Alaska State Fair** in August, featuring the Interior's best rodeo and horse show; and the **Fall Frolic Square Dance Festival** in October.

   No time is more active than the two weeks in late July and early August when the annual **Fairbanks Summer Arts Festival** is held. Workshops and concerts in classical music, jazz, dance, theater, and the visual arts are presented by well-known guest artists from all over the United States. Events are held on the University of Alaska campus. For information, write to P.O. Box 80845, Fairbanks, AK 99708; or call 907/479-6778.

WORLD ESKIMO INDIAN OLYMPICS   If you happen to be in Fairbanks in late July, don't miss this. Alaskan Natives have met here each year since 1961 to celebrate not only their sports, but also their dance, art, and culture.

   In recent years, events have been held over four days at the Big Dipper Recreation Arena, 19th Avenue and Lathrop Street. Among the 26 events are the ear pull, in which a loop of string is placed over the same ear of two contestants, who then stage what amounts to a tug-of-war; and the blanket toss, in which contestants try to jump the highest with the best form. There are also competitions in knuckle hopping, muktuk eating, fish cutting, seal skinning, greased pole walking, sewing, team dancing, and high-kicking. A Miss WEIO Queen contest, Native baby contest, and intertribal pow-wow are also part of the festivities.

   For more information and tickets, call the WEIO office (tel. 452-6646).

7. SPORTS & RECREATION

Well, you can't surf in the Fairbanks area and jai alai isn't a big crowd-pleaser. But virtually every other kind of sports activity is available here.

SPECTATOR SPORTS

AUTO RACING During the summer, there's stock car competition every Saturday at 7pm and/or Sunday at 2pm at the **Greater Fairbanks Raceway,** near the corner of Peger and Van Horn Roads (tel. 452-3500). The season runs from Memorial Day to Labor Day; admission is $5 for adults, $2.50 for students, $10 for families.

BASEBALL The **Fairbanks Goldpanners,** a nationally famous semipro team that has seen the likes of former major-league stars Tom Seaver, Chris Chambliss, and Dave Kingman in uniform, play their home games at 7:30pm in June, July, and August at Growden Field, at the corner of Wilbur Street and Second Avenue. Their archrivals in the Alaska Baseball League, the **North Pole Nicks,** play at their own field on Newby Road in North Pole. The Goldpanners are annual hosts to Alaska's most famous baseball tradition: a ✪ **midnight-sun baseball game,** played without artificial lights at midnight on June 21, the longest day of the year. The *News Miner* newspaper carries game schedules, or call the Goldpanners' office (tel. 451-0095).

BASKETBALL The **University of Alaska–Fairbanks** has men's and women's teams in NCAA Division II. Their rivals are schools like UA–Anchorage, the University of Puget Sound, and Eastern Montana University. Home games are played November to March at **Patty Athletic Center** (tel. 474-7205) on the UAF campus. Area high schools also have teams.

CURLING This European winter sport, something like shuffleboard on ice, has undergone a renaissance of popularity in Fairbanks. Their "Super Bowl," with numerous teams from Canada participating, is the International Bonspiel every April. Contact the **Fairbanks Curling Club,** 1962 Second Ave. (tel. 459-6209 or 452-3011).

DOG MUSHING If you're in Fairbanks in the winter, you'll have lots of opportunities to experience Alaska's official state sport. Local mushers practice at the **Jeff Studdert Racing Grounds** at Mile 4 on Farmers Loop Road, north of the university. There's a dog-mushing museum here (tel. 457-MUSH), with a comprehensive exhibit on sled-dog history and modern racing. The year's biggest event is the 1,000-mile **Yukon Quest International Sled Dog Race,** held annually in February and March between Fairbanks and Whitehorse (it starts in each city on alternate years). The **Yukon Quest General Store and Museum,** 552 Second Ave. (tel. 451-8985), has year-round videos and displays of historic and modern equipment.

    TIVI Kennels, at Mile 2 on Kallenberg Road in Ester (tel. 474-8702 or 456-4045), takes summer visitors on its ArfMobile, powered by 12 sled dogs. It also offers dinner, a show, and videos of winter racing from mid-June to mid-September. Dinner, show, and the ride cost $20 (discounts for children under 12 based on age).

ICE HOCKEY The **University of Alaska–Fairbanks** varsity hockey team, known as the Nanooks, and the **Gold Kings** semipro team play with the best in the country of their caliber. UAF plays its matches in winter at **Patty Ice Arena** (tel. 474-7602). Such major university teams as Michigan and Princeton are on the schedule. For the Gold Kings' schedule, call 456-7825.

VOLLEYBALL The **University of Alaska** women's volleyball team competes against the likes of the Air Force Academy and the University of California from September to November at **Patty Gym** (tel. 474-7205).

RECREATION

BICYCLING There's an extensive bike-path system all over Fairbanks. You can obtain a map at the Visitors Information Center at 550 First Ave. **Beaver Sports,** 3840 College Rd. (tel. 479-2494), rents touring and mountain bikes at $15 per day, including helmets; rentals can also be arranged from **Campbell Sports** (tel. 452-2757).

BOWLING Try the lanes at **Arctic Bowl,** 940 Cowles St. (tel. 456-7719).

CANOEING The extensive system of lakes, creeks, and rivers in the Interior makes this an exceptionally popular sport here. For rentals, contact **Wilderness Canoe Adventures** (tel. 452-8968), **Charley River Canoe Sales** (tel. 488-6990), or **Backcountry Logistical Services** (tel. 457-7606).

FISHING Your first contact should be the **Alaska Department of Fish and Game,** 1300 College Rd. (tel. 452-1531), for full information on licensing restrictions and local regulations. Fish and Game also has a year-round recorded hotline of hunting and fishing locations (tel. 452-1525).

The waters of the Interior produce grayling, sheefish, salmon, northern pike, and rainbow and lake trout. Drop a line straight into the Chena River, meander to a proven nearby fishing hole like Chena Lake (19 miles east) or the Chatanika River (39 miles north), or take advantage of the packages offered by numerous outfitters in the Fairbanks area.

You might consider **Bob Elliott Guide Service,** 5920 Airport Way, Fairbanks, AK 99707 (tel. 907/479-6323), with fly-in northern pike and trout fishing from $125 for a full day. For an extra $25 you can have a 24-hour (overnight) trip. **Alaska River Charters** (tel. 455-6827) offers customized remote trips by river or air. The guide services generally provide equipment, but if you need to rent, **Backcountry Logistical Services,** 469 Goldmine Trail (tel. 457-7606), has what you need.

GOLF Play a round at the nine-hole, par-35 **Fairbanks Golf and Country Club,** at Yankovich and Ballaine Roads (tel. 479-6555), and you'll be given a certificate verifying that you've tackled the world's northermost golf course. The **Chena Bend Golf Course** at Fort Wainwright (tel. 353-6749) is the best in the area. Both are open for summer business, and they welcome visitors. **Alaskaland** has an 18-hole miniature golf course (tel. 452-7888).

HEALTH CLUBS The most complete modern facilities are at the **Fairbanks Athletic Club,** 747 Old Richardson Hwy. (tel. 452-6801), and **The Athletic Club,** 150 Eagle St. (tel. 456-1914), both with excellent racquetball and handball courts.

HIKING & BACKPACKING After making a stop for information and maps at the **Public Lands Information Center,** Third Avenue and Cushman Street (tel. 451-7352), day and overnight hikers would do well to drive 40–50 miles east on the Chena Hot Springs Road to the **Chena River Recreation Area.** Popular tracks include the 6-mile Granite Tors Trail and the 29-mile Chena Dome Loop Trail. Another fine walk is the 20-mile White Mountains Trail, leaving the Elliott Highway at Wickersham Dome, 30 miles northwest of Fairbanks.

Wilderness backpacking expeditions of one to two weeks, many of them in the Brooks Range, are operated by a number of Fairbanks-based agencies. Some options are **ABEC's Alaska Adventures,** 1304 Westwick Dr. (tel. 457-8907); **Arctic Treks,** P.O. Box 73452, Fairbanks, AK 99707 (tel. 907/455-6502); and **Alaska Backcountry Guides Cooperative,** P.O. Box 81533, Fairbanks, AK 99708 (tel. 907/457-8907 or 479-2754).

HORSEBACK RIDING Trail rides are offered by **Wynfromere Farms,** Mile 0.2 on Bennett Road, off Chena Hot Springs Road (tel. 457-7902), and **Two Rivers Stables,** Mile 23, on Chena Hot Springs Road (tel. 488-2174). Expect to pay about $25 an hour.

HUNTING Again, contact the **Alaska Department of Fish and Game,** 1300 College Rd. (tel. 452-1531), for full information on licensing restrictions and local regulations, and for their year-round recorded hotline of hunting and fishing locations (tel. 452-1525).

For guide service to reach the best hunting grounds for bear, moose, caribou, and sheep, you won't go wrong in contacting **Alaska Backcountry Guides Cooperative,** P.O. Box 81533, Fairbanks, AK 99708 (tel. 907/457-8907 or 479-2754).

ICE SKATING If you have your own skates, you won't need to be told what to do.

Even the Chena River is frozen over in midwinter, although it's not regarded as safe for skating. If you're at the mercy of rental equipment, try the **Big Dipper Ice Arena**, 19th Avenue and Lathrop Street (tel. 456-6683), or the **UAF Patty Ice Arena** (tel. 474-6888 or 474-6868). **Chena Hot Springs Resort** (tel. 452-7867) also has great ice and rentals.

LUGE This perilous Olympic sport, relatively unknown except in the European Alps, has recently established a foothold in Fairbanks. Alaska's only luge course is at the **Birch Hill Recreation Area,** northeast of downtown off City Lights Boulevard. Lessons and rentals are available from late October to early April, snow permitting. The luge, for the uninitiated, is an open one-man bobsled.

MOUNTAINEERING Fairbanks itself isn't a mountaineering center, although it does offer some interesting rock climbs at the Granite Tors in the **Chena River Recreation Area,** 40 miles east of the city. Numerous alpine organizations are based here, however, and outfitters frequently travel to peaks in Denali National Park and the Brooks Range. Check with **Clem's Backpacking Sports,** 315 Wendell St. (tel. 456-6314), for information.

RAFTING From Fairbanks, you can arrange trips of a few hours to a week or longer, on rivers as slow and silty as the Chena to streams with Class IV white water. Some outfitters emphasize the aspect of adventure, others are oriented toward wildlife viewing and photography, and still others are geared mainly for fishermen. Shop around to find the firm that meets your particular needs.

Rainbow Riverrunners, P.O. Box 74202, Fairbanks, AK 99708 (tel. 907/479-5859), takes 55-mile fishing raft trips down the Gulkana River, starting 170 miles south of Fairbanks. **Alaskan Outback Expeditions,** P.O. Box 80281, Fairbanks, AK 99708 (tel. 907/895-4886), offers rafting and canoe adventures. There are many others; check with the Visitor Information Center.

RIVERBOATING A real network of boats operates on the Chena and Tanana Rivers, for commercial and fishing purposes as well as for touring and sightseeing. You can travel downstream to Nenana, for example, with **Alaska River Charters,** P.O. Box 81516, Fairbanks, AK 99708 (tel. 907/455-6827).

A proper riverboat is 22 feet long. Powered by a 60-horsepower engine, it can travel more than 60 m.p.h. On the summer solstice in June, Fairbanks riverboats compete in the Yukon 800 Marathon, a 24-hour race down the Chena, Tanana, and Yukon Rivers to Galena and back. The Mayor's Cup races are held in July.

ROLLER SKATING If you prefer wheels to blades, you can practice your pirouettes at **Skate Country,** 1087 Dennis Rd. in North Pole (tel. 488-9444).

SHOOTING Contact the **Tanana Valley Sportsman's Association,** P.O. Box 70669, Fairbanks, AK 99707 (tel. 479-4425), for information on rifle ranges, skeet shooting, and matches.

SKIING Cross-country skiers have a virtual paradise in Fairbanks, especially after the long December and January nights give way to much longer hours of daylight in February and March. On the **University of Alaska campus** alone there are 35 miles of cross-country trails, and there are many more at **Birch Hill Recreation Area** (site of the 1984 World Cup championships), Chena Lakes Recreation Area, Chena Hot Springs, and other nearby spots.

Overnight cross-country ski tours are organized by **Alaska Fish & Trails Unlimited,** 1177 Shypoke Dr., Fairbanks, AK 99709 (tel. 907/479-7630). You can rent equipment from a number of local sporting-goods stores, including **Beaver Sports,** 3480 College Rd. (tel. 479-2494).

The best downhill facilities close to Fairbanks are at the **Cleary Summit Ski Area,** Mile 21 on the Steese Highway (tel. 456-5520). The views from here are terrific at any time of year. The smaller **Skiland** area (tel. 389-3624 for the lodge or 488-9518 weekdays), a better spot for beginners, is on a hilltop accessible from Mile 13 on the Steese Highway.

SLEIGH RIDES The same folks who took you horseback riding in the summer will hook up Old Nell to the proverbial one-horse sleigh for a high-stepping trip through the countryside or downtown Fairbanks when winter comes. Also check with the **Pleasant Valley Animal Park** (tel. 488-3967) or **Helgeson Livestock** (tel. 457-6539).

SWIMMING Summer swimmers usually head for the **Chena Lakes Recreation Area,** 19 miles east of Fairbanks via North Pole, or the **Chena Hot Springs Resort.** Four heated indoor pools are open year round; call for times and prices: **Hamme Pool,** 901 Airport Way (tel. 459-1085 or 459-1469); **Mary Siah Recreation Center,** 1025 14th Ave. (tel. 459-1081 or 459-1469); **Patty Gym Pool,** University of Alaska (tel. 474-7205); and **Wescott Pool,** Eighth Avenue in North Pole (tel. 488-9402).

TENNIS The Fairbanks North Star Borough Parks and Recreation Department has six outdoor courts open on a first-come, first-served basis at the **Big Dipper Courts,** 19th Avenue and Lathrop Street (tel. 459-1070), and at the **Mary Siah Recreation Center,** 1025 14th Ave. (tel. 459-1081 or 459-1469).

8. SAVVY SHOPPING

With the sole exception of Anchorage, Fairbanks has the best selection of souvenir items of any settlement in Alaska.

SHOPPING A TO Z
ARTS & CRAFTS

Handcrafts of the Interior and Arctic are what you should look for here. Athabaskan art forms, designed and created by the Native peoples of the Yukon River basin, are worth seeking out. Unlike Eskimo crafts, they're hard to find elsewhere. (Look for a tag with an open hand, indicating an authentic handcrafted Alaskan Native product.) In particular, you might seek these out:

Tanned caribou- and moose-skin products, often decorated with fine beadwork: These include purses, pouches, gloves, slippers, parkas, and key rings.

Furs and products made from furs—caribou, wolf, wolverine, beaver, fox, and ground squirrel: Slippers, hats, and collars are good examples.

Jewelry made from moose skin, beads, feathers, porcupine quills, and shells.

Baskets: Birch-bark baskets in particular are beautiful. Willow may be used on top or as a reinforcement, and spruce roots are used for stitching. Grass, willow, or spruce roots may also be woven into complete baskets. Some baskets are decorated with beads and moose skin.

Walrus ivory carvings, masks, and jewelry: Most of these items come from Bering Sea islands—King, St. Lawrence, and Little Diomede—and from Nome and various coastal villages.

ALASKA HOUSE AND XANADU II, 250 3rd St. Tel. 479-6736 or 452-3714.
   This shop has a good collection of Native crafts. It has another store at the North Pole Plaza (tel. 488-0574) and an outlet at Alaskaland.

ARCTIC TRAVELERS GIFT SHOP, 201 Cushman St. Tel. 456-7080.
   You'll also find good collections of Native Alaskan crafts here, and at the store's other location in Alaskaland.

INSTITUTE OF ALASKA NATIVE ARTS, 524 Third Ave. Tel. 456-7491.

This is a good place to find all the items mentioned above. It features exclusively Native handcrafted goods.

BOOKS

Among the most interesting bookstores in Fairbanks is **Baker & Baker Booksellers,** open seven days a week at Eagle Plaza, 418 3rd St. (tel. 456-2278). In addition, **Waldenbooks,** the nationwide chain store, is represented at 32 College Rd. (tel. 456-8088).

CAMERAS & FILM

Fairbanks Fast Foto has an excellent selection of photographic equipment and supplies. There are two locations: in the Gavora Mall at 250 Third Ave. (tel. 456-3397), and in the Shopper's Forum at 1255 Airport Way (tel. 456-8896). **Northern Exposure** is located in the North Pole Plaza (tel. 488-1970). **Alaskan Photographic Repair Service,** 551½ Second Ave. (tel. 452-8819), carries used equipment and parts.

FINE ARTS

There are some fine artists in the Fairbanks area, both in traditional painting forms and in cottage industries.

Several galleries deal in modern adaptations of Native designs. I like the **New Horizons Gallery,** 211 Cushman St. (tel. 456-2063). You'll also find excellent collections at **Eye Appreciation Gallery,** 122 N. Turner St. (tel. 456-7015), and **The Artworks,** 3677 College Rd., at University Avenue (tel. 479-2563).

For other types of art—carvings, weaving, and pottery—check out the **House of Wood,** 411 Sixth Ave. (tel. 456-7958), and **Log Cabin Fibers,** 1074 McGrath Rd. (tel. 457-2786).

THE CRAFT MARKET, 401 Fifth Ave. at Noble St. Tel. 452-5495.

This is a good place to get an overview of Interior artisans' work. More than 100 different artists are represented here.

FURS & QIVIUT

Weavers might like to purchase some qiviut, the soft underwool of the musk-ox. The University of Alaska's Large Animal Research Station offers one-pound lots of qiviut for (at last notice) $110 plus $5 postage and handling. (If you think that's a lot, take a look at what qiviut scarves and hats sell for!) If interested, write to Muskox Research, Institute of Arctic Biology, University of Alaska, Fairbanks, AK 99775.

FUR FACTORY, 121 Dunkel St. Tel. 452-6240.

This place deals in raw hides as well as finished products.

GERALD VICTOR FURS, 212 Lacey St. Tel. 456-6890.

Here you'll find high-quality coats of fox, mink, beaver, muskrat, otter, and fur seal, and hats of sable, coyote, lynx, and marten.

GAME

REINDEER SHOP OF THE ARCTIC, No. 208 Regency Court, 59 College Rd. Tel. 456-4800.

This shop sells Indian Valley Meats gift packs with reindeer sausage, "squaw candy" (smoked salmon), and many other items.

GEMS

You won't have to look far in Fairbanks to find the mineral the town was built upon. Any jeweler will be happy to show you a wide selection of gold-nugget jewelry. In addition to the listing below, good bets are **A Touch of Gold,** in the Bentley Mall,

Old Steese Highway and College Road (tel. 451-7965); **Alaskan Gold Rush Fine Jewelry,** 531 Second Ave. (tel. 456-4991); **Larson's Jewelers,** 405 Noble St. (tel. 456-4141); and **Matrix Jewelers,** 208 Wendell St. (tel. 452-5939).

ALASKAN PROSPECTORS AND GEOLOGISTS SUPPLY, 504 College Rd. Tel. 452-7398.

Alaskan Prospectors store doubles as a dealer in recreational mining equipment. Gold, jade, ivory, and other minerals can be purchased.

GIFTS

Aside from hotel gift shops, souvenir hunters can browse at the **Pick 'n Poke Gift Shop,** 3175 College Rd. (tel. 479-5880 or 456-1680), and **TCR's Ivory,** 555 Second Ave. (tel. 452-1817). **JC Penney,** 610 Cushman St. (tel. 452-5131), also offers gifts and souvenirs at reasonable prices.

9. EVENING ENTERTAINMENT

For a city on the edge of the frontier, Fairbanks has a surprisingly active cultural life.

You can find out what's happening in Fairbanks at any time of year by calling the Fairbanks Convention and Visitor Bureau's **24-hour information line** (tel. 456-4636). The *Fairbanks Daily News-Miner* carries more detailed information in its Thursday "Arts/Entertainment" section and its Sunday supplement, "The Weekender."

THE PERFORMING ARTS

THEATER It's not serious theater, but it's lots of fun to catch the *Golden Heart* revue at Alaskaland's ✪ **Palace Theater and Saloon** (tel. 456-5960) nightly from late May to mid-September. Billed as a portrayal of "the comic life and musical times of Fairbanks," the sometimes-slapstick show takes its audience from the city's gold-rush era to modern times. There are two shows daily, at 7:30 and 9pm. Admission is $9.50. The bar opens at noon daily (at 2pm on Sunday).

Another rollicking repertoire is offered summer nights at the Cripple Creek Resort's ✪ **Malemute Saloon,** made famous by the Robert Service ballad "The Shooting of Dan McGrew." The Malemute looks like a converted barn with classic swinging doors and a sawdust floor. Tables are mere boards on kegs; a sign at the bar urges patrons to PLEASE USE SPITTOON. The show *Service with a Smile,* complete with ragtime music and Service poetry, begins at 9pm Monday through Saturday (on Friday and Saturday in July there is also a 7pm show). The show costs $5 for adults, $3 for children. The dinner buffet, featuring chicken, halibut, or reindeer stew, costs $13.95, and for an extra $5 you can have Dungeness crab too. Children pay 50¢ per year of age for the buffet, with crab $9.

Also at Cripple Creek, in the **Fire House Theater,** the *Crown of Light* multimedia program combines concert music with spectacular slides of the aurora borealis. It is presented at 6 and 8pm nightly in July, only at 8pm in June and August, by Photo Symphony Productions (tel. 479-2130). Adult admission is $5; children, $3.

Cripple Creek Resort (tel. 479-2500), a 1906 gold camp, is in Ester, eight miles west of Fairbanks. It's reached via a short dirt road that turns off the George Parks Highway at Mile 351.7.

For more serious theater, several local troupes have seasons that occasionally extend into summer. Contact any of the following for schedules and ticket information: **Fairbanks Drama Association,** 558 Gaffney Rd. (tel. 456-7529); **Fairbanks Light Opera Theater** (tel. 456-4631); and the **UAF Drama Department,** Fine Arts Building, University of Alaska–Fairbanks (tel. 474-7751).

CLASSICAL MUSIC & DANCE The **Fairbanks Symphony Orchestra** (tel.

479-3407), with headquarters at the Fine Arts Building on the University of Alaska campus, has an active October-to-April season. Year-round presentations by visiting artists in music, dance, ballet, opera, and other performing arts are hosted by the **Fairbanks Concert Association** (tel. 452-8880) and are presented at the UAF's Davis Concert Hall or at the Alaskaland Civic Center. Native shows are sometimes offered by the **Institute of Alaska Native Arts** (tel. 456-7491).

THE CLUB & MUSIC SCENE

To begin with, Fairbanks liquor laws are hardly "strict." They go to the limit allowed by the state: Every establishment serving alcoholic beverages must close for at least one hour at 5am. That relaxed attitude sets the scene for an effusive nightlife.

COUNTRY & WESTERN MUSIC

If you're a country music or square dancing aficionado, you'll have lots of company in this city, especially on the south side. There are several local groups that keep Alaskaland's Square and Round Dance Hall occupied every Thursday, Friday, and Saturday night with square dancing.

GREYHOUND LOUNGE, 1351 Cushman St., at Airport Way. Tel. 452-7977.

Stetson-hatted patrons from their 20s through their 60s dance in this dimly lit, low-ceilinged club Monday through Saturday from 9:30pm to 5am.

Admission: $2 Fri–Sat until 2am.

THE SILVER SPUR, 285 Old Richardson Hwy. Tel. 456-6300.

Behind the frontier facade of the Silver Spur is Fairbanks's newest country club, with live music Monday through Saturday nights starting at 9:30pm, and a big dance floor made for Texas two-stepping.

Admission: Free.

ROCK MUSIC

CABARET, 410 Second Ave. Tel. 456-1663.

The Cabaret is on the notorious downtown Fairbanks strip known during the Pipeline days simply as "Two Street." Every worker from Prudhoe Bay to Valdez knew that Two Street was where the action was: If you had the money, you could get anything you wanted. Today it's considerably tamer, but the reputation clings. This club features live music for dancing Monday through Saturday from 10pm to 4am; the bar is open from 9pm to 5am.

Admission: Free.

SUNSET INN, 345 Old Richardson Hwy. Tel. 456-4754.

This is the biggest hangout for Fairbanks's large population of single military men. Hard-rock or Top-40 acts perform nightly except Monday from 9:30pm, closing at 4am on Friday and Saturday, at 2:30am on other nights. The lounge itself, remarkable only for its large size and almost total lack of atmosphere, is open from 10pm to 5am seven days a week. Lip-sync contests and tequila night (Tuesday) are big occasions.

Admission: Free Sun and Tues–Thurs, $2 Fri–Sat.

BURLESQUE

For strip-show entertainment, visit **The Lonely Lady,** 4625 Old Airport Way (tel. 479-4162). There's never a cover charge.

THE BAR SCENE

HOWLING DOG SALOON, Mile 11.5, Steese Hwy. Tel. 457-8780.

For some true local color, make the drive out to Fox and drop in on this rustic remnant of better days. It's packed to the rafters most nights, especially Thursday through Saturday, when a neighborhood band plays its version of rock 'n' roll. In midsummer the volleyball net in the backyard is in use all night.

PIKE'S LANDING, Mile 4.5, Airport Way. Tel. 479-6305.

This bar is best known locally as the launching point for the annual Tanana Raft Race to Nenana in early June, but this riverside tavern is a popular hangout year-round. Open daily from before noon to 5am.

CINEMA

Moviegoers in Fairbanks can choose from eight first-run films at **Goldstream Cinemas,** 1855 Airport Way (tel. 456-5113).

Revivals and some first-run films are presented weekly at the **University of Alaska;** call for titles and schedules (tel. 474-7037). Free Alaska documentaries can be seen daily at the **Alaska Public Lands Information Center,** 250 Cushman St. (tel. 451-7352), and at 7pm on Monday at **Alaskan Prospectors and Geologists Supply,** 504 College Rd. (tel. 452-7398).

10. EXCURSIONS FROM FAIRBANKS

Beyond Fairbanks is the bush. The **Dalton Highway,** better known as the North Slope Haul Road, struggles nearly 500 miles through the Brooks Range to Prudhoe Bay on the Beaufort Sea. The Dalton is gravel all the way, but it does offer the only opportunity in Alaska to drive north of the Arctic Circle (which you'll cross 200 miles out of Fairbanks). Wildlife is prolific and the scenery is spectacular, especially after **Coldfoot,** a tiny way station 260 miles from Fairbanks. It has a restaurant, motel, grocery, and gas station. The owners are an Iditarod sled-dog musher, Dick Mackey, and his wife, Cathy.

THE STEESE HIGHWAY Few visitors make the one-way-and-turn-around drive to Prudhoe Bay. Most travelers join a tour if they're traveling that route. For drivers, there are numerous worthwhile destinations within shorter driving distance of Fairbanks. The Steese Highway, for instance, runs 162 miles from Fairbanks to Circle, on the banks of the Yukon River. En route it passes through the town of Central, with a side road to the popular Arctic Circle Hot Springs.

There are several campsites and numerous abandoned mining camps along the Steese Highway beyond Chatanika (Old F.E. Company) Gold Camp (see "Attractions," above). On the divide of the Yukon and Tanana River drainages, between Miles 85 and 108, you're likely to see a carpet of wildflowers in May and June, or herds of migrating caribou in August and September. **Eagle Summit** (elevation 3,624 feet) at Mile 108 is a popular place for Fairbanksans to view the summer solstice.

It's downhill from there—over 2,600 feet in less than 20 miles—to **Central.** The permanent population of some 100 grows to around 800 in summer In town you'll find the interesting **Circle District Museum,** a couple of restaurants, a motel, and a campground.

Eight miles southeast of Central via a side road, 136 miles from Fairbanks, is **Arctic Circle Hot Springs,** Central, AK 99730 (tel. 907/520-5113). The highly mineralized springs, flowing at a rate of 386 gallons per minute and a temperature of 139°F, are considered very medicinal. They have a high sodium and chloride content, and significant amounts of sulphate and silica. The resort hotel, built in 1930, offers year-round lodging at $45 single and $62 double, or $20 per bed (bring your own sleeping bag or bedding) in the hostel-style dormitory. Many of the vegetables served in the restaurant, which is open for breakfast, lunch, and dinner, are grown in greenhouses heated by the springs. Meal prices are moderate: For example, a steak dinner costs $13.50.

At **Circle** (pop. about 100), another 34 miles northeast of Central, you'll find a virtual ghost town that from 1894 to 1897 was the biggest boomtown the Far North had (to that time) ever seen. Circle City, as it was known, was a log-cabin metropolis with an opera house, hospital, and library, plus myriad hotels and bars. It was soon surpassed by Dawson City in the Klondike, but the town hung on as supply center for the mining camps of the Circle Mining District until the Steese Highway connected it with Fairbanks in 1927. The **Yukon Trading Post** (tel. 907/773-1217) houses a café and general store, and books flightseeing and charter-boat expeditions.

THE ELLIOTT HIGHWAY   Manley Hot Springs is almost exactly as far west of Fairbanks as Circle is northeast—163 miles. It's located at the end of the Elliott Highway, which forks the Steese Highway at Fox, 11 miles north of Fairbanks. The road turns to gravel 17 miles farther on.

This route offers spectacular views, access to good river fishing, and side trips to the communities of Livengood and Minto. **Livengood** (pop. about 100), 86 miles from Fairbanks, is little more than a ghost town, but it thrived between 1914 and 1920, when miners sluiced $9.5 million in gold out of the nearby hills.

The Athabaskan Indian residents of **Minto** (pop. about 230), 131 miles from Fairbanks and 11 miles off the Elliott Highway on the banks of the Tolovana River, are mainly hunters and fishermen. An arts-and-crafts center displays their birch-bark basketry and items of fur and skin clothing. Accommodations and meals are available at the **Minto Lakeview Lodge** (tel. 907/798-7112) for $45–$60 per night.

Manley Hot Springs, where Baker Creek empties into the Tanana River, has a permanent population of 88 that swells to almost 200 in summer. Frank Manley built a resort hotel here in 1907 when the settlement was the principal mining-supply center for the Eureka and Tofty gold districts, but today it's the hot springs—located about three-quarters of a mile east of the town itself—that attract the most attention. Bubbling out of the earth at a temperature of around 136°F, they are unusual in that they have no sulfur content, and thus none of the acrid smell that usually characterizes hot springs.

Manley's old hotel is now the **Manley Roadhouse,** 100 Front St., Manley Hot Springs, AK 99756 (tel. 907/672-3161 or 672-3221), a veritable "period piece" furnished with antiques and prehistoric artifacts. Open May 15 to October 1, it has a restaurant and saloon, plus rooms and cabins priced at $50–$65. Or pay $5 at the roadhouse to use the Manley Hot Springs Park Association's nearby campground.

The new **Manley Hot Springs Resort,** Old Manley Highway and Spring Drive, Manley Hot Springs, AK 99756 (tel. 907/672-3611), offers year-round swimming in a pool at the springs. The main lodge, housing the restaurant and lounge, is a lovely log building with a jade fireplace and a cozy, rustic feeling. There are 24 rooms with private bath; prices range from $70 to $115 (based on double occupancy) and some rooms have their own Jacuzzi. The resort also has an RV park, laundry, and gift shop. It arranges fishing trips and riverboat charters, and books tours to fishing camps, gold mines, and sled-dog kennels.

FORT YUKON   The largest Athabaskan village in Alaska is Fort Yukon, a settlement of about 650 people eight miles north of the Arctic Circle, some 140 air miles northeast of Fairbanks. It's a fascinating, friendly community with a subsistence lifestyle (note the fish wheels, traps, and garden plots) amid the accouterments of the late 20th century (telephones, satellite television, and off-road vehicles).

The Hudson's Bay Company first established a trading post here in 1847, on a great bend of the Yukon River near its confluence with the Porcupine. The community's subsequent missionary, gold-rush, and riverine commercial history is eloquently told at the **Dinji Zhuu Enjit Museum.** The **old fort** houses the Fort Yukon Native Council. Nearby are the **Old Mission House,** listed on the National Register of Historic Places, and Alaska's first Episcopal church, with its beaded moosehide altar cover. The Gwitchyaa Athabaskans are noted for their fine beadwork. It can be purchased at the museum.

Lodging and food are available year-round in riverside log cabins at the **Elderly Lodge,** P.O. Box 10, Fort Yukon, AK 99740 (tel. 907/662-2468 or 662-2634). Room rates are $40–$55 a night. For a change of scene, you can dine at the old **Sourdough Inn,** at First and Sled Streets (tel. 662-2402). Fort Yukon has been "dry" since its residents voted in 1984 to ban the sale and importation of alcoholic beverages.

Flights and tours are offered by **Frontier Flying Service,** 3820 University Ave. S., Fairbanks, AK 99709 (tel. 907/474-0014); **Wright Air Service,** P.O. Box 60142, Fairbanks, AK 99706 (tel. 907/474-0502); and **Fairbanks Floatplane Tours,** P.O. Box 61661, Fairbanks, AK 99706 (tel. 907/479-8778).

11. THE ALASKA HIGHWAY

Southeast of Fairbanks, the Richardson and Alaska Highways coincide as far as Delta Junction, a distance of 98 miles. From here, the Richardson Highway turns south toward Glennallen and Valdez (266 miles away), while the Alaska Highway continues in a southeasterly direction. The Canadian border is another 200 miles; Dawson Creek, B.C., is 1,422 miles on.

DELTA JUNCTION

A farm center of about 1,200 people serving an area population of some 5,700, Delta Junction lies in a stretch of fertile land between the Delta and Tanana Rivers. The town proudly calls itself the end of the Alaska Highway: A sign outside the Visitor Information Center underscores that declaration; inside, you can pay $1 for a certificate stating that you've driven the highway.

The **Visitor Information Center,** is a log cabin at the junction of the two major highways (tel. 907/895-9941), is open daily from 9am to 6pm, late May to Labor Day.

WHAT TO SEE & DO

The **Delta Agricultural Project,** started in 1978, has created 37 farms on 85,000 acres in the Delta Junction area. Farms grow mainly barley and forage crops. You can see many of the farms by driving out Clearwater and Jack Warren Roads. Ask directions locally. The agricultural community celebrates at the **Deltana Fair,** held annually over the first weekend of August.

Fort Greely, five miles south of Delta Junction off the Richardson Highway, contains the U.S. Army's Northern Warfare Training Center—which emphasizes arctic survival, military snow skiing, mountaineering, glacier crossing, and inland waterway navigation—and the army's Cold Regions Test Center for food, clothing, and equipment. Visitors can get a pass at the front gate. Call the Fort Greely Public Affairs Office (tel. 873-4161 or 872-4206) for more information.

Big Delta State Historic Park is 9½ miles north of Delta Junction toward Fairbanks. In the park is **Rika's Roadhouse** (tel. 895-4201), an early 20th-century lodge at an important ferry landing on the Tanana River. The Alaska Division of Parks has restored the roadhouse, with 1920s period furnishings, as a bed-and-breakfast that also serves meals. There's also a barn, the ferryman's house, and a blacksmith's shop.

Don't be surprised to see a large **herd of American bison** in this area. A herd of 23 was transplanted in 1928 from the National Bison Range in Moiese, Mont.; that group has grown to about 375, and hunting is permitted on a restricted basis from October to March.

WHERE TO STAY

ALASKA 7 MOTEL, Mile 270.3, Richardson Hwy. (P.O. Box 1115), Delta Junction, AK 99737. Tel. 907/895-4848. 16 rms (all with bath). TV TEL
$ Rates: $49 single; $55 double. Children under 10 stay free in parents' room. AE, DC, DISC, MC, V.

The Alaska 7 offers better quality for price than any other accommodation in the Delta Junction area. All the well-kept rooms, decorated in earth tones with wood paneling, have two double beds, a large desk, television, and hot-water heating. Half the rooms have kitchenettes.

DELTA YOUTH HOSTEL, Mile 3, Tanana Loop Rd. (P.O. Box 971), Delta Junction, AK 99737. Tel. 907/895-5074. Directions: Follow the highway toward Fairbanks to Mile 271.8, turn right on Tanana Loop Road, and follow the signs another three miles.
$ Rates: $10 for hostel association members, $13 for nonmembers. **Closed:** Sept 2–May.

Located nine miles from Delta Junction, this youth hostel is open from June 1 to September 1.

PIONEER CABINS, Mile 1,404, Alaska Hwy., Delta Junction, AK 99737. Tel. 907/895-4157. 8 cabins (all with bath).
$ Rates: $45 per cabin, for one to six guests. No credit cards.

⑤ In the heart of buffalo country is one of the great lodging bargains in Alaska. Each pine-construction cabin has charcoal-gray wall-to-wall carpeting, full bathroom with shower and sauna, full kitchen with four-burner stove and refrigerator, a sleeping loft, and propane heat. Up to six can stay in one unit for the same low price. The catch is that you must bring your own utensils or drive eight miles west to the nearest restaurant. The Silver Fox Roadhouse next door sells groceries, and The Nearest Bar is literally a stone's throw away. Owner Dan Splain is also an outfitter who arranges horse-pack trips into the Granite Mountains and McComb Plateau to look for buffalo and caribou.

SUMMIT LAKE LODGE, Mile 195, Richardson Hwy. (P.O. Box 1955), Fairbanks, AK 99707. Tel. 907/822-3969. 20 rms (all with bath).
$ Rates: Mid-May to mid-Sept, $60–$85 single or double. Mid-Sept to mid-May, $50–$75 single or double. AE, MC, V.

This popular summer vacation spot is also a takeoff point for snow machining and cross-country skiing in the winter. In addition to the comfortable guest rooms, the lodge has a laundry, gift shop, lounge, and restaurant. The restaurant serves a full breakfast and lunch, then slips into high gear at dinnertime with a wide choice of entrees, including steak and lobster. Food-and-lodging packages are available, and fishermen can buy gas for their boat or floatplane here.

WHERE TO DINE

PIZZA BELLA, Mile 266, Richardson Hwy. Tel. 895-4841.
Cuisine: ITALIAN/AMERICAN. **Reservations:** Recommended.
$ Prices: Appetizers $4–$6; main courses $8–$17. MC, V.
Open: Daily 11am–midnight.

You can sit at a red tablecloth in the spacious new dining room or place an order to go. Spaghetti and meatballs, and baked lasagne with Italian sausage, are popular Italian entrees. A 12-inch pepperoni-and-mushroom pizza costs about $12. Soups, salads, sandwiches, steaks, prime rib, and seafood are also on the menu, in case you don't fancy Italian food. Pizza Bella is licensed for beer and wine.

TOK

Located 206 miles from Fairbanks and 125 miles from the Canadian border near Beaver Creek, Yukon Territory, this unincorporated settlement of about 1,200 summer residents (less than half that in winter) spreads around the junction of the Alaska Highway and Glenn Highway. Travelers coming from Canada make a decision here: Do they continue straight ahead to Fairbanks or turn south toward Anchorage? As a result, it's a popular overnight stop for independent and package tourists.

Your first stop in town should be the state-operated **Alaska Public Lands Information Center,** Mile 1,314.1 on the Alaska Highway (tel. 883-5667). It has excellent exhibits of regional history and wildlife and a huge number of brochures from sites all over the state of Alaska. The information center is open Memorial Day through September, daily from 8am to 8pm, and in winter, Monday through Friday from 8am to 4:30pm. The Tok Chamber of Commerce operates a **visitor center** adjacent to the Alaska Public Lands Information Center and the **U.S. Fish and Wildlife Service** welcomes visitors at its office directly across the highway.

WHAT TO SEE & DO

Tok calls itself the "Sled-Dog Capital of the World." It's estimated that every third resident is in some way involved with raising dogs—breeding, training, or mushing.

Members of the **Tok Dog Mushers Association** (tel. 883-6874) are actively involved in the Race of Champions, the last major race of the Alaskan winter season, held here over the third weekend of March.

The **Burnt Paw,** a gift shop just west of the Glenn Highway junction with the Alaska Highway (tel. 883-4121 or 451-8256), presents sled-dog demonstrations at 7:30pm daily except Sunday during the months of June, July, and August.

WHERE TO STAY & DINE

GOLDEN BEAR MOTEL AND CAMPER PARK, Mile 124.4, Glenn Hwy. (P.O. Box 276), Tok, AK 99780. Tel. 907/883-2561. 62 rms (all with bath). TV
$ Rates: Memorial Day–Labor Day, $60 single; $65 double. Rest of the year, $55 single; $60 double. AE, MC, V.

The rooms at the Golden Bear—58 new rooms and four older log units with kitchenettes—are decorated in autumn tones with double or queen-size beds, large desk/dressers and tables, electric baseboard heating, and satellite TV with radio. Bathrooms are huge: Through the swinging saloon-style doors are a sink, dressing table, and wardrobe closet; the toilet and shower/bath are in a second room. The site also has a full-service restaurant, open from 6am to 10pm, and a large and complete gift shop.

The camper park has 15 full hookups and 12 partial, with tent sites, firepits, canopied tables, a heated bathhouse, and a laundry. Full hookups are $16 (based on double occupancy), water and electric sites are $14, and tent sites are $10.

SNOWSHOE GATEWAY MOTEL, Mile 1,314, Alaska Hwy. (P.O. Box 559), Tok, AK 99780. Tel. 907/883-4511. 24 rms (none with bath), 14 suites (all with bath). TV
$ Rates: Memorial Day–Labor Day, $25 single without bath, $50 single with bath; $30 double without bath, $55 double with bath. Labor Day–Memorial Day, $20 single without bath, $45 single with bath; $25 double without bath, $50 double with bath. MC, V.

The 14 new two-room suites have private baths and television. The 24 additional units in pipeline trailers share a large central bath; small and spartan, they have twin beds and little else. A fine-arts and gift shop is also on the site.

TOK INTERNATIONAL YOUTH HOSTEL, Pringle Rd. (P.O. Box 532), Tok, AK 99780. Tel. 907/883-5113. 10 beds.
$ Rates: June–Sept, $8 for American Youth Hostels members, $10 for nonmembers. No credit cards. **Closed:** Oct–May.

This small hostel, off Mile 1,322.5 on the Alaska Highway, 7½ miles west of Tok junction, has 10 beds in a wall tent and additional tent space. The toilet facilities, needless to say, are outhouses.

WESTMARK TOK, P.O. Box 130, Tok, AK 99780. Tel. 907/883-5174, or toll free 800/544-0970. 72 rms (all with bath).
$ Rates: $120 single; $130 double. $59 rates may be available on selected rooms and dates. AE, DC, MC, V. **Closed:** Last week of Sept to Memorial Day weekend.

Tok's largest (and most expensive) hotel operates only during the tourist season, is owned by outside interests, and is geared primarily to handling the busloads of tourists who stop here overnight. This hotel comprises a series of eight-plexes centered around rock gardens. The long, narrow rooms were once pipeline trailer units; the shape has resulted in awkwardly placed bathroom facilities. Otherwise, the rooms are very nice: wall-to-wall blue-gray carpeting, checkered covers on double or twin beds, dresser and table, clock radio, and electric baseboard heat. There's no TV or phone, but you can watch a video of *Never Cry Wolf* in the lobby at night, and there are pay phones near reception.

The warm lobby has a propane fireplace, lots of sofa and chair seating, and piped-in classical music. A friendly dining room with a garden decor serves breakfast daily from 6 to 9:30am and dinner daily from 5 to 10pm (no lunch). Help yourself to a 20-item salad bar for $7, or order a full dinner of halibut ($15) or broiled rib-eye steak ($18). The lounge is open from 4pm to midnight.

Ask about the special summer value rates from $49.

YOUNG'S MOTEL, Mile 1,313.3, Alaska Hwy. (P.O. Box 482), Tok, AK 99780. Tel. 907/883-4411. 25 rms (all with bath). TV

$ Rates: June–Aug. $55 single; additional person $5 extra. Sept–May, $45 single or double. MC, V.

The spacious rooms here are appointed in shades of brown, with double beds, desk/dressers, satellite TVs, fluorescent ceiling lamps, and hot-water baseboard heating. Register in adjoining Fast Eddy's Restaurant, which offers everything from omelets and pizzas to steak and lobster at reasonable prices. Fast Eddy's is open year-round, from 6am to midnight. There's also a guest laundry.

EAGLE

Situated on the banks of the Yukon River, 175 miles north of Tok via the narrow, winding Taylor Highway, Eagle (pop. 168) is a worthwhile stop for travelers en route to or from Dawson City, the capital of the Yukon's Klondike district. Founded in 1898 by Klondike gold miners as the nearest American settlement to the rush, it rapidly grew in importance, being established as the first incorporated city in the Alaskan Interior by declaration of President Theodore Roosevelt in 1901.

There's a lot to see in Eagle. The original **Wickersham Courthouse,** built in 1901 to establish the federal court in the Interior, today houses one of the city museums. Another museum occupies the old **Customs House** on the banks of the Yukon River. Reconstructed **Fort Egbert,** a U.S. Army post from 1899 to 1911, offers an interpretive exhibit and photo display, and a 58-stall mule barn (with name plates for each mule). Walking tours are conducted at 10am daily, Memorial Day to Labor Day, by the Eagle Historical Society ($2 per person).

Eagle is also the headquarters for the 2.5-million-acre **Yukon-Charley Rivers National Preserve,** comprising 128 miles of the Yukon River between Eagle and Circle and the entire 88-mile-long drainage of the Charley River. The preserve encompasses scenic beauty, gold-rush relics and ghost towns, ancient archeological sites, and a plethora of wildlife. Float trips are the most popular means of access. For information, contact the National Park Service, P.O. Box 64, Eagle, AK 99738 (tel. 907/547-2233).

Yukon River Cruises re-create the gold-rush era in summer cruises down the Yukon River between Dawson City and Eagle, aboard the M.V. *Yukon Queen.* Fully narrated, one-day bus-cruise round-trips are offered most days in summer. Contact **Gray Line of Alaska,** 1980 Cushman St., Fairbanks, AK 99701 (tel. 907/456-7741).

There is no road access to Eagle in the winter when the Taylor Highway is closed, but air taxis, snow machines, and dog teams make the trip easily. Meals and lodging are available in town.

CHAPTER 10

THE ARCTIC

- **WHAT'S SPECIAL ABOUT THE ARCTIC**
1. **NOME**
2. **KOTZEBUE**
3. **BARROW**
4. **PRUDHOE BAY**
5. **THE BROOKS RANGE**

North of the Arctic Circle, the longest day has no night and the longest night has no day. The landscape is mostly frozen desert, a region underlain by permafrost, where little precipitation falls but what does remains on the ground all winter. Myriad lakes, from a few feet to 35 miles long, reveal the unseen action of permafrost's summer thaw. There are no trees—only sparse bushes and colorful wildflowers that seasonally speckle the earth. The sea itself is frozen 10 months of the year, and even during the brief July-August period when it is not, there's no noticeable tidal shift, no wave action to speak of, leaving only an eerie flatness. This is a stark land. Human adaptability to the Arctic is one of the great survival stories to be discovered in Alaska.

Temperatures in the Arctic are not as extreme as in Alaska's Interior, but are definitely lower on average. Barrow, for instance, has an average July high of 44°F (over 50°F is tropical) and an average January low of −24°F. Nome and Kotzebue, farther south and west-facing, expect highs and lows 10°–15°F higher. Barrow gets 4 inches of precipitation annually (10 inches of snow equal 1 inch of rain), Kotzebue gets 8 inches, Nome 15 inches.

Who lives in the Arctic? Traditionally, it's the hardy Inupiat Eskimos. In settlements scattered along the coasts and rivers, they originally earned their living from the sea, fishing and sealing and whaling. Today no place is safe from the influence of "progress"; in most villages, snowmobiles have taken the place of dog sleds and satellite television has replaced tribal councils. In the two largest Eskimo communities, Kotzebue and Barrow, no visitor can avoid observing the conflict between old and new.

Most Native villages have wisely banned the sale and importation of alcoholic beverages, addressing another problem that has assailed Native populations throughout Alaska. Prudhoe Bay, founded in the 1970s as the northern terminus of the Trans Alaska Pipeline, also limits alcohol sales. Nome, though, has no such restrictions. The turn-of-the-century gold-rush town can still be the wildest community in the north, especially in March when the Iditarod dog-sled racers arrive from Anchorage.

Towns, of course, aren't representative of the Arctic as a whole. An enormous chunk of the landscape, mainly in the Brooks Range, has been set aside by the federal government as national park, preserve, or wildlife refuge. The extra effort it takes to reach this wilderness repays backpackers, canoeists, and other outdoor enthusiasts with the experience of a lifetime.

GETTING THERE

The only practical way to reach Alaska's Arctic is by air. **Alaska Airlines** (tel. toll free 800/426-0333) operates regular daily flights from Anchorage to Nome and Kotzebue, and from Anchorage and Fairbanks to Prudhoe Bay. **MarkAir** (tel. toll free 800/426-6784, 800/478-0800 in Alaska) operates the concession to Barrow from Anchorage and Fairbanks, and also visits Prudhoe Bay. Several air taxis, listed under the appropriate gateway city, service the region.

Most visitors travel to the Arctic as part of a summer tour. A number of options are available. Most popular are an overnight Nome-Kotzebue excursion ($472 from

WHAT'S SPECIAL ABOUT THE ARCTIC

Natural History

- [ ] North America's largest caribou herd, tenuously protected in the Arctic National Wildlife Refuge, in the face of threatened mineral exploitation.
- [ ] Marine mammals like whales and walruses, the subjects of annual native harvest festivals in Barrow and Savoonga, on St. Lawrence Island.
- [ ] Natural phenomena like permafrost and the aurora borealis.

History

- [ ] Archeological remnants of North America's earliest immigrants, protected in the Bering Land Bridge National Preserve and Cape Krusenstern National Monument.
- [ ] Sod igloo sites and dwelling mounds, uncovered at the Uqiagvik and Birnirk digs at Barrow.

- [ ] Humorist Will Rogers and pilot Wiley Post, who died in a 1935 plane crash near Barrow; a memorial marks their demise.

Towns

- [ ] Nome, famous for its turn-of-the-century gold rush and the finish line for the annual Iditarod sled-dog race in March.
- [ ] Barrow, the northernmost town on the North American continent.
- [ ] Kotzebue, where many of the Inupiat people who live in Alaska's largest Eskimo community, still pursue traditional subsistence lifestyles.
- [ ] Prudhoe Bay, the oil-company settlement that ships its "black gold" south via the Alaska Pipeline; visitors can observe the operation.

Anchorage) and a full-day trip to Prudhoe Bay ($315 from Anchorage). Since you cross the Arctic Circle on both trips, your airline provides a certificate stating such. For information, contact the airlines or your travel agent. **Alaska Airlines Vacations** (tel. toll free 800/468-2248) handles most trips.

1. NOME

539 miles NW of Anchorage, 102 miles S of the Arctic Circle

GETTING THERE   By Plane   Nome Airport, about a mile west of downtown via Seppala Drive, is served by **Alaska Airlines** (tel. toll free 800/426-0333) and **MarkAir** (tel. toll free 800/426-6784, 800/478-0800 in Alaska), with regular daily flights connecting Nome with Anchorage and Kotzebue. Several smaller airlines provide service within the Norton Sound region, including **Bering Air** (tel. 907/443-5464), **Cape Smythe Air** (tel. 907/443-2414), **Olson Air** (tel. 907/443-2229), and **Ryan Air** (tel. 907/443-5482).

There is no access to Nome by road or rail.

ESSENTIALS   Orientation   Almost everything is within walking distance of your accommodation. Front Street, where most businesses are located, sprawls along the waterfront in an east-west direction. Numbered avenues (First through Sixth) parallel it to the north. Near the western end of Front Street, Bering Street branches north as the main thoroughfare inland.

Climate   Average July temperatures range from 44°F to 55°F; average January

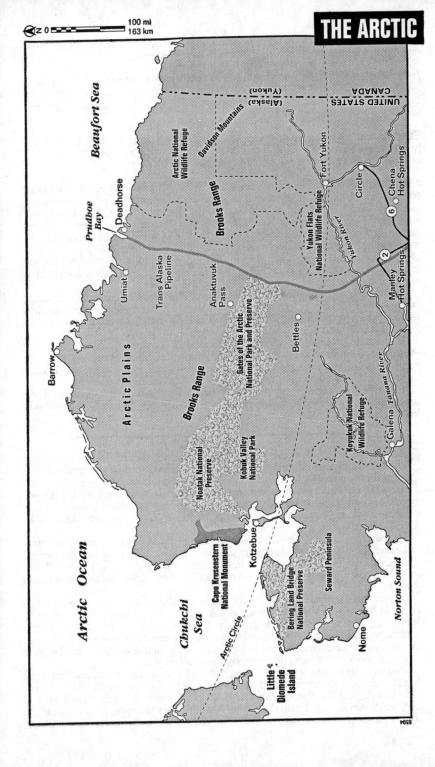

THE ARCTIC

temperatures from −3°F to 12°F. Average annual precipitation is 15 inches, about one-third of which drops as winter snow (56 inches annually).

Information The **Nome Convention and Visitors Bureau,** P.O. Box 251, Nome, AK 99762 (tel. 907/443-5535), maintains an efficient office with plenty of brochures and a free slide show at Front Street and Division Street. Its slogan is a natural: "There's no place like Nome!"

Fast Facts Nome's weekly newspaper, the *Nome Nugget,* has been continuously published since 1901. The city has a 20-bed hospital (tel. 907/443-3311), a community college, one bank, and 14 churches.

SPECIAL EVENTS The year's big event is the ◯ **Iditarod Trail Sled Dog Race,** which begins in Anchorage on the last Saturday in February and ends some two weeks and 1,100 miles later in Nome. Sometimes called "The Last Great Race," more commonly just "The Iditarod," it challenges 60–80 men and women—and over 1,000 dogs—with a snow- and ice-covered obstacle course of mountains and rivers, windswept tundra, and ice-locked seacoast. The top 20 finishers (in a good year, 70% of the starters will finish) share a $375,000-plus purse. Iditarod watchers can get recorded race updates by calling 907/248-5355, or straight information from 6am to midnight daily during the race by calling 907/248-MUSH.

Nome's **Month of Iditarod** also includes shorter dog-sled races, snow machine races, ice golf on the frozen Bering Sea, basketball and volleyball tournaments, Eskimo sports competitions, crafts exhibits and sales, special receptions, and an awards banquet for the Iditarod mushers.

In the week of June 21, when Nome receives 22½ hours of direct sunlight, the **Midnight Sun Festival** is held. Highlights are the Nome River raft race (the perpetual trophy is a fur-lined honey bucket), a softball tournament, and Eskimo cultural events including the Miss Alaska Native Brotherhood Pageant.

Other important annual events are the **Polar Bear Swim,** a Memorial Day dip in the Bering Sea; the **Fourth of July** parade and street games; and the hilarious **Great Bathtub Race** down Front Street on Labor Day.

Nome isn't technically in the Arctic. It's spread along the flat, barren Bering Sea coast 150 miles south of the Arctic Circle. Its climate can be downright balmy compared to that of Barrow. (On the other hand, no visitor would mistake Nome for the tropics.) But the city is isolated from most sizable Alaskan towns, and it has more in common with the Arctic than with any other region. Besides, many tourists combine a visit to Nome with one to Kotzebue, which is north of the Arctic Circle. And so Nome winds up in this Arctic chapter.

Whether intentionally or not, Nome is a living relic of a bygone era. Prospectors still search for gold along the shores and in the low, rolling hills of the Seward Peninsula. The dog sled remains a form of winter transportation. There are probably more bars per capita—at least nine in a town of 4,500 people—than anywhere else in Alaska.

Nome owes its establishment to the discovery of gold on Anvil Creek in 1898. News of the strike reached the Klondike goldfields that winter, and by the following spring "Anvil City" (soon to be renamed "Nome") had a population of 10,000 fortune seekers. When the beach sands were found to contain a little gold themselves, steamships from Seattle and San Francisco braved the Bering ice to assault the place where, according to rumor, "the beaches are made of gold."

No trees grew here, so there was no way to build log cabins without importing lumber. Tents soon dotted the landscape and lined a 30-mile stretch of beach. The U.S. Census of 1900 showed that one-third of all whites living in Alaska were in Nome: Its official population then was 12,488, though estimates ranged upward to 20,000. So sophisticated was Nome that it even had a French lingerie shop and four piano movers. But several violent storms and major fires, coupled with the increasing difficulty of finding easy wealth from gold, drove the population down near its current level after World War I.

Whence the name Nome? Credit it to a spelling mistake. A British naval officer charting this coast in the 1850s wrote the inscription "? Name" next to a prominent unnamed point. Another draftsman later took that to be "C. Nome," and it appeared on a map as "Cape Nome."

Today about 60% of the population is Native, mainly Yupik Eskimo. But Nome remains much more a "white man's town" than any other in western Alaska. One major gold-mining company is still in operation, along with many family-run operations, and Alaska's reindeer industry is based in Nome. Oil and gas leases in Norton Sound could bring additional wealth to the city.

GETTING AROUND

You can rent a pickup truck ($65 a day) or van ($75 a day) from **Stampede Rent-A-Car** (tel. 443-5252); or a van or four-wheel-drive pickup ($80 per day) from **Bonanza Car Rentals** (tel. 443-2221). **Alaska Cab Garage** (tel. 443-2939) rents trucks ($75–$85 per day), suburbans ($95 per day), and vans ($110 per day).

Nome has three 24-hour taxi companies—**Checker Cab** (tel. 443-5211), **Gold Rush Taxi** (tel. 443-5922), and **Nome Cab** (tel. 443-3030)—whose fares run approximately $3 to anywhere in town.

WHAT TO SEE & DO

SIGHTS & ATTRACTIONS

The **Carrie McLain Memorial Museum,** on Front Street opposite Lane's Way (tel. 443-2566), is a good place to start your exploration of downtown Nome. It's located in the Kegoayah Kozga Library building. A wealth of historical photographs show how the city looked during its glitzy heyday. Various artifacts and exhibits provide a glimpse both of the area's Native heritage and gold-rush past. Hours vary seasonally; call ahead. Admission is free.

The visitors bureau will provide you with a thoughtfully produced pamphlet to guide you on a 30- to 45-minute historical **walking tour.** The tour visits the former red-light district, whose working residents paid a $10 monthly "fine" (in lieu of arrest) which funded the Nome fire department; remnants of the Wild Goose Railroad, which ran from the city to tundra goldfields beginning in 1900; and the seawall that kept Nome from being "washed away" by a terrible storm in 1974. The seawall extends the entire length of Front Street to the Bering Sea beachfront at its east end. (Nome's oldest standing building, a log cabin dating from 1898 or 1899, was the sole structure to escape a devastating 1934 fire caused by the explosion of a whisky still during Prohibition. As of this writing, it was being restored and was not on the tour.)

I enjoy poking my head into the local **butcher shop,** on Front Street, to see what the Eskimo population eats. The meat of the *oogruk,* the bearded seal, is a favorite—along with its flippers, liver, and kidneys. You'll also find *coak* (walrus meat), *muktuk* (whale blubber), and reindeer steaks.

Many of the gift shops in downtown Nome specialize in ivory carvings. This is probably the best place in Alaska to buy ivory articles: Prices may be 50%–100% lower than in Anchorage. Gold-nugget jewelry, furs, and Eskimo handcrafts are also good buys. There are several shops on Front Street; I like **Maruskiya's Gift Shop** (tel. 443-2686), next door to the visitor center, and the **Arctic Trading Post** (tel. 443-2955), between Bering and Division Streets.

The nearest working reminders of Nome's gold rush are found near town at the **Little Creek Mining Station,** an original mining claim where visitors can keep the gold they pan. Tour buses make a stop here.

The beach for miles east of Nome is cluttered with the rusted litter of nine decades of gold mining. In the summer months you may see miners camped on the beach, sluicing for gold. The mineral is not as plentiful as it once was, but if you're a scavenger you may get lucky: In 1985 a tourist found a 3¼-inch gold nugget (1.29 ounces, valued at about $520) right at the end of the city seawall!

ORGANIZED TOURS

Nome Tour & Marketing (tel. 443-2651), with an office at the Nome Nugget Inn, is the major summer tour operator. The $40 half-day package includes a tour of town, a visit to the Little Creek Mining Station with an introductory slide show, and a visit to Howard Farley's dog camp. Meals and accommodation are not included.

Other local tour operators include **Camp Bendeleben** hunting and fishing guide service (tel. 443-2880); **Jade's Arctic Grizzlies** hunting trips (tel. 443-5187); **Tours by Taxi** (tel. 443-5136), which provides tours of town and the vicinity; and **Cape Wooley Tours and Native Fish Camp** (tel. 443-5701).

SPORTS & RECREATION

In a huge new building at 425 E. Sixth Ave., near Steadman Street, the **Nome Recreation Center** (tel. 443-5431) has a variety of facilities, including a six-lane bowling alley, racquetball courts, gymnasium, weight equipment, and aerobic dance classes. It's open in the summer Monday through Saturday from 11am to 9:30pm and on Sunday 1 to 9:30pm. In winter, hours are 10am to 10pm weekdays and 1 to 10pm weekends.

Nomeites go ga-ga over **softball** in the summer. The City League fields are two miles west of town near the airport.

Birdwatchers also love Nome. Merely sitting on the city seawall, you can spot migratory Asiatic species and various Beringian birds—those that breed only in the Bering Sea. The visitor center will provide a free checklist of birds found in this area.

FISHING After getting your Alaskan fishing license at the country store or the **Alaska Department of Fish and Game,** both on Front Street, you can go after salmon, northern pike, grayling, or arctic char on the Seward Peninsula's inland waterways. Peak fishing times are June through September. Some of the best fishing is on the Nome River north and east of the city and on the Snake River a few miles west.

GOLD MINING Most productive mining areas near Nome have been staked and are off-limits. Unstaked areas may be panned, but it's up to the individual to research possible ownership of the land, whether it be state, city, federal, private, or Native owned.

No permit is required for mining of a recreational nature—which means that you're limited to panning or using a small rocker box or portable dredge with an intake of less than two inches. Specific mining questions in Nome may be directed to the **Bureau of Land Management** (tel. 443-2177).

SWIMMING When the Bering Sea warms to 45°F in the middle of the summer, locals deem it warm enough for swimming. Some even allow their nerves to be numbed by waterskiing and windsurfing. Visitors are welcome to join in the fun—but most prefer the warmth of the indoor pool at **Nome-Beltz High School** (tel. 443-5717), three miles north of town. The fee for public pool use is $4.

WINTER SPORTS The Nome Kennel Club—the oldest **dog-mushing** organization in the world—sponsors local races for the Nome area's 40 teams every Sunday from January through March. Visitors can participate in the sport year-round. Richard and Linnea Burmeister's **Flat Dog Kennels,** 914 E. Sixth Ave. (P.O. Box 1103), Nome, AK 99762 (tel. 907/443-2958), offers sled trips in winter, and simulated sled trips on a wheeled rig in summer. The cost is about $25 for a half hour, which may seem like a lot . . . but in that time you can travel six to eight miles.

Cross-country skiing, sledding, and snow machining are all popular on the Seward Peninsula. Skis can be rented from the Nome Recreation Center (tel. 443-5431) for around $5 a weekend, with a $20 refundable deposit.

WHERE TO STAY

Accommodations in Nome range from small hotels to bed-and-breakfast inns and apartment-suite complexes. All the following establishments are in the moderate range.

If you're planning to be in Nome during Iditarod Month (March), it's essential that you book well in advance. If you still can't find a room, contact the Convention and Visitors Bureau: Local families often make extra space for guests at this time if the hotels are full.

Tax The city tax on lodging and meals is 4%.

BETTY'S IGLOO, 1st St. at K St. (P.O. Box 1784), Nome, AK 99762. Tel. 907/443-2419. 3 rms (none with bath). TEL
$ Rates (including breakfast): $50 single; $60 double. Weekly and monthly rates available. No credit cards.

Nome's newest bed-and-breakfast is within three blocks of the downtown core and one block of the waterfront, so it has a good view of the Bering Sea. A generous continental breakfast with fruit, yogurt, and pastries is provided.

NANUAQ MANOR [SITNASUAK VIP APARTMENTS], King's Place at Spokane St. (P.O. Box 905), Nome, AK 99672. Tel. 907/443-5296. 20 apts (all with bath). TV TEL
$ Rates: $80 single; $100 double; $150 triple or quad. For stays of a week or longer, $60 single; $80 double; $120 triple or quad. AE, DC, MC, V.

These are a bargain, especially for business travelers or couples. The two- and three-bedroom apartments are homes away from home. Furnished with a couch, chairs, and coffee table, each unit has 1¾ baths, satellite TV, washer-dryer, and a full kitchen with a refrigerator, four-burner stove, double sink, electric dishwasher (the only one I saw in Alaska), a dining table with six chairs, and lots of cabinet space (kitchenware provided). The bedrooms have double or twin beds, large closets, and dressers.

Register in the corporation's office at 223 E. Front St. While you're there, admire their display of Native ivory crafts.

NOME NUGGET INN, Front St. at Bering St. (P.O. Box 430), Nome, AK 99762. Tel. 907/443-2323. Fax 907/443-5966. 47 rms (all with bath).
$ Rates: May–Sept and Iditarod, $85 single; $95 double. Other times, $50 single; $60 double. AE, DC, MC, V.

Most tour groups lodge their guests here. In fact, between mid-May and mid-September, 35 rooms are reserved strictly for tour groups. Most of the small rooms in this hotel have twin beds (only one has a queen-size). Wood paneled and carpeted, they contain basic furnishings (no TV or phone) and a private bathroom with shower.

The lobby of this hotel is its most impressive feature. An antique organ and Victrola, a beautiful sideboard, and wrought-iron railings around the circular staircase give it a real Gay '90s feel. The theme is carried into the nice Gold Dust Lounge, where a big-screen TV is located. Fat Freddie's restaurant adjoins the hotel. Outside are life-size carvings of a prospector with his shovel and an Eskimo with his dog and harpoon.

OCEAN VIEW MANOR, 490 E. Front St. (P.O. Box 65), Nome, AK 99762. Tel. 907/443-2133. 8 rms (1 with bath). TV TEL
$ Rates (including breakfast): $45–$55 single; $50–$60 double. MC, V.

Nome's first bed-and-breakfast is right on the seacoast. Shirley Bronston has a spacious and comfortable home which offers better facilities for the price than the hotels. Guests have kitchen privileges, and the makings of continental breakfasts are provided. The living room, library, and outside deck offer a seemingly endless view of the Bering Sea.

POLAR ARMS APARTMENTS, Front St. at Federal St. (P.O. Box 880),

Nome, AK 99762. Tel. 907/443-5191 or 443-2661. 5 apts (all with bath). TV TEL

$ Rates: $80–$95 single; $90–$110 double. Additional person $10 extra. MC, V.
The Polar Arms Apartments comprise four fully furnished one-bedroom units and one two-bedroom suite with kitchen facilities. Maid service is provided and there are laundry facilities. There's a cocktail lounge on the premises.

POLARIS HOTEL, First Ave. at Bering St. (P.O. Box 741), Nome, AK 99762. Tel. 907/443-2000. Fax 907/443-2217. 29 rms (16 with bath). TV
$ Rates: $40 single without bath; $80 single or double with bath. No credit cards.
This is a lower-standard lodging that caters mainly to village travelers. Its new wing, which contains double or twin rooms off wide, well-lit corridors, offers private baths and showers, nice wood furnishings, and satellite television. The single units in the old section are a last resort, with communal bathrooms, metal furnishings, and paper-thin walls. All units are wood paneled and carpeted, with hot-water heating. The red-carpeted Polaris Bar has a jukebox and dance floor, pool tables, and dartboards.

During Iditarod, the Polaris can also arrange for a small house rental at a cost of $90 per day.

PONDEROSA INN, Third Ave. at Spokane St. (P.O. Box 125), Nome, AK 99762. Tel. 907/443-2368 or 443-5737. Fax 907/443-3542. 5 rms, 6 suites (all with bath). TV TEL
$ Rates: $65–$75 single; $75–$85 double; $110 suite. Weekly and monthly rates available. No credit cards.
The Ponderosa has deluxe suites and smaller rooms, all with full baths. Guests can use the kitchen, laundry, and living room (with its stereo and other furnishings).

WHERE TO DINE
MODERATE

FAT FREDDIE'S, Front St. Tel. 443-5899.
   Cuisine: STEAK/SEAFOOD. **Reservations:** Not required.
$ Prices: Appetizers $4–$6; main courses $10–$18; breakfast/lunch $5–$10. MC, V.
   Open: Daily 6am–10pm.
New York steak and coho (silver salmon) are among the lunch and dinner specials at Freddie's, which also features chicken dishes. The restaurant is also known for Nome's best salad bar (salad and soup costs $5.75).

MILANO'S PIZZARIA, Front St. at Federal St. Tel. 443-2924.
   Cuisine: ITALIAN. **Reservations:** Recommended.
$ Prices: Appetizers $5–$9; main courses $9–$22. MC, V.
   Open: Mon–Fri 11am–11pm, Sat–Sun 4–11pm.
This Korean-owned and -operated eatery in the Old Federal Building has low-lit Italian decor, with imitation brick walls and hanging stained-glass lamps, and a menu of pizzas, pastas, and veal parmigiana.

NACHO'S, Front St. at Federal St. Tel. 443-5503.
   Cuisine: MEXICAN. **Reservations:** Recommended.
$ Prices: Appetizers $3–$7; main courses $6–$18; breakfast $4–$9. MC, V.
   Open: Mon–Fri 7am–10pm, Sat 8am–9pm, Sun 8am–7pm.
Nacho's has a south-of-the-border atmosphere with stuccoed walls and private booths. Menu offerings include standard taco-enchilada combinations and an excellent steak picado (diced and simmered in salsa and vegetable sauce) at the top of the price range.

PIZZA NAPOLI, Front St. Tel. 443-5300.
   Cuisine: ITALIAN. **Reservations:** Not required.
$ Prices: Appetizers $4–$7; main courses $5.95–$9.95 at lunch, $12.95–$21.95 at dinner. MC, V.

Open: Mon–Sat 11am–11pm, Sun 4–11pm.

Pizza Napoli is one of Nome's newest restaurants and it comes highly recommended by the locals. It offers a good selection of Italian dishes, sandwiches, burgers and pizza.

POLAR CUB CAFE, Front St. Tel. 443-5191.

Cuisine: AMERICAN. **Reservations:** Not required.

$ Prices: Appetizers $3–$6; main courses $6–$20; breakfast $5–$12. MC, V.

Open: Daily 24 hours.

A clean, comfortable coffee shop, the Polar Cub offers pancake breakfasts from $5 (with coffee), a burger and fries for $6, and daily lunch specials, including soup, salad bar, dessert, and coffee or tea, for $9. Fresh baked goods from the Billikin Bakery are always on the menu. For dinner you can have anything from a burger to a steak dinner with all the trimmings. You'll find the café behind the Polar Gift Shop and Polar Bar and Liquor Store.

TWIN DRAGON, Bering St. at Second Ave. Tel. 443-5552.

Cuisine: CHINESE. **Reservations:** Recommended.

$ Prices: Appetizers $2–$8; main courses $10–$18. MC, V.

Open: Lunch daily 11:30am–2:30pm; dinner daily 5–10pm.

This Chinese restaurant is surprisingly authentic for its remote location. The tiny main dining room (four tables seat 15) is nicely decorated with ornate mirrored walls, dragon-and-phoenix motifs on the ceiling, and a large central hanging lantern. (There's additional seating upstairs and downstairs.) Lunch specials, such as pork chow mein and various beef, chicken, and shrimp dishes, are priced from $7 including soup, rice, eggroll, tea, and fortune cookie. Family-style dinners—take your pick of Mandarin, Szechuan, Cantonese, or Peking cuisine—start at $12 per person.

BUDGET

GLUE POT, Front St. at Division St. Tel. 443-5474.

Cuisine: AMERICAN/FAST FOOD. **Reservations:** Not required.

$ Prices: $4–$9. No credit cards.

Open: Summer, Mon–Fri 6am–3am, Sat–Sun 24 hours; winter, Mon–Fri 10am–3am, Sat–Sun 10am–6am; during Iditarod, daily 24 hours.

Fast-food fanatics head to this place, where they can get a double-bacon burger for $7, a small pizza for $6, or ham and eggs for $6.

EVENING ENTERTAINMENT

Despite the proliferation of saloons, there's a lot of sameness in this category: dingy bars and drunks. Your best bet for a nice evening out is the **Nome Nugget Inn.** If you really want to soak up some atmosphere, try the **Board of Trade (BOT) Saloon** on Front Street. The BOT has a big dance floor and live rock band nightly, but a largely inebriated clientele.

EASY EXCURSIONS FROM NOME

Although it's impossible to drive to Nome from other parts of Alaska, if you have a car at your disposal here ($2-per-gallon gas notwithstanding), there are over 350 miles of roads to travel. Three main (dirt and/or gravel) highways lead east 72 miles to Council, west 71 miles to Teller, and north 85 miles to Taylor.

Nome is also the gateway to 100-mile-long St. Lawrence Island, tiny Little Diomede Island, and the Bering Land Bridge National Preserve.

THE NOME–COUNCIL HIGHWAY Tour buses often drive four to six miles east, toward Cape Nome to **Farley's Camp,** from which there's an expansive shoreline view. Several fish camps are near here: Dried fish can be seen hanging from driftwood racks during salmon season. Also near here is a dog camp where musher Howard Farley, an Iditarod veteran, gives an excellent overland demonstration with his team. He'll welcome you to pet his pups and he'll encourage your photography, but don't get too friendly with his adult dogs. (Follow that rule wherever you see sled dogs chained outside small houses in the Nome area. The dogs' temperaments are unpredictable, and they may become territorial and overprotective.)

The road follows the coast for 30 miles, then turns inland to **Solomon,** a once-prosperous community with an active railroad, now a virtual ghost town with just four families resident. As you drive northeast across the Seward Peninsula from here, you're in prime wildlife country. Wild musk-oxen are occasionally seen near Hastings Creek and elsewhere. You may also spot reindeer, moose, or grizzly bears. If you do, don't get out of your vehicle!

When you pass into an area of trees—the nearest trees to Nome—you'll know you're only seven miles from **Council.** This village has a population of two families in winter, but 30–40 in summer. You'll have to park across the Niukluk River from the village and hitch a ride on a local boat.

THE NOME–TELLER HIGHWAY   Teller became famous in 1985 when resident Libby Riddles became the first woman ever to win the Iditarod Trail Sled Dog Race. About 200 people live here on Port Clarence year-round. There's no restaurant or lodging, but you'll find a small gift shop and general store.

THE NOME–TAYLOR HIGHWAY   Eight miles north of Nome, a small community called **Dexter** has a popular roadhouse and seasonal fishing camps. This route traverses many old mining areas, remembered by abandoned log cabins, water ditches, and railroad bridges. The **Salmon Lake** campground at Mile 38 is a popular weekend excursion site for Nomeites. This highway is locally known as Beam Road or Kougarok Road. **Taylor,** a tiny settlement at the head of the road, gives overland access (by trail) to Serpentine Hot Springs and Bering Land Bridge National Preserve. The terrain is very rough and not often attempted, even by locals.

ST. LAWRENCE ISLAND   The Yupik Eskimos of St. Lawrence Island cling to many of their ancient traditions, especially the reliance on the bounty of the sea. Visitors are welcomed to the main town, **Gambell** (formerly Sivuqaq), on tours from Nome.

A good time to visit is when the annual **Savoonga Walrus Carnival** is held in May or June in the island's only other community of size, Savoonga. Accommodation is available in Gambell. Inquire at the City of Gambell offices (tel. 907/985-3112) for details.

LITTLE DIOMEDE ISLAND   Little Diomede Island has the distinction of being the U.S. landmass closest to Russia. The two-square-mile rock, 125 miles northwest of Nome in the middle of the Bering Strait, is a mere three miles from Big Diomede Island, across the International Date Line in Russia. Most of the island's 150 Yupiks live in rudimentary plywood houses built in the mid-1970s by the Bureau of Indian Affairs. **Olson Air Service** (tel. 443-2229) has a Siberian Sightseer tour and flights between the Diomede Islands.

BERING LAND BRIDGE NATIONAL PRESERVE   Bering Land Bridge National Preserve covers much of the northern part of the Seward Peninsula. This 2½-million-acre parkland protects a wealth of features of geographical and archeological importance. The early North Americans who crossed the prehistoric land bridge (now beneath the Bering Strait) left sparse but priceless clues of their having passed this way. Birdlife is prolific in the gently rolling tundra, and nearly 250 varieties of wildflowers have been identified (best seen in late August and early September). Hot springs and lava beds are a reminder of ancient volcanic activity.

The only accommodation in the preserve is a simple shelter with cots, but planes can be chartered to numerous subsistence Eskimo villages like **Shishmaref** (pop. 425) or to **Serpentine Hot Springs,** a lovely oasis on the south-central side of the preserve. For information, contact the park superintendent at P.O. Box 220, Nome, AK 99762 (tel. 907/443-2522).

RUSSIAN FAR EAST   The City of Nome has become a gateway to the Russian Far East since the Russian–U.S. border was reopened in 1988. You can fly from Nome to Russia in about an hour and tour a city or participate in a wilderness adventure. Tours take place around the community of **Provideniya** (pop. 5,000), situated on the Bay of Provideniya, a natural deep-water harbor. The mountain, tundra, and fjord landforms provide a spectacular natural setting.

Bering Air (tel. 443-5464) provides two-, three-, or four-night Provideniya city tours, ranging in price from $975 to $1,300 per person. The tour introduces guests to the city and people of Provideniya via trips to industries (leather factory, dairy, and brewery), meetings with local residents, and cultural entertainment. Trips to nearby Native villages are included in the longer (three- and four-day) trips. All meals, transportation, customs and immigration fees, and most entertainment is included in the tour price.

Bering Air also offers a five-night adventure tour that includes traveling by boat to Native villages, camping in reindeer-hide tents, viewing wildlife from the ground and helicopter, and visiting Native dance groups. The cost for this tour is $2,400 per person.

FLIGHTSEEING Flightseeing tours and charters (usually $180–$200 an hour) can be arranged with the following: **Bering Air** (tel. 443-5464), **Foster's Aviation** (tel. 443-5292), **Ryan Air** (tel. 443-5482), and **Evergreen Helicopters** (tel. 443-5334). **Olson Air** (tel. 443-2229) has a feature sightseeing trip over the Diomede Islands and Siberia; **Cape Smythe Air** (tel. 443-2414) offers flightseeing trips to St. Lawrence Island and along the Norton Sound and north Seward Peninsula coastlines.

---

2. KOTZEBUE

550 miles NW of Anchorage, 26 miles N of the Arctic Circle

GETTING THERE By Plane Alaska Airlines (tel. 907/442-3474, or toll free 800/426-0333) has three flights a day connecting Kotzebue with Anchorage and Nome. Several smaller carriers that provide air service within the region include **Cape Smythe Air** (tel. 442-3040), **Ryan Air** (tel. 442-3347), and **Bering Air** (tel. 442-3943).

There is no access by road or rail.

ESSENTIALS Orientation Front Street, alternatively called Shore Road, is the main street in town, running south to north for about 1½ miles along the waterfront. It's paralleled to the east by numbered avenues. Second Avenue passes the NANA Regional Corporation offices en route to Kotzebue Airport. Named streets, including Lagoon Street and Tundra Way, connect Front Street with the avenues. The airport—whose runway is the only stretch of pavement this side of Nome—divides Kotzebue town from the rest of the Baldwin Peninsula. One road leads a few miles south across the tundra to a World War II air force station.

Climate The climate in Kotzebue is similar to that in Nome, but a little cooler and drier. Annual average temperatures range from a July high of 58°F to a January low of –11°F, with extremes of 85°F and –52°F. The annual precipitation is 8 inches, half of which equivalent is recorded as snow (47 inches).

Information The closest things Kotzebue has to visitor information offices is the NANA Museum (see "What to See and Do," below). But you can contact **Tour Arctic**, P.O. Box 49, Kotzebue, AK 99752 (tel. 907/442-3301; fax 907/442-2866), for information.

Fast Facts Kotzebue has a modern 50-bed Public Health Service Hospital (tel. 442-3321), a bank (Bank of the North), a community college and vocational training school, eight churches, and a library.

SPECIAL EVENTS The year's most festive period extends for a week beginning the **Fourth of July.** The nation's birthday observance includes a beluga whale-hunting celebration, beauty pageants, and Eskimo games such as seal-hook throwing and muktuk eating. It's followed by the **Northwest Native Trade Fair,** which draws Native peoples from throughout Arctic and Bering Alaska to participate in more cultural demonstrations, feasting and dancing, handcraft trading, and Eskimo games.

Alaska's most appealing Eskimo village, as well as its largest, with a population nearing 4,000, Kotzebue is located a mere 26 miles north of the Arctic Circle. It's situated on a barren gravel-and-tundra spit at the end of the Baldwin Peninsula, a long finger of land extending into the Chukchi Sea opposite the mouths of the Noatak, Kobuk, and Selawik Rivers.

Because of its location near the deltas of several important inland trading routes, the Inupiat Eskimo village called Kikiktagruk ("land that is almost an island") had been a thriving commercial center for a full three centuries when it was visited in 1816 by a Russian navy lieutenant named Otto von Kotzebue. Today, despite the importation of 20th-century culture in the form of TVs and snowmobiles, many Inupiat (80% of the population) still pursue traditional subsistence lifestyles. Indeed, until hunting of the animal was banned in 1972, Kotzebue was known as the "polar bear capital of the world." You can still look out the window of your hotel on Front Street to see fish drying on crude racks and handmade sealskin fishing boats braving the early-summer float ice.

The 21st century, however, may be upon Kotzebue before the townspeople know what hit them. In 1986, the world's largest lead-zinc mine, the Red Dog Mine, opened 90 miles north of Kotzebue in the DeLong Mountains on the edge of Noatak National Preserve. The $490-million construction bill included a seaport and 52-mile access road. Today the mine, owned by the Northwest Alaska Native Association (NANA) and operated in partnership with Cominco Alaska, employs 350 people. More than 50% of them are Eskimos or their spouses; by 2001, according to a NANA-Cominco pact, the mine will have 100% Native employees. Voters have approved a new Northwest Arctic Borough, which will detach the mine from the oil-rich North Slope Borough and ensure that the local government will control and benefit from taxation and land-use regulations.

GETTING AROUND

Kotzebue supports a 24-hour taxi company, **Midnight Sun Cab** (tel. 442-3394). **Tour Arctic** (tel. 907/442-3301) provides ground tours year-round.

WHAT TO SEE & DO
SIGHTS & ATTRACTIONS

Stroll around town at leisure, appreciating the different cultural perspective of these hard-working Eskimo people. Some of the earliest homes are at the north end of Front Street.

NANA MUSEUM OF THE ARCTIC, Second Ave. Tel. 442-3301.

Kotzebue's "must" attraction is located next to the regional corporation's headquarters. Don't expect an impersonal collection of artifacts. This is a living museum, a place built—according to the directors—so "generations of Eskimos would know who they were and why. So would the rest of America."

The full presentation takes 1½ hours. Upon arrival, you are ushered into an indoor diorama of Arctic wildlife complete with a soundtrack of the different animal calls. After a visit to the adjoining Jade Mountain factory, you return to the diorama room for a multimedia show, *The Roots of Kotzebue.* Finally, Inupiat natives offer a cultural demonstration of such time-honored crafts as skin sewing and ivory carving. The Kotzebue Native Dancers perform several traditional dances, inviting the audience to join in. The show concludes with an Eskimo blanket toss. Various handcrafts are offered for sale.

A viewing window atop a flight of carpeted steps next door to the NANA Museum lets visitors peer into the jade factory. NANA owns all mineral rights to Jade Mountain, Alaska's chief source of jade, 130 miles up the Kobuk River. Fire is used to dislodge boulders from permafrost during the summer; the rocks are then barged to Kotzebue. (When the icepack is frozen, summer fishermen become winter jade workers.) The factory sells its jade tiles worldwide.

Admission: General admission free; full show, $20 adults, $12.50 children.
Open: June–Aug, daily 9am–8pm; Sept–May, museum open on-call.

ORGANIZED TOURS

The tour offered by **Alaska Airlines Vacations** (tel. 442-3331 at the Nullagvik Hotel) includes round-trip airfare from Anchorage, a tour of the city, lengthy stops at the museum, an inspection of the tundra and permafrost layer, and a visit to "Kotzebue National Forest." (The tongue-in-cheek designation refers to a single, desperate spruce tree, the only tree for a good 100 miles, planted outside the former U.S. Air Force station south of town.) The tour costs $315, with airport pickup and dropoff. For ground tours, without the air transportation, contact **Tour Arctic,** P.O. Box 49, Kotzebue, AK 99752 (tel. 907/442-3301; fax 907/442-2866).

SPORTS & RECREATION

Fishing and hunting are popular in summer, mainly in the surrounding wilderness. **Walker Air Service,** 503 Front St. (tel. 442-3592), is a registered guide-outfitter. If you have questions, consult the **U.S. Fish and Wildlife Service** (tel. 442-3799).

In winter, dog-sled races and snow-machine competitions are big local events, and cross-country skiers find endless tundra to trek across.

WHERE TO STAY

NULLAGVIK HOTEL, 308 Front St. (P.O. Box 336), Kotzebue, AK 99752. Tel. 907/442-3331. 75 rms (all with bath). TV TEL
$ Rates: $110 single; $135 double. AE, MC, V.
This is the only accommodation in town, at this writing. Owned and operated by NANA, the Nullagvik—its name means "overnighting place" in the Inupiat dialect—is the nicest hotel in Alaska's Arctic. Its spacious rooms have full baths, thermostat-controlled hot-water heating, and even orange shag carpeting. On the oceanfront side of the hotel are second- and third-floor sitting rooms where you can watch the Kobuk ice floes crunching and tinkling their way down the coast of Kotzebue Sound long after the winter icepack has broken up and disappeared.

Dining/Entertainment: The restaurant—open from 6am to 10pm in summer, 7am to 9pm in winter—features such local specialties as grilled arctic sheefish (a full dinner for $15) and reindeer stew ($8 for lunch).

Services: Maid service (the hotel does not provide local transportation).

Facilities: Gift shop with good prices on local crafts, barbershop and beauty parlor, coin-op guest laundry, travel agency.

WHERE TO DINE

For fast-food fanatics, there's the **Kotzebue Pizza House** (tel. 442-3432 for delivery). If you're not dining at the Nullagvik Hotel, you can try the following restaurant:

ARCTIC DRAGON, Front St. Tel. 442-3770.
Cuisine: CHINESE. **Reservations:** Recommended.
$ Prices: Appetizers $3–$8; main courses $6–$13 at lunch, $10–$20 at dinner. AE, MC, V.
Open: Mon–Sat 11am–10pm, Sun noon–10pm.
A Korean-owned Mandarin Chinese restaurant, the Arctic Dragon features combination dinners from $13 and lunch specials in the $8 range. The decor is far from

elaborate, but it's quite comfortable, with a large aquarium against one wall and hanging Oriental lanterns.

EASY EXCURSIONS FROM KOTZEBUE

Kotzebue is the principal gateway to numerous federally protected lands. Chief among them are the 540,000-acre Cape Krusenstern National Monument, the 1.7-million-acre Kobuk Valley National Park, and the 6.5-million-acre Noatak National Preserve. Also nearby are the Selawik and Koyukuk National Wildlife Refuges. Gates of the Arctic National Park and Preserve are only slightly farther away. You can get full information on all these destinations and view an exhibit of their wildlife at the Northwest Alaska Areas headquarters of the **National Park Service,** P.O. Box 287, Kotzebue, AK 99752 (tel. 907/442-3573 or 442-3890). The offices are lodged in the NANA Regional Corporation building on Second Avenue.

Cape Krusenstern National Monument, whose closest point is only about 10 miles from Kotzebue across the Hotham Inlet, is important as a living archeological repository of 6,000 years of Eskimo history. Its 114 lateral beach ridges, formed by wind and wave action and by changing sea levels, contain various artifacts that recall marine mammal hunts when Mediterranean cultures were in their infancy. Eskimo men still hunt seals along the cape's outermost beach, only now they use rifles instead of harpoons. The women still trim and render the catch for the hides, meat, and seal oil vital to their diet.

The centerpiece of **Kobuk Valley National Park** is its 25 miles of shifting sand dunes, the largest active dune field in Arctic latitudes in the world. Summer temperatures can exceed 100°F. Most of the park is a vast tundra steppe supporting great herds of caribou, plus moose, bears, fish, waterfowl, and many edible and medicinal plants. Signs of human habitation date back 12,500 years at Onion Portage, the oldest-known site in the North American Arctic. The Kobuk River and its tributary, the Salmon, offer easy canoeing and kayaking.

Noatak National Preserve protects the largest virgin river basin in the United States. So important is the 425-mile Noatak River as a corridor between subarctic and arctic environments for plants and animals that it has been designated an International Biosphere Reserve by the United Nations Educational, Scientific and Cultural Organization (UNESCO). The river runs from glacial melt atop Mount Igikpak in the Brooks Range out to Kotzebue Sound, en route cutting the scenic Grand Canyon of the Noatak. Except for its headwaters, the entire route is slow moving and gentle, making it popular with wilderness canoeists and kayakers. Large mammals are prolific in the preserve, among them grizzly and black bears, caribou, wolves, lynx, and dall sheep. The Noatak abounds in arctic char, whitefish, grayling, and salmon.

Unless one or more of them has folded, all the following Kotzebue-based air services offer charter flights to federal lands: **Arctic Air Guides** (tel. 442-3030), **Baker Aviation** (tel. 442-3108), **Bering Air** (tel. 442-3943), **Cape Smythe Air** (tel. 442-3020), **Ryan Air** (tel. 442-3347), and **Walker Air Service** (tel. 442-3592).

---

3. BARROW

840 miles N of Anchorage, 330 miles N of the Arctic Circle

GETTING THERE By Plane Means of traveling to Barrow are, for all practical purposes, limited to one: **MarkAir** (tel. 907/852-7377 in Barrow, or toll free 800/426-6784, 800/478-0800 in Alaska). The carrier offers several flights daily to and from Anchorage (tel. 907/243-6275) and Fairbanks (tel. 907/452-7577). Connecting service to villages and locations near Barrow is provided by **Cape Smythe Air** (tel. 852-8333) and **Barrow Air** (tel. 852-2334).

ESSENTIALS Orientation Barrow's 3,000 people actually live in two adjoining settlements on either side of the freshwater Isatkoak Lagoon. Most businesses and visitor services are on the south side of the lagoon in Barrow proper. Many citizens live north of the lagoon in the residential neighborhood known as Browerville. The Barrow Airport faces on Ahkovak Street. Opposite the airport, at the intersection of Momegana Street, is the chamber of commerce office. Momegana leads north five blocks into the main part of town, ending in a T junction at Agvik Street. To your right (east) are the borough offices, hospital, and Isatkoak Lagoon; to your left (west) are the big Alaska Commercial Co. department store and the Top of the World Hotel. Stevenson Street, which follows the coast north to Browerville, intersects Agvik at the hotel.

Climate   The city is located in a veritable Arctic desert with average annual precipitation of just 4.9 inches (10 inches of snow equal 1 inch of precipitation). The average July high is 46°F (though a record high of 78°F was once attained), and the average January low is -24°F.

Information   The **Barrow Chamber of Commerce,** P.O. Box 942, Barrow, AK 99723 (tel. 907/852-5211 to city offices), has a visitor center across from the MarkAir terminal, at the corner of Ahkovak and Momegana Streets. Local crafts are also sold.

Fast Facts   The weekly newspaper is called *Ukpiagvik's Edgington Unedited.* Modern Barrow Hospital is at the east end of Agvik Street (tel. 852-4611). The city's only bank, the Bank of the North, at Agvik and Kiogak Streets (tel. 852-6200), is open Monday through Thursday from 9am to 2:30pm and on Friday from 11am to 6pm. There are six churches but no bars—Barrow is dry. While you're permitted to import alcoholic beverages for your own consumption, you can't buy or sell them here.

SPECIAL EVENTS   The year's biggest festival is **Nalukataq,** held in June following a successful whaling season. If you're in Barrow between mid-April and the end of May when the bowhead whales migrate through this area (depending on the ice pack), you'll likely be greeted by businesses with signs reading: CLOSED, GONE WHALING. Alaska's nine whaling communities from Barrow to St. Lawrence Island together are allowed 32 strikes a year with no more than 52 in two years. When village whalers in their walrus-skin umiaks (boats) harpoon a whale, they haul it onto the ice and drag it back to their settlement by dog sled. No part of the creature goes to waste. The meat and muktuk (inner skin and blubber) are eaten and used for oil; the bones were traditionally used in shelter construction. Even baleen—a long black fiber which hangs like a plate from certain whales' mouths to strain out plankton, their dietary mainstay—is used in etching and basket weaving. (New Englanders once used it for corset stays.)

The **Piuraagiaqta** spring festival in mid-April bids farewell to long winter nights with a parade and a variety of Native competitions, from dog-sled and cross-country ski races to speed contests with the participants toting tea and wearing mukluks (moccasins). Special observances are also scheduled on the Fourth of July and New Year's Eve, and there's a big home-lighting contest every Christmas.

Contrary to what you may read or be told, Barrow is not the northernmost point on the North American continent. That honor belongs to Canada's Boothia Peninsula, which extends to 71°58′ North Latitude. (Point Barrow reaches to 71°23′N). But that minor discrepancy doesn't diminish the value of a visit to the self-proclaimed "Top of the World."

There are few more memorable experiences than to stand in utter silence by the edge of the Arctic Ocean on a summer night and stare across a virtually frozen sea. Away from the city, with little contour to the barren earth, it can be hard to tell where land ends and water begins. Only for a few weeks at the peak of the summer does the ice pack drift away from shore enough for barges to navigate their way here.

When the sun rises here on May 10, it doesn't set again until August 2—bringing 84 days of continuous daylight. But when it sets on November 18, another 67 days pass before the sun rises again on January 24.

It takes a special breed of person to adapt to these unusual conditions. Few white settlers are able to last more than a couple of years here before midwinter depression takes a severe toll. Yet Inupiat Eskimos have lived here for 1,500 years, subsisting mainly on the bounty of the sea. Their culture is evident everywhere you turn.

Charted by the Royal Navy in 1825 and named for Sir John Barrow of the British Admiralty, Barrow became an important supply station for Boston whalers working the Arctic Ocean at the turn of the 20th century. It was incorporated as a first-class city in 1974, just in time to benefit from the oil boom at Prudhoe Bay. Barrow's position as seat of the 88,000-square-mile North Slope Borough—the world's largest municipal government—left it with millions of dollars to invest in modern schools, offices, stores, and health services. Despite its alien climate, the city has modern electric, water, and sewer systems.

GETTING AROUND

The efficient city bus service—the **Inuich Commuter Express** (tel. 852-2611, ext. 368)—operates Monday through Saturday year-round, every 20 minutes from 6:20am to 10pm. The adult fare is 50¢ (children 12 and under pay 25¢; under 6, free) within Barrow and Browerville.

If you don't mind paying upward of $2.50 a gallon for gas, you can rent a vehicle from **Julie's and Chuck's Trucks** (tel. 852-6732). Taxi service is provided by **Arcticab** (tel. 852-2227) and **Tundra Taxi** (tel. 852-4444).

WHAT TO SEE & DO
SIGHTS & ATTRACTIONS

The most interesting thing to do in Barrow is to wander with your eyes open, observing how painfully the old Eskimo culture is adjusting to the 9-to-5 society forced on it by Americanization. Here, 330 miles north of the Arctic Circle, you'll see a multi-million-dollar high school with fish and caribou hides hanging to dry outside, and modern racquetball courts and a tanning salon only a few blocks from a centuries-old archeological site.

The old village, **Uqiagvik** ("high place with good view"), was discovered in 1982 on a city bluff overlooking the Arctic Ocean. Subsequently excavated by University of Washington archeologists, its sod igloo sites have been dated back five centuries. These early Eskimos dug holes in the ground and covered them with canopies of skins on frames of whalebone and driftwood. You can walk to the site, which faces Apayauk Street opposite Ogrook Street, but respect tribal traditions by not treading on homesites and not taking souvenirs. Sixteen dwelling mounds have been uncovered at the earlier (A.D. 500–900) **Birnirk** archeological site about three miles up the coast at Pignaq (see below).

North of Barrow a couple of miles and inland a few more is the site of the **Naval Arctic Research Laboratory,** built by the federal government in 1955 as an operations base for the 23-million-acre Naval Petroleum Reserve no. 4, and to study Arctic survival and adaptation. The lab closed a few years ago and is now owned by an Inupiat corporation and used for storage and housing. A small weather station remains. The site is adjacent to the Distant Early Warning (DEW) radar system, which during the cold-war period served as a reminder of the proximity of Soviet Siberia.

Non-Eskimos normally aren't welcome to stop at **Pignaq,** a summer shantytown three miles north of Barrow where many Inupiats maintain second homes on Birnirk sacred ground. It's known as the Duck Camp Shooting Station to Native hunters who base themselves here while pursuing waterfowl. This area is beautiful in July, when the tundra grass turns green and speckled with wildflowers. By August annoying mosquitoes have taken much of the joy out of an excursion.

Point Barrow, the northernmost point in the United States, is four miles beyond Pignaq, out a long gravel-and-tundra spit. The point has a 50-foot tower and little more. All-terrain vehicles negotiate the spit with ease.

Fifteen miles southwest of Barrow is a **Wiley Post–Will Rogers Memorial,** erected where the famed pilot and the great humorist were killed in a 1935 airplane crash. En route from Fairbanks to Siberia, they stopped to ask directions to Barrow, stalled on takeoff, and plunged 50 feet into a river. A newer monument, dedicated in 1982, is directly opposite the Barrow Airport beside the chamber of commerce office.

ORGANIZED TOURS

Out-of-town visitors inevitably are greeted at the airport by **Tundra Tours,** owners of the Top of the World Hotel (tel. 852-3900). The prebooked package tour includes a whirl around city points of interest, a stop for Eskimo doughnuts, and an excellent show of Inupiat dancing and handcrafts. Dancers perform to chanting and a chorus of flat drums (from various animal skins and membranes), the only musical instruments. Native elders demonstrate how seal, caribou, polar bear, and other hides are worked to make warm clothing. Every body part is used, from sinews (which become threads) to bones (used for needles, especially the polar bear leg bone and walrus tusk).

Tundra Tours is represented outside of Barrow by **MarkTours** in Anchorage (tel. toll free 800/476-6784, 800/478-0800 in Alaska).

Flightseeing enthusiasts can contact **Cape Smythe Air,** P.O. Box 549, Barrow, AK 99723 (tel. 907/852-8333), about its 30-minute excursions to Point Barrow and the Post-Rogers Memorial. The charter rate for a Cessna 207 is $300 an hour; for a Cessna 185, $200 an hour. Find four other visitors to split the cost.

SPORTS & RECREATION

The obvious pursuits are outdoor recreations. Cross-country skiing, snow-machining, and ice skating are winter favorites, while camping and boating are popular in the short summer season.

Fishing and hunting licenses can be purchased in Barrow, but sportsmen should be aware that, first of all, no guide services are available; and second, only Native Alaskans are allowed to take marine mammals.

Swimmers can earn a membership certificate in the Polar Bear Club by being "willfully submerged in the Arctic Ocean." The water temperature in mid-August is typically 28°F (salt water has a lower freezing point); the air is around 45°F. Submersion must be total, though you can wear whatever clothes you want. Search and Rescue officials are present. If you're not that hardy, **Barrow High School,** at Okpik and Takpuk Streets (tel. 852-8950), has an indoor pool.

Facilities at the new **Piuraagvik Recreation Center,** on Ahkovak Street east of the airport, include racquetball and basketball courts and a sauna. Call the adjacent city hall (tel. 852-5211) for information and hours.

SHOPPING

Stroll from the ancient to the modern by browsing in a couple of Barrow's stores, like the **Arctic Cash and Carry supermarket,** on Pisokak Street at Apayauk Street (open from 11am to 1am daily), or the **A.C. Stuaqpak department store,** on Agvik Street near Kiogak Street (open Monday through Saturday from 1 to 9pm and on Sunday from noon to 5pm). You'll wonder how anyone can afford to live in Barrow after pricing milk at $7 a gallon and eggs just over $2 a dozen. The steep prices extend to the shortage of decent housing: Studio apartments were renting in 1992 for an average of $700 a month, not counting an additional utility bill of about $300 a month. Native handcrafts, on the other hand, can be purchased quite reasonably. Look for articles of carved walrus-tusk ivory and etched baleen, plus leather-and-fur masks, mittens, mukluks, and parkas. You can call **The Eskimo Shop** (tel. 852-5523) for custom orders.

WHERE TO STAY

Utility prices and the cost of importing all construction materials has resulted in high prices on hotel rooms in Barrow. Then again, everything in Barrow costs at least twice what you'd pay in Anchorage.

Tax Tag a 6% tax on quoted room rates.

BARROW AIRPORT INN, 1815 Okpik St. (P.O. Box 933), Barrow, AK 99723. Tel. 907/852-2525. 16 rms (all with bath). TV TEL
$ Rates: $110 single; $130 double. Children stay free in parents' room. AE, DC, MC, V.

This homey place is just a block from the airport on the bus line. A typical well-lit room has brown carpeting, a double bed with autumn-pattern cover, standard furnishings, 12-channel cable television, free local phone, a three-quarter bath, and hot-water baseboard heat. Nine units have kitchenettes with stoves, refrigerators, and cabinet space. The cozy lobby has couches and chairs amid standing plants and a large bookshelf, with complimentary coffee.

TOP OF THE WORLD HOTEL, Agvik and Stevenson Sts. (P.O. Box 189), Barrow, AK 99723. Tel. 907/852-3900. Fax 900/852-6752. 40 rms (all with bath). TV TEL
$ Rates: $120 single; $310 double. AE, DC, MC, V.

If you arrive on an organized tour, you'll be lodged here. The hotel is operated by Tundra Tours, a wholly owned subsidiary of the Arctic Slope Regional Corporation. Each rust-carpeted room has queen-size or twin beds, a desk/dresser, reclining chair, 11-channel cable TV, free (local) direct-dial telephone, electric baseboard heat, and full bath. Some also have a small refrigerator. The spacious lobby, with its huge mounted polar bear, has a 24-hour desk, plush seating, a gift counter, and a snack corner. Airport shuttle and guest laundry services are also provided. Room service is available from Pepe's North of the Border (see "Where to Dine," below).

WHERE TO DINE

ARCTIC PIZZA, 125 Apayauk St. Tel. 852-4222.
   Cuisine: ITALIAN/GREEK. **Reservations:** Not required.
$ Prices: Appetizers $5–$10; main courses $13–$20; pizzas $14–$45. No credit cards.
   Open: Mon 5–11pm, Tues–Sat 11am–11pm, Sun 2–11pm.

The pizzas range from the small cheese-only variety, at $14, to large ones with "the works," at $45. (For that price, you might expect caviar.) Greek-style gyros are $13; Italian spaghetti dinners run $17.

MATTIE'S ESKIMO CAFE, Simmonds St. Tel. 852-3435.
   Cuisine: AMERICAN/ALASKAN. **Reservations:** Not required.
$ Prices: Appetizers $6–$12; main courses $6–$10 at breakfast/lunch, $14–$18 at dinner. No credit cards.
   Open: Mon–Sat 8am–8pm, Sun 9am–7pm.

This café may be the major point of interest in Browerville. Mattie is a granddaughter of Barrow's first white settler, Charles Brower, who was a prolific gentleman: His Eskimo wives gave him 14 children. The café is decorated with paraphernalia of whaling days past—rusty harpoons and dramatic oil paintings on wood-paneled walls. Omelets cost around $8 for breakfast, cheeseburgers run $8 for lunch, and a reindeer or arctic fish steak is around $16 at dinnertime. Between meals you can snack on caribou soup or Eskimo doughnuts.

Be sure to drop in next door at Charles Brower's store, the Cape Smythe Whaling and Trading Post, established in 1886 and still in the family.

PEPE'S NORTH OF THE BORDER, Agvik St. at Kiogak St. Tel. 852-8200.
   Cuisine: MEXICAN. **Reservations:** Recommended.
$ Prices: Appetizers $6–$14; main courses $14–$42. MC, V.
   Open: Mon–Sat 6am–10pm, Sun 9am–8pm.

Visitors are always surprised to find a highly reputable Mexican restaurant in a location as isolated as Barrow. But the fame of Pepe's has spread far and wide. Its zealous owner, Fran Tate, appeared on "The Tonight Show" with Johnny Carson and other national telecasts; besides Pepe's, she also runs a fast-food diner, a water-delivery service, and Elephant Pot Sewage Haulers.

Fran's crustiness is typical of Barrow, though the restaurant doesn't reflect it (other than to warn diners who find a rock in their pinto beans that there are "not enough rocks for everyone"). Each of three dining rooms has fine decor, including the spacious El Toro room with bullfighting paintings and matador jackets on the walls around a tiled fireplace. Meal prices reflect the expense of decoration: A simple cheese enchilada, with rice, beans, and salad, costs $14. You can pay $24 for a crab Louis or up to $42 for a steak-and-seafood combination dinner.

SAM AND LEE'S, Kiogak St. at Aivik St. Tel. 852-5555.
   Cuisine: CHINESE. **Reservations:** Recommended.
$ Prices: Appetizers $5–$12; main courses $12–$35. MC, V.
   Open: Daily 6am–3am.
This Korean-owned Chinese restaurant is locally praised for its Mongolian beef. The extensive menu has a wide range of traditional Chinese dinners. The restaurant is open 21 hours a day, starting at 6am.

EASY EXCURSIONS FROM BARROW

There's little to see of tourist interest close to Barrow. The nearest village, **Atkasuk** (pop. 200), 70 miles south on the Meade River, has good fishing but no visitor accommodations.
   Wainwright (pop. 450), another Inupiat village, 95 miles southwest along the coast, is famed statewide for its superb craftsmen and Native dance troupe. The **Olgoonik Hotel,** Wainwright, AK 99782 (tel. 907/763-2514), has 12 basic rooms; rates are $105 per night without meals, $155 with meals. Fly there by commuter aircraft from Barrow.

---

4. PRUDHOE BAY

400 miles N of Fairbanks

GETTING THERE   By Plane   Alaska Airlines (tel. toll free 800/426-0333) and **MarkAir** (tel. 478-0800, toll free 800/426-6784) both fly daily to Deadhorse from Anchorage and Fairbanks. The 6,500-foot paved airstrip is on the southeastern side of the Prudhoe Bay field, within easy walking distance of several hotels and construction camps.

By Bus   Tour companies serving Prudhoe Bay include **Tour Arctic,** 1001 E. Benson Blvd., Anchorage, AK 99508 (tel. 907/265-4100), offering guided sightseeing focusing on wildlife and the Trans Alaska Pipeline; and **Prudhoe Bay Adventure,** P.O. Box 82991, Fairbanks, AK 99708 (tel. 907/474-8600), with a two-day guided journey to the shores of the Arctic Ocean, featuring the Brooks Range, the Trans Alaska Pipeline and an Athabaskan fish camp.

By Car   The Dalton Highway, otherwise known as the Haul Road, connects Prudhoe Bay with Fairbanks, a rugged 510-mile drive south. The northernmost 205 miles of the gravel road above Disaster Creek are restricted to drivers who hold commercial or industrial permits. (There have been efforts to open this portion of the highway to all motorists, but as of press time, this had not occurred.) In an average month, 150 trucks carrying seven million pounds of goods move over the road, which is kept open year-round. It's not normally accessible to tourists, although Princess Tours began taking trips down the Haul Road in 1987 (see "Organized Tours" in "What to See and Do," below).

By Boat   Barges, tugboats, and lighters may visit Prudhoe Bay during the six-week period in August and September when the shore ice has broken up and the polar ice shelf has moved away from the coast, but they have no provision for passengers.

ESSENTIALS   Orientation   The Prudhoe Bay field is operated by Arco and Sohio on behalf of all 15 oil companies with North Slope oil and gas leases. (Lease owners share the costs of developing and maintaining the field to minimize cost, maximize efficiency, and reduce negative environmental effects.) Security clearance is required to pass the checkpoints to the Arco Prudhoe Bay Operations Center, a complete village with a population of 560, or the Sohio Base Operations Center, which numbers its residents at 476. Each self-contained community, constructed on pilings above the permafrost, has a hospital, theater, library, and full sports facilities, including gymnasiums and running tracks. Sohio even has a heated swimming pool which doubles as a water reservoir and a glass arboretum landscaped with trees and flowers. In addition to the operations centers, Sohio has three construction camps for 500 workers each and Arco has a single construction camp housing another 1,900 workers.

Deadhorse, where the airport and hotel facilities are located, is the headquarters of highly specialized oilfield contractors—folks who haul water and treat sewage, who manufacture mud and cement, who stabilize oil temperatures, cap wells, and recover spills.

Climate   Located near the mouth of the Sagarvanirktok River, Prudhoe Bay has a climate similar to that of Barrow. Very sparse precipitation (a seven-inch annual average) falls mainly as snow in the late fall and early spring months. Winter temperatures average –20° to –30°F, and not infrequently drop to –60°F, with a high wind-chill factor of –115°F. Normal summer temperatures are 40°–50°F, but occasionally climb above 70°F. Winters see 56 consecutive days of darkness, but summers enjoy 75 days of continual daylight.

Information   There's no chamber of commerce or visitors center. **Sohio Alaska Petroleum Co.**, Pouch 6-612, Anchorage, AK 99502, or **Alyeska Pipeline Service Co.**, 1835 S. Bragaw St., Anchorage, AK 99512, have excellent brochures on their operations and general information on Prudhoe Bay. The hotels, especially the facility operated by the Northwest Alaska Native Association (NANA), also have information.

Fast Facts   The *Prudhoe Bay Journal* is published biweekly in Anchorage and distributed in Prudhoe Bay.

The most famous oil-drilling site in the United States, and perhaps the world, was built in the early 1970s on a permanently frozen desert 280 miles north of the Arctic Circle. The story of the discovery and exploitation of the vast petroleum reserve, and the subsequent pipeline boom, have been recounted elsewhere (see "History" in Chapter 1).

Modern history comes alive with a visit to Prudhoe Bay. Enormous controversy over its environmental impact preceded the industrialization of the North Slope, but today pump stations and drill pads share the tundra ecosystem with myriad nesting migratory birds and a herd of 10,000 caribou. It was truly a technological triumph to be able to tap the oil reserve while preserving the delicate Arctic environment.

Prudhoe Bay and its adjoining service village of Deadhorse are strict working communities with a combined population, transient but stable, of around 5,000. Most of the workers—90% of them men—live at Prudhoe eight days a fortnight and elsewhere in Alaska the other six. Although the population is down from about 18,000 during the mid-'70s pipeline construction era, the town is remarkable for a remote area which had no settlement whatsoever prior to 1967, when exploratory drilling began.

The Prudhoe Bay oilfield is the largest in North America and the 18th largest on earth. It pumps 1.9 million barrels of oil a day and accounts for 85% of Alaska's revenues (the state takes a 12.5% royalty interest). More than 700 offshore wells have been drilled in the 400-square-mile field. Each cost about $2.9 million, compared to $250,000 per well in Texas. The cost difference is attributable to the difficulty of drilling through a 2,000-foot layer of permafrost.

By 1992 the Prudhoe Bay field's estimated reserves of 9.6 billion barrels of crude oil and 26 trillion cubic feet of natural gas had been more than half depleted. Intensive exploration is continuing in offshore areas and in the 23-million-acre National Petroleum Reserve, west of Prudhoe Bay, to locate and exploit new oil reserves. Several smaller fields are now being developed.

The North Slope tundra is very flat and pockmarked with small lakes created by permafrost thaw. If you arrive in midsummer, don't be surprised to find it extremely beautiful. An astonishing variety of plant and animal life call this vast tundra home.

GETTING AROUND

Within the Prudhoe Bay oilfield itself are some 200 miles of interconnecting gravel roads. Most of them are off-bounds to all but oil-company-approved drivers. There are no vehicle-rental agencies in Deadhorse, although one contractor has developed a vehicle with low-pressure tires for traveling on the tundra with minimal environmental impact. It's called the Rollagon. Even that, however, is forbidden from traversing the tundra until the waterfowl have completed their spring nesting cycle, about mid-July.

WHAT TO SEE & DO
SIGHTS & ATTRACTIONS

Most visitors to Prudhoe Bay are anxious to look at the oil-production and pipeline facilities. Unless you're a working visitor or a guest of the oil companies, you'll have to join a ✪ **half-day tour** in order to be cleared to pass the security checkpoints. I enjoyed the tour offered by NANA (tel. 659-2368 or 659-2840); MarkAir has a similar four-hour tour in conjunction with the Arctic Caribou Inn (tel. 659-2536). Both tours cost about $70 per person. The NANA tour begins with a 30-minute film at the NANA Hotel. Then you'll proceed by van to the massive Arco operations center on the east side of the oilfield and the Sohio complex on the west. Their raised construction minimizes environmental impact on the permafrost. Both companies have three oil-gas separation plants located in strategic locations around the field. Your guide will point these out, as well as drill pads and the vital satellite communications system.

Between the two operating centers, but nearer the Sohio complex, is **Pump Station One,** the beginning of the 800-mile Trans Alaska Pipeline. Two 34-inch-diameter transit lines deliver 1.6 million barrels of oil daily to the pump station, one from each half of the field. Alyeska, the pipeline operator, meters the oil and pumps it south through a 48-inch-diameter pipeline. It takes the oil about six days to reach Valdez on Prince William Sound. An interpretive pavilion at Pump Station One helps explain its facilities and operation.

Aside from the industrial tour, the most popular activity at Prudhoe Bay is enjoying nature. The **tundra** here is thickly carpeted with some 250 species of colorful wildflowers, berries, and fully grown alder and willow trees that stand barely knee high. The Central Arctic caribou herd, 10,000 strong, migrates through the region, and some 200 different birds, mainly shorebirds and waterfowl such as snow geese and tundra swans, have been identified in the Prudhoe Bay summer nesting grounds. Polar bears and musk-oxen are rarely seen, but grizzly bears, arctic foxes, arctic hares, ground squirrels, lemmings, wolves, and other wildlife roam the coastal plain, and moose sometimes come in from the Brooks Range foothills.

The oil companies have invested a great deal of money to minimize their environmental impact on the North Slope. Sohio engineers, for example, address air and water quality, solid-waste disposal, hazardous-waste handling and disposal, spill cleanup, recovery and contingency planning for oil and hazardous substances, archeological site assessment, tundra vegetation monitoring, and gravel site restoration.

ORGANIZED TOURS

Princess Tours, 2815 Second Ave., Seattle, WA 98109 (tel. 206/728-4200), offers tours of Prudhoe Bay combined with a two-day, 510-mile bus trip down the Haul

Road. Participants fly from Fairbanks to Deadhorse, get a tour of oilfields, then head back south over the two-lane gravel road, stopping overnight at Coldfoot. Or they can do the four-day/three-night trip (including a night in Fairbanks) in reverse. Either way, the price tag is $949 from mid-June to September.

MarkAir (tel. toll free 800/426-6784, 800/478-0800 in Alaska) offers a two-day Barrow–Prudhoe Bay tour, with an overnight in Barrow, for $434 from Fairbanks or $585 from Anchorage. The trip is available June through August.

SPORTS & RECREATION

Fishing for arctic char, grayling, and Dolly Varden is good on the Sagarvanirktok and Kuparuk Rivers. Licenses can be purchased at the Trading Post. The river ice breaks up around the first of June, and the river doesn't freeze again until about mid-September. No hunting is permitted in the Prudhoe Bay field.

In winter the vast, open tundra is ideal for **cross-country skiing** and **snow-machining.** But white-out blizzard conditions and gale-force winds can arise quickly, so sportsmen should always let others know the direction they're headed in.

Hardy scuba-divers with highly efficient wetsuits will be fascinated by **"The Boulder Patch,"** a unique site discovered in 1971 in 20 feet of water off the mouth of the Sagarvanirktok River. Whereas most of the Arctic Ocean seafloor is rather barren, these boulders—which, scientists speculate, ice-rafted here from elsewhere—harbor a rich marine life of colorful coral, anemones, sponges, and algae. It's not far from an Exxon drilling site.

WHERE TO STAY & DINE

All facilities for overnight visitors, except those invited by Sohio or Arco, are in Deadhorse. Each hotel is a self-contained city providing accommodation, dining facilities, and living space for employees of smaller companies—mainly independent contractors—that don't have "camps" of their own. In every case, hotels are of modular construction, trailer units strung together on pilings in the permafrost. None of them is fancy and all are expensive, but they're extremely functional for their alien environment. In their favor, all have public cafeterias with all-you-can-eat meal hours three times daily. Unless otherwise noted, they're within a stone's throw of the airport terminal.

ARCTIC CARIBOU INN, Pouch 340010, Prudhoe Bay, AK 99734. Tel. 907/659-2368. Fax 907/569-2289. 100 rms (50 with bath).
$ Rates (including full board): $80 single without bath, $120 single with bath; $65 per person double without bath. DC, DISC, MC, V. **Closed:** Sept 16–May 14.
The Arctic Caribou Inn is operated in summer only by NANA for the benefit of Princess Tours' package travelers. It has 208 beds in a variety of single- and double-room configurations, some with private or semiprivate baths, a few with room/office combinations. Hotel facilities include TV rooms with satellite reception, a recreation room with pool and Ping-Pong, a weight room with a Universal gym, laundry rooms, and public pay phones. Next door to the hotel is the Trading Post, Prudhoe Bay's largest retail store, with clothing, office supplies, nonprescription drugs, and a variety of gifts and souvenirs. It's open daily from 9am to 10pm.

The dining room is warm and cozy, with a menu that changes nightly. Meals are served from 5:30 to 7:30am, noon to 1pm, and 6 to 8pm. Also offered are a salad bar and homemade dessert carousel. Prices are equivalent to other hotels. Beverages, snacks, and sandwiches are available anytime.

NANA OILFIELD SERVICES HOTEL, Pouch 340112, Prudhoe Bay, AK 99734. Tel. 907/659-2840. Fax 907/569-2289. 150 rms (10 with bath).
$ Rates (including full board): $80 single; $65 double. DC, DISC, MC, V.
This hotel is owned and operated by the Northwest Alaska Native Association, based in Kotzebue. (NANA also operates Prudhoe Bay's local tour service.) Many of the rooms are more or less permanently occupied by Prudhoe Bay employees. The rooms are basic, with twin beds, dresser, desk, and wardrobe cabinet, plus electric heat (the

hotel has its own powerhouse). Toilet and shower facilities are shared. Within the hotel are a TV room with satellite reception and a VCR, a weight room and sauna, and a recreation room with pool, Ping-Pong, darts, and video games. Pay-phone booths are in some corridors.

The cafeteria is open 24 hours, with breakfast ($10) served from 5 to 8pm, lunch ($12.50) from 11:30am to 1pm, and dinner ($15) from 5 to 8pm. Substantial snacks are available at all other times. Nonresidents can buy meal chits at reception.

PRUDHOE BAY HOTEL, Pouch 340004, Prudhoe Bay, AK 99734. Tel. 907/659-2449. 187 rms (24 with bath). TV

$ Rates (including all meals): $75 single without bath, $90 single with bath; $65 per person double without bath. AE, DC, V.

The Prudhoe Bay is a full-service accommodation opposite the airport. Its rooms have a double bed or two twin beds, a wardrobe closet, dresser and desk, and electric heat. The hotel also has a TV room, a weight room, a sauna, a sun room, a 24-hour commissary, and pay phones. A limited number of rooms with private baths must be reserved far in advance.

The dining room serves breakfast from 5:30 to 8am, lunch from 11:30am to 1pm, and dinner from 5:30 to 9pm, with snack service between meal hours and until 10pm.

5. THE BROOKS RANGE

The Brooks Range, spanning Alaska north of the Arctic Circle from the Chukchi Sea to the border of Canada's Yukon, has been called "one of the world's last true wildernesses." The northernmost extension of the Rocky Mountains, it has an austere beauty and grandeur, with magnificent views down pristine river valleys and across treeless, sedge-covered slopes.

Most of the range is contained within federally protected lands. Gates of the Arctic National Park and Preserve, 7.95 million acres straddling the range's crest, is the centerpiece. To its west are Noatak National Preserve and Kobuk Valley National Park (see "Easy Excursions from Kotzebue" in Section 2 of this chapter); to its east is the 18-million-acre Arctic National Wildlife Refuge. The only break in the protected belt is the narrow Trans Alaska Pipeline corridor.

The Brooks Range is not a particularly high mountain range—its highest point, Mount Isto near the Canadian border, is only 9,058 feet—but its sheer isolation makes it forbidding. From its spruce-and-taiga southern flank facing the Interior to its semi-arid and frigid North Slope, this wilderness is inhospitable to humankind. Grizzly bears, wolves, caribou, and dozens of other mammals range the fragile tundra. A few scattered tribes of Native Alaskans—Athabaskan Indians on the south, Inupiat Eskimos on the north—eke a meager subsistence living from hunting and fishing.

Though it's possible to walk into **Gates of the Arctic National Park and Preserve** directly off the Haul Road, most park visitors climb aboard scheduled flights on **Frontier Flying Service** (tel. 907/474-0014) from Fairbanks to the villages of Anaktuvuk Pass or Bettles, and hire outfitters and/or charter aircraft there to take them deeper into the wilderness. Get full information on park access and services from the Superintendent, Gates of the Arctic National Park and Preserve, P.O. Box 74680, Fairbanks, AK 99707 (tel. 907/456-0281).

Anaktuvuk Pass (pop. about 300), an Eskimo village in a historic 2,200-foot pass connecting the Interior with the Arctic, has some overnight accommodations and a pleasant little Native-crafts museum. Trips to the Endicott Mountains, Chandler Lake, and other North Slope destinations often begin here. The pass is 260 miles from Fairbanks. The name Anaktuvuk, incidentally, is Inupiat for "caribou droppings."

Bettles (pop. about 100), also known as Evansville, began in 1899 as a trading post on the south bank of Upper Koyukuk River in the Brooks Range foothills, 185 miles northwest of Fairbanks. There's still a trading post here, and year-round accommodation is available at the **Bettles Lodge,** Bettles, AK 99726 (tel. 907/692-5111 in summer, 907/455-9131 in winter), with 10 rustic units at $85 single or double. Trails lead 85 miles north to Anaktuvuk Pass and 35 miles southwest to the Athabaskan village of Allakaket. In addition to air and foot, Bettles is accessible by boat in summer and by snow machine in winter.

Bettles-based outfitters offer a wide variety of wilderness experiences, from combination backpack-river trips (in kayak or canoe) in summer, to dog sled and cross-country ski excursions in winter. Contact Dave Schmitz's **Brooks Range Wilderness Trips,** Bettles, AK 99726 (tel. 907/692-5312), or Dave Ketscher's **Sourdough Outfitters,** Bettles, AK 99726 (tel. 907/692-5252, or toll free 800/288-8293). Prices typically run from $1,000 for a seven-day trip to $2,500 for a three-week expedition. Private air-charter service is available in Bettles from **Bettles Air Service** (tel. 907/692-5111 in summer, 907/455-9131 in winter).

One of the few fishing lodges in Gates of the Arctic National Park is about 70 air miles northwest of Bettles. Nick and Susan Jennings's **Walker Lake Wilderness Lodge,** Bettles, AK 99726 (tel. 907/692-5252), is a modern three-story lodge overlooking 17-mile-long Walker Lake. It's open June 10 to September 15; rates begin at $950 per person for four days/three nights, including meals, guide service, and round-trip air transportation from Bettles. The lodge also has several remote log cabins for rental scattered through the Brooks Range.

Some of the best prices for summer backpacking and canoeing/kayaking expeditions are offered by **Brooks Range Adventures,** 1231 Sundance Loop, Fairbanks, AK 99709 (tel. 907/479-8203 or 452-1821). **Arctic Treks,** P.O. Box 73452, Fairbanks, AK 99707 (tel. 907/455-6502), has a wide selection of trips, while Roger Rom's **Alaska Wilderness** offers study treks into the Brooks Range in conjunction with the University of Alaska (contact Conferences and Continuing Education, 117 Eielson Building, University of Alaska, Fairbanks, AK 99775; tel. 907/474-7800).

If you're a river runner, see what **Alaska Treks 'n' Voyages,** P.O. Box 625, Seward, AK 99664 (tel. 907/224-2960 in summer, 907/288-3610 in winter), has planned. Kayaking trips of 10–13 days, priced about $1,500–$2,500, take in the John and Kobuk Rivers, as well as the Hulahula River in **Arctic National Wildlife Refuge.** The latter is a combination of rafting, kayaking, and hiking from the mountains to **Kaktovik,** an Eskimo village on Barter Island in the Arctic Ocean. The refuge, the northernmost and most remote refuge in the United States, supports the 180,000 caribou of the Porcupine herd. Increasing oil exploration is progressing on its Arctic plain.

CHAPTER 11

SOUTHWEST ALASKA

Southwest Alaska is at once the state's vastest region and its most difficult to categorize. Stretching from Cook Inlet to the Yukon River Delta to the tip of the 1,000-mile-long Aleutian archipelago, it contains bustling fishing communities and wind-ravaged wastelands, lush lowlands and smoldering volcanoes. Its tortured, rocky coastline limits boat landings but has created a paradise for marine mammals and birds.

If any two threads can be said to bind this region, they are the Russian heritage and fishing, both commercial and sport.

Kodiak Island was the site of the first Russian settlement in North America in the late 18th century, and the headquarters for the Russian American Company until its later move to Sitka. The company established numerous fur-trading outposts through the Alaska Peninsula, the Aleutians, and even the Pribilofs, simultaneously absorbing the Native Aleut people into their old-world culture. Today virtually every Aleut settlement—all of them in southwest Alaska—is centered around its own Orthodox church.

Fishing, which grew in importance after the American purchase of Alaska, provides the modern economic base. Bristol Bay, on the north side of the Alaska Peninsula, is considered by many to be the world's richest salmon ground, and the waters around Kodiak Island were once famed for their king crab. The Bristol Bay–Kodiak fishery has been restricted to permit holders since 1922. Additionally, the rivers and lakes of the Alaska Peninsula attract sport fishermen from all over the world to cast their lines for trophy-size salmon, trout, northern pike, arctic char, and grayling. The dozens of lodges that accommodate these anglers frequently charge $3,000 a week and more. The rates normally include not only room and board, but also round-trip transportation from Anchorage, use of boats and small planes from the lodge, guide service, all sports equipment—in short, virtually everything you'll need but your own alcoholic beverages.

---

1. KODIAK

260 miles SW of Anchorage

GETTING THERE **By Plane** **Kodiak State Airport** is efficiently served several times daily from Anchorage by **MarkAir** (tel. 907/487-2424, or toll free

WHAT'S SPECIAL ABOUT SOUTHWEST ALASKA

Wildlife

☐ Alaska Maritime National Wildlife Refuge, encompassing Round Island, a sanctuary for over 10,000 walruses, and 72 of the 80 named Aleutian Islands, where some 20,000 sea otters live.

☐ The Pribilof Islands, famous for their 211 species of marine bird life and a thriving colony of northern fur seals.

☐ The Kodiak brown bear, the world's largest carnivore, found in Kodiak National Wildlife Refuge on Kodiak Island.

☐ Large colonies of musk-oxen and reindeer, on boggy Nunivak Island in the Yukon Delta National Wildlife Refuge.

☐ The world's richest salmon ground, Bristol Bay.

Scenery

☐ Katmai National Park, including the fabled Valley of Ten Thousand Smokes, created by the cataclysmic 1912 eruption of Mount Katmai.

☐ Lake Iliamna, Alaska's largest lake (1,000 square miles of surface area), adjacent to Lake Clark National Park, with another huge lake wedged between towering volcanic peaks.

☐ Aniakchak National Monument, on the Alaska Peninsula, with a 30-square-mile dormant volcanic caldera.

☐ Wood-Tikchik State Park, the state's largest, with a dozen fjordlike lakes in two neighboring water systems.

History

☐ Kodiak, first capital of Russian Alaska, featuring the Baranov Museum in an 18th-century commissary and St. Herman's Seminary, the only Russian Orthodox seminary in the state.

☐ Remnants of World War II skirmishes on Kiska, Unalaska, and other Aleutian Islands.

☐ Fort Abercrombie State Historic Park, on Kodiak Island.

800/426-6784, 800/478-0800 in Alaska). **ERA Aviation** (tel. toll free 800/426-0333) also offers passenger service to Kodiak from Anchorage, Kenai, and Homer. Four air-charter services are based on Kodiak Island (see "Easy Excursions from Kodiak," below).

To get the five miles from the airport to town, you must opt for the **Ace Mecca Taxi Cab Service** (tel. 486-3211), with a rather steep fare of $3 at flagfall and $1.50 per mile. That should make the run from the airport about $10.50.

By Ferry Kodiak is served by the ferries of the Alaska Marine Highway System (tel. 907/486-3800, or toll free 800/526-6731). The M.V. *Tustumena* plies the waters between Kodiak, Port Lions (a village on the north side of Kodiak Island), the Kenai Peninsula, and Prince William Sound three times weekly throughout the year, except for a week-long trip to Dutch Harbor in the Aleutians once a month between May and September, and a 10-week maintenance period in Seattle beginning January 1. Under its normal schedule, the ferry leaves Kodiak for Homer and Seldovia every Monday at 3pm and Tuesday at 9pm, and for Seward, Valdez, and Cordova every Thursday at 8:15am. The passenger fare is $48 to Homer, $52 to Seward—vehicle, berth, and meals not included. The terminal is on Marine Way at the end of Center Avenue.

ESSENTIALS Orientation The city is laid out southwest to northeast, with the main street, **Rezanof Drive,** extending from the airport (five miles southwest of downtown) to Fort Abercrombie State Park (four miles northeast). **Marine Way,** the center of most activity, branches off Rezanof Drive just as it reaches the Small Boat

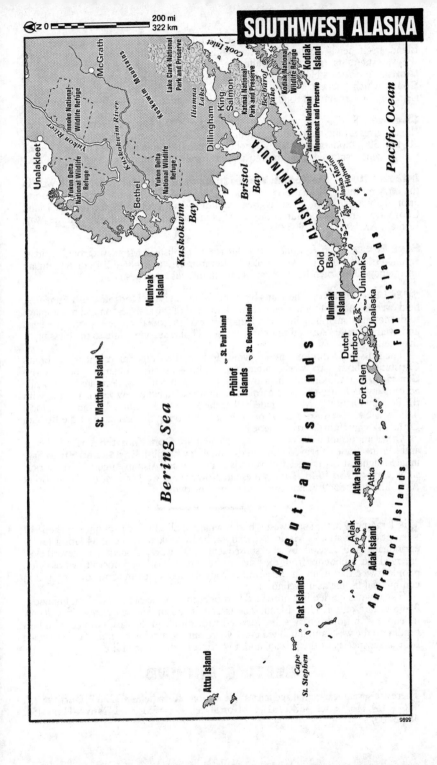

Harbor at the head of St. Paul Harbor and winds along the narrow strait facing Near Island, itself newly connected to the Kodiak Island mainland by a bridge. Many shops, restaurants, government buildings, and private offices are on Marine Way or **Center Avenue,** a block north. Rezanof Drive is paralleled to the east by **Mission Road,** which starts at Marine Way, and to the west by Mill Bay Road. The entire island has a very limited road system, only 87 miles in length—all in the northeast.

Climate Kodiak lies virtually in the middle of the Japan Current. Its maritime climate gives it mild temperatures (summer days in the 50s and 60s, winter days in the 20s and 30s), moderate rainfall (70 inches annually, especially in the fall, with several feet of winter snowfall), and more than its share of fog and wind.

Information The **Kodiak Visitor Information Center,** 100 Marine Way (in the ferry terminal), Kodiak, AK 99615 (tel. 907/486-4070), is open from 8:30am to 5pm: daily in summer, weekdays year-round. It's maintained by the Kodiak Island Convention and Visitor Bureau, downstairs in the same building: 100 Marine Way, Kodiak, AK 99615 (tel. 907/486-4782).

Fast Facts The *Kodiak Daily Mirror* is published Monday through Friday. Kodiak Island Hospital is at 1920 E. Rezanof Dr. (tel. 486-3281, or 911 in an emergency). The town has five banks and numerous churches.

SPECIAL EVENTS The year's biggest celebration is the **Kodiak Crab Festival,** held over Memorial Day weekend to mark the end of the crab season and pay homage to the commercial fishing industry. Parades, the Miss Kodiak contest, sporting events, and even the state "survival suit championships" play second fiddle to the blessing of the fleet.

The Russian Orthodox Church, which follows the Gregorian calendar, celebrates Christmas about two weeks after most folks—usually January 7 or 8—with **Starring,** a tradition in which a child twirls a beautifully decorated star while accompanying house-to-house carolers. One week later the new year is rung in with the Russian Orthodox Masquerade Ball at the Kodiak Elks Club. An important local holiday is **St. Herman's Day,** on August 9, honoring the first saint of the Russian Orthodox church in North America.

Other important dates on Kodiak's calendar are **Com Fish** (the Alaska Fisheries and Marine Trade Fair) in March and the three-day **Kodiak Rodeo and State Fair** in late August at the Jaycees Fairgrounds in Bell's Flats. Also in August, the theatrical show *Cry of the Wild Ram* is presented over three weekends at the Frank Brink Amphitheater (see "Evening Entertainment," below).

The largest city in the southwest is hardly a metropolis. Buried in pumice by the 1912 eruption of Katmai's Mount Novarupta, badly shaken by the 1964 Good Friday earthquake and leveled by the subsequent tidal wave, Kodiak has nevertheless emerged like a phoenix from the ashes to become a bustling modern town of 6,700 people (twice that many in the island borough), most of them somehow engaged in commercial fishing as a livelihood.

The town is nestled in a protected harbor at the northeastern end of mountainous 3,588-square-mile Kodiak Island. The largest island in Alaskan waters, it is deeply indented with fjords on all sides, forested with spruce in the east, covered with lush tundra on the west, and inhabited everywhere but the city by the great Kodiak brown bear (a subspecies of the grizzly) and a wealth of other animal life.

GETTING AROUND

There are several car-rental agencies at the airport: **Avis** (tel. 487-2264), **Budget** (tel. 486-5815), **Hertz** (tel. 487-2261), **National** (tel. 486-4751), and **Rent-a-Heap** (tel. 486-5200).

WHAT TO SEE & DO

An excellent way to get acquainted with the town of Kodiak is to take the walking tour detailed in the "Kodiak Island Visitors Guide," available at the Visitor Information Center.

SIGHTS & ATTRACTIONS
The Top Attractions

BARANOV MUSEUM, in the Erskine House, 101 Marine Way at Center Ave. Tel. 486-5920.

The Baranov Museum is one of the state's outstanding small museums. The oldest standing Russian building in Alaska, it was constructed around 1792 of logs and was used as a warehouse for sea otter pelts and a commissary in Alexander Baranov's capital. It subsequently belonged to the Alaska Commercial Company (1867–1911) and to W. J. and Nellie Erskine, who lived in the house until 1948. In 1962 it was declared a national historic landmark. The museum's collection includes fine samovars and other memorabilia from the Russian era, 18th- and 19th-century period furnishings, and artifacts from Aleut and Koniag Eskimo prehistory. Many authentic Russian and Native crafts are sold in the museum's sophisticated gift shop.

Admission: $1 adults, free for children under 12.

Open: May to mid-Sept, Mon–Fri 10am–3pm, Sat–Sun noon–4pm; mid-Sept to Apr, Mon–Wed and Fri 11am–3pm, Sat noon–3pm.

HOLY RESURRECTION ORTHODOX CHURCH, at Kashewarof Ave. and Mission Rd. Tel. 486-3524.

This church is the focus of much of Kodiak's spiritual life. It was, in fact, the first Christian parish in Alaska. Within the sanctuary are precious icons, rare paintings, and handmade brass works. Note the remains of eight bells beside a small bell tower in the churchyard. A plaque on the tower wall tells how the bells were cast at a Kodiak foundry in 1794–96, but were destroyed, along with the church, by fire in 1943. The church was rebuilt immediately after the war, but it was 1980 before the congregation could afford to have new bells cast and shipped from France.

Admission: Free.

Open: By appointment.

ST. HERMAN'S THEOLOGICAL SEMINARY, Mission Rd. past Third Ave.

Any young Alaskan who wants to become a Russian Orthodox priest will spend several years at St. Herman's. One of only three Orthodox training institutes in the United States, and the only one in Alaska, it also houses the St. Innocent Veniaminov Research Institute museum, containing many important items from church history in Kodiak and elsewhere in Alaska.

Admission: Free.

Open: June–Sept, Mon–Sat 10am–5:30pm, Sun 1–5:30pm.

Other Attractions in Town

While the church may be Kodiak's spiritual center, the **Small Boat Harbor** is unquestionably its economic hub. Stroll through and chat with the fishermen working on their boats or mending their nets. Most will be pleased to point out the different types of gear and rigs for salmon fishing, bottom fishing, and crab or shrimp fishing. You can watch the boats come and go from the loading dock in front of the Harbormaster Building on Marine Way. Directly in front is the heart-rending **Fishermen's Memorial,** dedicated to the dozens of Kodiak fishermen lost at sea. It's a grim reminder that commercial fishing is one of the world's most dangerous professions. As the largest commercial fishing port in the United States, Kodiak is bound to have its casualties.

If you wander up Rezanof Drive past Center Avenue and the Y junction, you'll spot a plaque marking the spot where the 86-foot crab boat M.V. *Selief* came to rest following the 1964 earthquake and tidal wave (the boat was repaired and is still operating as a fishing vessel). Another block uphill on Lower Mill Bay Road, a plaque on the outer wall of the police station marks the high-water level of that same '64 tsunami, which wiped out Kodiak's business district.

While most fishing vessels have slips in the Small Boat Harbor, pleasure craft generally are found across the strait in the **St. Herman Boat Harbor** on Near Island. A ferry shuttled to and from Near Island until the bridge was completed in 1986.

A surplus World War II liberty ship, the **Star of Kodiak,** was set beside Marine Way near the ferry dock as an emergency cannery following the disaster of 1964. Intended as a temporary facility, it has long since become a permanent feature of the city.

Nearby Attractions

Just over four miles north of downtown Kodiak is the rain forest–clad site of an important World War II outpost. **Fort Abercrombie State Historic Park** was built in 1941 as a top-secret radar station, with artillery added in 1943 (after the Japanese attack on Attu) to protect the Fort Greely Garrison at Naval Air Station Kodiak. Between 150 and 200 men were stationed here on 780 acres until the spring of 1944. Wander the trail and road system and see the radar tower, observation posts, strategic spotting and plotting room, war reserve magazine, and other facilities. Plans are under way to develop an interpretive museum in the ready ammunition bunker, beneath the gun emplacements, at Miller Point devoted to the World War II Aleutian Campaign.

In addition to being a site of historic value, the fort is a lovely spot to enjoy nature. The rugged coastline is rife with seabird rookeries and tidepools. Virgin Sitka spruce cloak the peninsula, ash from the 1912 eruption of Mount Novarupta still observable on their branches; flowering plants, berries, and lush moss carpet the forest floor. The ranger's office and visitor center near the park entrance has historical displays and interpretive literature. Contact the Alaska State Parks System, Southwest District, Kodiak Area Ranger, Star Route, Box 3800, Kodiak, AK 99615 (tel. 907/486-6339), for more information.

The navy turned its air station over to the U.S. Coast Guard in 1972. Today the **USCG Support Center Kodiak** (tel. 487-5267)—the Coast Guard's North Pacific operations base—occupies the entire Nyman Peninsula near the state airport, six miles west of downtown Kodiak, and additional surrounding land, making it the largest in area of any Coast Guard base. About 3,000 Coast Guardsmen and their families live here. Their duties extend from patroling Alaska's waters for illegal (inside the 200-mile limit) foreign fishing to performing search-and-rescue services.

Visitors are welcome but must make prior arrangements to be met by a Coast Guard bus. Call the Public Affairs Office (tel. 487-5259) for details on this, or on how to schedule a boat tour or hangar inspection.

Also in the Buskin River area, but on the city side of the airport opposite Lake Louise, is the **Kodiak National Wildlife Refuge Visitor Center.** The western two-thirds of Kodiak Island and three smaller islands are part and parcel of this 1,865,000-acre reserve. The variety and quantity of wildlife here are remarkable: The Kodiak brown bear, the world's largest carnivore (males range up to 1,500 pounds), is the central attraction of the refuge; all five species of Pacific salmon spawn in its streams and lakes; and at least 200 pairs of American bald eagles have been counted, among 200 other bird species. But dense vegetation and a mountainous spine make the land virtually impenetrable by trail, so that boat and float plane are the only practical means of arrival. Nine recreational cabins in different parts of the refuge are available for use on a reservation basis.

The visitor center, at 1390 Buskin Beach Rd. (tel. 907/487-2600), offers displays, interpretive programs, and trip-planning information. Free films on the island's wildlife are shown at 1, 2, and 3pm on Saturday and Sunday through the summer. The center is open Monday through Friday from 8am to 4:30pm and on Saturday and Sunday from noon to 4:30pm.

ORGANIZED TOURS

Travelers who prefer to have the arrangements made for them will find a variety of Kodiak tour packages offered from Anchorage.

One local Kodiak operator is also in on the package business. MarkAir books its visits with **Island Terrific Tours,** P.O. Box 3001, Kodiak, AK 99615 (tel. 907/486-4777). You're met at the airport by a driver/guide who will introduce you to all the major attractions. The cost is $199 for one day, $239 overnight (double occupancy), plus tax. If you're already in Kodiak, you can book the tour alone for $45.

SPORTS & RECREATION

Baranof Park, off Baranof Street between Powell and 14th Avenues near Kodiak High School, is operated as a recreation ground by the Kodiak Parks and Recreation Department. It contains lighted tennis and basketball courts, a sports field surrounded by a track, and two children's playgrounds. The high school **swimming pool** is open to the public for a small fee after school and on weekends during the school year.

There's **bowling** at Tropic Lanes, 120 Marine Way (tel. 486-6257); **horseback riding** and pack trips at Northland Ranch on Chiniak Road (tel. 486-5578); **stock-car races** at the fairgrounds on summer weekends; and **weight equipment** at Doc's Nautilus Fitness Center, 326 Center Ave. (tel. 486-4971).

FISHING Freshwater fishing is excellent any time of year. Many of the island's lakes have been stocked with rainbow trout, silver (coho) salmon, or grayling. All five species of Pacific salmon, steelhead, and Dolly Varden spawn in major streams between May and November, with the particular run depending on the species. Kodiak also has many enthusiastic ice fishermen.

Deep-sea charter vessels, working out of St. Herman's (formerly Dog Bay) Small Boat Harbor on Near Island, bring in fine catches of salmon, halibut, black bass, and cod year round. **Kodiak Sea Charters,** P.O. Box 2156, Kodiak, AK 99615 (tel. 907/487-2683), is one of half a dozen charter services that offer fishing, hunting, and sightseeing trips around the island. The Visitor Information Center will recommend charters.

Remember to get your Alaskan fishing license before you drop your first line. A nonresident sport-fishing license can be purchased at **Mack's Sport Shop,** 117 Lower Mill Bay Rd. (tel. 486-4276). Ask at the **Alaska Department of Fish and Game** office, 211 Mission Rd., at Kashewarof Avenue (P.O. Box 686), Kodiak, AK 99615 (tel. 907/486-4791), for their thorough "Kodiak Area Sport Fishing Guide." Fish and Game operates a 24-hour **"fishing hotline"** (tel. 486-4559) to answer up-to-the-minute questions about what's hot and what's not.

You needn't charter a boat or plane to take you fishing. The **Buskin River,** which empties into the Gulf of Alaska right beside the state airport, is one of the best fishing streams on the island, with spawning runs of Dolly Varden, sockeye, pink, and silver salmon. The island's best fishing stream, however, is the **Karluk River** (see "Easy Excursions from Kodiak," below).

HIKING The visitors bureau's Kodiak map lists no fewer than 24 recommended hiking trails within easy reach of the town of Kodiak by road or boat. A good start might be to walk up the road to the communication saucer atop 1,270-foot **Pillar Mountain,** overlooking Kodiak town. The road starts just above downtown. The five-mile **Termination Point** trail is quite popular; it starts at the end of the Monashka Bay Road beyond Fort Abercrombie. Or get a boat to drop you off on **Woody Island,** only a couple of miles due east of downtown. The site of a Christian summer camp, it also harbors an old Russian cemetery, sawmill, and ice-packing plant.

HUNTING If it's the Kodiak brown bear you're seeking, and if you're not a resident of Alaska, it'll cost you. Be prepared to part with an $85 license fee, a brown bear permit fee of several hundred dollars, and—unless you're hunting with a close relative who *is* an Alaska resident—$5,000 or so for an experienced guide. Bears are in season April 1 to May 15 and October 25 to November 30. You can also go after elk, Sitka black-tailed deer, or reindeer, as well as ducks.

You can get licenses and information in the same places as noted under "Fishing," above. In addition to the charter services listed in that category, **Kodiak Island Charters,** P.O. Box 1396, Kodiak, AK 99615 (tel. 907/486-5380 or 486-5140), handles hunting expeditions with great efficiency.

KAYAKING The jagged, sheltered coastline of Kodiak Island offers superb conditions for this sport. You can rent kayaks from **Shuyak Backcountry Sports,** 1314 Mill Bay Rd. (tel. 486-3771), for $30–$40 per half day or $45–$55 for a full day.

WINTER SPORTS Where there's snow, there are skiers and skaters. The island trails are ideal for cross-country skiers, while skaters find ample ice on several ponds—including Lilly Lake and Potato Patch Lake—within the city limits.

WHERE TO STAY

Kodiak city has three hotels and a motel. **Kodiak Bed and Breakfast,** 308 Cope St., Kodiak, AK 99615 (tel. 907/486-5367), places guests in island homes for $50 single, $60 double (MC, V accepted). Write or phone coordinator Mary Monroe for details.

Tax The borough bed tax is 10%.

KODIAK BUSKIN RIVER INN, 1395 Airport Way, Kodiak, AK 99615. Tel. 907/487-2700, or toll free 800/544-2202. 45 rms, 6 suites (all with bath). TV TEL

$ Rates: June–Sept 15, $76 single; $84 double; from $115 suite. Sept 16–May, $60 single or double; from $115 suite. Children under 12 stay free in parents' room. AE, DISC, MC, V.

This inn is removed from the city but a short walk from the airport. Its spacious rooms and suites have been newly renovated with a bright color scheme. Each room has queen-size or double beds and other standard furnishings, cable television, direct-dial phone (local calls are 25¢), and electric baseboard heat. If you're without a car, you can make arrangements to be dropped in town.

The inn's Eagle's Nest Restaurant overlooks the salmon-rich Buskin River, so it's appropriate that a catch of the day be its dinnertime specialty, at $13. Breakfast prices start at $4, and lunch sandwiches start at $4.50. It's open weekdays for lunch from 7am to 2pm and for dinner from 6 to 10pm, on Saturday and Sunday from 8am.

SHELIKOF LODGE, 211 Thorsheim Ave. (P.O. Box 774), Kodiak, AK 99615. Tel. 907/486-4141. 39 rms (all with bath). TV TEL
$ Rates: $60 single; $66 double. MC, V.

The Shelikof Lodge is a nondescript but adequate accommodation a quiet three blocks from Marine Way. Its dimly lit rooms, with blue carpeting and orange spreads on the double beds, have ample furnishings, including cable TV, telephone (free local calls), and electric baseboard heat. In the hotel, but under separate ownership, is the Fox Inn restaurant, open Monday through Saturday from 5am to 2pm and 5 to 9pm and on Sunday from 9am to 3pm.

WESTMARK KODIAK, 236 S. Rezanof Dr. (P.O. Box 1547), Kodiak, AK 99615. Tel. 907/486-5712, or toll free 800/544-0970 outside Alaska. Fax 907/486-3430. 81 rms (all with bath). TV TEL
$ Rates: Summer, $98 single; $108 double. Winter, $78 single; $88 double. AE, CB, DC, DISC, ER, MC, V.

Kodiak's best hotel has rooms decorated in muted masculine tones of navy blue and lavender. Each standard unit has two queen-size beds, a four-drawer dresser and other natural-wood furnishings, a large closet with sliding mirror doors, 17-channel cable TV, a direct-dial phone (local calls are 50¢), and thermostat-controlled electric heat.

CAMPGROUNDS

All three state parks on Kodiak Island have camping and RV facilities (without hookups). There are 18 sites at **Buskin River State Recreation Site** (four miles southwest of Kodiak), 15 at **Fort Abercrombie State Historic Park** (four miles north of Kodiak), and 9 at **Pasagshak River State Recreation Site** (47 miles south of Kodiak). All have fireplaces, latrines, and water.

WHERE TO DINE

CHART ROOM, in the Westmark Kodiak Hotel, 236 S. Rezanof Dr. Tel. 486-5712.
   Cuisine: CONTINENTAL. **Reservations:** Recommended.
$ Prices: Appetizers $6–$10; main courses $11–$25; breakfast/lunch $4–$7. AE, CB, DC, DISC, ER, MC, V.
   Open: Daily 6:30am–10pm.
For formal dining, this is unquestionably Kodiak's top choice. It's located on the second floor of the Westmark, facing the harbor, at the top of a circular staircase leading from the lobby. A personal favorite is the scampi flamed in Pernod, at $19.

CHINA HOUSE, 202 N. Rezanof Dr. Tel. 486-8589.
   Cuisine: CHINESE. **Reservations:** Not required.
$ Prices: Lunch $6–$10; dinner $11–$18. MC, V.
   Open: Sun–Thurs 11:30am–10pm, Fri–Sat 11:30am–11pm.
Young immigrants from Hong Kong operate Kodiak's original Asian restaurant, where Oriental art hangs on the walls, red lanterns are suspended over the tables, and even the wallpaper has a Chinese calligraphy pattern. The service is Hong Kong efficient, and the food—Cantonese, Mandarin, and Szechuan—is quite good. There's also a children's menu.

EL CHICANO, 104 Center Ave. Tel. 486-6116.
   Cuisine: MEXICAN. **Reservations:** Not required.
$ Prices: Lunch $6–$7; dinner $8–$10. MC, V.
   Open: Mon–Sat 11am–10pm.
Some of the best Mexican food in Alaska can be found here. A campy concrete fountain depicting a little Mexican boy in a sombrero greets diners to this spacious second-floor restaurant in the Center Avenue Plaza Building. Seating is in imitation brick alcoves, with basket shades over hanging lamps. Chicken mole ($8.25) is one of my favorite Mexican dishes, and this is one of the few places north of California I've been able to find it. Several imported Mexican beers are on the menu to douse the fire from the chili sauce, homemade with real chiles.

EVENING ENTERTAINMENT

The event of the year in Kodiak is a historical drama presented every August in Alaska's only outdoor theater. As the sun sets over Monashka Bay and balalaikas play spirited Russian folk music, *Cry of the Wild Ram* begins in the Frank Brink Amphitheater (named for the playwright) near Fort Abercrombie. Since 1967 this acclaimed play has traced the history of the first Russian colony in America through the eyes of its enigmatic and beleaguered governor of 30 years, Alexander Baranov. Most of the cast is local, though some professionals from the Lower 48 are brought in to direct the play and take several major roles.

Ten evening performances are spread over the first three weekends of August. Reserved seats are $15, general admission is $12, and student tickets are $10. The production plays rain or (moon) shine, so the audience is advised to dress warmly and bring raingear . . . just in case. Russian food is served during intermission. Contact the **Kodiak Arts Council,** P.O. Box 1792, Kodiak, AK 99615 (tel. 907/486-5291), for more information.

The rest of the year, nightlife is pretty much what you might expect in a fishing town: casual and lively, sometimes crossing the fine line to rowdy. Most of the action is within a couple blocks of the Harbormaster's Building. In the Mall on Marine Way you'll find **Solly's Office,** a large, dimly lit lounge with live rock bands playing Tuesday through Saturday nights. **The Mecca,** on the opposite side of the Mall (tel. 486-3364), has live music Tuesday through Saturday and a very spacious dance floor. Nearby are **The Village,** with a country-and-western soloist Thursday through Sunday nights, and the **Ship's Bar,** a traditional fishermen's watering hole.

EASY EXCURSIONS FROM KODIAK

Beyond the state airport, Rezanof Drive—now known as **Chiniak Road**—zigs and zags around several bays to Cape Greville, 47½ beautiful miles from downtown Kodiak. En route, it passes the residential district of Bell's Flats at the head of Women's Bay, skirts Holiday Bay on Middle Bay, and traverses the Olds River where it flows into Kalsin Bay. The **Kalsin Inn Ranch,** P.O. Box 1696, Kodiak, AK 99615 (tel. 907/486-2659), and the **Northland Ranch Resort,** P.O. Box 2367, Kodiak, AK 99615 (tel. 907/486-5578), both offer lodging and meals: Cabins are $35–$62 at the inn, $59–$145 at the ranch; and steak dinners run $10–$15 at both. (The beef is local: This is open range country.)

From Kalsin Bay the road weaves down a rugged coastline to **Road's End,** P.O. Box 1305, Kodiak, AK 99615 (tel. 907/486-2885), another friendly and casual lodge with excellent steak and seafood lunches ($6–$8) and dinners ($10–$15). Year-round room rates are $50–$55. It's not far from here to Cape Greville and Cape Chiniak, Kodiak Island's easternmost point. In March and April you may see folks gazing to sea in the hope of spotting a migrating gray whale.

Pasagshak Bay Road branches south off Chiniak Road at the Northland Ranch and climbs 16½ miles over the Mann Range to Fossil Beach at Pasagshak Bay State Recreation Area. Near the airport, Kodiak Island's only other road, **Anton Larsen Bay Road,** leaves Rezanof Drive/Chiniak Road for a scenic 11½-mile trip to its namesake. Bears are occasionally spotted at Anton Larsen Bay, a quiet cove on the island's north shore.

The city of Kodiak is not the only settlement on Kodiak Island. There are, in fact, five other villages on the island and another just offshore.

Ouzinkie (pop. 233), on the west coast of Spruce Island, is the closest to Kodiak city. Spruce Island is only about five miles from Fort Abercrombie, and easily visible from there; Ouzinkie nestles in a grove of spruce trees on its western shore. St. Herman is buried on this island, where he lived in a hermitage; today the New Valaam Monastery and a Russian Orthodox church are the foci of villagers' social lives. Chris and Kathy Opheim's **Pleasant Harbor Lodge,** P.O. Box 8049, Kodiak, AK 99615 (tel. 907/486-6526), is a great place for a getaway at $250 a day per person, including full board. The island is a favorite of hunters, fishermen, beachcombers, and nature lovers.

Port Lions (pop. 291), 19 miles northwest of Kodiak city on Kizhuyak Bay, may be the only community in the world named for a Lions Club. When the 1964 earthquake and tidal wave destroyed 28 of the 33 homes in the village of Afognak and caused salt water to contaminate the freshwater supply, villagers relocated here at Settler Cove with the assistance of several service organizations, including the Mennonites, the Salvation Army, the U.S. Navy, and, yes, Kodiak's 49th District Lions Club. Today the village—which is served by the state ferry system—has schools and churches, a library and a medical clinic, two grocery stores, and a café. The **Lions Den Lodge,** P.O. Box 66, Port Lions, AK 99550 (tel. 907/454-2301), has rooms for $85 a night per person, $125 with full board, May to September; and $55 a night, $95 with full board, the rest of the year.

The Native fishing village of **Karluk** (pop. 102), 75 miles southwest of Kodiak on Shelikof Strait, actually consists of three village sites near the mouth of the salmon-rich Karluk River. Archeologists have found many prehistoric artifacts at two of them. An Orthodox church, left over from a former Russian trading post, overlooks a massive abandoned cannery. Accommodation is available at Rob and Martha Sikes's **Aleut Fishing Village,** Karluk, AK 99608 (tel. 907/241-2229). Full fishing packages, including food, lodging, boats, and guides, vary according to season, but run $200–$300 a day.

There's another large cannery at **Larsen Bay** (pop. 180), 15 miles east of Karluk on Uyak Bay, built at the turn of this century by the Alaska Packers Association. It operated until 1984. As at Karluk, prehistoric artifacts such as ulus, spearpoints, and oil lamps have been found in this area. Visitors who want to shoot bears with rifle or camera will find **Mike Munsey's Bear Camp** not far from Larsen Bay. Contact Munsey at Amook Pass, Kodiak, AK 99615 (tel. 907/847-2203). His rates start at $1,700 for five days.

On the south shore of Kodiak Island are **Akhiok** (pop. 102), 90 miles southwest of Kodiak city, and **Old Harbor** (pop. 355), 50 miles southwest. Akhiok was established as a sea otter–hunting settlement on the barren, grassy shores of deep Alitak Bay. Old Harbor, which faces Sitkalidak Island, is the closest settlement to Three Saints Bay, site of Grigori Shelekhov's first Russian America colony in 1784. Old Harbor villagers erected a cross on the site in 1984 to celebrate its bicentennial.

Afognak Island, just north of Kodiak Island and part of the borough, is a wilderness island with no permanent settlements. But you can stay in the **Afognak Cabins** by contacting the office in Seal Bay, AK 99697 (tel. 907/486-6442; fax 907/486-2217). All-inclusive rates run $350 per person during the peak summer season, as low as $50 at other times. Also available is a 14-foot skiff with an outboard motor. The cabins sleep six. They're available on Kazakof Bay year-round.

Shuyak Island, immediately north of Afognak Island, is a state park. A popular stop for sea kayakers en route from Homer to Kodiak (or vice versa), it can also be reached by boat or plane from either city. Four rustic cabins on the island can be reserved for $20 a night by contacting Alaska State Parks (tel. 486-6339 in Kodiak). There's a puffin rookery on the island, and many sea otters and sea lions.

All of Kodiak's small air companies perform a variety of services, from air-taxi shuttles to flightseeing, fishing, and hunting expeditions to freight hauling. **Peninsula Airways,** P.O. Box 890, Kodiak, AK 99615 (tel. 907/487-4014), regularly flies a Grumman Goose to King Salmon and Cold Bay. **Island Air Service,** P.O. Box 125, Kodiak, AK 99615 (tel. 486-6196), serves Chignik from June to September. **Uyak Air Service,** P.O. Box 4188, Kodiak, AK 99615 (tel. 486-3407), flies Cessnas back and forth to Larsen Bay, where it has cabins for rent. A newer service is **Sea Hawk Charters,** P.O. Box 500, Kodiak, AK 99619 (tel. 907/487-2477).

2. THE ALASKA PENINSULA

The 450-mile-long Alaska Peninsula, from huge Iliamna Lake to False Pass, contains some of Alaska's most rugged wilderness and most prolific fishing grounds. Its terrain is everywhere mountainous, although the spruce forests of the northeast are replaced by barren tundra in the southwest. By stretching the peninsula's boundaries just slightly to the north of Iliamna, it can be said to contain two national parks (Lake Clark and Katmai) and a national monument (Aniakchak). Population is sparse: No town on the peninsula has as many as 1,000 residents.

LAKE CLARK

A maze of jagged peaks, smoldering volcanoes, and high alpine lakes, four-million-acre **Lake Clark National Park and Preserve** encompasses the territory where the Alaska Range meets the Aleutian Range. The awesome, granite-spired Chigmit Mountains, formed by violent earth movement and sculpted by glaciers, provide the link; they have been called the Alaskan Alps. Looming over the western shore of Cook Inlet, with a broad view across the Kenai Peninsula, are the great twin volcanoes Mount Redoubt (10,197 feet) and Mount Iliamna (10,016 feet). Behind the range, fed by hundreds of waterfalls, is turquoise, 50-mile-long Lake Clark, a key spawning ground for red salmon in the Bristol Bay fishery.

The park's features vary from fossil-rich cliffs and marshy lowlands on the Cook Inlet coast to tundra-covered foothills and boreal spruce forest on the mountains' western flanks. Brown and black bears, moose, caribou, dall sheep, wolves, and smaller mammals inhabit the environs. Most visits are made between June and August, after the spring thaw and before the first snow. Float trips on three designated wild rivers (the Chilikadrotna, the Mulchatna, and the Tlikakila), backpacking, and fly-in fishing and hunting (the last in the preserve only) are popular activities.

Port Alsworth, within the preserve on the eastern shore of Lake Clark, is the headquarters of the park and preserve. Air charters from Anchorage, Kenai, and Iliamna land here, and a variety of lodging, from primitive to modern, is available. You can get a list of lodges, air charters, and outfitters licensed to operate in the park and preserve by contacting the Superintendent, Lake Clark National Park and Preserve, 701 C St. (P.O. Box 61), Anchorage, AK 99513 (tel. 907/271-4224).

Among the wilderness lodges on Lake Clark are Chuck and Sara Hornsberger's unique **Koksetna Wilderness Lodge,** Port Alsworth, AK 99653 (tel. 907/781-2227), open year-round at an all-inclusive rate of $250 a day per person; Glen and Jean Alsworth's **Farm Lodge,** P.O. Box 1, Port Alsworth, AK 99653 (tel. 907/781-2211; fax 907/781-2215), with four cabins at $150 a night from June to September; and **Alaska's Wilderness Lodge,** Wilderness Point, Port Alsworth, AK 99653 (tel. 907/781-2223 in summer, 206/863-6795 in winter, or toll free 800/835-8032 year-round), with packages starting at $1,600 per week.

ILIAMNA LAKE

By far Alaska's largest natural freshwater lake, with a surface area of an even 1,000 square miles, Iliamna Lake bridges the gap between the Chigmit Mountains and the Bristol Bay lowlands.

There are two villages on the lake's north shore, **Iliamna** (pop. 100) and **Newhalen** (pop. 150). Inhabitants of Newhalen are mainly Tanaina Indians, a branch of Athabaskan. Iliamna village, on the other hand, is a bustling resort community in the summer months with large numbers of fishermen and hunters staying at its lodges.

Among the wilderness lodges on or near Lake Iliamna are the **Igiugig Lodge,** P.O. Box 4022, Igiugig, AK 99613 (tel. 907/533-3216), in summer, or P.O. Box 871395, Wasilla, AK 99687 (tel. 907/376-2859), in winter, charging $350 daily per person from June 10 to October 15 for modern accommodation at the lake outlet; **Iliaska Lodge,** P.O. Box 228, Iliamna, AK 99606 (tel. 907/571-1221), in summer, or P.O. Box 30, Homer, AK 99603 (tel. 907/235-6188), in winter, at $4,000 weekly per person, with three float planes and 10 jet boats available for guest use, early June through September; and the **Copper River Lodge,** Pope Vanoy Landing, Iliamna, AK 99606 (tel. 907/571-1248), in summer, or P.O. Box 200831, Anchorage, AK 99520 (tel. 907/344-3677), in winter, with rates of $350 daily, $2,200 weekly, per person from early June through September.

KING SALMON

This small town (pop. 550) is the gateway to Iliamna Lake and numerous other lakes, to Katmai National Park and Preserve, and to Aniakchak National Monument. King Salmon is served twice daily by commercial flights from Anchorage via **MarkAir** (tel. toll free 800/426-6784) and from Kodiak and Cold Bay via **Peninsula Airways** (tel. 907/246-3372). Many state and federal agencies are located here, including a small U.S. Air Force base (with a complement of 375 men and women), the National Park Service (tel. 246-3305), and the Alaska Department of Fish and Game (tel. 246-3340).

King Salmon is the main town, but not the governmental seat, of the Bristol Bay Borough. That honor falls to the fish-processing center of **Naknek** (pop. 320), 15 miles down the Naknek River on Bristol Bay. The village has hotels, restaurants, schools, a medical clinic, and a civic center.

A 25-mile, all-weather road connects Naknek with King Salmon and the western boundary of Katmai National Park, near the point where the Naknek River empties out of Naknek Lake. The river, ice free from May to October, has some minor rapids and is a popular spot for float and fishing trips.

Local fishing charters typically run $150 per person per day. Rainbow trout from 8 to 15 pounds run in the Naknek River in the spring and fall; Dolly Varden, arctic grayling, and northern pike are also common in Naknek Lake, as well as the five species of Pacific salmon. Full fishing packages, including round-trip transportation from Anchorage, lodging, lunches, and guided fishing, are widely available. More specific information can be obtained by writing the **Bristol Bay Borough,** P.O. Box 189, Naknek, AK 99633.

Local air-taxi service is offered June through mid-October by the **Branch River Air Service** (tel. 907/246-3437), and May through September by the **Katmai Air Service** (tel. 907/243-5448).

If you're staying in King Salmon and drop into Brooks Lodge (tel. 907/243-5448, or toll free 800/544-0551), in Katmai National Park and Preserve (see below) for the day, you're still welcome to join the 22-mile bus tour to see the valley from a National Park Service cabin on Overlook Mountain. The tour runs $50 with lunch, $43 without. Flightseeing tours are also offered for $70 a head.

WHERE TO STAY & DINE

KING KO INN, P.O. Box 346, King Salmon, AK 99613. Tel. 907/246-3378 or 907/562-4052. Fax 907/561-5868. 10 rms (2 with bath).

$ Rates: $65 single without bath, $75 single with semiprivate bath; $90 double without bath, $100 double with semiprivate bath. Deluxe trailer units, $85 single; $125 double. AE, MC, V.

This full-service hotel-restaurant is open year-round. Manager Jacques Marshall or staff will pick you up at the airport, arrange car or boat rentals, send you on guided hunting, fishing, or rafting trips, provide jet-boat service to Brooks Lodge in Katmai National Park, then urge you to relax at night in front of the lounge's big-screen satellite TV. The rooms are simple but comfortable, and there are deluxe trailer units with separate bedroom, kitchen, and private bath available.

PONDEROSA INN, P.O. Box 234, King Salmon, AK 99613. Tel. 907/246-3444 or 246-3360. 25 rms (all with bath).

$ Rates (including full board): $495 per person for three nights, $990 per person per week. AE, MC, V.

Open mid-May to mid-October, the Ponderosa specializes in all-inclusive packages for fishermen. Guests get three family-style meals a day, a boat, motor, gas, and transfers. There's a TV in the lounge.

QUINNAT LANDING HOTEL, P.O. Box 418, King Salmon, AK 99613. Tel. 907/246-3000 in summer. Fax 907/246-6200. (In winter, write 5520 Lake Otis Pkwy., Suite 101, Anchorage, AK 99507; tel. 907/246-3000; fax 907/561-1700.) 48 rms (all with bath). TV TEL

$ Rates: Summer, $150 single; $170 double. Winter, $98 single; $108 double. AE, CB, DC, JCB, MC, V.

The Katmai area's new luxury hotel has big-city amenities but a fishing-lodge atmosphere. Rooms have television, phones, and private baths. A conference room appeals to corporate getaways. There's also a fine restaurant and lounge. Guided and independent fishing and hunting tours can be arranged, as well as boat rentals and tours of Katmai National Park.

Wilderness Lodges

There are many of these in the King Salmon–Katmai area. On the Kvichak River is the **Alaska Rainbow Lodge,** P.O. Box 190166, Anchorage, AK 99519 (tel. 907/248-2880, or toll free 800/451-6198), charging $3,800 weekly per person (no credit cards). On the Alagnak River is **Katmai Lodge,** P.O. Box 421, King Salmon, AK 99613; contact 2825 90th Ave. N.E., Everett, WA 98208 (tel. 206/337-0326; fax 206/337-0335). Both are open from early June to late September. The **Battle River**

Wilderness Retreat is on the fringe of the national park; contact 8076 Caribbean Way, Sacramento, CA 95826 (tel. 916/381-0250). Rates include three meals and guide service, and run $250 per person per day, July through September.

KATMAI NATIONAL PARK & PRESERVE

The 1980 eruption of Mount St. Helens was nothing compared to the blast that shook the Alaska Peninsula on June 6–7, 1912. In one of the most violent cataclysms ever recorded, Mount Katmai collapsed into itself, while a side vent called Novarupta spewed seven cubic miles of flaming ash and sand, burying a 50-square-mile valley up to 700 feet deep. The sparse Native population in the area weathered about 60 hours of total ash-induced darkness. Some 1,500 miles away, in Vancouver, B.C., rain laden with sulfuric acid ate away linens hung outside to dry, and all that summer northern hemisphere temperatures were unusually low because of the high concentration of dust particles in the atmosphere.

Today the **Valley of Ten Thousand Smokes** that Novarupta created is the best-known attraction of the 4.2-million-acre Katmai National Park and Preserve—created as a national monument in 1918 at the behest of the National Geographic Society, which sent four separate expeditions to explore the eruption site during the interim years. At that time the valley contained millions of fumaroles which issued steam hot enough to melt zinc. Only a few fumaroles remain active today, and Mount Katmai's crater holds a lake.

Elsewhere in the park and preserve, however, is pristine wilderness relatively unaffected by the great eruption. A coastline of plunging cliffs and islets is home to seals and sea lions, sea otters, and a rich birdlife, including puffins, auklets, and kittiwakes. West of the Aleutian Range, where creeks and rivers tumble as waterfalls from the mountain glaciers, are numerous large lakes—Naknek, Brooks, Grosvenor, Coville, Nonvianuk, Kulik, and Kukaklek.

This is prime territory for the Alaska brown bear, the grizzly, which feasts all summer on migrating salmon in park streams. Katmai National Park and Preserve has the world's largest population of unhunted brown bear; in fact the park's boundaries have been expanded four times, most recently in 1978, primarily to protect the habitat of these bears through their annual cycle. Other land mammals found in the park are the moose, caribou, wolf, fox, wolverine, porcupine, lynx, beaver, otter, marten, weasel, hare, squirrel, and vole.

At the Katmai National Park and Preserve **visitor center,** on the lakeshore near Brooks Lodge, you can watch nightly slide presentations. There's also a campground with tables, fireplaces, wood, water, shelters, and a food cache (to deter bears). Space is limited, so if you plan to stay—or if you need more information—contact the Superintendent, Katmai National Park and Preserve, P.O. Box 7, King Salmon, AK 99613 (tel. 907/246-3305).

Don't expect to see the sights of Katmai National Park under sunny skies, by the way. Wind and rain are the norm here, where weather systems from the Bering Sea and Gulf of Alaska collide. Summer temperatures average in the 50s and 60s in the daytime, but tempests can arise very quickly. Don't go on an outing, no matter how brief, without being prepared for the worst.

WHERE TO STAY & DINE

The park's most popular destination is the **Brooks Lodge,** operated by Katmailand, Inc., 4700 Aircraft Dr., Suite 2, Anchorage, AK 99502 (tel. 907/243-5448, or toll free 800/544-0551; fax 907/243-0649). Located on the short stream connecting Lake Brooks with Naknek Lake, the lodge was established by pioneer aviator Ray Petersen in 1950. Today it has 16 modern guest cabins with hot and cold running water, private baths and showers, and electric heat. Most cabins have twin bunk beds. Family-style meals are served three times a day in the dining hall, and the lodge bar allows guests to relax around a large circular fireplace. Standard rates in 1992 for a three-day/two-night visit—including a round-trip flight from Anchorage and a bus tour to the Valley of Ten Thousand Smokes—were $565–$675 per adult ($20 more in July), plus another $42 a day for meals. One- and three-night packages are also available, and children under 12 are discounted.

Katmailand, Inc., the folks who operate Brooks Lodge, also have the only other two lodges in the park—all of which operate from late May into September only. Both the deluxe **Kulik Lodge,** between Kulik and Nonvianuk Lakes, on the edge of the preserve, and the more rustic **Grosvenor Camp,** on the narrows between Lakes Coville and Grosvenor, are fly-in wilderness fishing lodges. All-inclusive rates, which cover round-trip air transportation from Anchorage, are $2,050 for three nights or $3,850 per week per person at the Kulik Lodge; and $1,250 for three nights, $2,075 per week, at the Grosvenor Camp. Contact Katmailand, Inc., 4700 Aircraft Dr., Suite 2, Anchorage, AK 99502 (tel. 907/243-5448). There are a few other lodges in the preserve on Nonvianuk and Kukaklek Lakes; contact the park service for a list.

MCNEIL RIVER

If it's bears you want to see, it's bears you'll get at the **McNeil River State Game Sanctuary.** Surrounded on the south and west by Katmai National Park and Preserve, on the east by Cook Inlet, and on the north by the rugged Chigmit Mountains, this sanctuary offers a unique opportunity for wildlife photographers, amateur as well as professional. The large concentration of brown bears here don't seem to mind that humans watch them: They go about their business as usual, tolerant of humans as long as their actions fall within an established pattern of noninterference.

That established pattern requires that no more than 10 people a day accompany armed rangers to McNeil River Falls (the prime viewing spot) in July and August. A lottery held May 15 determines who will be included in these daily visits. Apply by May 1 to the Alaska Department of Fish and Game, Game Division, 333 Raspberry Rd., Anchorage, AK 99502, enclosing a completed questionnaire (which you must request in advance) and a $5 fee.

It's a short hike or boat ride from the river's mouth to the falls. You can arrive by plane or boat from Homer at high tide, and you can camp at the river's mouth for up to a week.

WHERE TO STAY & DINE

The **Chenik Wilderness Camp,** an outpost of the Kachemak Bay Wilderness Lodge, P.O. Box 956, Homer, AK 99603 (tel. 907/235-8910), is the only permanent facility near the sanctuary. The minimum stay here is five days, with arrival on Saturday and departure on Thursday; the price of $2,250 per person includes the $300 round-trip floatplane trip to and from Homer. A maximum of six guests stay in tent cabins with sun porches and outside "privies"; the lodge, where all meals are served, also has a library, big fireplace, and—nearby—a wood-heat sauna. Hosts Michael and Diane McBride will gladly put your name in the McNeil River lottery pool; they point out that the permit system is not in effect in June, and even if you miss out in July or August, there's a good chance that a no-show will leave a space open for you. When you're not watching the bears, there's excellent hiking, fishing, and beachcombing. Only a few miles offshore, in the Cook Inlet, is the recently active Augustine Island volcano.

ANIAKCHAK NATIONAL MONUMENT & PRESERVE

If Mount Katmai's 1912 eruption was colossal, there are few words to describe what might have happened at Aniakchak at some point in the distant past. Sometime since the last Ice Age, the caldera exploded and collapsed, creating a crater six miles wide and 30 square miles in area. That's half again as big as Oregon's Crater Lake. But here the only water is in small (and aptly named) Surprise Lake. Hot springs heat the lake, which feeds the Aniakchak River, which cascades through a 1,500-foot rift in the crater wall to empty into Bristol Bay. Sockeye salmon spawning up the river have a distinctive flavor of soda and iron. Aniakchak last erupted in 1931 from its caldera cone, Vent Mountain. The 586,000-acre national park and preserve was established in 1980.

For information, contact the Superintendent, Aniakchak National Monument and Preserve, P.O. Box 7, King Salmon, AK 99613 (tel. 907/246-3305). It's a singular experience to cruise over Aniakchak's moonscape in a floatplane from King Salmon, 150 miles north, or **Port Heiden** (pop. 100), the nearest village, and land on Surprise Lake.

THE WESTERN EXTREMITY

West of Aniakchak, the Alaska Peninsula is mainly cold, rainy, windswept tundra, dotted with scattered Aleut villages and fish-processing plants. **Chignik** (pop. 180), **Sand Point** on Popof Island (pop. 800), **King Cove** (pop. 530), and **Cold Bay** (pop. 250), all served by the Alaska state ferry system five times between May and September, are the major settlements.

From Katmai National Park and Preserve south, all the land on the Gulf of Alaska side of the peninsula is owned by the federal government. The 1.2-million-acre **Becharof National Wildlife Refuge**, P.O. Box 277, King Salmon, AK 99613 (tel. 907/246-3339), abuts Katmai on the south and contains 458-square-mile Becharof Lake, Alaska's second largest. The 3.5-million-acre **Alaska Peninsula National Wildlife Refuge** (same address as Becharof) flanks Aniakchak National Monument and Preserve on either side. The tip of the long, snakelike peninsula comprises 320,000-acre **Izembek National Wildlife Refuge**, P.O. Box 2, Cold Bay, AK 99571 (tel. 907/532-2445).

3. BRISTOL BAY

The most productive red (sockeye) salmon fishery on earth is this 170-mile-wide bay where the Togiak, Wood, Nushagak, Kvichak, and King Salmon Rivers, among others, enter the Bering Sea after tumbling from alpine lakes and mountain glaciers. This is an angler's paradise, land not only for the commercial fishermen who ply their trade in the often-foggy waters of the bay. Sportspeople flock here from around the world to test the freshwater lakes and rivers for rainbow and lake trout, arctic char, Dolly Varden, grayling, steelhead, northern pike, and sheefish.

DILLINGHAM

Spread across lush tundra on the shore of Bristol Bay, near the confluence of the Wood and Nushagak Rivers, this growing town of 2,000 people, 320 miles west of Anchorage, is the home of a 500-boat salmon fleet and a center for sport fishing and hunting.

Few towns in Alaska have a longer history. A Russian fort, known as Aleksandrovski Redoubt but later renamed Nushagak, was built at the mouth of the Nushagak River in 1818 and an Orthodox mission established in 1837. American entrepreneurs built the first salmon cannery in the Bristol Bay region at Nushagak in 1884 and another in 1886 on the site of modern Dillingham. U.S. Sen. W. P. Dillingham of Vermont visited the cannery in 1903. His name was bestowed on the town the following year when a post office was established.

Dillingham has a climate called "marine transitional": Bristol Bay's warmer air collides with cool weather fronts from the Interior, bringing mild temperatures but almost perpetually cloudy skies, strong winds, and moderate precipitation. Average temperatures are in the 50s and 60s in summer, between 0° and 20°F in winter, with annual extremes of 92° to −36°F. Average annual precipitation is 25 inches, including 71 inches of snow.

Dillingham is best regarded as a base for visiting the outdoors rather than a destination in itself. The town does have a **Heritage Museum** (tel. 842-5610) with a varied collection of Native Yupik Eskimo arts and crafts. The **Bristol Bay Native Corporation** has its headquarters here. And in March there's a three-day festival called the Beaver Roundup, which celebrates the end of the winter trapping season with dog-sled and snowmobile races, a Miss Dillingham pageant, and other activities.

ORIENTATION & ESSENTIAL INFORMATION

The **Alaska Department of Fish and Game** (tel. 842-5925) maintains an office in Dillingham. For further information about the area, contact the **Dillingham Chamber of Commerce,** City of Dillingham, P.O. Box 191, Dillingham, AK 99576.

Local air-taxi services include **Armstrong Air Service** (tel. 842-5940) and **Yute Air Alaska** (tel. 842-5333). Cars can be rented for the 20-mile drive to **Aleknagik** (pop. 250), a Native village on Lake Aleknagik in Wood-Tikchik State Park.

WHERE TO STAY & DINE

BRISTOL INN, P.O. Box 196, Dillingham, AK 99576. Tel. 907/842-2240. 30 rms (all with bath). TV TEL
$ Rates: $79–$125 single or double. MC, V.
The rooms at Bristol Inn all have cable television and in-room phones. The Cannery restaurant and lounge is open daily for all meals. Courtesy-van service is offered to and from the airport year-round.

DILLINGHAM HOTEL, P.O. Box 194, Dillingham, AK 99576. Tel. 907/842-5316. 32 rms (all with bath). TV TEL
$ Rates: $62–$69 single; $69–$76 double. MC, V.
Bristol Bay's original hotel has a convenient location in the center of town. Several rooms have kitchenettes. Courtesy car from airport.

WOOD-TIKCHIK STATE PARK

Alaska s largest state park is a wilderness wonderland of two separate water systems, each with half a dozen long, fjordlike lakes interconnected by cascading rivers and streams, all emptying into Nushagak Bay (an arm of Bristol Bay) at Dillingham. Its 1.4 million acres are one of the state's lesser-known secrets. The tundra-cloaked slopes of the Kilbuck Mountains enclose the western shores of the Tikchik lakes and some of the Wood River lakes, while spruce forests tickle the eastern shores. Contact the **Alaska Division of Parks,** 619 Warehouse Ave., Suite 210, Anchorage, AK 99501 (tel. 907/274-4676), to learn more.

WHERE TO STAY & DINE

As might be expected in a rich natural area, there are numerous fishing lodges in the park. They include **Bristol Bay Lodge,** Rte. 1, Box 580, Ellensburg, WA 98926 (tel. 509/964-2094), charging $3,795 weekly per person, June through September; the **Tikchik Narrows Lodge,** P.O. Box 220248, Anchorage, AK 99522 (tel. 907/243-8450; fax 907/248-3091), charging $4,100 weekly per person, June to October; and the **Wood River Lodge,** 4437 Sanford Dr., Fairbanks, AK 99701 (tel. 907/479-0308, or toll free 800/456-8925; fax 907/479-2858), at $3,900 weekly per person, mid-June to late September.

NATIONAL WILDLIFE REFUGES

Togiak National Wildlife Refuge, 4.1 million acres, with nearly every major wildlife species in Alaska represented, covers the Ahklun Mountains and most of the western shore of Bristol Bay adjoining Wood-Tikchik State Park. Its headquarters are at P.O. Box 10201, Dillingham, AK 99576 (tel. 907/842-1063). Offshore, the Walrus Islands and Round Island are part of the expansive **Alaska Maritime National Wildlife Refuge.** Round Island in particular is a rare and highly restricted sanctuary for walrus, of which as many as 10,000 bulls may congregate on its rocky shores at once. Contact the Alaska Maritime NWR, 202 Pioneer Ave., Homer, AK 99603 (tel. 907/235-6546).

No visitors are allowed without permits, but you can expect to see a lot of marine life if you go out with **Trapper Don's Round Island Boat Charters,** General Delivery, Togiak, AK 99678 (tel. 907/493-5927).

4. THE YUKON-KUSKOKWIM DELTA

Alaska's two greatest river systems, the Yukon and the Kuskokwim, empty into the Bering Sea. Though their mouths are about 200 miles apart, they come as close as 30 miles to one another as they flow from the vast Interior onto the barren, flat tundra of the western plains. The final 150–200 miles of their courses are marshy and meandering, and an ideal environment for birdlife. Indeed, the nation's largest wildlife refuge—the Yukon Delta National Wildlife Refuge—covers most of this boggy tundra.

BETHEL

The largest town in western Alaska lies along the northern bank of the Kuskokwim River, 90 miles from the Bering Sea at the head of narrow Kuskokwim Bay. The trade and transportation center for the 57 villages of the delta region, this town of 3,700 people also has a substantial commercial fishing business and a sizable service sector. Yet it's at the mercy of the river, which annually tears large chunks of land from the city waterfront, and nearly as often floods its banks.

Once known as Mumtrekhlagamute, Yupik for "smokehouse village," Bethel got its name from Scripture in 1885 when a Moravian mission was established near a trading post. The climate, similar to but drier than that at Bristol Bay, has mean temperatures in summer of 53°F (record high: 86°F) and in winter of 11°F (record low: −46°F). Annual precipitation is 17 inches, including 50 inches of snow.

GETTING THERE & ESSENTIAL INFORMATION

Alaska Airlines (tel. 907/543-3905, or toll free 800/426-0333) serves Bethel twice daily on weekdays, and once daily on weekends, with flights from Anchorage.

For information, contact the **Bethel Chamber of Commerce,** P.O. Box 329, Bethel, AK 99559, or call the city offices (tel. 907/543-2097). District and superior courts are here, as well as a regional hospital (tel. 543-3711) and offices of the Alaska Department of Fish and Game, the U.S. Fish and Wildlife Service, and the federal Bureau of Indian Affairs. Bethel has a weekly newspaper, the *Tundra Drums,* 13 churches, Kuskokwim Community College, and head offices of the Native Calista Corporation.

WHAT TO SEE & DO

Bethel's long, dreary winter is made survivable by the **Yukon-Kuskokwim State Fair,** which runs from mid-January to mid-February annually. The highlight is the Kuskokwim 300 Sled Dog Race; other events include a one-dog sled race for children, a fishing derby for village elders, a Native olympics, Yupik dance contests, and the exhibit and sale of traditional handcrafts from throughout the delta region. Write P.O. Box 388, Bethel, AK 99559, for more information. Spring is ushered in with the **Kuskokwim Ice Classic,** modeled on the more famous Nenana Ice Classic: Lottery entrants must try to guess the precise day and minute that the ice will move on the Kuskokwim River at Bethel. Contact P.O. Box 271, Bethel, AK 99559 (tel. 907/543-4239).

Bethel's pride and joy is the **Yugtarvik Regional Museum,** in a log building on Third Avenue (tel. 543-2098). Dedicated to the preservation of Yupik Eskimo culture, its purpose is twofold: to display artifacts from the past (such as kayaks, hunting implements, household items, and clothing) and to encourage modern works. To the latter end, this is a living museum where master artisans and apprentices shape works of ivory and wood, weave grass baskets, and design skin clothing, while bantering in their native Yupik tongue and talking freely (in English) to visitors who ply them with questions about the "old way" of life. Works are sold in the excellent museum shop. Admission to the collection is free.

WHERE TO STAY & DINE

Bed-and-breakfast may be the way to go here. **Porterhouse Bed and Breakfast,** P.O. Box 868, Bethel, AK 99559 (tel. 907/543-3551 or 543-3552), charges $50 single, $75 double. There are cable TVs in every room, full breakfasts served on fine china, and a river view. The upscale **Pacifica Guest House,** P.O. Box 1208, Bethel, AK 99559 (tel. 907/543-2484 or 543-4305; fax 907/543-3403), has rates of $90 in winter (single or double), $100 in summer.

KUSKOKWIM INN, P.O. Box 818, Bethel, AK 99559. Tel. 907/543-2207. Fax 543-2228. 35 rms (all with bath). TV TEL
$ Rates: $65 single; $85 double. MC, V.
Recent travelers have found the town's long-established and only hotel in need of a major renovation. Rooms have cable TVs, and there's a restaurant on the premises. A 10% discount is given to military personnel and government employees.

AN EXCURSION TO YUKON DELTA NATIONAL WILDLIFE REFUGE

The 19.6-million-acre Yukon Delta National Wildlife Refuge, larger than several states in the Lower 48, is home to more than 100 million migratory waterfowl. It also harbors a large colony of reindeer and musk-oxen on huge Nunivak Island, just across the Etolin Strait. Between May and September, Nunivak Island Guide Service, P.O. Box 31, Mekoryuk, AK 99630 (tel. 907/827-8213), offers a rare opportunity to visit the offshore island for wilderness trips, photography, fishing, or hunting. (Limited hunting for musk-oxen is permitted in season.) Refuge offices are at P.O. Box 346, Bethel, AK 99559 (tel. 543-3151).

---

5. THE PRIBILOF ISLANDS

The Pribilofs are one of Alaska's most isolated enclaves and one of its most fascinating, both for their Russian heritage and for their thriving colonies of northern fur seals and sea birds.

Here on these barren rocks, 880 miles west of Anchorage and 350 miles from the North American mainland in the middle of the Bering Sea, fortunate visitors can peer over the edges of cliffs directly into the rookeries of puffins, auklets, and 209 other species of avian life. And two blinds have been set up—accessible by permit or with a tour guide—for a closeup view of up to a million seals in their rookeries. It's a wildlife photographer's dream.

Slaughtered nearly to extinction by the 18th- and 19th-century Russians, the fur seals have come back from the brink, protected by an international treaty barring their harvest on the high seas. Today they are harvested in limited numbers (typically 2,500–3,000) by the Aleut population of the Pribilofs as part of their subsistence lifestyle, under the management of the federal Department of Commerce.

Neither of the main islands of **Saint Paul** (pop. 600) and **Saint George** (pop. 220)—there are also three smaller islets—was inhabited until 1786, when Russian fur traders founded the communities with Aleuts from the Aleutians. The Aleut inhabitants of these tiny villages, which cling like limpets to the tundra, still bear Russian names and other signs of the European lifestyle. None is so evident as their churches, both on the National Register of Historic Places—Saints Peter and Paul Russian Orthodox Church on Saint Paul and Saint George the Great Martyr Russian Orthodox Church on Saint George.

The climate in the Pribilofs is cool and wet, with heavy fog expected between May and August. Temperatures are typically in the 40s in summer (record high is 63°F), in the teens in winter (record low is −7°F on Saint George, −19°F on Saint Paul). Annual precipitation is 23–30 inches (heavier on Saint Paul), with around 50 inches of snow.

Both islands have telephone, radio, and television, as well as electricity and water and sewage systems.

Reeve Aleutian Airways (tel. 907/243-4700 in Anchorage) serves St. Paul five times weekly from Anchorage via Cold Bay. Most Pribilof visitors, however, go to the islands as part of a package tour.

Midnight Sun Tours, P.O. Box 103355, Anchorage, AK 99510 (tel. 907/276-8687, or toll free 800/544-2235), operates the primary Pribilof tour in conjunction with Reeve Airways. The three-day/two-night trips depart from Anchorage on Tuesday and Thursday, June through August. Packages include round-trip transportation, shared hotel accommodations, and full guide services, but no meals. The tour costs $799 plus 3% tax; week-long tours cost as much as $1,449.

WHERE TO STAY & DINE

As the larger of the two villages, Saint Paul has the more complete visitor facilities. There are several restaurants, a clinic, a general store, and four gift shops, but no banks. Off-road vehicles can be rented. For more information, write City of St. Paul, P.O. Box 1, Saint Paul Island, AK 99660 (tel. 907/546-2331, or 907/278-2312 in Anchorage; fax 907/546-2365 or 278-2316).

KING EIDER HOTEL, P.O. Box 88, Saint Paul Island, AK 99660. Tel. 907/546-2312, or toll free 800/544-2248. 45 rms (none with bath).
$ Rates: $80–$100 single or double. AE, MC, V.
Owned by the Native Tanadgusix Corp., the King Eider has a handful of clean, spartan rooms with shared baths, and the island's most popular restaurant.

ST. GEORGE HOTEL, Saint George Island, AK 99660. Tel. 907/859-2255. 20 rms (none with bath).
$ Rates: $80–$100 single or double. MC, V.
The historic St. George Hotel is operated by the Saint George Tanaq Corp., with most rooms going to participants in the corporation's naturalist tours from mid-June to Labor Day. Contact the corporation at 4000 Old Seward Hwy., Suite 302, Anchorage, AK 99503 (tel. 907/562-3100), for details.

6. THE ALEUTIAN ISLANDS

Perpetually buffeted by violent winds, fog, and rain, the bleak and barren 1,000-mile-long Aleutian archipelago sweeps in a broad arc from the tip of the Alaska Peninsula nearly to the Kamchatka Peninsula of Russia. As the submarine extension of the Aleutian Range, the islands are mountainous and volcanic, with a high degree of seismic activity.

Extending beyond 173° East Longitude—the International Date Line must make an abrupt dogleg to keep the Aleutians in the same day as the rest of Alaska—they represent both the westernmost (179°10′ West, Amatignak Island) and easternmost (179°46′ East, Semisopochnoi Island) points in the United States.

There are 80 named islands in the Aleutian chain, 72 of them uninhabited except for the sea birds and marine mammals protected by the **Alaska Maritime National Wildlife Refuge.** They are covered with a tundra vegetation of tussock grasses and heath, with some dwarf trees and occasional taller shrubs along streambeds. Nearly 20,000 sea otters, bouncing back from near extinction, make their principal home in

Aleutian waters. For general information, contact the Alaska Maritime NWR, Aleutian Islands Unit, P.O. Box 5251, FPO Seattle, WA 98791 (tel. 907/592-2406).

Dutch Harbor and **Unalaska** on Unalaska Island, near the eastern end of the archipelago, are the largest settlements, with a combined population of about 4,000 people. A U.S. Navy base on **Adak,** an air force base on Shemya, and a Coast Guard station on **Attu,** the farthest-west island, together employ about 2,250 military personnel.

Aleut villages at **Atka** (pop. 100) and **False Pass** on Unimak Island (pop. 70) are the only surviving Native villages from an island chain that once supported thousands of Aleuts. There are other small fishing communities at **Akutan** (pop. 200) and **Nikolski** on Umnak Island (pop. 50).

Even on the uninhabited islands—**Kiska,** in particular—there are traces of the battles fought with the Japanese for control of this archipelago during World War II. Miles of abandoned military installations, including landing strips and roads, warehouses, and Quonset huts, are reminders of a time not so long past.

That time is well recalled in the "1000 Mile War Tours" offered by **Alaskabound,** 1621 Tongass Ave., Ketchikan, AK 99901 (tel. 907/225-8800, or toll free 800/544-0808). As the agent fits the itinerary to the particular desire of the traveler, this tour is suited for veterans of the Aleutian campaign who want to sneak a latter-day look at the grim battlefield of the 1940s. Prices vary from $795 to $1,195; tours are offered only from April 14 to October 20.

Reeve Aleutian Airways (tel. 907/243-4700 in Anchorage), which has been flying to this island chain since 1932, provides regular service on Boeing 727s from Anchorage to Adak, False Pass, and Shemya. Unalaska (Dutch Harbor) is served from Anchorage by **MarkAir** (tel. toll free 800/426-6784) and from Kodiak and Dillingham by **Peninsula Airways** (tel. toll free 800/544-2248). The **Alaska Marine Highway System** (tel. toll free 800/544-0552) takes the ferry M.V. *Tustumena* as far as Dutch Harbor from Kodiak monthly, May to September.

DUTCH HARBOR/UNALASKA

These thriving twin fishing villages on the eastern side of Unalaska Island, 920 miles southwest of Anchorage, are seeing an increasing trade in tourism.

The best way to tour the island is with **Aleutian Experience Tours,** 3400 Kvichak Circle, Anchorage, AK 99515 (tel. 907/522-1323), between mid-June and mid-September. Tours vary, but may include Bunker Hill and Mount Ballyhoo, the site of Fort Mears and a Japanese prisoner-of-war camp, and the hulk of the S.S. *Northwestern.* They may also visit Alaska's oldest Russian Orthodox church, where tourists can sample Russian tea and learn about the Aleut culture.

Flightseeing and inter-island transport can be arranged through **Aleutian Air Ltd.,** P.O. Box 330, Dutch Harbor, AK 99692 (tel. 907/581-1686), or **Maritime Helicopters,** P.O. Box 597, Dutch Harbor, AK 99692 (tel. 907/581-1771).

WHERE TO STAY & DINE

CARL'S MOTEL, 100 Bayview Ave. (P.O. Box 109), Unalaska, AK 99685. Tel. 907/581-1230. 12 rms (all with bath). TV TEL
$ Rates: $55–$75 single; $65–$85 double. MC, V.
Rooms here have cable TVs, kitchens, and full baths.

UNISEA INN, P.O. Box 503, Dutch Harbor, AK 99692. Tel. 907/581-1325. 46 rms (all with bath). TV TEL
$ Rates: $71–$81 single; $82–$92 double. MC, V.
The hotel has a restaurant and lounge, a gift shop, games room, and beauty salon.

GLOSSARY OF ALASKANA

English, of course, is the common tongue of nearly all Alaskans, with a smattering of Inupiat, Yupik, Tlingit, and other Native tongues thrown in. But that doesn't mean you'll understand every word an Alaskan says. The following glossary is supplied to help you cope with some uniquely Alaskan words and concepts:

Akutak Eskimo ice cream, traditionally made of whipped soapberries, seal oil, and snow.

Alaxsxag An Aleut word meaning "mainland" or "great country."

Baleen The black, fringed, bonelike substance that lines the mouth of baleen whales, straining plankton and krill from the water. It is often used in Native crafts.

Billiken A smiling, pot-bellied good-luck charm with a pointed head, commonly carved from ivory by Yupik Eskimos.

Blanket toss Also called the *nalukatag,* this Eskimo game requires a dozen or more people to grasp the edges of a circular walrus-hide blanket and toss an individual as high as 20 feet into the air, as on a trampoline.

Breakup The end of an Alaskan winter, when the ice that has frozen the major rivers thaws, pounding its way downstream as the spring snows melt. It typically occurs in the Yukon River in early May. In the Nenana Ice Classic, Alaska's biggest lottery-style pool, Alaskans each year buy tickets to guess the exact minute of breakup of the Tanana River at Nenana, with over $100,000 paid to winners.

Bush Any part of Alaska not accessible by road or ferry.

Cabin fever What you get if breakup is late. Even "sourdoughs" (see below), housebound during the long, dark, cold winter months, may suffer depression, discontent, or fits of violence.

Cache A miniature log-cabin storage bin, mounted on stilts and reached by a ladder, to keep food and other goods safe from animal invasions.

Cheechako A newcomer or greenhorn, similar to the Hawaiian word *malihini.* Specifically, a cheechako is one who has not spent a full winter in Alaska, until breakup.

Hooligan Small smelt caught by dip-netting as they swim upriver to spawn.

Ice fog An unpleasant weather phenomenon that occurs in the Interior and arctic during winter. Clear skies allow heat to rise from the earth's surface, trapping ice crystals in a dry fog at lower elevations. In Fairbanks this may take the form of ice smog.

Iceworm A black, segmented worm, usually the size of a straight pin, that lives near the surface of glaciers and icefields. Its myth, perpetuated by the annual Cordova Iceworm Festival (see "Prince William Sound" in Chapter 6), has outgrown its reality.

Igloo A traditional Eskimo dwelling made of sod, driftwood, and whalebone. The stereotypical ice-block igloo was built mainly by Canadian Eskimos as an emergency bivouac.

Lower 48 The contiguous 48 states of the Union.

Mukluks Eskimo moccasins, very warm but lightweight. They are usually made with sealskin soles and caribou tops, and trimmed with fur.

Muktuk A favorite Eskimo delicacy: whale blubber, specifically the outer layers of skin.

Muskeg Boglike areas underlaid by permafrost or periodically frozen ground, where little vegetation except scrub trees, shrubs, and moss can grow.

North Slope The frigid north side of the Brooks Range, where the oil and natural gas (and money) are. Also referred to merely as "The Slope."

No-see-ums Tiny gnats, almost microscopic in size, seen all too often in pesky swarms, especially in the summer. Good insect repellent and netting may deter them.

Outside Anywhere but Alaska.

Qiviut The warm underwool of the musk-ox, knitted into scarves, caps, and other clothing items.

Scrimshaw The traditional art of etching designs and pictures into walrus-tusk ivory. Look for the distinctive cross-hatch pattern to distinguish walrus tusks (which only Native Alaskans are allowed to craft) from illegally imported elephant tusks.

Skookum Strong or hearty, as in *a skookum meal* or *a skookum baby.*

Skookum chuck A narrow passage between the open sea and a tidal lagoon. It may take on the appearance of river rapids when the tide changes.

Soapstone Compact talc, an extremely soft and greasy-feeling mineral used in carving art objects.

Sourdough An Alaska old-timer, often someone whose granddaddy arrived during the gold rushes and stayed. The name comes from the high-yeast bread so popular in the bush.

South The Lower 48 (contiguous) states.

Squaw candy Dried or smoked salmon, a staple winter food for bush Alaskans and their dogs.

Ulu A traditional, fan-shaped Eskimo knife with a handle of bone or wood, used for scraping (mainly animal skins) and chopping.

Umiak A skin-covered Eskimo boat, lightweight but hardy for dragging across sea ice; usually made of walrus or oogruk (bearded seal) skin.

Williwaws Sudden windstorms that can exceed 100 m.p.h.

INDEX

GENERAL INFORMATION

DESTINATIONS

Key to abbreviations: *B* = Expensive; *I* = Inexpensive; *M* = Moderate; *VE* = Very expensive; *B&B* = Bed-&-Breakfast; *CG* = Campground; *FR* = Fishing Resort; *YH* = Youth Hostel; *WL* =Wilderness Lodge; *$* =Super-value Choice; * = Author's favorite.

Please Send Me the Books Checked Below:

FROMMER'S COMPREHENSIVE GUIDES
(Guides listing facilities from budget to deluxe,
with emphasis on the medium-priced)

	Retail Price	Code		Retail Price	Code
☐ Acapulco/Ixtapa/Taxco 1993–94	$15.00	C120	☐ Jamaica/Barbados 1993–94	$15.00	C105
☐ Alaska 1994–95	$17.00	C130	☐ Japan 1992–93	$19.00	C020
☐ Arizona 1993–94	$18.00	C101	☐ Morocco 1992–93	$18.00	C021
☐ Australia 1992–93	$18.00	C002	☐ Nepal 1994–95	$18.00	C126
☐ Austria 1993–94	$19.00	C119	☐ New England 1993	$17.00	C114
☐ Belgium/Holland/ Luxembourg 1993–94	$18.00	C106	☐ New Mexico 1993–94	$15.00	C117
☐ Bahamas 1994–95	$17.00	C121	☐ New York State 1994–95	$19.00	C132
☐ Bermuda 1994–95	$15.00	C122	☐ Northwest 1991–92	$17.00	C026
☐ Brazil 1993–94	$20.00	C111	☐ Portugal 1992–93	$16.00	C027
☐ California 1993	$18.00	C112	☐ Puerto Rico 1993–94	$15.00	C103
☐ Canada 1992–93	$18.00	C009	☐ Puerto Vallarta/Manzanillo/ Guadalajara 1992–93	$14.00	C028
☐ Caribbean 1994	$18.00	C123	☐ Scandinavia 1993–94	$19.00	C118
☐ Carolinas/Georgia 1994–95	$17.00	C128	☐ Scotland 1992–93	$16.00	C040
☐ Colorado 1993–94	$16.00	C100	☐ Skiing Europe 1989–90	$15.00	C030
☐ Cruises 1993–94	$19.00	C107	☐ South Pacific 1992–93	$20.00	C031
☐ DE/MD/PA & NJ Shore 1992–93	$19.00	C012	☐ Spain 1993–94	$19.00	C115
☐ Egypt 1990–91	$17.00	C013	☐ Switzerland/Liechtenstein 1992–93	$19.00	C032
☐ England 1994	$18.00	C129	☐ Thailand 1992–93	$20.00	C033
☐ Florida 1994	$18.00	C124	☐ U.S.A. 1993–94	$19.00	C116
☐ France 1994–95	$20.00	C131	☐ Virgin Islands 1994–95	$13.00	C127
☐ Germany 1994	$19.00	C125	☐ Virginia 1992–93	$14.00	C037
☐ Italy 1994	$19.00	C130	☐ Yucatán 1993–94	$18.00	C110

FROMMER'S $-A-DAY GUIDES
(Guides to low-cost tourist accommodations and facilities)

	Retail Price	Code		Retail Price	Code
☐ Australia on $45 1993–94	$18.00	D102	☐ Mexico on $45 1994	$19.00	D116
☐ Costa Rica/Guatemala/ Belize on $35 1993–94	$17.00	D108	☐ New York on $70 1992–93	$16.00	D016
☐ Eastern Europe on $30 1993–94	$18.00	D110	☐ New Zealand on $45 1993–94	$18.00	D103
☐ England on $60 1994	$18.00	D112	☐ Scotland/Wales on $50 1992–93	$18.00	D019
☐ Europe on $50 1994	$19.00	D115	☐ South America on $40 1993–94	$19.00	D109
☐ Greece on $45 1993–94	$19.00	D100			
☐ Hawaii on $75 1994	$19.00	D113	☐ Turkey on $40 1992–93	$22.00	D023
☐ India on $40 1992–93	$20.00	D010	☐ Washington, D.C. on $40 1992–93	$17.00	D024
☐ Ireland on $40 1992–93	$17.00	D011			
☐ Israel on $45 1993–94	$18.00	D101			

FROMMER'S CITY $-A-DAY GUIDES
(Pocket-size guides with an emphasis on low-cost tourist accommodations and facilities)

	Retail Price	Code		Retail Price	Code
☐ Berlin on $40 1994–95	$12.00	D111	☐ Madrid on $50 1992–93	$13.00	D014
☐ Copenhagen on $50 1992–93	$12.00	D003	☐ Paris on $45 1994–95	$12.00	D117
☐ London on $45 1994–95	$12.00	D114	☐ Stockholm on $50 1992–93	$13.00	D022

FROMMER'S WALKING TOURS
(With routes and detailed maps, these companion guides point out
the places and pleasures that make a city unique)

	Retail Price	Code		Retail Price	Code
☐ Berlin	$12.00	W100	☐ Paris	$12.00	W103
☐ London	$12.00	W101	☐ San Francisco	$12.00	W104
☐ New York	$12.00	W102	☐ Washington, D.C.	$12.00	W105

FROMMER'S TOURING GUIDES
(Color-illustrated guides that include walking tours, cultural and historic
sites, and practical information)

	Retail Price	Code		Retail Price	Code
☐ Amsterdam	$11.00	T001	☐ New York	$11.00	T008
☐ Barcelona	$14.00	T015	☐ Rome	$11.00	T010
☐ Brazil	$11.00	T003	☐ Scotland	$10.00	T011
☐ Florence	$ 9.00	T005	☐ Sicily	$15.00	T017
☐ Hong Kong/Singapore/			☐ Tokyo	$15.00	T016
Macau	$11.00	T006	☐ Turkey	$11.00	T013
☐ Kenya	$14.00	T018	☐ Venice	$ 9.00	T014
☐ London	$13.00	T007			

FROMMER'S FAMILY GUIDES

	Retail Price	Code		Retail Price	Code
☐ California with Kids	$18.00	F100	☐ San Francisco with Kids	$17.00	F004
☐ Los Angeles with Kids	$17.00	F002	☐ Washington, D.C. with Kids	$17.00	F005
☐ New York City with Kids	$18.00	F003			

FROMMER'S CITY GUIDES
(Pocket-size guides to sightseeing and tourist accommodations and
facilities in all price ranges)

	Retail Price	Code		Retail Price	Code
☐ Amsterdam 1993–94	$13.00	S110	☐ Montreál/Québec		
☐ Athens 1993–94	$13.00	S114	City 1993–94	$13.00	S125
☐ Atlanta 1993–94	$13.00	S112	☐ New Orleans 1993–94	$13.00	S103
☐ Atlantic City/Cape			☐ New York 1993	$13.00	S120
May 1993–94	$13.00	S130	☐ Orlando 1994	$13.00	S135
☐ Bangkok 1992–93	$13.00	S005	☐ Paris 1993–94	$13.00	S109
☐ Barcelona/Majorca/			☐ Philadelphia 1993–94	$13.00	S113
Minorca/Ibiza 1993–94	$13.00	S115	☐ Rio 1991–92	$ 9.00	S029
☐ Berlin 1993–94	$13.00	S116	☐ Rome 1993–94	$13.00	S111
☐ Boston 1993–94	$13.00	S117	☐ Salt Lake City 1991–92	$ 9.00	S031
☐ Cancún/Cozumel 1991–			☐ San Diego 1993–94	$13.00	S107
92	$ 9.00	S010	☐ San Francisco 1994	$13.00	S133
☐ Chicago 1993–94	$13.00	S122	☐ Santa Fe/Taos/		
☐ Denver/Boulder/Colorado			Albuquerque 1993–94	$13.00	S108
Springs 1993–94	$13.00	S131	☐ Seattle/Portland 1992–93	$12.00	S035
☐ Dublin 1993–94	$13.00	S128	☐ St. Louis/Kansas		
☐ Hawaii 1992	$12.00	S014	City 1993–94	$13.00	S127
☐ Hong Kong 1992–93	$12.00	S015	☐ Sydney 1993–94	$13.00	S129
☐ Honolulu/Oahu 1994	$13.00	S134	☐ Tampa/St.		
☐ Las Vegas 1993–94	$13.00	S121	Petersburg 1993–94	$13.00	S105
☐ London 1994	$13.00	S132	☐ Tokyo 1992–93	$13.00	S039
☐ Los Angeles 1993–94	$13.00	S123	☐ Toronto 1993–94	$13.00	S126
☐ Madrid/Costa del			☐ Vancouver/Victoria 1990–		
Sol 1993–94	$13.00	S124	91	$ 8.00	S041
☐ Miami 1993–94	$13.00	S118	☐ Washington, D.C. 1993	$13.00	S102
☐ Minneapolis/St.					
Paul 1993–94	$13.00	S119			

Other Titles Available at Membership Prices

SPECIAL EDITIONS

	Retail Price	Code		Retail Price	Code
☐ Bed & Breakfast North America	$15.00	P002	☐ Marilyn Wood's Wonderful Weekends (within a 250-mile radius of NYC)	$12.00	P017
☐ Bed & Breakfast Southwest	$16.00	P100	☐ National Park Guide 1993	$15.00	P101
☐ Caribbean Hideaways	$16.00	P103	☐ Where to Stay U.S.A.	$15.00	P102

GAULT MILLAU'S "BEST OF" GUIDES
(The only guides that distinguish the truly superlative from the merely overrated)

	Retail Price	Code		Retail Price	Code
☐ Chicago	$16.00	G002	☐ New England	$16.00	G010
☐ Florida	$17.00	G003	☐ New Orleans	$17.00	G011
☐ France	$17.00	G004	☐ New York	$17.00	G012
☐ Germany	$18.00	G018	☐ Paris	$17.00	G013
☐ Hawaii	$17.00	G006	☐ San Francisco	$17.00	G014
☐ Hong Kong	$17.00	G007	☐ Thailand	$18.00	G019
☐ London	$17.00	G009	☐ Toronto	$17.00	G020
☐ Los Angeles	$17.00	G005	☐ Washington, D.C.	$17.00	G017

THE REAL GUIDES
(Opinionated, politically aware guides for youthful budget-minded travelers)

	Retail Price	Code		Retail Price	Code
☐ Able to Travel	$20.00	R112	☐ Kenya	$12.95	R015
☐ Amsterdam	$13.00	R100	☐ Mexico	$11.95	R128
☐ Barcelona	$13.00	R101	☐ Morocco	$14.00	R129
☐ Belgium/Holland/ Luxembourg	$16.00	R031	☐ Nepal	$14.00	R018
☐ Berlin	$13.00	R123	☐ New York	$13.00	R019
☐ Brazil	$13.95	R003	☐ Paris	$13.00	R130
☐ California & the West Coast	$17.00	R121	☐ Peru	$12.95	R021
☐ Canada	$15.00	R103	☐ Poland	$13.95	R131
☐ Czechoslovakia	$15.00	R124	☐ Portugal	$16.00	R126
☐ Egypt	$19.00	R105	☐ Prague	$15.00	R113
☐ Europe	$18.00	R122	☐ San Francisco & the Bay Area	$11.95	R024
☐ Florida	$14.00	R006	☐ Scandinavia	$14.95	R025
☐ France	$18.00	R106	☐ Spain	$16.00	R026
☐ Germany	$18.00	R107	☐ Thailand	$17.00	R119
☐ Greece	$18.00	R108	☐ Tunisia	$17.00	R115
☐ Guatemala/Belize	$14.00	R127	☐ Turkey	$13.95	R027
☐ Hong Kong/Macau	$11.95	R011	☐ U.S.A.	$18.00	R117
☐ Hungary	$14.95	R118	☐ Venice	$11.95	R028
☐ Ireland	$17.00	R120	☐ Women Travel	$12.95	R029
☐ Italy	$18.00	R125	☐ Yugoslavia	$12.95	R030